THE ROUTLEDGE INTERNATIONAL HANDBOOK OF DEINDUSTRIALIZATION STUDIES

The Routledge International Handbook of Deindustrialization Studies is a timely volume that provides an overview of this interdisciplinary field that emerged in response to the widespread decline of manufacturing and heavy industry from the 1980s onward. Edited by prominent figures in the field, the volume brings together many of the leading scholars from a range of countries across the globe to offer a multifaceted overview of deindustrialization and its impact.

Deindustrialization has been cited as one of the factors behind the rise of the far right, and to a lesser extent the far left, across Europe, the rise and success of Trumpism in the US, and the Brexit vote as well as the more recent and sudden erosion of UK Labour's 'Red Wall' of the North of England. This collection brings together scholars of deindustrialization around the globe and from a wide variety of academic disciplines including history, sociology, politics, geography, economics, anthropology, literature, arts practice, photography, heritage, and cultural studies. In doing so, the volume explores the roots of deindustrialization across the world, highlights the key themes and issues in the field, illustrates the intersectional and interdisciplinary character of the field, and shows how deindustrialization lies at the heart of many of the key political, cultural, social, and economic issues of our time.

Written in a clear and accessible style, the *Handbook* is a comprehensive interdisciplinary volume for this young but maturing field. The volume is a valuable resource for students, teachers, and researchers interested in industrial decline, closure, and the multifaceted impacts they cause. It speaks to readers across the arts, humanities, and social and political sciences concerned with deindustrialization broadly defined.

Tim Strangleman is Emeritus Professor of Sociology at the University of Kent, UK, where he is also Director of the Work, Employment and Economic Life research cluster. He has researched and published widely on issues of work, class, community, and deindustrialization. He has carried out work in the coal mining, rail, health, shipbuilding, engineering, papermaking, and brewing industries, drawing on oral history, archives, and visual material. He is the author of *Work Identity at the End of the Line? Privatisation and Culture Change in the UK Railway Industry* (2004) and *Voices of Guinness: An Oral History of the Park Royal Brewery* (2019). He is also the co-author of *Work and Society: Sociological Approaches, Themes and Methods* (2008) and the co-editor of *The Routledge Handbook of Working-Class Studies*

(2021). He is also a co-investigator on the Deindustrialization and the Politics of Our Time (DéPOT) project.

Sherry Lee Linkon is Professor of English and American Studies at Georgetown University, USA, where, with campus and community colleagues, she developed the Steel Valley Voices digital archive of interviews and artifacts reflecting the experiences of 24 racial and ethnic groups in the Youngstown area. Her most recent book, *The Half-Life of Deindustrialization* (2018), examines early twenty-first century working-class narratives reflecting the continuing effects of economic restructuring in the US. With John Russo, she also co-authored *Steeltown USA: Work and Memory in Youngstown* (2002) and co-edited *New Working Class Studies* (2005). Her current research examines literature and photography reflecting Black women's perspectives on the legacies of deindustrialization. She is also a co-investigator on the Deindustrialization and the Politics of Our Time (DéPOT) project.

Steven High is Professor of History at Concordia University, Canada and Principal Investigator of the Deindustrialization and the Politics of Our Time (DéPOT) project. He has published extensively on the history and politics of deindustrialization in the US and Canada. His book, *Industrial Sunset: The Making of North America's Rust Belt* (2003), won prizes from the American Historical Association and other organizations. He is also the author of *Corporate Wasteland: The Landscape and Memory of Deindustrialization* (with photographer David Lewis, 2007) and *One Job Town: Work, Memory and Betrayal in Northern Ontario* (2018), and the co-editor of *The Deindustrialized World: Confronting Ruination in Postindustrial Places* (2017).

Jackie Clarke is Senior Lecturer in French Studies at the University of Glasgow, UK, where she is also a member of the Centre for Gender History. She is also a co-investigator on the Deindustrialization and the Politics of Our Time (DéPOT) project. Her research explores questions about work, consumption, deindustrialization, and gender in contemporary France. She is the co-editor of a special issue on gender and deindustrialization in *International Labor and Working Class Studies* (2024).

Stefan Berger is Professor of Social History and Director of the Institute for Social Movements at Ruhr-Universität Bochum, Germany. He is also Executive Chair of the Foundation History of the Ruhr and Honorary Professor at Cardiff University, UK. He is the author of *History and Identity: How Historical Theory Shapes Historical Practice* (2022) and editor of *Constructing Industrial Pasts: Heritage, Historical Culture and Identity in Regions Undergoing Structural Economic Transformation* (2020). He is a co-investigator on the Deindustrialization and the Politics of Our Time (DéPOT) project, an international partnership project funded by the Canadian Social Sciences and Humanities Research Council (SSHRC).

THE ROUTLEDGE INTERNATIONAL HANDBOOK OF DEINDUSTRIALIZATION STUDIES

Edited by Tim Strangleman, Sherry Lee Linkon, Steven High, Jackie Clarke, and Stefan Berger

LONDON AND NEW YORK

Designed cover image: 'A poster by Fred Wright protesting plant closures'

First published 2025
by Routledge
4 Park Square, Milton Park, Abingdon, Oxon OX14 4RN

and by Routledge
605 Third Avenue, New York, NY 10158

Routledge is an imprint of the Taylor & Francis Group, an informa business

© 2025 selection and editorial matter, Tim Strangleman, Sherry Lee Linkon, Steven High, Jackie Clarke, and Stefan Berger; individual chapters, the contributors

The right of Tim Strangleman, Sherry Lee Linkon, Steven High, Clarke, and Stefan Berger to be identified as the authors of the editorial material, and of the authors for their individual chapters, has been asserted in accordance with sections 77 and 78 of the Copyright, Designs and Patents Act 1988.

All rights reserved. No part of this book may be reprinted or reproduced or utilised in any form or by any electronic, mechanical, or other means, now known or hereafter invented, including photocopying and recording, or in any information storage or retrieval system, without permission in writing from the publishers.

Trademark notice: Product or corporate names may be trademarks or registered trademarks, and are used only for identification and explanation without intent to infringe.

British Library Cataloguing-in-Publication Data
A catalogue record for this book is available from the British Library

Library of Congress Cataloging-in-Publication Data
Names: Strangleman, Tim, 1967– editor.
Title: Routledge international handbook of deindustrialization studies / edited by Tim Strangleman, Sherry Lee Linkon, Steven High, Jackie Clarke, Stefan Berger.
Description: Abingdon, Oxon ; New York, NY : Routledge, 2025. | Series: Routledge international handbooks | Includes bibliographical references and index.
Identifiers: LCCN 2024049109 (print) | LCCN 2024049110 (ebook) | ISBN 9781032311524 (hardback) | ISBN 9781032311531 (paperback) | ISBN 9781003308324 (ebook)
Subjects: LCSH: Deindustrialization. | Industries—History.
Classification: LCC HD2329 .R679 2025 (print) | LCC HD2329 (ebook) | DDC 338.09—dc23/eng/20241213
LC record available at https://lccn.loc.gov/2024049109
LC ebook record available at https://lccn.loc.gov/2024049110

ISBN: 978-1-032-31152-4 (hbk)
ISBN: 978-1-032-31153-1 (pbk)
ISBN: 978-1-003-30832-4 (ebk)

DOI: 10.4324/9781003308324

Typeset in Galliard
by Apex CoVantage, LLC

CONTENTS

List of Figures	*ix*
List of Tables	*xi*
List of Contributors	*xii*
Acknowledgments	*xviii*

Introduction	1

PART I
Concepts and Theories — 7

Introduction: Concepts and Theories *Tim Strangleman*	9
1 Theorizing Deindustrialization *Steven High*	18
2 Reflections on the Half-Life *Sherry Lee Linkon*	33
3 Deindustrialization as Global History *Jim Tomlinson*	46
4 Moral Economy and Industrial Culture *Andrew Perchard*	63
5 Racializing Deindustrialization Studies *James Rhodes*	76

Contents

PART II
Political Economy of Deindustrialization   **93**

Introduction: Political Economy of Deindustrialization   95
Steven High

6 Uneven Development, the World-System, and Lumpenization: Bringing Marxian Political Economy Back Into Deindustrialization Studies   102
Fred Burrill and Matthew Penney

7 The Racial Dimensions of (De)industrialization   116
Jason Hackworth

8 The Region as an Analytical Framework for Deindustrialization Studies: Regional Economic Development in Atlantic Canada   126
Lachlan MacKinnon

9 Deindustrialization and Nationhood   138
Ewan Gibbs

10 Challenging and Politicizing Deindustrialization?   154
Marion Fontaine and Xavier Vigna

11 Anticipating Just Transitions: Ecological Crisis and Future Deindustrialization   169
Alice Mah

PART III
Communities, Identities, Affects   **179**

Introduction: Communities, Identities, Affects   181
Jackie Clarke

12 Community, Affect, and Deindustrialization   189
Valerie Walkerdine

13 Deindustrialization and Racialized Communities: A Historical Perspective   202
Christopher Lawson

Contents

14 Class, Gender, and Industrial Structures of Feeling After Socialism: Post-Industrial Lives in the Post-Yugoslav Space 218
Chiara Bonfiglioli

15 Metallic Vitalities: Smog, Steel, and Stigma in a Deindustrial Town 232
Anoop Nayak

16 Deindustrialization, Leisure, and Feeling Communities 248
Julia Wambach

17 "Dad, Why Did You Bring Me to a Gay Steel Mill?": Notes Toward a Queer Study of Deindustrialization 262
Liam Devitt

PART IV
The Critical Cultural Work of Representations 277

Introduction: The Critical Cultural Work of Representations 279
Sherry Lee Linkon

18 Black Spatial Agency and Cultural Justice: Race, Ruins, and Gentrification in Detroit 287
Dora Apel

19 Uncovering the Discovery of the Ruhr: Representations of Deindustrialization in Germany's Former Industrial Heartland 305
Helen Wagner

20 Making the Human Wreckage Visible: Deindustrialization in Kate Beaton's *Ducks* 320
Peter Thompson

21 The Sound of Deindustrialization 335
Giacomo Bottà

22 Garment Workers Through the Lens of Loss: The Long Shadow of Deindustrialization in South Asian Films 347
Piyusha Chatterjee

Contents

PART V
Memories, Memorialization, and the Heritage of Deindustrialization   **361**

Introduction: Memories, Memorialization, and the Heritage
of Deindustrialization   363
Stefan Berger

23 Industrial Memory Landscapes in Urban Planning Processes:
Comparative Perspectives from Germany, Luxembourg,
and France   381
Christa Reicher and Liliana Iuga

24 Memorialization of Industrial Pasts in Post-Socialist Countries   398
Juliane Tomann

25 The Memorialization of Class in Industrial Heritage Initiatives   419
Laurajane Smith

26 Uncovering Gender Tracks: Erasure and Railway Industrial Heritage
Initiatives Across the World   436
Lucy Taksa

27 Industrial Heritage From the South: Decolonial Approaches
to the Social Construction of Heritage and Preservation
Practices   459
Marion Steiner

Conclusion   484
*Tim Strangleman, Sherry Lee Linkon, Steven High,
Jackie Clarke, and Stefan Berger*

Index   486

FIGURES

1.1	Fred Wright, "Full Speed Ahead!" President Nixon allowing runaway plants to drive over a worker on their way to a non-union low-wage area	20
1.2	Fred Wright, "It Looks Like We Are Victims of An International Conspiracy!"	21
1.3	Fred Wright, "Stop Runaway Shops." 25 March 1966	21
1.4	Fred Wright, "Jobs For Export"	26
1.5	Fred Wright, "How Foreign Is 'Foreign' Competition?"	27
1.6	Fred Wright, "Jobs Truck."	28
3.1	Percentage of working population in industry	47
3.2	Sectoral employment in India, 1991–2020	57
9.1	Scottish employment, 1901–2021	144
18.1	Packard Plant with placards spelling *Arbeit macht Frei* on the production line bridge, 2013	289
18.2	Tyree Guyton, The Dotty Wotty House, The Heidelberg Project	291
18.3	Shepard Fairey mural on the right, 2015; How & Nosm on the left, 2016 on One Campus Martius	294
18.4	Dave Jordano, *Michael, Poletown, Detroit, 2011*	297
18.5	Dave Jordano, *Woman Sleeping in a Parking Lot, Eastside, Detroit, 2010*	298
18.6	Isaac Diggs & Edward Hillel, *Sterling Toles #2, 2017*	299
18.7	Isaac Diggs & Edward Hillel, *United Sound Systems Recording Studios*	300
19.1	KVR-campaign motif, 1985	311
19.2	KVR-campaign motif, 1988	312
19.3	KVR-campaign motif, 1998	313
19.4	KVR-campaign motif, 1998	313
19.5	Final publication of the IBA Emscher Park, 1999	314
19.6	Ruhr.2010-campaign motif, 2010	315
20.1 and 20.2	From *Ducks: Two Years in the Oil Sands*	325
23.1	Zollverein: UNESCO World Heritage Site	387
23.2	Zollverein as tourist destination	387
23.3	Blast furnace A and City of Science Belval	390

Figures

23.4	Luxembourg Learning Centre/University Library Belval	391
26.1	National Railway Museum, York, UK, Locomotives	439
26.2	National Railway Museum, York, UK, Rail Clocks	440
26.3	California State Railroad Museum Locomotive, Sacramento USA	441
26.4	California State Railroad Museum Carriage, Sacramento USA	442
26.5	California State Railroad Museum Sacramento USA. Male rail workers	443
26.6	California State Railroad Museum Sacramento USA. Historical sign regarding the laying of tracks	444
26.7	Whangarei Steam Club. Whangarei Museum and Heritage Park, Northland, New Zealand	445
26.8	Railway Memorabilia Museum, Northland, New Zealand	446
26.9	Whangarei rail artifact. Whangarei Museum and Heritage Park, Northland, New Zealand	446
26.10	Whangarei diesel. Whangarei Museum and Heritage Park, Northland, New Zealand	447
26.11	California State Railroad Museum Sacramento USA. Technological artifact	448
27.1	The machine hall of the El Sauce hydropower plant in the outskirts of Valparaíso, Chile	464
27.2	The Historical Museum of Placilla after its expansion	466
27.3	Aerial view of the La Luz water reservoir built 1907–1910 by Berlin companies	467
27.4	Map of Chile around 1810, before the national territory was expanded to the South and the North	468
27.5	Railway heritage on Indigenous lands: San Rosendo railway complex on the confluence of the Biobío and Laja Rivers	469
27.6	The Arpillera "Memories of the Lota Woman": presentation at the international congress in Concepción in October 2023	471
27.7	Women survivors at Bhopal fighting for Justice and Repair in 2022, 38 years after the tragedy	474
27.8	Contamination mapping of soil and waste samples at the former Union Carbide India Ltd. site in Bhopal	475
27.9	Conceptual landscape strategy for the future Bhopal memorial site	476

TABLES

1.1	Industrial employment (as % of total employment)	23
3.1	Structural change in employment in England, 1600–c.1817 (percentage of males)	47
3.2	Sectoral shares of labor in Britain, 1856–1973	50
3.3	A common European pattern: industrial employment peaks	55
9.1	Scottish industrial employment since 1901	144
10.1	Unemployment crisis in France by gender	159
25.1	Heritage sites and numbers of interviews	422

CONTRIBUTORS

Dora Apel is an art historian, cultural critic, and author whose work engages visual culture and politics, including issues of trauma and memory, sex and gender, racial and ethnic oppression, class, war, capitalism, cities, and ruins. She has authored six books as well as numerous articles and book chapters. Her most recent book, *Calling Memory Into Place* (2020), reflects on the role of memory in processing personal and cultural narratives through images, monuments, and stories. Her other books include *Memory Effects: The Holocaust and the Art of Secondary Witnessing* (2002); *Imagery of Lynching: Black Men, White Women, and the Mob* (2004); *Lynching Photographs* (co-authored with Shawn Michelle Smith, 2008); *War Culture and the Contest of Images* (2012); and *Beautiful Terrible Ruins: Detroit and the Anxiety of Decline* (2015). She has published in journals such as *Jacobin*, *Journal of Visual Culture*, *Oxford Art Journal*, *American Quarterly*, and *Mississippi Quarterly* and has chapters in ten edited volumes. She is a professor emerita at Wayne State University.

Chiara Bonfiglioli is Associate Professor of Contemporary History at Ca' Foscari University of Venice, Italy. She is the Principle Investigator of an ERC Consolidator grant titled "Women and Non-Alignment in the Cold War era: Biographical and intersectional perspectives (WO-NAM)," 2023–2028. She previously taught Gender & Women's Studies at University College Cork. She is the author of *Women and Industry in the Balkans: The Rise and Fall of the Yugoslav Textile Sector* (I.B. Tauris, 2019).

Giacomo Bottà is currently a senior researcher at the University of the Arts Helsinki within the Diversity of Music Heritage in Finland project. He holds titles of docent (habilitation, adjunct professorship) in urban studies at the University of Helsinki and in music research at Tampere University. He is a fellow of the Humboldt Foundation and has written extensively about musical urbanism, especially on deindustrializing European cities.

Fred Burrill is a postdoctoral researcher at Cape Breton University, having recently completed his PhD in history at Concordia. He is a Core Affiliate of Concordia's Centre for Oral History and Digital Storytelling and splits his time between Nova Scotia and Montreal.

Contributors

Fred grew up in rural Nova Scotia, in the heart of Eastern Canada's lumber industry, and witnessed the dire consequences of deindustrialization on his community. In Montreal, he has been an active participant in a variety of grassroots struggles against capitalist exploitation, particularly in tenants' movements and in migrant justice organizing. This political work has shaped his commitment to public-facing historical scholarship that challenges power structures and despecializes the pursuit of serious historical inquiry.

Piyusha Chatterjee works on gender and labor from a Global South perspective. She is currently Research Associate with the Deindustrialization and the Politics of Our Time project at the School of Modern Languages and Cultures, University of Glasgow.

Liam Devitt is a writer and public historian based in Tiohti:áke/Montréal, Canada. They are a recent graduate of the MA history program at Concordia University, where they examined how Cape Breton's queer community was affected by deindustrialization as a part of the Deindustrialization and the Politics of Our Time (DéPOT) initiative. Liam's popular work can be found in *Jacobin*, *THIS Magazine*, and *Briarpatch*.

Marion Fontaine is a professor at Sciences Po (Paris) and a researcher at the Centre Norbert Elias. Her early work focused on the relationship between sport and the construction of working-class identity (*Le Racing Club de Lens et les gueules noires*, 2010). Her work now focuses on deindustrialization and the crisis of working-class worlds, particularly with regard to coal miners in France and Europe (*Fin d'un monde ouvrier. Liévin 74*, 2014).

Jason Hackworth is a professor of planning and geography at the University of Toronto. He writes broadly about urban political economy with a focus on North American cities. He is the author of many books and articles about land abandonment in Rust Belt cities. His most recent book is titled *Manufacturing Decline: How Racism and the Conservative Movement Crush the American Rust Belt* (2019).

Liliana Iuga is a research associate at RWTH Aachen University, Institute for Urban Design and European Urbanism. Her research focuses on the history of architecture, urban design, and heritage preservation in twentieth-century Eastern and Central Europe. She is currently working on the topic of residential heritage in Eastern Europe after socialism, as well as on a project exploring the legacy of Soviet nuclear infrastructure and deindustrialization in Romania. She received her PhD in comparative history from the Central European University, Budapest, Hungary (2017), with a thesis on the politics of built heritage and urban design in socialist Romania.

Christopher Lawson is a historian of imperial and post-imperial Britain. His work focuses on the intersection of decolonization, deindustrialization, the transformation of cities, and the rise of 'neo-liberalism' in the mid-to-late twentieth century. He is particularly interested in tracing how structural economic changes interact with preexisting inequalities of class, race, and gender to produce segregation, exclusion, and exploitation. He completed his PhD in history at the University of California, Berkeley, in 2020. He holds degrees from McGill University and the University of Toronto. He lives in Toronto, Ontario.

Lachlan MacKinnon is the Canada research chair (Tier II) in Post-Industrial Communities at Cape Breton University. His recent book *Closing Sysco: Industrial Decline in Atlantic*

Canada's Steel City uses oral history to explore the intersections of political economy, bodily health, and environmental changes wrought by deindustrialization. MacKinnon's research relates to the history of capitalism and deindustrialization, with special focus on environment and ecology, labor and occupational health, oral history, and state policy.

Alice Mah is a professor of sociology at the University of Warwick, UK. She is the author of *Industrial Ruination, Community, and Place* (2012), *Port Cities and Global Legacies* (2014), and *Toxic Truths: Environmental Justice and Citizen Science in a Post-Truth Age* (with Thom Davies, 2020). Her research has been awarded the Leverhulme Prize in Sociology, the SAGE Prize for Innovation and/or Excellence, and the British Sociological Association Philip Abrams Memorial Prize. She is currently writing two books drawing on her European Research Council-funded project 'Toxic Expertise: Environmental Justice and the Global Petrochemical Industry.' For the SSHRC-funded 'Deindustrialization and the Politics of our Time' partnership grant, Alice is contributing to the thematic research initiatives on 'Race and the Populist Politics of Deindustrialization' and 'Deindustrialization and the Environment.'

Anoop Nayak is a professor in social and cultural geography at Newcastle University, UK. His research explores issues of race, class, masculinities, and youth inequalities in deindustrial locations. Anoop is the author of *Race, Place and Globalization: Youth Cultures in a Changing World*; *Gender, Youth and Culture: Global Masculinities and Femininities* (with Professor Mary Jane Kehily); and *Geographical Thought: Thought and Ideas in Human Geography* (with Professor Alex Jeffrey). He is the co-editor of *Thinking Technologies: Young People and the Anthropocene* (2022) and *Social Geographies* (2020) (with the Newcastle Social Geographies Collective).

Matthew Penney is a specialist in postwar Japanese history at Concordia University. His early research focused on war memory, popular culture (especially manga and anime, mass market historical writing, and film), historiography, and nationalism. He is currently writing on the global political economy of deindustrialization, bringing Japan into the conversation within the field.

Andrew Perchard is an honorary research professor at the University of Otago, New Zealand, and a visiting professor at Birkbeck, University of London. He is the author of two monographs, *The Mine Management Professions in the Twentieth-Century Scottish Coal Mining Industry* (EMP, 2007) and *Aluminiumville: Government, Global Business and the Scottish Highlands* (Carnegie, 2012), and co-editor of *Tin and Global Capitalism, 1850–2000: A History of the "Devil's Metal"* (with Mats Ingulstad and Espen Storli) (Routledge, 2014) and *The Deindustrialized World: Confronting Ruination in Postindustrial Places* (with Steven High and Lachlan MacKinnon) (University of British Columbia Press, 2017), as well as contributing to numerous journal articles and chapters in edited collections. Aside from deindustrialization, his research interests lie in business–government–labor relations; occupational and organizational culture; industrial and regional policy and development; natural resource governance; music and class; and environmental and occupational health. Andy is also an editor of *History Workshop Journal*.

Christa Reicher is an architect and urban planner and professor and chair of urban planning and design in the Faculty of Architecture at RWTH Aachen University. Since 2023, she is also the holder of the UNESCO Chair for Cultural Heritage and Urban Development. In 2022, she was awarded the Grand Prize for Building Culture by the Association of German Architects' and Engineers' Associations (DAI). Her research and teaching focuses on urban renewal and district development, urban and landscape design, cultural heritage and transformation, and housing and strategies for urban development. Her numerous publications include *Internationale Bauausstellung Emscher Park: Impulse: lokal, regional, national, international* (2011), *Städtebauliches Entwerfen* (1st edition 2012, 5th edition 2017), and 'Urban development under conditions of deindustrialization. Approaches from the Ruhr Region in Germany' (2022, book chapter).

James Rhodes is a sociologist with affiliations at the University of Manchester and Hiram College in Ohio. He has previously spent time as a visiting scholar at the Center for Working-Class Studies at Youngstown State University. James has a long-standing interest in deindustrialization, particularly in terms of its relationship to place, identity, and inequality. His work focuses on the situated, lived experiences of deindustrialization and related processes such as depopulation and urban decline. Informed by this interest, he has examined far-right politics and explored the conception of the 'left behind' in the North West of England while also examining forms of urban decline and depopulation in the Rust Belt and policies related to urban shrinkage. His work within the context of the Deindustrialization and the Politics of Our Time (DéPOT) project will explore the relationship between deindustrialization, place, and racialized and classed political identities and subjectivities in the American Rust Belt.

Laurajane Smith is a professor of heritage and museum studies at the Centre of Heritage and Museum Studies, Australian National University in Canberra. She is also a fellow of the Society for the Academy of the Social Sciences in Australia, founder of the Association of Critical Heritage Studies, and editor of the *International Journal of Heritage Studies* (since 2009). In 2021, she was the recipient of the European Archaeology Association Heritage Prize, and in 2019 she was awarded a Doctor honoris causa from the University of Antwerp in Belgium. Between 2023 and 2025, she has been a French CNRS Fellow-Ambassador. Together with Gönül Bozoglu, she is the co-editor of the Routledge *Key Issues in Cultural Heritage* series. Among her numerous publications are *Uses of Heritage* (2006), *Emotional Heritage* (2021), and the co-edited volumes *Intangible Heritage* (2009), *Safeguarding Intangible Heritage* (2019), and *Emotion, Affective Practices and the Past in the Present* (2018).

Marion Steiner is an independent researcher affiliated with the University of Chile, director of the ESPI Lab for Critical Industrial Heritage Studies in Valparaíso, and Secretary General of The International Committee for the Conservation of the Industrial Heritage (TICCIH). As a cultural geographer with academic titles from Humboldt University Berlin, University Paris 8, and Bauhaus University Weimar, she has specialized in global industrial heritage interpretation working across continents and at the interface of academia and local communities. Her research focuses on entangled urban history, European imperialism, and emerging decolonial heritage perspectives from the South. Her current project 'Luz, Poder y Progreso. La electrificación urbana alemana de América Latina en su contexto geopolítico y cultural, 1880–1920' is financed by the Chilean Research and Development Agency ANID via its FONDECYT Iniciación program from 2023 to 2026.

Contributors

Lucy Taksa is a professor of management at Deakin University Business School. She has published on the history of working people and management, gendered workplace cultures, and labor, migrant, and gender dimensions of industrial heritage. She chaired the Board of the NSW State Archives (2007–2012), was the secretary and president of the Australian Society for the Study of Labour History (1990–2009), and an editorial board member of the *Journal of Transport History (1997–2015)*. She is on the editorial boards of *Labour History* (since 1993) and the *Journal of Management History* (since 2018).

Peter Thompson is a professor in the department of English at the University of New Brunswick. His research focuses mainly on representations of deindustrialization in contemporary literature and popular culture, with a particular emphasis on the regions of Appalachia and Atlantic Canada. His work has appeared in *Acadiensis, Studies in Canadian Literature*, and *Journal of Appalachian Studies.*

Juliane Tomann is a junior professor for public history at Regensburg University, Germany. Her research interests revolve around performative practices in historical culture as well as deindustrialized spaces and landscapes. She has published journal articles in *The Public Historian, International Public History* and *Docupedia Zeitgeschichte online*. Her books include *The Routledge Handbook of Reenactment Studies* (2020, with Vanessa Agnew and Jonathan Lamb), and *Transcending the Nostalgic: Landscapes of Postindustrial Europe Beyond Representation* (Berghahn Books, 2021, with George S. Jaramillo). She received her PhD from Freie Universität Berlin with a thesis on historical culture in times of structural change after 1989 in Katowice, Poland. This work was awarded the Scientific Award of the Ambassador of Poland in 2015.

Jim Tomlinson is a professor emeritus of economic and social history at the University of Glasgow, having been Bonar Professor of Modern History at Dundee University from 2004 to 2013. He has published widely on the historical political economy of modern Britain, including on postwar reconstruction in *Democratic Socialism and Economic Policy: The Attlee Years 1945–1951.* (Cambridge University Press, 1996). Most recently, he published *Deindustrialisation and the Moral Economy in Scotland Since 1950* (with Jim Phillips and Valerie Wright) (Edinburgh University Press, 2021) and *Managing the Economy, Managing the People: Narratives of British Economic Life From Brexit to Beveridge* (Oxford University Press, 2017). From 2021 to 2023, he had a Leverhulme Major Research Fellowship, and the book from this project, *Churchill and Industrial Britain. Liberalism, Empire and Employment, 1900–1929,* will be published by Bloomsbury Academic in later 2024.

Xavier Vigna is a professor of contemporary history at the University of Paris-Nanterre and a member of the IDHES laboratory. His thesis work explored workers' strikes in France in the wake of May–June 1968 (*L'insubordination ouvrière dans les années 68*, 2007). Following this, he published a survey of 1968 (*Histoire des ouvriers en France au XXe siècle*, 2012) before broadening his research into workers' writings and those devoted to them (*L'espoir et l'effroi. Luttes d'écritures et luttes de classes en France au XXe siècle*, 2016).

Helen Wagner studied history, philosophy, and public history at the Universities of Münster, Berlin, and Amsterdam. She received a PhD from the University of Duisburg-Essen in 2021. After working in the history departments at the Universities of Duisburg-Essen and

Erlangen-Nürnberg, she joined the Team of Industrial Culture at the Ruhr Regional Association in 2023.

Valerie Walkerdine is a distinguished research professor emerita in the School of Social Sciences, Cardiff University, UK. She has worked on issues of subjectivity, gender, and class for many years and on affective and psychosocial research on work, neoliberalism, and deindustrialization for more than 20 years. She is currently working on an affective history of Britain from the postwar period to the present based around fieldwork with the families of a group of working- and middle-class women born in the UK in the 1970s.

Julia Wambach is a researcher at the Center for the History of Emotions at the Max Planck Institute for Human Development Berlin. She is working on the deindustrialization in Germany and France with a special focus on the quest for community and solidarity in two deindustrialized cities, Lens and Gelsenkirchen. In the context of this work, she published a book chapter: 'Feeling Political Through a Football Club: FC Schalke 04, 1904–2020,' in: Ute Frevert et al.: Learning How to Feel Political. Emotions and Institutions since 1789 (London: Palgrave, 2022).

ACKNOWLEDGMENTS

As always, a collection like this incurs many debts along the way. All the team would like to thank the many staff at Routledge for their help and support, especially Chris and Lakshita. We would like to acknowledge the wonderful copy editing undertaken by Halima Bensaid. This handbook emerges out of many discussions at various in-person and online events over the last two decades or more. This field's strength lies in its ability to draw on academic and nonacademic material, insights, and encounters. It rightfully draws on established scholars but also is exciting as newer generation younger scholars' voices are heard. We thank you all.

We gratefully acknowledge the support of the DéPOT (Deindustrialization and the Politics of Our Time) project led by Steven High and funded by Social Sciences and Humanities Research Council (SSHRC) of Canada. This volume received funding for copy editing work undertaken by Halima. More widely, all of the editors are involved in the DéPOT program and gratefully acknowledge how important it has been to this volume.

Tim would like to thank Claudia, Max, Maddy, and Pip for all their love and support.

Sherry would like to thank Tim for creating space here for arts and culture, the contributors to the representations section for their patience and enthusiasm, and John for his never-ending encouragement and support.

INTRODUCTION

Deindustrialization as a field of study emerged in the late 1970s and early 1980s when scholars and activists began to recognize a pattern of industrial job loss over and above 'ordinary' closures and layoffs. In many of the 'developed' countries of the world, traditional industrial manufacturing sectors were experiencing massive downsizing or even systematic eradication. This destructive process united North America, the UK, and Western, Central, and Eastern Europe, but it has also occurred in economies as varied as India, Tanzania, China, and Australia. Scholars studying deindustrialization recognized that its effects went far beyond the immediate economic impact of job loss, generating a host of social, cultural, health, and political challenges for individuals and their families, communities, and nation-states. Since the turn of the millennium, the field has matured and expanded, becoming increasingly interdisciplinary and international. This handbook offers a guide to the range of scholarship and thinking about deindustrialization for those new to the field as well as more established scholars.

Why Deindustrialization Studies?

Scholars have been writing about the process of deindustrialization for over four decades. Early work sought to understand change in the context of the crisis in Fordism and the end of the long postwar boom in 'western' industrial nations. Prosperity for these countries was built around a regime of manufacturing and consumption that was celebrated and seen as open-ended. A strong welfare industrial state could be built on this model buttressed by consensus on the need for a managed economy and full employment. By the 1970s, this consensus was breaking down politically, economically, and socially. The heavy and light industries, which had been the bedrock of the long boom era, were increasingly shedding jobs, and corporations were disinvesting from the industrialized countries of the Global North and setting up facilities in the Global South.

The brunt of deindustrialization in the US, for example, fell on the Industrial Midwest, which saw nearly one in five manufacturing jobs disappear between 1979 and 1986 (Markusen and Carlson, 1989, pp. 30–31). The unemployment rate in Detroit, the US's 'motor city,' climbed from 8.3% in 1978 to 20.3% in 1982. It was even worse in nearby Flint,

DOI: 10.4324/9781003308324-1

which saw its unemployment rate jump from 8.8% to 27.1% (Clark, 1986, p. 129). The impact on industrial workers, their families, and their communities was enormous. Undertaking anthropological research in the former auto-manufacturing town of Kenosha, Wisconsin, Kathryn Marie Dudley describes plant closures as rites of passage where displaced workers were not only "stripped of their workplace identities" but unmasked as middle-class imposters (Dudley, 1994, p. 134). While this pattern repeated in many places, as studies of closings in different locations and industries have shown, recent scholarship has made clear that deindustrialization unfolded unevenly even within the same country.

We see this in parts of the Global South, which is often treated as a single mass with a vague destination point for runaway plants. Yet offshoring is an uneven process, and the economic trajectories of countries vary enormously. Much attention has been given to the rise of the newly industrialized nations on the Pacific Rim such as South Korea and Taiwan, but, since the 1980s, South America has experienced a manufacturing decline similar to what occurred in Europe and North America (Rodrik, 2016, p. 2). Deindustrialization was a strong trend throughout much of the region, with Brazil serving as its poster child, given the loss of 1.7 million industrial jobs between 1988 and 1998. The rate of unionization in Brazil was also cut in half during that terrible decade (Anner, 2008, p. 38). China and India have likewise seen the deindustrialization of older industrial areas such as Harbin and West Bengal respectively, while newly industrialized regions have emerged with the liberalization of trade (see Neethi and Rao, 2023; Xie, 2024).

In part, the purpose of this volume is to chart this process but also to reflect on the historiography around the study of deindustrialization. It raises questions about how scholars attempted to frame these processes conceptually, theoretically, methodologically, and historically. Bluestone and Harrison's *The Deindustrialization of America* was something of a foundational text for the field and is a touchstone drawn on throughout the volume. Bluestone and Harrison argued that the industrial change being witnessed at scale in the 1970s and early 1980s had to be seen as a process that went beyond economics. The consequences of large-scale closure and loss were profound, long-lasting, and ongoing. As important as economics were to the story, they argued, it was also vital to understand deindustrialization socially, geographically, politically, and morally. This process was the consequence and outcome of choices made by corporations and by national, regional, and local politicians faced with globalization and increased international competition.

As this volume shows, deindustrialization can and should be studied in multiple ways and through multiple disciplines. While there have been significant and largely separate threads of scholarship by historians, geographers, and sociologists, the field has been increasingly marked by cross- and interdisciplinary work. One of the distinctive features of this collaboration is how it straddles the arts, humanities, and social sciences. This has led to genuinely inclusive learning, allowing scholars to think in new and imaginative ways about industry and the ideas that attach to it. As social scientists such as sociologists, geographers, and political scientists use and adopt visual and literacy approaches, humanities scholars draw on concepts and theories developed in the human and social sciences. One theme connecting research across disciplines – and running through this volume – is the temporal. Many scholars here consider ideas about history, memory, nostalgia, and the past. We cannot ignore how things came to be, but at the same time, many of the contributions here also examine the crucial role of the past in shaping how individuals, communities, and nations think about the present and their futures. As deindustrialization continues to evolve, it reshapes our understanding of the temporal. In some places such as the UK, the closures of the 1980s may have been met

Introduction

with radical opposition on the left, while in the first three decades of the new millennium deindustrialization is generating social conservatism and divisive politics. This speaks to our own time, but it also calls for deindustrialization scholars to ponder how these ideas and imaginaries are deploying the past to cast the future and its possibilities.

For many of us who have been studying deindustrialization, much of what has unfolded since the 1980s was entirely predictable. If industry disappears from a town, city, or region, it leaves in its wake a whole series of legacies. Some of these are noble and positive – including what some might capture in the phrase an "industrial structure of feeling," often reduced to the phrase a good work ethic. But, too often, these positive traits are swamped by multiple problems: lack of education, poor health (mental and physical), alcohol and drug problems, and housing and transport issues. Politically, deindustrialized places have often felt forgotten and marginalized. Oftentimes, industrial areas that played vital roles in forging regional or national identities now find themselves stigmatized and neglected. Too often, deindustrialized places have had to make the best of their lot, advised to get over their past without being given the capacity or resources to do just that.

French historians Marion Fontaine and Xavier Vigna have recently suggested that deindustrialization represents an especially promising pathway to understanding contemporary societies (Fontaine and Vigna, 2019, p. 3). With the emergence of new currents of national populism – Trump, Brexit, AfD in Germany, the Front National/Rassemblement National in France, and radical politics elsewhere – deindustrialization began to move to the top of the political agenda. Often, progressive parties whose base had been the places now deindustrialized sought to broaden their appeal, moving on to emerging social issues but leaving a political vacuum in their wake. Deindustrialization, like industrialization before, continues to shape and reshape the politics and meanings of class, race, and gender. In many ways, these issues speak to larger questions of what the transition from the previous industrial order is likely to mean, how it is to be handled, and what kind of society we would like to see in the future. One of the biggest challenges to have emerged since the 1970s is the environment, especially the ongoing consequences of a carbon-based industrial society. The idea of just transitions goes to the heart of deindustrialization studies, which has examined transitions that have been far from just. Communities have been left to themselves to 'get over' their industrial pasts, to move on, and forget, and many continue to struggle decades after industrial closures. At the same time, just transitions have to involve more than economic justice. They should also take account of the physical environment, social and moral terrains, and the multiple legacies of an industrial past. Justice for deindustrialized areas need not disrupt us in tackling climate change; indeed, the two are inextricably linked.

The Structure of the Handbook

In the parts and chapters that follow we explore these issues. We have organized the volume into five parts, each with an introduction. We have tried to represent a range of scholars and scholarship to showcase the state of the art of the field in all its richness. Inevitably, there are gaps and absences here. We address some of these in the part introductions and the conclusion to the volume. As in any handbook, what follows can be dipped into selectively or read part by part. Inevitably, some themes and even examples appear multiple times, underscoring the shared knowledge of the field while also highlighting the diversity of approaches.

In *Part I Concepts and Theories*, editor Tim Strangleman provides an overview of definitional challenges of the field, followed by Steven High's discussion of the theoretical underpinnings of deindustrialization studies. High explores the historiography of the field and how it has emerged since the beginning of widespread closures of the 1970s. Sherry Lee Linkon's chapter reflects on how her concept of the half-life of deindustrialization has been taken up but also adapted by others in the field. Economic historian Jim Tomlinson considers how we might think more historically about deindustrialization and how we are now witnessing a contraction in industrial jobs across the globe. In 'Moral Economy and Industrial Culture,' business oral historian Andrew Perchard traces the idea of the moral economy, which has its roots in E. P. Thompson's famous use of the phrase to reveal preindustrial ways of being and understanding. Moral economy is useful in thinking about how deindustrialized communities make sense of past, present, and future. Finally, sociologist James Rhodes looks at questions of race and ethnicity and deindustrialization studies, providing a wide-ranging account of how race has shaped deindustrialization and how deindustrialization has in turn shaped race.

Part II Political Economy of Deindustrialization, edited by Steven High, comprises six chapters on the 'how' and 'why' of the political economy of deindustrialization. It begins with the fiery appeal of Fred Burrill and Matthew Penney for researchers to break out of their national silos and reengage with Marxist theory to study the workings of global capitalism itself. Jason Hackworth then pushes us to consider the ways that race and class play off against each other, pointing to the experience of Black-majority neighborhoods in the US as a case in point. Lachlan MacKinnon considers how a regional development mindset structured the state's early understanding and response to deindustrialization, using the 'have-not region' of Atlantic Canada as an example. Ewan Gibbs challenges, using the Scottish counterexample, the assumption that the economically left behind in deindustrialized areas have always veered toward right-wing populism. Marion Fontaine and Xavier Vigna then interrogate the underlying reasons for working-class resistance or passivity to industrial closures, grounding their analysis in France. Finally, Alice Mah explores the labor movement origins of the 'just transition,' which has become central to organizing around global warming today.

Part III Communities, Identities, Affects, explores further the human implications of deindustrialization with a focus on communities, identities, and affects. After an introduction by Jackie Clarke outlining the salience of these categories for deindustrialization studies, the part opens with a chapter by Valerie Walkerdine. Walkerdine adopts a psychosocial approach, arguing that to understand the full impact of deindustrialization on communities we must attend to its affective and gender implications. Christopher Lawson then offers a transnational historical assessment of the implications of deindustrialization for Black and ethnic minority communities and for community relations, focusing particularly on the US and the UK. Chiara Bonfiglioli's chapter examines the class and gender implications of deindustrialization in the post-socialist context of the former Yugoslavia, identifying a distinctive 'industrial structure of feeling' in the post-Yugoslav space. In doing so, she draws on the concept of structures of feeling first developed by Raymond Williams and introduced to many scholars of deindustrialization through the work of Tim Strangleman (Williams, 1977; Strangleman, 2017; Strangleman, 2012). Julia Wambach turns to the history of emotions and the concept 'feeling communities' to argue for the significance of leisure activities such as football clubs as spaces in which community can be reconstructed in deindustrialized places from Detroit to the Ruhr. A contribution from geographer Anoop Nayak draws on fieldwork in the English town Middlesbrough to demonstrate how place-based stigma attaches to deindustrialized

Introduction

places but also how it can be resisted through local acts of 'rescripting' place. Finally, in a return to questions of gender and sexuality, Liam Devitt asks what a queer study of deindustrialization might look like and sketches some paths for future researchers to follow.

Part IV The Critical Cultural Work of Representations, edited by Sherry Lee Linkon, examines representations of deindustrialization. It opens with a chapter on public art and photography in Detroit, Michigan, a place that has often served as a visual icon of deindustrialization. Art historian Dora Apel argues that Black artists have used community arts projects, public art commissioned as part of redevelopment projects, and photography as tools for Black spatial agency to resist racialized erasure in a slowly gentrifying city. Picking up on Apel's themes of redevelopment and visual representations, historian Helen Wagner traces how community identity campaigns in the German Ruhr used photographs to redefine the region's relationship with the industrial past and imagine a post-industrial future. Turning to music, Giacomo Bottà's chapter, "The Sound of Deindustrialization," argues that while punk did not originate as a response to deindustrialization, it was embraced by musicians in deindustrialized communities in several countries as an expression of the pain, grief, and rage caused by the loss of industrial work and identities. Also, Bottà shows how this music extended the deindustrialization imaginary, providing listeners who had not experienced significant declines a resource for critiquing the broader economic, social, and political changes of the late twentieth and early twenty-first centuries. Literary scholar Peter Thompson considers how Kate Beaton's award-winning graphic memoir *Ducks* captures the multiple tensions and contradictions of a changing Canadian economy. His analysis highlights themes of place, memory, the nature of work, and the environmental impacts of industry while also noting the particular power of the graphic narrative as a form. The final chapter of Part IV, by historian Piyusha Chatterjee, considers the implications of three films about South Asian women garment workers. Although the films focus on an industry that is growing, Chatterjee's analysis highlights how industrial labor and deindustrialization share a common cause: the exploitative engine of capitalism.

Part V Memories, Memorialization, and the Heritage of Deindustrialization on industrial heritage, begins with an opening chapter by Stefan Berger on the heritage of deindustrialization and its links to memory activism. Bringing a range of theoretical perspectives to bear from memory studies and the theory of history, he argues that a global comparison of industrial heritage constructions will have to relate the politics of deindustrialization to diverse memory regimes and forms of nostalgia. This is followed by Christa Reicher and Liliana Iuga's account on how urban planners in the Ruhr, Germany; Belval, Luxembourg; and the Nord-Pas-de-Calais, France have integrated industrial heritage into innovative and constructive forms of urban planning and how a transregional dialogue has fostered these developments. Following on from this West-European perspective, Juliane Tomann analyses the development of industrial heritage in the post-communist states of East-Central and Southeastern Europe tracing a development from neglect to nostalgic forms of remembrance. Lucy Taksa focuses on the global forms of railway heritage to underline how gendered this heritage is and how women have often been excluded from it. Laurajane Smith subsequently deals with the exclusion of working-class perspectives from industrial heritage initiatives focusing on the reception of labor and working-class heritage by visitors to labor museums. Finally, Marion Steiner provides important decolonial perspectives on industrial heritage from the Global South, arguing that the view from the South necessitates a complete reconceptualization of our understandings of industrial heritage.

Reference List

Anner, M. (2008). Meeting the Challenges of Industrial Restructuring: Labor Reform and Enforcement in Latin America. *Latin American Politics and Society*, p. 38.

Clark, G.L. (1986). The Crisis of the Midwest Auto Industry. In Scott, A.J. and Storper, M. (eds.) *Production, Work, Territory: The Geographical Anatomy of Industrial Capitalism*. Boston: Allen and Unwin, p. 129.

Dudley, K.M. (1994). *The End of the Line: Lost Jobs, New Lives in Postindustrial America*. Chicago: University of Chicago Press, p. 134.

Fontaine, M. and Vigna, X. (2019). La désindustrialisation, une histoire en cours. *20&21: Revue d'histoire*, 144, p. 3.

Markusen, A.R. and Carlson, V. (1989). Deindustrialization in the American Midwest: Causes and Responses. In Rodwin, L. and Sazanami, H. (eds.) *Deindustrialization and Regional Economic Transformation: The Experience of the United States*. Boston: Unwin Hyman, pp. 30–31.

Neethi, P. and Rao, Deeksha. (2023). Memory, Identity and Deindustrialization: Reflections from Bygone Mill-Scapes of Bangalore, India. *Development and Change*, 54(6).

Rodrik, D. (2016). Premature Deindustrialization. *Journal of Economic Growth*, 21, p. 2.

Strangleman, T. (2012). Work Identity in Crisis? Rethinking the Problem of Attachment and Loss at Work. *Sociology*, 46(3), pp. 411–425. https://doi.org/10.1177/0038038511422585

Strangleman, T. (2017). Deindustrialisation and the Historical Sociological Imagination: Making Sense of Work and Industrial Change. *Sociology*, 51(2), pp. 466–482. https://doi.org/10.1177/0038038515622906

Williams, R. (1977). *Marxism and Literature*. Oxford and New York: Oxford University Press, pp. 131–132.

Xie, W. (2024). Generations at the Crossroads: Biographical Experience and Working-Class Politics in China. *Labor History*, 65(3), pp. 337–351.

PART I

Concepts and Theories

INTRODUCTION
Concepts and Theories

Tim Strangleman

Introduction

At the beginning of the now accepted 'classic' period of deindustrialization, from the late 1970s onward, it was difficult to both think of this area as an academic field and, arguably, define what we meant by deindustrialization. One of the major contributions that deindustrialization studies can make as a field is in terms of conceptual definition. This part introduction shows how the concept of deindustrialization changes across time and space as scholars, activists, and politicians try to describe a complex economic and social process evolving around them. It serves also to examine how more abstract ideas emerge and help to shape an ongoing, developing discussion in a field. Finally, this short introduction discusses the shortcomings and potential future developments in the fields through a reflection on the chapters that follow.

Defining Deindustrialization

As soon as one looks in detail at any concept or idea, its complexity becomes apparent. This is perhaps especially true of deindustrialization. To begin, what do we mean by the concept? For many years I taught my sociology students the topic of deindustrialization as part of a much larger discussion of work and employment. In their *Dictionary of Sociology*, Jary and Jary define deindustrialization as "the process in which a previously industrialized or industrializing economy, or society, or region, reverts partly or wholly to a preindustrialized form" (Jary and Jary, 1991, p. 149).

In an attempt to historicize my students' understanding I tried to show them how work and industry had emerged, evolved, changed, and declined across years, decades, and even millennia. Separating out decline and closure from outright loss is complex and confusing. The question really is this: when was deindustrialization? Or, perhaps, what is distinct about deindustrialization as opposed to, say, a case of closure(s) or downsizing(s)? The loss of an individual place of work, however devastating for the individuals and communities involved, is not necessarily deindustrialization. It is only really when we can see individual cases as part of a wider trend or pattern that we can fully grasp the phenomenon.

DOI: 10.4324/9781003308324-3

Marx and Engels famously summed up the ephemeral nature of capitalist society in their *Communist Manifesto* with the phrase "All that is solid melts into air," observing that capitalism involved the

[c]onstant revolutionizing of production, uninterrupted disturbance of all social conditions, everlasting uncertainty and agitation distinguish the bourgeois epoch from earlier ones. All fixed, fast-frozen relations, with their train of ancient and venerable prejudices and opinions are swept away, all new-formed ones become antiquated before they can ossify.

(Marx and Engels, 1967)

For Marx and Engels then, deindustrialization was part and parcel of the earliest stages of modernity itself, not something that would first occur in the late twentieth century. Change, decline, eradication, and erasure were the fundamentals of capitalism itself, a constant process of emergence, obsolescence, and reinvention. Over 60 years ago, social historian E. P. Thompson completed what was to become his classic *The Making of The English Working Class* (Thompson, 1963). Thompson argued that between 1780 and the early 1830s, a significant class consciousness emerged among English working people as a result of proto and then early industrialization. Thompson's book attempted to piece together fragmentary evidence left by this emerging working class in contemporary England; a mixture of cultural and political writings, of observations and other ephemera including poetry and song. In his famous *Preface* to *The Making*, he writes:

I am seeking to rescue the poor stockinger, the Luddite cropper, the obsolete hand-loom weaver, the "utopian" artisan, and even the deluded follower of Joanna Southcott, from the enormous condescension of posterity. Their crafts and traditions may have been dying. Their hostility to the new industrialism may have been backward-looking. Their communitarian ideals may have been fantasies. Their insurrectionary conspiracies may have been foolhardy. But they lived through these times of acute social disturbance, and we did not. Their aspirations were valid in terms of their own experience: and, if they were casualties of history, they remain, condemned in their own lives, as casualties.

(Thompson, 1963, p. 12)

Thompson alerts us to the obvious fact that industrialization itself changed or destroyed earlier forms of industry and preexisting technology and, with it, its cultures, communities, and practices. Just as technology can be understood as a continuum from AI going back, in extremis, to a simple stone age axe, then we have to conceive of deindustrialization as having occurred across the span of human history as new technologies and organization of production and consumption emerge, adapt, ossify, and die. The Roman world, and its decline, is full of examples of the stimulation of industries and their decline, often as a result of imperial arrival or withdrawal. Classical historian Robin Fleming, for instance, uses the term deindustrialization to describe fifth-century post-Roman Britain (Fleming, 2010, p. 9).

These issues illustrate how questions of chronology and history are an important in defining and locating in time deindustrialization. We are forced then to confront deindustrialization's conceptual slipperiness; what do we mean by the phrase, when did deindustrialization begin, and how is it different from industrial change more widely? To these questions, we could add how useful it is if it is attached to so many instances of industrial change. Tomlinson's

Introduction

chapter (Chapter 3) addresses many of these issues from an international perspective in this part. In particular, Tomlinson makes the distinction between deindustrialization as in the loss of industry and deindustrialization in the sense of a global loss of industrial jobs in totality.

To take the issue of chronology first, the classic era of deindustrialization is assumed to date from the mid-to-late 1970s and the widespread shutdowns of basic heavy industry in the US and Europe. But as soon as that marker is placed, we begin to see far earlier examples of this trend. In the UK, we could see closures occurring in the mining industry in the 1960s or earlier during the interwar depression as an era of widespread industrial loss (Linehan, 2003). In the US economics historians have identified these processes occurring from the Second World War and before that during the Great Depression. Koistinen's *Confronting Decline*, for example, is a historical account of deindustrialization on the Eastern seaboard of the US, although one that again casts back much further than the 1970s to capture evidence of this trend (Koistinen, 2013). Koistinen studies the New England textile industry arguing that the process of industrial retrenchment began during the 1920s, as mills in the North-east states came under intense competition from the newly industrializing South, driven by newer technology, low wages, and anti-union politics. Thus, the relatively high wages of the North were progressively undermined through the 1920s and the Depression era of the 1930s. Koistinen suggests that the first signs of this structural weakness of the sector in New England were detected as early as the 1890s, which brought the response of investment in textile schools to train workers and especially managers in improved industrial techniques (Koistinen, 2013). In another example, Johnson's book on the woolen textile manufacture in the Languedoc region of France argues for the use of that phrase in the nineteenth century to describe industrial eclipse (Johnson, 1995).

In its modern meaning, deindustrialization as a term can be dated from postwar planning undertaken by the allies during the latter stages of the Second World War. Serious consideration was given to the complete eradication of industry in postwar Germany as a way of permanently preventing the rise of a militaristic state once again. The plan involved Germany reverting to a wholly agrarian economy. While there was some forced dismantling of German industry by the victors, especially the Soviets, the plan was quickly eclipsed by the emergence of the Cold War (Gareau, 1961; Tøllefsen, 2016).

It is now nearly four decades since what has come to be described as the modern process of deindustrialization began. The most important early academic portrayal of the process was the seminal *The Deindustrialization of America* by Bluestone and Harrison, where they defined deindustrialization as

> a widespread, systematic disinvestment in the nation's basic productive capacity. Controversial as it may be, the essential problem with the U.S. economy can be traced to the way capital – in the forms of financial resources and of real plant and equipment – has been diverted from productive investment in our basic national industries into unproductive speculation, mergers and acquisitions, and foreign investment.
>
> *(Bluestone and Harrison, 1982, p. 6)*

As High points out in the upcoming chapter, the phrase had been used in academic circles in the 1970s and 1980s in the UK to try to label emerging trends in the economies of the West. There were various reasons for this. One stimulus came from futurologists attempting to think about how industrial economies would move further toward the tertiary economy away from manufacturing. Harvard sociologist Daniel Bell, for example, wrote in

1973 *The Coming of the Post-Industrial Society*, while slightly later Krishan Kumar published his *Prophecy and Progress: The Sociology of the Industrial and Post-Industrial Society*. On the whole, these accounts tended to adopt a positive reading of this shift (Bell, 1973; Kumar, 1978). Others, however, were more pessimistic in their outlook and sought the tools to explain trends that captured what was occurring at the time. In the UK, sociologists such as Jay Gershuny and Ray Pahl's writings are a good illustration of sensemaking in the midst of change. In his 1978 book *After Industrial Society*, Gershuny suggested a retreat for some former industrial workers into self-provisioning (Gershuny, 1978). Pahl's *Divisions of Labour* is a really fascinating account of industrial and deindustrializing society seen through the lens of his extensive research on the relatively isolated Isle of Sheppey, off the North Kent coast (Pahl, 1984). Pahl referred to Sheppey as his post-industrial laboratory. As I have written elsewhere, Pahl understood the variety and complexity of the deindustrial transition, and his work deserves greater attention for that early insight (Strangleman, 2017a). Gershuny and Pahl, along with other researchers, recognized something more profound was happening than the simply working out of the economic cycle.

Deindustrialization as a term itself was contentious and controversial for a number of reasons during the 1970s and 1980s. Deindustrialization, as a label, is almost by definition political, as to use it in some cases is to accept the permanent loss of industry. This acceptance brings with it the logical position that industries which close, or are left to whither on the vine, are therefore not worth subsidizing or restructuring. Many of the closures of the 1980s were in part due to market-driven philosophies of the Conservatives in the UK under Margaret Thatcher and in the US as part of the Reagan era. Job loss and plant, even industry closure was, for them, a necessary and inevitable part of market logic – however painful. Whatever the rights and wrongs of the policies of industrial and economic restructuring at this time, many on the left – community or union activists – hoped to resist job loss and avoided using the term deindustrialization (see Bensman and Lynch, 1987). As has been noted often in this volume, early academic research into the process tended to focus, completely understandably, on specific struggles over individual plant closures. Early studies were often engaged in what Cowie and Heathcott describe as the "body count," where the numbers of laid-off workers were compiled while others attempted to record the struggle over closure and resistance to it (Cowie and Heathcott, 2003). Both of these approaches had their value. We could also see a long and continuing tradition of monograph studies of single plants and their closure, which I think was a necessary part of the emergence of the field of deindustrialization. In telling multiple stories of decline and closing, academics and journalists produced the first version of the modern story of deindustrialization. In itself we could see a powerful moral argument informing these narratives, an aspect of which Perchard elaborates on in this part.[1] Perchard's contribution (Chapter 4) illustrates how ideas of moral economy have developed through preindustrial, industrial, and then in to deindustrial accounts of work. We see that on both sides of industry, and indeed in the political realm, morality is a powerful way in which to understand the framing and reception of closures and industrial loss.

The Creation of a Field

From the late 1990s, scholars in a number of disciplines started to stand back from the immediacy of the story in front of them to identify patterns, attempting to construct a language that might capture the full complexity of this process of deindustrialization. One of

Introduction

the features in deindustrialization literature was an attempt to provide just such a synthetic account of the process with historical and comparative techniques, often deploying inter- and multidisciplinary techniques (High, 2013; Cowie and Heathcott, 2003; Strangleman and Rhodes, 2014; Strangleman, Rhodes, and Linkon, 2013; Altena and Van der Linden, 2002). Each of the contributions in this part poses wider, broader questions about the meaning and value of the term deindustrialization and the longer-term consequences of such industrial upheaval. Vital to this trend was how this questioning of the meaning of deindustrialization was in turn casting new light on older industrial culture itself, prompting questions about environment, economy, social relations, social divisions, class, gender, race, and the meaning of work. The most important of these synthesizing accounts was Cowie and Heathcott's *Beyond the Ruins*, a collection of studies prefaced with an important reflective editorial introduction, 'The Meanings of Deindustrialization.' Cowie and Heathcott used their introduction to, in their words, "move the terms of the discussion 'beyond the ruins'" (Cowie and Heathcott, 2003, p. 1). While they made clear their purpose was not to dismiss the important testimonies from workers caught in the midst of plant shutdowns, they instead argued that

> the time is right to widen the scope of the discussion beyond prototypical plant shutdowns, the immediate politics of employment policy, the tales of victimization, or the swell of industrial nostalgia. Rather, our goal is to rethink the chronology, memory, spatial relations, culture and politics of what we have come to call "deindustrialization."
>
> *(Cowie and Heathcott, 2003, p. 1–2)*

Cowie and Heathcott's introduction to *Beyond the Ruins* has been conceptually and theoretically very important for the emerging field. It is at once sensitive to empirical evidence – the importance of detailed study of individual closures – while simultaneously recognizing the weakness and limitations inherent in such accounts. As such it builds on Bluestone and Harrison's *The Deindustrialization of America* in its insistence on the bigger picture while opening up still further the breadth of material upon which one might study industrial change (Bluestone and Harrison, 1982). For this scholar, the liberating tendency in deindustrialization studies is in its openness to multi and interdisciplinary dialogue. Speaking personally, one of the reasons I was attracted to this field was that cross-/inter and multidisciplinary scholarship was not unusual but rather the norm. This disciplinary mixing is also true of another relatively new of field of Working-Class Studies, where, at least initially, deindustrialization was one of the main foci of interest. Many of us who attended the Working-Class Studies conferences of the late 1990s onward grew used to hearing from literary scholars and poets as much as from social and political scientists. For me, this was liberating from a rather stale set of debates within UK work sociology/ study which were dominated by labor process theorists who saw discussions of "culture," "identity," and meaning as imagined diversions from the class struggle (Fazio, Launius, and Strangleman, 2021).

The timing of this conceptual and theoretical maturing of the field was no accident. After two decades there was enough quantitative and qualitative evidence to start drawing out themes and trends. There was a sense that while the process was ongoing, patterns of response can be discerned in the round. There is also the fact of a generation of scholars who had been socialized into an era where there had been a consistent decline in industry, where

Fordism with all that entailed had been in decades-long crisis. There was then fertile ground in that a cohort of scholars and successive ones were open to novel approaches to these issues and new ways of interrogating them.

Conceptually, one of the most important and fruitful developments within the field of deindustrialization studies has been Sherry Lee Linkon's idea of the half-life of deindustrialization. Linkon explores in this part (Chapter 2) how the concept developed out of her thinking about various strands of deindustrial literature and fictional writing. There are a number of things to note about the half-life idea. Linkon's 2018 landmark book, *The Half-Life of Deindustrialization: Working-Class Writing About Economic Restructuring,* has as its focus creative, mostly fictional, responses to deindustrialization (Linkon, 2018). As readers will see, not only from this part but across the collection, in a relatively short space of time, Linkon's work has become a conceptual touchstone for scholars in the field. Linkon notes her ideas have been refined precisely because, as a literary scholar, she has been in dialogue with social science scholars, as well as those in arts and humanities closer to her own field. This cross-fertilization has been crucial to both the origin of the idea and its widespread adoption. Its success, I believe, lies in how it opens up an abstract conceptual and theoretical space for thinking about processes of industrial change; of different experiences of that change across distinct generations, places, regions, countries, and industry. Like all the best abstractions, it allows other scholars to populate the model with their own ideas and compare and contrast their own cases with others. So, for example, how one experiences loss in an isolated former company town in North America will be different from displaced workers in more urban environments in Europe and so on. However, the power of the half-life is that often those displaced workers share more in common with other similar workers elsewhere in the world. Further, the long-term effects of deindustrialization are often felt just as keenly by subsequent generations. In essence, then the half-life underpins and describes processes which are shared.

There is perhaps another sense of value to the half-life: the temporal aspects it opens up. On one level it describes processes that have happened. We could talk of the half-life of coal communities in the UK or steel communities in Ohio, USA. We can track the initial closure process and the subsequent remedial attempts by local economic development and job creation agencies. We can examine community response and generational agency and reflection. We can use the half-life as a historical probe or deploy it in real time as these events unfold. But the half-life can also be used as a policy tool, as a piece of futurology where the threat of closure hanging over a plant might be made sense of by showing the likely challenges such communities might face if deindustrialization unfolds. The policy value then of the concept is high in the immediate confrontation of the problems of a displaced workforce, but perhaps more recently we have come to see its value in evidentially underpinning responses to the challenges of 'just' transitions – away from polluting carbon economies. The half-life then allows us to think through new policy challenges.[2]

In my own work, I have seen the value of the concept of the half-life in a number of ways, and it has helped me develop my thinking no end. One way we can use it is in thinking historically about change. This can be as simple as retrospectively looking at how previous instances of deindustrialization can be reviewed through the prism of the half-life. I have used it in rethinking the period of industrialization itself, as it allows us to understand how preindustrial cultures themselves folded into industrial ones (Strangleman, 2017b; Strangleman, 2022). As E. P. Thompson recognized, in his case, the English working class were present at their

Introduction

own birth, by which he meant they responded to the process of industrialization with a set of morals, ethics, and intellectual ideas formed from preindustrial ways of life and being. In the same way that industrial culture doesn't just disappear with plant closure, cultures, norms, and values have their own half-life and trajectory; they display what Raymond Williams would describe as a residual quality, continuing to structure ways of being – a half-life by another name (Williams, 1977). Again, Perchard's chapter here explores many of these points.

Thinking Theoretically About the Future of Deindustrialization Studies

The power of the theoretical and conceptual approaches to the study of deindustrialization are, I hope, by now obvious. They facilitate more abstract critical thinking. They allow us to compare and contrast different instances of the same phenomenon. Theoretical and conceptual approaches also let us think about absence, what is not currently being studied, or included in mainstream thinking. One of the long-standing criticisms of the field of Working-Class Studies is that it marginalizes race and ethnicity. While this argument has some merit for our purposes, here it is useful to think about how deindustrialization studies might equally be race/ethnicity blind. There are two components here. One is that historically the study of deindustrialization has emerged and matured in the Global North. The second feature is that the assumption is often that deindustrialization is something associated with white male workers. As James Rhodes's chapter (Chapter 5) highlights, this second critique is unfair and that when we add race and ethnicity into the unfolding story of deindustrialization we come away with a far more complex, contradictory, and richer picture. Again, here the conceptual importance of the half-life comes to the fore in being able to see the way race and ethnicity are implicated in industrial areas and the process of decline and eventual closure. More abstract ideas about deindustrialization have also helped to build a distinct field of study and with it shared literatures and understanding.

The strength of deindustrialization studies then is the way it combines theory and conceptualisation with empirically rich material. Part by choice and part by accident, the field has grown up as a genuinely inter and cross-disciplinary one. This is true in terms of empirical material, its methods, and also in its choice and deployment of conceptual ideas. The attraction for many scholars working in the field is how license is given to social science to borrow ideas and concepts from the humanities and arts and vice versa. A feature of the field is that this borrowing goes on to stimulate new ways of seeing the unfolding process of deindustrialization. The power here is the way in turn we think about how artistic and cultural reflections and manifestations shape and structure responses to change and how these in turn help shape how we might think about policy response to change.

In my own work, I have often thought of deindustrialization as providing what sociologists call a breaching experiment – where a change from the norm goes to highlight the everyday, taken for granted in life. Deindustrialization can be conceived as a gigantic breaching experiment, working simultaneously at multiple levels. It shows us how individuals, their families, and communities react to change and think about past, present, and future. It allows us to look at these reactions at a regional level as well as at the level of the nation state. Deindustrialization then makes us rethink and evaluate what must happen in the immediate future but also makes us cast a critical eye on what went before – what the experience of industrialization was. The power of the field then is that in looking at something in the past, we are also always looking to the future, asking, what next?

Notes

1 For an interesting thematic attempt to pull together a range of material on industrial change, see Sovacool, B.K., Iskandarova, M. and Hall, J. (2023). Industrializing Theories: A Thematic Analysis of Conceptual Frameworks and Typologies for Industrial Sociotechnical Change in a Low-Carbon Future. *Energy Research & Social Science*, 97, p. 102954.
2 For a discussion on futurology, work, and deindustrialization, see Strangleman, T. (2023). Sociological Futures and the Importance of the Past. *Sociology*, 57(2); Strangleman, T., (2024). The Future of Work: A History. In MacLeavy, J. and Pitts, F.H. (eds.) *Routledge Handbook for the Future of Work*. Abingdon: Routledge.

Reference List

Altena, B. and Van der Linden, M. (2002). Preface. *International Review of Social History*, 47, pp. 1–2.

Bell, D. (1973). *The Coming of the Post-Industrial Society: A Venture in Social Forecasting*. Penguin Books.

Bensman, D. and Lynch, R. (1987). *Rusted Dreams: Hard Times in a Steel Community*. McGraw Hill.

Bluestone, B. and Harrison, B. (1982). *The Deindustrialization of America: Plant Closing, Community Abandonment, and the Dismantling of Basic Industry*. Basic Books, p. 6.

Cowie, J. and Heathcott, J. (eds.). (2003). *Beyond the Ruins: The Meanings of Deindustrialisation*. Cornell University Press.

Fazio, M., Launius, C. and Strangleman, T. (eds.). (2021). *Routledge International Handbook of Working-Class Studies*. Routledge.

Fleming, R. (2010). *Britain After Rome: The Fall and Rise 400 to 1070*. Penguin Books, p. 9.

Gareau, F.H. (1961). Morgenthau's Plan for Industrial Disarmament in Germany. *Western Political Quarterly*, 14(2), pp. 517–534.

Gershuny, J. (1978). *After Industrial Society: The Emerging Self-Service Economy*. MacMillan.

High, S. (2013). 'The Wounds of Class': A Historiographical Reflection on the Study of Deindustrialization 1973–2013. *History Compass*, 11(11), pp. 994–1007.

Jary, D. and Jary, J. (1991). *Collins Dictionary of Sociology*. Harper Collins, p. 149.

Johnson, C.H. (1995). *The Life and Death of Industrial Languedoc 1700–1920*. Oxford University Press.

Koistinen, D. (2013). *Confronting Decline: The Political Economy of Deindustrialization in Twentieth-Century New England*. University Press of Florida.

Kumar, K. (1978). *Prophecy and Progress: The Sociology of the Industrial and Post-Industrial Society*. Penguin Books.

Linehan, D. (2003). Regional Survey and the Economic Geographies of Britain 1930–1939. *Transactions of the Institute of British Geographers, New Series*, 28(1), pp. 96–122.

Linkon, S. (2018). *The Half-Life of Deindustrialization: Working-Class Writing about Economic Restructuring*. Michigan University Press.

Marx, K. and Engels, F. (1967). *The Communist Party Manifesto*. Penguin Books.

Pahl, R. (1984). *Divisions of Labour*. Blackwell.

Strangleman, T. (2017a). Portrait of a Deindustrialising Island. In Crow, G. and Ellis, J. (eds.) *Revisiting Divisions of Labour: The Impacts and Legacies of a Modern Sociological Classic*. Manchester University Press.

Strangleman, T. (2017b). Deindustrialization and the Historical Sociological Imagination: Making Sense of Work and Industrial Change. *Sociology*, 51(2), pp. 466–482.

Strangleman, T. (2022). Contextualising the Coalfields: Mapping the Socio-Economic and Cultural Loss of the Coal Industry. In Simmons, R. and Simpson, K. (eds.) *Education, Work and Social Change in Britain's Former Coalfield Communities: The Ghost of Coal*. Palgrave.

Strangleman, T. and Rhodes, J. (2014). The 'New' Sociology of Deindustrialisation? Understanding Industrial Change. *Sociology Compass*, 8(4), pp. 411–421.

Strangleman, T., Rhodes, J. and Linkon, S. (2013). Introduction to Crumbling Cultures: Deindustrialisation, Class and Memory. *International Labor and Working-Class History*, 84, pp. 7–22.

Introduction

Thompson, E.P. (1963). *The Making of the English Working Class*. Penguin Books.
Tøllefsen, T.O. (2016). *The British-German Fight over Dismantling the Removal of Industrial Plants as Reparations and its Political Repercussions*. Unpublished PhD Thesis. European University Institute.
Williams, R. (1977). *Marxism and Literature*. Oxford University Press.

1

THEORIZING DEINDUSTRIALIZATION

Steven High

The sweeping economic changes of the 1970s and 1980s, which saw millions of factory workers lose their jobs to industrial closures, and the crashing end of the postwar boom, demanded that we come up with a new vocabulary for understanding what was happening around us. As Stuart Hall once wrote,

> Ruling or dominant conceptions of the world do not directly prescribe the mental content of the illusions that supposedly fill the heads of the dominant classes. But the circle of dominant ideas does accumulate the symbolic power to map or classify the world for others. . . . It becomes the horizon of the taken-for-granted: what the world is and how it works, for all practical purposes.[1]

The evolutionary theory that the most advanced capitalist economies of Western Europe and North America were transitioning to a new post-industrial stage of human development was formulated in a series of articles published by sociologist Daniel Bell in the late 1960s and early 1970s.[2] The capstone was the publication of Bell's *The Coming of Postindustrial Society* in 1973. In this theoretical framework, the structural violence being inflicted on working-class communities could be explained away as a natural and necessary step forward in human progress. One could no more resist the post-industrial revolution than one could the industrial or agricultural revolutions before it.[3] We all know what happened to the Luddites, a movement of English craft workers who destroyed the industrial machinery that were replacing them in the early nineteenth century: their opposition to economic change has lived on as a scornful term for those misguided or backwards enough to oppose new technologies and new ways of working.[4] Postindustrialism, sometimes under the guise of the knowledge economy or creative class, is now firmly coupled with the wider meritocratic idea that one's worth can be measured by professional credentials or the university that one attended. But the post-industrial viewpoint has always been contested.

Forged in the fires of political struggle, the deindustrialization idea provided an alternative reading of these catastrophic changes. I have written elsewhere about the radical origins of deindustrialization studies in North America, suffice it to say here that the earliest articulation of the deindustrialization thesis in Canada (1973) and the US (1982) were in books

DOI: 10.4324/9781003308324-4

generated by left-wing and progressive movements against mine, mill, and factory closures.[5] New concepts do not simply get invented by great men and women out of thin air, though this is often the conceit of intellectual history, but also flow out of collective action and the political need for an alternative interpretative framework to sustain and legitimate resistance. The concepts we use are thus an integral part of the histories we study. British literary scholar Raymond Williams found in such keywords "a history and complexity of meanings; conscious changes, or consciously different uses; innovation, obsolescence, specialization, extension, overlap, transfer; or changes which are masked by a nominal continuity so that words seem to have been there for centuries."[6] They "typically carry unspoken assumptions and connotations that can powerfully influence the discourses they permeate."[7] These incisive observations ring true to me.

"What the post-industrialists have ignored or played down is the changing spatial division of labor," political economists Barry Bluestone and Bennett Harrison argued in 1980.[8] The lowering of tariff walls with the Kennedy and Tokyo rounds of the General Agreement on Tariffs and Trade (GATT) led to the radical restructuring of the international division of labor. Manufacturing industries quickly moved the most labor-intensive work offshore to lower wage areas of Latin America and Asia. This represented a geographic extension of a long-term trend within nation-states, as industries fled unions to more rural or remote regions. Runaway shops and capital flight are therefore at the core of the conceptualization of deindustrialization, even if factories close for other reasons as well. Neighborhoods, towns, and regions were hollowed out and left behind by departing manufacturers intent on maximizing profits and ridding themselves of bothersome trade unions. As Jefferson Cowie wrote in his classic study of RCA's history of shifting television production from one town to the next: the "[c]ommand of spatial relations, therefore, becomes a crucial weapon in management's arsenal."[9] It is a story as old as industrial capitalism itself.

In the US context, with which I am most familiar, the pressing problem of the interregional 'runaway plant,' emerged in the 1920s in the female-dominated clothing and garment sectors, expanded to the textile and electrical industries in the 1950s, and then to auto-parts, tires, and other industries that employed mainly men thereafter. What all of these industrial sectors had in common was the fact that they were labor-intensive, with relatively modest capital investments and were therefore more apt to move. The 1947 Taft-Hartley Act enabled some jurisdictions in the US, especially in the South, to declare themselves 'right to work' states, making it considerably harder for trade unions to establish themselves there. By the 1960s and 1970s, runaway plants were increasingly crossing international borders and oceans in search of low-waged and unorganized workers (see Figure 1.1). This longer history of employers weaponizing geography had a profound influence on the conceptualization of deindustrialization in North America, where laissez-faire savage capitalism reigned supreme and few legal or statutory limitations infringed on management rights.

British Marxist geographer Doreen Massey's *Spatial Division of Labour* (1984) remains essential reading in deindustrialization studies. Geography, she writes is "fundamental to understanding an economy and a society," and with it "spatial inequality."[11] She makes the case that "social and spatial changes were interwoven," and as such we need to recognize the importance of "spatial restructuring."[12] The restructuring of the international division of labor therefore has had profound consequences and reverberates down to the local level. Indeed, "[a] country's internal economic geography reflects its place in the international political economy, the international division of labour."[13]

19

Figure 1.1 Fred Wright, "Full Speed Ahead!" President Nixon allowing runaway plants to drive over a worker on their way to a non-union low-wage area.[10] (Copyright: Wright, UE13.1.0389)

In Fred Wright's cartoons we see the graphic history of the US trade union movement's struggle against runaway plants and capital flight. Employed by the left-wing United Electrical, Radio and Machine Workers of America (UE) from 1949 to 1984, Fred Wright drew cartoons that appeared regularly in the *UE News*, in the newsletters of local unions, on pamphlets, posters, and picket signs, as well as being widely syndicated through the Federated Press.[14] Wright is said to have "reinvented the labor cartoon," as he broke with the old "symbolic muscular giant" to represent the working class and depicted instead the "average Joe who took the punishment without being broken, going on day after day, as in real life."[15] I have included several of his cartoons here, as they help us visualize the centrality of capital flight in the making of the deindustrialization idea (see Figures 1.2 and 1.3). What follows is not a Foucaultian genealogy of the concept but rather an effort to historicize and learn from its emergence in struggle.

Tentative Beginnings in Europe

Starting in the 1960s, we begin to see passing references to deindustrialization in different countries. For some, deindustrialization offered a useful "short form for the serious structural problem in the economy" and signaled the sheer enormity of the crisis unfolding in working-class communities.[17] As the geographies of economic rise and decline under global capitalism are uneven, as are governmental responses to the social dislocation that results, the

Figure 1.2 Fred Wright, "It Looks Like We Are Victims of An International Conspiracy!"[16] (Copyright: Wright, UE13.1.1350)

Figure 1.3 Fred Wright, "Stop Runaway Shops."[26] 25 March 1966. (Copyright: Wright, UE13.8.0016)

conceptualization of the problem differed to varying degrees from one national or linguistic context to another.[18] As historians Stefan Berger and Paul Pickering put it, "the clock of deindustrialization ticked differently in each country/region."[19] In Germany, for example, the language of deindustrialization has largely failed to take hold due to the degree to which industrial closures, before German unification at least, was successfully managed. There, the dominant term was "strukturwandel," roughly translated as restructuring, which better reflected the predominant experience with industrial decline.[20] The privatizations and mass industrial closures in the East that followed German unification is another matter entirely, and we see the political ramifications of this today in the rise of the populist right there.

A similar pattern could be seen in Italy, which was slower to deindustrialize than elsewhere and where the state was compelled by a militant trade union movement to soften the social blow on those displaced. Even trade unions, historian Gilda Zazzara notes, have "long contributed to the failure to legitimise the idea of an 'Italian deindustrialisation'," as they associated the term with political and economic defeat.[21] This strong stance began to change only in the 2000s as industrial closures accelerated, government supports for workers were rolled back, and right-wing populism took hold in former bastions of the Italian Communist Party or the center-left.[22]

Industrial decline was far steeper in France. Most agree that "désindustrialisation" first appeared in French in the 1963 book *Villes et Campagnes en Bas-Languedoc* by geographer Raymond Dugrand, but the term did not begin to take hold until well after the 1989 publication of Elie Cohen's *L'Etat brancardier. Politiques du déclin industriel*.[23] Like Germany, industrial decline in key sectors such as state-owned coal mining was extensively managed to soften the blow, deferring the economic price of industrial closures to the next generation. Of course, coal mining employed men almost exclusively, other female-dominated industries such as clothing and textile did not receive the same special treatment. As a result, deindustrialization entered everyday language in France only in the early 2000s with growing public concern over factory closures. According to historian Jean-Claude Daumas, "it was also at this moment that the government recognized the deterioration of French industry and the necessity of restoring a strong industrial base."[24] Before then, the language of industrial decline was mainly expressed in the technical terms of 'mutations industrielles' and 'reconversion,' or, more generally, as the more critical 'délocalisation.' The last of these keywords articulated the bitter trade union struggle against capital mobility on par with the runaway shop in the US. According to geographer François Bost, "well before that of désindustrialisation, the question of délocalisations established itself in public debate – notably within politics and unions."[25]

Meanwhile, across the English Channel in the UK, British economists came together for a conference organized by the National Institute of Economic and Social Research in 1978 to discuss the efficacy of the deindustrialization concept. Conference-goers tied deindustrialization to the "general economic sickness" being experienced by ailing British manufacturers suffering, some said, from the "British disease."[27] Attendees agreed on the significance of the term, though the resulting report called it "a new label for an old problem."[28] More critical voices such as Alec Cairncross wondered if deindustrialization was too "ambiguous" in definition and measurement to be practically useful.[29] Geographers Ron Martin and Bob Rowthorn later wryly suggested that the deindustrialization idea had in effect "gate-crashed" the economics literature.[30] But the concept spoke to many in Britain, especially on the Left, and the term entered everyday language by the time that Margaret Thatcher ruthlessly crushed the miner's union in the mid-1980s.[31] Historian Jim Tomlinson recently made

Theorizing Deindustrialization

Table 1.1 Industrial employment (as % of total employment)[34]

Country	1970	2016
Germany	50	27
Belgium	45	19
France	39	18
Italy	44	23
UK	46	17
USA	31	17
Japan	34	24

the case for the centrality of deindustrialization in post-1945 British history.[32] In doing so, he challenged the earlier tendency to equate the problem with regional disparities and the North–South economic divide in England (see Table 1.1). Instead, Tomlinson suggested that deindustrialization is as much about the failure to create new industrial jobs as it is about the loss of old ones, as factory closures are nothing new. Albeit skeptical, mainstream British economists were initially more open to the deindustrial idea than their counterparts in the US. Writing in *the Washington Post* in May 1984, economist Robert J. Samuelson suggested that " 'Deindustrialization' is one of these mongrel words that has crept into the language and ought to be kicked out."[33] The strong reaction from mainstream US economists reflected the radical political origins of the concept in North America.

Radical Origins of the Deindustrialization Thesis

The Canadian articulation of the deindustrialization thesis emerged out of the Waffle Movement for an Independent Socialist Canada, a left-nationalist formation that was strongly opposed to the economic domination of the US.[35] At first, the Waffle was focused on foreign direct investment and the ways that Canada's dependent relationship on the US may have stunted industrial development and resulted in the underdevelopment of the country. For many, Canadians remained 'drawers of water and hewers of wood.' US manufacturing firms had been enticed to set up branch plants in Canada with the erection of a high tariff wall in the 1870s and 1880s.[36] By the 1960s, there was growing concern about the corporate structure of US multinational corporations and how few high-end managerial or engineering jobs were located in these branch plants. Vital decisions were made elsewhere. Writers like Kari Polanyi Levitt, the daughter of renowned political economist Karl Polanyi, spoke of American corporate dominance in Canada as a 'new mercantilism' such were its distortive effects on the country's economic development. Dependency theory, then coming out of Latin America and the Caribbean, further bolstered this left-nationalist argument of external linkages in imperial chains.

The tsunami of mine, mill, and factory closures that swept across Canada in the early 1970s, combined with the protectionist policies of US President Richard Nixon, and the sense that something had fundamentally changed, led the Waffle to the conclusion that this economic dependency was now causing Canada to deindustrialize. In *(Canada) Ltd: The Political Economy of Dependency*, edited by Gordon Laxer in 1973, the "thesis of de-industrialisation receives its first treatment . . . within the broader context of a developed anti-imperialist analysis."[37] Political economist Mel Watkins, one of the contributors, made the case that

Canada's dependency on resource extraction has contributed to its underdevelopment as an industrialized nation, citing dependency theorist Andre Gunder Frank in arguing that "capitalist economic development is a dialectical process simultaneously creating development and under development."[38] For his part, Jim Laxer argued that

> [d]e-industrialization is the price workers pay for Canada's dependent status. . . . As the American empire enters a period of decline, the costs of the decline are passed in disproportionately high amounts to workers in dependent countries like Canada and to minorities like the blacks within the United States.[39]

These Wafflers went so far as to suggest that the deindustrialization of Canada was the "strategic aim" of US government policy under Richard Nixon, which aggressively sought to repatriate industrial jobs.[40] American corporations, said to be more loyal to American workers, closed their Canadian branch plants before their American home plants. While this nationalist reasoning has been successfully challenged, as American corporations have proven to be loyal to no one, just visit Detroit: the idea that Canada's branch plant economy, built to serve the local market, was particularly vulnerable to trade liberalization is a compelling one.

Not everyone on the Canadian Left, however, agreed with the left-nationalist deindustrialization thesis.[41] Canadian labor historians, in particular, were critical of the left-nationalist emphasis on external heartland and hinterland relationships as it obscured the class struggle inside Canada and denied that industrial capitalism took hold here.[42] Steve Moore and Debi Well went so far as to call deindustrialization a myth that was "symbolic of the theoretical poverty of left-nationalism."[43] Other historians, meanwhile, pointed to earlier examples of made-in-Canada regional deindustrialization in the Maritimes and the West.[44] For her part, political economist Rianne Mahon, who was sympathetic to left-nationalism, showed that Canada's declining textile industry was not due to Canada's dependent relationship with the US, as the industry was largely Canadian-owned. She therefore formulated the notion of "dependent industrialization"[45] that led to the 'tariff-induced deindustrialization' of that industry. These early debates tainted the deindustrialization thesis for many Canadian labor historians, leading few to take up the concept until recently.

In the US, employers had long used their ultimate power to move production somewhere else, to threaten workers contemplating joining a union or, once established, to dampen their demands for higher wages and benefits. Writing in 1963, legal scholar Michael Frenkel confirmed that

> [c]ertainly, one of the most drastic economic weapons in managements' arsenal in battles with labor unions is the runaway shop. This is the device whereby an employer either prevents unionization, or escapes bargaining with an established union, by ceasing operations at his original location and relocating in another, usually distant community.[46]

There was intense competition between US jurisdictions for industrial jobs, leading southern states to offer incentives such as tax exemptions, free or reduced power costs, and, most importantly, the promise of cheap and unorganized labor to convince existing employers in the Northeast and Midwest to relocate. Taft-Hartley's allowance of 'right to work' legislation at the state level made it considerably harder for unions to follow these runaways to the US South. To make matters even worse, in a series of important decisions, the US Supreme

Court eliminated whatever little protection labor law provided unionized workers faced with this anti-union impulse. An employer had no duty whatsoever to negotiate the decision to close its factory and terminate a collective agreement, no matter the reason and no matter if it was another runaway shop.[47]

This was the deteriorating political situation in which cartoonist Fred Wright found himself drawing political cartoons in support of the United Electrical (UE) workers. Wright came to the UE after quitting his job with the National Maritime Union in 1949, having been "asked to draw red-baiting cartoons."[48] His archived papers at the University of Pittsburgh offer us a rich archive of thousands of cartoons, all of which are now available digitally online.[49] According to Gary Huck, who succeeded Wright after his death,

> Fred's cartoons defined, documented, challenged, and combated the attacks from corporate and government forces during the Red Scare. His cartoons fought off raids by other unions, organized new workers and gave vision to a progressive political agenda. Until his death in 1984, Fred almost singlehandedly supplied the labor movement in the United States with cartoons that so defined working class life and are so timeless that they continue to organize workers and promote social causes around the world today.[50]

At least 32 of these cartoons focused explicitly on runaway shops and plant closures, offering us a rich visual archive of one union's fight against industrial closures. Many of these cartoons feature cigar-smoking capitalists as thieves stealing away factories. The focus here is on the how and why of deindustrialization rather than on its socioeconomic effects on workers thereafter. It was clear what the problem was and who was to blame: capital flight. Only a few of the cartoons featured the locked factory gate motif, which became popular in the mainstream media. There were signs of resistance, too, such as a union hand holding back the thief trying to get away or a worker opening the padlocked factory gate. There is also a clearly visible progression from interregional runaway shops to international ones. The globalization of the problem is represented as runaways crossing border and being welcomed in distant low-wage areas, usually in Asia, or giant shipping containers labelled 'jobs' being loaded onto ships for 'export' (see Figure 1.4). Without exception, the American worker is represented as white and male as are their employers. But Fred Wright clearly sought to avoid racist tropes of the foreign worker and blaming foreign imports. Foreign workers were usually represented as ordinary joes, too. "How foreign is foreign competition," read one caption (see Figure 1.5). There was nothing inevitable in the process of job theft: it was a product of US corporate greed.

The shift from interregional to international runaway plants represented a political opportunity to nationalize the plant closure problem in the US, which had hitherto been viewed as a regional problem largely contained to the US Northeast and Midwest. As long as capital flight was between regions within the US, there was little likelihood of political intervention. The globalization of the problem provided the opportunity for a unified response but risked letting employers off the political hook by blaming foreign imports rather than disinvestment. It was at this point that Barry Bluestone and Bennett Harrison, founding members of the Union of Radical Political Economics, were commissioned by the Progressive Alliance of trade unions and civic groups opposed to plant closures to write a report on the problem. Their 1980 study, titled 'Capital and Communities: The Causes and Consequences of Private Disinvestment,' blamed capital flight for community abandonment. Their analysis effectively

Figure 1.4 Fred Wright, "Jobs For Export"[51] (Copyright: Wright, UE13.1.2142)

combined the old trade union concern with runaway plants with the American New Left's fixation on the virtues of local community.[53] This was no coincidence as Bluestone was the son of a United Auto Workers Vice-President and had thus grown up in the union movement. He was also politically active in New Left organizations such as the Students for a Democratic Society. They opened the report by declaring that "You don't have to be an economist or an unemployed worker to be aware of the epidemic of plant closings and other forms of capital flight now sweeping the country"[54] or the 'economic and social wreckage' left behind. It was framed as a life-or-death struggle between capital and community. They blamed "large, absentee profit-maximizing corporations" for the nationwide problem.[55] Yet the word deindustrialization itself was not even mentioned.

Two years later, Bluestone and Harrison revised and expanded their analysis in *The Deindustrialization of America: Plant Closings, Community Abandonment and the Dismantling of Basic Industry (1982)*. As the book's title suggests, deindustrialization was the new name given to their existing analysis on capital flight. Their definition of deindustrialization as "a widespread, systemic disinvestment in the nation's productive capacity" remains the standard one in the field today.[56] Industrial capital during these years was increasingly being directed into mergers and acquisitions, other sectors, and foreign investment. "At the root of all this is a fundamental struggle between capital and community," they argued. "Deindustrialization does not just happen," they added, but was made to happen: "Conscious decisions have to be made by corporate managers to move a factory from one location to another, to buy up a

Theorizing Deindustrialization

Figure 1.5 Fred Wright, "How Foreign Is 'Foreign' Competition?"[52] (Copyright: Wright, UE13.1.1385)

going concern or to dispose of one, or to shut down a facility altogether."[57] What was missing from their analysis, however, was a wider transnational or global perspective, as the US was not alone in experiencing deindustrialization.

Bluestone and Harrison's work was influential across the US and around the world in the years that followed. For example, in their book *The Geography of De-Industrialization* (1986), British geographers Martin and Rowthorn sought to "introduce a similar geographical perspective into the discussion of British de-industrialisation."[58] For US historians Jefferson Cowie and Joseph Heathcott, who published their influential edited volume *Beyond the Ruins: The Meaning of Deindustrialization*, with a foreword from Bluestone, precisely 20 years after *The Deindustrialization of America*: "What was labelled deindustrialization in the intense political heat of the late 1970s and early 1980s turned out to be a more socially complicated, historically deep, geographically diverse, and politically perplexing phenomenon than previously thought."[59] They saw deindustrialization as a process, a "historical transformation that marks not just a quantitative and qualitative change in employment, but a fundamental change in the social fabric on a par with industrialization itself."[60] Both the Canadian and American variants of the deindustrialization thesis thus emphasized the importance of geography, corporate (dis)investment decisions, and capital flight in their formulation of the concept. There was nothing inevitable in the new economic order taking shape: it was made to happen (see Figure 1.6).

Figure 1.6 Fred Wright, "Jobs Truck."[61] (Copyright: Wright, UE13.1.0580)

Conclusion

Those who study deindustrialization have come to understand it is "an essential element in the functioning of capitalism" and that it is "not an orderly or smooth transition."[62] However, in keeping with the micro-historical approach of the 'New Labour History,' this field of research remains dominated by local and regional studies grounded in the lives of displaced workers and working-class communities. These studies have revealed the lived interior of this destructive process, bearing witness to the pain and hardship produced. Very few researchers, however, have geographically scaled-up their analysis to the nation-state much less cross international borders to study the changing international division of labor itself.[63] The focus, overwhelmingly, has been on the socioeconomic, environmental, and health *effects* over 'deindustrialization's half-life' or its cultural significance rather than the how and why of deindustrialization. As there has not been much cause to critically engage with the deindustrialization concept, the field risks reinforcing the evolutionary idea that industrialism is now a thing of the past. I therefore disagree with my good friend Tim Strangleman when he argues that the industrial revolution and our current transitional moment are "two historically discrete epochs [that] can be thought of as two bookends of what was an industrial era."[64] It is essential to remind ourselves that the world has not deindustrialized, everything is made somewhere. Where things are made, however, has dramatically changed. While deindustrialization involves the decline of industrial production, according to Marion Fontaine and Xavier Vigna, it "is therefore not synonymous with the end of industry. It signals instead the loss of its centrality."[65] The how and why of the restructuring of the international division of labor has yet to receive the attention it deserves from deindustrialization scholars.

Public historian Cathy Stanton argues that we need to make a clean break with the linearity implied in the deindustrialization framework and "grapple in a really serious way with what it means to operate within that paradox."[66] In doing so, we can learn much from the early scholarship of Doreen Massey, Barry Bluestone, and Bennett Harrison, as well as Jefferson Cowie, who highlighted the importance of geography and capital flight. It is not enough to say that deindustrialization is a global phenomenon. In extending our analysis beyond the industrial heartlands of Western Europe and North America, we need to heed Andy Pike's cautionary message when he urges us against simply rolling out "global North perspectives in new geographical or temporal settings or diffuse 'leading edge' ideas from the 'core' to the 'periphery.'"[67] The Global South needs to be something more than serve as "a non-descript destination for runaway factories."[68] Historian Ian McKay is surely right when he wrote that "a more fully theorized account of de-industrialization would surely have to take fuller measure of dependency theory and models from Latin America."[69]

Notes

1 Hall, Stuart. (1988). The Toad in the Garden: Thatcherism among the Theorists. In Nelson, C. and Grossberg, L. (eds.) *Marxism and the Interpretation of Culture*. Chicago: University of Illinois Press, p. 44.
2 Block, Fred. (1990). *Postindustrial Possibilities: A Critique of Economic Discourse*. Berkeley, CA: University of California Press, p. 5.
3 Block, *Postindustrial Possibilities*, p. 6.
4 Thompson, E.P. (1964). *The Making of the English Working Class*. London: Victor Gollancz.
5 High, Steven. (forthcoming). The Radical Origins of the Deindustrialization Thesis: From Dependency to Capital Mobility & Community Abandonment. *Labour/le Travail*; and High, Steven. (2013, November). 'The Wounds of Class': A Historiographical Reflection on the Study of Deindustrialization. *History Compass*, 11(11), pp. 994–1007.
6 Williams, Raymond. (1983). *Keywords*. 2nd edn. London: Fontana Press, p. 17.
7 Fraser, Nancy and Gordon, Linda. (1994). A Genealogy of Dependency: Tracing a Keyword of the US Welfare State. *Signs*, 19(2), p. 310.
8 Bluestone, Barry and Harrison, Bennett. (1980). *Capital and Communities: The Causes and Consequences of Private Disinvestment*. Washington: The Progressive Alliance, p. 154.
9 Cowie, Jefferson. (1999). *Capital Moves: RCA's 70-Year Quest for Cheap Labor*. Ithaca, NY: Cornell University Press, p. 185.
10 UE13.1.0389. Fred Wright Original Cartoons (Subgroup 13.1), Fred Wright Papers (UE.13), Archives & Special Collections, University of Pittsburgh Library System.
11 Massey, Doreeen. (1984). *Spatial Division of Labour: Social Structures and the Geography of Production*. London: Macmillan, p. viii.
12 Massey, Doreeen. (1984). *Spatial Division of Labour: Social Structures and the Geography of Production*. London: Macmillan, pp. 2, 8.
13 Massey, Doreeen. (1984). *Spatial Division of Labour: Social Structures and the Geography of Production*. London: Macmillan, p. 82.
14 Huck, Gary and Konopacki, Mike. (2001, Fall). What Happened to the Labor Movement's Sense of Humor? The Rise and Fall of Labor Cartooning. *New Labor Forum*, 9, p. 37.
15 Buhl, Paul. (1992). Fred Wright. In Buhle, M.J., Buhle, P. and Georgakas, D. (eds.) *Encyclopedia of the American Left*. Urbana, IL: University of Illinois Press, p. 908; Buhle, Paul. (2013). Book Review of 'Course of Action: A Journalist's Account from Inside the American League Against War and Fascism and the United Electrical Workers Union (UE), 1933–1978'. *Socialism and Democracy*, 27(2), pp. 197–199.

16 UE13.1.1350. Fred Wright Original Cartoons (Subgroup 13.1), Fred Wright Papers (UE.13), Archives & Special Collections, University of Pittsburgh Library System.

17 Windsor, Hugh. (1980, June 25). Differences on Halting a Decline. *Globe and Mail.*

18 Our research project, "Deindustrialization and the Politics of Our Time (DePOT)," organized a series of virtual keyword roundtable in its first year of activity on "deindustrialization," "ruination," "brownfields," "greening," and "moral economy." At the time of writing, the recordings are available at deindustrialization.org. We sought to understand to what extent the language of industrial decline differed across Western Europe and North America. Quite a lot it turns out. These early discussions profoundly shaped my analysis here as has my ongoing collaboration with the members of this project.

19 Berger, Stefan and Pickering, Paul. (2018). Regions of Heavy Industry and their Heritage – Between Identity Politics and 'Touristification'. In Wicke, Christian, Berger, Stefan and Golombek, Jana (eds.) *Industrial Heritage and Regional Identities.* London: Routledge, p. 220.

20 Berger, Stefan. (2019). Industrial Heritage and the Ambiguities of Nostalgia for an Industrial Past in the Ruhr Valley, Germany. *Labor,* 16(1), pp. 37–64.

21 Zazzara, Gilada. (2020). Making Sense of the Industrial Past: Deindustrialisation and Industrial Heritage in Italy. *Italia Contemporanea Yearbook,* p. 168.

22 Zazzara, Gilda. (2018). 'Italians First': Workers on the Right Amidst Old and New Populisms. *International Labor and Working-Class History,* 93, pp. 101–112. See also: Garruccio, Roberta. (2016). Chiedi alla ruggine. Studi e storiografia della deindustrializzazione. *Meridiana,* 85, pp. 35–37.

23 Raggi, Pascal. (2019). Un demi-siècle de désindustrialisation en Lorraine du fer (1963–2013). *Revue du Rhin Superiéur* (Special Issue on 'Cinquante ans de désindustrialisation'), 1, p. 92; and, Cohen, Elie. (1989). *L'Etat brancardier. Politiques du déclin industriel (1974–1984).* Paris: Calmann-Lévy.

24 Daumas, Jean-Claude. (2019). Désindustrialisation et politique industrielle en France (1974–2012). *Revue du Rhin Superiéur* (Special Issue on 'Cinquante ans de désindustrialisation'), 1, p. 75.

25 Bost, François. (2011–12). Désindustrialisation, délocalisation: les mots et les choses. *BAGF – GÉOG-RAPHIES,* p. 121.

26 UE13.1.0612a. Fred Wright Original Cartoons (Subgroup 13.1), Fred Wright Papers (UE.13), Archives & Special Collections, University of Pittsburgh Library System.

27 Blackaby, Frank (ed.). (1978). *De-industrialisation.* London: Heinemann, p. 1.

28 Blackaby, Frank. (1978). Report of the Discussion. In Blackaby, F. (ed.) *De-Industrialisation.* London: Heinemann, pp. 263–268.

29 Cairncross, Alec. (1978). What is De-industrialisation?. In Blackaby, F. (ed.) *De-Industrialisation.* London: Heinemann, p. 5.

30 Martin, Ron and Rowthorn, Bob. (1986). *The Geography of De-Industrialisation.* London: Macmillan, p. xv.

31 See the various publications of Jim Phillips, Andrew Perchard, and Ewan Gibbs.

32 Tomlinson, Jim. (2020). De-industrialization: Strengths and Weaknesses as a Key Concept for Understanding Post-War British History. *Urban History,* 47, pp. 199–219.

33 Samuelson, Robert J. (1984, May 30). 'Deindustrialization' is Disinformation. *Washington Post.*

34 Lomba, Cédric. (2018). *La restructuration permanente de la condition ouvrière: De Cockerill à ArcelorMittal.* Vulaines sur Seine: Editions du Croquet, p. 27.

35 For more on the Waffle, see Blocker, David G. (2019). 'To Waffle to the Left:' The Waffle, the New Democratic Party, and Canada's New Left during the Long Sixties. *Electronic Thesis and Dissertation Repository,* p. 6554. https://ir.lib.uwo.ca/etd/6554.

36 Bliss, Michael. (1977 [1970]). Canadianizing American Business: The Roots of the Branch Plant. In Lumsden, Ian (ed.) *Close the 49th Parallel: The Americanization of Canada.* Toronto: University of Toronto Press, pp. 29–31.

37 Laxer, Robert. (1973). Foreword. In Laxer, Robert M. (ed.) *(Canada) Ltd: The Political Economy of Dependency.* Toronto: McClelland and Stewart, p. 7.

38 Watkins, Mel. (1973). Resources and Underdevelopment. In Laxer, Robert M. (ed.) *(Canada) Ltd: The Political Economy of Dependency.* Toronto: McClelland and Stewart, p. 111.

39 Laxer, Jim. (1973). Canadian Manufacturing and US Trade Policy. In Laxer, Robert M. (ed.) *(Canada) Ltd: The Political Economy of Dependency.* Toronto: McClelland and Stewart, p. 146.

40 Laxer, Foreword, p. 9.

41 Niosi, J. (1983). The Canadian Bourgeoisie: Towards a Synthetical Approach. *Canadian Journal of Political and Social Theory*, 7(3), p. 128.

42 Mahon, Rianne. (1984). *The Politics of Industrial Restructuring: Canadian Textiles*. Toronto: University of Toronto Press, p. 7.

43 Moore, S. and Wells, Debi. (1977). The Myth of Canadian De-industrialization. In Heron, Craig (ed.) *Imperialism, Nationalism and Canada*. Toronto: New Hogtown Press, p. 45.

44 Acheson, T.W. (1972). The National Policy and the Industrialization of the Maritimes, 1880–1910. *Acadiensis*, 1(2), pp. 191–202; Forbes, E.R. (1977). Misguided Symmetry: The Destruction of Regional Transport Policy for the Maritimes. In Bercuson, D. (ed.) *Canada and the Burden of Unity*. Toronto: Macmillan of Canada; and, Clow, Michael. (1984). Politics and Uneven Capitalist Development: The Maritime Challenge to the Study of Canadian Political Economy. *Studies in Political Economy*, 13; and Lutz, John. (1988). Losing Steam: The Boiler and Engine Industry as an Index of British Columbia's Deindustrialization, 1880–1915. *CHA Historical Papers*, 23(1).

45 Mahon, *The Politics of Industrial Restructuring*, p. 4.

46 Frenkel, Michael. (1963). The Runaway Shop, 12 *Clev.-Marshall L. Rev.* 523, p. 523.

47 Collingsworth, T. (1993). Resurrecting the National Labor Relations Act Plant Closings and Runaway Shops in Global Economy. *Berkeley Journal of Employment and Labor Law*, 14(1), pp. 89–90.

48 Huck, Gary. (1996, July–August). Art in the Movement. *Resist Newsletter*.

49 Fred Wright Original Cartoons (Subgroup 13.1), Fred Wright Papers (UE.13), Archives & Special Collections, University of Pittsburgh Library System.

50 Huck, Gary. (2006, July–August). Art in the Movement. *Resist Newsletter*. See also Kercher, Stephen E. (2006). *Revel with a Cause: Liberal Satire in Postwar America*. Chicago: University of Chicago Press, p. 34.

51 UE13.1.2142 and UE13.1.1385. Fred Wright Original Cartoons (Subgroup 13.1), Fred Wright Papers (UE.13), Archives & Special Collections, University of Pittsburgh Library System.

52 UE13.1.2142 and UE13.1.1385. Fred Wright Original Cartoons (Subgroup 13.1), Fred Wright Papers (UE.13), Archives & Special Collections, University of Pittsburgh Library System.

53 For more on the fight against plant closures, see High, Steven. (2003). *Industrial Sunset: The Making of North America's Rust Belt, 1969–1984*. Toronto: University of Toronto Press.

54 Bluestone, Barry and Harrison, Bennett. (1980). *Capital and Communities: The Causes and Consequences of Private Disinvestment*. Washington: The Progressive Alliance, p. i.

55 Bluestone, Barry and Harrison, Bennett. (1980). *Capital and Communities: The Causes and Consequences of Private Disinvestment*. Washington: The Progressive Alliance, p. iv.

56 Bluestone, Barry and Harrison, Bennett. (1982). *The Deindustrialization of America: Plant Closings, Community Abandonment and the Dismantling of Basic Industry*. New York: Basic Books, p. 5.

57 Bluestone and Harrison, *The Deindustrialization of America*, p. 15.

58 Martin and Rowthorn, *The Geography of De-industrialisation*, p. xix.

59 Cowie, Jefferson and Heathcott, Joseph (eds.). (2003). *Beyond the Ruins: The Meaning of Deindustrialization*. Ithaca, NY: Cornell University Press, p. 2.

60 Cowie and Heathcott, *Beyond the Ruins*, pp. 5–6.

61 UE13.1.0580. Fred Wright Original Cartoons (Subgroup 13.1), Fred Wright Papers (UE.13), Archives & Special Collections, University of Pittsburgh Library System.

62 Johnson, Christopher H. (2002). Introduction: De-industrialization and Globalization. Altena, Bert and van der Linden, Marcel (eds.) *De-industrialization: Social, Cultural and Political Aspects*. *IRSH*, 47, p. 29; and, Dudley, Kathryn Marie. (1994). *The End of the Line: Lost Jobs, New Lives in Postindustrial America*. Chicago: University of Chicago Press, p. 26.

63 Among those works that have crossed national borders are Cowie, Jefferson. (1999). *Capital Moves: RCA's 70-Year Quest for Cheap Labor*. Ithaca, NY: Cornell University Press; High, *Industrial Sunset*; Raggi, Pascal. (2019). *La Désindustrialisation de la Lorraine du fer*. Paris: Classiques Garnier; and the comparative volumes edited by Stefan Berger such as *Constructing Industrial Pasts: Heritage, Historical Culture and Identity in Regions undergoing Structural Economic Transformation*. London: Berghahn, 2020.

64 Strangleman, Tim. (2017). Deindustrialisation and the Historical Sociological Imagination: Making Sense of Work and Industrial Change. *Sociology*, 51(2), p. 467.

65 Fontaine, Marion and Vigna, Xavier. (2019). La désindustrialisation, une histoire en cours. *20&21: Revue d'histoire*, 144, p. 6. More than elsewhere, the French historiography has taken the political economy of deindustrialization seriously.

66 Stanton, Cathy. (2018). Keeping 'the Industrial': New Solidarities in Postindustrial Places. In High, Steven, Mackinnon, Lachlan and Perchard, Andrew (eds.) *The Deindustrialized World: Confronting Ruination in Postindustrial Places*. Vancouver: University of British Columbia Press, p. 156.

67 Pike, Andy. (2020). Coping with Deindustrialization in the Global North and South. *International Journal of Urban Sciences*, p. 15.

68 Schindler, Seth, Gillespie, Tom, Banks, Nicola, et al. (2020). Deindustrialization in cities of the Global South. *Area Development and Policy* 5(3), p. 285.

69 Ian McKay review of Donald Reid's The Miners of Decazeville, *Labour/Le Travail* 20 (1987), pp. 221–228. In addition to Latin American dependency theory, Immanuel Wallerstein's world-systems theory may help us in this regard, given its close attention to an integrated global capitalist system and the international division of labor.

2
REFLECTIONS ON THE HALF-LIFE

Sherry Lee Linkon

Introduction

"The half-life of deindustrialization" names a multilayered set of ideas and themes that have become increasingly central to deindustrialization studies. When the phrase first appeared in print in 2013,[1] deindustrialization studies had already pivoted from a focus on the causes and immediate responses to shutdowns to the continuing consequences of deindustrialization. Emerging themes included the simple but significant insight that deindustrialization was not a discrete event but a longer-term shift with problematic economic, social, cultural, and political impacts. Second, the effects of deindustrialization extend far beyond those who were displaced by closings; it remained significant for the next generation (or more) of families and communities as well as for the broader culture. Third, the half-life makes itself visible in memories of industrial work and its loss and in informal, unofficial ways as well as in cultural heritage efforts and representations.

The half-life of deindustrialization is not so much an explanatory theory as a metaphor. Metaphor uses one, often fairly concrete object to represent the qualities of another, often abstract thing. As a rhetorical move, metaphor not only clarifies an abstract idea. It also facilitates complex, nuanced understanding. As the *Cambridge Guide to Literature in English* phrases it, metaphor invites "openness to a common idea" and implies "an aura of suggestion and implication" (Ousby, 2000). If the metaphor "the half-life of deindustrialization" offers more than a nice turn of phrase for referencing the post-shutdown era, it should invite analyses that expand and complicate our understanding of the long-term effects of deindustrialization. The metaphor of the half-life has been in circulation for over a decade, so now is a good time to consider how it has been used and what it offers. The metaphor has been widely cited, and of course I'm pleased that so many colleagues have found it useful. But the real measure of the value of the half-life of deindustrialization lies in what it generates. What does it offer to deindustrialization studies, and what are its limitations?

To answer that question, this chapter traces the history of the half-life as an approach to the study of deindustrialization, in my own work and across the field. While the term has circulated widely, across multiple disciplines and is often used only briefly,[2] about a dozen articles or books apply it more fully, and their work suggests productive insights about what

DOI: 10.4324/9781003308324-5

the metaphor generates. At the same time, even the most generative metaphor has limitations. By characterizing deindustrialization through the comparison with radioactive waste, we close off some important alternative approaches. I close this chapter by considering the gaps that the metaphor creates or reinforces.

A Brief History of the Half-Life

I remember very distinctly the first time I thought to describe deindustrialization as having a half-life. As part of a panel about working-class communities at the 2011 Working-Class Studies Association conference, Christine Walley discussed her then-forthcoming autoethnography of East Chicago, *Exit Zero,* which explored how steelmaking shaped the life of her family and community and how toxic waste from that industry contributed to the cancer that struck her in her twenties (Walley, 2013). Walley highlights how toxins from the steel industry remain dangerous long after mills have been torn down, and listening to her, I was struck by the similarity between the chemical toxins of steelmaking and the economic, social, and cultural effects of deindustrialization. Among other things, both have long-term consequences, but their influence is often indirect. That the parallel emerged during a conversation about the toxic residue left by the operation of a steel mill, not by the effect of its closing, reinforces the impossibility of separating the industrial from the deindustrial. In the physical environment, social patterns, and memory, they are inextricably linked.

While *half-life* can be applied to any decreasing but measurable thing, its most familiar usage comes from nuclear physics, where it refers to the time it takes for a radioactive isotope to deteriorate by half. It came into common usage in the mid-twentieth century, amid public anxiety about the dangers of nuclear meltdowns prompted by accidents at Three Mile Island in 1979, Chernobyl in 1986, and Fukushima in 2011. From early on, anti-nuclear activists also emphasized the long-term dangers of radioactive waste, which could have a half-life lasting thousands of years. This makes the very idea of measuring the half-life ironic, since such measurements predict phenomena that we will not live to observe or document. Invoking the half-life as a metaphor for deindustrialization makes two obvious implicit claims: that deindustrialization is harmful and that its effects may well continue for decades and have no identifiable end. On the other hand, while the longevity of radiation surprises no one at this point, the persistent toxicity of deindustrialization contradicts the predictions and expectations of many policymakers, journalists, and analysts. As John Russo remembers, reporters started asking him if Youngstown had recovered from the closing of its steel mills within just a few years, as closings continued to occur. Almost 50 years later, the question has taken on an almost resigned tone: will Youngstown ever recover?

The metaphor's link with radioactive waste highlights another theme central to deindustrialization studies: the importance and complications of memory. Starting in the 1980s, as regulatory agencies developed guidelines for storing radioactive waste, they also designed ways of marking disposal sites that would transcend languages, cultures, and time (Trauth, Hora, and Guzowski, 1993). While it would be a stretch to define industrial heritage or cultural representations of deindustrialization as comparable to warning signs at nuclear sites, they do serve as markers that commemorate what came before and have drawn considerable critical attention as scholars, curators, and cultural producers consider how – and why – we should remember the industrial and deindustrial pasts. Memory weaves through the economic, political, and social effects of deindustrialization. Some scholars have noted how heritage sites and communities deploy memories of eras of industrial productivity and strong working-class families and institutions to promote redevelopment, though some discussions of heritage note how the environmental degradation left behind by shutdowns limit or prevent efforts to memorialize and complicate redevelopment efforts.[3]

The idea that both industries and their closings could be toxic was nothing new in 2011. By that time, Russo and I had been researching, writing, and organizing community projects about Youngstown, Ohio, for nearly 15 years, and much of our work focused on the paradox that the steel industry had first contaminated the region with soot, heavy metals, and chemicals and then generated social contamination as it shut down. Russo recalls using the language of toxicity and even the term *half-life* in fights against the mill closings in the 1980s and in addressing the problems of deindustrialization in the early 1990s. For Russo, as for many local residents and activists, and even a few reporters and academics who covered the shutdowns, the emotional injuries of the first decade of deindustrialization were powerful. As he puts it, it took until the late 1990s, two decades after Youngstown Sheet and Tube announced the first major shutdown, for him to move from grieving to thinking critically about the longer-term impacts of deindustrialization.

Given trends in deindustrialization studies, Russo was probably not alone. During the 1990s, deindustrialization studies increasingly shifted attention from the immediate causes, responses to, and outcomes of plant closings to the complex long-term effects of deindustrialization. As Jefferson Cowie and Joseph Heathcott phrased it in *Beyond the Ruins* in 2003, we came to see deindustrialization not as an event but rather a "socially complicated, historically deep, geographically diverse, and politically perplexing phenomenon" (Cowie and Heathcott, 2003, p. 12). The complexity of deindustrialization guided the research that yielded *Steeltown USA*. Russo and I saw how the rise and fall of the steel industry had affected far more than the material conditions or lived experiences of workers. It had first shaped Youngstown's culture and communal memory and inflicted serious injuries to its identity and agency long after the mills closed. Our initial inspiration for that project was Bruce Springsteen's 1995 song, which functioned as a refraction point for a dozen representations of the Jeannette blast furnace produced across more than 50 years from the 1930s to the 1990s. As that idea expanded into a book, tracing narratives and images of work in Youngstown, we incorporated materials produced over more than a century. The final chapter traced how the community's identity shifted during the 20 years between the closing of the first mill and the time we were writing. In *Steeltown USA* and elsewhere, Russo and I argued that the toxicity of deindustrialization was, as Cowie and Heathcott suggest, multifaceted and long-lasting (Linkon and Russo, 2002).[4]

I have continued exploring the half-life of deindustrialization for almost two decades. In 2009, Russo and I cataloged the toxic effects of shutdowns on communities across the US. "The Social Costs of Deindustrialization" considered both immediate effects – economic decline, physical and mental health outcomes, deterioration of the built environment, struggling local governments – and longer-term cultural injuries like loss of trust in institutions, lowered expectations for individual and community trajectories, and political resentment (Russo and Linkon, 2009). In *The Half-Life of Deindustrialization: Working-Class Writing About Economic Restructuring*, I turned more directly to cultural representations, tracing how writers and filmmakers interpreted working-class experience in deindustrialized places. Most of the texts discussed in that book were written by people who did not themselves work in manufacturing or mining. Some were the children or grandchildren of industrial workers, while others had grown up in deindustrialized communities or even moved to such places as adults. Their narratives make clear how economic restructuring, including deindustrialization, unsettled and harmed working-class people and communities. They tell stories about how the structures and nature of work have changed, but they also reflect the experience of growing up in places marked by material and social deterioration.

As Russo's reflections about his own grief after the struggles of the 1980s suggest, for many scholars in this field, the half-life is personal as well as intellectual. This is true for me, too, though I didn't move to Youngstown until 1990. By then, most of the steel mills had been torn down, but the physical landscape and local culture kept steel and its loss palpably present. From boarded-up storefronts and abandoned homes to the lived experiences and attitudes of my students, some of whom still worked in the mills or were the children of displaced workers, I could not ignore the power of the half-life. Youngstown in the 1990s was still struggling to adapt to the loss of that industry. It still is.[5]

That deindustrialization has its own history and remains a force in shaping the present and future is clear in the range of work that constitutes deindustrialization studies today. We are interested not only in what caused shutdowns but also in how deindustrialization changes working-class places and cultures over time. We have considered how shutdowns harm working-class people and their communities, immediately and over time. We have documented the injuries of economic devastation, social disruption and displacement, and feelings of despair and confusion. Scholars have traced deindustrialization's effects on gender roles, employment and education patterns, uses and adaptations of the built environment, political discourse, and more. As the half-life metaphor implies, most of this work traces the persistent negative effects of deindustrialization, including its role in the growth of populist politics and white supremacist organizing since 2016, though a few studies point to potentially positive outcomes.[6] Only some of this work uses the metaphor overtly, but the bigger idea that the half-life references – that deindustrialization is not a discrete event of the past but a continuing and problematic force in contemporary life – has come to dominate this field.

Toxic Variations

Scholars most often use the phrase "the half-life of deindustrialization" to indicate their emphasis on long-term outcomes rather than the causes and immediate effects of shutdowns. Many articles use the phrase once, without exploring its implications, and brief references like this have helped make the term familiar. However, the articles and books that explore the half-life as a concept suggest its potential. Studies of the continuing costs of deindustrialization have become increasingly central to this field, and critical work that develops the metaphor of the half-life points us to some important themes – including several that suggest nuances and complications of the metaphor.

One especially powerful implication of the metaphor is that deindustrialization is an environmental issue, a link that is embedded in its basis in physics. Radioactivity leeches into land and water, so that its toxicity becomes materially embedded in the environment in ways that expose people to its dangers through ordinary activities and over long periods of time. This takes us back to the paradox of Walley's discussion of her town's steel industry, which provided both a common livelihood and an unseen danger. As her story suggests, there is an irony in using half-life to talk about deindustrialization, since closing factories and mines is often a first step toward environmental remediation. Toxins generated by heavy industry can be removed, or people can be protected from exposure to them, when industrial sites are closed. Yet, as Gilda Zazzara has pointed out, that process operates in tension with efforts to preserve or repurpose such sites. Dismantling factories often improves environmental conditions in deindustrialized communities, and clean-up efforts can reveal new information about industrial sites that can, in turn, be incorporated into cultural heritage projects (Zazzara, 2021, p. 166). Yet while deindustrialization can improve the quality of land, air, and water, it also disrupts and contaminates cultural ecologies, the systems of thinking, feeling, and acting that shape how people relate to their material settings.

The metaphor of the half-life can help us untangle the connections between literal and figurative contamination to the cultural ecologies of deindustrialized places. As Russo and I wrote in *Steeltown,* Youngstown's post-industrial possibilities were hampered by literal toxins, which left remaining industrial structures and significant stretches of public and private land unusable. Yet efforts to address these dangers by tearing down mills that were too dangerous to repurpose disrupted Youngstown's community of memory. That, in turn, fostered resentment over the failure of various institutions to protect laid-off steelworkers, their families, and the community from the ravages of mill closings, which contributed to acceptance of political corruption (Linkon and Russo, 2002).[7] Our argument proved more significant than we understood at the time: almost 15 years later, the slow contamination had deepened to the point that a metro area that had been a Democratic Party stronghold for most of a century embraced Donald J. Trump in the 2016 presidential election. In 2020, Youngstown continued its shift to the right, with even more residents voting for Trump than in the previous election, even though his promises to revive the steel industry had clearly proven false. Interviews with area voters suggest that the politics of resentment had spread far beyond displaced steelworkers, revealing how the toxicity of deindustrialization had infected many who had were not immediately harmed by the mill closings.[8]

Alistair Fraser and Andy Clark examine a similar situation in their study of local attitudes toward organized crime in a small city in Scotland (Fraser and Clark, 2021).[9] They show how the ruination and contamination of deindustrialization – both physical and social – enabled especially significant and 'volatile' organized crime. Fraser and Clark articulate the degradation of the local community after deindustrialization in explicitly environmental terms, linking material conditions – "very visible signs of abandonment and decay," including derelict buildings and land too polluted by a demolished foundry to be used for new construction (Fraser and Clark, 2021, p. 1068) – with the feelings, perceptions, and attitudes of residents. Several of their interviewees link crime, addiction, and other social problems with the deterioration of the built environment as well as with the hopelessness felt by people living amid so much evidence of abandonment and poverty. Further, these are the views not of people displaced by shutdowns but of the next generation. "As the impacts of deindustrialization have become more subtle," Fraser and Clark write, people "born in the period after closure have been brought up in a community that seemingly offers little opportunity for work, and where drugs are readily available" (Fraser and Clark, 2021, 1070).

In this context, and perhaps especially for 'those born after closure,' crime represents not only an alternative economy but in some ways – though Fraser and Clark note that this is less true now than it might once have been – an alternative site for demonstrating masculine toughness. All this makes working in the illegal drug industry attractive for workers and acceptable in the community, despite the damages of addiction and the fact that the profits made do not go back into the local area. Notably, they argue, the environment that fosters the growth of organized crime results from the toxicity of the half-life of deindustrialization but also contributes to its continuation.

I find two ideas from this study especially helpful in thinking about what the metaphor of the half-life offers us. First, Frasier and Clark's phrasing of the damaged culture of a local community in environmental terms, like Zazzara's attention to the relationship between environmental clean-up and industrial heritage projects, deepens and complicates our thinking about the toxicity of deindustrialization. As such work makes clear, toxicity is chemical and material but also psychological, social, and cultural, and these variations of toxicity are interconnected. The contamination of land obstructs redevelopment, the deterioration of the built environment fosters psychological despair, and the loss of social institutions and economic options helps to make once-denigrated groups and activities acceptable. Equally important, in arguing that the harms of deindustrialization actually generate further toxic outcomes that have the effect of "amplifying and extending the half-life," Fraser and Clark offer an insightful explanation of persistence of the toxicity of deindustrialization (Fraser and Clark, 2021, 1064).

While Fraser and Clark's attention to crime links the toxicity of the half-life with physical violence, deindustrialization itself has been described as a form of economic violence rooted in conflicts over power and inflicting injuries and damages. The metaphor of the half-life sidesteps this attention to violence in one sense, because it focuses on effects rather than on the contested interests that lead to deindustrialization. Yet while the half-life itself is a period of passive threat rather than active violence, nuclear weapons have clear associations with state violence, and nuclear reactions involve an atomic nucleus being 'bombarded' or 'colliding' with other particles. It is appropriate, then, for Steven High to draw our attention to the violence of deindustrialization by using the language of the half-life alongside environmental historian Rob Nixon's idea of "slow violence." Nixon describes the "structural violence of capitalism" as something that "occurs gradually and out of sight, a violence of delayed destruction that is dispersed across time and space, an attritional violence that is typically not viewed as violence at all" (High, 2021, 98). By linking these terms in his analysis of the debates over the character and development of a Montreal neighborhood, High demonstrates the value of attention to conflict in thinking about the half-life. It is not only injuries that get "dispersed across time and space," he suggests. It is also conflict. Those whose lives have been disrupted shift the focus of their anger and resentment from the corporations responsible for the initial violence of shutdowns toward other social actors – politicians, immigrants, the elite, even as they are themselves scorned and denigrated for holding on too tightly to nostalgia for the industrial past. Like Fraser and Clark, High shows how the half-life is at once a result of economic violence and an environment that fosters continuing conflict.

Where High examines conflicts between people of different classes, sociologist Emma Pleasant considers conflict across generations within the working class. She compares attitudes about work and self among workers displaced when the Chatham Dockyard in Kent, England, closed in 1984 and younger workers entering apprenticeship programs in the area in the 2010s. Pleasant identifies the first as members of the "craft-skill community," while the younger generation, whose views of class, masculinity, and work have been shaped by "communal memories" of industrial labor and its loss, are "the half-life community." She traces "intergenerational discourses of value," captured and shared through stories and artifacts. This "communicative cultural remembering" helps to shape generational identities (Pleasant, 2019, p. 50), but younger workers do not simply adopt inherited memories. Pleasant riffs on the metaphor "utilising the language of the atomic bomb . . . enables us to see the 'craft-skill community' acting as a fallout shelter to protect the workers who experienced deindustrialisation first hand and bridge the gap between industrial and deindustrial" (Pleasant, 2019, p. 46). To see industrial culture as a protective site makes a powerful claim about the relationship between the past and the present, yet it is also a nuanced link. After all, a fallout shelter protects people from radioactive debris only if they remain in the shelter, and given the length of the half-life of radioactive material, it would be impossible for people to remain inside a shelter long enough to be safe. As Pleasant shows, the protection afforded by the "craft-skill community" cannot extend to the "half-life community." She extends the fallout shelter idea by describing the "craft-skill community" as an "underground memory movement, keeping alive the histories and cultural resources," but she also shows how communal memories and their meanings "can be challenged" as younger generations redefine what constitutes "good" character in relation to work (Pleasant, 2019, p. 49). The "half-life character," she writes, is the result of "negotiation" about the meaning of the past, with younger workers "selecting what is useful and renegotiating the terrain of what is valuable" (Pleasant, 2019, p. 46). Pleasant draws on Beverly Skeggs's analysis of how value is attached to social ideas about the self but also how, when working-class people are excluded from "the traditional forms of capital that accrue the self's value," they may "reject or renegotiate" established ideas about value (Pleasant, 2019, p. 36). Her attention to exclusion as part of generational shifts adds an important layer to our thinking about the half-life, because it reminds us that the erasure and forgetting that High identifies is not only an injury to the working class but one that can occur within it.

As these examples illustrate, the half-life metaphor can yield complex and varied analyses of how deindustrialization acts on people and communities and how responses to its effects can reinforce those harms and contribute to new injuries. By linking aspects of radioactivity such as deindustrialization's multiple environmental impacts, its connections with violence, and the fallout shelter as a problematic site for protection, these scholars show that the half-life of deindustrialization can foster 'openness to a common idea' and inspire new 'suggestions and implications' about the toxicity of deindustrialization.

Memory and (In)visibility in the Half-Life

While deindustrialization generates very real material and environmental outcomes, the half-life is perhaps even more significantly a matter of culture, which is, in turn, intertwined with memory. Deindustrialization affects how people think, feel, and interact not only because it changes material conditions but because it disrupts expectations, identities, and relationships. In the simplest sense, deindustrialization challenges long-established patterns and thus violates how memory tells us things should be. It remakes the landscape, which Dolores Hayden describes as a "storehouse for memory" (Hayden, 1995, p. 8). Whether industrial sites are torn down or transformed into museums or offices, people's relationship with those spaces shift. Memory becomes more abstract and more reliant on cultural artifacts and representations. Artifacts, photos, oral histories, and other materials help to preserve memory in ways that enable it to shore up the memories of those who did the work that has disappeared. Those sources also serve to pass memory on to others, including later generations who draw on inherited memory to create novels, films, and other representations. All of these sources help to extend the half-life, keeping industrial work and deindustrialization present through and in culture. Preserving memory requires not only documenting the past but also making – or keeping – it visible. As scholars of deindustrialization, whether we seek to understand how the past shapes working-class lives in the present or to ensure the continuing visibility of working-class culture for the future, we are all at once examining memory and, in the process, ensuring the continuation of the half-life.

People can remember toxicity, and memory can itself be toxic. Some criticize deindustrialized communities for clinging to a futile nostalgia for a past that will never return. Holding on to the fantasy that industrial work will somehow magically return can make the continuing economic and social struggles of deindustrialized communities all the more painful. So, too, can idealized visions of the industrial era that erase conflicts and difficulties of class and labor. But the half-life is only partially about holding on to rosy memories. As Russo and I have noted, the memory of loss and struggle is also central to the half-life. As a scholar of deindustrialization literature, I am especially attuned to how the stories we tell reflect tensions and contradictions of memory, because these are central themes in fiction and film. But social science and history scholars have found evidence that the memories of industrial work and its loss influence how displaced workers, their children, and others in their communities understand their experiences, interact with each other, and engage with political and social life.

Pleasant's work on intergenerational conflicts around work recognizes the centrality of memory, which she articulates in part in terms of *visibility*. As she writes, the industrial generation has not yet been "destroyed," but it has "become less visible," and if that trend continues, "they will not be able to pass on their histories, find value and keep their community alive" (Pleasant, 2019, p. 222). This slow decrease in the visibility of the earlier generation's experience highlights one of the affordances of the half-life metaphor: anxieties around the invisibility of radiation. The half-life of radioactivity matters not only because its effects can manifest over thousands of years but also because it cannot be seen, raising questions of how to design storage sites to prevent future harm. This might seem irrelevant for deindustrialization, since its material effects often remain painfully visible, as communities continue to struggle with economic loss. However, erasure of the memory of industrial work and of the experience of deindustrialization can itself damage working-class people and communities, in part because the causal relationship between deindustrialization and the social, cultural, and psychological injuries it generates can become invisible over time. As Russo and I argued in *Steeltown*, working-class people may come to blame themselves for the failure to fully recover from deindustrialization if the slow violence of economic change is allowed to fade into the background.

That we should value the industrial past and understand its influence on the present are central themes of deindustrialization studies, but the half-life metaphor reminds us that memory should extend to deindustrialization itself. Many artifacts and representations focus on the experience of job loss, community deterioration, disruption of local identities, and challenges to long-held cultural values and expectations. These have long been part of the toolkit for deindustrialization studies, especially in public history and cultural heritage efforts, which seek to preserve not only the memory of workers' experiences but also the memory of decline – memories that, for many, feel painful but also necessary. As the half-life of deindustrialization unfolds, remnants of the industrial past and the experience of loss can fade. As High writes about Montreal, in some places, "the half-life . . . is at once too diffuse and too localized to be noticed" (High, 2021, p. 98). The effects of economic loss deserve to be "publicly recognized," he argues, because they enable us to see and understand structures of power and conflict that otherwise remain hidden or can be seen as givens. High traces how residents of the gentrifying Pont Saint-Charles neighborhood speak nostalgically about an earlier time when their community was better off, even as they view deindustrialization as "pre-history," and their "activist narrative" ignores "the persistence of urban loss or industrial work" (High, 2021, p. 109). Unlike those who experienced deindustrialization and still feel 'anger and bitterness' about it, anti-gentrification activists, most of them newer residents of the area, ignore the neighborhood's history of fighting to keep a glass factory open. Instead, they focus on a version of Pont Saint-Charles as represented in a mural that depicts "the postindustrial present . . . as a liberatory moment worthy of being celebrated" (High, 2021, p. 110). The mural's "uplifting message," however, does not include any visible reference to "loss, capital flight, or even a recognition of the structural violence experienced by so many local residents." For High, this is "a history shorn of its class politics," a version of "displacement" in which the working class "are rendered invisible" (High, 2021, p. 111). Invisibility is a form of toxicity that harms working-class people.

Industrial heritage and cultural representations resist this invisibility by documenting and narrating the significance of industrial work and its loss. But the half-life metaphor reminds us that documentation and representation serve to warn people of still-potent contamination, though for deindustrialization, the challenge of this is quite different than for radioactive waste. We do not have to communicate across barriers of language and time to protect people living thousands of years from now. Rather, our challenge is presenting industrial work and the effects of deindustrialization in ways that respect and value working-class experience in all its complexity. This requires balancing preservation, commemoration, and critique and considering the full range of cultural resources. The typical sources of historical and social science research – oral histories, written documents, news and government reports, and so on – are usefully complemented by creative sources like art, music, and literature. While such works of imaginative engagement make no pretense to accuracy, their imaginative qualities reveal how their creators understand history and place. They offer affective and perspectival accuracy, so to speak, that helps to make the experience of the half-life visible.

Interpretive research, heritage sites, and representations also make visible threads of conflict and influence that extend into the period of the half-life, threads that are not only visible in these projects but also often implicated in their development. High and Stefan Berger point out that heritage efforts link deindustrialization with gentrification, both shaped by economic and political interests (Berger and High, 2019, p. 5). As Zazzara puts it, the ways that we commemorate the industrial and deindustrial past reflect "material and symbolical selections and negotiations between social, political and economic actors." Indeed, she argues, both heritage and deindustrialization itself are sites of conflict, "battlefields where opposing values and interests regularly confront one another" (Zazzara, 2021, p. 156). Including deindustrialization in industrial heritage can, as Zazzara puts it, enable us to "move beyond politics of requalification (which often coincide with gentrification processes), beyond the linear history of scientific progress, and beyond a sweetened or nostalgic narrative" (Zazzara, 2021, p. 163). While Zazzara does not use the half-life in making this argument, the metaphor could help advance the claim that we must not only commemorate the past but also make visible its continuing conflicts, including the costs of 'progress.' Heritage sites and cultural representations are products of the half-life, emerging in the context of the experiences of individuals and communities dealing with economic and social disruptions, but unlike many of the effects of deindustrialization, they are deliberate interventions. They interpret and comment on the past and its continuing influence. They make the toxicity of the half-life visible and may function as warnings about economic violence, even as they also ensure the continuation of the half-life itself by insisting that audiences and scholars keep thinking and talking about it.

The Limits of the Half-Life

The projects discussed here, like the dozens of other pieces that use the metaphor in more limited ways, suggest that the half-life can be a productive metaphor for deindustrialization studies. But like any theory, it also has limitations, and these reflect challenges for our field. Most important, while the half-life rightly emphasizes the toxicity and persistence of deindustrialization, it can also focus our attention too narrowly on harm and danger. To be sure, injury and loss, and responses to these effects, are primary concerns of deindustrialization studies, however, as High points out in his study of Pont Saint-Charles, our fixation on damage can lead us to ignore or to discount evidence of the resilience and adaptability of deindustrialized communities. The metaphor of the half-life can discourage us from considering – to adapt Herbert Gutman's familiar line – not only what was done to deindustrialized communities but what they did with what was done to them (Gutman, 1987). And for all of the injuries of deindustrialization, it has also generated some productive adaptations. My work on "rust belt chic" reflects the problem with focusing too insistently on harm: I have viewed efforts to reframe the industrial working-class past and the potential for creative redevelopment of the deindustrialized built environment with skepticism (see Linkon, 2018, pp. 131–162). We should critique projects that seek to capitalize on working-class history while failing to help – and sometimes even exploiting – workers in the present. We have a responsibility to highlight how deindustrialization contributes to a politics of resentment that can generate support for fascism. Yet we should also embrace and examine narratives that reveal the persistence of working-class communities and perspectives.

Two specific American examples illustrate the productive potential of deindustrialization's half-life. Belt Publishing began in 2013, in Cleveland, as an effort to promote positive stories about the Rust Belt region. Its creators both embraced and resisted the idea that deindustrialized places could be cool, and its publications at once tapped into and critiqued nostalgia for the region's working-class roots. The company has published anthologies of essays, neighborhood guides, and map collections by residents of deindustrialized cities. These books often combine fond, even idealized, personal memories with more critical takes on the character, history, and challenges of these places. Belt also sells a Rust Belt Arcana tarot deck and 'Rust Belt Chic' T-shirts and publishes an online magazine with articles and photo essays that consider current developments in the region, including discussions of how local politics reflect broader concerns. The press's work clearly recognizes the continuing influence of economic change and represents the region and its people as resilient and creative. Its products make a provocative case that these places matter not only because of their industrial histories but also because of their deindustrial persistence. That the press has expanded its list far beyond writing about the Rust Belt demonstrates the potential for innovation and growth emerging from a focus on deindustrialization. Belt has gained national recognition as a "worker-owned and woman-led" company[10] that produces award-winning books and advocates for a collaborative and supportive business model that pushes back against the exploitative practices of the mainstream industry. While many of its books reflect the toxicity of the half-life, Belt Publishing also reminds us that the half-life is not only about loss and harm.

Utica, New York, represents a different kind of adaptation. I learned about its story from a student writing his undergraduate American Studies thesis about that city's renewal (Debraggio, 2016). My interests in the long-term damage of deindustrialization led me to push back on Andrew Debraggio's optimism about his hometown, but I was also taken with the story he told. He argued that Utica's embrace of refugees from Africa, Asia, and Europe helped to shore up its residential neighborhoods, created opportunities for new small businesses, including some in redeveloped former warehouses and factories, and enabled the founding of a major new company, Chobani yogurt, which employs many of those refugees (Debraggio, 2016, p. 26; See also Hartman, 2022). I am too much of an academic not to view such good news stories with a critical eye, and I am sure there are nuances in Utica's story, but we should not ignore examples of working-class communities that have adapted to and even gained strength despite – or even because of – economic change. How might our understanding of deindustrialization's half-life change if we included stories like this alongside examinations of places and people who have struggled to recover? If the half-life metaphor has the effect of limiting our ability or willingness to recognize productive change in working-class communities or working-class culture, then we should, at the very least, be careful how we use it.

Happily, the half-life is only one of several articulations of the long-term effects of deindustrialization, so we should understand it as part of a vocabulary for articulating the central concerns of the field as we tackle the question of why deindustrialization matters decades after shutdowns. The half-life can complement and complicate other terms, as we see in High's combination of this metaphor with Nixon's idea of slow violence or in Pleasant's use of Geoff Bright's adaptation of Avery Gordon's theory of haunting in her discussion of older workers being "half-alive" (Pleasant, 2019, p. 224). Tim Strangleman incorporates the half-life metaphor into his framing of industrialization and deindustrialization not as discrete events but as transitional periods of cultural resistance and adaptation to economic and structural change. Also, he draws on historical and sociological theories to identify parallels between what Raymond Williams calls 'residual structures of feeling' in the transition into industrialization and the cultural overlap between the industrial and deindustrial periods. This approach highlights the interconnections between industrialization and deindustrialization, reminding us that the vectors of historical change move in two directions: earlier research on industrialization offers models for thinking about deindustrialization, just as our studies of the effects of deindustrialization invite us to think more critically about "older industrial culture itself, prompting questions about environment, economy, social relations, divisions of class, gender, race and the meaning of work" (Strangleman, 2017, p. 473). As this suggests, the half-life is just one of several concepts through which deindustrialization studies has taken up the challenge that Cowie and Heathcott posed in 2003: that we should expand our work beyond the immediate impact of shutdowns and "rethink the chronology, memory, spatial relations, culture and politics of what we have come to call 'deindustrialization'" (Cowie and Heathcott, 2003, pp. 1–2). As a metaphor, the half-life of deindustrialization enables interpretation and adaption that may, in conversation with other approaches and concepts, help us consider nuances of our shared object of study.

Notes

1 See my article (2013), "Narrating Past and Future: Deindustrialized Landscapes as Resources," in "Crumbling Cultures," a special issue of *International Labor and Working-Class History*, Strangleman, T., Rhodes, J., and Linkon, S.L. eds., My 2018 book, *The Half-Life of Deindustrialization: Working-Class Writing about Economic Restructuring* (Michigan) extended that analysis across several themes and a wide range of texts. As of January 2023, Google Scholar indicates that these have been cited more than 145 times. The phrase has probably been used without formal citation additional times, and by this time, it is likely being used without being linked to me – as it should be.

2 I use figures from Google Scholar here, which provide an incomplete measure. It lists reviews and citations that make no direct reference to deindustrialization or its half-life. This also counts only materials in print, not conference papers or other scholarly work.

3 For example, a plan to locate a museum documenting the history of the steel industry in an abandoned mill in Youngstown proved impossible because of the cost of removing asbestos and cleaning up the polluted ground. In his study of redevelopment in Anaconda, Montana, Kent Curtis (in Cowie and Heathcott, pp. 91–111) describes how a golf course built on the site of a former mine and smelter had to bar golfers from walking off the landscaped part of the course to protect them from exposure to toxins and to limit erosion that could release dangerous chemicals into the local drinking water.

4 *Steeltown USA: Work and Memory in Youngstown* (Kansas, 2002) offers our fullest examination of the half-life, a more focused analysis of how the city's image changed over time can be found in "Collateral Damage: Deindustrialization and the Uses of Youngstown," in Cowie and Heathcott.

5 In 2022, Russo and I argued that Youngstown's continuing struggles do not reflect the community's failures but rather the limitations of revitalization efforts in the absence of good, stable working-class jobs. See 'Recalibrating Expectations: Lessons from Youngstown, OH,' in *The Future of Cities*, edited by Ryan Streeter and Joel Kotkin, from American Enterprise Institute.

6 During and soon after the 2016 election, I published several commentaries on BillMoyers.com, linking deindustrialization and the politics of resentment with Trump's support from many white working-class voters in deindustrialized areas. Lois Weis's 2004 *Class Reunion: The Remaking of the American White Working Class.* (New York: Routledge) suggests that, for some, deindustrialization led to more balanced gender roles among younger adults.

7 See chapter 4 of *Steeltown USA*.

8 See, for example, Jacqueline Alemany's September, 2016 report from CBS News, 'On a Street in Ohio, Defiant Democrats Flock to Trump' or Trip Gabriel's *New York Times* article from May, 2019, 'There's No Boom in Youngstown, but Blue-Collar Workers are Sticking with Trump.'

9 As they note early on, this piece is one outcome of a large-scale study of organized crime in Scotland; they have published several articles from that study, some with other colleagues.

10 Founder Anne Trubek has led the way with creativity, insight, and a commitment to an alternative economic model. See "About Belt (n.d.)" for more in the history and goals of this project.

Reference List

About Belt. (n.d.). Belt Publishing. https://beltpublishing.com/pages/about (Accessed: 27 May 2024).

Alemany, J. (2016, September 21). On a Street in Ohio, Defiant Democrats Flock to Trump. *CBS News.* https://www.cbsnews.com/news/on-a-street-in-ohio-defiant-democrats-flock-to-trump/ (Accessed: 27 May 2024).

Berger, S. and High, S. (2019). (De-)Industrial Heritage: An Introduction. *Labor (Durham, N.C.),* 16(1), pp. 1–27. https://doi.org/10.1215/15476715-7269281 (Accessed: 27 May 2024).

Cowie, J. and Heathcott, J. (2003). *Beyond the Ruins: The Meanings of Deindustrialization.* Ithaca, NY: ILR Press.

Debraggio, A. (2016). *(Re)Imagine all the (Rust Belt) People: Living Life in Today's Postindustrial Utica, New York.* Georgetown University.

Fraser, A. and Clark, A. (2021). Damaged Hardmen: Organized Crime and the Half-Life of Deindustrialization. *The British Journal of Sociology,* 72(4), pp. 1062–1076. https://doi.org/10.1111/1468-4446.12828 (Accessed: 27 May 2024).

Gabriel, T. (2019). A Blue-Collar City Sticks with Trump. *The New York Times.*

Gutman, H. (1987). Labor History and the 'Sartre Question'. In *Power and Culture: Essays on the American Working Class.* New York: Pantheon Books, pp. 326–328.

Hartman, S. (2022, June 3). How Refugees Transformed a Dying Rust Belt Town. *New York Times.* https://www.nytimes.com/interactive/2022/06/03/realestate/utica-burma-refugees.html (Accessed: 27 May 2024).

Hayden, D. (1995). *The Power of Place: Urban Landscapes as Public History.* Cambridge, MA: MIT Press.

High, S. (2021). The 'Normalized Quiet of Unseen Power': Recognizing the Structural Violence of Deindustrialization as Loss. *Urban History Review*, 48(2), pp. 97–115.

Linkon, S.L. (2013). Narrating Past and Future: Deindustrialized Landscapes as Resources. *International Labor and Working Class History*, 84, pp. 38–54. https://doi.org/10.1017/S0147547913000240 (Accessed: 27 May 2024).

Linkon, S.L. (2016). *BillMoyers.com*.

Linkon, S.L. (2018). *The Half-Life of Deindustrialization: Working-Class Writing about Economic Restructuring*. Ann Arbor: University of Michigan.

Linkon, S.L. and Russo, J. (2002). *Steeltown U.S.A.: Work and Memory in Youngstown*. Lawrence, KS: University Press of Kansas.

Linkon, S.L. and Russo, J. (2023). Recalibrating Expectations: Lessons from Youngstown, OH. In Streeter, R. and Kotkin, J. (eds.) *The Future of Cities*. American Enterprise Institute.

Ousby, I. (ed.). (2000). Metaphor. In *The Cambridge Guide to Literature in English*. 2nd edn. Cambridge: Cambridge University Press. https://proxy.library.georgetown.edu/login?url=https://search.credoreference.com/content/entry/cupliteng/metaphor/0?institutionId=702 (Accessed: 7 June 2022).

Pleasant, E. (2019). *Beyond the Dockyards: Changing Narratives of Industrial Occupational Cultures in Medway*. Doctor of Philosophy (PhD) thesis, University of Kent.

Russo, J. and Linkon, S.L. (2009). The Social Costs of Deindustrialization. In McCormack, R.A. (ed.) *Manufacturing a Better Future for America*. Alliance of American Manufacturers, pp. 149–174.

Strangleman, T. (2017). Deindustrialisation and the Historical Sociological Imagination: Making Sense of Work and Industrial Change. *Sociology (Oxford)*, 51(2), pp. 466–482. https://doi.org/10.1177/0038038515622906 (Accessed: 27 May 2024).

Strangleman, T., Rhodes, J. and Linkon, S.L. (eds.). (2013). Crumbling Cultures' Special Issue. *International Labor and Working Class History*, 84.

Trauth, K.M., Hora, S.C. and Guzowski, R.V. (1993, November 1). *Expert Judgment on Markers to Deter Inadvertent Human Intrusion into the Waste Isolation Pilot Plant*, report. Albuquerque, NM. https://digital.library.unt.edu/ark:/67531/metadc1279277/ (Accessed: 27 May 2024).

Walley, C.J. (2013). *Exit Zero: Family and Class in Postindustrial Chicago*. Chicago: The University of Chicago Press.

Weis, L. (2004). *Class Reunion: The Remaking of the American White Working Class*. New York: Routledge.

Zazzara, G. (2021, July). Making Sense of the Industrial Past: Deindustrialisation and Industrial Heritage in Italy. *Italia Contemporanea Yearbook 2020*, pp. 155–181.

3

DEINDUSTRIALIZATION AS GLOBAL HISTORY

Jim Tomlinson

Introduction

The global spread of industry is one of the key narratives of modern history. For most countries the expansion of industry has been central to economic growth and to "development" broadly conceived (O'Rourke and Williamson, 2017; Allen, 2014). It is almost banal to assert that "our modern world is in many ways the product of industrialization" (Rodrik, 2016).

But between the Great Financial Crash of 2007–2008 and the onset of COVID-19 something remarkable in world history occurred, measured by the share of industrial employment in total employment, we entered a phase of *global* employment deindustrialization, with the proportion falling 0.4% between 2012 and 2019 ((Rodrik, 2016, pp. 2–4; Tregenna, 2009, pp. 433–436; See Figure 3.1). Of course, the trend of industrial *output* continues upwards – but given the rate of increase in industrial productivity, this increased output requires proportionally fewer workers. Even in a slow-growing country like the UK, labor productivity growth in manufacturing (which constitutes by far the larger portion of the industrial sector) has grown on trend at around 4% per annum (Broadberry and Leunig, 2013, Table 3.1). That means if industrial output is growing at less than 4% per annum (a rate that few countries have sustained for a long period), employment will shrink in *absolute* terms. But as a proportion of the total economy, industrial output has commonly shrunk, so the *proportion* of industrial workers has been even more contractionary. While there are a small number of countries bucking the trend, for the world as a whole it is clear that the weight of industrial workers in the total workforce is declining for the first time since the industrial revolution.

In fact, the global figure had been falling in the 1990s, until the extraordinary industrial transformation of China, with such a large weight in the global total, drove that figure up to its peak in 2012–2014, before decline again set in. A fall of 0.4 per cent by 2019 might seem a small number to put much weight upon, but in absolute terms it amounted to a fall of almost three million workers. In addition, given the striking fall in the Chinese figure (c.2 per cent) over the same period, it seems clear that the main driver of the global expansion of the previous decade has exhausted itself. Neither of these aggregates is likely to be a blip.

DOI: 10.4324/9781003308324-6

Deindustrialization as Global History

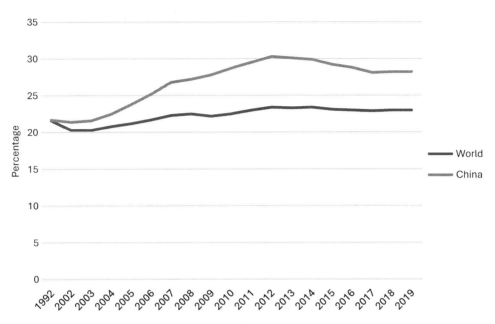

Figure 3.1 Percentage of working population in industry

Table 3.1 Structural change in employment in England, 1600–c.1817 (percentage of males) (Wrigley, 2016, p. 71)

	1600	c.1710	c. 1817
Primary	71	50.8	39.4
Secondary	21.0	37.2	42.1
Tertiary	8.0	12.0	18.4
Male population aged 15–64 (000)	1,242	1,576	2,910

The long-run global decline up to 2002 reflected the employment deindustrialization of the world's biggest economies outside China – the US, Germany, Japan, which dates back decades, and extended to the whole OECD area from the 1960s (see Figure 3.1). In China it was an explicit aim of the 13th Plan (2016–2020) to bring about a small fall in the share of the labor force in industry. The current Plan may aim to make China a world leading manufacturing country, but that aim is linked to rapid technological and productivity increase, not more industrial workers (State Council, 2015).

Employment is defined as persons of working age who were engaged in any activity to produce goods or provide services for pay or profit, whether at work during the reference period or not at work due to temporary absence from a job or to working-time arrangement.

The industry sector consists of mining and quarrying, manufacturing, construction, and public utilities (electricity, gas, and water), in accordance with divisions 2–5 (ISIC 2) or categories C-F (ISIC 3) or categories B-F (ISIC 4) (World Bank, 2024).

Employment deindustrialization has long been recognized in mature industrial economies, but it has increasingly been seen in many of the "late-comers" to development, who are suffering what some development economists call "premature deindustrialization," meaning a loss of industrial employment at much lower levels of industrialization and income per head than in the history of mature economies (Rodrik, 2016; Tregenna, 2015). Some of this downward pressure in poorer countries has been conjunctural, driven by the impact of China's recent explosive growth in driving up demand and prices for commodities and, in consequence, drawing resources away from the industrial sector in commodity-exporting countries (Wood and Mayer, 2011). But some of it may be secular, as global demand for industrial products does not expand fast enough to leave enough room for major output expansions in countries currently with small industrial populations.

Of course, 'deindustrialization' is not a neutral, purely descriptive term. Just like all terms used to describe historical processes, it is itself the product of a complex and controversial history. This chapter addresses the historical underpinnings, meanings, and deployment of the term. The story of industrialization is commonly one of intellectual, social, and political, as well as economic transformation; its reversal poses similar questions about the significance of deindustrialization.

The first section traces the underpinning idea of the economy as constituted by different 'sectors,' showing how the centrality of one sector, industry, became the dominant understanding of economic and social change from the eighteenth century to the twentieth century. The second looks at the emergence of ideas that diagnosed a supposed transition to a new kind of nonindustrial society. Various terminologies were attempted to characterize the outcome of this shift, with 'deindustrialization,' with its negative connotations, emerging only late in the day, following earlier discussions which used terms such as the 'service economy' and the 'post-industrial society.' The third section looks at the historical evolution of the term deindustrialization and its deployment as a historical category. The final section looks at the causes and consequences of the spread of deindustrialization in the recent historical past.

Economy and industry

A tripartite division of the economy, with the designation of a separate industrial sector, can be traced back to the seventeenth century when William Petty, often regarded as the founder of national income accounting, wrote: "there is much more to be gained by Manufacture than by Husbandry, and by Merchandize than Manufacture," an assertion linked to an attempt to understand the prosperity of the Netherlands (Hull, 1899, p. 256).

Over the succeeding two centuries, the emergent discipline of (classical) political economy talked a great deal about industry and rather less about services. When it did discuss the latter, much of what was said was framed by questions about the productiveness, or otherwise, of service activity. Illustrative of this kind of linkage was Adam Smith, who wrote that there were two types of labor:

> The former produces a value, may be called productive, the latter, unproductive. Thus, the labor of a manufacturer (i.e. an industrial worker) adds generally to the value of the materials, which he works upon, that of his own maintenance, and of his master's profit. The labor of a menial servant, on the contrary, adds to the value of nothing.

Yet Smith was wrestling with this, adding the argument later in the same passage that the labor of the menial servant "has its value, and deserves its reward" (Smith, 1976, p. 330). The terminology of 'productiveness,' which often treated industrial activity as in some important sense more productive than other forms, was to cast a long shadow.

In the late nineteenth century, the neoclassical revolution in economics undermined all the debate about 'productiveness' and value as something linked to the character of the activity producing economic goods, in favor of the view that 'value' should be seen as something imparted to any kind of commodity only by the *demand* for that commodity. In this version of the world, how much labor was embodied in a commodity and whether or not the commodity took the form of a tangible, physical entity were both irrelevant considerations (Delaunay and Gadrey, 1992, p. 64). Paradoxically, this shift in economic theory was taking place at a time when industry was seen as more important than ever in the world of politics and policy because of its perceived centrality to the two great intertwined projects of the nineteenth and twentieth centuries – nation-building and economic prosperity.

The idea that industrialization was the key to national prosperity arose in the wake of the industrial revolution in Britain, seen by many as the harbinger of modernity. For Hobsbawm, "The Industrial revolution marks the most fundamental transformation of human life in the history of the world recorded in written documents" (Hobsbawm, 1968, p. 1). This formulation not only became the common sense of most historians but, more importantly, became embedded in the beliefs of rulers of most existing or fledgling nation-states by the middle of the nineteenth century (Gellner, 1983). In the broadest terms, industrialization has been integral to the creation and persistence of most nation-states, and in the nineteenth century all the ascending powers sought to industrialize. Britain, of course, was the 'first industrial nation,' but its rivals, most obviously the US and then Germany, sought to follow suit. Friedrich List, who analyzed the possibilities for both countries, famously founded a genre of "National Political Economy" whose central concern was how these countries could industrialize in the face of the competition from the British pioneer (Levi-Faur, 1997). In the US, Alexander Hamilton, the first Secretary of the Treasury from 1789 to 1795, was the key political actor in seeking to transform the new state's economy. Like the leaders of all 'late-industrializers,' Hamilton was happy to deploy all means, legal or otherwise, to gain the knowledge of new industrial processes. After unification, Germany became synonymous with a nation-building project centered on state-guided industrialization (Gerschenkron, 1962).

Factory-based manufacturing spread from Western Europe through much of the rest of the world, peaking in the "Golden Age" of c.1960–1973 (O'Rourke and Williamson, 2017, pp. 2–3). The belief that industrialization was central to national prosperity (and security) continued to be powerful through the twentieth century. It was embodied in the extraordinary Soviet industrialization effort from 1928, the efforts of the "Asian Tigers" later in the twentieth century, and, of course, Communist China (Davies, 1974–2018; Chang 2006).

In Britain, the pioneer industrializer, the shift out of agriculture long pre-dated the industrial revolution. Table 3.1 suggests how early the proportion of those employed in agriculture began to fall.[1] The corollary of this was the shift into secondary and tertiary occupations. The growth of secondary occupations – industrial in other words – was striking even before 1710 and emphasizes how much the changes we link to the industrial revolution involved switches in *types* of industrial jobs rather than their overall increase. So a simple historical stage theory based on the statistical predominance in turn of agriculture, industry, and services can be highly misleading. Industrialization in Britain was accompanied, and indeed

Table 3.2 Sectoral shares of labor in Britain, 1856–1973 (Matthews, Feinstein, and Odling-Smee, 1982, pp. 223–224)[2]

	1856	1873	1913*	1924	1937*	1951	1964	1973
Agriculture Fishing and Forestry	29.6	21.4	10.4	8.1	5.6	5.6	4.1	2.9
Mining and Quarrying	3.6	4.1	6.2	6.2	4.1	3.7	2.6	1.5
Manufacturing	32.5	33.5	32.3	32.9	31.7	35.1	36.1	34.7
Construction	4.0	4.8	4.9	4.5	6.0	6.9	8.5	8.7
Gas, Electricity, and Water	0.1	0.2	0.7	1.1	1.3	1.6	1.7	1.4
Transport and Communication	4.1	5.6	8.0	8.6	7.7	8.1	7.5	7.5
Commerce	20.8	24.7	29.3	29.2	34.0	23.4	24.5	25.4
Public and Professional Services	5.3	5.7	7.9	9.4	9.9	16.6	15.0	18.0

greatly facilitated, by the growth of services in transport and communication, in finance, and in retail and wholesale trade.

Three important points emerge from Table 3.2. First, the very long-run decline of agriculture was at its peak in the decades immediately before 1913, and thereafter the sector was too small to make a major contribution to the change in the labor force. This contrasts with most of the rest of Western Europe, where the agricultural labor shrinkage was rapid after 1945 and was crucial to the various 'economic miracles' in those countries during the three decades after the war. It is also noticeable that after 1924 the decline in agricultural employment is broadly paralleled by that in mining, emphasizing how important employment in that sector – especially in coal – had grown by the First World War.

Second, the other most striking change in the period was the growth of public and professional services, greatly expanding forms of employment requiring high levels of formal education, a trend with not only major economic but also cultural and social implications. A significant part of this was the growth of public sector services, especially health and education, again linked to one of the key persistent changes in the twentieth-century world: the growth of state expenditure and of tax regimes to finance this growth.

Third, and most directly important in the discussion of deindustrialization, was the strikingly *stable* share of manufacturing, by far the biggest industrial sector. Apart from the impact of the two world wars, there is remarkably little variation in this figure. The wartime and postwar shift to a more distinctly industrial economy is rightly emphasized by Edgerton (Edgerton, 2018).

From the mid-1960s the trend in manufacturing employment, and because of its weight in the total, the whole of industry, was unambiguously downwards. Around the end of the twentieth century, Britain passed the 80% figure for those employed in the service sector, the industrial sector falling below 20%.[3]

Beyond industrial society?

As argued later, the specific term 'deindustrialization' was not significant in public discussion until the 1970s and 1980s, but the idea that some economies were beginning to move beyond the industrial stage has a much longer history. A key author in beginning the analysis of 'post-industrial' society (without himself using that terminology) was A.G.B. Fisher. In his *Clash of Progress and Security* of 1935, he started from the paradox that many commentators in Australia and New Zealand in the 1930s believed their countries' futures depended upon an indefinite expansion of their rural populations, while what was actually happening was a growing urban population fed from an increasingly efficient agriculture. His conclusion was clear: "To complain about the world-wide drift to the towns is to complain that the whole world is growing richer" (Fisher, 1935, p. vi). A simple moral followed: "Material progress means change, and change frequently inflicts much inconvenience and suffering upon individuals directly affected." He stressed the importance of education in allowing people to adjust to the demand for new skills as new types of employment expanded (Fisher, 1935, pp. 7, 66–68, 204).

Fisher saw structural change as following three 'stages,' echoing much older, Enlightenment-era thinking, but also feeding forward into many subsequent accounts. So there was a 'primary producing stage' when agricultural and pastoral occupations were most important; a 'manufacturing or industrial or secondary producing stage,' which he conventionally dated as beginning in Britain at the end of the eighteenth century; and a 'tertiary' stage (which) begins in the twentieth century. Fisher noted that "It has been a well-known feature of modern economic development that the proportion of total population engaged in 'tertiary' production has been rapidly growing," and he cited evidence for this trend since 1920, in both the US and the UK (Fisher, 1935, pp. 25–28, 30–31). Such broad ideas about tertiary growth were indeed in general circulation among economists in the 1930s.

Another key figure was Colin Clark, a pioneer of national income accounting but with a broad interest in structural change which marked him out from others working on constructing such accounts.[4] His *Conditions of Economic Progress*, drafted in the late 1930s, was influential in post-1945 concerns with economic development and growth in a Cold War context (Clark, 1953). It fed into Kuznet's foundational text on *Modern Economic Growth*, which stressed the importance of structural change, especially shifts in the composition of *output* toward industry, while noting the rising share of labor in services in a number of countries (Kuznets, 1966).

Concern about structural change was returned to in several registers in the 1960s. The post-Second World War revolution in international economic statistics fed into the first detailed comparative analyses of the rise of the service sector, with Lengelle's OECD study. This noted that, among the richest countries, especially in North America, the trend to a shift of employment from industry to services was unmistakable and that Western Europe overall would follow the same trajectory over the next decades (Lengelle, 1966, pp. 18–20).

The possible impact of the sectoral shift on overall productivity became a huge issue in ensuing decades because of fears that productivity in services was necessarily slower-growing than in industry. This issue was addressed at a theoretical level by Baumol, who argued that it was inherently difficult to improve productivity in many areas of the service sector. He used an example which became famous: the 30-minute Mozart quartet, which would take two hours of labor to provide whether performed in 1700 or 1965. Also, Baumol pointed to the growing weight of health and education within the service sector and again emphasized the difficulties of raising productivity where the provision of a service requires personal contact with the customer (Baumol, 1967; Baumol, 1993). This question about the productivity implications of service expansion has continued to be central to the work of economists and economic historians who are concerned with economic growth (Broadberry, 2006).

Baumol's approach to the service sector emphasized the supply side aspects, with low productivity growth in services compared with industry inescapable because of less dramatic technological possibilities. This contributed to the funneling of more and more workers into the former activity. Shifting emphasis to the demand side allows for a more optimistic interpretation. This suggests that the income elasticity of demand is lowest for agricultural products (food), higher for tangible industrial goods, and highest for services. Thus rising incomes are seen as closely allied with sectoral shifts (Wrigley, 2016; Wren, 2013, p. 3). This broad idea is crucial to many accounts of long-run sectoral change and implies a rather more benign process at work than where the emphasis is on supply side *constraints* (Fuchs, 1968).

The sense of epochal shift was evident elsewhere in the 1960s in the sociological debate about the 'post-industrial society.' This was influenced by economists such as Clark, but also by sociological thinking about the 'future of work,' especially among French neo-Marxists concerned with the existence and character of the working class as an agent of revolutionary change (Touraine, 1974). In Britain in the 1970s, there was a similar pessimism that the Labour Party was in long-term electoral decline because of the transformation of the industrial structure since 1945 and especially the decline of the industrial working class (Hobsbawm, 1978, pp. 279–280). Psephologists were by no means universally convinced by these arguments, but their appearance in strong form in the mid-1970s coincides, as discussed later, with the emergence of public discussion of deindustrialization and helped animate that discussion (Crewe, 1991).

The potentially radical impact of structural change on the gender composition of the workforce was increasingly recognized from the 1960s. Mingelle's OECD study was unambiguous: the expansion of services was favoring women's employment even though this was not uniform across all service subsectors (Lengelle, 1966, pp. 21–22). A more emphatic iteration of such claims was later made by Delaunay and Gadrey:

> The social prominence of men over women, once a pillar of the traditional social structure, is a thing of the past, largely as the result of the rise of the services sector and its reliance on a female labor force.
>
> *(Delaunay and Gadrey, 1992, p. 1)*

Whether patriarchy has been decisively uprooted and 'largely' by employment change may well be doubted, but that the rise of the service sector has transformed women's labor market experience across much of the world is clearly the case and a key element in any discussion of deindustrialization (Horrell, 2000).

Not all theorists of 'post-industrialism' have direct political concerns or much engagement with the gendered implications. The American sociologist Daniel Bell's *Coming of Post-Industrial Society* was focused on the changing structure of occupations, and he saw the decline in industrial work, pioneered in the US, as leading to a fundamental change in social structure. For him, the future was one of especially rapid growth of services in the form of health, education, research, and government, leading to the creation of a 'new intelligentsia' and the 'pre-eminence of the professional and technical class.' While drawing on ideas that had come to have wide circulation by the end of the 1960s, Bell was also a precursor to much later discussions of the "information society" (Bell, 1973).

Many of those who have written about "the rise of the service economy" or the coming of "post-industrial society" have attached broadly positive connotations to this shift, in contrast to those who speak of "deindustrialization," with its sense of a damaging and even dangerous historical turn (Rowthorn and Wells, 1986, pp. 24–25).[5] Somewhere between these poles of argument have been the political scientists who debate the "political economy" of the service transition (Wren, 2013). This literature is especially useful because of its focus on the labor market effects of the expansion of services and the potential implications these have for political allegiances. In particular, it points to dilemma arising in a political economy characterized by the growth of low productivity and often publicly funded employment. The reconciliation of demands for egalitarian wage structures and expectations of full employment with political constraints on taxation and state expenditure becomes much harder to achieve (Iversen and Wren, 1998).

The invention of 'deindustrialization'

The idea of a shift to an economy where industry and industrial employment was less important was well-established in academic debate in advanced countries by the 1960s. While the idea of a transition to a service economy was viewed through both optimistic and pessimistic lens, the invention of the term 'deindustrialization' to describe this structural shift undoubtedly embedded a negative sense of its implications – something was clearly being lost rather than gained.

Reductions in industrial activity and employment in particular localities or regions can be found throughout modern history, but before the 1970s the term deindustrialization was largely confined to the analysis of the historical impact of European industrialization on "Third World" countries, especially colonies of European Empires (Johnson, 2002). The classic case was India, where it was widely argued that a significant part of Britain's 'early start' in industrialization (especially in the key area of cotton textiles) was directly at the expense of India, whose textiles had succumbed first to Britain's barriers to their export and then from competition in the home market from British factory goods, unhindered by any protection because of imperially imposed free trade (Clingingsmith and Williamson, 2008). The nature and significance of this process is a highly contentious topic in Indian and imperial history, but the particular industrial trajectory of India means that it remains a key country in current debates about the industrialization and deindustrialization.

Deindustrialization also figured in debates about postwar Germany, with specific proposals with this end in mind famously put forward in the Morgenthau plan for depriving the country of its war-making capacity by stripping back its major industries. This, of course, was never implemented (Gareau, 1961).

Deindustrialization as a term to describe contemporary changes in industrial structure and employment emerged prominently into public discourse for the first time in a specific national context, that of Britain in the mid-1970s, so it is worth examining this particular context in some detail. The groundwork had been laid in debates in the 1960s, when, in the context of declinist debates about Britain's economic performance, the economist Nikolas Kaldor developed general economic models that argued that manufacturing was crucial to economic growth, and that, simultaneously, Britain's economic failings derived from poor industrial performance (Kaldor, 1966).

Kaldor then deserves to be seen as the academic originator of the term deindustrialization to describe a *pathological* weakening of industrial performance and a decline in industrial employment (Singh, 1989, p. 103). In his view, manufacturing was central to the growth performance of the economy, especially because of the importance of the sector for productivity. Kaldor's argument had an unusually direct impact on government policy. As economic adviser to the Labor governments from 1964 to 1970, Kaldor initiated the Selective Employment Tax, which incentivized employment in the manufacturing sector at the expense of services (Tomlinson, 2004, pp. 132–134, 225–226). Kaldor also influenced Ajit Singh, author in 1977 of one of the first academic articles that sought to define deindustrialization. For Singh, this was the inability of the economy to generate enough manufacturing exports to finance a full employment level of imports (Singh, 1977).

The initial public use of the term in Britain followed the end of the international post-war boom in 1973/1974, marked by the surge in global oil prices (OPEC 1) and the first significant economic recession since 1945. While most British arguments on deindustrialization have come from the Left of center, the initial public debate originated from a more conservative position, when, in 1974, *the Sunday Times* ran a series of articles by economists Bacon and Eltis which argued that "Britain's difficulties . . . largely result from a structural shift away from industry since 1962." Bacon and Eltis then published a book arguing that the unwelcome structural move out of industry was the result of an excessive growth of the 'non-marketed sector' of the economy: the culprit, in other words, was the state, with government services provided in kind "crowding out" private investment in manufacturing (Bacon and Eltis, 1976).[6] This was arguably a proto-Thatcherite position (Barnett, 1987).[7] But the Left soon reclaimed the agenda, with the Labor government's Secretary of State for Industry, Tony Benn, lamented in April 1975 the "devastating trend to contraction of British industry." In the budget speech that same month, the Chancellor of the Exchequer, Denis Healey, explicitly used the word 'deindustrialization.' Referencing Benn's influence, Healey urged: "We must reverse the process of deindustrialization – of a steady loss of jobs and factory capacity year after year – which my right hon. Friend the Secretary of State for Industry described so convincingly in a recent article" (Parliamentary Debates, Commons, 1975).

In 1978, a landmark conference largely followed Singh – and Kaldor – in agreeing a macroeconomic view of the problem, linked to Britain's trading performance. Frank Blackaby, editor of the resulting book, opined: "In 'Deindustrialization' we had a new label for an old problem-the relatively poor competitive performance of British manufacturing industry" (Blackaby, 1979, p. 268). But this macroeconomic focus, while not disappearing from debate, became less central in the early 1980s when 'employment deindustrialization' came into new prominence. This was the result of the extraordinary contraction of both employment and output in manufacturing which followed the election of the Thatcher government in 1979. There followed an unprecedented deindustrializing shock, leading to the loss of almost two million industrial jobs in the space of four years from 1979 to 1983 (Britton, 1991, 248). This loss of jobs was accompanied by a much more widespread use of the term deindustrialization, but the prime focus was no longer on the macroeconomic aspects but directly on industrial closures, job losses, and unemployment. This literature proliferated in Britain in the early 1980s (Martin and Rowthorn, 1986; Levie, Gregory, and Lorentzen, 1984; Foster and Woolfson, 1986; Dickson, 1987).

But although much British discussion was framed as if the process of deindustrialization was recent and confined to that country, in fact, the trend was much older and Western European wide (Table 3.3). From the 1980s, it became a commonplace in Britain that deindustrialization was the result of "Thatcherism," but although the early 1980s saw a major acceleration of industrial job losses, this was imposed on a much longer trend (Phillips, 2013; Gibbs, 2018).[8]

The use of the term deindustrialization to denote pathology of the mature economy proved to be an export product. In the early 1980s in the US, in the face of both the

Table 3.3 A common European pattern: industrial employment peaks (Feinstein, 1999, p. 39)

	Peak year	*% in industry in peak year*
UK	1955	47.9
Belgium	1957	47.0
Switzerland	1964	48.8
Netherlands	1965	41.1
Sweden	1965	42.8
West Germany	1970	49.3
Italy	1971	39.7
France	1973	39.5

immediate economic downturn and longer-term contraction of industrial employment, its use proliferated. As in Britain, contemporary literature was preoccupied with recent employment loss in industry but was distinct in exploring the migration of jobs from the 'rust-belt to the sun-belt,' from Northeastern US to the South and Southwest. Deindustrialization in these accounts reflected especially the impact of capital flight, linked to wage levels and trade union strength, and low-cost 'business-friendly' offers from state 'booster' governors in the south and the west.[9]

Also, like Britain, use of the term deindustrialization to describe a pathological state was linked to notions of national economic decline, albeit 'decline' was framed in a distinctly American fashion. In a panic akin to the 'Made in Germany' furor in Britain in the 1890s, US concerns about Japanese competition led to overblown prognostications about the future damage to American industry from foreign competition if the rising Asian power was not effectively responded to.[10] But, as in Britain, deindustrialization in the US was a long-term trend. The scale of the depression in interwar America makes it especially difficult to disentangle cycles from trends, but it seems likely that the long-run process began in the 1920s (Fuchs, 1968, p. 19). But, as in several other countries like Britain and Germany, the Second World War temporarily reversed the pattern until the 1950s.

From these origins in the 1980s, there has grown a large, especially British/North American, literature on deindustrialization, which has been especially concerned with job loss and its consequences. As it has grown, this literature has diversified both conceptually and methodologically, with, for example, substantial use of oral history methods and a burgeoning concern with the gendered consequences of employment change (High, MacKinnon, and Perchard, 2017; Bracke, 2019). The impetus for this growth has come partly from widespread perceptions of economic failure in the advanced countries of the West, especially since the GFC, perhaps especially with the concern with growing inequality. Among social and political historians of contemporary Western Europe and North America, therefore, loss of industrial employment has overwhelmingly been framed with the negative connotations of 'deindustrialization,' focusing, as Steven High notes, "on those left behind when mills and factories closed . . . leaving towns, regions, and countries without an industrial base" (High, 2013, 994). This focus on the negative aspects of employment change has led in turn to much debate about the dangers of a too nostalgic approach to industrial work (Clarke, 2015; Strangleman, 2013; Gibbs, 2021). This literature, it should be noted, has been much more concerned with the *effects* rather than the *causes* of deindustrialization.

Causes and consequences of a 'deindustrializing world'

Why has deindustrialization spread across the globe? In line with the arguments of Clark and Baumol, two large forces have been at work, albeit working at highly variable temporalities and with greatly uneven geographies. First, changes in the composition of demand, with rising incomes not matched by a proportionate rise in the demand for industrial products. Second, the rapid rise in industrial (especially manufacturing) productivity, a rise not paralleled in most of the service sector.

Recent debate in rich countries has focused on a third cause, the impact of 'globalization' in shifting employment from those countries to poorer countries, especially in Asia. This was undoubtedly important in the first years of the twenty-first century, above all with the rise of Chinese manufacturing exports and with especial impact on manufacturing employment in the US. Estimates suggest that up to 2.5 million jobs in American manufacturing could have been lost as a result of Chinese competition (Autor, Dorn, and Hanson, 2013). But, as we have seen, this was an acceleration of a much longer-term trend in American employment, driven not by international competition but by domestic demand shifts and relative productivity. The rise of industrial China was a hugely important historical event, but its occurrence should not obscure the greater importance of demand and productivity trends in shaping the long-run trend to global deindustrialization.

Arguments set out in the 1980s about deindustrialization's seriously damaging effects (focused on the rich countries) were remade with greater force in the twenty-first century. Economists and others pointed to a fundamental problem in the labor market. Where industry had historically provided large-scale, relatively stable, and well-paid employment to workers with little formal education, the new service-dominated economy offered very little to those without substantial educational qualifications. The result was a growing polarization of the labor market between those who could take up the expanding number of well-paid and relatively secure jobs in such areas as professional services, health care, and education and those whose lack of qualifications confined them to poorly paid and often precarious employment. These changes were detected in a range of rich countries, including Western Europe, the US, and Australia (Goos and Manning, 2007; Standing, 2011; Borland and Coelli, 2016).

While (state-led) industrial development had dominated in substantial parts of East Asia, including China, the problem of an absence of industrial employment was a particular worry for India, where national economic growth had accelerated from the 1980s, largely on the back of the growth of the service sector (Bosworth and Collins, 2008). This occasioned wide debate among development economists about the viability of this route to development.

Much of this was framed by the contrast with China, which from the 1980s underwent classic "Lewis-style" growth, drawing on unlimited supplies of labor from the agrarian sector to become industrial workers, this structural shift being central to China's rapidly rising GDP (Lewis, 1954). Lewis's model does not apply to recent developments in India, where agrarian employment decline has been much slower, and many agriculturalists have moved into services rather than industry (Figure 3.2). Even more serious for the overall development trajectory was that India has an almost unique bifurcated industrial sector, divided between a high productivity/high-skilled 'registered' sector and a low productivity/low-skilled 'unregistered' sector. If only the former is taken into account, India has not experienced even the slow industrialization as suggested by Figure 3.2 but employment deindustrialization. This "modern" industrial sector has been too small to act as the main driver of Indian growth, which has largely relied on the service sector (Dagsputa and Singh, 2005).

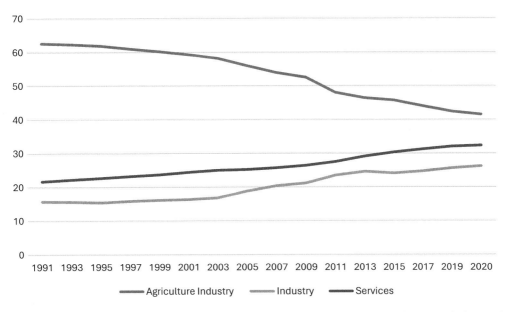

Figure 3.2 Sectoral employment in India, 1991–2020. (Source: https://data.worldbank.org/indicator/SL.IND.EMPL.ZS).

The Indian economy, measured by GDP growth, has performed well since the early 1980s, despite the performance of manufacturing – but it remains a low-income country, whereas China has ascended to middle-income status. Most analysts see India's distinctive path as problematic, given the enormous number of poorly educated Indians who in a Lewis world would be able to access industrial jobs and so escape agrarian poverty. Some jobs in the Indian service sector are high productivity/high wage like those in the 'organized' industrial sector, but most of these require highly educated workers. The transition out of agriculture for millions of Indians has been so slow because the 'traditional' route into an expanding industrial labor market has not been available.

Africa, alongside Latin America, has been a major continent of premature industrialization. The experience has not been homogenous across the continent, but most African nations have experienced 'premature' deindustrialization in Rodrik's sense and have confronted major problems parallel to those in India, of absorbing into productive work those with limited education and skills (Jalilian, Tribe, and Weiss, 2000). Some of this has been a by-product of rapid Chinese growth. In a fashion parallel to the enrichment of agrarian exporters like Australia, Argentina, and Denmark in the first great globalization circa 1870–1914, many countries had commodity export booms based on the rapid rise in Chinese demand for food and raw materials.[11] Brazil is one example where the growth in export of primary products, especially to China, has led to the decline in the relative economic role of industry. But China also competed with the industrial products of other developing economies as well as the developed, and this constrained their route to industrial expansion. A striking feature of Chinese development has been its ability to compete with not only the US and the West, where wages are higher, but also with poorer countries. Higher wages in China have been effectively offset by lower unit costs (Tregenna, 2015, p. 106).

Conclusions

It remains an apt conclusion on the history of the last 70 years that "for the vast majority of countries, successful industrialization (in the sense of developing the capacity to produce a high per capita output of manufactures) is an essential condition for the attainment of a high level of development" (Rowthorn and Wells, 1986, p. 69). But such success, where achieved, no longer carries the implication of an increasing number of industrial workers.

Employment deindustrialization is a long-term phenomenon, widely experienced across first-mover industrial economies in the third quarter of the twentieth century and increasingly apparent across most 'late-industrializers' in the final quarter. By the early twenty-first century, it was a global phenomenon, with even the 'factory of the world,' China, beginning to move in this direction.

This trajectory puts to bed any lingering, nineteenth-century notion that one day the whole world would be industrialized and that industrial workers would be numerically and potentially politically dominant. The peaks of industrial employment experienced in Western European countries in the postwar Golden Age now look like exceptions rather than presaging similar-sized sectors spreading across the world.

The narrative of industrialization and deindustrialization is often linked with stage theories in which first agriculture, then industry, and then services are the dominant employing sectors. But beyond the almost universal contraction of agriculture, such stage theories require heavy qualification. While historically most countries have experienced growth in industrial employment, this has commonly *coincided* with a growth in services rather than preceding it. Precisely because industrial expansion is accompanied by rising incomes, it reshapes patterns of demand, which commonly favor the service sector. 'The rise of the service sector' in most countries has not had to await upon deindustrialization.

Deindustrialization has not typically resulted directly from policies with that aim in mind. The drivers have largely been macro-level demand changes and productivity increases. Policy has been used, of course, to expand the size of individual industries, but no country appears to have reversed the aggregate trend. The response to this underlying trend has not been uniform, but generally worries and regrets have given way to policies that have mainly focused on *managing* its effects, with very varying levels of success (see Strath, 1987).[12]

In developing countries, deindustrialization has owed more to policy choices, with the broad trend of the last quarter of the twentieth century toward trade and financial liberalization exposing many countries to greater international competition. Some have lost out in this competition and seen their industries decline. More common has been not the displacement of "mature" industries but the failure to break into the manufacturing "club" (Tregenna, 2009, p. 106). Others have succeeded in this liberalized environment, and among the competitively successful, expansion of industrial output has been strong, not only in China but also in countries like Bangladesh and Vietnam. But success in this open environment has necessitated fast-rising productivity, increasing the gap between output increase and its employment consequences.

Deindustrialization has had no necessary outcomes for the welfare of the countries that experienced it. Where it has been accompanied by a significant rise in industrial productivity and an increase in competitiveness, this has aided a less painful transition of workers between sectors, though in no country have such pains been wholly avoided. In less dynamic economies, or where employment transitions have been less well-managed, the negative impacts on economic welfare have been very much greater and the social consequences often grave.

In that regard the negative connotations of the term 'deindustrialization' are appropriate to frame the sectoral shifts in employment that have occurred.

Notes

1 The early census used occupational distinctions, but these paralleled the three sectors: Wrigley, E.A. (2022). The PST System for Classifying Occupations. *The Cambridge Group for the History of Population and Social Structure*, paper 20. www.geog.cam.ac.uk/research/projects/occupations/abstracts/ (Accessed: 12 August 2022).
2 *For 1913 and 1937, the authors often supply two estimates, and where that is the case, the figure here is simply the mean of those two figures, rounded up.
3 International Labour Organization. (2024). *ILO Modelled Estimates Database*. ILOSTAT. https://ilostat.ilo.org/data (Accessed: 7 February 2024). https://data.worldbank.org/indicator/SL.IND.EMPL.ZS; World Bank. (2024). *Employment in Industry (% of Total Employment)*. https://data.worldbank.org/indicator/SL.IND.EMPL.ZS (Accessed: 26 May 2024).
4 On Colin Clark, see Tribe, K. (2015). *Economy of the Word*. Oxford University Press, pp. 89–107.
5 One important work in the field distinguished "positive" deindustrialization (driven by increasing efficiency in industry reducing the demand for labor) from "negative," (driven by inefficiency): Rowthorn, R. and Wells, D. (1986). *De-industrialization and Foreign Trade*. Cambridge: Cambridge University Press, pp. 24–25.
6 This work was part of a much wider attack on the growth of the public sector which was central to British politics in the 1970s.
7 Many conservatives have seen talk of "deindustrialization" as dangerous because of related calls for the state to act to reverse the process: for example, Crafts, N. (1993). *Can De-industrialisation Seriously Damage Your Wealth?* London: Institute of Economic Affairs. On the other hand, conservatives of a "Prussian" bent have been willing to embrace the term: Barnett, C. (1987). *The Audit of War*. London: Macmillan.
8 Coal mining is an important example, where postwar employment loss began in the 1950s, and in absolute numbers losses peaked in the 1960s: Phillips, J. (2013). Deindustrialization and the Moral Economy of the Scottish Coalfields, 1947 to 1991. *International Labour and Working-Class History*, 84(1), pp. 99–115; Gibbs, E. (2018). The Moral Economy of the Scottish Coalfields: Managing Deindustrialization under Nationalization c.1947–1983. *Enterprise and Society*, 19(1), pp. 214–252.
9 The most important American work was Bluestone, B. and Harrison, B. (1982). *The Deindustrialization of America. Plant Closings, Community Abandonment, and the Dismantling of Basic Industry*. New York: Basic Books. For the context of this work see Bluestone, B. (2003). Foreword. In Cowie, J. and Heathcott, J. (eds.) *Beyond the Ruins: The Meanings of Deindustrialization*. Ithaca, NY: Cornell University Press.
10 Fears of industrial Japan can be traced back to Kahn, H. (1970). *The Emerging Japanese Super-State*. New York: Prentice-Hall.
11 Australia did well in both periods, with some continuity in the products exported, especially wool.
12 Comparative studies on deindustrialization in Western Europe are surprisingly sparse, but see Strath, B. (1987). *The Politics of De-industrialisation. The Contraction of the West European Shipbuilding Industry*. London: Croom Helm.

Reference list

Allen, R. (2014). The Spread of Manufacturing. In Neal, L. and Williamson, J. (eds.) *The Cambridge History of Capitalism, Vol. II the Spread of Capitalism*. Cambridge: Cambridge University Press.
Autor, D., Dorn, D. and Hanson, G. (2013). The China Syndrome: Labor Market Effects of Import Competition in the United States. *American Economic Review*, 103(6), pp. 2121–2168.
Bacon, R. and Eltis, W. (1976). *Britain's Economic Problem: Too Few Producers*. London: Macmillan.
Barnett, C. (1987). *The Audit of War*. London: Macmillan.
Baumol, W. (1967). Macroeconomics of Unbalanced Growth: The Anatomy of Urban Crisis. *American Economic Review*, 57, pp. 415–426.

Baumol, W. (1993). Health Care, Education and the Cost Disease: A Looming Crisis for Public Choice. *Public Choice*, 77(1), pp. 17–28.

Bell, D. (1973). *The Coming of Post-industrial Society: A Venture in Social Forecasting*. New York: Basic Books.

Blackaby, F. (ed.). (1979). *De-industrialisation*. London: Heinemann, p. 268.

Bluestone, B. and Harrison, B. (1982). *The Deindustrialization of America. Plant Closings, Community Abandonment, and the Dismantling of Basic Industry*. New York: Basic Books.

Borland, J. and Coelli, M. (2016). Labour Market Inequality in Australia. *Economic Record*, 92(4), pp. 517–547.

Bosworth, B. and Collins, S. (2008). Accounting for Growth: Comparing China and India. *Journal of Economic Perspectives*, 22(1), pp. 45–66.

Bracke, M. (2019). Labour, Gender and Deindustrialisation in Fiat (Italy 1970–1980s). *Contemporary European History*, 29, pp. 484–499.

Britton, A.J.C. (1991). *Macroeconomic Policy in Britain 1974–1987*. Cambridge: Cambridge University Press.

Broadberry, S. (2006). *Market Services and the Productivity Race, 1850–2000. British Performance in International Perspective*. Cambridge: Cambridge University Press.

Broadberry, S. and Leunig, T. (2013). *The Impact of Government Policies on UK Manufacturing since 1945*. London: Government Office for Science.

Chang, H.-J. (2006). *The East Asian Development Experience: The Miracle, the Crisis and the Future*. London: Zed Books.

Clark, C. (1953). *The Conditions of Economic Progress*. London: Macmillan.

Clarke, J. (2015). Closing Time: Deindustrialization and Nostalgia in Contemporary France. *History Workshop Journal*, 79, pp. 107–125.

Clingingsmith, D. and Williamson, J. (2008). Deindustrialization in 18th and 19th Century India: Mughal Decline, Climate Shocks and British Industrial Ascent. *Explorations in Economic History*, 45(2), pp. 209–234.

Cowie, J. and Heathcott, J. (eds.). (2003). *Beyond the Ruins. The Meanings of Deindustrialization*. Ithaca, NY: Cornell University Press.

Crafts, N. (1993). *Can De-industrialisation Seriously Damage Your Wealth?* London: Institute of Economic Affairs.

Crewe, I. (1991). Labour Force Changes, Working Class Decline and the Labour Vote: Social and Electoral Trends in Postwar Britain. In Piven, F. (ed.) *Labour Parties in Postindustrial Societies*. Oxford: Oxford University Press.

Dasgupta, S. and Singh, A. (2005). Will Services be the New Engine of Indian Economic Growth?. *Development and Change*, 36(6), pp. 1035–1057.

Davies, R.W. (1974–2018). *The Industrialization of Soviet Russia*, Vols. 1–7. Cambridge, MA: Harvard University Press.

Delaunay, J.-C. and Gadrey, J. (1992). *Services in Economic Thought. Three Centuries of Debate*. Boston: Kluwer.

Dickson, T. and Judge, D. (eds.). (1987). *The Politics of Industrial Closure*. Basingstoke: Macmillan.

Edgerton, D. (2018). *The Rise and Fall of the British Nation*. London: Allen Lane.

Feinstein, C. (1999). Structural Change in the Developed Countries in the Twentieth Century. *Oxford Review of Economic Policy*, 15, p. 39.

Fisher, A.G.B. (1935). *Clash of Progress and Security*. London: Macmillan.

Foster, J. and Woolfson, C. (1986). *The Politics of the UCS Work-in: Class Alliances and the Right to Work*. London: Lawrence and Wishart.

Fuchs, V. (1968). *The Service Economy*. New York: NBER.

Gareau, F. (1961). Morgenthau's Plan for Industrial Disarmament in Germany. *The Western Political Quarterly*, 14(2), pp. 517–534.

Gellner, E. (1983). *Nations and Nationalism*. Oxford: Oxford University Press.

Gerschenkron, A. (1962). *Economic Backwardness in Historical Perspective*. Cambridge, MA: Belknap.

Gibbs, E. (2018). The Moral Economy of the Scottish Coalfields: Managing Deindustrialization under Nationalization c.1947–1983. *Enterprise and Society*, 19(1), pp. 214–252.

Gibbs, E. (2021). *Coal Country: the Meaning and Memory of Deindustrialization in Post-war Scotland*. London: UCL Press.

Goos, M. and Manning, A. (2007). Lousy and Lovely Jobs: The Rising Polarisation of Work in Britain. *Review of Economics and Statistics*, 89(1), pp. 118–133.

High, S. (2013). 'The Wounds of Class': A Historiographical Reflection on the Study of Deindustrialization, 1973–2013. *History Compass*, 11(11), p. 994.

High, S., MacKinnon, L. and Perchard, A. (eds.). (2017). *The Deindustrialized World. Confronting Ruination in Postindustrial Places*. Vancouver: UBC Press.

Hobsbawm, E. (1968). *Industry and Empire*. London: Allen Lane.

Hobsbawm, E. (1978, September). The Forward March of Labour Halted?. *Marxism Today*, pp. 279–280.

Horrell, S. (2000). Living Standards in Britain 1900–2000: Women's Century?. *National Institute Economic Review*, 172(1), pp. 62–77.

Hull, C. (ed.). (1899). *The Economic Writings of Sir William Petty*. Cambridge: Cambridge University Press, p. 256.

Iversen, T. and Wren, A. (1998). Equality, Employment and Budgetary Restraint: The Trilemma of the Service Economy. *World Politics*, 50(4), pp. 507–546.

Jalilian, H., Tribe, M. and Weiss, J. (2000). *Industrial Development and Policy in Africa: Issues of De-industrialisation and Development Strategy*. Cheltenham: Edward Elgar.

Johnson, C. (2002). Introduction: De-industrialization and Globalization. *International Review of Social History*, 47(S10), pp. 3–33.

Kahn, H. (1970). *The Emerging Japanese Super-State*. New York: Prentice-Hall.

Kaldor, N. (1966). *Causes of the Slow Rate of Growth of the United Kingdom*. Cambridge: Cambridge University Press.

Kuznets, S. (1966). *Modern Economic Growth*. New Haven, CT: Yale University Press.

Lengelle, M. (1966). *The Growing Importance of the Service Sector in Member Countries*. Paris: OECD, pp. 18–20.

Levi-Faur, D. (1997). List and the Political Economy of the Nation State. *Review of International Political Economy*, 4(1), pp. 154–178.

Levie, H., Gregory, D. and Lorentzen, N. (eds.). (1984). *Fighting Closures: Deindustrialisation and the Trade Union*. Nottingham: Spokesman Books.

Lewis, A. (1954). Economic Development with Unlimited Supplies of Labour. *Manchester School*, 22(2), pp. 139–191.

Martin, R. and Rowthorn, R. (eds.). (1986). *The Geography of Deindustrialisation*. London: Macmillan.

Matthews, R., Feinstein, C. and Odling-Smee, J. (1982). *British Economic Growth, 1956–1973*. Oxford: Oxford University Press, pp. 223–224.

O'Rourke, K. and Williamson, J. (eds.). (2017). *The Spread of Modern Industry to the Periphery since 1871*. Oxford: Oxford University Press.

Parliamentary Debates. (1975, April). *Commons*, Vol. 890, Col. 288, 15 April 1975; Tony Benn Writes about Industrial Policy. *Trade and Industry*. London: HMSO.

Phillips, J. (2013). Deindustrialization and the Moral Economy of the Scottish Coalfields, 1947 to 1991. *International Labour and Working-Class History*, 84(1).

Rodrik, D. (2016). Premature deindustrialisation. *Journal of Economic Growth*, 21(1).

Rowthorn, R. and Wells, D. (1986). *De-industrialization and Foreign Trade*. Cambridge: Cambridge University Press, pp. 24–25.

Singh, A. (1977). UK Industry and the World Economy: a Case of Deindustrialisation?. *Cambridge Journal of Economics*, 1(2), pp. 113–136.

Singh, A. (1989). Third World Competition and De-industrialisation in Advanced Countries. *Cambridge Journal of Economics*, 13(1), p. 103.

Smith, A. (1976). *The Wealth of Nations*, Vol. 1. Oxford: Clarendon.

Standing, G. (2011). *The Precariat: The New Dangerous Class*. London: Bloomsbury.

State Council. (2015, July). *Made in China 2025*. http://www.cittadellascienza.it/cina/wp-content/uploads/2017/02/IoT-ONE-Made-in-China-2025.pdf

Strangleman, T. (2013, Fall). Smokestack Nostalgia, Ruin Porn or Working-Class Obituary: The Role and Meaning of Deindustrial Representation. *International Labor and Working-Class History*, 84, pp. 23–37.

Strath, B. (1987). *The Politics of De-industrialisation. The Contraction of the West European Shipbuilding Industry*. London: Croom Helm.

Tomlinson, J. (2004). *The Labour Governments 1964–70, Vol. 3: Economic Policy.* Manchester: Manchester University Press, pp. 132–134, 225–226.

Touraine, A. (1974). *The Post-Industrial Society.* London: Random House.

Tregenna, F. (2009). Characterising Deindustrialisation: An Analysis of Changes in Manufacturing Employment and Output Internationally. *Cambridge Journal of Economics*, 33(3), pp. 433–436.

Tregenna, F. (2015). Deindustrialisation. An Issue for Both Developed and Developing Countries. In Weiss, J. and Tribe, M. (eds.) *The Routledge Handbook of Industry and Development.* New York: Routledge, pp. 97–113.

Wood, A. and Mayer, J. (2011). Has China Deindustrialised other Developing Countries?. *Review of the World Economy*, 147(3), pp. 325–350.

World Bank. (2024). Employment in industry (% of total employment) (modeled ILO estimate). https://data.worldbank.org/indicator/SL.IND.EMPL.ZS

Wren, A. (ed.). (2013). *The Political Economy of the Service Transition.* Oxford: Oxford University Press.

Wrigley, E.A. (2016). *The Path to Sustained Growth. England's Transition from an Organic Economy to an Industrial Revolution.* Cambridge: Cambridge University Press, p. 71.

Wrigley, E.A. (2022). The PST System for Classifying Occupations. *The Cambridge Group for the History of Population and Social Structure*, paper 20. www.geog.cam.ac.uk/research/projects/occupations/abstracts/ (Accessed: 12 August 2022).

4
MORAL ECONOMY AND INDUSTRIAL CULTURE

Andrew Perchard

Introduction

This chapter explores the development of moral economy in relation to industrial culture and deindustrialization. It first explores evolving ideas of industrial culture and then of moral economy, with a predominant focus on the work of literary scholar Raymond Williams and social historian Edward Palmer (E. P.) Thompson, and alongside them those of political economist Karl Polanyi, anthropologist James C. Scott, and social theorist Andrew Sayer. The chapter then explores how moral economy has been applied to the subject of deindustrialization before concluding with suggestions for ways in which it might be further used to enrich the application of this concept within the current literature.

Industrial Culture

What do we mean by industrial culture? Let us in the first place consider what we mean by culture. In this chapter, I employ Raymond Williams's notion of culture as "residual," "experiences, meanings and values, which cannot be verified or cannot be expressed in terms of the dominant culture, are nevertheless lived and practiced on the basis of the residue – cultural as well as social – of some previous social formation"; and "emergent," "new meanings and values, new practices, new significances and experiences," which for him were "constantly being created" (Williams, 1977, pp. 40–41). Ultimately, Williams considered culture to be "a record of our reactions, in thought and feeling, to our changed lives" (Williams, 1983, p. 285). In E. P. Thompson's work, the emergence of industrial capitalism was accompanied by an alteration of time, family, and community life – and consequently to culture – but the "residual" to which Williams referred is to be found alongside the "emergent" in the moral economy of the crowd, as we will see (Thompson, 1967, pp. 56–97). The combination of inherited and evolving industrial culture was acknowledged by sociologist David Byrne in his comparative study of the northeast of England and Katowice, Poland:

> Industrial systems were more than just systems of economic production. They were also systems of social production and reproduction. In particular, they generated new and

DOI: 10.4324/9781003308324-7

distinctive cultural forms. We generally, and in many ways correctly, have understood these cultural forms in terms of working class economic and political consciousness but that has never been a complete or adequate description. First, industrial culture went beyond the specific proletarian experience, even if we employ the most extensive definition of proletariat. Second, industrial culture transcended the "simply economic" in terms of content and implication.

(Bryne, 2002, pp. 279–280)

Thompson underlined, albeit loosely, the importance of understanding culture in its broadest communal sense: "And this culture includes the systems of power, property-relations, religious institutions, etc., inattention to which merely flattens phenomena and trivializes analysis" (Thompson, 1967, p. 80). The importance of appreciating this heritable, as well as emergent, aspect to industrial culture was underlined by Byrne, writing of areas reeling from the prolonged effects of deindustrialization he noted: "In other words, 'industrial' must be considered to cover more than just production. It too has been a component of identity. As old industrial become post-industrial regions, we have large populations with multi-generation experience of industrial life" (Bryne, 2002, p. 280). Bryne dissects that through Williams's notion of Williams's 'structures of feeling.' Keith Gildart in his work on working-class identity and music deploys Williams's understanding of cultural manifestations of class identity "as attempts to understand a social experience which is still in process . . . and their connections in a generation or period." This is evident, for example, in Bruce Springsteen's oeuvre, for example, in songs like 'Youngstown' influenced by the process of closures in 'Steeltown USA,' Youngstown, Ohio; a song that was itself influenced by Dale Maharidge and Michael Williamson's 1985 *Journey to Nowhere: The Saga of the New Underclass*, and the establishment of the Center for Working Class Studies (CWCS) at Youngstown State University (Bryne, 2002; Williams, 1977, p. 97; Gildart, 2013; Perchard, 2018, pp. 77–92). This was a process subsequently captured in *Steeltown USA: Work and Memory in Youngstown*, with acute sensitivity to culture and identity, by two of the founders of CWCS, Sherry Lee Linkon and John Russo (Linkon and Russo, 2003). Linkon has characterized that process of living through the protracted death of industries and the impact across multiple generations and its evocation in popular culture as the "half-life of deindustrialization" (Linkon, 2018).

The use of moral economy within deindustrialization studies has tended to define industrial culture in communal terms, in keeping with their focus on the defense of community assets, although this has been focused on specific occupational communities and traditions (e.g., coal mining and railways) or companies with strong and often patrician organizational cultures (Strangleman, 2001, pp. 253–267; Strangleman, 2004; Perchard, 2012; Perchard, 2013, pp. 78–98; Phillips, 2019; Strangleman, 2019). In the cases of coal mining and railways, these have been identified with "genealogies of coal" and railway families, including for managers and their families (Gildart, 2009, pp. 139–161; Strangleman, 2004; Strangleman, 2018, pp. 18–38; Perchard and Gildart, 2023, pp. 230–261). This was often the case with more patrician firms like the British Aluminum and Guinness, too, and in the steel and other resource towns of North America, often further cemented by a sense of geographical and symbolic distinctiveness and peripheralization by policymakers (Linkon and Russo, 2003; High and Lewis, 2007; Perchard, 2012; High, 2018; Strangleman, 2019; MacKinnon, 2020). While aspects of this work have focused on the symbolism of the destruction of industrial plant, few barring Keith Gildart and Steven Catteral have explored this in relation to broader popular culture (see High, MacKinnon, and Perchard, 2017; Gildart, 2013; Gildart and Catteral, 2021; Perchard, 2013).[1]

Moral Economy and Industrial Culture

The concept, if not the roots, of moral economy was first introduced through the work of social historian and activist, E. P. (Edward Palmer) Thompson (1924–1993) and the anthropologist James C. Scott (1936–), through the former's influential 1971 article in the historical journal *Past & Present* and the latter's 1976 book, *The Moral Economy of the Peasant: Rebellion and Subsistence in Southeast Asia* (Thompson, 1971b, pp. 76–136; Scott, 1976). These works represent different traditions in the development of discourse around moral economy. It is principally to the former's work that ongoing debates around moral economy, industrial culture, and deindustrialization are most indebted. Thompson's work was itself grounded within broader schools of thought and ideas around citizenship, welfarism, and social and cultural change, which are given some explanation here. This chapter moreover explores the work of two other influential contributors to these debates, anthropologist and economic sociologist Karl Polanyi (1886–1964) and political economist Andrew Sayer (1949–). Carolyn Steedman observed that, "specificity of place and politics has to be reckoned with in making an account of anybody's life, and their use of their own past"; in both Polanyi and Thompson's cases, their political activism was also intrinsic to the development of their ideas (Steedman, 1986, p. 6; Rogan, 2018; Palmer, 1994; Hamilton, 2010; Dale, 2016).

E. P. Thompson's treatment of moral economy and the rise of industrialism was first aired in his hugely successful and influential book, *The Making of the English Working Class*, published in 1963, in which he famously set out to:

[r]escue the poor stockinger, the Luddite cropper, the obsolete hand-loom weaver, the "utopian" artisan, and even the deluded follower of Joanna Southcott, from the enormous condescension of posterity. Their crafts and traditions may have been dying. Their hostility to the new industrialism may have been backward-looking. Their communitarian ideals may have been fantasies. Their insurrectionary conspiracies may have been foolhardy. But they lived through these times of acute social disturbance, and we did not. Their aspirations were valid in terms of their own experience: and, if they were casualties of history, they remain, condemned in their own lives, as casualties.

(Thompson, 1963, p. 12)

This would serve as a rallying call to those who would come to study history from below, as epitomized by the History Workshop movement and Raphael Samuel (Hamilton, 2010). In its recognition of history from below and erasure, Thompson's call also lends itself well to the study of deindustrialization (once again highlighting the importance of the cultural and emotional, as well as power relations in that process). That focus and giving voice to the dispossessed in unequal power relations are pivotal in a process in which policymakers and influencers purposefully ignored the multigenerational effects of deindustrialization, as symbolized by the apathy in such utterances from the International Monetary Fund in 1997: "Deindustrialization is not a negative phenomenon, but a natural consequence of further growth in advanced economies" (Rowthorn and Ramaswamy, 1997). Writing around the same time, Judith Stein detected that such complacency had made US voters and policymakers "anaesthetized . . . to industrial decline" (Stein, 1998, p. 320).

Thompson started to articulate his notions of moral economy in *The Making* but explicitly developed these further in his article, 'The moral economy of the English crowd': "In eighteenth-century England and France . . . the market remained a social as well as an economic nexus . . . The market was a place where the people because they were numerous, felt for a moment that they were strong" (1971b, p. 135). Fundamental to this for the emergent working class was: "the notion of legitimation . . . men and women in the crowd were informed by the belief that they were defending traditional rights or customs; and, in general, that they were supported by the wider consensus of the community" (1971b, p. 78).

Thompson continued to be astounded by the success of this article even while it caused him some discomfort (Hamilton, 2010; Thompson, 1993). In that article, Thompson provided further definition to what he termed the moral economy of a crowd enraged by the abandonment of patrician Elizabethan welfare rights for the liberal market:

[A] consistent traditional view of social norms and obligations, of the proper economic functions of several parties within the community . . . An outrage to these moral assumptions, quite as much as actual deprivation, was the usual occasion for direct action. While this moral economy cannot be described as "political" in any advanced sense, nevertheless it cannot be described as unpolitical either, since it supposed definite, and passionately held, notions of the common weal – notions which, indeed, found some support in the paternalist tradition of the authorities.

(Thompson, 1971b, p. 79)

It is important to contextualize the evolution of these ideas in Thompson's mind in terms of both his disciplinary and political journey. At the time of writing the *Making*, Thompson thought predominantly of himself as a poet and not a historian. He was teaching literature and history as a Workers Educational Association tutor in England's West Yorkshire, an area that at the time was starting to experience deindustrialization (in coal and textiles) but was profoundly affected by romantic notions and poetry of William Blake, Wordsworth, and Morris, and D. H. Lawrence, among others, and even acquired and learned how to use a weaver's loom to experience what that craft involved. Yet his romantic assumptions were culturally at odds with the working-class students he was teaching who were predominantly either more interested in Americana or more focused on the need for lessons in working-class history and political economy. Indeed, he had not intended on writing the *Making* (Palmer, 1994; Hamilton, 2010). His development of the idea of moral economy drew on the ideas of the Irish-born Chartist leader Brontierre O'Brien (1805–1864) and his 1837 account of a Chartist meeting explored by Dorothy Thompson the same year as E P published the 'moral economy' (see Thompson, 1971a; Perchard et al., 2024b). Scott Hamilton attributes the development of Thompson's moral economy to the ideological crisis after his departure from the Communist Party of Great Britain in 1956 and contusions in the New Left, and his departure from dialectical materialism and the categorization of social class as a "thing" rather than as fluid and relational (Palmer, 1994; Hamilton, 2010). Bryan Palmer locates it in experiences of people, as well as literary texts, and their warmth; "[a] refusal to concede that the class culture that consolidated in the backcountries of English capitalism could be written off as somehow inadequate" (Palmer, 1994, p. 395).[2] Both explanations find

Moral Economy and Industrial Culture

resonance in the *Making* and in Thompson's 1965 essay, 'Peculiarities of the English.' In the latter, Thompson observes:

> Class is a social and cultural formation (often finding institutional expression) which cannot be defined abstractly or in isolation, but only in terms of relationship with other classes; and ultimately the definition can only be made in the medium of time – that is, action and reaction, change and conflict . . . class itself is not a thing, it is a happening.
> *(Thompson, 1965, p. 357)*

This echoed his insistence in the *Making* that, "the notion of class entails the notion of historical relationship" (Thompson, 1963, p. 9). It was a view intensely informed by culture and critical of what he perceived as the rigidity of dialectical materialism as advanced by Marxist theoreticians like Louis Althusser, as articulated in Thompson's *Poverty of Theory* (1978) and the History Workshop debates of November 30–December 2, 1979 (Thompson, 1978; Parks, 2012). Crucially, Thompson was concerned with an understanding of the cultural as a corrective to the 'crass economic reductionism' of extant explanations of the actions of the crowd; "The weakness which these explanations share is an abbreviated view of the economic man" (Thompson, 1971b, p. 78). Thompson's was both breaking ossified notions of dialectical materialism and profoundly concerned with the cultural (and emotional), even while his definition of culture in these senses were underdeveloped in the original work. His view also privileged 'history from below,' the lay perspective. Conceptually, if not ideologically, Thompson's views were similar to those articulated by historical sociologist Philip Abrams in his posthumous work, *Historical Sociology* (1982): "the social world is essentially historical. Process is the link between action and structure" (Abrams, 1983, p. 3).

Tim Strangleman has suggested it is in this, "historical moment in which Thompson was concerned with, the experience of communities emerging into an industrial age," that "can be usefully compared and contrasted with contemporary researchers studying communities experiencing deindustrialization" (Strangleman, 2017, p. 467). Strangleman going on to suggest: "These two historically discrete epochs can be thought of as two bookends of what was an industrial era" (Strangleman, 2017, p. 467). Certainly, for those studying community responses to deindustrialization, there is much resonance to be found in Thompson's observation of the social dislocation caused by industrialization: "The stress of the transition falls upon the whole culture: resistance to change and assent to change arise from the whole culture" (Thompson, 1967, p. 80). Strangleman's suggestion brings with it complexities, not least of the ongoing debates about the relationship between history and sociology, but for the purposes of this chapter and collection focuses on questions around the transferability of Thompsonian notions of moral economy from the eighteenth century to the twentieth and twenty-first centuries.[3] Strangleman and others seek to bridge this through the convergence of moral economic thinking as expounded by Karl Polanyi and Andrew Sayer (Gibbs, 2018; Perchard and Gildart, 2018, 2023).

The complementarity of the work of Polanyi and Sayer to Thompson's work has lain in their ability to bridge a greater sense of the balance of social forces (Polanyi), evolving societal moral and political mores (Sayer), and the agency and moral interpretation of the crowd (Thompson), within the context of historicity.

While Thompson remained concerned about the ahistorical use of moral economy, his understanding of how the moral economy of the crowd emerged in contradistinction to the new political economy is congruent with Polanyi's explanation of the social forces and the "embeddedness" and "disembeddedness" of markets over time and Sayer's understanding of changing moral and political values: "to some extent moral-political values regarding economic activities and responsibilities co-evolve with economic systems" (Polanyi, 1957; Sayer, 2000, p. 81).

Thompson's views on the application of the specific historical context of applying moral economy also evolved over time between the writing of the 'moral economy of the crowd,' and his response to critics published after his death in *Customs in Common*. Norbert Götz's suggested that:

> as Thompson used it, moral economy remained bound to a specific epoch and a particular historical context. It served as an umbrella term for obsolete customary titles and ways of life prior to the great leap from traditional society to the modern market system.
>
> *(Götz, 2015, p. 147)*

However, this fails to recognize both the evolution of his ideas and the conceptual currency of his ideas about social relations and historical processes. Sayer, like Thompson, has also been particularly concerned with "relating morality to everyday life and the experience of well-being and ill-being without reducing it to a matter of individual subjectivity or social convention" (Sayer, 2007, p. 261). Also, like Thompson, that stems from Sayer's profound interest in the human condition, that "we are sentient beings who can flourish or suffer" (Sayer, 2011, p. 3). Indeed, Sayer has been concerned with impressing upon social science the importance of recognizing the emotive and subjective. Something that is implicit in the Thompsonian canon.

Perhaps, given his focus on agrarian societies, James C. Scott's study of moral economy in colonial Southeast Asia has not been picked up in relation to industrial culture and deindustrialization, though his studies of the high modernist state have (Scott, 1976; Scott, 1999; High, MacKinnon, and Perchard, 2017). As outlined at the end of this chapter, his work does deserve the attraction of those studying industrial culture and politics and deindustrialization.

Moral Economy and the Political Economy of Deindustrialization

Thompson, Polanyi, and Sayer have attracted considerable explicit attention in the literature of deindustrialization in Scotland and the British coal industry, in what has almost become an industry in itself. That work has focused predominantly on the period after 1945 and nationalization and privatization. Though that has been both geographically and temporally focused (primarily twentieth-century Britain), this demonstrates what carefully considered historicity can offer to the application of moral economy outside of the eighteenth and nineteenth centuries that Thompson originally applied, and contiguous with Sayer's work, capturing both lay morality and shifting national political trends. This focus on moral and political views governing the political economy of Britain between 1945 and the 1990s (and the contestation of those views) is particularly apposite. Jim Tomlinson characterized 1940s Britain at a moment in which the political imperatives of the war economy combined with a greater balance of social forces:

> What marked the nineteen-forties was not a new awareness of the moral issues of economic life among intellectuals and policymakers, but a new political imperative

Moral Economy and Industrial Culture

to improve the performance of the economy at a time of full employment and with a citizenry empowered and energized by the exigencies of war.

(Tomlinson, 2011, p. 360)

There is a particular resonance to this in terms of some of the foundational ideas governing industrial citizenship and the welfare state at this time, with the currency attached to the ideas of sociologist T. H. Marshall on industrial citizenship and the influence of G. D. Cole, John Maynard Keynes, and William Beveridge on welfare economics and the welfare state (Marshall, 1950; Bulmer and Rees, 1996; Keynes, 1936; Beveridge, 1944). Crucially, much of this was influenced by observations of the preceding decades, and in practical ways, his observations in the East End of London shaped the thinking of Britain's first postwar Labour Prime Minister Clement Attlee (Harris, 1995; Bew, 2017). As Tim Strangleman has noted, such ideas of industrial citizenship were to be found in Britain's nationalized railways and the large Anglo-Irish brewer, Guinness, while Perchard has identified this in another patrician British company, British Aluminium, and Perchard and Gildart identify this in the management of the publicly owned National Coal Board (NCB) (Strangleman, 2004; Strangleman, 2019; Perchard, 2012; Perchard and Gildart, 2023).

Studies of deindustrialization in Scotland and in the British coalfields, such as those of Ewan Gibbs, Keith Gildart, Andrew Perchard, Jim Phillips, Jim Tomlinson, and Valerie Wright, have expressly utilized the work of Thompson, Sayer, and Polanyi to demonstrate both in communities and nationally how closures were contested during the postwar period both under a more welfarist state and with the moral and political sea change after 1979 with the New Right Conservative administrations of Margaret Thatcher and John Major (Phillips, 2008; Perchard and Phillips, 2011; Phillips, 2012; Perchard, 2013; Phillips, 2013; Gibbs, 2021; Perchard and Gildart, 2018, pp. 79–110; Perchard and Gildart, 2023, pp. 230–261; Phillips, Wright, and Tomlinson, 2021; Perchard et al., 2025). Community contestation of closures under the accepted norms and practices of the nationalized coal industry deployed a clear articulation of the moral economy of the crowd, as Gibbs, Gildart, Perchard, and Phillips's work demonstrates in relation to the Scottish coalfield. Perchard, Gildart, Curtis, and Millar advance this further with their study of deindustrialization in the nationalized British coalfields of England, Scotland, and Wales, which demonstrates the cross-coalfield dynamics of this and the damage to the ideal of public ownership (Perchard et al., 2024). Perchard and Gildart demonstrate how the undermining of moral economic norms and practices by government was also contested by management in the industry, so often missing from analysis of the impact of deindustrialization or assumed simply to be vassals of the employer. As they indicate, managers and their union occupied, in the words of sociologist Erik Olin Wright, "contradictory" and "contested locations," as employees and skills exploiters, not least given their social locations and background (Perchard and Gildart, 2018, 2023). In the 1980s and 1990s, Conservative administrations sought to roll back the state, with the UK accounting for 40% of state assets privatized between 1980 and 1996 (Peck and Tickell, 2002, p. 386). These years were part of what Peck and Tickell have described as the 'roll-out of neoliberalism' in the 'North Atlantic Zone':

A commitment to the extension of markets and logics of competitiveness with a profound antipathy to all kinds of Keynesian and/or collectivist strategies. The constitution and extension of competitive forces is married with aggressive forms of state downsizing, austerity financing, and public service "reform." And while rhetorically antistatist, neoliberals have proved adept at the (mis)use of state power in the pursuit of these goals.

(Peck and Tickell, 2002, p. 381)

As Tomlinson and Florence Sutcliffe-Braithwaite underline, the policies of the Thatcher and Major administrations, though socially disruptive, divisive, and harmful, were guided by equally strong moral convictions as those opposing them (Sutcliffe-Braithwaite, 2012; Tomlinson, 2021). The effects of the deindustrialization and these assaults on the welfare state (and public sector more broadly), often using the full force of state power, as Avner Offer put it:

[Cast] workers as consumers rather than citizens or producers punished those with low purchasing power, de-legitimized producer collective action and justified low wages. Poverty increased and relative wages fell . . . The majority continued to identify as working class, but their culture was discredited by market liberalism and consumerism.

(Offer, 2008, p. 537)

As Gildart, Perchard, Phillips, and Strangleman have all pointed out, managers in nationalized industries like coal and railways (often because of their occupational culture and social background), contrary to stereotypes, did not always conform to this vision and did resist these public service reforms and closures (Strangleman, 2004; Perchard, 2007; Perchard and Phillips, 2011; Perchard and Gildart, 2018, 2023). In Scotland, moral economic protests to closures inflected the politics of self-determination and the cultural politics of a resurgent national identity, strongly influenced by sections of the labor movement, notably the National Union of Mineworkers (NUM), Scottish Area, from the late 1960s onward (Phillips, 2008; Perchard, 2013; Phillips, Wright, and Tomlinson, 2021). Ben Curtis similarly has noted the importance of closures and the NUM South Wales Area on the politics of devolution for Wales (Curtis, 2013). In Canada's Rust Belt, there were nationalist stirrings, expressed in moral economic terms, in response to US multinationals (High, 2003). As Strangleman suggests, the Thompsonian moral economic lens offers much to understand deindustrialization. As the next section sets out, there is considerable scope for expanding that in different ways in relation to the 'half-life of deindustrialization.'

Concluding Remarks and Speculative Suggestions on Areas for Expansion

If moral economic perspectives have proved valuable to exploring deindustrialization, there is much capacity for extending those both conceptually and methodologically. Commenting on a well-established literature, chiefly anthropological, on the moral economy of water, Beresford et al. urge a clearer definition of what moral economy approaches incorporate, citing concerns that the term has become too interchangeably deployed in relation to studies of ethics and markets. They define moral economy, according to Thompson and Scott's traditions, as "a body that investigates how shared understandings of morality instigate normative human behaviors that ensure survival and uphold notions of justice when vital resources for subsistence are insecure" (Beresford et al., 2022). While some degree of precision on the essential characteristics and historical context is desirable to ensure not just that the term is not ill-deployed (something which both Thompson and Sayer warned against in terms of historical context) but also to aid multidisciplinary working (which I come to in due course), there is a risk in applying strictures to a concept, which Thompson intended to capture the nebulous nature of culture as evolving and complex (Thompson, 1971b; Sayer, 2000). Crucially, as in Williams's explanations, culture is inflected with human emotion (trying to make sense of that change against both established and emerging traditions); as with the artisans, stockingers, and weavers contending with the industrial revolution, so too with those contending with the long drawn-out process of deindustrialization. Emotions have been both implicit and yet little talked about in much literature on the moral economy of deindustrialization. Indeed, this is one aspect which is deserving of far greater attention in future explorations of the moral economy of deindustrialization, engaging with the long-established literature on the history of emotions and more broadly of cultural manifestations.[4] Uncovering the interchange of popular culture and emotions in relation to deep multigenerational harm caused by deindustrialization begs for more study, in a situation in which, as psychologist Hank Greenspan put it, "survivors" were left "confronting the reality of being disposable *en masse*," with any sense of "predictable history gone" (High, MacKinnon, and Perchard, 2017, p. 415).

Beresford et al.'s suggestions for what moral economy does not constitute deserve consideration:

> [T]he moral economy is *not* an evaluation of or judgment on the morality of economic systems. Values and morals undergird all economic systems, thus values and morals alone do not constitute a moral economy. . . . A moral economy is *not* defined by any legal codification; rather, it is normative and consistently evolving. . . . A moral economy is *not* restricted to nonmarket arrangements; moral economies often govern market interactions. . . . A moral economy is not always equitable; it spans elite and nonelite ranks of society. . . . A moral economy is not a conflict-free utopia; it is a site of ongoing struggle and social conflict.
>
> *(Beresford et al., 2022)[5]*

While these certainly capture Thompson, Sayer, and Scott's explanations of the characteristics of moral economy, it is worth discussing the ontological conundrums implicit in the basis certainly of Polanyi, Thompson, and Scott's work; all three were activists, as well as scholars, and that bled into their work. That much is also discernible in Sayer's work (Sayer, 2015, pp. 291–293). So that while all these authors, to a greater or lesser extent, were committed to understanding the social forces at play, any discussion of moral economy does require a recognition of those motivations. Indeed, it is such humanistic sensibilities that lend themselves to the persuasion to explore moral economic frameworks. And yet, Thompson and Sayer empirically sought, without judgment, to comment on the morality of the changing societies and social forces they were engaging with. Subsequent work on industrial culture and deindustrialization has sought to emulate this in different ways, including recognizing that different systems of nonmarket interactions may coexist alongside different varieties of capitalism over time, but once again this provides ongoing scope for investigation (Thompson, 1963; Scott, 1976; MacKenzie et al., 2023).

If Thompson was unfairly criticized for insufficient attention to women in his original studies – who were neither entirely absent nor did he fail to acknowledge women's underrepresentation – then there is nonetheless considerable scope for better understanding the intersections of gender more broadly within moral economic studies of deindustrialization, though considerable gains have been made in this area, such as studies of women workers' protests and the crisis of masculinity.[6] Moral economic analysis of deindustrialization would also benefit from far greater attention paid to the intersections of race and youth, and methodologically with a great engagement with the study of popular culture as an expression, as Thompson acknowledged himself, he was not always observant of and, like sections of the Left of his generation, attuned to it.[7] One further area deserving of far greater symbiosis between the extant literatures on deindustrialization and moral economy is around the subject of occupational and public health and environmental legacies of industrialization and deindustrialization, absorbing these discussions of the various social forces and norms and practices over time.[8] This is all the more pressing given decarbonization initiatives (Eadson, van Veelan, and Backius, 2023). Equally, there is far greater scope for the use of James Scott's work both in different systems and around protest forms.

This glimpse into industrial culture and moral economy, with a particular focus on deindustrialization, is necessarily illustrative but is intended to demonstrate both the resonance of moral economy frameworks and what it still has to offer.

Notes

1 See discussions of the symbolism of the destruction of industrial plant in High, Linkon and Russo, Strangleman, and Russo. For broader material cultural analyses, see Gildart, Keith. (2013). *Images of England through Popular Music. Class, Youth and Rock n'Roll, 1955–1976.* Basingstoke: Palgrave Macmillan; Keith Gildart and Steven Catteral. (2021). *Keeping the Faith: A History of Northern Soul.* Manchester: Manchester University Press; Perchard explores the feeding of closures into national narrative in Scotland in 'Broken Men.'

2 Some of this and the impact of West Yorkshire, as well as the influence of Blake, can be detected on his interview on the BBC's Desert Islands Discs interview, 8 November 1991: https://www.bbc.co.uk/programmes/p0093yq.

3 For debates around the convergence of history and sociology, for example, Steadman-Jones, Gareth. (1976). From Historical Sociology to Theoretic History. *British Journal of Sociology*, 27, pp. 295–305; Abrams, Philip. (1980). History, Sociology, Historical Sociology. *Past & Present*, 87, pp. 3 16; Abrams, Philip. (1983). *Historical Sociology.* Ithaca, NY: University of Cornell Press.

4 For some exceptions: Gildart, *Images of England*; Perchard, 'Broken Men'; Waddington, Lee. (2023). Rethinking Camaraderie as Emotional Practices: Deindustrialisation and Deskilling in South Yorkshire Coalfields, 1980s-2000s. *Contemporary British History*, 37, pp. 432–464; On the history of emotions: Febvre, Lucien. (1941). La sensibilité et l'histoire: Comment reconstituer la vie affective d'autrefois. *Annales d'histoire sociale*, 1, pp. 5–20; Boddice, Rob. (2017). *The History of Emotions.* Manchester: Manchester University Press.

5 Gildart, *Images of England*.

6 For the original debates over Thompson's treatment of women, see those between Joan Scott, Anna Clark, Sheil Rowbotham, and Barbara Winslow; Perchard, 'Broken Men'; Clarke, Jackie. (2015). Closing Time: Deindustrialization and Nostalgia in Contemporary France. *History Workshop Journal*, 79, pp. 107–125; Fraser, Alistair and Clark, Andy. (2021). Damaged Hardmen: Organized Crime and the Half-Life of Deindustrialization. *British Journal of Sociology*, 72, pp. 1062–1076; Phillips et al., *Deindustrialization and Moral Economy*; Clark, Andy. (2023). *Fighting Deindustrialisation: Scottish Women's Factory Occupations, 1981–1982.* Liverpool: Liverpool University Press; Pierson-Webber, Emily. (2021). Mining Men: Reflections on Masculinity and Oral History during the Coronavirus Pandemic. *History Workshop Journal*, 92, pp. 242–250; Waddington, Lee. (2023). Rethinking Camaraderie as Emotional Practices: Deindustrialisation and Deskilling in South Yorkshire Coalfields, 1980s-2000s. *Contemporary British History*, 37, pp. 432–464; Curtis, Ben, Gildart, Keith, Perchard, Andrew and Millar, Grace. (forthcoming). 'Be a Man': Masculinity, Class, and Popular Culture in the British Coalfields, c.1970–1983. *International Review of Social History.*

7 For excellent work on this subject, see that by Keith Gildart and other members of the subcultures network: https://research.reading.ac.uk/subcultures-network/.
8 For example, Mah, Alice. (2012). *Industrial Ruination, Community and Place: Lanscape and Legacies of Urban Decline*. Toronto: University of Toronto Press; Mah, Alice. (2023). *Petrochemical Planet: Multiscalar Battles of Industrial Transformation*. Durham, NC: University of North Carolina Press; See Arthur McIvor, Lachlan MacKinnon and Robert Storey's contributions in *The Deindustrialized World*.

Reference List

Abrams, Philip. (1980). History, Sociology, Historical Sociology. *Past & Present*, 87, pp. 3–16.

Abrams, Philip. (1983). *Historical Sociology*. Ithaca, NY: University of Cornell Press.

Beresford, Melissa, Wutich, Amber, Garrick, Dustin and Drew, Georgina. (2022). Moral Economies for Water: A Framework for Analyzing Norms of Justice, Economic Behavior, and Social Enforcement in the Contexts of Water Inequality. *WIREs Water*, 10. https://doi.org/10.1002/wat2.1627

Beveridge, William H. (1944). *Full Employment in a Free Society*. London: Allen & Unwin.

Bew, J. (2017). *Citizen Clem: A Biography of Attlee*. London: Riverrun.

Boddice, Rob. (2017). *The History of Emotions*. Manchester: Manchester University Press.

Bryne, David. (2002). Industrial Culture in a Post-Industrial World: The Case of the North East of England. *City*, 6, pp. 279–289.

Bulmer, Martin and Rees, Anthony M. (eds.). (1996). *Citizenship Today: The Contemporary Relevance of T.H. Marshall*. London: UCL Press.

Clark, Andy. (2023). *Fighting Deindustrialisation: Scottish Women's Factory Occupations, 1981–1982*. Liverpool: Liverpool University Press.

Clarke, Jackie. (2015). Closing Time: Deindustrialization and Nostalgia in Contemporary France. *History Workshop Journal*, 79, pp. 107–125.

Curtis, Ben. (2013). *South Wales Miners 1964–1985*. Cardiff: University of Wales Press.

Dale, Gareth. (2016). *Karl Polanyi: A Life on the Left*. New York: Columbia University Press.

Eadson, William, van Veelan, Bregje and Backius, Stefan. (2023). Decarbonising Industry: A Places-of-work Research Agenda. *The Extractive Industries and Society*, 15. https://doi.org/10.1016/j.exis.2023.101307

Febvre, Lucien. (1941). La sensibilité et l'histoire: Comment reconstituer la vie affective d'autrefois. *Annales d'histoire sociale*, 1, pp. 5–20.

Fraser, Alistair and Clark, Andy. (2021). Damaged hardmen: Organized Crime and the Half-Life of Deindustrialization. *British Journal of Sociology*, 72, pp. 1062–1076.

Gibbs, Ewan. (2018). The Moral Economy of the Scottish Coalfields: Managing Deindustrialization under Nationalization, c.1947–1983. *Enterprise & Society*, 19, pp. 124–152.

Gibbs, Ewan. (2021). *Coal Country: The Meaning and Memory of Deindustrialization in Postwar Scotland*. London: University of London Press.

Gildart, Keith. (2009). Mining Memories: Reading Coalfield Autobiographies. *Labor History*, 50, pp. 139–161.

Gildart, Keith. (2013). *Images of England through Popular Music. Class, Youth and Rock n'Roll, 1955–1976*. Basingstoke: Palgrave Macmillan.

Gildart, Keith and Catteral, Steven. (2021). *Keeping the Faith: A History of Northern Soul*. Manchester: Manchester University Press.

Götz, Norbert. (2015). 'Moral Economy': Its Conceptual History and Analytical Prospects. *Journal of Global Ethics*, 11, pp. 147–162.

Hamilton, Scott. (2010). *The Crisis of Theory: E. P. Thompson, the New Left and Postwar British Politics*. Manchester: Manchester University Press.

Harris, Keith. (1995). *Attlee*. London: Orion.

High, Steven. (2003). *Industrial Sunset: The Making of North America's Rust Belt, 1969–1984*. Toronto: University of Toronto Press.

High, Steven. (2018). *One Job Town: Work, Belonging, and Betrayal in Northern Ontario*. Toronto: University of Toronto Press.

High, Steven and Lewis, David W. (2007). *Corporate Wasteland: The Landscape and Memory of Deindustrialization*. Ithaca, NY: ILR Press.

High, Steven, MacKinnon, Lachlan and Perchard, Andrew (eds.). (2017). *The Deindustrialized World: Confronting Ruination in Postindustrial Places*. Vancouver: University of British Columbia Press.

Keynes, John Maynard. (1936). *The General Theory of Employment, Interest and Money*. Cambridge: Cambridge University Press.

Linkon, Sherry Lee. (2018). *The Half-Life of Deindustrialization: Working-Class Writing about Economic Restructuring*. Ann Arbor: University of Michigan Press.

Linkon, Sherry Lee and Russo, John. (2003). *Steeltown U.S.A.: Work and Memory in Youngstown*. Lawrence: University of Kansas Press.

MacKenzie, Niall G, Perchard, Andrew, Miller, Christopher, and Forbes, Neil. (eds.). (2023). *Varieties of Capitalism Over Time*. London: Routledge.

MacKinnon, Lachlan. (2020). *Closing Sysco: Industrial Decline in Atlantic Canada's Steel City*. Toronto: University of Toronto Press.

Mah, Alice. (2012). *Industrial Ruination, Community and Place: Lanscape and Legacies of Urban Decline*. Toronto: University of Toronto Press.

Mah, Alice. (2023). *Petrochemical Planet: Multiscalar Battles of Industrial Transformation*. Durham, NC: University of North Carolina Press.

Marshall Thomas H. (1950). *Citizenship and Social Class and other Essays*. Cambridge: Cambridge University Press.

Offer, Avner. (2008). British Manual Workers: From Producers to Consumers, c.1950–2000. *Contemporary British History*, 22, pp. 537–571.

Palmer, Bryan B. (1994). *E. P. Thompson: Objections and Oppositions*. New York: Verso.

Parks, L. (2012). History Workshop 13. *History Workshop*. https://www.historyworkshop.org.uk/public-history/history-workshop-13/ (Accessed: 10 March 2023).

Peck, Jamie and Tickell, Adam. (2002). Neoliberalizing Space. *Antipode*, 34, pp. 380–404.

Perchard, Andrew. (2007). *The Mine Management Professions in the Twentieth Century Scottish Coal Mining Industry*. Lampeter and Lewiston: The Edwin Mellen Press.

Perchard, Andrew. (2012). *Aluminiumville: Government, Global Business and the Scottish Highlands*. Lancaster: Carnegie Publishing.

Perchard, Andrew. (2013). 'Broken Men' and 'Thatcher's Children': Memory and Legacy in Scotland's Coalfields. *International Labor and Working-Class History*, 84, pp. 78–98.

Perchard, Andrew. (2018). Workplace Cultures. In Walkowitz, D. (ed.) *A Cultural History of Work in the Modern Age, Vol. 6: 1920 – Present*. London: Bloomsbury Academic, pp. 77–92.

Perchard, Andrew and Gildart, Keith. (2018). 'Run with the Fox and Hunt with the Hounds': Managerial Trade-Unionism and the British Association of Colliery Management, 1947–1994. *Historical Studies in Industrial Relations*, 39, pp. 79–110.

Perchard, Andrew and Gildart, Keith. (2023). Managerial Ideology and Identity in the Nationalised British Coal Industry. *Economic and Industrial Democracy*, 44, pp. 230–261.

Perchard, Andrew and Phillips, Jim. (2011). Transgressing the Moral Economy: Wheelerism and Management of the Nationalised Coal Industry in Scotland. *Contemporary British History*, 25, pp. 387–405.

Perchard, Andrew, McGuire, Darren, Laaser, Knut, Gildart, Keith, Kaufman, Anya, McMaster, Robert and Curtis, Ben C. (2024a). Moral Economy at the Crossroads of History and Social Science: Finding Customs in Common? *Economic and Industrial Democracy*.

Perchard, Andrew, Gildart, Keith, Curtis, Ben and Millar, Grace. (2024b). Fighting for the Soul of Coal: Colliery Closures and the Moral Economy of Nationalization in Britain, 1947–1994. *Enterprise and Society*. https://doi.org/10.1017/eso.2024.6

Phillips, Jim. (2008). *The Industrial Politics of Devolution: Scotland in the 1960s and 1970s*. Manchester: Manchester University Press.

Phillips, Jim. (2012). *Collieries, Communities and the Miners' Strike in Scotland, 1984–85*. Manchester: Manchester University Press.

Phillips, Jim. (2013). Deindustrialization and the Moral Economy of the Scottish Coalfields 1957 to 1991. *International Labor and Working Class History*, 84, pp. 99–115.

Phillips, Jim. (2019). *Scottish Coal Miners in the Twentieth Century*. Edinburgh: Edinburgh University Press.

Phillips, Jim, Wright, Valerie and Tomlinson, Jim. (2021). *Deindustrialization and the Moral Economy in Scotland since 1955.* Edinburgh: Edinburgh University Press.

Pierson-Webber, Emily. (2021). Mining Men: Reflections on Masculinity and Oral History during the Coronavirus Pandemic. *History Workshop Journal*, 92, pp. 242–250.

Polanyi, Karl. (1957 [1944]). *The Great Transformation: The Political and Economic Origins of our Time*, this edition. Boston: Beacon Books.

Rogan, Tim. (2018). *The Moral Economists: R. H. Tawney, Karl Polanyi, E. P. Thompson, and the Critique of Capitalism.* Princeton: Princeton University Press.

Rowthorn, Robert and Ramaswamy, Ramana. (1997). *Deindustrialization: Causes and Implications.* IMF Research Department. https://www.imf.org/external/pubs/ft/wp/wp9742.pdf

Sayer, Andrew. (2000). Moral and Political Economy. *Studies in Political Economy*, 61, pp. 79–104.

Sayer, Andrew. (2007). Moral Economy as Critique. *New Political Economy*, 12, pp. 261–270.

Sayer, Andrew. (2011). *Why Things Matter to People: Social Science, Values and Ethical Life.* Cambridge: Cambridge University Press.

Sayer, Andrew. (2015). Time for Moral Economy?. *Geoforum*, 65, pp. 291–293.

Scott, James C. (1976). *The Moral Economy of the Peasant: Rebellion and Subsistence in Southeast Asia.* New Haven, CT: Yale University Press.

Scott, James C. (1999). *Seeing Like a State: How Certain Schemes to Improve the Human Condition have Failed.* New Haven, CT: Yale University Press.

Steadman-Jones, Gareth. (1976). From Historical Sociology to Theoretic History. *British Journal of Sociology*, 27, pp. 295–305.

Steedman, Carolyn. (1986). *Landscape for a Good Woman.* London: Virago.

Stein, Judith. (1998). *Running Steel, Running America: Race, Economy Policy, and the Decline of Liberalism.* Chapel Hill: University of North Carolina Press.

Strangleman, Tim. (2001). Networks, Place and Identities in Post-industrial Mining Communities. *International Journal of Urban and Regional Research*, 25, pp. 253–267.

Strangleman, Tim. (2004). *Work Identity at the End of the Line? Privatisation and Culture Change in the UK Rail Industry.* London: Palgrave.

Strangleman, Tim. (2017). Deindustrialisation and the Historical Sociological Imagination: Making Sense of Work and Industrial Change. *Sociology*, 51, pp. 466–482.

Strangleman, Tim. (2018). Mining a Productive Seam? The Coal Industry, Community and Sociology. *Contemporary British History*, 32, pp. 18–38.

Strangleman, Tim. (2019). *Voices of Guinness: An Oral History of the Park Royal Brewery.* Oxford: Oxford University Press.

Sutcliffe-Braithwaite, Florence. (2012). Neoliberalism and Morality in the Making of Thatcherite Social Policy. *Historical Journal*, 55, pp. 497–520.

Thompson, Dorothy. (1971a). *The Early Chartists.* Columbia, SC: University of South Carolina Press.

Thompson, E.P. (1963). *The Making of the English Working Class.* London: Victor Gollancz.

Thompson, E.P. (1965). The Peculiarities of the English. *Socialist Register*, pp. 311–362.

Thompson, E.P. (1967). Time, Work-Discipline, and Industrial Capitalism. *Past & Present*, 38, pp. 56–97.

Thompson, E.P. (1971b). The Moral Economy of the English Crowd in the Eighteenth Century. *Past & Present*, 50, pp. 76–136.

Thompson, E.P. (1978). *The Poverty of Theory & Other Essays.* London: Merlin.

Thompson, E.P. (1993). *Customs in Common.* London: Merlin.

Tomlinson, Jim. (2011). Re-inventing the 'Moral Economy' in Post-War Britain. *Historical Research*, 84, pp. 356–373.

Tomlinson, Jim. (2021). Deindustrialisation and 'Thatcherism': Moral Economy and Unintended Consequences. *Contemporary British History*, 35, pp. 620–642.

Waddington, Lee. (2023). Rethinking Camaraderie as Emotional Practices: Deindustrialisation and Deskilling in South Yorkshire Coalfields, 1980s-2000s. *Contemporary British History*, 37, pp. 432–464.

Williams, Raymond. (1977). *Marxism and Literature.* Oxford: Oxford University Press.

Williams, Raymond. (1983). *Culture and Society, 1780–1950.* New York: Columbia University Press.

5

RACIALIZING DEINDUSTRIALIZATION STUDIES

James Rhodes

Introduction

The examination of deindustrialization emerged in the midst of the mass of industrial closures across advanced capitalist societies in the 1970s and 1980s, subsequently forming as a vibrant and increasingly vital area of interdisciplinary academic inquiry. What has been termed "deindustrialization studies" (High, 2013) has rapidly expanded over the past quarter of a century, addressing in a range of innovative ways the ongoing economic, political, social, and cultural consequences of deindustrialization. A key feature of contemporary scholarship has been a move toward a more thorough foregrounding of the deep and enduring relationships between "race" and deindustrialization (Hackworth, this volume; Lawson, 2020; High, 2022; Matera et al., 2023).

This shifting focus has been driven by a number of interrelated developments; these include ongoing processes of deindustrialization and deepening socio-spatial inequalities; conceptual work on racial capitalism; and finally deindustrialization and the politics of whiteness. First, the unfolding of deindustrialization has continued to highlight its role in shaping persistent racial inequalities in areas including employment, housing, income and wealth, health, and environmental justice. Second, emergent work on racial capitalism has highlighted the need to foreground the central role that race and racialization play within the development of capitalist structures and relations (Virdee, 2019; Robinson, 2021). Third, the rise of far right and right-wing populist politics of resentment – often evident within deindustrialized communities – has drawn attention to the complex interplay between 'race' and class and economics and culture. The outcome of these developments has been the prompting of critical appraisals of deindustrialization studies themselves, which have problematized the relative neglect of considerations of race and racialization, the privileging of the experiences of white communities and workers, and the tendency for 'race' and class to remain bifurcated within analysis of the impacts of deindustrialization. Steven High has recognized the need to "challenge the deepening divergence of class and race analysis and recognize the intimate relationship between capitalism, class struggles, and racial inequality" (High, 2022, p. 5).

This chapter explores the growing attentiveness to 'race' and racialization, creating deeper analyses of deindustrialization. It focuses on three distinctive themes: first, the way processes

DOI: 10.4324/9781003308324-8

Racializing Deindustrialization Studies

of racialization and forms of racialized inequality are embedded in deindustrialization. Second, exploring how the connections between 'race' and deindustrialization articulate with other social, economic and political processes. Finally, the chapter considers how 'race' shapes both wider imaginaries of deindustrialization and its more cultural and affective impacts, informing experiences, subjectivities, and identities.

The Racialization of Deindustrialization

The increasing focus on race and racialization within deindustrialization studies starts from the premise that economic restructuring at its heart involves a reconfiguration of "relations between bodies, work and capital" (Hamera, 2017, p. 6), organized through forms of both class and racial stratification. While working-class communities have been broadly impacted, it is clear that the process of deindustrialization itself is a racialized one with racial minorities being particularly impacted. The racially uneven impacts of deindustrialization are illustrative of the racial constitution of industrial capitalism itself (Robinson, 2021). Work on racial capitalism has highlighted "capitalism's inherently racializing capacities" (Virdee, 2019, p. 9), as capitalism works on and through forms of racial categorization, differentiation, and hierarchization, which connect with specific modes and relations of exploitation, requiring us to "[think] race and class together" (Virdee, 2019, p. 4).

Bonilla-Silva identifies societies as constituting "racialized social systems," "in which economic, political, social, and ideological levels are partially structured by the placement of actors in racial categories or race" (Bonilla-Silva, 1997, p. 469). However, the precise form this takes varies by nation, region, industry, and group identity. Deindustrialization studies' task is to examine the specific ways in which this process works through and upon "race," as racial capitalism operates differently across time and space (Virdee, 2019). As Hall notes, there is no singular form of racism but rather "historically-specific racisms," which manifest "difference [and] . . . specificity rather than . . . a unitary, transhistorical or universal 'structure'" (Hall, 1980, p. 336). The ways in which forms of capitalism – and deindustrialization itself – were variously shaped by forces such as plantation slavery, colonialism and settler colonialism, formal and informal segregation, economic structures, and the broad ideologies and governance of "racial difference" are all pertinent to tracing the racialized contours of deindustrialization (Matera et al., 2023).

As Hackworth shows, the interplay between racism and capitalism assumed a number of forms within the Western industrial order, including the concentration of racialized minorities in low-wage work, greater exposure to poor and degrading work conditions, and the fermentation of racial division and conflict. This reflected different forms of incorporation within industrial capitalism and meant racially minoritized communities were generally positioned more marginally in relation to it (Hackworth, this volume). Echoing this, Gabriel Winant, in his analysis of the fall of the steel industry in Pittsburgh in the US points to how the New Deal-era marked a comprehensive political and economic investment in whiteness, as principally white, male unionized workers benefited most fully from the introduction of the welfare state and collective bargaining rights (Winant, 2021). This privileging of white workers, particularly, male, and unionized workers, within industrial capitalism emphasizes how deindustrialization has represented a diminishing in the "wages of whiteness" (Du Bois, 1935). As Hosang and Lowndes state, the loss of industrial work, declining unionism, deregulation, and capital mobility have "eroded the political standing and material security of an increasing percentage of white middle- and low-income workers" (HoSang and Lowndes, 2019, p. 53).

However, deindustrialization has impacted social groups unevenly as "race unmistakably structures these dispossessions" (HoSang and Lowndes, 2019, p. 53). Racially minoritized groups were adversely impacted through deindustrialization because of this more insecure incorporation. Indeed, a persistent and fair criticism of deindustrialization studies has been the tendency to assess the impacts of deindustrialization through the lens of the white male worker, obscuring the racially disparate forms that this assumed (Hamera, 2017; Matera et al., 2023). The delayed entry to industrial jobs, the lesser economic security in work, greater risk of layoffs, and heightened marginalization within service-oriented employment, all illustrate the racialized character of deindustrialization.

This is evident in the UK, where in the wake of the Second World War and an acute labor shortage, racialized minorities were sought through British colonies and imperial relations, reflecting what Sivanandan (1982) has termed 'new circuits of imperialism.' Migrants from Africa, the Caribbean, and the Indian subcontinent frequently found themselves concentrated in jobs marked by low rates of skill, pay, and poor conditions, subject to racial discrimination and union opposition to the recruitment of non-white workers. This labor market marginalization intensified through deindustrialization and declining employment opportunities (Fryer, 2018). In the UK, as Sivanandan explains, the colonial legacy determined that immigrants to the UK found work in poorer, more marginal sectors and industries. Also, they were confronted with restricted training and welfare opportunities and often worked unattractive shifts and roles, those which white workers were more reluctant to occupy in textiles, engineering and foundry work, and service industries (Sivanandan, 1982).

Kalra elaborates further in his analysis of the experiences of post-imperial migrant workers of South Asian heritage within the textile industry in the north of England. Here from the mid-1960s workers entered into an industry already experiencing protracted decline and with significantly lower levels of pay relative to other manufacturing work. South Asian male workers in particular were recruited into textile manufacture as white women – who predominated in the industry – took advantage of new opportunities including within emergent light manufacturing industries from the 1970s. These workers were concentrated within nightshift work and subject to the worst working conditions and low pay. The onset of significant redundancies and closures in the 1980s, a lack of union support, racial discrimination, and greater concentration in manual and semi-skilled work made South Asian workers significantly more vulnerable to deindustrialization. This was exacerbated further by wider industrial decline – concentrated particularly in the north of England (Kalra, 2000).

The racialized dimensions of deindustrialization are also clearly visible across the US, particularly within the Rust Belt. Sugrue's study of Detroit (1996), Sides's analyses of Los Angeles (2006), and Gabriel Winant's study of Pittsburgh (2021) all reveal the racialized impacts of deindustrialization. Here societal and labor market racism and racial marginalization worked to concentrate Black workers in lower-paid, lower-skilled occupations with lower-levels of seniority (due to the restrictive practices of labor unions and employers and a lack of governmental protections) placing them at the sharp end of industrial decline from the 1950s onward. This led to Black workers often experiencing deindustrialization earlier than white workers. Highlighting how this operated within the steel industry, Winant notes how

> [j]ob loss was racialized because it tracked the industrial workplace's internal labor market hierarchy. Seniority in the mill accrued within a worker's department rather

than plant-wide, meaning that the confinement of African Americans to undesirable departments institutionalized the pattern of who was likely to be hired and laid of first, as well as who would be exposed to the most dangerous and difficult work.

(Winant, 2021, pp. 102–103)

A 1968 study conducted by the Equal Employment Opportunity Commission found Black workers were "almost twofold overrepresented in the lowest classification and equally disproportionately underrepresented in the most skilled blue-collar work" (Cited in Winant, 2021, p. 103). The passage of federal consent decree within the steel industry in 1974, influenced through grassroots campaigning by Black steelworkers, was an attempt to promote more inclusive approaches to hiring, enhance access to more skilled, higher paid positions, and institute plant-wide seniority lists that would offer more protections to minority workers. However, as Winant shows, this decision occurred in the midst of the large-scale contraction of industrial work, providing greater access to more stable blue-collar work at the very moment it was undermined by "economic decline and disinvestment," with any employment gains largely offset by wider layoffs and contraction (Winant, 2021, pp. 124–125).

Despite these exclusions and delayed entry, manufacturing jobs represented an important avenue for economic security and social mobility for racially and ethnically minoritized groups in a wider context of educational inequalities, housing segregation, and labor market discrimination, which limited access to other forms of secure and well-paid employment (Bettis, 1994). Access to manufacturing jobs – which despite ongoing discrimination – increased during the 1940s in the context of the Second World War, allowing minority workers to share albeit to lesser degrees in the postwar expansion of the US economy, which saw marked economic and wage growth between the 1940s and early 1970s. Indeed, by the late 1970s, white workers secured upward social mobility during postwar economic expansion, often meaning their children were relatively less reliant on industrial work. This was not the case for significant portions of Black workers, whose entry into manufacturing had both come later and with lesser economic rewards, and this was particularly evident with the advent of plant closures that hit during the 1970s (Wilson, 2012; Parks, 2011). Bettis reports that during 1979, in the midst of deindustrialization 30% of Chrysler's workforce, concentrated heavily in the Rust Belt, consisted of African Americans, despite making up only around 12% of the national population (Bettis, 1994, p. 79). Parks also found that both Black and Latino men were proportionally more reliant than white men on manufacturing employment in Chicago in both 1970 and 1980. In fact, between 1950 and 1970, the number of white men employed in manufacturing in the city declined by 9%, while it increased by 57% for Black men and 154% for Latino men (Parks, 2011, pp. 117–118).

Across the industrial centers of the Rust Belt and beyond, the impacts of manufacturing job losses on Black workers were profound, with Black employment in manufacturing falling by 50% during the 1980s (Hinshaw, 2002). This was driven by the heavy concentration of Black workers within the steel industry, significantly outnumbering white workers as a proportion of industry workers by 1980. During the 1980s, steel losses accounted for 40% of all Black manufacturing losses (Parks, 2011, p. 119). The impacts on Black men were particularly devastating. Oliver and Shapiro state that "from 1979 to 1984 one-half of Black males in durable goods-manufacturing in five Great Lakes cities lost their jobs" (Oliver and Shapiro, 2006, p. 26 cited in Golash-Boza, 2022, p. 288). Detroit lost 70% of its manufacturing jobs between 1969 and 1989 (Golash-Boza, 2022, p. 288), significantly impacting

Black male employment. In Chicago, the number of Black men employed in manufacturing also declined by 36% between 1980 and 1990 (Parks, 2011, p. 118).

The effect on employment rates was not just due to the impacts of the loss of industrial work but the challenges Black workers faced in accessing new jobs within the emerging service industries, registering significantly higher levels of unemployment. Bettis notes that African Americans had difficulty accessing new service sector jobs for a number of reasons. Institutionalized racism in the housing market had worked to concentrate Black workers in areas away from where new jobs were located, and additionally they experienced ongoing labor market discrimination. This particularly impacted Black men, "because self-presentation skills are imperative here, and white owners were less willing to hire blacks for jobs in which they interacted with the public" (Bettis, 1994, pp. 79–80; Wilson, 2007). The effects of this labor market marginalization on poor Black men particularly those who were younger and residing in more impoverished urban neighborhoods were stark. In 1985, 51% of African American men aged 16–24 and 35% of those aged 25–64 who lived in a central city area were unemployed, while only 20% and 17% of white men were unemployed in the same age groups (Bettis, 1994, p. 80). William Julius Wilson too documents a dramatic increase in Black male unemployment in Chicago, where by 1990, across the Bronzeville neighborhoods, only 37% of males aged 16 and over were employed (Wilson, 1996, p. 19). Squires noted how among workers displaced through deindustrialization, "blacks are unemployed for longer periods of time and when these workers do find jobs, blacks earn a lower percentage of their previous wages than do whites" (Squires, 1994, p. 21).

The particularly harsh impact of deindustrialization on Black communities in the US highlights the need for deindustrialization studies to parse both the common and the distinctive experiences of industrial change for racialized groups located differently within systems of racial stratification. For instance, in examining the economic experiences of Black and Latinx communities in South Los Angeles, Stephens and Pastor note that despite both groups having high rates of poverty and low median household incomes, "Economic precarity for the black community has been undergirded by rampant black unemployment, spanning several decades, linked to the decline in manufacturing . . . as well as to continued practices of employment discrimination" (Stephens and Pastor, 2020, p. 17). In contrast, Latino workers have higher median household incomes and higher rates of labor market participation relative to Black workers. Kalra too observes the distinctive challenges that South Asian male workers faced in the wake of deindustrialization in the textile towns of the north of England. Concentrated in areas marked by emergent low-wage service-based economies, factors such as age, work history, education, and language combined with racial discrimination and inequality saw South Asian men come to occupy distinctive niches in areas such as taxi driving and food retail (Kalra, 2000).

The experiences outlined here highlight how in investigating the relationship between deindustrialization and race, it is clearly necessary to both explore interracial differences and examine intra-racial variation forged along lines of class, gender, and ethnicity (Hall, 1980; Virdee, 2019). As already illustrated, deindustrialization exerted a particularly profound impact on working-class Black men, particularly those residing in poorer areas and with lower levels of education (Sugrue, 1996; Wilson, 2012). It is also the case that women of color suffered disproportionately. In both the UK and the US, Black women have historically had higher employment rates, making them more exposed to industrial job loss relative to white women (particularly middle-class white women). Brewer in her analysis of Black women in the textile industry in North Carolina highlights how as white women left the industry for more desirable jobs, Black women increasingly filled semi- and unskilled positions. By the mid-1980s, Black women comprised a majority of operative workers in many southern textile plants, "bear[ing] the brunt" of "lay-offs," "plant mobility and closedowns" (Brewer, 1999, p. 40). As Brewer argues in understanding processes such as deindustrialization, "pivotal here is the intersection of race/gender hierarchies" and the 'class fractioning' that is also at play. Brewer notes, for instance, how economic restructuring is linked to class bifurcation among Black women, with the integration of more affluent and educated Black women into white-collar work, rising unemployment among the most marginal, while working-class women heavily concentrated in blue-collar occupations including, "nondurable goods, operatives, private household workers, service workers" (Brewer, 1999, pp. 37–38).

The importance of this is further evident within the service-based economy that has emerged in the wake of deindustrialization marked by sharp bifurcations along the lines of skill, reward, and security. This process has marked a reconfiguration of the working classes, with women, racialized minorities, and particularly minoritized women comprising heavily this new working class (Brewer, 1999; Winant, 2021). Brewer notes that within the service economy in the US, working-class Black women have become concentrated in "public reproductive work in the form of nurses' aides and age-old assistants, and in fast food outlets and cafeterias" (Brewer, 1999, p. 37). Here, "disproportionate numbers of black women are at the bottom of this division of labor, rooted in social meaning systems which get remade in the material context of social practices as well as the calculus of profit" (Brewer, 1999, p. 36). Affirming this, Winant traces the emergence of low-wage care work in the wake of deindustrialization. He notes that since the 1980s the care sector has accounted for the majority of job growth in the US economy, with this trend being particularly pronounced in "the old industrial zones of the northern and Midwestern United States," where on average one in five jobs are located in this sector (Winant, 2021, p. 5).

The task for deindustrialization studies is to illuminate specifically the ways in which deindustrialization has worked through and upon 'race' and existing racial hierarchies, exploring too how its intersections with class and gender produced divergent trajectories through deindustrialization, despite a common pattern in terms of the exacerbation of existing racial inequalities. However, the racialized impacts of deindustrialization should and cannot be understood as narrowly economically determined but also sociopolitical and spatial in character. As Hall reminds us, the significance of 'race' is not determined solely through economic relations, nor solely within the confines of the labor market rather it possesses a relative autonomy shaped also by social, cultural, and importantly political processes not reducible or internal to capitalism alone. This becomes evident in thinking through the wider community-level consequences of deindustrialization (Hall, 1980).

The Racialized Consequences of Deindustrialization

A key contribution of deindustrialization studies has been to broaden the analysis of the impacts of deindustrialization beyond simply job losses to also encompass its profound impacts on communities and community resources through the loss of employment, income, tax revenues, and the subsequent effects in terms of social provision (Bluestone and Harrison, 1982). In tracing these impacts, it is clear again that the consequences of deindustrialization have adversely impacted upon racialized minorities. However, reckoning with this requires a consideration of the ways in which deindustrialization intersects with social and spatial processes such as residential segregation and suburbanization, changing forms of governance and patterns of urban redevelopment.

Perhaps, the most significant factor in shaping the racialized consequences of deindustrialization is the pernicious problem of residential segregation. In both the UK and the US, the residential concentration of racialized minorities in areas of heightened social and economic disadvantage exacerbated the impacts of deindustrialization and shaped experiences of it. Not only were minorities disproportionately located in regions adversely impacted by the loss of industry, they were also concentrated in central-city areas – and within marginalized neighborhoods – that magnified the impacts of deindustrialization and the disinvestment associated with it (Hackworth, this volume). In 1990, for instance, almost 58% of Blacks lived in central city areas compared with just 26% of whites (Squires, 1994, p. 21).

Across the American Rust Belt, as Black residents moved in significant numbers from the 1910s onward through the Great Migration from the southern states to northern industrial cities, they encountered institutionally racist housing systems reinforced through an array of public and private mechanisms, including zoning practices, realtor steering, and the existence of racially restrictive covenants, which served to concentrate Black residents in the poorest-quality housing within the most deprived zones of the city. This relative fixity in place meant that when these central city areas began hemorrhaging industrial jobs from the 1950s, and especially the 1970s onward, residents were increasingly cut adrift from emergent employment opportunities, which tended to be located in smaller cities or the newly forming suburbs (Wilson, 2012; Wilson, 1996; Bettis, 1994; Sugrue, 1996; Wilson, 2007; Winant, 2021). Here, cheaper taxation rates, greater availability of land, favorable federal subsidies, newer infrastructure, lower rates of unionization, but also antipathy toward Black urban residents were key factors shaping this relocation. Sugrue notes the emergence of this industry decentralization during the 1940s, as companies relocated out of the central-city areas of Detroit into newer suburban zones (Sugrue, 1996). Bettis too observes how in California, the vast majority of employment growth during the 1980s occurred in areas with small Black populations (Bettis, 1994, p. 79).

This spatial redistribution of work was particularly harmful for Black, inner-city residents who experience particularly higher rates of residential segregation from white communities, much higher rates than Latinx and Asian American groups. Massey and Denton argue that Black Americans experience a form of "hypersegregation," with spatial concentration not just a result of but also a vehicle for racial stratification, linked to higher rates of Black poverty and unemployment (Massey and Denton, 1993). Housing segregation created what has been termed a "spatial mismatch" with Black working-class residents increasingly located at a geographical remove from new jobs emerging in the wake of deindustrialization (Wilson, 2012; Sugrue, 1996). Similar patterns of residential segregation also shaped the racialized consequences of deindustrialization in the UK. Postwar immigrants encountered limited housing options through processes of racial discrimination in both employment and housing. While redlining restricted private housing opportunities, racial exclusion in the public sector limited access to social housing, concentrating racial minorities in disadvantaged inner-city areas in poorer quality housing (Phillips and Harrison, 2010; Wetherell, 2020). This residential concentration compounded the impacts of deindustrialization, as newer manufacturing and service opportunities were often located away from central urban areas in peripheral and suburban industrial estates and retail zones. As Kalra notes these "sites tended to be closer to where skilled and white collar labor was available" (Kalra, 2000, p. 126).

In the US, not only residential segregation exacerbated racial minorities' experiences of industrial change, but deindustrialization in conjunction with processes such as suburbanization represented a significant form of economic disinvestment from inner urban areas. It contributed to a worsening of conditions within poor, inner-city neighborhoods as suburbanization marked a form of both 'white' and 'capital' flight out of cities, resulting in significant levels of depopulation and disinvestment. This worked to further concentrate social and economic disadvantage while at the same time reducing the fiscal resources available to tackle it. The civil rights movement and Fair Housing Act of 1968 intensified class segregation within the Black community as an outcome of increased residential mobility, particularly for the Black middle class (Wilson, 2012, 1996, 2007). Mallach notes how between 1970 and 2009, segregation by income among Black families grew four times faster than the rates for white families (Mallach, 2017), exacerbating the effects of industrial restructuring.

However, to attribute deepening social and economic marginalization solely to deindustrialization – to see it as driven purely by economic factors – would be wrong according to Wacquant (Wacquant, 2007). He argues that the deepening marginalization of poor, minoritized urban residents in Southern Chicago and the Parisian *banlieues* is not straightforwardly the result of economic restructuring alone but is rather better understood as being primarily political in its character. What has exacerbated the loss of manufacturing jobs for him and created growing racial and class segregation in urban cores is a shift in urban governance under conditions of post-Fordism, marked by the rise of neoliberal policies of deregulation, cuts to public spending and welfare retrenchment, and increasingly punitive approaches to law and order evident, for instance, in the rise of mass incarceration through the 1970s to the early 2000s. Here, "advanced marginality" within the post-industrial city is a result of the "refusal or reticence of their ruling classes converted to neoliberalism to check the social and spatial accumulation of economic hardship, social dissolution and cultural dishonor in the deteriorating working-class, and/or ethnoracial enclaves of the dualizing metropolis" (Wacquant, 2007, p. 7). Indeed, in both the UK and the US, the post-1970s have seen significant changes in urban governance marked by the retrenchment of public resources through policies of neoliberal governance and fiscal austerity.

In both of these places, the "inner city" became a target of these reforms, both materially and symbolically, through what Wacquant has termed "territorial stigmatization" (Wacquant, 2007). The conflation of the 'inner city' with class and particularly racial otherness, a process which preceded deindustrialization in both countries, undoubtedly increased through economic and state restructuring. Urban racialized minorities and the spaces they disproportionately inhabited served as an ideological justification for state retrenchment (Wilson, 2007; High, 2022; Hackworth, 2019; Rhodes and Brown, 2019). Detroit became paradigmatic of this, uniting a range of political actors through its representation of the city as a pathologized, Black space of danger and disinvestment, which served to legitimate structural disinvestment and which was seen to highlight the failures of the "overregulation" of liberal state intervention (Hackworth, 2019, pp. 99–100; Hamera, 2017).

Jason Hackworth's recent analysis of the decline of the American Rust Belt also argues that to locate this solely as a consequence of deindustrialization simplifies the processes that have produced decline and works to obscure the central role that 'race' and cultural ideologies of 'racial threat' played within this. Rather than being simply an outcome of the loss of work, Hackworth argues that Rust Belt cities have experienced sustained disinvestment as an outcome of a process of "organized deprivation" which "involves direct state actions to reduce social welfare, liberate corporations from local regulation, and punish 'unruly people'" (Hackworth, 2019). This deprivation has resulted in systemic disinvestment within 'black spaces' through decades-long processes of decline. He notes, for instance, that the most significant predictor of land abandonment across Rust Belt cities is not manufacturing

83

job losses but size of Black population, with neighborhoods experiencing the most shrinkage also having significantly larger shares of black residents. While not dismissing the role that deindustrialization played, the foregrounding of 'race,' and specifically anti-Blackness, highlights the complex factors driving urban decline and also helps to explain regional and local variations within it, for instance, in terms of abandonment (Hackworth, 2019; High, 2022). Beyond the neighborhood level, Hackworth also illustrates that decline has been most pronounced in cities with larger historic Black populations, where Blacks constitute a majority, and cities with histories of Black political leadership (Hackworth, 2019).

It is also the forms of urban development that have emerged to revitalize purportedly 'post-industrial' cities that have exacerbated the racialized dimensions of deindustrialization. As David Harvey (1989) has noted, neoliberal reforms since the 1970s have shifted urban governance and development away from "managerial" approaches which are oriented toward public provision and redistribution, toward more "entrepreneurial" models, in which political actors pursue growth-based strategies to attract more flexible forms of capital investment in the context of heightened interurban competition (Harvey, 1989). This has involved both a material and symbolic re-envisioning of urban space in the wake of deindustrialization, with an emphasis on leisure, consumption, and tourism to court more affluent visitors and residents. Again, these processes have often adversely impacted poorer, racially minoritized groups through increased marginalization and threats of displacement. Zimmerman in this analysis of the redevelopment of Milwaukee in the early 2000s noted that investment in the downtown area, cultural amenities, and select neighborhoods was accompanied by ongoing manufacturing job losses, economic contraction, and high rates of unemployment and racialized poverty (Zimmerman, 2008).

David Wilson has argued that these types of approaches to urban redevelopment have become commonplace across the Rust Belt in cities such as Chicago, Cleveland, Detroit, St. Louis, and Indianapolis, intensifying in the 1990s. These strategies which work to "fully shift local politics to a concern with resource attraction and forge land- and property vibrant cities," are deemed essential for "economic survivability" in an era of global capital (Wilson, 2007, p. 36). For Wilson, this targeting of investment has worsened the social and economic marginalization of poor communities, particularly poor, Black communities. This has occurred through this redirecting of resources, which include significant tax abatements for new development rather than simply through the threat of residential displacement via rising property prices. As Wilson states, "Businesses, corporations, and real-estate agents gained but at the expense of depleting a central funding source for the creation of housing, jobs, drug-treatment programs and facilities, after-school programs" (Wilson, 2007, p. 38). This resource-switching again is especially evident and harmful within more heavily Black-populated cities in the Rust Belt, as renewed investment in urban cores has occurred alongside the proliferation of approaches aimed at 'rightsizing' declining cities in places such as Detroit, Cleveland, Youngstown, and Flint. Here the rationalization of resources that these approaches represent most often target heavily Black and historically disinvested neighborhoods, furthering the retraction of social and economic resources (Wilson, 2007; Hackworth, 2019).

Focusing on the broader consequences of deindustrialization reveals a process which works to exacerbate race and class inequalities and existing forms of socio-spatial division. However, to focus solely on deindustrialization obscures the ways in which it intersects dynamically with processes such as segregation and suburbanization and shifting forms of urban governance characterized by a prioritizing of entrepreneurial growth-oriented strategies and austerity. The task for deindustrialization studies is to trace the consequences of industrial change in ways that are attentive to intersecting social, spatial, and political processes that shape its racially uneven legacies.

Deindustrialization as Race-Making

Deindustrialization is racialized in terms of its character and consequences, but 'race' also shapes and is shaped by wider cultural imaginaries of industrial decline and its more micro-level impacts upon experiences, subjectivities, and identities. Deindustrialization studies has to reckon with the processes of race-making, -thinking, -being, and -feeling. In understanding this, it is useful to draw on Hamera's distinction between *deindustrialization* as the process of industrial loss and the 'deindustrial' which captures the cultural frames – the 'figural economies' – through which deindustrialization is understood and navigated. As Hamera elaborates, "Figural economies [represent]. . . a way to track and analyze the affective, aesthetic, rhetorical and above all racial dynamics shaping and powering the way we experience deindustrialization" (Hamera, 2017, p. xiv). For Hamera, deindustrialization is not simply racialized, but rather it is race-making; 'race' frames how we apprehend industrial change, but this shift itself also informs meanings of 'race' and racial hierarchies, as well as the lived experiences of racialized identities and relations.

Hamera argues that deindustrialization has played a key role in producing new meanings and forms of 'blackness' and 'whiteness,' just as the rise of industrial capitalism did. For instance, she argues that "African-Americans are both repeatedly evident and often absent in the figural economies of the deindustrial," not viewed as "creative agents" (Hamera, 2017, p. 7). In the wake of deindustrialization, Black Americans have been subjected to an array of stigmatizing representations of irrationality, dependency, often blamed for urban and economic decline through the pathologization of Black bodies and spaces, depictions that have intensified in the neoliberal era. Relatedly, the cultural meanings of 'whiteness' have also been shaped by deindustrialization and organized through ideas of increasing insecurity and a loss of privilege, "as it generated an increasing sense of precarity and anxiety that the Fordist good life, sustained by work in the plant, would soon be a thing of the past" (Hamera, 2017, p. 8). HoSang and Lowndes argue that economic restructuring has been accompanied by a "racialization of white precarity" (HoSang and Lowndes, 2019). They note during the 1980s and 1990s the rise of stigmatizing tropes (i.e., 'white trash,' 'hillbilly') regarding the disintegration of the white working class and the emergence of a 'white underclass,' characterized by dysfunction, failure, and forms of cultural otherness.

The UK has also seen parallel narratives evident in the rise of the designation "chav" in the early 2000s (Jones, 2011). More recently, in the US and the UK, the trope of the 'left behind' has emerged in response to the election of Donald Trump and the support for Brexit. Within this more structurally oriented narrative, the "white working class" are cast as uniquely disadvantaged through deindustrialization and globalization, whose purported political resentment is deemed a legitimate response to societal change (Bhambra, 2017). These currents point to a politicization of increased white insecurity, as deindustrialization has been identified as pivotal to the ways in which "white political identity becomes mobilized, inhabited, contested, and transformed in the context of material crisis and abandonment" (HoSang and Lowndes, 2019, pp. 47–48). Research has suggested that the salience of race as a basis for political mobilization and affinity has likely increased due both the material and symbolic losses of deindustrialization itself but also due to the ways in which deindustrialization has eroded more racially inclusive forms of class-based political organization (i.e., unions) and discourse, which at times has offered a means for cross-racial solidarity (Lamont, Park, and Ayala-Hurtado, 2017; Makin-Waite, 2021). Deindustrialization has paralleled transitions in racial demography, the decline of traditionally leftist political movements, and the rise of identity politics rooted in race and ethnicity (Holmes, 2000; McQuarrie, 2017). Rogaly, for instance, situates the contemporary appeal of racial politics among often more marginalized sections of the white population as being due to what he terms an "ethnicization" of class relations (Rogaly, 2020).

Much of the renewed focus on race within the field of deindustrialization studies has developed in response to the rise of a politics of white resentment and the marked increase in sympathy for right-wing populist and far-right political sentiment across formerly industrialized nations. This body of work has sought to explain the concentration of such political sentiments within significant sections of the 'white working classes' across deindustrialized territories. It has indicated problems with pursuing analyses that separate out and seek to rank the importance of economic or cultural factors (for instance, through a privileging of either 'race' or class), imposing a false and misleading dichotomy upon them. Gest, Reny, and Mayer, for instance, note how support for such political ideas in both the UK and the US is driven by a simultaneous sense of economic, political, and social marginalization and a broadly defined sense of a loss of racial and class privileges and status (Gest, Reny, and Mayer, 2018). So, too, Gest in his study of white working-class residents in Youngstown, Ohio and Barking and Dagenham also observed a heightened sentiment of marginalization and an emergent, "transatlantic politics of white working-class people defined by their senses of economic obsolescence and social relegation" (Gest, 2016, p. 15). Hochschild in her analysis of Tea Party supporters in Louisiana notes that this politics of white resentment is rooted in the entanglements of a perceived and deeply felt economic and cultural degradation (Hochschild, 2016). So too in the UK context, in seeking to explain the widespread support for Brexit, Virdee and McGeever note the ways in which protracted economic decline and its 'class injuries' find expression through an insular, racialized sense of Englishness. This identity becomes a vehicle for the articulation of a set of simultaneously racial, national, and economic malaises, which capture the coalescence of the forces of deindustrialization, decolonization, and the rise of neoliberal policies which have worked to heighten social insecurity (Virdee and McGeever, 2018).

In establishing the significance of deindustrialization, therefore, it is also clearly imperative to tease out how this process has and is reshaping the entangled "modalities" of racialized and classed subjectivities (Hall, 1980; Virdee, 2014). Issues of racial conflict and division and the political salience of 'race' precede deindustrialization, and class formation has always worked through racial demarcations (Cowie, 2010; HoSang and Lowndes, 2019; Virdee, 2019). However, deindustrialization has evidently exerted a profound impact on how racial categories are understood and inhabited. Research indicates that for sections of white communities in particular, deindustrialization has been understood and experienced as a threat to (racial) identity itself, producing senses of loss, anger, anxiety and nostalgia (Virdee and McGeever, 2018; Baccini and Weymouth, 2021; Schofield, 2023).

An emergent body of work has sought to more fully understand these dynamics considering how deindustrialization has been refracted and responded to through racialized moral economies grounded in specific places and communities. In avoiding the construction of easy associations between deindustrialization and racial resentment and the imputation of any linear or causal relationship between them, emerging work is also beginning to wrestle more thoroughly with the intersections of race, class, and nation and the way these acquire salience within situational contexts shaped by deindustrialization. In the UK, Makin-Waite in documenting the appeal of far-right and right-wing populist politics in the former textile town of Burnley notes how deindustrialization has been pivotal in producing a form of demoralization which expresses itself through locally embedded structures of feeling, which rest on racially exclusionary forms of belonging and entitlement and a deeply felt political alienation (Makin-Waite, 2021; Pattison, 2022).

This greater reckoning with the way deindustrialization is experienced through 'race' has also highlighted how the process has disrupted material but also 'affective economies' – what Ahmed describes as the ways in which emotions "work, in concrete and particular ways, to mediate the relationship between the psychic and the social, and between the individual and the collective" (Ahmed, 2004, p. 119). In the US, Newman's excellent analysis of the views of white workers in the immediate aftermath of the closure of a Singer plant in Elizabeth, New Jersey, found that the contraction of jobs and the perceived decline of the town were experienced by workers as a loss of a moral universe and their central place within it. This exacerbated hostility toward both employers and minorities via a "'politics of blame' for the closure that was racially and ethnically loaded" (Newman, 1985, p. 137). Hinshaw and Modell (1996) in their interviews with Black and white residents in Homestead, Pennsylvania, argued that racial conflict increased in the context of urban decline, competition for resources, and pessimism about the future. Here senses of loss and lament – driven in part by deindustrialization – are identified as producing powerful responses at the levels of individual and collective that sustain local reserves of racialized resentment and nostalgia (Gest, 2016). However, equally important here – and something which deindustrialization studies must illuminate – are the more positive forms of racial meaning and association that persist within the context of industrial change (Rogaly, 2020).

While this work has been vital to the development of deindustrialization studies, in some instances it reproduces familiar failings, namely the overwhelming focus on the 'white working class' subject, which embodies a number of problems. First, the tendency toward what Bhambra has termed "methodological whiteness" in centering the experiences and views of white communities, risks framing deindustrialization as singularly and disproportionately impacting this group, eliding the impacts upon racially minoritized groups (Bhambra, 2017). A second problem is that in much popular analysis there is a tendency to identify the "white working class" as uniquely and endemically drawn to the politics of resentment (for a critique of such analyses, see: Pied, 2018). Indeed, such narratives which are prominent in both the US and the UK tend to portray the "white working class," particularly within deindustrialized communities, as a group both unified in its political outlook and predisposed to right-wing populist appeals rooted in racism and anti-immigrant sentiment (Rogaly, 2020). Fortunately, in the wake of the rise of Brexit and Trump, emerging scholarship has begun to reckon with the high concentrations of such political outlooks within more marginal sections of the white population while also illustrating the cross-class appeal of such sentiments (Pied, 2018). Indeed, a task for deindustrialization studies is to explore how the process has impacted upon racialized identities and subjectivities beyond simply the 'white working class,' considering instead its relevance to the thoughts and actions of a wider range of classed groups and actors.

While the focus on how deindustrialization has animated meanings and experiences of "race," the predominant focus on white communities risks reaffirming "deindustriality's presumptive whiteness" (Hamera, 2017, p. 30). Indeed, much more remains to be uncovered about the way in which deindustrialization has impacted upon the experiences and subjectivities of racialized minorities. In the UK, for instance, Kalra notes how deindustrialization saw South Asian males, largely segregated and excluded from white institutional spaces, invest more fully in family and religious life and ideology which provided a way of dealing with job loss and the development of moral accounts that lamented a perceived decline in British society and Muslim youth in particular (Kalra, 2000). Mah in her analysis of the lived experience of industrial ruination points to the way in which Black residents of Niagara Falls, while also lamenting the loss of industry and what was remembered as a time of greater social and economic stability, expressed an "ambivalent nostalgia" (Mah, 2012). Here positive memories of the industrial past coexisted with inequality, deprivation, and bearing the disproportionate burdens of environmental pollution. Interestingly, research also suggests that rising inequality and deindustrialization are not experienced as a threat to racial identity by minoritized workers who despite facing greater economic insecurity exhibit greater optimism about their future prospects relative to white Americans (Silva, 2019; Hanley and Branch, 2022). Indeed, while much work has focused on the turn to right-wing populism as a key reflex response for many white Americans, it would be interesting to explore how deindustrialization might be informing Black political subjectivities, particularly in the case of the rise of movements such as Black Lives Matter, identified by some as a form of left populism and which again has secured support in territories reconfigured through deindustrialization and responses to it. Despite important advances in the field, there remains a pressing need to explore more broadly and deeply how deindustrialization matters within the racialized classes and microsocial spaces of everyday lives, psyches, and relations.

Conclusion

This chapter has sought to set out the ways in which foregrounding 'race' can help to deepen our approach to the study of deindustrialization, highlighting three key avenues through which we might achieve this. First, there is a need to recognize how deindustrialization itself is a racialized process. The racial hierarchies that inhere within industrial capitalism have been selectively disturbed, acted upon, and reinforced via the loss of manufacturing and the ascendancy of the service economy. Deindustrialization studies must illuminate the racial character of this process examining the racial unevenness of the loss of manufacturing work, the impacts of rise of service industries, and processes of race and class reconfiguration. It must also remain attentive to how this has impacted racialized groups differentially due to the different forms of racial stratification that exist across different social and historical contexts. At the same time, deindustrialization works through 'race' but always also at its intersections with class and gender. It is important that the field captures the complex ways in which class and gender hierarchies animate and alchemize racial trajectories through deindustrialization.

This focus not only helps to better illuminate the complex contours of deindustrialization as it works through racialized bodies and spaces, but it also challenges some of the grander narratives which deindustrialization studies can at times endorse. For instance, the racialized precarity experienced by minorities prior to the onset of deindustrialization raises questions about the newness of this issue when incorporating the experiences of a more racially and gender-diverse working class (Winant, 2021). This forces the field to consider what – when viewed through a more racially attuned lens – the impacts of deindustrialization have been.

It is through this attunement that we can heed Cowie and Heathcott's call to "rethink the chronology, memory, spatial relations, culture, politics of what we have come to call 'deindustrialization'" (Cowie and Heathcott, 2003).

Second, the field of deindustrialization studies must be attentive to how the consequences of deindustrialization are also racialized as the impacts of industrial decline intersect with processes of residential segregation and suburbanization, the advent of neoliberal governance and fiscal authority, and patterns of urban redevelopment. This occurs in ways which persistently disadvantage racially minoritized spaces and communities, with deindustrialization but one dimension of a broader process of disinvestment. Being aware of these compounding and interconnected forces helps ward against a tendency to isolate industrial change from its wider social, spatial, and political embeddedness. Also, it again helps to highlight the complexity of the impacts of deindustrialization and define the parameters of the process less narrowly. It is only through rigorous analyses of the coarticulation of these processes that deindustrialization can be more fully reckoned with.

Third, deindustrialization has and is continuing to play an important role in reconfiguring the saliency and meanings of 'race,' as it reforms racial meanings, racialized experiences, identities, and subjectivities. The ways in which it does this require ongoing explication and accounting. The scholarship which has emerged as a means of exploring the relationship between deindustrialization and the rise of a politics of resentment has generated important insights that must be further built upon. In rejecting the assertion of a direct and inescapable relationship between deindustrialization and such political sentiments, work has drawn attention to the entangled modalities of race and class and the ways in which industrial decline comes to be navigated via deep-rooted and dynamic, situated moral economies. This forces us to consider more concretely how and why deindustrialization is impacting racialized experiences and subjectivities in ways that embrace nuance and complexity and attempt to capture the simultaneity of social and spatial identities. However, a danger within this work is the ongoing foregrounding of the experiences of white communities in ways which obscure and limit the agency and experiences of racially minoritized groups. Much remains to be known about how deindustrialization has impacted the racialized experiences and sentiments of racially diverse actors. By centering 'race' we can more fully comprehend the character and costs of deindustrialization, formulating richer accounts of its complicated past and its ongoing legacies.

Reference List

Ahmed, S. (2004). Affective Economies. *Social Text*, 22(2), pp. 117–139. https://doi.org/10.1215/01642472-22-2_79-117

Baccini, L. and Weymouth, S. (2021). Gone for Good: Deindustrialization, White Voter Backlash, and US Presidential Voting. *American Political Science Review*, 115(2), pp. 550–567.

Bettis, P. (1994). Deindustrialization and Urban Schools: Some Theoretical Considerations. *The Urban Review*, 26(2), pp. 75–94.

Bhambra, G. (2017). Brexit, Trump, and 'Methodological Whiteness': On the Misrecognition of Race and Class. *The British Journal of Sociology*, 68(1), pp. S214–S232. https://doi.org/10.1111/1468-4446.12317

Bluestone, B. and Harrison, B. (1982). *The Deindustrialization of America: Plant Closings, Community Abandonment, and the Dismantling of Basic Industry*. New York: Basic Books Inc.

Bonilla-Silva, E. (1997). Rethinking Racism: Toward a Structural Interpretation. *American Sociological Review*, 62(3), pp. 465–480. https://doi.org/10.2307/2657316

Brewer, R. (1999). Theorizing Race, Class and Gender: The New Scholarship of Black Feminist Intellectuals and Black Women's Labor. *Race, Gender and Class: African-American Perspectives*, 6(2), pp. 29–47.

Cowie, J. (2010). *Stayin' Alive: The 1970s and the Last Days of the Working Class*. New York: The New Press.

Cowie, J. and Heathcott, J. (eds.). (2003). *Beyond the Ruins: The Meanings of Deindustrialization*. Ithaca, NY: ILR Press.

Du Bois, W.E.B. (1935). *Black Reconstruction in America: An Essay Toward a History of the Part which Black Folk Played in the Attempt to Reconstruct Democracy in America, 1860–1880*. New York: Simon and Schuster.

Fryer, P. (2018). *Staying Power: The History of Black People in Britain*. London: Pluto Press.

Gest, J. (2016). *The New Minority: White Working Class Politics in an Age of Immigration and Inequality*. Oxford: Oxford University Press.

Gest, J., Reny, T. and Mayer, J. (2018). Roots of the Radical Right: Nostalgic Deprivation in the United States and Britain. *Comparative Political Studies*, 51(13), pp. 1694–1719. https://doi.org/10.1177/0010414017720705

Golash-Boza, T. (2022). *Race and Racisms: A Critical Approach*. 3rd edn. Oxford: Oxford University Press.

Hackworth, J. (2019). *Manufacturing Decline: How Racism and the Conservative Movement Crush the American Rust Belt*. New York: Columbia University Press.

Hall, S. (1980). Race, Articulation and Societies Structured in Dominance. In UNESCO (ed.) *Sociological Theories: Race and Colonialism*. Paris: UNESCO, pp. 305–345.

Hamera, J. (2017). *Unfinished Business: Michael Jackson, Detroit, and the Figural Economy of American Deindustrialization*. Oxford: Oxford University Press.

Hanley, C. and Branch, E.H. (2022). *Work in Black and White: Striving for the American Dream*. New York: Russell Sage Foundation.

Harvey, D. (1989). From Managerialism to Entrepreneurialism: The Transformation in Urban Governance in Late Capitalism. *Geografiska Annaler. Series B, Human Geography*, 71(1), pp. 3–17. https://doi.org/10.2307/490503

High, S. (2013). 'The Wounds of Class': A Historiographical Reflection on the Study of Deindustrialization, 1973–2013. *History Compass*, 11(11), pp. 994–1007. https://doi.org/10.1111/hic3.12099

High, S. (2022). *Deindustrializing Montreal: Entangled Histories of Race, Residence, and Class*. Montreal and Kingston: McGill-Queen's University Press.

Hinshaw, J. (2002). *Steel and Steelworkers: Race and Class Struggle in Twentieth Century Pittsburgh*. Albany, NY: State University of New York Press.

Hinshaw, J. and Modell, J. (1996). Perceiving Racism: Homestead from Depression to Deindustrialization. *Pennsylvania History: A Journal of Mid-Atlantic Studies*, pp. 17–52.

Hochschild, A.R. (2016). *Strangers in their Own Land: Anger and Mourning on the American Right*. New York: The New Press.

Holmes, D. (2000). *Integral Europe: Fast-Capitalism, Multiculturalism, Neofascism*. Princeton, NJ: Princeton University Press.

HoSang, D. and Lowndes, J.E. (2019). *Producers, Parasites, Patriots: Race and the New Right-Wing Politics of Precarity*. Minneapolis: University of Minnesota Press.

Jones, O. (2011). *Chavs: The Demonization of the Working Class*. London: Verso.

Kalra, V. (2000). *From Textile Mills to Taxi Ranks: Experiences of Migration, Labour and Social Change*. Aldershot: Ashgate.

Lamont, M., Park, B.Y. and Ayala-Hurtado, E. (2017). Trump's electoral speeches and his appeal to the American white working class. *British Journal of Sociology*, 68(S1), pp. S153–S180. https://doi.org/10.1111/1468-4446.12315

Lawson, C. (2020). Making Sense of the Ruins: The Historiography of Deindustrialization and Its Continued Relevance in Neoliberal Times. *History Compass*, 18(8), pp. 1–14. https://doi.org/10.1111/hic3.12619

Mah, A. (2012). *Industrial Ruination, Community and Place: Landscapes and Legacies of Urban Decline*. Toronto: University of Toronto Press.

Makin-Waite, M. (2021). *On Burnley Road: Class, Race and Politics in a Northern English Town*. London: Lawrence and Wishart.

Mallach, A. (2017). *The Divided City: Poverty and Prosperity in Urban America*. Washington: Island Press.

Massey, D. and Denton, N. (1993). *American Apartheid: Segregation and the Making of the Underclass*. Cambridge, MA: Harvard University Press.

Matera, M., Natarajan, R., Perry, K.H., Schofield, C. and Waters, R. (2023). Marking Race: Empire, Social Democracy and Deindustrialization. *20th Century British History*, 34(3), pp. 552–579. https://doi.org/10.1093/tcbh/hwad035

McQuarrie, M. (2017). The Revolt of the Rust Belt: Place and Politics in the Age of Anger. *British Journal of Sociology*, 68(S1), pp. S120–152. https://doi.org/10.1111/1468-4446.12328

Newman, K.S. (1985). Turning Your Back on Tradition: Symbolic Analysis and Moral Critique in a Plant Shutdown. *Urban Anthropology and Studies of Cultural Systems and World Economic Development*, 14(1/3), pp. 109–150.

Oliver, M. and Shapiro, T. (2006). *Black Wealth/White Wealth: A New Perspective on Inequality*. 2nd edn. New York: Routledge.

Parks, V. (2011). Revisiting Shibboleths of Race and Urban Economy: Black Employment in Manufacturing and the Public Sector Compared, Chicago 1950–2000. *International Journal of Urban and Regional Research*, 35(1), pp. 110–129.

Pattison, J. (2022). "There's Just Too Many": The Construction of Immigration as a Social Problem. *British Journal of Sociology*, 73(2), pp. 273–290.

Phillips, D. and Harrison, M. (2010). Constructing an Integrated Society: Historical Lessons for Tackling Black and Minority Ethnic Housing Segregation in Britain. *Housing Studies*, 25(2), pp. 221–235.

Pied, C.M. (2018). Conservative Populist Politics and the Remaking of the 'White Working Class' in the USA. *Dialect Anthropol*, 42, pp. 193–206. https://doi.org/10.1007/s10624-018-9501-1

Rhodes, J. and Brown, L. (2019). The Rise and Fall of the "Inner City": Race, Space and Urban Policy in Postwar England. *Journal of Ethnic and Migration Studies*, 45(17), pp. 3242–3259.

Robinson, C. (2021). *Black Marxism: The Making of the Black Radical Tradition*. 3rd edn. Chapel Hill: North Carolina University Press.

Rogaly, B. (2020). *Stories from a Migrant City: Living and Working Together in the Shadow of Brexit*. Manchester: Manchester University Press.

Schofield, C. (2023). In Defence of White Freedom: Working Men's Clubs and the Politics of Sociability in Late Industrial England. *Twentieth Century British History*, 34(3), p. 515.

Silva, J.M. (2019). *We're Still Here: Pain and Politics in the Heart of America*. Oxford: Oxford University Press.

Sivanandan, A. (1982). *A Different Hunger*. London: Pluto Press.

Squires, G.D. (1994). *Capital and Communities in Black and White: The Intersections of Race, Class and Uneven Development*. Albany, NY: State University of New York Press.

Stephens, P. and Pastor, M. (2020). What's Going On? Black Experiences of Latinization and Loss in South Los Angeles. *Du Bois Review: Social Science Research on Race*, 17(1), pp. 1–32.

Sugrue, T. (1996). *The Origins of the Urban Crisis: Race and Inequality in Postwar Detroit*, Princeton, NJ: Princeton University Press.

Virdee, S. (2014). *Racism, Class and the Racialized Outsider*. Basingstoke: Palgrave.

Virdee, S. (2019). Racialized Capitalism: An Account of its Contested Origins and Consolidation. *The Sociological Review*, 67(1), pp. 3–27.

Virdee, S. and McGeever, S. (2018). Racism, Crisis, Brexit. *Ethnic and Racial Studies*, 41(10), pp. 1802–1819.

Wacquant, L. (2007). *Urban Outcasts: Towards a Sociology of Advanced Marginality*. Cambridge: Polity.

Wetherell, S. (2020). 'Redlining' the British City. *Renewal*, 28(2).

Wilson, D. (2007). *Cities and Race: America's New Black Ghetto*. New York: Routledge.

Wilson, W.J. (1996). *When Work Disappears: The World of the New Urban Poor*. New York: Knopf.

Wilson, W.J. (2012 [1987]). *The Truly Disadvantaged: The Inner City, the Underclass, and Public Policy*, 2nd edn. Chicago: University of Chicago Press.

Winant, G. (2021). *The Next Shift: The Fall of Industry and the Rise of Health Care in Rust Belt America*. Cambridge, MA: Harvard University Press.

Zimmerman, J. (2008). From Brewtown to Cooltown: Neoliberalism and the Creative City Development Strategy in Milwaukee. *Cities*, 25(4), pp. 230–242.

PART II

Political Economy of Deindustrialization

INTRODUCTION
Political Economy of Deindustrialization

Steven High

Introduction

Questions of political economy have been central to the study of deindustrialization since the field's emergence in the 1970s and 1980s. With the crashing end of the postwar boom, Western Europe and North America, once highly industrialized, grappled with the enormity and long-term significance of the economic transformation underway. The 'how' and 'why' of these changes were fiercely debated, and competing explanatory frameworks quickly emerged. Sociologist Daniel Bell's 1973 book *The Coming of Postindustrial Society* cast these changes as an evolutionary step forward into a bright new post-industrial era. Resistance was futile: remember the Luddites who broke the machines that were replacing them during the industrial revolution? They became a punch line for a joke. In many ways, the deindustrialization thesis emerged to counter the desirability and inevitability of post-industrial theory. For deindustrialization scholars, industrial closures were primarily the result of capital flight and driven by the greed and anti-unionism of multinational corporations. Moving to lower-wage areas was thus a political and economic choice and not a linear stage of development. During this period, the dismantling of international trade barriers by the General Agreement on Tariffs and Trade (GATT) and the insulating of the market from democratic interference, key aspects of the new neoliberal order taking shape, triggered the radical restructuring of the international division of labor. Runaway shops and the outsourcing of production have now become a global phenomenon.

Three of the earliest studies in the field emerged directly out of the political struggle against industrial closures. Robert Laxer's edited volume *(Canada) Ltd: The Politics of Dependence*, published the same year as Bell's tome, was written by left nationalists in the Canadian 'Waffle' movement who equated deindustrialization with dependent industrialization – namely, the dominance of US capital in that country. Turning to Latin American dependency theorist André Gunder Frank, contributor Mel Watkins noted that "capitalist economic development is a dialectical process simultaneously creating development and under development" (Watkins, 1973, p. 111). The metropolitan-hinterland relationship is thus characterized by 'hierarchical links in long imperial chains.' Here, concluded Laxer, "the

DOI: 10.4324/9781003308324-10

thesis of de-industrialization receives its first treatment in this volume, within the broader context of a developed anti-imperialist analysis" (Laxer, 1973, p. 7).[1]

A few years later, radical political economists Barry Bluestone and Bennett Harrison were commissioned by the Progressive Alliance, a coalition of groups fighting plant closures in the US, to write a 1980 report on the "social violence" of capital flight (Bluestone and Harrison, 1980, p. v). "What the post-industrialists have ignored or played down," they argued: "is the changing spatial division of labor" (Bluestone and Harrison, 1980, p. 154). This report was essentially the first draft of their classic 1982 book *The Deindustrialization of America*, a foundational text in the field, which depicted the struggle as one pitting capital against community (Bluestone and Harrison, 1982). Finally, radical historian Staughton Lynd's 1983 book *The Fight Against Shutdowns* tells the story of community resistance to three steel mill closings in Youngstown Ohio. Fired from Yale for his anti-war activism and blacklisted, Lynd became a lawyer and represented these workers as general counsel of the local Ecumenical Coalition and later attempted to get an injunction to prevent another closure. "After our struggle ended, it was natural to think of telling the story as best as I could," he wrote (Lynd, 1983, p. 11). These activist beginnings set the agenda and tone for the field.

Capital's weaponization of geography against trade unions and working people was the central contribution of British Marxist geographer Doreen Massey's 1984 *Spatial Division of Labour* and American historian Jefferson Cowie's 1999 *Capital Moves*. Massey argued that geography is "fundamental to understanding an economy and a society" and, with it, "spatial inequality" (Massey, 1984, p. viii). Her book sought to connect the "changing geography of industry" to the "wider context of the development of capitalist society" (Massey, 1984, pp. 5–6). Hence, deindustrialization was fundamentally a process of spatial restructuring. For his part, Cowie followed RCA as it moved TV production from one US locality to the next until it crossed into Mexico to Ciudad Juarez (Cowie, 1999, pp. 10–11). His key insight: "Command of spatial relations, therefore, has become a crucial weapon in management's arsenal" (Cowie, 1999, p. 185). Cowie then went on to question the "ambivalent inheritance" of the community study which has been the "stock and trade of the so-called new labor history" – a point that could be directed at deindustrialization scholarship as well (Cowie, 1999, p. 7). Local studies are essential, especially as they center the experience of working-class people, but there is a danger that we lose sight of the how and why of structural change. A political economy approach therefore invites us to geographically scale up our analysis from the local case study.

Since the 2008 financial crisis, the center of gravity in deindustrialization studies has shifted decisively from the US to Europe. The UK, in particular, has seen the publication of an impressive number of books, articles, and PhD dissertations. Much of this recent scholarship has focused on the destruction of coal mining communities and the National Union of Mineworkers by Margaret Thatcher in the 1980s. Ewen Gibbs's *Coal Country: The Meaning of Deindustrialization in Postwar Scotland*, which excavates the willful destruction of the moral economy of the Scottish coalfields, and Huw Beynon and Ray Hudson's *The Shadow of the Mine: Coal and the End of Industrial Britain*, which compares the destruction of coalfield communities in South Wales and County Durham, stand out (Gibbs, 2021; Beynon and Hudson, 2021). In France, the black and yellow "faces" of coal and iron miners have also loomed large in the field.[2] The coal mining basin of Nord-Pas-de-Calais, the symbol of French mining since Emile Zola's 1885 novel *Germinal*, saw its last mine close in 1990 (see, e.g., Fontaine, 2018; Fontaine, 2019, p. 65). France's "Lorraine de fer" has also received

Introduction

attention, given the region's iron mines and steel mills, as well as its history of resistance to industrial closures (Raggi, 2019). The coal mines of Germany's Ruhr Valley have likewise received enormous attention, reinforced by the emergence of the region as an industrial heritage superpower.

If steelmaking has taken a back seat to mining in the European scholarship, the study of the automotive sector has barely made it into the car's back trunk. Europe's inattention stands in sharp contrast to North America, where the crisis in the automotive industry has been a central focus of the scholarship, alongside steelmaking. The agony of the 'Motor City' of Detroit has served as the Rust Belt's ground zero. In *The Origins of the Urban Crisis*, historian Thomas J. Sugrue asked, "What explains the emergence of persistent, concentrated, racialized poverty in Rust Belt cities?" (Sugrue, 1996, p. 4). His answer to that question speaks to the "mutual reinforcement" of race, economics, and politics (Sugrue, 1996, p. 5). Cities like Detroit were thus "overwhelmed by the combination of racial strife and economic restructuring" (Sugrue, 1996, p. 5). It is one of the few studies that tries to bridge the historiographic and political divide between the study of race and class in the context of deindustrialization.

Much of the scholarship remains anchored in well-known deindustrializing localities or regions. Regional and local identity are historical processes and, as such, very much entangled in the history of capitalist development, underdevelopment, and deindustrialization. Christopher Johnson's book on the decline of France's Languedoc region over the eighteenth and early nineteenth centuries is a case in point (Johnson, 1995). So, too, is my own work on the late twentieth-century "making" of the US Rust Belt (High, 2003). As social historian John Cumbler once observed: "depressions do not manifest themselves only at moments of national economic collapse, but also recur in scattered sites across the nation in regions, in industries, and in communities" (Cumbler, 1989, p. 182). Christopher Johnson drew a similar conclusion a few years later when he wrote: "One of the great ironies of differential regional deindustrialization, which is the standard form of capitalist 'crisis,' is that it hardly leads to revolution, but rather engenders quiescence, the internalization of despair" (Johnson, 1995, p. 259). While most regional and local studies zoom in on a single heartland area in isolation, there has been a recent move to draw cross-national comparisons. The most sustained of these efforts, so far, is Stefan Berger, Stefano Musso, and Christian Wicke's edited volume *Deindustrialization in Twentieth-Century Europe,* which compares Germany's Ruhr Valley and Italy's Golden Triangle (Berger, Musso, and Wicke, 2022). If Marion Fontaine and Xavier Vigna could write in 2019 that "rare are the true comparisons or transnational analyses" in deindustrialization studies, we are now seeing signs that this is finally changing (Fontaine and Vigna, 2019, p. 10).

That said, the scholarship has yet to truly recognize the historic nonrecognition of female-dominated sectors such as textiles, clothing, and electrical equipment. Industrial heartland regions, almost always, are formed around the classic male proletarians of lore. It is their history, given its perceived centrality to regional and national identity, that is deemed worthy of heritage preservation. Not so industrial sectors where women were concentrated. This long-standing derecognition had far-reaching consequences for displaced women. Doreen Massey notes that no regional policy assistance was given to the deindustrializing cotton towns of Lancashire, while the decline of male-dominated industries elsewhere received Developed Area status – this "was due in part to a more general political blindness to questions of women's employment" (Massey, 1994, p. 206). Germany's much heralded social compact under Rhenish capitalism, which saw the managed decline of some industrial sectors to minimize hardship, did not extend to textiles or other female-dominated industries. I am finding much the same in my own research on labor adjustment in Canada.

If gender is an important structuring force, the twentieth century's prevailing regional development response to deindustrialization troubled trade unionists and anti-plant shutdown activists; at least in the US, corporations regularly whipsawed one community against another and one political jurisdiction against the next (Barker, 1981, p. 455). One town or region's loss was often another's gain. In *The Deindustrialization of America*, Bluestone and Harrison therefore discounted the idea that it was a regional problem in their effort to politically nationalize the issue. Only then, they believed, would federal politicians be compelled to act. For his part, British historian Jim Tomlinson has made the case for the centrality of deindustrialization in postwar British history (Tomlinson, 2020). He notes that the scholarship of the 1980s had framed industrial decline in terms of regional disparities and the North–South divide in England (Tomlinson, 2020, p. 202). Tomlinson rejects this framing as deindustrialization began in the big cities, including London. However, we have only just begun to study how deindustrialization played out in larger metropolitan cities.[3]

Scholars of race have usefully pushed back at Tomlinson's suggestion that deindustrialization can frame the post-1945 history of the UK, noting the ways the field has contributed to the coding of working class as white. It is imperative, they argue, that any return to historical materialism "not go down the same intellectual cul-de-sac of social histories past – by relating 'race'" to the margins. A first step would be for us to expand our view of the geography of deindustrialization to account for diverse metropolitan cities and port cities (Matera et al., 2023, pp. 571–74). There is more to deindustrialization than the pit-village.

Most of the contributors to the Political Economy part of this handbook are members of the transnational research project, Deindustrialization and the Politics of Our Time (DéPOT), which is seeking to make wider cross-national comparisons and transdisciplinary linkages. None of the six chapters that follow are therefore local studies. Their aim is transnational even if their national anchoring remains visible. The how and why of deindustrialization is their primary focus as is working-class resistance. The part begins with an impassioned appeal from Fred Burrill and Matthew Penney, a historian of Canada and Japan respectively, for the field to break out of our national silos and examine the overriding logic of capitalism itself. Industrial closures are not the result of a few bad corporate apples or some failure of capitalism to function properly, indeed deindustrialization is literally capitalism at work. To understand deindustrialization as political and economic process, we must go beyond its effects on those left behind and analyze the structural forces that caused, and continue to cause, widespread displacement. In other words, they are calling on researchers in the field to reengage with Marxist theory and praxis.

Drawing for his part from the Black radical tradition in North America and the Caribbean, geographer Jason Hackworth speaks to how anti-Blackness was baked into industrialism in the US and around the world and, thereafter, profoundly structured the process of deindustrialization. As he writes, the "landscapes of abandonment in Detroit and Cleveland are disproportionately located in Black majority neighborhoods" (Hackworth, this volume), Capital flight and white flight were thus two sides of the same coin. Black communities have likewise, disproportionately, been urban renewed out of existence while simultaneously being blamed for urban decline. Hackworth's piece asks us to consider how race and class intersect and reinforce each other. His discussion of moral panics and backlashes reminds me of Loïc Wacquant's earlier work on American Black ghettos and French banlieues in the

Introduction

"deindustrializing Red Belt," which invited us to think more about territorial stigmatization and the spatial relations of injustice and inequality (Wacquant, 2008, p. 9). The slow decomposition of working-class territories and the pauperization of those left behind are real, but underclass discourse has been politically appropriated by neoconservatives, Third Way social democrats, and others who prefer to blame cultures of poverty and the poor themselves for their circumstances rather than the underlying structural violence of capitalism and racism (Gans, 1995). Deindustrialization studies has much work to do, if we are going to understand the ways that Empire, racial capitalism, and settler colonialism infuse industrialism and its loss.

Given the geographic unevenness of economic rise and decline, the promotion of regional economic diversification emerged as a key policy response to twentieth-century deindustrialization. In the US, we see this with the creation of a regional rehabilitation board for Minnesota's Iron Range in the 1940s and in the establishment of the Area Redevelopment Administration for Appalachia during the 1960s, to name just two (Manuel, 2015; Wilson, 2009). The regional development impulse was even stronger in Canada, at least until the 1980s, when the community economic development paradigm took hold. In his contribution to this part, Canadian historian Lachlan MacKinnon considers the role of the state in countering regional industrial decline. His chapter is anchored in Atlantic Canada, a peripheral region of the country that was historically dependent on the fisheries, forestry, and mining, though there were also pockets of heavy industry such as the integrated steel mill in Sydney, Nova Scotia. Mackinnon's contribution speaks to the ways that regional development ideas crisscrossed the Atlantic and across national borders.

The contribution from Ewan Gibbs invites us to consider the relationship between deindustrialization and national feeling, using the intriguing case of Scotland. In the wake of Brexit and the rise of right-wing populism in many countries, the assumption is often made that those economically left-behind are prone to nationalist xenophobia. Scotland reveals a different pattern with the rise of center-left Scottish nationalism in the wake of deindustrialization. It therefore shares much in common with the Canadian example insofar as deindustrialization is blamed on an external other, be it Margaret Thatcher or Uncle Sam, that works to nationalize the plant closing issue. National identity is very much bound up with deindustrialization, but its significance remains contested.

For their part, French historians Marion Fontaine and Xavier Vigna examine the history of political struggle to deindustrialization. What are the factors driving working-class resistance in certain contexts and why are industrial closures mostly met with silent despair? Drawing from social movement theory, they consider the factors that contribute to a politics of resistance to industrial restructuring and closure. Grounding their analysis in France, they offer a political periodization of resistance since the 1950s. Why did the towns of Decazeville and Logwy emerge as veritable symbols of working-class defiance? Resistance also underpins the contribution from sociologist Alice Mah, who explores how the "just transition" idea, like deindustrialization itself, has its origins in the US labor movement during the 1980s, when it sought to reconcile the 'jobs versus environment' conundrum. Best known for her centering of ruination as a key framework for understanding deindustrialization, Mah modifies this idea in proposing 'toxic industrial ruination.' What can we learn from past transitions to ensure that the coming life-or-death global transition away from fossil fuels is considerably fairer to those being economically and climatically displaced? We can and must do better. Thinking critically about 'anticipatory' or 'future' deindustrialization, in relation to past experiences, is essential going forward.

The Routledge Handbook of Deindustrialization Studies

Notes

1 For an analysis of these early years, see High, S. (2023). The Radical Origins of the Deindustrialization Thesis: From Dependency to Capital Mobility & Community Abandonment. *Labour/le travail*, 91 (Spring), pp. 31–56.
2 A key early work is Reid, D. (1985). *The Miner of Decazeville: A Genealogy of Deindustrialization*. Cambridge: Harvard University Press. The important forthcoming monographs by Fontaine, M. and Castellesi, R. represent the coming of age of the French deindustrialization historiography.
3 An exception is High, S. (2022). *Deindustrializing Montreal: The Entangled Histories of Race, Residence and Class*. Montreal: McGill-Queen's University Press.

Reference List

Barker, L. (1981). There is a Better Way. *Labor Law Journal*, 32(8), p. 455.

Berger, S., Musso, S. and Wicke, C. (eds.). (2022). *Deindustrialisation in Twentieth-Century Europe: The Northwest of Italy and the Ruhr Region in Comparison*. Switzerland: Palgrave-Macmillan.

Beynon, H. and Hudson, R. (2021). *The Shadow of the Mine: Coal and the End of Industrial Britain*. London: Verso.

Bluestone, B. and Harrison, B. (1980). *Capital and Communities: The Causes and Consequences of Private Disinvestment*. Washington: The Progressive Alliance.

Bluestone, B. and Harrison, B. (1982). *The Deindustrialization of America: Plant Closings, Community Abandonment and the Dismantling of Basic Industry*. New York: Basic Books.

Cowie, J. (1999). *Capital Moves: RCA's 70-Year Quest for Cheap Labor*. Ithaca, NY: Cornell University Press.

Cumbler, J.T. (1989). *A Social History of Economic Decline: Business, Politics and Work in Trenton*. New Brunswick, New Jersey: Rutgers University Press.

Fontaine, M. (2018). Regional Identity and Industrial Heritage in the Mining Area of Nord-Pas-de-Calais. In Wicke, C., Berger, S. and Golombek, J. (eds.) *Industrial Heritage and Regional Identities*. London: Routledge, pp. 56–73.

Fontaine, M. (2019). From Myth to Stigma? The Political Uses of Mining Identity in the North of France. *Labor*, 16(1), p. 65.

Fontaine, M. and Vigna, X. (2019). La désindustrialisation, une histoire en cours. *20&21: Revue d'histoire*, 144, p. 10.

Gans, H. (1995). *The War Against the Poor: The Underclass and Antipoverty Policy*. New York: Basic Books.

Gibbs, E. (2021). *Coal Country: The Meaning and Memory of Deindustrialization in Postwar Scotland*. London: University of London Press.

High, S. (2003). *Industrial Sunset: The Making of North America's Rust Belt*. Toronto: University of Toronto Press.

Johnson, C.H. (1995). *The Life and Death of Industrial Languedoc, 1700–1920*. New York: Oxford University Press.

Laxer, R. (1973). Foreword. In Laxer, R.M. (ed.) *(Canada) Ltd: The Political Economy of Dependency*. Toronto: McClelland and Stewart, p. 7.

Lynd, S. (1983). *The Fight Against Shutdowns: Youngstown's Steel Mill Closings*. San Pedro, California: Singlejack Books.

Manuel, J.T. (2015). *Taconite Dreams: The Struggle to Sustain Mining on Minnesota's Iron Range, 1915–2000*. Minneapolis: University of Minnesota Press.

Massey, D. (1984). *Spatial Division of Labour: Social Structures and the Geography of Production*. London: Macmillan.

Massey, D. (1994). *Space, Place and Gender*. Minneapolis: University of Minnesota Press.

Matera, M., Natarajan, R., Perry, K.H., Schofield, C. and Waters, R. (2023). Marking Race: Empire, Social Democracy, Deindustrialization. *Twentieth Century British History*, 34(3), pp. 571–74.

Raggi, P. (2019). *La Désindustrialisation de la Lorraine du fer*. Paris: Classiques Garnier.

Reid, D. (1985). *The Miner of Decazeville: A Genealogy of Deindustrialization*. Cambridge: Harvard University Press.

Introduction

Sugrue, T.J. (1996). *The Origins of the Urban Crisis: Race and Inequality in Postwar Detroit.* Princeton: Princeton University Press.

Tomlinson, J. (2020). De-industrialization: Strengths and Weaknesses as a Key Concept for Understanding Post-War British History. *Urban History,* 47, pp. 199–219.

Watkins, M. (1973). Resources and Underdevelopment. In Laxer, R.M. (ed.) *(Canada) Ltd: The Political Economy of Dependency.* Toronto: McClelland and Stewart, p. 111.

Wacquant, L. (2008). *Urban Outcasts: A Comparative Sociology of Advanced Marginality.* Cambridge: Polity.

Wilson, G.S. (2009). *Communities Left Behind: The Area Redevelopment Administration, 1945–1965.* Knoxville: University of Tennessee Press.

6
UNEVEN DEVELOPMENT, THE WORLD-SYSTEM, AND LUMPENIZATION

Bringing Marxian Political Economy Back Into Deindustrialization Studies

Fred Burrill and Matthew Penney

There is a specter haunting deindustrialization studies – the specter of Marxian political economy. The overarching direction of the field in the Anglosphere over the last 40 years has been from the general to the specific, helping us to gain an impressive oral history and memory-based understanding of the long-term "wounds of class" lived out in the Global North towns and neighborhoods abandoned by industrial capital (High, 2013).[1] But this has entailed a marked national siloing: the process of "moving beyond the body count" has also been one of enclosure; industry "left," leaving us to study the "left behind" rather than adjusting our gaze to follow the dynamics of capital accumulation continuing just over the horizon (Cowie and Heathcott, 2005).[2]

In this chapter, we ask historiographical questions about the tools that have been adopted for understanding shutdowns. Which aspects of Marxist thinking are part of the canon of the field, and why? And why so little focus on the global?[3] With these questions in mind, we propose a return to the critique of political economy through an engagement with the literature on three interrelated concepts: uneven development, the world-system, and lumpenization. Thinking these three together can help us understand the ways in which de- and re-industrialization are integrally tied on both local and international scales and concomitantly how the process of class fragmentation and disintegration which we are observing in many parts of the Global North is not simply the product of specific political decisions and free-trade regimes or particular examples of predatory financialization, but rather an integral function of capitalism itself. A return to the tools of Marxian critique, in short, can be one important way to "shift our attention back to theorizing deindustrialization instead of simply documenting it" (Clark, 2022, p. 30).

There are, of course, perfectly legitimate non-Marxist ways to engage with the study of deindustrialization. But the question of which Marx and why is begged by both the theoretical inclinations of the field's progenitors and the continued recourse of many of its practitioners to the insights of the Marxist critical lineage. As historian Steven High has shown, early North American work in the field was certainly rooted in materialist political economy, either

DOI: 10.4324/9781003308324-11

Uneven Development, the World-System, and Lumpenization

in the dependency theory of left nationalists in Canada or in Barry Bluestone and Bennett Harrison's focus on capital flight in the US (High, 2023). Much as Jim Tomlinson points out with respect to the first 1970s writings on deindustrialization in the UK, however, these works conceived of shutdowns as a national problem – the global was an abstraction against which the domestic plight of workers could be measured or upon which it could be blamed (Tomlinson, 2020, pp. 199–200; See Bluestone and Harrison, 1982, pp. 4–5; Laxer, 1973). And in both of these North American cases, while the tools of Marxist political economy were important to their respective analyses, they were modulated by the preceding decades of Cold War repression. Jim Laxer and Mel Watkins, the central figures behind Canadian left nationalism's concern with deindustrialization, were criticized by some on the radical left as being simply a few more "liberals in a hurry" (Bullen, 1983, p. 189). The political movement of which they were a part, the Waffle, was a short-lived New Left formation whose most significant accomplishment was to be the first of many attempts at drawing radical youth energy into the inevitable cul-de-sac of the New Democratic Party, founded by left intellectuals and the labor movement in 1961 with the hope of occupying a similar political position to the left wing of the American Democrats (McKay, 2005, pp. 173–174). In the US, Bluestone and Harrison were part of the nexus of heterodox economists in the Union for Radical Political Economics that emerged out of New Left campus organizing in the late 1960s and early 1970s, the 'radical' label seen as having less baggage, especially after the lean professional prospects of the McCarthyist 1950s than 'Marxist' or 'socialist.' The important thing was that one needed to be critical of American capitalism, which in theory could be done from a Marxist, institutionalist, Keynesian, or neoclassical theoretical standpoint. In practice, this resulted in a trending toward social democracy, mirroring the overall tendency in the post-1960s white American New Left (see Lee, 2004; Kim, 2018; Rosenfeld, 2012). In 1972, Bluestone was predicting the inevitable downfall of capitalism; by 1982, he and Harrison were arguing for "early warning systems" and "re-industrialization with a human face," focused on social justice within American capitalism (Bluestone, 1972, p. 82; Bluestone and Harrison, 1982). In fact, political scientist Clyde W. Barrow goes as far as to argue that their recommendation of "liberal and progressive workforce development programs" laid the groundwork for the subsequent decades of failed Democratic strategies for countering deindustrialization (Barrow, 2020, p. 11).[4]

When the nascent field of deindustrialization studies began to turn away from political economy in the early 2000s in favor of explorations of the longer-term social and cultural impacts of shutdowns, it maintained this basically social-democratic, national(ist) approach to the question. Certain strands of Marxism fit easier than others within these parameters. Within the UK and Canada, for example, historians and sociologists of deindustrialization have turned to the thinking of E. P. Thompson and Raymond Williams. The use of this humanist strain within British Marxism, while obviously relevant for understanding the making and unmaking of working-class worlds, has in many ways followed the tendency within the works themselves to foreclose the possibility of considering race and empire (see Gregg, 1998; Viswanathan, 1991).[5] The field engages much less with the thinking of contemporary figures like Dobbs or Hobsbawm, who provide us with potentially important tools for thinking through the transition of one mode of accumulation (if not production) to another.[6] Other heterodox Marxist thinkers of the period who worked across national boundaries also have largely gone by the theoretical wayside in our field, even though we might well benefit from the work of someone like, say, Immanuel Wallerstein, in thinking through the relation between production at home and what Cowie and Heathcott referred to in 2003 as the "far-flung points of the globe" (Cowie and Heathcott, 2005, p. 4).[7] And, as a result, as Schindler et al. pointed out recently, we operate within a body of scholarship wherein "the Global South remains a vague construct, which, when it appears at all, is a homogenized recipient of offshored industry" (Schindler et al., 2020, p. 287). Parts of the Global North outside 'the West' like Japan, South Korea, and Taiwan, some of the original boogeymen of 'offshoring' but also 'value added' industrial competitors and the origin point of powerful multinationals, are left equally vague despite their theoretical potential to challenge simple assumptions about outsourcing and cheap labor and the possible comparative value of their own internal processes of deindustrialization (Cowie, 2001).

To counter these dynamics, we need to bring the spatial dimensions of the problem out of the footnotes, where we in deindustrialization studies often make gestures to the work of thinkers like Doreen Massey, David Harvey, and Neil Smith. While these scholars obviously worked in tension with one another, they were united in their attempt to understand capitalism's construction of space through the process of uneven development. The key insight of uneven development is not just that capital concentrates in some zones at the expense of others (à la Leninist understandings of imperialism, or even how mainstream business journalists tend to write about the rise of Chinese manufacturing vis-à-vis the American heartland) but that within the accumulation process there exists a simultaneous and connected push toward both spatial uniformity – equalization across regions via capital's restless circulation throughout the world market – and territorial differentiation, through the necessary social and geographical divisions of labor, the sinking value of immobile, fixed capital, and a tendency toward sectoral crises or, in other words, "absolute space" where equalization is largely achieved but only through the ever-increasing hyper differentiation of "relative space" (Harvey, 1978; Smith, 2008, p. 196). This is not just a transnational process, although obviously there is a marked North–South division of labor in many if not most forms of global manufacturing in primary and secondary industries. It is a constantly shifting, intra- and supranational dynamic; not so much a matter, as Massey put it, of "more jobs/investment/income here than there" as a conceptualization of space as a "product of the stretched-out, intersecting and articulating social relations of the economy" (Massey, 1995, p. 2).

The example of the textile industry is instructive. Canadian companies like Dominion Textile were broadly understood by both workers and scholars as having gradually been forced to close in the 1980s and 1990s due to trade liberalization and "penetration of the Canadian market by low-wage textile imports," notably from China (Mahon, 1984, pp. 50–51). But within the latter country, and largely within the same time frame, the textile industry was also affected by the downward trend of the Northeastern Chinese Rust Belt, with deindustrialization destroying the relative stability of the "Iron Rice Bowl" in favor of the southern Sunbelt with its workforce of dispossessed, formerly rural migrant workers. Textile workers in Montreal and Liaoning faced much the same fate, and for broadly similar material reasons of competition and technological innovations in production and labor processes, if refracted through the local particularities of political systems and grounded moral economies (see Lee, 2007). Now, decades later, rising wages and diverse social factors in China led to the country's own bout of 'outsourcing' carried out by supply chain intermediaries owned partly by Chinese and European funds, with greater-than-ever amounts of fixed capital sunk into the colossal container ships that make this all possible. The 'fast fashion' textiles of H&M and Uniqlo and the seemingly endless stocks of Walmart or Amazon Essentials are more likely to be made in Bangladesh or Cambodia, while Chinese factories in all sectors roll out industrial robots and other automation technology at a rate that equals the rest of the world combined (Douglas, 2022). Chinese workers, both north and south, are themselves thrown into precarious service work propping up their version of the information economy transition (Jiang, 2023). Refocusing on the political–economic geography of deindustrialization would require us to remove our hemispheric blinders in favor of this more complicated and connected approach, thinking about the variegated "regional pathways to deindustrialization" within countries the world over (see Pike, 2022).

Much like a serial killer in a Hollywood film, capital is constantly fleeing ahead of its own atrocities, yet drawn inexorably to return to the scene of the crime. Preliminary European research in fact suggests a post-pandemic firming up of the shift that began after 2008 toward 're-shoring,' or industrial capital reopening or strengthening existing manufacturing facilities in 'home' countries due to challenges with global supply chains, rising transportation costs, and, notably, the reduction in the global wage gap: the homogenization or absolute space brought about by capital circulation once again generating differention or relative space (Medina, 2022). As this 're-shoring' takes place, it finds individuals and communities devastated by capital's initial departure and social relations destabilized by financial capital. In this context, we see the abuse of temporary foreign workers and undocumented migrants, millions of whom toil for less than the legal minimum wage in countries like Canada and the US, and even the sundering of the achievements of the nineteenth-century worker's movement like the elimination of the most open forms of child labor in the industrial core. Following 2023 legislation, 14-year-olds in Iowa can now work six-hour night shifts, a move presented as a boon for local manufacturing (Roscoe, 2023). 'Deindustrialization,' as we have tended to understand it in the field, perhaps fails as a conceptual tool to fully grasp the dynamic nature of these processes and their shifting local manifestations within global regimes of accumulation.

This is partly due to a confusion between form and content of commodity production, as Michael Heinrich might argue, or between the disarticulation of certain types of industrial social relations and class identities, as Sylvie Contrepois's work on France demonstrates, with the disappearance of industry as whole (Heinrich, 2004; Contrepois, 2017). But it is also due to the nationalist paradigms written into the study of shutdowns from the very beginning, resulting in a tendency to point the finger at recent phenomena such as 'globalization' or 'neoliberalism' in lieu of a *longue durée* critique of capitalist political economy. Pursuing the relational focus of uneven development, instead, we can profitably understand the cycles of investment and disinvestment driving industrial dislocation from the historical perspective of the capitalist world-system (High, MacKinnon, and Perchard, 2017).

World-systems theory, developed by Wallerstein and others like Andre Gunder Frank and Samir Amin beginning in the 1970s, began as a reaction to the developmentalist modernization theory predominant under postwar American hegemony (Wallerstein, 1974). As an alternative, world-systems theory drew upon the Marxian critical lineage while breaking with ossified versions of Marxism that only looked at relations of production within separate, clearly delineated states. It brought in innovations from the Annales School of historiography and a rethinking of Marxian categories to stress uneven interconnection in interstate, regional, and global balance under capitalism, a world-spanning historical system with its roots in the sixteenth century characterized by long-term, materially relational realignments of core, semi-peripheral, and peripheral zones (Wallerstein, 1991). These zones, in turn, are defined not simply by concentration of wealth but rather by unequal exchange generated by different forms of production processes: "What we mean by core-periphery is the degree of profitability of the production processes. Since profitability is directly related to the degree of monopolization," Wallerstein wrote, then "what we essentially mean by core-like production processes is those that are controlled by quasi-monopolies. Peripheral processes are then those that are truly competitive" (Wallerstein, 1983, p. 28).

The long-term shift in focal points in historical capitalism is difficult to understand solely through the traditional lens of job losses and low-wage competition, categories that fit comfortably within bourgeois political economy. When we consider 'capital flight,' in other words, we should also consider patterns of relationality and instrumentalization. It is important to not see this process through the ontology of either the job *or* the commodity that is produced.

Let's use the example of Apple's iPhone as a nodal point in the complicated dance of core–periphery relations. China is a site of hyper-competition among local parts manufacturers, with some processes carried out in countries like Japan and Taiwan that now enjoy core status under US hegemony. Apple can dictate terms, with the winners expected to produce at high quality and rapid pace for a low price. They receive a tiny share of the profits realized at the end point of sale; their workers receive far less. Apple has a monopoly – its phones and proprietary software and related digital infrastructure like the App Store tie consumers to it and a brand developed by activities like advertising that are considered 'unproductive' in the interpretative lineage of the labor theory of value.

It is important to note, however, that core monopolies like Apple, are not drawn to China only because of wage scales. Apple CEO Tim Cook, speaking at the 2017 Fortune Global Forum in China:

> The popular conception is that companies come to China because of low labor cost. I'm not sure what part of China they go to, but the truth is China stopped being the low labor cost country many years ago. And that is not the reason to come to China from a supply point of view. The reason is because of the skill, and the quantity of skill in one location, and the type of skill it is. The products we do require really advanced tooling . . . and the tooling skill is very deep here. In the US you could have a meeting of tooling engineers, and I'm not sure we could fill the room. In China you could fill multiple football fields.
>
> *(Quoted in Hammond, 2023)*

These skills as 'job' – process toward the rendering of a distinct commodity produced through repeated application of the same individual's labor power – did not simply depart what was the American, European, or Japanese manufacturing core for China. They were shaped in their local expression through a meeting of global forces and an equally important malleability of relationality when it came to social reproduction, including concentration of vocational education and the movement of young women accustomed to fine and repetitive work – things like weaving bamboo, paper making, picking – from the agricultural periphery to cities that were burgeoning not just through foreign investment but also national class dynamics creating internal migrant workforces of rural laborers ("No Way Forward, No Way Back," 2023). Crucially, China did not simply 'start over,' taking American or European industrial practice and building up to its full realization (but for lower wages, creating 'competitive advantage') in what is a teleological, progress-based understanding of 'development.' The start is with different forms of relationality which then develop *differently*. So, while the ontological return of the job is thinkable, the return of relations of production in an 'original' form is not. This has its most dramatic manifestation in the development of just-in-time production and the 'supply chain,' the movement of commodities between different sites of specialty (points of relational intersection) during the production process.

The result of these processes which have been underway since the 1980s has been not only the concentration of production in China but also the transformation of Chinese social relations according to the priorities of global production. Chinese support underpins US consumerism through bond purchases, which in turn secures a market for Chinese products (Drezner, 2009). This has seen China transition from merely 'peripheral,' a simple site of cheap labor in abstraction, to 'semi-peripheral' – or perhaps more accurately 'semi-core' – status in the capitalist world-system and amass a level of accumulated capital and develop a level of productive power (which has allowed China to create a massive arms industry – underpinning many of its own high-valued exports) and outflow of capital investments to countries that are systemically peripheral, and finally to complete with American tech giants in much of the world; challenging American technological, military, and increasingly geopolitical hegemony. The US and China may yet share a symbiotic position at the hegemonic core, or the 'rise' of China and 'decline' of the US by various measures could lead to the type of shift that Wallerstein and other world-systems theorists have identified at important historical junctures – from the Italian city-states to the Dutch empire to the English in the eighteenth century and from England to America in the twentieth, driven by unprecedented levels of speculation and financialization (see Arrighi, 2008). The deindustrialization of the Northwestern Euro-American core, in other words, cannot be understood apart from the *longue durée* of historical capitalism and the distinct forms of spatialization and local exploitation that together make up the global mode of accumulation.

Finally, what does this all mean for class relations, structures, and experience? Here, we need to explore in greater depth the process of lumpenization – a concept which, despite its historically pejorative overdetermination by bourgeois stereotypes about poverty, criminality, and social dysfunction, can help us to draw connections between the broader structural mechanisms of the capitalist economy and the sociocultural unmaking of working-class worlds that has preoccupied the field of deindustrialization studies.

Marx and Engels, for instance, described the nineteenth-century lumpenproletariat as a "passively rotting mass thrown off by the lowest layers of the old society" (Marx and Engels, 1998, p. 48). In his recent book on the subject, however, Clyde W. Barrow urges us to look beyond Marx's more well-known polemical writing on the lumpenproletariat to his treatment of the question within the critique of political economy laid out in *Capital*. There, Marx grapples with the lumpen as an economic category, part of his discussion of the various subsets of the ever-increasing "relative surplus population" generated by capitalist development (see Barrow, 2020). For Marx, the periodic expulsion of vast segments of the working class from production and distribution is a basic "condition for the existence of the capitalist mode of production," triggered by the competitive drive toward centralization and the increased organic composition of capital (the ratio of constant capital, machines, etc., to variable capital – i.e., the wage paid to labor) (Marx, 2013, p. 440). This expulsion acts as a means of transfer of labor power from mature to emerging industries and as a way of creating a "reserve army of labour," allowing firms to weather the vagaries of industrial capitalism's expanding and contracting business cycles (Barrow, 2020, pp. 35–38). This 'relative surplus' is made up of 'floating, latent, and stagnant' categories, including everyone from the downsized older worker to the former agricultural laborer to the pauper/lumpenproletariat.

Underlining the fluidity with which dispossessed people move between work and non-work, remaining "parts of the same class" but experiencing different social statuses through increased pauperization, criminalization, age, race, etc., Barrow argues that the shifting category of the lumpenproletariat is "constantly undergoing a process of dynamic recomposition as elements of the relative surplus population and the industrial reserve army are spun off from the proletariat as a result of the continuous de-composition and re-composition of the working class" (Barrow, 2020, pp. 35–38). In other words, the idea of the lumpenproletariat is not simply relevant to us because the withdrawal of industrial capital is often accompanied by the encroachment of less legal forms of exploitation and underground economies (see Fraser and Clark, 2021). Instead, as an end point of sorts on a shifting scale of proletarian material positions tied to shifts in the mode of accumulation, it demonstrates that the disintegration of formerly industrial working-class towns and neighborhoods and associated long-term joblessness is not accidental or capricious but instead fundamental to capitalism's functioning.

Deindustrialization and joblessness, especially when it stretches out across years, drives proletarians downward through the lumpenization process. This has myriad expressions that also tie to capitalism's world-systemic expression. For example, the lumpen at present should not simply be written off as 'wild' or 'undisciplined' but rather understood as people created as 'deviant' as they are placed outside of 'normal' productive relations. Violent, increasingly militarized policing and private prisons have become a vector of accumulation that brings manifold colonial and neo-imperial practices home, profiting from what can be understood as forms of 'uneven development' within, as capital turns the landscapes of deindustrialization into new sites of primitive accumulation (Gilmore, 2007). At the same time, the technologies of violent maintenance of core hegemony and global surveillance find their training grounds and monopolist profits for manufacturers. Police are not static in their modern positioning as guardians of capitalist property relations – they are also a mechanism of public to private transfer of surplus, exemplified by the largesse of military-style equipment and training in core countries, and marshaling of labor power at meagre captive wages. Inmates in US federal prisons make around 23 cents to $1.15 an hour, far lower than wages at some major "offshoring" sites (Federal Bureau of Prisons, 2023). Members of the lumpenproletariat, made deviant, are finally rendered productive.

Of course, in many ways the 'de-composition and recomposition' pointed out by Barrow is nothing new for scholars of deindustrialization. We have long been attuned to the changing technical composition of the working class wrought by capital flight, emphasizing things like the move from male-dominated, unionized industrial jobs to increasingly feminized, precarious service-sector work, and have of course paid particular attention to the sociopolitical aspects of class decomposition through the process of making residual industrial structures of feeling and industrial working-class lifeways – as Michael Denning points out, "Under capitalism, the only thing worse than being exploited is not being exploited" (Denning, 2010, p. 79). But thinking about class decomposition in the dynamic way described by Marx can help us to make links with the political economic theory described in the first two parts of the paper, analyzing class fragmentation in terms of its relationship to the complicated global processes of capital accumulation and highlighting the dialectic relationship of national working-class composition to the global class structure.

The constant push-pull axis of homogenization and differentiation caused by the restless circulation of capital is mirrored by the simultaneous pulling into and spitting out of populations from wage labor – pairing with financialization to facilitate the switching of capital flows between industries and localities that becomes necessary during the crisis-ridden capitalist accumulation cycle. Marx laid out in *Capital* what he referred to as the 'general law of capitalist accumulation':

> The greater the social wealth, the functioning capital, the extent and energy of its growth, and therefore also the greater the absolute mass of the proletariat and the productivity of its labor, the greater is the industrial reserve army. The same causes which develop the expansive power of capital, also develop the labor-power at its disposal . . . But the greater this reserve army in proportion to the active labor-army, the greater is the mass of a consolidated surplus population, whose misery is in inverse ratio to the amount of torture it has to undergo in the form of labor.
>
> *(Marx, 2013, p. 450)*

In the twenty-first century, with the scale and intensification of capitalist production outstripping even Marx's dreams and nightmares, political economists David Neilson and Thomas Stubbs argued that the acceleration of the process of uneven development under neoliberal globalization had resulted in an unprecedented situation wherein "a clear majority of the world's labouring population (was) now relatively surplus to the functioning of capitalism" (Neilson and Stubbs, 2011, p. 450). On the one hand, rendered surplus by the growing organic composition of capital of core-like, monopolistic production processes, and especially by the associated financialization of the core economies, formerly industrial towns, neighborhoods, and regions across North America and Western Europe form capitalism's "lumpen-geography" (Walker, 1978, pp. 28–38), what J. Sakai called

> zone[s] of the dispossessed . . . charged by the duology of the lower working class and the lumpen/proletariat living together ambidextrously side by side, being family, being inside each other's lives and struggling with and against each other to stay alive.
>
> *(Sakai, 2017, pp. 2–3)*

As we know too well, life in these zones is not easy.

However, wrote Neilson and Stubbs,

> as long as research, development, marketing, advanced assembly processes and major shareholdings are located in the developed economies, then the high-paid, high-skilled core productive workforce and the independently wealthy can continue to underwrite a much less desperate form and composition of the relative surplus population.
>
> *(Neilson and Stubbs, 2011, p. 449)*

Moreover, the reproduction of this lumpenizing section of the Global North proletariat is eased by the steady flow of cheap consumer goods made in places like China, India, and Bangladesh. On the other side of the hemisphere, this can be contrasted with what Samir Amin describes as the 'lumpen-development' of emerging Global South economies like India, where massive state and capital investment in industrial capacity and the resulting growth of technological capacity, education, and the middle class are matched by stark pauperization for two-thirds of the population due to heightened processes of enclosure and environmental/agricultural destruction or the massive forced informalization of labor sparked by trade liberalization (Amin, 2014, p. 143; see also Breman, 2004). The sheer scope and scale of this labor reserve serves as a mighty check on Global South wages, facilitating the hyper-competitive production processes of the periphery. In turn, the relatively lower reproductive costs of Global South industrial workers facilitate the general shift of industrial production out of the North and, with it, the finance-driven hegemonic status of core economies. The current capitalist world order, in other words, depends on the untenable process of making billions of people surplus, with little access to the means of reproduction (see Hansen, 2015). As John Bellamy Foster and Robert McChesney point out, deindustrialization in countries like Canada, the US, and the UK "is only the tip of the iceberg where the growing worldwide destabilization and overexploitation of labour is concerned" (Foster and McChesney, 2018, p. 499). The process of lumpenization, considered globally, demonstrates the interrelated ties between class composition and decomposition nationally and their broader structural outlines on a world stage, both creating and created by imperialist competition and driving unprecedented environmental destruction, forced migration, and war in the push to produce absolute space.

As is brought into stark relief by these billions made surplus, the 'wounds of class' are real. They shape and twist lives and communities. It is important, however, in considering radical alternatives to widespread acceptance of industrial decline to avoid presenting working-class communities as simply damaged, their disintegration terminal. Deindustrialization leaves potential relations of production and reproduction intact; they are just seldom recognized as such by capital. In some contexts, especially in the most urban areas, industrial expertise and working-class communality were subsumed into poorly paid service industry work. In the 'one job towns' of the former industrial heartland, welfare arrived, propping up the profits of 'big retail' like Walmart on both the side of consumption and subsistence and subsidizing the wages of the minority of local workers who made the transition to what was now a "big employer," as much as it paled in comparison to vital industry, with programs like Medicaid and food stamps in the US (Dube and Jacobs, 2004). What money does circulate is prey for things like the most monopolistic of monopoly practices – addiction. The opioid epidemic, which has devastated countless lives, has also been a source of astronomical profits for pharmaceutical manufacturers like OxyContin dealer Purdue Pharma. This, like the violent, militarized policing that has targeted former sites of industry that are now adrift between lumpenization, 'reserve army' oscillation, and what can be called 'primitive accumulation' at home, is yet another form of public-to-private transfer at a time when the rate of profit, if not falling, appears stymied in systemic exhaustion. This is the context of the 'deaths of despair' in deindustrialized communities in North America and beyond. The bodies of these working-class people, no longer seen as a source of labor power, are nevertheless still mapped as sites of accumulation.

How then to 'grow' buried potentialities into something that can sustain lives and communities at a time when 'degrowth' philosophies appear as the only solution to apocalyptic climate change scenarios, with mass heat deaths, desertification, ever more destructive wildfires that mock stopgaps like carbon taxes, as the flames themselves release huge amounts of carbon into the atmosphere, and 'freak' weather events having already exited the realm of dire prediction and become an annual reality? Working-class communities, the struggling, the lumpenized, and the undocumented, sundered from the relations of world-systemic industrial production can still shape their own solutions.

Seeing possibility and potential before the crisis we are facing, the implications of which for the capitalist world-system we can only begin to fathom, may seem a utopian gesture. But as we can imagine the end of the world (and not, it seems, the end of capitalism) ever more starkly, we should be reminded that Marx's critique of political economy started with his passionate defense of the commons, of the basic right of German peasants to pick up wood for heating and cooking from the forest floor, practices going back to the beginnings of human collectivity that were now, in the 1840s, being met with the violence of enclosure (Bensaid, 2021).[8] Marx continued to hold that in attention to capitalism's crises and contradictions there is a glimpse of a way forward, to commons new or renewed, and new visions of possible community. This did not have to be the centralizing, sanguinary, and relentlessly productivist drive of the state capitalism of the Soviet Union (James, Dunayevskaya, and Boggs, 2013). As Japanese Marxist Saito Kohei, among many others, argues, there was little justification for this approach in Marx's writings, especially his late work that began to reckon more with the environmental devastation wrought by industry (Saito, 2023).

Within the liberal capitalist states of the Global North there has been political and cultural room for 'make work projects' or public cash for private capital to 'bring back jobs' – as in Canada's Maritime Provinces and Newfoundland and Labrador – after the decline of industry, exhaustion of extraction, and the economic and social devastation of the 1992 cod moratorium. These projects, which represented massive government spending, seemingly bucking the trends of neoliberalism and austerity, instead can be seen as another side of it, as they were heavily tied to fantasies of return – of industrial capital and of the fish "stocks" decimated by corporate fishing practices (Bavington, 2011; see MacKinnon, 2023). That forms of state spending helped people make a living for a year or two should not simply be dismissed, but as we have argued in this chapter, relations of production are complex, global, and intersect in vital but unpredictable ways with forms of social reproduction. Temporary cash becomes just that, and often a 'gift' to capitalists, absent acknowledgement that depleted resources are not coming back. And if they did, capitalist priorities of extraction, instrumentalization, exchange, and accumulation would soon see them pushed to the brink again. Production-based stopgaps prefigure new deindustrialization.

As Kirstin Munro has argued, social reproduction is multi-layered (Munro, 2019, pp. 451–468). It encompasses the day-to-day reproduction of labor power as commodity from the point of view of capital, the reproduction of populations and the carrying on of forms of social life, and the reproduction of capitalism, its relations, and world-systemic character. The dominant form of aid to deindustrialized communities under neoliberal policy regimes forces a liminal temporality: capitalism, having abandoned stable community, is always seen as on the cusp of return, even if that return would simply prefigure new forms of departure. This is a new version of the old Whig development teleology that sees stable prosperity and limitless growth as capital's natural consequence. Indeed, if there is a form of 'return,' it could be through a hitherto unseen technology with unpredictable social effects or, more likely, it could be a return to earlier patterns of exploitation. Normative ways of thinking about the economy place progress as a sort of civilizational 'level' that once reached brooks no retreat. The only change comes from more, and indeed, endless progress. The blame for any backslide is placed on individuals and communities for not living up to the level. Maybe they should have abandoned union protections and embraced the 'right to work.' Maybe they should have learned to code.

What now? In contrast to capital's grand narrative, we have little choice but to turn to smaller stories for glimmers of hope in the wake of deindustrialization and the wounds of class that have often been left to fester, finding expression in the forces of right-wing populism so effective at giving abandoned communities a story, any story, to make sense of a future obscured by present darkness. Some efforts may seem barely incrementalist as praxis in a world where value in the capitalist core and beyond is nearly always conceived of in terms of trillion-dollar GDPs, but these practices have power through new manifestations of the commons. It is this type of rethinking of normative exchange relations and ruthless competition as norm or human 'essence' that could bolster solidarities beyond the bounds of nationalisms ensconced in the competitive inter-state system that has proven incapable of seeing beyond capital's good as global good. 'Degrowth,' directing productive power to reproductive forms and the rethinking of valuation, is one way forward.

As an example, Japanese communities facing depopulation due to population decline and outmigration to the megalopolises, which are the nexus of the service industry that now makes up around 70% of national output, are seizing abandoned houses, storefronts, and even small factories and selling them to newcomers for a token one yen (about one cent). There are also grants for repairs and renovations, active support for transformation of 'dead labor,' in its guise as the ruins of abandoned relations, into the potential for community vitality. This incentive model conceives of the buildings as private assets, and some homes have been passed on in this way only to be turned into Airbnb cash grabs in scenic locales, but there is no reason why this model could not be followed for cooperative, collective, or otherwise 'social' housing, community kitchens, 'libraries of things,' and so on. And if these efforts, fundamentally reproductive of community as well as productive, just outside of the limiting frame of capital's self-valorization, are seeing local and situational success, other reproductive work, child and elder care, attention to disability and access, communal gardens and meals could also be sites of universalized support – a share of surplus that conceives of the labor of community making, devalued by forms of capitalist instrumentality like deindustrialization, without expanding the power of the state over people in their multiplicity of relations and possibilities for social life.

Deindustrialization studies, and Marxian critique within it, can play a role in thinking these possibilities. Taking up again the tools of Marxian political economy, either vis-à-vis the spatial aspects of deindustrialization or with respect to the systematic process of de- and remaking of the working class, can move the field not only toward the global but beyond the fantasy of simple return of jobs lost into new ways of thinking relations of production and reproduction. Doing this pushes us to move beyond the underlying, social democratic, and nation-bound politics at the heart of the field, which an exclusive focus on the cultural and social allows us to pass over sometimes too neatly. The point is not that deindustrialization scholars have to adhere to Marxist ideas, but rather that in abandoning the field of political economy, we also abandon the hope of developing a revolutionary praxis.

Notes

1 For other national/linguistic corpuses on deindustrialization, see Fontaine, M. and Vigna, X. (2019). La désindustrialisation, une histoire en cours. *20&21. Revue d'histoire*, 4, pp. 2–17; Zazzara, G. (2020). Making Sense of the Industrial Past: Deindustrialisation and Industrial Heritage in Italy. *Italia Contemporanea*, 294, supplemento, pp. 155–181; Moitra, S. and Nogueira, K. (2020). (Post-) Industrial Memories. Oral History and Structural Change. Introduction. *BIOS–Zeitschrift für Biographieforschung, Oral History und Lebensverlaufsanalysen*, 31(2), pp. 3–4.

2 The honorable exception, of course, is Cowie's (2001) *Capital Moves: RCA's Seventy-Year Quest for Cheap Labour*. New York: New Press.

3 Debates about deindustrialization and the global are more robust for historians of earlier periods. See Johnson, C.H. (2002). Introduction: De-industrialization and Globalization. *IRSH*, 47, pp. 3–33.

4 For the recommendations he's referencing, see in particular the last chapter of Bluestone, B. and Harrison, B. (1988). *The Great U-Turn: Corporate Restructuring and the Polarizing of America*. New York: Basic Books.

Uneven Development, the World-System, and Lumpenization

5 Of course, it is possible to use these theorists otherwise. See Virdee, S. (2019). Racialized Capitalism: An Account of its Contested Origins and Consolidation. *The Sociological Review*, 67(1), pp. 3–27.
6 On transition debates, see Kaye, H.J. (1995). Maurice Dobb and the Debate on the Transition to Capitalism. In Kaye, H.J. (ed.) *The British Marxist Historians: An Introductory Analysis*. New York: St. Martin's Press, pp. 23–69.
7 On the relevance of Wallerstein's thinking about mercantilism in the early modern world-system for the global economic situation in which we find ourselves today, see Lenger, F. (2021). Wallerstein on Early Modern Capitalism and Global Inequality: A Re-evaluation. *Socio: La nouvelle revue des sciences sociales*, 15, pp. 49–70.
8 Bensaid's work (2021) contains translations of Marx's early writings on enclosure in Germany with trenchant commentary by Bensaid.

Reference List

Amin, S. (2014). *Samir Amin: Pioneer of the Rise of the South*. Springer Briefs on Pioneers in Science and Practice, Vol. 16. Heidelberg, New York, Dordrecht, London: Springer, p. 143.

Arrighi, G. (2008). *Adam Smith in Beijing: Lineages of the 21st Century*. London: Verso.

Barrow, C.W. (2020). *The Dangerous Class: The Concept of the Lumpenproletariat*. Ann Arbor: University of Michigan Press, pp. 11, 30–54, 35–38, 42, 47–50.

Bavington, D. (2011). *Managed Annihilation: An Unnatural History of the Newfoundland Cod Collapse*. Vancouver: UBC Press.

Bensaid, D. (2021). *The Dispossessed – Karl Marx's Debates on Wood Theft and the Right of the Poor*. Trans. Nichols, R. Minneapolis: University of Minnesota Press.

Bluestone, B. (1972). Economic Crises and the Law of Uneven Development. *Politics and Society*, 3(1), p. 82.

Bluestone, B. and Harrison, B. (1982). *The Deindustrialization of America: Plant Closings, Community Abandonment, and the Dismantling of Basic Industry*. New York: Basic Books, pp. 4–5, 231–264.

Breman, J. (2004). *The Making and Unmaking of an Industrial Working Class: Sliding Down the Labour Hierarchy in Ahmedabad, India*. Amsterdam: Amsterdam University Press.

Bullen, J. (1983). The Ontario Waffle and the Struggle for an Independent Socialist Canada: Conflict within the NDP. *Canadian Historical Review*, 64(2), p. 189.

Clark, J. (2022). Reframing Deindustrialization. *International Journal of Urban Sciences*, 26, p. 30.

Contrepois, S. (2017). Regeneration and Class Identities: A Case Study in the Corbeil-Essonnes-Évry Region, France. In High, S., MacKinnon, L. and Perchard, A. (eds.) *The Deindustrialized World: Confronting Ruination in Postindustrial Places*. Vancouver: UBC Press, pp. 173–189.

Cowie, J. (2001). *Capital Moves: RCA's Seventy-Year Quest for Cheap Labour*. New York: New Press.

Cowie, J. and Heathcott, J. (2005). Introduction. In Cowie, J. and Heathcott, J. (eds.) *Beyond the Ruins: The Meaning of Deindustrialization*. Ithaca, NY: Cornell University Press, p. 5.

Denning, M. (2010, November–December). Wageless Life. *New Left Review*, 66, p. 79.

Douglas, J. (2022, September 18). China's Factories Accelerate Robotics Push as Workforce Shrinks. *The Wall Street Journal*. https://www.wsj.com/articles/chinas-factories-accelerate-robotics-push-as-workforce-shrinks-11663493405 (Accessed: 15 September 2023).

Drezner, D.W. (2009). Bad Debts: Assessing China's Financial Influence in Great Power Politics. *International Security*, 34(2), pp. 7–45.

Dube, A. and Jacobs, K. (2004, August 2). Hidden Cost of Wal-Mart Jobs: Use of Safety Net Programs by Wal-Mart Workers in California. *UC Berkeley Labor Center*. https://laborcenter.berkeley.edu/hidden-cost-of-wal-mart-jobs-use-of-safety-net-programs-by-wal-mart-workers-in-california-2/ (Accessed: 15 September 2023).

Federal Bureau of Prisons. (2023). Program Details. https://www.bop.gov/inmates/custody_and_care/unicor_about.jsp (Accessed: 15 September 2023).

Fontaine, M. and Vigna, X. (2019). La désindustrialisation, une histoire en cours. *20&21. Revue d'histoire*, 4, pp. 2–17.

Foster, J.B. and McChesney, R.W. (2018). The Global Reserve Army of Labor and the New Imperialism. In Aronowitz, S. and Roberts, M.J. (eds.) *Class: The Anthology*. Hoboken, NJ: Wiley Blackwell, p. 499.

Fraser, A. and Clark, A. (2021). Damaged Hardmen: Organized Crime and the Half-Life of Deindustrialisation. *The British Journal of Sociology*, 72, pp. 1062–1076.

Gilmore, R.W. (2007). *Golden Gulag: Prisons, Surplus, Crisis, and Opposition in Globalizing California.* Berkeley, CA: University of California Press.

Gregg, R. (1998). Class, Culture and Empire: E.P. Thompson and the Making of Social History. *Journal of Historical Sociology*, 11(4), pp. 419–460.

Hammond, S. (2023, Summer). The China Shock Doctrine. *National Affairs*, 56. https://www.nationalaffairs.com/publications/detail/the-china-shock-doctrine (Accessed: 15 September 2023).

Hansen, R.B. (2015, October 31). Surplus Population, Social Reproduction, and the Problem of Class Formation. *Viewpoint Magazine.* https://viewpointmag.com/2015/10/31/surplus-population-social-reproduction-and-the-problem-of-class-formation/ (Accessed: 15 September 2023).

Harvey, D. (1978). The Urban Process Under Capitalism: A Framework for Analysis. *International Journal of Urban and Regional Research*, 2(1–3), pp. 101–131.

Heinrich, M. (2004). *An Introduction to the Three Volumes of Karl Marx's Capital.* New York: Monthly Review Press.

High, S. (2013). 'The Wounds of Class': A Historiographical Reflection on the Study of Deindustrialization, 1973–2013. *History Compass*, 11(11), pp. 994–1007.

High, S. (2023). The Radical Origins of the Deindustrialization Thesis: From Dependency to Capital Mobility and Community Abandonment. *Labour/Le Travail*, 91(1), pp. 31–56.

High, S., MacKinnon, L. and Perchard, A. (2017). Introduction. In High, S., MacKinnon, L. and Perchard, A. (eds.) *The Deindustrialized World: Confronting Ruination in Postindustrial Places.* Vancouver: UBC Press, p. 4.

James, C.L.R., Dunayevskaya, R. and Lee Boggs, G. (2013). *State Capitalism and World Revolution.* San Francisco: Charles H. Kerr Library and PM Press.

Jiang, B. (2023, August 5). China's Vulnerable Gig Workers Grapple with Lower Pay and Longer Hours as Beijing Touts Benefits of Platform Economy. *South China Morning Post.* https://www.scmp.com/tech/tech-trends/article/3229888/chinas-vulnerable-gig-workers-grapple-lower-pay-and-longer-hours-beijing-touts-benefits-platform (Accessed: 15 September 2023).

Johnson, C.H. (2002). Introduction: De-industrialization and Globalization. *International Review of Social History*, 47, pp. 3–33.

Kaye, H.J. (1995). Maurice Dobb and the Debate on the Transition to Capitalism. In Kaye, H.J. (ed.) *The British Marxist Historians: An Introductory Analysis.* New York: St. Martin's Press, pp. 23–69.

Kim, M. (2018). URPE at Fifty: Reflections on a Half-Century of Activism, Community, Debate (and a Few Crazy Moments). *Review of Radical Political Economics*, 50(3), pp. 478–486.

Laxer, J. (1973). Introduction to the Political Economy of Canada. In Laxer, R. (ed.) *(Canada) Ltd.: The Political Economy of Dependency.* Toronto: McClelland and Stewart Ltd., pp. 26–41.

Lee, C.K. (2007). *Against the Law: Labor Protests in China's Rustbelt and Sunbelt.* Berkeley, CA and Los Angeles, CA: University of California Press.

Lee, F.S. (2004). History and Identity: The Case of Radical Economics and Radical Economists, 1945–1970. *Review of Radical Political Economics*, 36(2), pp. 177–195.

Lenger, F. (2021). Wallerstein on Early Modern Capitalism and Global Inequality: A Re-evaluation. *Socio: La nouvelle revue des sciences sociales*, 15, pp. 49–70.

MacKinnon, L. (2023). Importing the Clairtone Sound: Political Economy, Regionalism, and Deindustrialization in Pictou County. *Labour/le Travail*, 91, pp. 147–168.

Mahon, R. (1984). *The Politics of Industrial Restructuring: Canadian Textiles.* Toronto: University of Toronto Press, pp. 50–51.

Marx, K. (2013). *Capital: A Critical Analysis of Capitalist Production*, Vol. 1. Hertfordshire, UK: Wordsworth Editions, pp. 440, 450.

Marx, K. and Engels, F. (1998). *The Communist Manifesto: A Modern Edition.* London: Verso, p. 48.

Massey, D. (1995). *Spatial Divisions of Labour: Social Structures and the Geography of Production.* 2nd edn. New York, NY: Routledge, p. 2.

McKay, I. (2005). *Rebels, Reds, Radicals: Rethinking Canada's Left History.* Toronto: Between the Lines, pp. 173–174.

Medina, X.S. (2022). From Deindustrialization to a Reinforced Process of Reshoring in Europe. Another Effect of the COVID-19 Pandemic? *Land*, 11(12), p. 2109. https://doi.org/10.3390/land11122109 (Accessed: 15 September 2023).

Moitra, S. and Nogueira, K. (2020). (Post-) Industrial Memories. Oral History and Structural Change. Introduction. *BIOS–Zeitschrift für Biographieforschung, Oral History und Lebensverlaufsanalysen*, 31(2), pp. 3–4.

Munro, K. (2019). 'Social Reproduction Theory,' Social Reproduction, and Household Production. *Science and Society*, 83(1), pp. 451–468.

Neilson, D. and Stubbs, T. (2011). Relative Surplus Population and Uneven Development in the Neoliberal Era: Theory and Empirical Application. *Capital & Class*, 35(3), pp. 450, 449.

Pike, A. (2022). Coping with Deindustrialization in the Global North and South. *International Journal of Urban Sciences*, 26(1), pp. 1–22.

Roscoe, J. (2023, April 18). Iowa Senate Pulls All-Nighter to Roll Back Child Labor Protections. *Vice*. https://www.vice.com/en/article/5d9bwx/iowa-senate-pulls-all-nighter-to-roll-back-child-labor-protections (Accessed: 15 September 2023).

Rosenfeld, H. (2012). American Social Democracy: Exceptional but Otherwise Familiar. In Evans, B. and Schmidt, I. (eds) *Social Democracy After the Cold War*. Edmonton: Athabasca University Press, pp. 99–147.

Saito, K. (2023). *Zero kara no Shihonron (Capital from Zero)*. Tokyo: NHK Shuppan.

Sakai, J. (2017). *The 'Dangerous Class' and Revolutionary Theory: Thoughts on the Making of the Lumpen/Proletariat*. Montreal: Kersplebedeb, pp. 2–3.

Schindler, S., Gillespie, T., Banks, N., Bayırbağ, M.K., Burte, H., Kanai, J.M. and Sami, N. (2020). Deindustrialization in Cities of the Global South. *Area Development and Policy*, 5(3), p. 287.

Smith, N. (2008). *Uneven Development: Nature, Capital, and the Production of Space*. 3rd edn. Athens and London: University of Georgia Press, Google Play edition, p. 196.

Tomlinson, J. (2020). De-industrialization: Strengths and Weaknesses as a Key Concept for Understanding Post-war British History. *Urban History*, 47, pp. 199–200.

Virdee, S. (2019). Racialized Capitalism: An Account of its Contested Origins and Consolidation. *The Sociological Review*, 67(1), pp. 3–27.

Viswanathan, G. (1991). Raymond Williams and British Colonialism. *The Yale Journal of Criticism*, 4(2), pp. 47–66.

Walker, R.A. (1978). Two Sources of Uneven Development Under Advanced Capitalism: Spatial Differentiation and Capital Mobility. *Review of Radical Political Economics*, 10(3), pp. 28–38.

Wallerstein, I. (1974). Dependence in an Interdependent World: The Limited Possibilities of Transformation Within the Capitalist World Economy. *African Studies Review*, 17(1), pp. 1–26.

Wallerstein, I. (1983). *Historical Capitalism*. London: Verso, p. 28.

Wallerstein, I. (1991). Beyond Annales?. *Radical History Review*, 49, pp. 7–15.

7

THE RACIAL DIMENSIONS OF (DE)INDUSTRIALIZATION

Jason Hackworth

Introduction

An important subset of the scholarly work on industrialization and deindustrialization emphasizes the ways that race has been constructed to justify lower wages, disinvestment, and profitable exploitation overall. There is no universal relationship, but this chapter will address some common patterns in the intersection of industrial employment and racism. The conceptual framework here is drawn from the American and Caribbean Black radical tradition.[1] Authors in this tradition were acutely aware of economics and industrial power but pushed their readers to take seriously social formations other than class. In particular, they described how anti-Blackness has been used to justify exploitation and colonial pillage. Importantly, they also pushed readers to understand the ways that the white working class not only absorbed these values of racialization but actively participated in their construction and reproduction. To supplement these conceptual insights, I will draw on examples presented in selected deindustrialization studies from the past 30 years.

Before proceeding, it is important to define how I am using the concept of race. I understand race to be a social construction. While there are no biologically tidy ways of separating humanity into races, there are of course phenotypic and ethno-cultural differences between individuals. The socially constructed assignment of these physical characteristics to moral or behavioral ones forms the basis for differential treatment. Race and racism cannot exist without a more powerful group creating and perpetuating this belief system (Omi and Winant, 2014). Racism can take a variety of forms and be deployed for different purposes. The racial capitalism school has emphasized how not only race is constructed to justify inequality but that in some forms capitalism could not exist without this construction (Robinson, 1983). This school suggests that not only do racism and capitalism coexist, they are co-dependent. This chapter will summarize some of the key insights and examples of where the construction of race has been used to advance or retard industrial capitalism. Specifically, I identify common modalities of race and the rise of industry, followed by common modalities of race and the fall of industry (deindustrialization).

DOI: 10.4324/9781003308324-12

The Racial Dimensions of Industrialization

During the rise of industrial capitalism, Black and other non-white laborers have been systematically devalued to justify exploitation. This exploitation has operated at a variety of scales and over different durations, but it has functioned to justify greater realized material benefit to white countries, neighborhoods, and people. Five prominent forms have been discussed in literature.

Justifying Low-Cost Inputs for the Industrial Economy

The original, and most commonly discussed, form is the creation of a moral justification for colonialism and slavery. The increase and consolidation of wealth in the Global North in the eighteenth century onward was significantly built on the rise of industry in places like Manchester and Lowell. Scholars describing the rise of garment production in such places rightly emphasize the combination of low-cost energy (e.g., the fall line in the Northeastern US) and low wage labor. But while exploitation was certainly present in such places, the profitability of such endeavors was built on an even more extreme form of exploitation elsewhere in the world. Garment manufacturing was built on the pillage of resources and humanity in Africa, North America, and South Asia in particular. One does not have the rise of garment manufacturing without inexpensive cotton from North America.

W.E.B. Du Bois compellingly argued that such exploitation was an afront to the stated values of Western civilization, so there developed a deep social need to justify it:

> Lying treaties, rivers of rum, murder, assassination, mutilation, rape, and torture have marked the progress of the Englishman, German, Frenchman, and Belgian on the Dark Continent. The only way in which the world has been able to endure the horrible tales is by deliberately stopping its ears and changing the subject of the conversation as the deviltry went on. . . . "Color" became the world's thought synonymous with inferiority, "Negro" lost its capitalization, and Africa was another name for bestiality and barbarism. Thus the world began to invest in color prejudice.
>
> *(Du Bois, 1915, p. 708; for a similar definition,*
> *see also Marable, 1983)*

Racist narratives were used to justify the pillage of African lands and people. Without that pillage the industrial power of the Global North could not have existed or at the very least would have been substantially different. Such narratives were not simply created by the beneficiaries of such logics: slave traders, industrial magnates, and planters. They were created and reproduced by a wider variety of figures with no clear material reason. National politicians discussed the 'white man's burden' of civilizing the uncivilized in Africa. Clergy spoke of bringing the lord to godless people. Artists, authors, and historians demeaned, belittled, and dehumanized non-white people as lesser than Europeans. One function of this was to justify the further pillage of humanity and resources. The low-cost inputs of labor and resources from the fifteenth century onward significantly fueled the rise of industrial power in the Global North. Racist narratives were crucial at minimizing the existential risk that such practices had to self-professed egalitarian societies (Mills, 1997).

Naturalizing Poorly Paid, Dangerous Work

Of course, conditions for workers in places like eighteenth-century Manchester were anything but idyllic. Workers, many of them children, toiled in hot, dangerous conditions for many hours a day. Many lost their lives as a direct result of industrial accidents. Even more had their life expectancies reduced from prolonged exposure to such working conditions. It is no coincidence, argues Cedric Robinson (1983), that many early industrial workers were recruited from groups racialized as lesser. Irish workers, for example, were recruited to fill the most dangerous and lowest paying jobs in early industrial England. As Robinson writes (1983, p. 39), "The Irish worker having descended from and inferior race, so his English employers believed, the cheap market value of his labor was but its most rational form." In this instance, racism provoked the English worker to believe that the most dangerous tasks were beneath him and justified the extreme exploitation of the Irish workers in Liverpool and Manchester to a society that deeply believed that it was built on the ethics of egalitarianism. A society cannot credibly be considered 'egalitarian' if workers routinely die on the job and have no viable alternative. But it can if those workers are framed as lesser, even subhuman, than others in society. The naturalization of lower paying dangerous industrial jobs continued into the twentieth century in a variety of forms. Thomas Sugrue's classic book on Detroit, *The Origins of the Urban Crisis*, depicts in great detail how Black workers from the American South were allowed only the most dangerous and low-paying jobs (e.g., painting, foundry) in auto assembly plants (Sugrue, 2005). Labor activist Branko Widdick describes in an interview with an auto-industry employer in the 1940s justifying this discrimination. "Yes," notes the employer, "there are some jobs that white people will not do; so, they have to take niggers in, particularly in duce work, spraying paint on car bodies. This soon kills a white man" (Widdick, 1976, p. 54).

When asked whether it would have the same effect on Black workers, he responded, "it shortens their life, it cuts them down but they're just niggers" (Widdick, 1976, p. 54). Not only did many unions accept this brutal arrangement, they actively reproduced it by impeding, ignoring, or opposing the efforts of Black workers to transfer into better-paid, less-dangerous work.

Limiting Industrial Employment to White Workers

The opening of a mill, factory, or important warehouse is often celebrated as a supplier of jobs in a town or city. But who receives those jobs was and remains anything but random. Exclusion on the basis of race occurs in multiple ways. Perhaps, the most common form was the simple refusal to hire non-white workers. Steven High's work on mill towns in Northern Ontario is instructive here (High, 2015; High, 2018). As mills opened in the 1940s and 1950s, nearby Indigenous residents were excluded from employment (Dunk, 2003). Union positions on non-white employment varied over time and space. Some unions were enthusiastically racist by refusing to allow non-white workers into their fold. Others were more casually racist, as in the case of the UAW segmenting social spaces for Black and white workers in Flint, Michigan (Highsmith, 2015). Still others fought to overcome the color line and actively participated in the passage of Civil Rights legislation. Some unions like the United Autoworkers performed all of these roles at one point in time. But the fact remains that the high-earning, career-advancing industrial work that changed so many lives did so disproportionately to the benefit of white workers over non-white workers. White industrial workers, writes Thomas Sugrue, "enjoyed preferential treatment at hiring gates, in personnel offices, in union halls, and in promotions to better positions" (Sugrue, 2005, p. 92).

Cities themselves also casually and assertively participated to uphold the color line and build an industrial economy for white workers only. Brian Alexander's *Glass House* focuses on the rise of Lancaster Ohio in the mid-twentieth century (Alexander, 2018). Lancaster was the home of Anchor Hocking, once the world's largest glass manufacturer. Alexander describes an almost idyllic existence in the town following the Second World War – plentiful employment, executives who sent their children to public schools, and very few labor disruptions. In 1947, *Forbes Magazine* devoted nearly all of its 30th-anniversary issue to Lancaster. They celebrated it as the ideal American town – peaceful, bucolic, and prosperous. But almost every person who lived in Lancaster and worked at Anchor Hocking was white. "Lancaster did have a few African Americans living within its borders," writes Alexander,

[B]ut from the time the first Black person arrived, they were treated as barely tolerated guests. . . . The mayor and sheriff were both Klan members, and the city gave Klan ideas the force of law. The few Black children attended the public schools, but they were permitted to swim in the Miller Park pool only on Fridays. Every Friday evening, the parks department drained the pool, then refilled it so whites would have "pure" water on Saturday. Cross burnings were routine. They occurred even when Malcolm Forbes lived there in 1941 – sometimes on the top of Mount Pleasant [the town's highest point], where the flames could be seen all over town. . . . If a Black man wanted to move to Lancaster but didn't have a job, he was told to move on.

(Alexander, 2018, pp. 33–34)

Lancaster was idyllic for white workers and their families – hostile to non-white people. It is unlikely that such places were unusual. In short, while the prevailing arc of many industrialization narratives emphasizes the benefits to workers, most firms, cities, and unions favored some workers at the expense of others. The benefits of industrial work were disproportionately white. Those without secure, safe, well-remunerated jobs were disproportionally non-white.

Pitting White and Non-White Workers Against One Another

It would be an overstatement to suggest that places like Lancaster were without intra-white class conflict or that its relative peace was typical in the annals of organized labor. The fight to achieve meaningful wages and benefits, even if disproportionately white, was hard fought, often violent. Simple exclusion was not the only way that employers exploited the socially justified discrimination of paying non-white workers less. As often, they used Black workers to undermine class solidarity, particularly to break the strikes of white workers and suppress wages when the latter became too powerful (Whatley, 1993). Black workers were often receptive to such actions because, as discussed earlier, they had been excluded by unions, firms, and the (white) labor movement in the first place. Some have suggested that this was a factor in which strikes they were willing to break. "American racism," writes Whatley, "made African American workers more willing to break strikes, especially when the targeted union had a history of racial discrimination" (Whatley, 1993, p. 526). Even when Black workers simply migrated to a region (i.e., not when they were deliberately escorted to break strikes), white violence often ensued (Anderson, 2016). Anti-Black riots Chicago, Detroit, and East

St. Louis occurred as factories hired Black migrants to fuel the industrial war machine during both world wars. Such actions have undermined the ability of the broader working class to build a labor movement in the US as strong as those in other more racially monolithic countries. It has also been a crucial component and tactic of employers. By increasing labor competition and exploiting white worker racism, industrial employers have been able to secure greater profits by keeping wages lower for all workers.

Geopolitical Maintenance of the Color Line

Finally, industrialized Global North countries have long used their militaries and immigration policy to maintain the global color line. While slavery was outlawed in the nineteenth century, and the formal colonial era declared dead in the twentieth century, white majority core capitalist countries have deployed a variety of mechanisms to maintain the racial hierarchy of the world's economy. This has involved military and economic interventions designed to advantage multinational companies in wealthy white majority countries (King, 2016).

When industrial production was more common in the Global North, functionaries like the IMF, World Bank, and American military made sure that foreign markets were open to their products, but that the US, Canada, and Western Europe were under no reciprocal obligation to open their economies to imports. As often, it involved the structuring of non-Global North economies in such a way that maintained their "underdevelopment" (Rodney, 2018). While colonialism may have formally ended in much of Africa and Latin America, large landowners were often sympathetic to the vacated colonial power. They were more than happy to continue lucrative monocrop cultivation that does not develop or industrialize the broader economy. When owners and political forces are not as sympathetic, strings-attached loans from the IMF and World Bank are used to reorient the economy toward Global North multinational company (MNC) interests. Walter Rodney has argued that it is precisely for this reason that the underdevelopment of Africa has occurred in direct proportion to the development of Europe (Rodney, 2018). Such measures were coupled with restrictive immigration policies, which kept non-white workers out of countries like the US and Canada at a time when industrial work was a viable path to the middle class (Hackworth, 2016).

Now that industrial production has become more global, such interventions also function to structure where benefits are gained and where exploitation is greatest. Global North firms have shifted industrial employment to key parts of the Global South but with careful attention (and assistance from Global North nation-states) at assuring that profits will be repatriated to wealthy countries. The deliberate underdevelopment of Africa, South and Southeast Asia, and Latin America thus continues after the formal abolition of slavery and colonialism. Many were thwarted initially from becoming industrial competitors. Now that industry is more widespread, Global North interests function to hasten the flow of profits to wealthy MNCs rather than the country where production actually takes place.

The Racial Dimensions of Deindustrialization

Discussing the rise of industry in the Global North is, in part, a historical exercise. No longer is the bulk of the world's manufacturing done there. Rather, the hearths of industrialization are shells of their former selves. The Rust Belts of the US, Germany, England, and France, among others are filled with small towns and major cities that are but a fraction of their former size and production. Abandoned factories are now more associated with places like Detroit than actual production. Though it is often not discussed, there is considerable overlap between the concentration of racialized populations and the most acute industrial ruins (Hackworth, 2019a). This pattern is most acute in the US, but it is not unique to it. Liverpool, for example, has seen post-industrial stress, but majority-Black Toxteith is the most abandoned and pathologized. Manchester is not the industrial powerhouse that it once was but the most pathologized space in the city is Moss Park – a majority Black Caribbean neighborhood. Little Burgundy in Montreal is the center of the city's Black population and the visible center of its post-industrial pain (High, 2022). Why would there be a close correspondence between the locations of Black (and other non-white residence) and urban abandonment? As with the rise of industry, there is no single pattern across time and space, but there are several tendencies that have accelerated and intensified the challenges of deindustrialization on non-white communities in the Global North.

Destructive "Fixes" to Neighborhood Decline

Global North urban development schemes have been common in the past 100 years. Whether for the purpose of architectural ideology, economic efficiency, or patronage to development interests, cities throughout the Global North have destroyed and rebuilt major portions of their landscapes. A key rationale of mid-twentieth-century urban renewal programs was to improve a city's economic position by rebuilding it to accommodate modern industry. This included, but was not limited to, expropriating and demolishing large portions of cities to make way for expressways, freight facilities, and land for factories.

It has been repeatedly noted, however, that the process of selecting which neighborhoods needed to be demolished, and which needed to be spared was racially biased. Both because non-white populations often occupied rigidly segregated neighborhoods where property values were low and because the mere presence of non-white people was sufficient for rational-scientific planners to assume that neighborhood was in decline, planners often targeted Black neighborhoods for removal and spared white ones (Rutland, 2018). Black (and other non-white) residents were displaced from the only neighborhood where they were permitted to live, often with little-to-no warning or compensation. This occurred in cities throughout North America during the mid-twentieth century. Black residents were often rehoused in newly built but poorly designed and funded public housing complexes. By the end of the twentieth century, those too were pathologized as 'in decline' and demolished to make way for a variety of purposes.

This cycle of community destruction disproportionately targeted black majority neighborhoods and had several consequences. First, as Mindy Fullilove argues, this continued cycle of pathologization and then destruction creates what she deems "root shock" – the production and reproduction of individual and familial instability (Fullilove, 2005). Second, and related, the home is often the greatest asset owned by middle-class white households. It provides not only emotional stability but an asset that can be lent against for other purposes such as major purchases, weathering unemployment, and university education for children. But the benefits of home ownership did not extend to Black families in North America in the same way. And to the extent that it did was undermined by this repeated cycle of unwanted, incomplete, or vengeful demolitions that wiped away the financial benefits. It is thus not terribly surprising that the most damaged sections of the post-industrial city are those that have been historically and currently occupied by non-white people (Hackworth, 2021a). The mere presence of non-white people has been repeatedly considered just cause for community destruction. This has weakened and destroyed Black spaces and cities far more frequently than similar white spaces and white-majority cities in the post-industrial era.

The Continued Flight of White People From Black Spaces

The continued refusal of white people to live or be schooled with Black people has fundamentally shaped the post-industrial urban landscape (Hackworth, 2022). Mixed-race neighborhoods continue to be the exception in American Rust Belt cities. This has a number of consequences for Black people and the spaces in which they reside. First, if the largest ethno-racial group with the greatest access to mainstream mortgage capital (white people) refuses to live near Black people, this, by definition, contributes to a punishing collapse of demand in the most non-white spaces. Black (and other non-white) families struggle to achieve equity gains, and eventually sell their properties unless they live in a white-majority space, or there is a substantial Black migration into their city (generating potential buyers) (Hackworth, 2021a). In extreme instances, houses go unsold for years and sometimes are forfeited to government authorities as part of tax auctions. The landscapes of abandonment in Detroit and Cleveland are disproportionately located in Black majority neighborhoods.

A second consequence can occur if an entire city becomes majority Black, and its political institutions are represented by Black people. Safford famously argued that for cities to make the transition from an industrial to post-industrial economy, there needs to be a socially invested elite willing and able to make difficult decisions and important investments (Safford, 2009). They are more likely to do this in places where they have deep social connections. White economic elites in places that become majority Black have displayed a pattern of not being willing to make those decisions. In fact, when places like Cleveland, Gary, and Detroit became majority Black and began to elect Black mayors and city councilors, firms generally abandoned the city or dealt with it like they were a hostile power (Hackworth, 2019a). The same has been shown to be true of elected officials at the state level. Political scientists refer to this as the "hollow prize" of Black municipal empowerment (Friesema, 1969; Reed, 1988). The promise of Black political leadership is punctured by the reality that state and surrounding municipal governments possess an extraordinary amount of power over the city they putatively abandoned. This power has largely been used to impose austerity not make difficult decisions that might benefit the people of a majority Black city or neighborhood.

The Long Shadow of (Post-Industrial) Employment Discrimination

The nature of employment has changed considerably in the post-industrial era, but the necessity of relying on employment income for most people has not. The pay scale and stability of a job is still the greatest determinant of economic stability for most people. As cities transition from an industrial to a post-industrial economy, this fact has generated a social polarization along racial lines. First, because of the aforementioned discrimination during the industrial era, a greater percentage of white workers now have residual benefits associated with industrial wealth. They were more likely to land a unionized job and be allowed access to white equity-gaining neighborhoods, so they were also more likely to have an equity-positive house, and a pension, even after the factory or mill or entire industry left. Because Black workers were denied access by unions, firms, and cities, they were disproportionally denied these benefits. It is also the case that Black families – deprived of these residual benefits – are less able to parlay them into university educations for their children that might enable them (their children) to thrive in the post-industrial economy. Second, audit studies continue to reveal racist employment discrimination. In one famous audit study, the late sociologist Devah Pager hired a young Black and a young white man to apply for poorly paid service work in Milwaukee (Pager, 2003). Not only did she show that service work overall is difficult to obtain and poorly paid; she found that the Black applicant was less than half as likely to be invited for an interview as the white applicant. This ongoing employment bias contributes to Black deprivation in the post-industrial city (Pager and Shepherd, 2008).

The Racial Politics of Post-Industrial Victim Blaming

The cumulative effect of the post-industrial transition has been disproportionately harsh to non-white people and spaces. Among other outcomes, this has led to non-white majority cities and neighborhoods being observably more abandoned and derelict than whiter spaces in the same cities (and elsewhere) (Hackworth, 2021a). The sociopolitical impact of these landscapes and their depiction has been profound. They have been deployed in ways that support policies that effectively reinforce, rather than ameliorate, deprivation in non-white post-industrial spaces.

Social psychologists have long documented how white people assign physical disorder to Black and other non-white residents. When asked, for example, to guess which ethno-racial group lived in a pictured neighborhood (with no people present in the image), white respondents routinely assume that the most visibly derelict spaces are occupied by Black people (Sampson and Raudenbush, 2004). Similarly, when asked to guess the value of a home, white respondents routinely assume that a home is worth more when a white family is present in the image (compared to when a Black family is present in front of the same house) (Bonam, Bergsieker, and Eberhardt, 2016). Assumptions about living environments are a key extension and producer of racial prejudice. These extant prejudices have been actively exploited by conservative political entrepreneurs – politicians, think tanks, and university-based academics – to advance the belief that Black (and other non-white) spaces are unsafe, poorly governed, and corrupt. In the US, fear of Black people has been produced and reproduced at the highest levels, and the invocation of derelict space has been a common method (Hackworth, 2019b). Depicting inner city spaces as dangerous, disorderly spaces have been used by reactionary politicians in Europe as well (Rhodes, 2012; Rhodes and Brown, 2019). The broader purpose of these efforts is to reinforce a racially prejudiced world view that, in effect, blames deprived people and spaces for their deprivation, thereby setting the framework for further punishing these spaces for their perceived misdeeds.

This political ethos has motivated moral panics about crime that enable targeted policing and the further over-incarceration of Black people in the US. Heather Ann Thompson has persuasively argued that these policies devastate not only the individuals incarcerated but the neighborhoods from which they come as well (Thompson, 2010). Other, less publicized outcomes include removing key economic development powers once a city is represented by Black mayors, state legislatures overturning city laws and ordinances that are unpopular with a state's white electorate, and state legislatures choosing white rural areas for economic development incentives (Kornberg, 2016; Hackworth, 2019a). Collectively, these policies undermine (sometimes destroy) a city's ability to make a turn toward a post-industrial future, thus leading to an exacerbation of the forces that created derelict landscapes. In effect, the imagery of post-industrial deprivation is used to justify the acceleration of forces that were created.

Conclusion

Racism is a series of practices and narratives that position some people beneath others. Racism has many functions, but in the economic realm it was (and remains) crucial for positioning some workers as beneath others to morally justify extracting maximum value from their labor. Class is very real but, seen within the prism of a racially monolithic workforce, often obscures other, often worse forms of exploitation nearby or around the globe. The wealth (and eventual political power) of Global North industry was and remains significantly built on the construction of some workers as more worthy than others. There is no singular pattern or force, but there are several ways that racism was used to advance the rise of industry in particular spaces. It was used, for example, to justify colonial pillage and enslavement upon which wealth was built. It was used to justify the mistreatment and underpayment of non-white workers and the exclusion of non-white workers from industrial work once it became more secure, safe, and a pathway to the middle class. It was used, finally, to justify the foreign policy and immigration practices of wealthy industrial countries. By the same token, deindustrialization has fallen unevenly upon non-white post-industrial spaces and workers. Racism in this context has functioned to build narratives that blame non-white post-industrial citizens for their own mistreatment and exploitation. These narratives have advanced policies that reinforce existing patterns and deepen deprivation for non-white people, neighborhoods, and cities.

Note

1 The following works have been particularly influential in my thinking: Du Bois, William Edward Burghardt. (2007 [1935]). *Black Reconstruction in America*. Oxford: Oxford University Press; James, Cyril Lionel Robert. (1989 [1963]). *The Black Jacobins: Toussaint L'Ouverture and the San Domingo Revolution*. New York: Vintage Books. For a more developed piece on the links between Black and white political economy, see Hackworth, J. (2021b). W.E.B. Du Bois and the Urban Political Economy Tradition in Geography. *Progress in Human Geography*, 45(5), pp. 1022–1039.

Reference List

Alexander, B. (2018). *The 1% Economy and the Shattering of the All-American Town*. New York: St. Martin's Press.

Anderson, C. (2016). *White Rage: The Unspoken Truth of our Racial Divide*. New York: Bloomsbury.

Bonam, C., Bergsieker, H. and Eberhardt, J. (2016). Polluting Black Space. *Journal of Experimental Psychology*, 145(11), pp. 1561–1582.

Dunk, T. (2003). *It's a Working Man's Town: Male Working Class Culture*. 2nd edn. Montreal: McGill-Queen's University Press.

Du Bois, W.E.B. (2007 [1935]). *Black Reconstruction in America*. Oxford: Oxford University Press.

Du Bois, W.E.B. (1915, May). The African Roots of War. *Atlantic Monthly*, p. 708.

Friesema, P. (1969, March). Black Control of the Central City: The Hollow Prize. *American Institute of Planners Journal*, 35, pp. 75–79.

Fullilove, M. (2005). *Root Shock: How Tearing up City Neighborhoods Hurts America and what We Can Do about it*. New York: Random House.

Hackworth, J. (2016). Why there is no Detroit in Canada. *Urban Geography*, 37(2), pp. 272–295.

Hackworth, J. (2019a). *Manufacturing Decline: How Racism and the Conservative Movement Crush the American Rust Belt*. New York: Columbia University Press.

Hackworth, J. (2019b). Urban Crisis as Conservative Bonding Capital. *City*, 23(1), pp. 53–65.

Hackworth, J. (2021a). Why Black-Majority Neighborhoods are the Epicenter of Population Shrinkage in the American Rust Belt. *Tijdschrift voor Economische en Sociale Geografie*, 112(1), pp. 44–61.

Hackworth, J. (2021b). W.E.B. Du Bois and the Urban Political Economy Tradition in Geography. *Progress in Human Geography*, 45(5), pp. 1022–1039.

Hackworth, J. (2022). Reaction to the Black City as a Cause of Modern Conservatism: A Case Study of Political Change in Ohio, 1932–2016. *Du Bois Review*, 19(1), pp. 85–105.

High, S. (2015). 'They Were Making Good Money, Just Ten Minutes from Home': Proximity and Distance in the Plant Shutdown Stories of Northern Ontario Mill Workers. *Labour/Le Travail*, 76, pp. 11–36.

High, S. (2018). *One Job Town: Work, Belonging and Betrayal in Northern Ontario*. Toronto: University of Toronto Press.

High, S. (2022). *Deindustrializing Montreal: Entangled Histories of Race, Residence, and Class*. Montreal: McGill-Queen's University Press.

Highsmith, A. (2015). *Demolition Means Progress: Flint, Michigan, and the Fate of the American Metropolis*. Chicago: University of Chicago Press.

James, C.L.R. (1989 [1963]). *The Black Jacobins: Toussaint L'Ouverture and the San Domingo Revolution*. New York: Vintage Books.

Kaye, H.J. (1995). Maurice Dobb and the Debate on the Transition to Capitalism. In *The British Marxist Historians: An Introductory Analysis*. New York: St. Martin's Press, pp. 23–69.

King, A. (2016). *Writing the Global City: Globalisation, Postcolonialism and the Urban*. London: Routledge.

Kornberg, D. (2016). The Structural Origins of Territorial Stigma: Water and Racial Politics in Metropolitan Detroit, 1950s-2010s. *International Journal of Urban and Regional Research*, 40(2), pp. 263–283.

Marable, M. (1983). *How Capitalism Underdeveloped Black America: Problems in Race, Political Economy, and Society*. Chicago: Haymarket Books.

Mills, C. (1997). *The Racial Contract*. Ithaca, NY: Cornell University Press.

Omi, M. and Winant, H. (2014). *Racial Formation in the United States*. 3rd edn. New York: Routledge.

Pager, D. (2003). The Mark of a Criminal Record. *American Journal of Sociology*, 108(5), pp. 937–975.

Pager, D. and Shepherd, H. (2008). The Sociology of Discrimination: Racial Discrimination in Employment, Housing, Credit, and Consumer Markets. *Annual Review of Sociology*, 34, pp. 181–209.

Reed, A. (1988). The Black Urban Regime: Structural Origins and Constraints. In Smith, M.P. (ed.) *Comparative Urban and Community Research: An Annual Review*. New Brunswick, NJ: Transaction, pp. 138–189.

Robinson, C. (1983). *Black Marxism: The Making of the Black Radical Tradition*. Chapel Hill, NC: University of North Carolina Press.

Rodney, W. (2018 [1972]). *How Europe Underdeveloped Africa*. New York: Verso.

Rhodes, J. (2012). Stigmatization, Space, and Boundaries in De-industrial Burnley. *Ethnic and Racial Studies*, 35(4), pp. 684–703.

Rhodes, J. and Brown, L. (2019). The Rise and Fall of the 'Inner City': Race, Space, and Urban Policy in Postwar England. *Journal of Ethnic and Migration Studies*, 45(17), pp. 3243–3259.

Rutland, T. (2018). *Displacing Blackness: Planning, Power and Race in Twentieth Century Halifax*. Toronto: University of Toronto Press.

Safford, S. (2009). *Why the Garden Club Couldn't Save Youngstown: The Transformation of the Rust Belt*. Cambridge, MA: Harvard University Press.

Sampson, R. and Raudenbush, S. (2004). Seeing Disorder: Neighborhood Stigma and the Social Construction of 'Broken Windows'. *Social Psychology Quarterly*, 67(4), pp. 319–342.

Sugrue, T. (2005). *The Origins of the Urban Crisis: Race and Inequality in Postwar Detroit*. Princeton Classic Edition. Princeton, NJ: Princeton University Press.

Thompson, H.A. (2010). Why Mass Incarceration Matters: Rethinking Crisis, Decline, and Transformation in Postwar American History. *Journal of American History*, 97(3), pp. 703–734.

Whatley, W. (1993). African-American Strikebreaking from the Civil War to the New Deal. *Social Science History*, 17(4), pp. 525–558.

Widdick, B. (1976). Black Workers: Double Discontents. In *Auto Work and its Discontents*. Baltimore, MD: Johns Hopkins Press, p. 54.

8

THE REGION AS AN ANALYTICAL FRAMEWORK FOR DEINDUSTRIALIZATION STUDIES

Regional Economic Development in Atlantic Canada

Lachlan MacKinnon

Introduction

Scholarship within the field of deindustrialization studies is increasingly recognizing the importance of adopting the region as a unit of analysis and pushing outward into cross-regional and transnational comparative studies. In a recent edited collection that explores the intersections of regionalism and industrial heritage, Christian Wicke makes the essential point that regional experiences of deindustrialization are instrumental in shaping the ways in which working-class communities have responded to industrial closure and loss. He writes, "Regions, like nations, not only are administrative or economic units; they are also imagined communities reliant on historical narratives and visions for the future that legitimize their continuous existence as spatial entities" (Wicke, 2018, p. 3). In areas described by Stefan Berger and Paul Pickering as "regions of heavy industry," these imagined communities contribute significantly to the historical memory of industry and deindustrialization in a variety of ways. In the Ruhr region of Germany, a convergence of factors has resulted in a state-supported historical narrative of deindustrialization that is "densely reclaimed, curated, and narrated." This approach firmly places the region's industrial past within the domain of "official" national historical narrative, often downplaying questions related to class struggle or conflict (Berger and Pickering, 2018, p. 232).

In contrast to the example of the Ruhr, regions that have not benefited from comparable levels of state-led heritage support are sometimes more able to include conflicting, radical, or activist-driven historical narratives (Berger and Pickering, 2018, p. 232). This is true in the UK, where regional industrial memories often correspond with resistance to British state-sanctioned industrial closures during the 1980s and the repression of the Miners' Strike, and in Spain, where Asturian music retains a strong cultural connection to the industrial experience (Dicks, Orange, and Vega Garcia, 2020). Although the specific details differ, there is a consistent sense that historical experiences related to industrialization and

DOI: 10.4324/9781003308324-13

deindustrialization are deeply embedded within conceptualizations of region, regional identity, and collective regional memory.

The primary argument of this chapter is that we must be more explicit in how we employ the concept of 'region' as an analytical lens to explore the historical experience of deindustrialization. While Berger et al. have demonstrated that regional sensibilities influence how working-class experiences and cultures are memorialized, commemorated, or expressed through industrial heritage, it is essential to recognize that, in many instances, regional identities evolved alongside industrialization and class formation. These identities played a role in shaping how various states chose to respond (or not respond) to uneven economic development, deindustrialization, industrial closure, or post-industrial revitalization. In this respect, there is a valuable opportunity for further research at the intersection of regional economic development policies and deindustrialization. Greg Wilson's examination of the Area Redevelopment Administration is an illustrative example of this sort of research, foregrounding how geographic and spatial disparities during the 1950s resulted in a host of regional responses to rural poverty and economic decline (Wilson, 2009, p. 34). Drawing upon the case study of the Atlantic region of Canada, this chapter traces the rise of regionalist sensibilities, rooted in the uneven development of the Canadian economy during the late nineteenth century, and explores the ways that these sentiments informed the emergence of regional economic development as an early state-led response to deindustrialization. This will be accomplished through an examination of development policies that were implemented in the four Atlantic provinces between the postwar years and the late 1960s.

Defining the concept of 'the region' as a unit of analysis in any such effort is an imprecise and complex process. Marxist geographers have long described the emergence of regions as a process by which subnational polities arise alongside uneven market allocation of resources in the advanced capitalist economies (Massey, 1978, pp. 106–107; Paasi, 1986, pp. 108–109; Paasi, 2009, pp. 126–128). As Xosé M. Núñez Seixas and Eric Storm describe, regionalism arose in many parts of Europe in the form of mass movements in the nineteenth century and represented "an imagined community . . . [which] may or may not make political claims but is located somewhere between the nation (subject of sovereignty and territorially broader) and the local sphere (the space of human experience and daily interaction)" (Núñez Seixas and Storm, 2018, p. 8). While underlying conceptions of political economy and uneven development often inform such constructions, regional identities lack the explicit orientation toward political independence that Benedict Anderson argued characterize the imaged communities of nationalist movements (Anderson, 2006). In Atlantic Canada, such constructions emerged along with the creation of the Canadian administrative state after the process of Confederation in 1867. The longer-term implications of regionalism in this case included wide-ranging political support for 'regional economic development' as an early, if largely ineffective, set of policy responses to another wave of deindustrialization in the 1960s and 1970s.

Deindustrialization and Regionalism in Atlantic Canada

In the field of deindustrialization studies, we are often urged to write about deindustrialization as a process of capital mobility that can manifest differently across various places and times (Johnson, 1995; High, 2013, p. 140). While the discipline has recently expanded to include elements of transnationality and deindustrialization across borders, becoming increasingly global in scope, much of our work still adheres to the periodization of deindustrialization that originated from its activist roots in the Global North. This observation was also high-lighted in a recent introduction to a special issue on deindustrialization in the Canadian labor journal *Labour/Le Travail*, co-authored by Steven High and myself. In the introduction, we underscored how certain areas in Canada, including parts of British Columbia, the Mari-times, and even segments of Southern Ontario, experienced deindustrialization as early as the 1920s (MacKinnon and High, 2023). While broader global patterns of political economy remain valuable, historians of deindustrialization must also be attuned to the ways in which smaller regions and localities may experience its processes along distinct timelines, deviating from those found in dominant national economic histories.

The early roots of regionalism in Atlantic Canada can be traced back to the significant economic shifts experienced along the Atlantic coast during the demographic and political upheavals of the nineteenth century. Consecutive waves of European settlement, coupled with the industrialization and centralization of the national economy, generated a host of economic pressures. These changes led to a fundamental reorientation of the Atlantic econ-omy, shifting it away from its traditional moorings in North–South coastal trade and pushing toward continental integration. This concept was central to T. W. Acheson's research on the nineteenth-century Maritimes.

Acheson argued that the expansion of transportation networks and the federal 'National Policy,' which dictated trade after 1879, reformulated the economy in ways that promoted centralization. This contributed directly to the Maritimes' inability to develop a "metro-pole" that could compete directly with central Canadian cities like Toronto and Montreal (Acheson, 1972). While these circumstances set the stage for the industrialization of the region between 1880 and 1910 through the maturity of industries like coal, steel, textiles, and manufacturing, it came at the expense of the existing wooden shipbuilding industry. In what has been called "the region's first substantial deindustrialization," the decline of firms within this sector and the associated impacts on affected communities were masked by the availability of other forms of industrial work and the late nineteenth-century pattern of urban migration (Reid and Reid, 2016, p. 94).

These shifts are often contextualized within Canadian history as indicative of sweeping changes in the British World, the growth of heavy industry, the perceived "natural" decline of wooden shipbuilding, or the expansion of the Canadian national economy concurrent with the displacement of Indigenous peoples from their lands and the opening of the continent for capital investment (see Acheson, Frank, and Frost, 1985; Nerbas, 2018). Despite our emphasis on a broader periodization of deindustrialization as an ongoing facet of capital-ist development and underdevelopment, the nineteenth-century sectoral deindustrialization in various regions of Canada has received limited attention. Nevertheless, comparisons to deindustrialized steel or coal towns of the 1970s are not far-fetched. As noted by Eric Sager and Gerald E. Panting, "ship-owning and shipbuilding in the Maritimes did not simply decline – these industries collapsed," with local fleets shrinking to a third of their 1880 size by 1900 (Sager and Panting, 1990, p. 4). While a concurrent manufacturing boom and the movement of rural populations reshaped this landscape, prevailing histories often convey a narrative of transition rather than offering substantial insight into the social and communal upheaval caused by deindustrialization. In certain respects, this mirrors more recent argu-ments about the visibility or invisibility of deindustrialization in urban spaces – where the rapid pace of capitalist redevelopment obscures certain aspects of the process. As factories are demolished, working-class neighborhoods gentrified, and new industries arise, key aspects of the process are made invisible (see High, 2022).

The Region as an Analytical Framework

Between 1880 and 1910, the Maritime provinces of Canada experienced a notable surge of industrialization in new sectors and an expansion of manufacturing. The coalfields in Nova Scotia and New Brunswick attracted workers from further afield as production increased during the early years of the twentieth century. Colin Howell describes the valuation of the manufacturing sector in the Maritime provinces increasing nearly 95% between 1900 and 1910 – a reflection of the significant economic and urban changes buffeting the region (Howell, 1993, p. 165). This growth would not be sustained.

The region soon entered the "second major deindustrialization" – a period beginning in the interwar years when the Maritime provinces of Canada suffered major plant closures, protracted unemployment, and the beginnings of an outmigration crisis that would continue for decades (Reid and Reid, 2016, p. 95; Burrill, 1992). David Frank has expertly traced the crisis in the Nova Scotia coal industry that erupted during the 1920s but also reflected upon the wider challenges in manufacturing that witnessed thousands of jobs lost across Nova Scotia in places like Amherst – where "industrial employment was virtually wiped out by shutdowns" (Frank, 1977, pp. 3–34; Frank, 1993, p. 256). In New Brunswick, the recession following the First World War bankrupted the majority of provincial lumber barons and provoked a sharp fiscal crisis that "resulted in mass unemployment for the more than 30,000 people who worked directly in the mills and woods" (Parenteau, 2013, p. 102). In Prince Edward Island, the province had not benefited from industrial growth in the aftermath of the nineteenth-century shipbuilding collapse that had helped to buoy its neighboring provinces. During the first half of the twentieth century, the island boasted fewer services than most other provinces in Canada and the lowest per-capita income in the country (MacDonald, 2003, p. 21). Despite robust attempts to grow shellfish, silver fox, and seed potato industries, the island moved into crisis alongside most of North America in 1920 with the advent of the Great Depression (MacDonald, 2016).

In the case of Newfoundland, despite its late entry into the Canadian project – not joining Confederation until 1949 – the province suffered similarly from the vicissitudes of political economy during the interwar years. Though Atlantic Canada as a political entity had not yet been "invented," Newfoundland experienced a protracted decline in its important saltfish industry (Slumkoski, 2011; Alexander, 1977). Margaret Conrad and James Hiller found that 242 businesses declared bankruptcy in Newfoundland between 1921 and 1923, placing a significant strain on public coffers that would result in debt crisis and the surrender of responsible government in 1934. These crises ultimately paved the way for Newfoundland's eventual entry into Canadian Confederation (Conrad and Hiller, 2010, pp. 175–176).

It was this period of multi-sectoral deindustrialization across the Atlantic region and the associated protracted economic crisis that gave rise to a variety of social movements that adopted regionalist language to articulate their dissatisfactions. One notable example is the 'Maritime Rights Movement,' which emerged during the 1920s. This movement relied on an explicitly regional argument to assert that structural forces within Confederation had led to economic underdevelopment and a lack of opportunities for entrepreneurs and workers in the region (Forbes, 1979). Simultaneously, many industrial workers in the Atlantic region turned to trade unionism and class politics as an opportunity to resist their dispossession. The Amherst general strike in 1919, the Cape Breton labor wars of 1923–1925, the Fishermen's Protective Union in Newfoundland, and trade unionism across New Brunswick signaled a broad working-class response to the wave of industrial closures (Frank, 1999; Reilly, 1980, pp. 56–77; O'Brien, 2011, pp. 45–69; Frank, 2013).

Federal and provincial governments responded in a variety of ways to these emerging forms of resistance. In the immediate aftermath of the Cape Breton coal wars, private capital was pushed into reorganization as the Dominion Steel and Coal Company Ltd. With the generational memory of these struggles close at hand, Nova Scotia was the first province to legislate a Trade Union Act in 1937 to avoid the same sorts of open conflict. In response to these and other labor issues across the country, the Government of Canada began enacting legislation that would form the basis for labor legalism and the capital-labor compact (Heron, 1989; McInnis, 2002). It is no coincidence that this is also the same time that different levels of government begin accepting the concept of 'regional underdevelopment' as an explanation for disparity – as opposed to Marxist explanations of spatial capital accumulation. If we reconsider the social movements, class politics, and open conflicts of the interwar period in the Atlantic region as bottom-up, regionally informed responses to the challenges of deindustrialization, it provides the material rationality for the later appearance of 'regional economic development' as a particular set of state responses to the reemergence of crisis in the mid-century.

The deindustrialization of certain sectors of the Atlantic economy during late nineteenth and early twentieth centuries, coupled with the failure of Canadian and provincial governments to address the emerging crisis, led to protracted social conflict, the rise of movement politics, regionalism, and class struggle. Regionalism directly informed these social movements, and underdevelopment was increasingly accepted at the federal and provincial levels as an explanation for disparity within Canada by the 1930s. Meanwhile, the expansion of state control over the Canadian economy that arose during the Second World War provided evidence for the possibilities of economic planning within the market economy. As Canadian capitalism transitioned in the aftermath of the conflict, different levels of government responded to the continuation of regional disparity through more direct, state-led initiatives. The adoption of 'regional economic development' as a set of policy responses in the postwar period was therefore directly predicated upon a recognition of the historical context of these earlier periods of deindustrialization.

Regional Development as a Response to Deindustrialization

The Government of Canada proposed to solve the problems associated with the distinctly regional orientation of Canadian political economy as early as 1940, when the Royal Commission on Dominion-Provincial Relations, colloquially known as the Rowell-Sirois Commission, delivered its final report. While its recommendations were not immediately put into practice, the Rowell-Sirois Commission recognized the importance of enabling each Canadian province to offer comparable levels of services to their residents through similar taxation rates (Wardhaugh and Ferguson, 2021, p. 10). This principle lay at the core of the passage of Canada's equalization program in 1957, championed by the Liberal government of Louis St. Laurent. The Prime Minister saw it as a tax-sharing initiative that would "place the provinces in a more stable financial position to provide a minimum standard of provincial services" (Pickersgill, 1975, p. 310). The program's objectives were twofold; the federal government viewed equalization as a vehicle for nation-building and of countering the isolation of Quebec under Premier Maurice Duplessis. For their part, provincial governments in areas with sluggish economic growth recognized the immediate potential for expansion of services (Bryden, 2014, pp. 413–414). As a result, by the mid-1950s there was a broad political acceptance of the notion that Canada was fundamentally a nation of regions with distinct trajectories of development and that state action could be wielded to bring these areas together in terms of shared growth.

Political economists likewise provided explanations for regional underdevelopment. Harold Innis, a professor at the University of Toronto, delineated a "staples theory" of Canadian economic history in his early works *The Fur Trade in Canada* (1927) and *The Cod Fisheries: The History of an International Economy* (1940). Innis's writings propose that Canada's growth was shaped by the colonial extraction of staples products – fur, fish, lumber, and coal – which were transported to secondary sites of manufacture, refinement, and subsequent stages of production. Consequently, the Canadian economy remained economically wedded to the larger imperial powers to which it had become associated – first the British World and later the American Empire. These dynamics were mirrored internally, with the "Empire of the Saint Lawrence" of Southern Ontario and Quebec holding sway as the economic center and the "hinterlands" of the Maritimes, the North, or the West existing as rural resource frontiers (Drache, 1982, p. 36). This notion would go on to inform much left-nationalist activism in Canada and form part of the basis for what Steven High describes as the "Radical Origins of the Deindustrialization Thesis" (High, 2023, p. 36).

The historical experience of structural economic change and deindustrialization in the Atlantic region combined with an increasingly regionally informed political economy and an appetite for state-led economic intervention that survived the national experience during the Second World War to create an ideal environment for 'regional economic development' to emerge. Alongside equalization in the 1950s, the federal government leveraged this understanding to embark on numerous large-scale infrastructure projects and operate a variety of Crown corporations, including the Canadian Broadcast Corporation and Air Canada. These initiatives aimed to foster greater unity among the diverse regions of the country. In essence, the federal government engaged in a massive campaign of "nation-building," as described by Donald Savoie (Savoie, 1992, p. 16). Meanwhile, provincial governments adopted the rhetoric of 'regional development' to advocate for their own interests, secure additional funds from federal coffers, and to underpin a broad commitment to state-led economic growth. Drawing upon the example of the four Atlantic provinces after 1949 offers insight into how these sentiments translated into specific policy frameworks that would eventually inform the regional response to the deindustrialization crisis.

It was in Newfoundland, Canada's easternmost province which had joined Confederation only in 1949 that Liberal Premier Joey Smallwood staked out ground as the first major regional proponent of state-led industrial development. Following Confederation, Smallwood personally took on the Economic Development portfolio and aimed to secure support from both the federal government and external investors (Hiller, 1993, p. 381). Smallwood's 'New Industries' program, which began in July 1949, adopted the slogan 'develop or perish' as a rallying cry. Eager to fulfill promises of rapid industrialization, Smallwood sought deals with a variety of German and Latvian firms to relocate industries to the struggling province. These initiatives were largely supported by residents who were amid what Gerhardt Bassler describes as an ongoing 'social, cultural, and psychological revolution.' This transformation was prompted by the province's emerging ties with Canada and its wartime experience, during which Newfoundland workers interacted with tens of thousands of American and Allied servicemen stationed at bases in the province (Bassler, 1986, p. 97; High, 2003). Addressing the challenges of a modernizing fishery, the outmigration of young people from outport communities, and the increased liabilities assumed by the province after Confederation, Smallwood viewed the fight against underdevelopment as pivotal for the future of the province (Gwyn, 1999, p. 167).

Serving as Premier from 1949 until 1972, Smallwood oversaw the era of development in Newfoundland. Choosing Alfred Valdmanis as the Director General of Economic Development, Smallwood signaled that there would be an international dimension to his plan for escaping the regional underdevelopment trap. Valdmanis had worked previously for the Latvian finance and trade departments, where he had helped to diversify the economy away from agriculture and focus on technological and industrial growth. Smallwood drew clear parallels between this and the situation in Newfoundland, where reliance upon the fisheries had long been the province's economic bedrock. Over the following decade, the New Industries program attracted investment in gypsum, hardwood, and textile production through targeted efforts and collaboration with companies from Latvia and Germany (Bassler, 1986, p. 119). Complimenting this was a comprehensive initiative for reorganizing the fisheries, forcing the resettlement of outport communities and technological advancement (House, 2018, p. 444). This transformation brought about the swift destruction of the "rural way of life" as entire communities disappeared – prompting some degree of resistance and nostalgia among those who were displaced (Webb, 2016, p. 8). In this sense, Smallwood's policy endeavors to counter regional underdevelopment also targeted the foundations of what E. R. Forbes described as the "regional stereotype" – a set of perceptions surrounding the continued existence of rural populations throughout the region that sustain themselves through staples or agriculture (Forbes, 1989, p. 7; McKay, 1992).

In Nova Scotia, the Progressive Conservative Party under Robert Stanfield was the first to introduce the concept of state-led industrial development. This occurred while the party was in opposition during the run-up to an unsuccessful electoral bid in 1953. E. D. Haliburton, a member of Stanfield's cabinet after the party won the 1956 provincial election, later reflected:

> The Conservatives . . . had a philosophy completely unlike that of the old Tory reactionaries. Stanfield and his group believed in more government involvement in business and the economy generally, in putting new life into private enterprise by stepping up and activating assistance programs to spur businesses into new aggressiveness, new risk taking, and new responsibility.
>
> *(Haliburton, 1972, pp. 28–29)*

Although hailing from a staunch family of Tories, Stanfield, in fact, briefly identified as a socialist during his younger years – having become enamored with the writings of Fabian socialist G.D.H. Cole during a visit to Cambridge University in 1933 (Stevens, 1973, p. 31). It was not until Stanfield's ascendency to the Premier's office in 1956 that the scope of this project was truly revealed. In his campaign, he outlined a 9-point plan – detailing infrastructure investment, greater cooperation with the other three Atlantic premiers in support of a broader regional interest, the establishment of a "Maritime House" in Europe to attract direct investment, and a new Crown corporation – the "Nova Scotia Industrial Development Corporation" (see George, 1974; Stevens, 1973, p. 103).[1]

In power between 1956 and 1970, Nova Scotia's Progressive Conservatives executed various state planning initiatives to address perceived regional disparities within the framework of Canadian federalism. Alongside the proposals outlined during the 1956 campaign, Stanfield and his cabinet introduced a tripartite approach to industrial development. This approach encompassed alterations to the industrial relations structure, the establishment of Industrial Estates Limited as an exercise in attracting capital and industrial investment to the province, and the initiation of a voluntary sectoral planning program that would see state investment directed to specific areas of the provincial economy (Clancy, 1997; George, 1974). Although Stanfield left provincial politics in 1967 to become the leader of the federal Progressive Conservative Party and the leader of the Official Opposition, he was succeeded as Premier by cabinet minister G. I. Smith, who served in the role until 1970. Under Smith's leadership, the province continued its interventionist stance – culminating with the nationalization of the provincial steel industry and the creation of the Sydney Steel Corporation in response to the threatened closure of the mill in Sydney (Thiesen, 1995).

In New Brunswick, the shift toward development coincided with a broader series of political and cultural transformations, initiated with the election of Premier Louis Robichaud at the head of a Liberal provincial government on June 27, 1960. As the first elected Acadian premier of the province, Robichaud focused on improving the circumstances facing many of the underserved Francophone Acadian population. Among other achievements, Robichaud created the Université de Moncton in 1963 and legislated official bilingualism in the province with the Equal Opportunities Program in 1969 (Savoie, 2009, p. 70). Development was a key component of this overarching strategy. Tabling 130 bills, the Robichaud government undertook a comprehensive overhaul of the provincial bureaucracy, expanding education, social services, and sometimes challenging the economic influence of prominent industrialist K. C. Irving (Stanley, 1984).[2] Spearheading this initiative, Robichaud collaborated with a team of financial and economic advisors from Saskatchewan, brought in to bureaucratize the civil service and provide advice for the reorientation and modernization of provincial economic development (Passoli, 2009, p. 143).[3] These bureaucrats, known as the "Saskatchewan Mafia," had prior experience working with the Co-operative Commonwealth Federation in that province. As a result, they brought to the table the sort of transformative leadership that was being sought for the reconfiguration of New Brunswick society (Passoli, 2009, p. 142).

While Robichaud did not approach economic development with the same intensity and single-mindedness as Stanfield or Smallwood, the comprehensive reforms he implemented within the civil service and the financial framework of the provincial government established a foundation for state-led intervention by the time of the Equal Opportunities Program. As revealed by Lisa Passoli, Robichaud's administration began drafting reports and plans for a province-wide development strategy as early as 1967. Don Tansley, one of the staff imports from Saskatchewan, contributed to the New Brunswick Development Board, overseeing initiatives such as "the Grand Falls Industrial Complex, the Westmoreland Chemical Part, and especially the Noranda takeover of Brunswick Mining and Smelting" (Passoli, 2009, p. 142). In the final instance, this capped a long period of state intervention in the base metal industry along New Brunswick's north shore. Robichaud was central to these developments since the early 1960s, when he showcased the formation of the Brunswick Mining and Smelting Company as an example of a province-based growth strategy. At that time, the company was purchased from an American multinational by a consortium of local industrialists, including Irving, with a support of the provincial government. Throughout the decade, the Robichaud government extended substantial support to multiple companies through direct subsidies amounting to tens of millions of dollars (Kenny, 1997, p. 1; Kenny and Secord, 2001). Eventually, the province intervened to endorse a takeover of the firm by Noranda in contravention of Irving's wishes (McCutcheon and Walker, 2020, p. 152).

Just across the Northumberland Strait on Prince Edward Island, Canada's smallest province, much of the existing industry relied upon direct resource extraction. This was particularly evident in the two primary sectors – agriculture and the lobster fishery, which experienced growth after the 1940s (Stanley, 1993, pp. 421–459). The Progressive Conservative government under Walter R. Shaw, elected in 1959, was the first to join the path of industrial development. Initial attempts sought to bolster the island's existing economic strengths, with efforts like supporting the establishment of frozen food manufacturing plants serving as a form of modernization within the long-standing farming and seafood industries. In 1963, the province entered into an ill-fated agreement with Norwegian investor Jens Moe to develop an agricultural manufacturing and shipbuilding hub in Georgetown. Although this initiative, like many others, proved unsuccessful, it underscores that leaders in Charlottetown were equally willing to take calculated risks on economic development, akin to their counterparts in the neighboring provinces.[4]

The tourism industry also played a pivotal role in Prince Edward Island's industrial planning strategy. As outlined by Alan MacEachern and Edward MacDonald, the long-standing tourism sector was boosted significantly by state intervention during the 1960s. During these years, the province commissioned Acres International consultants to set out a longer-term plan for subsidy and development. In 1965, this resulted in the highest per-capita expenditure on tourism development of any province in Canada – with the Island's government allocating approximately 1.3% of its ordinary expenditures on the operations of the Department of Tourist Development (MacEachern and MacDonald, 2022, p. 141). The representation of the island as quaint, pastoral, and "Folk-ish" matches with similar tourist-focused efforts in Nova Scotia but clashes with the broader modernist trajectory of other development initiatives of the era (see MacEachern, 1999, p. 23; McKay, 1992).

In each of the Atlantic Provinces, these industrial revitalization and development programs of the 1950s and 1960s have traditionally been interpreted within Canadian scholarship as responses to regional underdevelopment and as indicators of a growing state acknowledgment that the benefits of Confederation had not been uniformly distributed. However, these efforts must also be viewed as a set of responses to an ongoing process of regional deindustrialization, grounded in the distinctive political economy of Canadian federalism. This process pre-dates the larger wave of industrial crises that devastated communities across North America and Europe during the 1970s and 1980s that comprise much of the scholarship within the field. In this sense, the activist states that responded to deindustrialization in the Nova Scotia coal and steel sectors during the 1960s – applying tools up to and including nationalization – were tapping into a much lengthier history of industrial decline. This history was interwoven with a political atmosphere that emboldened direct state-led intervention.

Viewing the rise of regional economic development from this perspective, as a set of policy responses that emerged in the aftermath of an earlier wave of deindustrialization, helps to explain some of the seemingly anachronistic actions taken during the early years of the industrial crisis of the late 1960s and early 1970s. In the case of the nationalization of the Cape Breton steel and coal industries, for example, it is not necessarily that the different levels of government were being entirely innovative and proactive in the face of an economic catastrophe but that the province had already learned the pitfalls of failing to act during the 1920s. The emergence of regional economic development discourse provided the grounding for the state to act in such cases. Digging into the historical roots of 'region' in Atlantic Canada reveals how the concept shaped protest and social movements and how its concurrent rise alongside consecutive waves of deindustrialization helped to orient the trajectories of the state responses that emerged in these four Canadian provinces. Considering region as a variable in our assessments of state responses to deindustrialization is a necessary step

The Region as an Analytical Framework

in understanding why its processes unfolded in strikingly different ways in different national contexts and may provide fruitful ground for future comparative work.

Notes

1 The idea of a specialized Crown corporation dedicated to industrial development in the province was predictive of the later creation of Industrial Estates Limited. See George, R.E. (1974). *The Life and Times of Industrial Estates Limited*. Halifax: Dalhousie University Institute for Public Affairs; Stevens, G. (1973). *Stanfield*. Toronto: McClelland and Stewart, p. 103.
2 At the time, the Irving companies owned more than 10% of the land in the province of New Brunswick and provided the same percentage of nongovernmental employment. Following Robichaud's reforms, Irving famously signaled strong support for the Progressive Conservatives and ran anti-Francophone racial cartoons in Irving-owned newspapers. See Cowan, E. (1971, June 20). Man in Business. *New York Times*, p. 7; Laxer, J. (2006). *The Acadians: In Search of a Homeland*. Toronto: Anchor Canada, p. 215.
3 Notably, and with direct comparison to the Nova Scotia and Newfoundland examples, Bliss White describes a study tour, wherein one author of an influential provincial development report traveled to Sweden to learn about the prevailing 'socialist' system. See White, B. (2020). Bringing the Commune to Canada. *Acadiensis*, 49(2), pp. 185–196.
4 Ultimately, a Royal Commission was formed to investigate the Moe debacle. See MacDonald, G.E. (2000). *If You're Stronghearted: Prince Edward Island In the 20th Century*. Charlottetown: Prince Edward Island Museum and Heritage Foundation, p. 275.

Reference List

Acheson, T.W. (1972). The National Policy and the Industrialization of the Maritimes, 1880–1910. *Acadiensis*, 1(2), pp. 3–28.

Acheson, T.W., Frank, D. and Frost, J.D. (1985). *Industrialization and Underdevelopment in the Maritimes, 1880-1930*. Toronto: Garamond Press.

Alexander, D. (1977). *The Decay of Trade: An Economic History of the Newfoundland Saltfish Trade, 1935–1965*. St. John's: Institute of Social and Economic Research.

Anderson, B. (2006). *Imagined Communities: Reflections on the Origin and Spread of Nationalism*. Revised edition. London: Verso.

Bassler, G.P. (1986). Develop or Perish: Joseph R. Smallwood and Newfoundland's Quest for German Industry, 1949–1953. *Acadiensis*, 15(2), pp. 97, 119.

Berger, S. and Pickering, P. (2018). Regions of Heavy Industry and their Heritage – Between Identity Politics and 'Touristification'. In Wicke, C., Berger, S. and Golombek, J. (eds.) *Industrial Heritage and Regional Identities*. London: Routledge, p. 232.

Bryden, P.E. (2014). 'Pooling our Resources:' Equalization and the Origins of Regional Universality, 1937–1957. *Canadian Public Administration*, 57(3), pp. 413–414.

Burrill, G. (1992). *Away: Maritimers in Massachusetts, Ontario, and Alberta*. Montreal and Kingston: McGill-Queen's University Press.

Clancy, P. (1997). Concerted Action on the Periphery? Voluntary Economic Planning in Nova Scotia. *Acadiensis*, 26(2), pp. 3–30.

Conrad, M. and Hiller, J. (2010). *Atlantic Canada: A Region in the Making*. Oxford: Oxford University Press, pp. 175–176.

Cowan, E. (1971, June 20). Man in Business. *New York Times*, Section F, p. 7.

Dicks, B., Orange, H. and Vega Garcia, R. (2020). Industrial Heritage as Place Making: The Case of Wales; Cornish Mining Heritage and Cornish Identity; Sounds of Decline: Industrial Echoes in Asturian Music. In Berger. S. (ed.) *Constructing Industrial Pasts: Heritage, Historical Culture and Identity in Regions Undergoing Structural Economic Transformation*. New York: Berghahn Books, pp. 68–90, 107–127, 216–227.

Drache, D. (1982). Harold Innis and Canadian Capitalist Development. *Canadian Journal of Political and Social Theory/Revue Canadienne de théorie politique et sociale*, 6(2), p. 36.

Forbes, E.R. (1979). *The Maritime Rights Movement, 1919–1927*. Montreal and Kingston: McGill-Queen's University Press.

Forbes, E.R. (1989). *Challenging the Regional Stereotype: Essays on the 20th Century Maritimes*. Fredericton: Acadiensis Press, p. 7.

Frank, D. (1977). The Cape Breton Coal Industry and the Rise and Fall of the British Empire and Steel Corporation. *Acadiensis*, 7(1), pp. 3–34.

Frank, D. (1993). The 1920s: Class and Region, Resistance and Accommodation. In Forbes, E.R. and Muise, D.A. (eds.) *The Atlantic Provinces in Confederation*. Toronto: University of Toronto Press, p. 256.

Frank, D. (1999). *J.B. McLachlan: A Biography*. Toronto: James Lorimer and Co.

Frank, D. (2013). *Provincial Solidarities: A History of the New Brunswick Federation of Labour*. Athabasca: Athabasca University Press.

George, R.E. (1974). *The Life and Times of Industrial Estates Limited*. Halifax: Dalhousie University Institute for Public Affairs.

Gwyn, R. (1999). *Smallwood: The Unlikely Revolutionary*. Toronto: McClelland and Stewart.

Haliburton, E.D. (1972). *My Years with Stanfield*. Windsor, NS: Lancelot Press, pp. 28–29.

Heron, C. (1989). *The Canadian Labour Movement: A Short History*. Toronto: Lorimer.

High, S. (2003). Working for Uncle Sam: The "Comings" and "Goings" of Newfoundland Base Construction Labour, 1940–1945. *Acadiensis*, 32(2), pp. 84–107.

High, S. (2013). Beyond Aesthetics: Visibility and Invisibility in the Aftermath of Deindustrialization. *International Labor and Working-Class History*, 84, p. 140.

High, S. (2022). *Deindustrializing Montreal: Entangled Histories of Race and Class*. Montreal and Kingston: McGill-Queen's University Press.

High, S. (2023). The Radical Origins of the Deindustrialization Thesis: From Dependency to Capital Flight and Community Abandonment. *Labour/Le Travail*, 91, p. 36.

Hiller, J.K. (1993). Newfoundland Confronts Canada, 1867–1949. In Forbes, E.R. and Muise, D.A. (eds.) *The Atlantic Provinces in Confederation*. Toronto: University of Toronto Press and Acadiensis Press, pp. 349–382.

House, D. (2018). Did Smallwood Neglect the Fisheries? *Newfoundland and Labrador Studies*, 33(2), p. 444.

Howell, C. (1993). The 1900s: Industry, Urbanization, and Reform. In Forbes, E.R. and Muise, D.A. (eds.) *The Atlantic Provinces in Confederation*. Toronto: University of Toronto Press and Acadiensis Press, pp. 155–191.

Johnson, C. (1995). *The Life and Death of Industrial Languedoc, 1700–1920: The Politics of Deindustrialization*. Oxford: Oxford University Press.

Kenny, J. (1997). A New Dependency: State, Local Capital, and the Development of New Brunswick's Base Metal Industry, 1960–70. *Canadian Historical Review*, 78(1), p. 1.

Kenny, J. and Secord, A. (2001). Public Power for Industry: A Re-examination of the New Brunswick Case, 1940–1960. *Acadiensis*, 30(2), pp. 84–108.

Laxer, J. (2006). *The Acadians: In Search of a Homeland*. Toronto: Anchor Canada, p. 215.

MacDonald, E. (2000). *If You're Stronghearted: Prince Edward Island In the 20th Century*. Charlottetown: Prince Edward Island Museum and Heritage Foundation, p. 275.

MacDonald, E. (2016). Economic Dislocation on Prince Edward Island: Small Producers, Distant Markets. *London Journal of Canadian Studies*, 31(31), pp. 19–34.

MacDonald, H. (2003). Doing More with Less: The Sisters of St. Martha (PEI) Diminish the Impact of the Great Depression. *Acadiensis*, 33(1), p. 21.

MacEachern, A. (1999). The Greening of Green Gables: Establishing Prince Edward Island National Park. *The Island Magazine*, 45, p. 23.

MacEachern, A. and MacDonald, E. (2022). *The Summer Trade: A History of Tourism on Prince Edward Island*. Montreal and Kingston: McGill Queen's University Press, p. 141.

MacKinnon, L. and High, S. (2023). Deindustrialization in Canada: New Perspectives. *Labour/Le Travail*, 91, pp. 13–30.

Massey, D. (1978). Regionalism: Some Current Issues. *Capital and Class*, 2(3), pp. 106–107.

McCutcheon, S. and Walker, J. (2020). Great Mining Camps of Canada 8. The Bathurst Mining Camp, New Brunswick, Part 2: Mining History and Contributions to Society. *Geoscience Canada*, 47(3), p. 152.

McInnis, P. (2002). *Harnessing Labour Confrontation: Shaping the Postwar Settlement in Canada, 1943–1950.* Toronto: University of Toronto Press.

McKay, I. (1992). *The Quest of the Folk: Antimodernism and Cultural Selection in Twentieth Century Nova Scotia.* Montreal and Kingston: McGill-Queen's University Press.

Nerbas, D. (2018). Empire, Colonial Enterprise, and Speculation: Cape Breton's Coal Boom of the 1860s. *The Journal of Imperial and Commonwealth History*, 46(6), pp. 1067–1095.

Núñez Seixas, X.M. and Storm, E. (2018). Introduction: Region, Nation, and History. In Núñez Seixas, X.M. and Storm, E. (eds.) *Regionalism and Modern Europe: Identity Construction and Movements from 1890 to the Present Day.* London: Blooms.

O'Brien, M. (2011). Producers versus Profiteers: The Politics of Class in Newfoundland during the First World War. *Acadiensis*, 40(1), pp. 45–69.

Paasi, A. (1986). The Institutionalization of Regions: A Theoretical Framework for Understanding the Emergence of Regions and the Constitution of Regional Identity. *Fennia*, 164(1), pp. 105–146.

Paasi, A. (2009). The Resurgence of the 'Region' and 'Regional Identity': Theoretical Perspectives and Empirical Observations on Regional Dynamics in Europe. *Review of International Studies*, 35(S1), pp. 121–146.

Parenteau, B. (2013). Looking Backward, Looking Ahead: History and the Future of the New Brunswick Forest Industries. *Acadiensis*, 42(2), pp. 92–113.

Passoli, L. (2009). Bureaucratizing the Atlantic Revolution: The "Saskatchewan Mafia" in the New Brunswick Civil Service, 1960–1970. *Acadiensis*, 38(1), pp. 126–150.

Pickersgill, J.W. (1975). *My Years with Louis St. Laurent: A Political Memoir.* Toronto: University of Toronto Press.

Reid, J. and Reid, J. (2016). The Multiple Deindustrializations of Canada's Maritime Provinces and the Evaluation of Heritage-Related Urban Regeneration. *London Journal of Canadian Studies*, 31, pp. 89–112.

Reilly, N. (1980). The General Strike in Amherst, Nova Scotia, 1919. *Acadiensis*, 9(2), pp. 56–77.

Sager, E. and Painting, G. (1990). *Maritime Capital: The Shipping Industry in Atlantic Canada, 1820–1914.* Montreal and Kingston: McGill Queen's University Press.

Savoie, D. (1992). *Regional Economic Development: Canada's Search for Solutions.* Second edition. Toronto: University of Toronto Press.

Savoie, D. (2009). *I'm from Bouctouche, Me. Roots Matter.* Montreal and Kingston: McGill-Queen's University Press.

Stanley, D. (1984). *Louis Robichaud: A Decade of Power.* Halifax: Nimbus.

Stanley, D. (1993). The 1960s: The Illusions and Realities of Progress. In Forbes, E.R. and Muise, D.A. (eds.) *The Atlantic Provinces in Confederation.* Toronto: University of Toronto Press and Acadiensis Press, pp. 421–459.

Stevens, G. (1973). *Stanfield.* Toronto: McClelland and Stewart.

Slumkoski, C. (2011). *Inventing Atlantic Canada: Regionalism & the Maritime Reaction to Newfoundland's Entry into Canadian Confederation.* Toronto: University of Toronto Press.

Thiesen, A. (1995). *G.I. Smith and Economic Development in Nova Scotia.* MA Thesis, Saint Mary's University. Halifax, Nova Scotia.

Wardhaugh, R. and Ferguson, B. (2021). *The Rowell-Sirois Commission and the Remaking of Canadian Federalism.* Vancouver: UBC Press.

Webb, J. (2016). *Observing the Outports: Describing Newfoundland Culture, 1950–1980.* Toronto: University of Toronto Press.

Wicke, C. (2018). Introduction: Industrial Heritage and Regional Identities. In Wicke, C. Berger, S. and Golombek, J. (eds.) *Industrial Heritage and Regional Identities.* New York: Routledge, pp. 1–12.

Wilson, G. (2009). *Communities Left Behind: The Area Redevelopment Administration, 1945–1965.* Knoxville: The University of Tennessee Press.

9

DEINDUSTRIALIZATION AND NATIONHOOD

Ewan Gibbs

Introduction

Since it was first popularized as a term by economists during the 1970s, deindustrialization has been inextricably linked to political nationhood. Within Canada, the US, and Britain, the closure of smelters, shipyards, mines, and factories was understood as highly threatening to the national interest. Industrial ruination came to symbolize American domination of the Canadian economy on the one hand and the relative decline of economies perceived to be losing ground to foreign competition within both Britain and the US on the other. In these early readings, deindustrialization was pathologized and viewed as rooted in the failings of national industrial economies. Those sentiments foregrounded a diverse range of folk villains who had transgressed the nation, including politicians, financial interests or multinational corporations, and organized labor.

As deindustrialization has progressed, and become a generalized experience across developed economies, its political meaning has continued to be contested within national framings. Scholars and journalists examining 'right-wing populism' have drawn attention to deindustrialization as an explanation for the election of Donald Trump and support for 'Brexit' (British exit from the European Union) as well as the subsequent election of a raft of Conservative MPs in former Labour Party 'heartlands' within the 'red wall' of ex-industrial constituencies in Northern and Central England. Studies of North Rhine Westphalia in Germany and the Northwest of Italy similarly reveal connections between the erosion of employment in mines, steelmaking, and car manufacturing and the growing support for anti-immigrant far-right parties. Often these parties use motifs associated with the labor movement, donning the rhetorical gab of class conflict to claim that they speak for a forgotten, rooted, nativist plebian electorate. Political scientists such as Brown and Mondon (2021, p. 284) have warned that academic research and journalism have reinforced "the simplistic association of the working class and the far right" by naturalizing claims by right-wing nationalists that they in fact represent the authentic voice of disaffected working-class constituencies. These developments were epitomized by the former Conservative British Prime Minister Theresa May's claim that her Brexit agenda privileged "the spirit of citizenship." For May, this "means you respect the bonds and obligations that make our society work," and it is an ethic juxtaposed

DOI: 10.4324/9781003308324-14

to the ruthless "citizen of nowhere," whose numbers notably included employers who hire migrants over British workers (May, 2016).

While there is a close association between deindustrialization and the decline of the labor movement and social democracy as it developed during the twentieth century, the contention that deindustrialization leads to the triumph of xenophobic politics requires a more critical inspection. This chapter begins with an overview of deindustrialization scholarship, emphasizing the long-standing importance of nationhood to assessments of seismic economic changes associated with the end of large-scale industrial employment. Such assessments have evolved from earlier attempts to explain deindustrialization where it was negatively received by the workers and communities affected through to the discussions of the particularities of national political economy. During the twenty-first century, following on from the increased salience of 'populist' forces on the right, deindustrialization has become associated with explaining why constituencies that were formerly associated with left, social-democratic, or progressive politics have shifted.

Economic change provides a materialist basis for those changes, but such explanations also overstate the power of political causation associated with deindustrialization. Rather than a causal factor, deindustrialization should be understood as a context whose meaning is contested by political forces. These can produce diverse and divergent outcomes but shifting politicized understandings of nationhood is a dominant feature of deindustrialization, which is an experience that fundamentally questions the dominant understandings of the economy of industrial nations. Those have not exclusively been shaped from the right, however. Contemporary Scottish nationalism provides a centrist to center-left contrast to the radical right politics which has exercised a strong influence over deindustrialization scholarship. The second and third sections of this chapter assess how Scottish nationalism has been shaped by the long experience of declining industrial employment since the 1960s. It begins by examining how arguments for both independence and a devolved Scottish Parliament within the UK were molded by trade union opposition to workplace closures between the 1960s and 1990s. The second section overviews the role that collective memory of late twentieth-century deindustrialization has played in shaping politics in Scotland under devolution. These sections draw on research from trade union archives and records of the Scottish National Party (SNP), the main pro-independence party which has governed Scotland since 2007. They are supplemented by oral history interviews recorded during 2020 and 2021 with pro-independence politicians and their advisors which were themed around how Scottish nationalists interpreted experiences of job loss and economic change.

The Nation in Deindustrialization Scholarship

Industry has been central to how nations are imagined and understood at both elite and popular levels. As Adam Tooze (1998, pp. 214–215) convincingly explains, production and employment data became a defining feature of 'official nationalism' within industrialized economies such as Germany, the UK, and the US during the twentieth century. Localized or regional trends and events fed into a "a wider narrative, that of the national economy," including its achievements and also its fragilities and failures. Deindustrialization, the sustained fall of industrial employment and the declining significance of industrial sectors to overall economic production, shook the assumptions that these perspectives were built around. The prolonged contraction of the industrial workforce was fundamentally different from earlier periodic cyclical recessions or the shifts between sectors, which were an enduring feature of industrial economies. The permanent shrinking of industry destabilized older ways of imagining the national economy, but these perspectives in turn also had a sustained impact upon how deindustrialization itself was understood.

When it was first popularized as a term in the 1970s, deindustrialization was associated in political terms with the failure of national government policies and firms in (former) leading industrial economies. These motifs were strongly visible in responses to the onset of sustained contractions in industrial employment on both sides of the Atlantic. Britain's Chancellor of the Exchequer, Dennis Healey, referred to "deindustrialization" when he defined the core economic objectives of the Labour government as he moved the national budget for 1975, explaining that "there is a vast task of regeneration ahead of us. We must reverse the process of deindustrialization – of a steady loss of jobs and factory capacity year after year."[1] Healey articulated a view that closely associated falling employment in manufacturing with the loss of national prestige, technological leadership, and worsening economic fundamentals, especially as these related to the balance of payments which depended on Britain's capacity to pay for raw materials with manufacturing exports. As Jim Tomlinson (2022) has emphasized, Healey was responding to an agenda defined by economists such as Bacon and Eltis, who had acted as key opinion formers through newspaper columns in advance of the budget. Month before, they had bluntly implored him to "get more people into factories" (*Sunday Times*, 10 November 1974, quoted in Tomlinson, 2022, p. 623). While the Conservative government that took power under Margaret Thatcher in 1979 adopted policies which encouraged the dramatic escalation of manufacturing job losses, this was not their objective. Union recalcitrance was blamed for making British firms unproductive (Tomlinson, 2022).

A preoccupation with economic decline had earlier characterized British economic and political debate following the Second World War. Deindustrialization was understood as a culmination of failure. These discussions centered on comparing the performance of Britain with other advanced capitalist economies. Industry was central to these debates, first through the onset of job losses within textiles, mining, railway, and the docks during the 1950s but more pronouncedly across manufacturing sectors in the 1960s (Edgerton, 2018). This context shaped early deindustrialization scholarship. An influential example was the *De-Industrialisation* collection of articles edited by Frank Blackaby. It was published in 1979, based on papers presented to a National Institute of Economic and Social Research conference the previous year. In the foreword, Charles Cater, an influential British economist, set the tone by underlining the negative and national nature of falling industrial employment and the diminishing significance of industrial output to overall production: "It was the general view of the conference, that in the circumstances of the United Kingdom, deindustrialization is associated with a general economic sickness which urgently calls for a cure" (Carter, 1979, p. v). Sir Alec Cairncross, a former adviser to Harold Wilson's 1960s Labour government and a prominent Keynesian economist, put forward a definition of deindustrialization which underlined relative economic performance rather than changes to the economic structure:

> De-industrialization is to be interpreted as a progressive failure to achieve a sufficient surplus of exports over imports of manufactures to keep the economy in general balance. . . . De-industrialization can be defined as involving the absence of an efficient manufacturing sector in this sense.
>
> *(Cairncross, 1979, p. 10)*

Deindustrialization and Nationhood

In the US, deindustrialization was also experienced in traumatic national terms. Bluestone and Harrison's (1982, p. 15) foundational study of plant closures within the emergent Rust Belt of the former "heartland" states in the Midwest and the Northeast explained that "deindustrialization does not just happen." This book, which stimulated the internationalization of "the deindustrialization thesis," was written during the height of catastrophic job losses and skyrocketing unemployment (High, 2014, p. 996). It pointed to the breakdown in shared interests between US-headquartered multinationals and their American workforces as the chief explanation for workplace closures. Territorial logics of industrial production changed as companies began pursuing 'runaway shop' tactics within the US, moving production to non-union workplaces in states with lower wages and more pliant workforces. Later, at the invitation of US government policy within the Cold War context, inward investment became the characteristic form of the runaway shop while firms such as US Steel abandoned iconic production centers like Youngstown, Ohio, and Pittsburgh, Pennsylvania (Bluestone and Harrison, 1982).

Bluestone and Harrison's emphasis on a broken social contract has been a characteristic feature of deindustrialization scholarship. Often this implicitly and sometimes explicitly features proletarian workers enjoying a venerated status within an industrial nation. These sentiments extended across the divide between the capitalist West and communist East during the Cold War. Guy Standing (2009) has characterized a shared shift from "industrial citizens," the predominantly male manufacturing, transport, or extractive workers who enjoyed economic security and cultural recognition towards the more diverse "precariat" employed on "flexible" insecure terms as shaping deindustrialization since the late twentieth century and characterizing its enduring political significance.

Scholarship from former socialist economies chimes with Standing's assessment by underlining the pertinence of the loss of status within societal hierarchies keenly felt by former and remaining industrial workers. Mrozowicki's (2011, p. 99) study of Silesian workers underlined "The devaluation of labor" in Polish public discourses. His respondents, encompassing male and female manual service staff as well as manufacturing workers and miners, felt constrained by "the shrinking structural and institutional foundations of work-related life projects." Archer (2018) found that former manual workers in Belgrade, who had shopfloor experiences from the 1970s and 1980s, shared a 'pan-Yugoslav' experience of diminishing economic and social rewards from employment. This was a long process, beginning from adverse economic impact of the 1979 oil shock and Tito's death soon after but extending through the breakup of Yugoslavia and to the war in Kosovo in the late 1990s. Respondents shared an affinity with graffiti in Croatian port city of Pula, which read "It was better when it was worse." The experience of new state formation for these workers was associated with accelerating inequality and employment law liberalizations that permitted layoffs and rising unemployment. Li (2015) concluded that employees of China's state-owned steel enterprises have internalized their own relegation in national life. Before the full weight of economic restructuring took force during the 1990s, workers enjoyed a privileged position which was celebrated in steelworks hooters blaring out anthems and the steelworker being depicted on national currency. Nationalized enterprises now rank behind the "market heroes" employed in export processing factories, who were even lionized in a new series of songs that replaced the old ones.

Vulnerability to decisions made by other agents, often located outside the nation, has been a powerful stimulant in nationalist responses to deindustrialization (High, 2005). National consciousness stimulated the sense of betrayal articulated by American manufacturing workers who lost their jobs to disinvestment during the 1970s and 1980s, but there were formative distinctions between the American Midwest and the Canadian Golden Horseshoe on either side of the Great Lakes. Canadian autoworkers were comparatively successful in their efforts to preserve manufacturing jobs through marshalling nationalist symbols and economic arguments. These rested on the implications of the Canadian economy being subject to the whims of American multinationals (Anastakis, 2007). By contrast, workers within the Midwest were dismissed as experiencing merely "a regional crisis" and not a national one in the US context (High, 2003, p. 35).

As deindustrialization has become a focus of historical research during the twenty-first century, it has also increasingly been held as an explanatory factor for political changes broadly associated with the crisis of the left and its failure to continue representing traditional working-class constituencies. For instance, the "Deindustrialization and the Politics of Our Time" (DéPot, n.d.) project, by far the largest transnational research project to have been undertaken on deindustrialization, states in its "About Us" explanation on its website that

> Brexit, the election of Donald Trump as US President, and the rise of right-wing populism across continental Europe have refocused attention on the connections between political events and deindustrialized working-class communities. . . . Decades of internalized despair have exploded into a populist revolt as many deindustrialized areas have seen a massive shift in voting patterns from centrist or leftist parties to the radical right.
>
> *(DéPot, "About Us," n.d.)*

Influential scholarly analyses that link deindustrialization with the emergence of 'right-wing populism' sustain these contentions. Alter and Zürn (2020, p. 556) have recently defined "backlash politics" as "retrograde, aiming to revert to a prior social condition." Opposition to economic and social liberalization is often held to be a central feature of right-wing populism. Assessments of electoral support for the Republican Party under Donald Trump's leadership by political scientists Baccini and Weymouth found a direct correlation between the likelihood of white voters supporting the Republicans and levels of recent local manufacturing job loss (Baccini and Weymouth, 2021). Sherry Lee Linkon's (2018, pp. xvi–7) "half-life of deindustrialization" provides a means to understand the long-term development of political changes. She theorizes that the "toxic" effects of job losses, disinvestment, and the environmental scarring of former industrial landscapes have shaped "the politics of resentment," which led former autoworker and steelworkers and their family members to vote for Trump in 2016. These "hidden injuries" stimulate regressive social attitudes, especially among white men who feel they have lost their economic and cultural standing, not suddenly but across a harder-to-define "liminal period."

Scholarship on the rise of far-right parties in Western Europe has often reached similar conclusions about the increasing salience of nationhood for disaffected constituencies that were formerly connected to strategic areas of industrial production. Garruccio's (2022) account of her oral history research in Sesto San Giovanni, a steel town on the edge of Milan, addresses its transformation from the 'Stalingrad of Italy' toward a settlement where racist nationalism has been on the rise in the twenty-first century. Local politicians attempted to block the building of a mosque, while a persisting sense of falling behind Milan has characterized reflections on the suburb's economy. In the Ruhr valley, the 'cradle' of Germany's industrial economy, the far right adopted a starker strategy of directly appropriating the region's history of working-class politics during the 2010s. Guido Reill, a former Essen councilor and trade unionist who moved to the far-right Alternative for Deutschland (AfD) party from the Social Democratic Party, was depicted in miners' clothing on his election material and explained his switch to the AfD because he was "at heart a Social Democrat" (Berger, Musso, and Wicke, 2022, pp. 1–10). In his autoethnography on growing up and leaving Reims in Northwestern France, Didier Eribon (2018) powerfully reflects on how male members of his family, who worked in manual working-class jobs and had previously identified with the Communist Party, now voted for the far right. They transferred existing regressive attitudes in terms of nationality, gender, and sexuality, especially where the latter could be held to accord to middle-class deviancy, but also communicated a sense of loss and despair at the direction of French society and their place within it.

These accounts demonstrate the need to avoid deterministic readings of the relationship between deindustrialization and the rise of the far right. Recent research has revised Baccini and Weymouth's (2021) conclusion on the direct relationship between manufacturing job losses and support for the Republican Party among white voters (Jeannet and Maneuvrier-Hervieu, 2022). Instead, a less deterministic understanding of how deindustrialization is politicized by varying tendencies in ways which connect the history of particular sectors, localities, and nations is essential. One example of this is the approach Mike Makin-Waite (2021) takes to understanding the riots in Burnley, Lancashire, during 2001 and the subsequent election of far-right British National Party councilors. Makin-Waite's analysis is founded upon the view that deindustrialization is a context rather than a causation in political terms:

> Although industrial ruination was a key contributing factor, such politics were never the only possible response to socioeconomic change. The decline in manufacturing provides an important backdrop to recent political developments in Burnley. But suggesting that far-right impulses were automatic in such circumstances is to accept as an explanation what has to be explained.
>
> *(Makin-Wait, 2021, p. 23)*

Deindustrialization is a fundamental challenge to dominant political understandings of the economy of industrial nations. Responses to deindustrialization within divergent capitalist and socialist contexts since the 1970s have commonly included dislocation and betrayal, often framed in strongly national terms. Recent scholarship from Europe and North America has tended to underline the link between former industrial localities and regions and support for the far right. Tracing and understanding links between the immediate and longer-term experience of economic change with shifts in political alignments and how these are connected to nationhood is important and characterized by significant agency. In the two-section discussion of Scottish nationhood and deindustrialization that follows, we will see a different set of outcomes flow from similar changes to the economic structure experienced in Burnley: the emergence of a broadly center-left and latterly increasingly pro-European Union form of nationalism.

Deindustrialization and Scottish Nationhood I: The 1950s to 1990s

Scotland was a maturing industrial economy in the middle of the twentieth century. As demonstrated in Figure 9.1 and Table 9.1, approaching 40% of the workforce, and nearing one million workers, were employed in manufacturing and mining and quarrying in 1951.

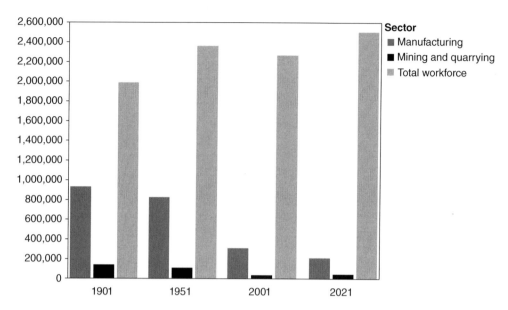

Figure 9.1 Scottish employment, 1901–2021

Table 9.1 Scottish industrial employment since 1901 (Population Census 1901; Digest of Scottish Statistics 1953; Population Census 2001l Scottish Government, Scotland's Labour Market: People, Places and Regions – background tables and charts (2021)

Year	Total workforce	Mining and quarrying	(%)	Manufacturing	(%)
1901	1,982,812	132,183	7	923,800	47
1951	2,357,000	100,000	4	818,000	35
2001	2,261,281	28,118	1	299,213	13
2021	2,500,000	33,980	1	202,396	8

Still more were employed in power generation and transportation among other sectors often considered as industrial. By the early twenty-first century, the industrial workforce stood at around a third of its previous level in absolute terms and accounted for less than 15% of Scottish workers. These trends have continued since the establishment of a devolved Scottish Parliament within the UK in 1999. During the twenty-first century, the industrial workforce has fallen to account for under a quarter of a million workers and to less than 10% of an expanding employed population. Deindustrialization has been the defining economic event of the past seven decades in Scotland. The closure of mines, mills, factories, and shipyards has been the economic substance behind the political changes associated with growing support for both independence and devolution.

Two referendums in 2014 and 2016 illustrate these changes but also demonstrate the distinctive nature of these developments within a broader UK setting. In 2014, a referendum on Scottish independence was held after the election of an SNP Scottish Parliamentary majority three years earlier. The result, a 45% vote for independence and 55% against, saw just four of 32 local authority areas voting in favor of independence. Notably, each of these was strongly associated with the impact of deindustrialization. They comprised the ex-manufacturing cities of Glasgow and Dundee, the former coal mining and steelmaking settlements of North Lanarkshire and West Dunbartonshire, where the largest population center is the former shipbuilding town of Clydebank (Scottish Electoral Commission, 2015). Two years later, Scotland voted to reject Brexit more decisively, with 62% of those voting favoring remaining within the European Union. All the local authority areas of Scotland voted in favor of Remain (The Electoral Commission, 2019). These outcomes contrasted with the strength of the Leave vote in former industrial regions elsewhere in the UK. As Beynon and Hudson's (2021, p. 320) recent study of the long-term impact of colliery closures emphasizes, "it was the working-class vote in the North of England and in South Wales that tipped the balance" by delivering a narrow victory for Brexit across the UK.

These distinctive outcomes were long in the making, with deep origins in the politicization of Scottish nationhood through the experience of deindustrialization and the popularization of devolution and independence. Industrial job losses, as well as the role of nationalized industries and of UK government policies in shaping these outcomes, were formative to the national nature of Scottish opposition to ostensibly local redundancies or workplace closures. These sentiments were first strongly articulated during the 1960s, which was also the SNP's first period of sustained electoral advance. SNP fortunes began to turn when the future party leader Billy Wolfe polled 20%, coming second, at the West Lothian by-election in 1962. A broad upswing lasted until the party obtained its best twentieth-century election result at the British general election in October 1974, winning over 30% of the Scottish popular vote and 11 seats (Lynch, 2013, p. 109). In 1962, Wolfe had forcefully articulated his opposition to what he termed the "economic and social murder" of West Lothian's shale oil industry by the terms of British entry to the European Free Trade Area and the greed of BP, who opted to import petroleum from the Middle East in place of shale. His perspective garnered support within the context of sustained coal mining closures in the area.[2]

SNP electoral and economic strategy centered upon the deleterious impact of Britain's increasingly centralized industrial structure and the view that Scotland was disadvantaged through decision-making that centered on London. These costs of the Anglo-Scottish Union were held to justify the case for independence. When the SNP had a significant parliamentary presence during the mid-1970s, its representatives put this message forward during instances of industrial closures. At this time, Douglas Crawford MP spoke in support of the party's Save Scottish Steel campaign, which denounced Scotland being "forced into dependence on outside sources for one of the most basic materials of industry" through the nationalized British Steel Corporation's decision to rationalize production and close large numbers of Scottish mills.[3] Earlier in the decade, the *SNP Research Bulletin* circular distributed to party members approvingly quoted Jimmy Reid, the leader of the Upper Clyde Shipbuilders (UCS) work-in, when he declared that "there is nothing wrong with nationalism – as long as it is a healthy nationalism – in which you love all that is good in your culture, in your history, in your traditions, and so in turn respect similar feelings held by those in other countries" (SNP, 1972, p. 3). The work-in was a successful campaign that saved three of the four UCS yards from closure and preserved jobs on the Clyde. Reid led the dispute as a shopfloor trade union representative and Communist Party of Great Britain (CPGB) activist. He adopted a left-wing nationalist orientation, contrasting the interests of Scottish industrial communities with the decisions of "faceless men" in Whitehall and the increasingly unpopular Conservative government they served (Knox and McKinlay, 2019).

There were important distinctions in constitutional politics between the capital-n Nationalists and labor movement supporters of devolution – more commonly known as 'home rule' – but they shared a commitment to using the economic levers of increased political autonomy to stem the impact of deindustrialization. When he unsuccessfully stood for parliament in Dunbartonshire Central, principally Clydebank, as a CPGB candidate in 1974, Jimmy Reid warned voters that Scotland faced a "Lowland Clearances" of "genocidal" proportions unless a devolved Scottish Assembly was established to preserve Scotland's economic and cultural fabric (Reid, 1976, pp. 121–122). Reid's party comrade, Michael McGahey, was also the President of the National Union of Mineworkers Scottish Area (NUMSA). McGahey had articulated similar sentiments in a less drastic tone a few years earlier during the 1968 annual congress of Scotland's union federation, the Scottish Trades Union Congress (STUC). In moving a motion which favored a devolved parliament, McGahey asserted a class-conscious case for "the decentralization of power" within the UK. Notably, this resolution was remitted rather than rejected, a significant marker in the Scottish labor movement's orientation toward devolution during the late twentieth century and shifting away from supporting a unitary British state.[4] McGahey's case was reinforced by the view that the centralized management of the National Coal Board had contributed to intensifying pit closures within the Scottish coalfields. When he addressed the National Energy Conference of producer and consumer organizations that the UK government's Department of Energy held in 1976, McGahey underlined the costs of closures and the distinctive national interests of Scotland's 27,000 remaining miners, who numbered less than a third of their total 20 years earlier. The impact of deindustrialization, McGahey asserted, was permanent and cumulative. Unlike other industrial workplaces, pits could not be mothballed: "No generation is entitled to deny future generations their original inheritance" (Department of Energy, 1976, p. 40).

The sense of finality in this statement grew with mass unemployment and the impact of increasingly adverse economic and political circumstances following the election of Margaret Thatcher's Conservative government in 1979. These led to a dramatic increase in plant closures and loss of manufacturing capacity but also to attacks on nationalized industries and eventual privatization (Tomlinson, 2022). The labor movement and SNP figures began to recognize these changes as amounting to deindustrialization rather than just job losses in particular sectors. In 1982, Alex Salmond, the future SNP First Minister from 2007 to 2014, emphasized that "a process of deindustrialization continues apace and the pillars of Scottish industry are systematically dismantled."[5] The next year, Michael McGahey used the same term at the NUMSA's annual conference when he called for workers in steel, rail, and shipbuilding to support the miners in campaigning against colliery closures and also in demanding that the Labour Party support a renewed campaign for devolution.[6] This logic was strengthened following Labour's defeat in the 1983 general election. Despite Labour winning a majority of seats and the most votes of any party in Scotland, English votes and seats delivered a Tory parliamentary majority. Decisive defeat for the miners in the 1984–1985 strike compounded these developments. Not long after the dispute ended, the NUMSA's Vice-President, George Bolton, who replaced McGahey following his retirement two years after, was critical of the NUM's President, Arthur Scargill and his prominent English supporters such as the Midlands Labour MPs Dennis Skinner and Tony Benn. Bolton argued that they expounded "a range of thinking in the movement that's not caught up with the reality of Thatcher and Thatcherism, and the state of British politics" (Priscott, 1985,

p. 24). His perspective was symptomatic of the failure of Britain-wide industrial action and electoral politics to deliver favorable outcomes which encouraged Scottish trade unionists and Labour Party politicians to support devolution.

After the miners' strike, campaigns against steel closures mobilized a growing political coalition behind preserving Scotland's industrial future and distinctive national economic interest. During 1986, nine men marched 450 miles to London from the threatened Gartcosh steelworks in North Lanarkshire. Their number included Iron and Steel Trades Confederation union officials, but they were joined by representatives from Labour, the SNP, and the Liberal Party. An SNP election leaflet produced soon after profiled the dispute in national terms, declaring that "this march is about truth, honesty and the rights of the people of Scotland."[7] In 1992, as Scotland's last major steelworks, Ravenscraig, not far from Gartcosh in Motherwell, faced closure, Kay Ulrich, the SNP's candidate for Motherwell South at the upcoming general election glibly insisted that "The Ravenscraig closure could not possible happen except in a country without a government."[8]

The SNP's insistence that only independence would save Ravenscraig, and their happiness to support Scottish workers against those in South Wales and the North of England whose futures were also threatened by privatization, divided them from the larger swathe of trade union and Labour Party-affiliated activists and politicians who led the campaign against closures. Nevertheless, the forming of a broad civil society campaign asserting Scottish national economic interests around Ravenscraig only further instilled labor movement support for devolution and a sense of divergent political consciousness between Scotland and England (Stewart, 2005).

A formative example was the Day for Scotland event hosted by the STUC in the grounds of Stirling Castle on July 14, 1990. The event combined culture and politics, including appearances from leading Scottish pop and rock bands. Industrial causes were arranged around the demand for a Scottish Parliament. Afterwards, the STUC hailed the event as "an outstanding success," claiming that 40,000 people had attended.[9] The contrasting influences which came together in the castle grounds are best summarized by the STUC's President, Clive Lewis, a Welsh steelworker who subsequently found work in Scotland, leading chants of 'Ravenscraig!' while dressed in his son's leather jacket. Keith Aitken's (1997, p. 296) history of the STUC underlines that "not many rock festivals cheer for steelmills," but one of the bands that appeared at the event, the folk-rock band, Runrig, had written a song about Ravenscraig. Their guitarist, Pete Wishart, went onto become an SNP MP in 2001 (UK Parliament, n.d.). The gathering in Stirling came nearly a decade before a Scottish Parliament was eventually realized. It demonstrated the pluralistic political and societal forces behind devolution while also confirming the central role played by the labor movement and responses to industrial job losses and workplace closures in shaping and popularizing the demand for a Parliament.

Deindustrialization and Scottish Nationhood II: Scotland Under Devolution

While the Scottish Parliament was an outcome of mobilizations against workplace closures, it arrived late in the period of major economic change. By 1999, Scotland had lost its last basic steel capacity, its shipbuilding industry was reduced to a small number of yards, and its last deep coal mine would close three years afterwards (Harvie, 2001, pp. 502–503; Gibbs, 2021a, p. 2). As Figure 9.1 and Table 9.1 demonstrate, by the opening years of the millennium, manufacturing employment had fallen sharply from its mid-twentieth-century level, but it has also continued to decline in both relative and absolute terms. The collective memory of industrial employment and deindustrialization has continued to play a significant role in molding politics under SNP Scottish governments since 2007, including through the framing of economic policy ambitions. These developments have not been without conflict. Clark and Gibbs (2020) found that within the Clydeside local authority areas of Inverclyde and North Lanarkshire, memorials to shipbuilding, coal mining, and steelmaking that have been unveiled within recent years are characterized by distinctions between regeneration initiatives and those erected by community groups. The former have tended toward memorializing a more abstract, passing, industrial era while the latter tend to commemorate specific events, including the loss of life in mining disasters or episodes of class struggle. This section considers the continued significance of deindustrialization within contemporary Scottish politics through assessing the development of the 'reindustrialization' agenda and related environmental 'just transition' ambitions along with the campaign by miners convicted of offences during the 1984–1985 strike which recently achieved important successes.

During the buildup to the 2014 referendum, the Scottish Government under Alex Salmond developed an agenda for economic change, which included a significant focus on responding to the legacy of deindustrialization. This included a proposal for *Reindustrialising Scotland*. The plan was built on assumptions which chimed with the arguments put forward by Dennis Healey around 40 years before. Manufacturing was cited as the key driver of economic growth and productivity as well as exports and balance of trade improvements. British failure, relative to other economies, closely echoing the analysis of Blackaby and other 1970s economists cited earlier, was another feature of the argument that Scottish industry would fare better under independence than by continuing to shed jobs in the Union. The plan centered on a proposal to create 100,000 new manufacturing jobs through increasing export volumes by half (Scottish Government, 2014). These were exceedingly ambitious objectives, especially given they related to competitive sectors with global supply chains such as wind turbine manufacturing. Recent analyses have revealed the sharp challenges facing Scottish yards engaged in cutthroat competition for labor-intensive fabrication work while often lacking the expertise in more advanced areas such as blade production and design (Gibbs, 2021b; Meek, 2021).

Phillips, Tomlinson, and Wright's (2021) monograph study concluded that the hopes invested in 'reindustrialization' by the SNP, the pro-independence Scottish Greens, as well as the Labour Party, were an understandable response to the long-term impacts of deindustrialization: insecure work and stagnating incomes. Nevertheless, these hopes were also misplaced in solving "central problem of deindustrialization," namely the "loss of relatively well-paid jobs that could be undertaken by citizens with rudimentary entry-level skills and qualifications" (Phillips, Wright, and Tomlinson, 2021, p. 243). Contemporary manufacturing sectors are increasingly capital- and knowledge-intensive, requiring levels of qualifications far beyond many of the jobs in more labor-intensive jobs which have been lost in recent decades. The faith placed in reindustrialization is though revealing of how the experience of deindustrialization was formative to contemporary nationalism. In an oral history recorded in 2021, which considered the role that energy resources have played in arguments for independence, Kevin Pringle, who acted as a senior Special Advisor to Alex Salmond and later advised First Minister Humza Yousaf, discussed being socialized within the party through collective memories of the 1962 West Lothian byelection and the campaign to save the shale industry. Pringle explained that although he had not even been born at the time, these experiences were key reference points to figures such as himself, and Alex Salmond, a West

Lothian native, in devising reindustrialization and viewing renewable energy as central to an independent Scotland's economy.[10]

These sentiments were shared by younger nationalists and have evolved as responding to climate change has replaced reindustrialization as a dominant SNP economic objective within recent years. Dan Paris, who became an SNP Press Officer later in the decade, recalled that he joined the party in the run-up to the 2011 Scottish Parliament election, which he characterized as "the period when Salmond, in particular, was talking about, sort of, the green reindustrialization of Scotland, which I did think was very attractive at the time."[11] Paris's insistence on the green character of reindustrialization has been reinforced in recent years as the Scottish Government has adopted a 'Just Transition' policy framework. This phrase, which has origins in the American labor movement, refers to planning industrial change in such a way that workers and communities who rely on employment in polluting industry are not adversely affected by their closure. These concerns are especially strongly felt with regard to North Sea oil and gas sector. In 2021, the Just Transition Commission, an independent advisory body to the Scottish government, published its National Mission, making explicit reference to the history of deindustrialization:

> The story of how Scotland lost much of its heavy industry through the 70s and 80s is well known and an example of how not to manage structural change. There was little in the way of a "just transition" for communities and families reliant on coal mining as pit closures swept the country. Decades later the impacts of this can still be felt.
>
> *(Just Transition Commission, 2021, p. 21)*

In an interview recorded with the author the previous year, Lorna Slater articulated the logic of a just transition in similar historical terms. Slater was then the co-leader of the Scottish Greens and an election candidate ahead of the 2021 Scottish Parliamentary election:

> That's what a Just Transition means. It means you plan it, in consultation with the people who are affected. The contrast is the sort of coal mining, the Thatcher era, where you closed down coal mines and devastate entire communities. And that's the problem because that's the model people have in their minds. And we say, we have to stop fossil fuels. People imagine their children going hungry. They imagine not having an income.[12]

Following her election as a Regional List MSP for the Lothians, Slater served as the Minister of Green Skills and Circular Economy from 2021 to 2024 in the new Scottish Government formed on the basis of partnership between the SNP and the Greens. Nicola Sturgeon, who succeeded Salmond in 2014 and served as First Minister until 2023, has also frequently drawn on the memory of deindustrialization to contrast her own beliefs and policy from those of past and current UK governments. Following the death of Margaret Thatcher in 2013, Sturgeon, who was then Deputy First Minister, referred to "The brutal deindustrialization she presided over, and the unemployment that resulted, [which] has left deep scars in every community in this city [, Glasgow,] and across Scotland" (STV, 2013). Eight years later, First Minister Sturgeon marshaled her own experience of growing up in industrial Ayrshire during the peak of coal and steel closures in the 1980s to reassure oil workers that she was concerned for their plight, explaining that: "I saw and remember first-hand the devastation that is done to people and communities when governments don't take care to take people along in a transition." Sturgeon said these experiences were "seared into her consciousness." Newspaper reporting by the *Press and Journal*, which covers the oil-reliant Northeast of Scotland, emphasized focus groups of locals also referring to fears that settlements dependent on offshore employment could be left in a comparable situation to ex-mining villages in the Central Belt (Ross, 2021).

Deindustrialization, especially the highly negative experiences of closures and job losses under the Thatcher governments of the 1980s, is an important dimension of national consciousness in Scotland and shapes contemporary economic debates. The framing of the unjust transition of the 1980s has been heightened by the recent campaign for just by Scottish miners who were convicted of offences related to the 1984–1985 strike. Their struggle for justice revealed both the complications and confluences between class and nation in Scotland, with echoes of the distinctions drawn between Clark and Gibbs in memories of Scotland's industrial past. Calls for a pardon and legal and political recognition of the deprivations striking miners suffered were initially resisted by SNP administrations keen to avoid accepting responsibilities for decisions that were taken by independent Scottish police forces and judiciary who nevertheless answered to a UK government before devolution (Phillips, 2015). In 2022, following on from the publication of a Scottish Government Independent Review into the policing of the strike during 2019, the SNP reversed this stance, leading to a parliamentary vote in favor of a pardon (Scottish Government, 2019). This was a victory for victimized miners, their families, and trade union comrades, as well as parliamentarians such as Neil Findlay, the Labour List MSP for the Lothians from 2011 to 2021, who had long campaigned for it. The Scottish Parliament and the Scottish Government recognized that Scottish miners had been victimized by politicized policing and judicial processes, leading to them being convicted and sacked in higher numbers than their strikers in England and Wales. This rendered their convictions unsafe and unjust (Phillips, 2023). These developments inform a broader perspective on the character of deindustrialization in the closing decades of the twentieth century, which acts as a powerful framing within contemporary politics even as the industrial sector of the Scottish economy continues to diminish.

Conclusion

Nationhood has been central to how deindustrialization has been experienced and interpreted. The closure of factories and mines and the shrinking of industrial workforces have often had a shuddering impact on industrial nations, challenging dominant understandings of the economy as well as the security and cultural standing enjoyed by workers and their families in manufacturing and mining regions. When deindustrialization began to fray at advanced economies in the closing decades of the twentieth century, it was interpreted as a national failing, revealing deficiencies within the economic structure in contrast to the performance of other nations. Even as those experiences have become generalized, these sentiments have not fully departed. Nationalist responses to workplace closures were common but varied in context. While Canadian workers rallied against the power of American corporations, workers in the US themselves struggled against what they saw as the disloyalty of their American employers who preferred to move production overseas. Disorientation within emergent economic structures and national cultural registers was also felt in the former planned economies of Eastern Europe and China. Here, heavy industry workers no longer enjoyed the enhanced economic citizenship or social standing that they had previously.

While much of the literature has assessed instances where the long-term impact of deindustrialization has been the erosion of support for social democratic parties and the growth of support for the far right, it is important to underline that this is far from a universal experience. Deindustrialization is better understood as a context whose meaning is contested and politicized in national terms by competing forces. The Scottish experience of the end of mass industrial employment over the second half of the twentieth century demonstrates that both the labor movement and nationalists sought to apply national framings to deindustrialization and were largely successful in doing so on broadly center-left terms. These outcomes have shaped a distinct trajectory from deindustrialized areas elsewhere within the UK in party and constitutional terms. Even into the 2020s, with industrial employment now running in single-digit percentages, the legacy of industrial employment and the experience of workplace closures during the 1980s are a powerful influence in politics. Collective memories of economic change exercise significant political power, and there is a strong tendency for historical narratives of deindustrialization to become a lasting feature of national consciousness.

Notes

1 Hansard, The Official Report: House of Commons, 5th ser., 15 April 1975, vol.890, col.288.
2 Billy Wolfe West Lothian 1962 by-election 40th anniversary celebration, Bathgate Golf Club, Saturday 15th June 2002. Scottish Political Archive (hereafter SPA) General Accession, Political Parties (hereafter GA/PP) 1 Strategy 50/3.
3 Press Release, 7 December 1975, National Library of Scotland, 10754, SNP, 26, Headquarters statements, 1974–1976.
4 STUC, Annual Report 1967–1968, p. 400.
5 Alex Salmond, "Introduction," *The Scottish Industrial Resistance* Paper 7 (1982): 1, SPA GA/PP/1 79 Group 2.
6 NUMSA, *Executive Committee Minutes, July 1982 to June 1983*, pp. 702–703, National Mining Museum of Scotland, Newton Grange.
7 "Introducing Ian Lawson" leaflet (1987), SPA GA/PP/1 Election Material/Falkirk.
8 "Steel and Freedom," *Scots Independent*, February 1992: 6, SPA, Scots Independent February 1992–January 1994.
9 Minutes of Meeting of the Finance and General Purposes Committee, 18 July 1990 in STUC General Council Minutes, April to May 1990, Records of the Scottish Trades Union Congress, Glasgow Caledonian University Archive Centre.
10 Kevin Pringle, remote interview with author, 22 January 2021.
11 Dan Paris, remote interview with author, 8 December 2020.
12 Lorna Slater, remote interview with author, 16 October 2020.

Reference List

Aitken, K. (1997). *The Bairns O'Adam: The Story of the STUC*. Edinburgh: Polygon.
Alter, K.J. and Zürn, M. (2020). Conceptualising Backlash Politics: Introduction to a Special Issue on Backlash Politics in Comparison. *The British Journal of Politics and International Relations*, 22, pp. 563–584.
Anastakis, D. (2007). Industrial Sunrise? The Chrysler Bailout, the State, and the Re-Industrialization of the Canadian Automotive Sector, 1975–1986. *Urban History*, 35, pp. 37–50.
Archer, R. (2018). 'It was Better when it was Worse': Blue-Collar Narratives of the Recent Past in Belgrade. *Social History*, 43, pp. 30–55.
Baccini, L. and Weymouth, S. (2021). Gone For Good: Deindustrialization, White Voter Backlash, and US Presidential Voting. *American Political Science Review*, 115, pp. 550–567.
Berger, S., Musso, S. and Wicke, C. (2022). The Unmaking of Industrial Landscapes – The North-Western Italian Industrial Triangle and the Ruhr Region in Germany. In Berger, S. Musso, S.

and Wike, C. (eds.) *Deindustrialisation in Twentieth-Century Europe The Northwest of Italy and the Ruhr Region in Comparison*. New York: Springer, pp. 1–10.

Beynon, H. and Hudson, R. (2021). *The Shadow of the Mine: Coal and the End of Industrial Britain*. London: Verso.

Bluestone, B. and Harrison, B. (1982). *The Deindustrialization of America: Plant Closings, Community Abandonment, and the Dismantling of Basic Industry*. New York: Basic Books.

Brown, K. and Mondon, A. (2021). Populism, the Media, and the Mainstreaming of the Far Right: The Guardian's Coverage of Populism as a Case Study. *Politics*, 41, pp. 279–295.

Cairncross, A. (1979). What is De-industrialisation? In Blackaby, F. (ed.) *De-Industrialisation*. London: Heinemann, pp. 5–17.

Carter, C. (1979). Foreword. In Blackaby, F. (ed.) *De-Industrialisation*. London: Heinemann, p. v.

Clark, A. and Gibbs, E. (2020). Voices of Social Dislocation, Lost Work and Economic Restructuring: Narratives from Marginalised Localities in the 'New Scotland'. *Memory Studies*, 13, pp. 39–59.

Deindustrialization and the Politics of Our Time (DePot). (n.d.). 'About Us', https://deindustrialization.org/about-us/

Department of Energy. (1976). *National Energy Conference June 22 1976: Volume 1: Report of Proceedings; Written Contributions*. London: HMSO.

Edgerton, D. (2018). *The Rise and Fall of the British Nation: A Twentieth-Century History*. London: Penguin.

The Electoral Commission. (2019, September 5). *EU Referendum Results by Region: Scotland*. https://www.electoralcommission.org.uk/who-we-are-and-what-we-do/elections-and-referendums/past-elections-and-referendums/eu-referendum/results-and-turnout-eu-referendum/eu-referendum-results-region-scotland

Eribon, D. (2018). *Returning to Reims*. London: Allen Lane.

Garruccio, R. (2022). 'The Master Director of all this is Time': An Oral History Project in Sesto San Giovanni. In Berger, S., Musso, S. and Wike, C. (eds.) *Deindustrialisation in Twentieth-Century Europe the Northwest of Italy and the Ruhr Region in Comparison*. New York: Springer, pp. 111–145.

Gibbs, E. (2021a). *Coal Country: The Meaning and Memory of Deindustrialization in Postwar Scotland*. London: University of London Press.

Gibbs, E. (2021b). Scotland's Faltering Green Industrial Revolution. *Political Quarterly*, 92, pp. 57–65.

Harvie, C. (2001). Scotland after 1978: from Referendum to Millennium. In Houston, R.A. and Knox, W.W. (ed.) *The New Penguin History of Scotland: From Earliest Times to the Present Day*. London: Penguin, pp. 494–531.

High, S. (2003). *Industrial Sunset: The Making of North America's Rustbelt*. Toronto: University of Toronto Press.

High, S. (2005). Capital and Community Reconsidered: The Politics and meaning of Deindustrialization. *Labor/Le Travail*, 55, pp. 194–195.

High, S. (2014). 'The Wounds of Class': A Historiographical Reflection on the Study of Deindustrialization, 1973–2013. *History Compass*, 11, p. 996.

Jeannet, A.-M. and Maneuvrier-Hervieu, P. (2022, July 9–11). *Reassessing the Backlash of Manufacturing Job Loss in US Presidential Elections*. Paper presented at the Annual Meeting, Society for Advancement of Socio-Economics (SASE), Amsterdam.

Just Transition Commission. (2021). *A National Mission for a Fairer, Greener Scotland*.

Knox, W.W.J. and McKinlay, A. (2019). *Jimmy Reid: A Clyde-Built Man*. Liverpool: Liverpool University Press.

Li, J. (2015). From 'Master' to 'Loser': Changing Working-Class Cultural Identity in Contemporary China. *International Labor and Working-Class History*, 88, pp. 190–208.

Linkon, S.L. (2018). *The Half-Life of Deindustrialization: Working-Class Writing about Economic Restructuring*. Ann Arbor: University of Michigan Press.

Lynch, P. (2013). *The History of the Scottish National Party*. Cardiff: Welsh Academic Press.

Makin-Wait, M. (2021). *On Burnley Road: Class, Race and Politics in a Northern English Town*. London: Lawrence and Wishart.

May, T. (2016, October 5). Full Text: Theresa May's Conference Speech. *The Spectator*. https://www.spectator.co.uk/article/full-text-theresa-may-s-conference-speech/

Meek, J. (2021). Who Holds the Welding Rod? *London Review of Books*, 43(14). https://www.lrb.co.uk/the-paper/v43/n14/james-meek/who-holds-the-welding-rod

Mrozowicki, A. (2011). *Coping with Social Change: Life Strategies of Workers in Poland's New Capitalism*. Leuven: Leuven University Press.

Phillips, J. (2015). Contested Memories: The Scottish Parliament and the 1984–5 Miners' Strike. *Scottish Affairs*, 24, pp. 187–206.

Phillips, J. (2023). Strategic Injustice and the 1984–85 Miners' Strike in Scotland. *Industrial Law Journal*, 52(2), pp. 283–311.

Phillips, J., Wright, V. and Tomlinson, J. (2021). *Deindustrialisation and the Moral Economy in Scotland since 1955*. Edinburgh: Edinburgh University Press.

Priscott, D. (1985). The Miners' Strike Assessed. *Marxism Today*, April 1985, pp. 21–27.

Reid, J. (1976). *Reflections of a Clyde-Built Man*. London: Souvenir Press.

Ross, C. (2021, May 5). Nicola Sturgeon Vows to Protect North-East from Post-Oil "Devastation". *Press and Journal*. https://www.pressandjournal.co.uk/fp/politics/scottish-politics

Scottish Electoral Commission. (2015). *Scottish Independence Referendum Electoral Data*.

Scottish Government. (2014). *Reindustrialising Scotland for the 21st Century: A Sustainable Industrial Strategy for a Modern, Independent Nation*.

Scottish Government. (2019). *Independent Review: Impact on Communities of the Policing of the Miners' Strike, 1984–85: Final Report*.

Stewart, D. (2005). Fighting for Survival: The 1980s Campaign to Save Ravenscraig Steelworks, *The Journal of Scottish Historical Studies*, 25, pp. 40–57.

SNP. (1972). *Research Bulletin*. October 1972.

STV. (2013, 17 April). Thatcher remembered: The Scottish Nationalist, Nicola Sturgeon. https://web.archive.org/web/20160722002348/http://stv.tv/news/west-central/221629-margaret-thatcher-remembered-by-nicola-sturgeon-msp-for-political-division/

Standing, G. (2009). *Work After Globalisation*. Cheltenham: Edward Elgar.

Tomlinson, J. (2022). Deindustrialisation and 'Thatcherism': Moral Economy and Unintended Consequences. *Contemporary British History*, 3, pp. 620–642.

Tooze, A. (1998). Imagining National Economies: National and International Economic Statistics, 1900–1950. In G. Cubitt (ed.) *Imagining Nations*. Manchester: Manchester University Press, pp. 212–228.

UK Parliament (n.d.). Pete Wishart. https://members.parliament.uk/member/1440/career

10

CHALLENGING AND POLITICIZING DEINDUSTRIALIZATION?

Marion Fontaine and Xavier Vigna

Introduction

Deindustrialization in the West, with its procession of factory closures, job destruction, and regional destructuring, has been marked by a number of significant and highly political conflicts. Among them, the UK miners' strike of 1984–1985 undoubtedly remains one of the most iconic.[1] The confrontation between coal workers and Margaret Thatcher's neoliberal government has been described by researchers, novelists (David Peace), and filmmakers (Ken Loach) as symbolizing the struggles linked to deindustrialization: the desperate resistance of miners seeking to safeguard their jobs, their way of life, and their community against the hard line of the state; the focus on working-class values, both political and moral, in the face of neoliberalism; the violence, along with the spectacle-driven and media-friendly nature of the struggle; the tragic consequences of defeat, etc. The hyper-visibility of this conflict, as well as its place in memory, should not obscure the issue: does it make up the standard, or at least a typical Western example, of the relationship between social conflict, the labor world, and politics in the era of mass closures? Or is it, on the contrary, an exception, a singular event that, on its own, does not represent the variability of workers' reactions, nor that of the states and the political forces linked to organized labor movements, when faced with such crises?

One must consider several types of parameters when responding to this issue. The first involves the visibility of protests, along with their power to take on a collective meaning, to hit a nerve within public opinion, and to resonate in the media. The miners' strike of 1984–1985, along with the steelworkers' movement in France at the end of the 1970s (Vigna, 2004), attest to such 'visibilization' and the ability of certain movements to become true symbols. However, a number of studies have shown that this increase in visibility is far from systematic and that a significant portion of closures took place quietly in the shadows; their impact was merely local, and at times individual, occurring under the shock and bitterness of the "half-lives" left behind by deindustrialization (High, 2019). These differences may result from temporal and geographical effects, along with the characteristics of industrial sectors, all of which are often linked to the composition of the labor world involved; thus, large bastions of heavy industry (steelmaking, e.g.) have often been shut down with

DOI: 10.4324/9781003308324-15

far more noise and fanfare than those of the textile industry, which was largely dominated by women.

The second parameter involves the evolution of "repertoires of collective action," a term summarized by political scientist Charles Tilly as "the set of established means that certain groups use to advance or defend their interests" (Tilly, 1984, p. 94). The social movements mentioned earlier, which are among the most spectacular, seem to present fairly homogeneous and standardized repertoires of action: the strong presence of labor unions, massive strikes, protests, and confrontations with law enforcement that varied in their degree of violence. But this is only one possible type of repertoire, one that is by no means immutable. Social struggles linked to deindustrialization span a relatively long period, from the 1950s to 1960s and almost to the present day. Thus, their forms have varied according to the evolution of the workers' group but also according to the mutations of social movements in general, as in the year of 1968. Strikes and protests can give way to more transgressive repertoires of action; they can be confined to the factory or, in contrast, spill over into the public arena; movements can emphasize their peaceful and 'respectable' nature to make their demands heard or, in contrast, deliberately take on more contentious and violent dimensions (sabotage, conflict with management representatives or the state).

The third and final parameter involves the political aspect, or rather the degree of politicization, always variable and random, surrounding protests involving deindustrialization. One way to define politicization involves the awareness of stakeholders outside the usual political games regarding the political dimension or scope of the activities involved and how these ordinary stakeholders intervene, act, or protest in political debates (Lagroye, 2003, pp. 365–366). But not every struggle involving factory closures has led to such awareness, nor have they all taken on a political scope: conflicts may be confined to a single site or a single locality, and they may involve nothing more than a face-to-face meeting between employer and employees to negotiate highly pragmatic objectives (timetable for the closure, number of jobs lost or preserved, compensation). Other times, these conflicts spill over and take on additional meaning for the stakeholders themselves: they can highlight the clash between certain attributes of the worker's "moral economy" (Phillips, 2013) – justice, stability, protection, concern for children's future – and representations of the world which, for example, value efficiency and competitiveness, as defined by dominant groups, whether employers or public authorities. Social movements involving deindustrialization can, at times, be linked to revolutionary aspirations or, at the least, radical protests of the capitalist system; they are also likely to focus on local national or social identities – an 'Us' versus a 'Them' with evolving contours (capitalists, the dominant, proponents of globalization, etc.) – while reshaping these identities in the process.

Once again, this dimension does not emerge naturally within all movements: it can saturate some but remain all but absent within others. While it is impossible for a single chapter to account for every form of politicization that surrounds deindustrialization-related protests, or their lack of politicization, we intend to focus on some of these forms while linking them to the two parameters mentioned earlier (visibility/invisibility; evolving repertoires of action).

We will do so within a relatively broad time frame, namely from the late 1950s to the 2000s. This period was marked by a culmination of left-wing forces and organized labor movements (Lutz, 2019), along with somewhat centralized relations between the culture of labor and the culture of militancy, which led to a golden age of struggles, especially between the 1960s and 1970s.[2] This political and oppositional dynamic eventually entered a state of dereliction, as the labor world and its movements weakened and fragmented. The role of the state at this time was undergoing considerable transformation, passing from the consolidation of the welfare state to its involution, primarily due to globalization and the imposition, at least in part, of new paradigms linked to 'neo-liberalism.' In this context, we will primarily focus on Western Europe and France in particular. This focus has not been chosen simply because the two authors of this chapter are more familiar with this terrain. The importance of the central government's role in social and economic life, along with the central role played by the communist movement for much of the period, as well as in political and union life, led to a rather peculiar twist in the relationship between deindustrialization, dissent, and politicization within this national context.[3] We will not, however, limit ourselves to this framework which, in any case, makes sense only in relation to other national cases, such as that of Great Britain, mentioned earlier, or Belgium and Italy.

From Growth to Crisis: The Genesis of Closure-Related Conflicts (Late 1950s–1970s)

The period of strong economic growth and modernization that took place between the 1950s and the 1970s is well known, both in France and elsewhere, as a time of significant social struggle and conflict.[4] These conflicts were both supported and fueled by traditional forces behind labor movements – the French Communist Party, General Confederation of Labour (CGT) but also, increasingly, by new political organizations (far left) and unions like the French Democratic Confederation of Labour (CFDT). Rooted in highly politicized contexts (the Cold War, anti-colonial struggles, the movements during the years of 1968), these struggles put forth the workers' desire for a greater share of the benefits of growth while increasingly challenging the traditional factory order: the pace of work, the relationship with lower management, the place of women and immigrant workers, etc. (Vigna, 2007).

While often obscured and lacking visibility in classic accounts of this period, the issues surrounding deindustrialization were very much present. As early as the 1950s, a number of small-scale industrial sectors rooted in rural areas (textiles, metallurgy, mining) appeared to be in crisis and gaining in years (Castellesi, 2019). Around this time, difficulties began to appear in several mining regions like Sardinia, in Southwest France and the Borinage region of Belgium. These difficulties have attracted sociologists seeking to investigate the response of workers in these "old" regions when faced with economic modernization (Barbichon and Moscovici, 1962), as well as that of national and even European institutions (European Coal and Steel Community), all of which were struggling to find remedies for the social problems caused by the industrial crises at hand (job destruction, territorial impoverishment etc.) (Verschueren, 2014).

The workers and residents of these territories did not, however, remain passive. Within a few years, several large-scale social movements broke out in the Borinage region in 1959, as well as at the Decazeville mines in Southwest France between December 1961 and January 1962; in March 1963, every miner in France went on strike demanding a wage increase while voicing their concerns regarding the future of their profession.[5] These movements appear fairly classical at first glance; they involve long-standing traditions of labor-related protest. They also involve a male-dominated profession and stem from regions with a strong militant heritage. They received strong support from local labor organizations, whether socialist (in the case of Belgium) or communist, but they also received support from the Young Christian Workers. They took on the anticipated forms, including mass strikes (in

March 1963, over 90% of miners went on strike in most mining pools), along with large-scale union and political meetings that included speeches, large crowds, and calls for solidarity from the entire working class.

But we should not let our thinking be skewed by apparent continuity. On the contrary, the protests that took place reveal that workers in these territories were aware of the stakes involved in a social and economic modernization process in which they felt victimized. In 1963, miners in the Nord and Lorraine regions used the slogan "We are the last," the last to grow, the forgotten; the miners of the Borinage region proclaimed "we want bread," while those of Decazeville, joined by nearby agricultural and factory workers, asserted their desire to "live and work in the country." The issue was not merely one of closures related to certain sites and mine shafts but very much a sense of marginalization within territories, the countryside, and traditional industries, where inhabitants felt abandoned by public authorities and technocratic elites. The journalist Pierre Belleville explicitly links worker protests, in Decazeville, for example, to a number of agricultural movements (in Brittany in 1961): in his view, both cases involve revolts from the "colonized," both inland and within dominated and dependent "backwater" regions and sectors that were hit hard by brutal, centralizing and unilateral modernization efforts (Belleville, 1963).

This type of representation, which includes a degree of condescension – miners and agricultural workers who remain "archaic" in the face of a transformation deemed inescapable – should not undermine the agency and adaptability of these working-class populations. Far from passive and closed to modernity, they were, on the contrary, part of it; they understood very well the need to publicize these movements as much as possible and to gain public support when confronted with the risk of becoming erased and made invisible. Most of the movements mentioned earlier can be interpreted through this desire: to deploy actions that are both peaceful and spectacular, like the Decazeville strikers, who celebrated Christmas mass at the bottom of the mine; the focus on the misery suffered and the dangerousness of their working conditions "we live as in the time of Germinal"; the support, or at least the interest, they finally obtained from a number of intellectuals, artists (photographers and filmmakers), and journalists who, with the help of new media (television), helped publicize their demands. The very "respectable" nature of these movements, which contrast with those of the Cold War, as did those of the years of 1968, can be understood only through this desire to obtain as much consensual public support as possible.

What was being sought on this basis? The challenge was not necessarily to prevent the closure of mine shafts or coal mines, whose decline in the face of oil and new energy sources seemed largely irreparable. By mobilizing public opinion, and by relying on workers' organizations and left-wing parties, the objective was to point government policies in two directions. To begin with, the mobilized miners and workers issued a demand for justice: their situation of economic decline, they argued, should not condemn them to misery, and they too have the right to enjoy the benefits of growth, along with access to consumption. Indeed, the dynamics of the welfare state, and the prevalence of progressive ideas, led to their partial satisfaction. Even the French technocrat Pierre Massé recognized this:

"Over the past few weeks, public opinion has shown its refusal to accept the fact that workers in a strenuous and dangerous occupation can be disadvantaged when sharing the fruits of expansion because they belong to a stagnating sector in decline."

(Massé, Bloch-Lainé, and Masselin, 1963, p. 13)

The other major demand involved retraining opportunities for those who work on sites undergoing difficulties, especially for their children and the future of the territory. The challenge was less about negotiating the principle behind the closures and more about negotiating the conditions under which these closures took place (Michel, 1988) and about the opportunities for young people to access new types of employment on site, as seen in the famous slogan by the Decazeville miners. Here, as in the British mines (Phillips, 2013), the overall economic growth of the 1960s represented an asset that provided hope for a less brutal transition and for the availability of new jobs in a variety of sectors, including automotive, steel, and consumer goods. The development of territorial planning policies, which invested heavily in establishing these new activities, also increased expectations in this regard (Dard, in Eck et al., 2006).

How did 'Les Années 1968' affect this type of configuration? First, they were marked by worsening and relatively expanding forms of industrial crisis. The impact was felt beyond the small mines in the south and west of France, for example, and also in the large mining pools, like those in the Nord region, as well as in other heavy industry sectors; one example is the long strike (1967) by iron miners in Lorraine, and the problems encountered by a number of steelworks in the same region.[6] But job losses and closures also became a concern beyond the rural areas and bastions of heavy industry: from the textile industry in the Nord region to factories in Seine-Saint-Denis, the fear of unemployment began spreading while simultaneously attracting greater attention from public authorities (the 1967 creation of the Agence nationale pour l'emploi (ANPE) [National employment agency]).

This gloomy outlook was combined with an explosion of social conflict and widespread unrest in the factories, in which the May–June 1968 strikes were but a single episode and which continued for much of the following decade (Vigna, 2007). Traditional workers' organizations, led by the French Communist Party and the CGT, saw their influence challenged by new militant groups (Maoists, Trotskyists). The myriad of movements and protests that erupted during this period were also marked by tougher confrontations with employers, law enforcement, and government representatives. This is also reflected by a shift in the repertoires of action that were mobilized. Strikes and mass demonstrations retained their significance, but strikers and militants invented – or rather reinvented (certain forms were already well established by the end of the nineteenth century) – more subversive forms of action: sabotage, occupying premises, kidnapping leaders, seizing the work tools, challenging managerial authority, etc. In December 1967, workers at the Rhodiacéta factory in Lyon-Vaise ransacked its offices after company managers announced close to 1,000 job cuts. Those at Usinor Longwy in Denain (Nord), and the Société métallurgique de Normandie [Normandy metallurgical company], kidnapped some of their managers in an attempt to unblock or relaunch negotiations.

This type of action was often primarily considered a fact of modern factories and growth sectors; above all, it sought better wages and a democratic transformation of working conditions and labor relations while nourishing hope for society's revolutionary transformation. But the situation was not so simple; it did not involve the first signs of a rising tide of deindustrialization on the one side, and the militant unrest of the years of 1968 on the other, since the two were very much intertwined. The case involving the Rhodiacéta factory clearly shows that the reasons behind the protests included employment-related concerns, along with fears surrounding wage losses and the erosion of identities attached to factory work. The old industrial mining pools, while not necessarily the most visible, also played a role in renewing these forms of protest. In 1971, at the Faulquemont mine in Lorraine, which was threatened with closure, miners kidnapped three engineers in charge of dismantling the installations, then occupied senior management offices for several days. At the time, small

(Maoist) militant groups were circulating in the mining pools of the Nord region, attempting to re-politicize miners around safety and reconversion issues (Fontaine, 2014; Artières, 2023). This was not merely a French phenomenon. In Belgium's former Borinage region, the closure of factories installed to compensate for difficulties in the coal industry (Siemens, Farah and Salik) gave rise to new forms of activism (Verschueren, 2011) from both male and female workers, forms that were strongly influenced by the cultural currents and dynamics of the years of 1968: plays were staged during factory occupations and strikers composed songs of struggle denouncing the irresponsibility and failures of management. Protests against the closures were therefore based on, and fueled by, new repertoires of militant action.

What were the results? Therein lies the main issue. Neither the consensual forms of mobilization, nor those appealing to the minority and subject to contention, seemed capable of halting the dynamics surrounding the closures. This is particularly true in the former coal mining areas between the Nord region and Southern France, which continued their slow extinction. Radical forms of protest remained very few in numbers and had no immediate impact, while negotiations between unions and coal company managers regarding the pace of closures predominated, along with negotiations surrounding the social compensation demanded by workers (early retirement, increasingly). Despite achieving a shift in the balance of power, at least temporarily, the workers' protests seemed incapable of stemming the rising tide of industrial crisis. This phenomenon also appeared in Great Britain, where the crisis also continued to deepen, despite a major increase in the number of strike days in the 1970s, along with a few remarkable episodes (the 1972 miners' strike, the 1978–1979 "Winter of Discontent") that reflected a hardening of the relationship between the working class and the state (Phillips, 2006). The election of Margaret Thatcher at the end of the 1970s, and of Ronald Reagan across the Atlantic, signaled a reversal of the welfare state, along with new policies that were far less protective and far more confrontational when addressing the failings of certain sectors.

Failed Hopes in an Alternative, Circa 1975–1985

The gradual onset of the economic crisis in the second half of the 1970s led to greater difficulties for industrial companies. Closures multiplied, sharpening a sense of crisis in France, all the more so under soaring unemployment, the main indicator. The year 1975 breached the threshold of one million unemployed, 1982 saw two million unemployed, and the three million mark was reached in 1993. Unemployment hit the working class hard but unevenly, and foremost by gender, as shown by the trend in unemployment rates (Maruani and Meron, 2012, p. 116).

It is striking to note how the gap between male and female workers widens to a massive ten points as the crisis deepens and lasts (see Table 10.1). Unemployment statistics, updated and publicized on a monthly basis, marked the passing of time and defined this period far

Table 10.1 Unemployment crisis in France by gender

	1975	1982	1990
Male workers	3.4	8.2	12
Female workers	6.9	14.8	22.1

more than any notion of deindustrialization, which was less clearly defined due to a lack of large-scale statistical indicators. Moreover, deindustrialization became increasingly difficult to grasp as a number of industrial branches continued to flourish – nuclear power, aeronautics, fine chemicals, etc. – and a number of offensive strikes impacted the automotive industry, among others, until 1983–1984.

It is the job cuts, occasionally accompanied by site closures, and even company closures, that reflected the crisis at both local and national levels. Locally, this may have involved an industrial branch beset by difficulties: the shoe industry in Romans-sur-Isère (Drôme), but also in Fougère (Île-et-Villaine), with a struggling and occasionally sinking flagship company: this was the case in 1980 with Manufrance in Saint-Etienne, or in 1984 with the bankruptcy of Creusot-Loire, heir group to the Schneiders, which overwhelmed the city of Le Creusot (Saône-et-Loire). One could expand this obituary with dozens of examples in an effort to grasp the magnitude of the shock and trauma. On a national level, France did not experience the enormous strikes that would symbolize a tipping point toward accelerated deindustrialization: there is no comparison with the Fiat strike at Mirafiori in 1980 or the 1984–1985 British miners' strike. The only functional equivalent, in terms of the impact and the intense mobilization that resulted, involved the plan to safeguard the steel industry, announced by Raymond Barre's government in December 1978, which included 21,750 job cuts, two-thirds of which affected the small towns of Longwy in Lorraine and Denain in the Nord region.

Thus, industrial workers and their unions were not fighting deindustrialization as such; they were attempting to oppose its consequences and build alternatives in ways that differed from the previous period. This response was deployed from three perspectives, which may be connected but are rarely articulated. The first, as well as the most massive and visible, consists of the on-site struggle to preserve jobs. In November 1975, the CFDT clothing, leather and textile federation (Hacuitex) organized a training session addressing "long conflicts over employment," most often marked by occupations. In the months that followed, the CFDT industrial action department began to take stock of these types of conflict, which numbered in the dozens by the summer of 1977. By the writers' own admission, this figure remains approximate, since conflicts limited to other labor confederations, primarily the CGT, were unknown (Archives Confédérales CFDT, 8 H 530). In February 1979, it listed 56 "occupied companies (long-term struggles)," a third of which involved the metals industry (Archives IHS-CGT, 7 CFD 65). Dozens of industrial plants were therefore occupied for months on end during the second half of the 1970s, with highly variable staffing levels that tended to decline as the occupation dragged on without any clear prospects. One of the most emblematic and long-running conflicts struck the Chaix printing plant in Saint-Ouen: facing job cuts involving 410 of the 640 book workers, the CGT launched a very long struggle that lasted 68 months before coming to an end in July 1981, with the company being taken over and winning back . . . only 47 jobs (CGT, 1981).

Holding their ground, the strikers committed for the long term. In doing so, they followed the example set by the LIP strikers (1973), turning to worker self-management whenever they could. They manufactured objects that could be sold to their supporters (according to the LIP slogan, "We produce, we sell, we pay ourselves") while feeding the hope that some factories could be saved by the seizing of power and worker autonomy (Reid, 2018). These productive strikes, as they are sometimes called, oxymoronically, number around 20; this model of action also appeared in Belgium, particularly in Wallonia (Verschueren, 2011). Such transgressive and often illegal practices were in line with transnational issues; in Great

Challenging and Politicizing Deindustrialization?

Britain, at least 200 company occupations took place in the 1970s, occasionally leading to the creation of cooperatives (Vigna, 2007; Gold, 2004). At times, these producers' cooperatives seemed to offer the ideal instrument to ensure long-term company viability, but some resounding failures – LIP in Besançon, along with Manufrance in Saint-Etienne – reveal the competitive difficulties faced by cooperatives in a context marked by crisis. In addition, and in continuity with the previous period, popularity became a significant issue in these strikes: public authorities could only be forced to intervene and mobilize reactivators if people were talking. These strikes were therefore widely photographed and recorded by filmmakers close to the workers' movement, especially in the Paris suburbs.[7]

The unions attempted to go beyond the local character of the strike through regional, and even national, mobilization. One of the most spectacular mobilizations involved the "Giscard sell-out rally" (Valéry Giscard d'Estaing was President of the Republic at the time), which took place in June 1976 in Saint-Etienne, the city of Michel Durafour, labor minister, a city hit especially hard by the crisis. The CGT invited delegations from at least 117 companies across 24 departments, with opening rallies held in Péage-de-Roussillon, Chalon-sur-Saône, Bordeaux, Nantes, and Orléans, then in Lyon and Clermont-Ferrand, before moving on to Saint-Etienne. A bus also ran a *Tour de France* for employment from June to September 1977, starting in Paris and ending in Rouen after 43 stages. These initiatives are reminiscent of the typical unemployment marches held in the 1930s in the UK and France, organized by the Communist galaxy (Perry, 2007). But the aim was more defensive, as explained in a preparatory memorandum:

> Thus, this clearly involves occupied companies already in liquidation, along with companies and branches under threat. The main objective is to provide the struggle with far greater popular support against liquidation and layoffs. For each company and branch, the idea is to present a kind of travelling exhibition illustrating the reasons for maintaining the activities, the absurdity, and the inhumanity of liquidation. For each protest, the goal is to create a crescendo that summarizes the extent of the problem, culminating in Saint-Etienne, and to indict the government, the employers, and the system in an effort to strengthen public support for our solutions.
>
> *(Archives IHS-CGT, 7 CFD 68, pp. 2–3)*

This argument promoted the emergence of a discourse defending French industry, which served as a clutch for nationalist rhetoric. One record involving the paper industry presents it as "an industry of national interest," stating, "As an essential part of French education and culture, the French paper industry must cover most of the country's needs." Also, it seeks to defend "large French forest tracts" with the following question: "Are we to understand that our national wealth is going to be used by foreign companies? A colonized France!" Hence the demand for nationalization and the reduction of paper and cardboard imports through "the implementation of a protective barrier."

This repertoire of actions could also be found at the local level: in the Valenciennes region, for example, a rally for the unemployed, followed by an automobile rally for employment, took place on May 4, 1977, and October 7, 1978. But the most significant innovation was the spread of union radio stations publicizing struggles while giving voice to strikers and the general public alike in a counter-information approach to a media landscape accused of being indifferent, or even hostile. These radio stations began with the struggles in the steel industry between 1978 and 1979. The first radio station, SOS-Emploi [SOS-employment] was set up by the CFDT section in Longwy, before the CGT launched a much larger structure: Lorraine Cœur d'Acier [Lorraine heart of steel], hosted by two professional journalists. The radio station's very name associates regional identity with steel production, contributing to its popularity (Hayes, 2018). It had its counterpart in Radio-Quinquin in the Nord region. These illegal radio stations mobilized the population to show its attachment to the steel industry. The mobilizations contested the consequences of the crisis, and unemployment in particular, but they were framed in a national context threatened by foreign companies while deindustrialization as such was not central to these mobilizations. For this reason, the interpretation promoted the emergence of a nationalist discourse targeting the US, and above all Germany, particularly with the 1978–1979 steel crisis, which ended with the repudiation of a supposedly German Europe. The CGT's short brochure, *Halte au massacre des industries! Nous voulons travailler* [Stop the massacre of industry! We want to work] also addressed these issues. A preface by Henri Krasucki denounces the perpetrators, namely "the capitalist monopolies and their government," and offers a simple solution. "To save jobs and revive the economy, we must attack the root of the problem: to truly remove the means of domination from the large capitalist monopolies by nationalizing them for good and without fuss."

Nationalization became part of the common government agenda signed by the socialist and communist parties in June 1972. The CGT was particularly attached to this tool. But the essential point, which refers to the common agenda, was to boost consumption, or "increase purchasing power," "reduce the work week to 40 hours, and lower the retirement age to 60 and 55," which was intended to promote job creation according to a classic Keynesian scheme (CGT, 1978, p. 15).

The election of Socialist François Mitterrand to the presidency of the Republic on May 10, 1981, followed by the formation of a left-wing parliamentary majority that brought together socialists and communists, appeared to delight CGT leaders, who believed that change was on the way. A chronology of the union struggles that began in May 1981 begins with the following ("Initiatives, bilans des luttes, 1978–1985," Archives IHS-CGT 7 CFD 65):

> Manufrance. Here we go again–the factory is back in operation under SCOPD management
> 12/5: Lardrecht miners celebrate victory
> 16/5: Chaix has restarted. The conflict is resolved after 68 months of fighting

The fact that the chronology was written at all speaks of the enthusiasm behind CGT militants, for whom a new period was emerging for the benefit of a working world, far beyond the workers themselves. While the enthusiasm lasted a few months, difficulties soon began to mount as social conflicts remained bitter, especially in car factories in the Paris region, and workers' gains were under threat. In February 1983, the CGT launched the Comité national des chômeurs [National committee for the unemployed]. In February 1984, the actions cataloged by the CGT indicated the scale of these difficulties:

> The prime minister met with unions: industrial restructuring, a central issue for the 30,000-strong CGT worker protest on the Canebière in Marseille, to maintain and renew industrial potential . . .
> Lorraine on the alert–the CGT calls for a day of action against industrial decline . . .

The 20th: National miners' strike calling on five labor and management federations opposing the anticipated job cuts.

The restructuring and decline were rejected, but deindustrialization was not effectively named. Similarly, while the threats in sectors with the strongest union traditions – steel, mining, books, metallurgy – were clearly identified, the cutbacks in textiles, clothing, and footwear, all sectors that massively employ women, further eluded union leaders.

On the government side, the ruling left faced new difficulties: the automotive sector, which had prospered until the end of the 1970s, scattering production sites across industrial regions like Lorraine and Nord-Pas-de-Calais, was in turn forced to undertake massive job cuts from 1983 onward, while the steel and coal industries continued to collapse. From then on, and regardless of its generosity regarding social measures, the governing left allowed companies, both private and nationalized, to shed jobs while limiting its efforts to the promotion of local reconversion: 14 conversion clusters were identified, including most of the steel basins, while unionist Jacques Chérèque, number two at the CFDT, became delegate reeve in charge of industrial redeployment in Lorraine (Tracol, 2019). This approach to identifying and helping regions in difficulty is part of a traditional policy that dates to the 1930s in Great Britain, along with the second postwar period in the US (Wilson, 2002). The involvement of a unionist-turned-reeve only muddied the waters by suggesting that no alternative was available for the labor movement.

The Outbursts of a Fragmented Group, From the Late 1980s to the Early Twenty-First Century

The CGT, struggling under its own isolation, but more so under its weakened state, continued to advocate a policy that would put an end to the "extroverted dynamic" of the national industry and intended to win back the domestic market while planning for the reconstitution of entire sectors rather than an attachment to a few niches (CGT, 1984, pp. 109, 120). The confederation clearly remained faithful to a national scheme that ignored the European scale and showed little concern for internal transformations in work processes, as opposed to the international division of labor. But these appeals fell on deaf ears as public authorities abandoned all industrial policy in favor of a "stretcher state," which seeks to restore an ailing industry's health through restructuring (Daumas, 2017). Worse still, the most senior politicians neglected the value of public companies, which they privatized at rock-bottom prices. This trend, which began in 1986 and reached spectacular proportions in the medium term, continued without pause until the most recent period. This removal of public power was accompanied by an acceptance of industrial decline (Margairaz and Tartakowsky, 2020). Shortly after taking office in 1997, socialist Prime Minister Lionel Jospin agreed to the closure of the Vilvorde factory in Belgium by Renault, in which the state was a shareholder. Then, in September 1999, when the Michelin tire group announced 7,500 job cuts, he explained that "we should not expect everything from the state" and that "everyone accepts the market."

This renunciation left workers and their unions even more helpless in the face of companies that were increasingly committed to financialization, some of which resorted to fraudulent bankruptcies, as seen in the spectacular cases of Daewoo – for which public authorities had truly rolled out the red carpet – and its factories in Longwy, or of

Metaleurop in Noyelles-Godault in 2003 (Galinier and Jakubyszyn, 2001; Mazade, 2013). This trend toward financialization further eroded the relationship with the territory, along with the sense of corporate responsibility toward employees. At the same time, the labor group contracted, weakened, and transformed. Numbering 6.9 million in 1982, one million workers disappeared by 1999 while still making up a quarter of the active population. This contraction went hand in hand with a decline in union membership, which remains poorly documented, however, since it depends entirely on confederal evaluations that lack data regarding the evolution of industrial federations: thus, the CGT went from around 1.3 million members in 1979, to just over 540,000 in 2004. However, the Montreuil-based labor confederation is said to have outstripped its CFDT rival, which still managed to contain its hemorrhaging: with 800,000 members in 1978, it retained 450,000 members 25 years later (Andolfatto and Labbé, 2009, p. 22). This deunionization was even more pronounced in the labor world. In the early 2000s, the unionization rate within private companies hovered at around 5%, compared with over 15% in public companies and the civil service. Worse still, the rate for workers stood at just over 6%, compared with 10% for intermediate occupations, and 14% for managers (Sirot, 2011, p. 328). The union framework, effective when developing and implementing collective responses, was being dismantled, aggravating a kind of worker disempowerment, all the more so as the group itself was transforming.

Deindustrialization, however severe, rarely leads to a complete eradication of production in a way that obliterates the working class in the fullest sense; rather, it implies its large-scale recomposition. Pascal Raggi eloquently demonstrated this fact for the Lorraine steel industry when, in 1989, workers were outnumbered by managers, employees, technicians, and executives combined. "The steel industry has statistically [ceased] to be a labor industry and become an industrial activity for technicians" (Raggi, 2019, p. 74). This observation applies to many other sectors that recruit workers with higher levels of initial training, so that these workers believe themselves to be technicians and are occasionally classified as such, especially when they have a vocational baccalaureate (created in 1985) (Beaud and Pialoux, 1999; Eckert, 2006). These transformations have led to a crisis in the group's internal reproduction. And yet, those who continued to work were required to show more commitment. The few ethnographic surveys available, particularly in the automotive industry, point to an intensification of work, especially since organizations now required complex forms of self-management, along with maximum commitment from workers (Hatzfeld, 2002, p. 44; Rot, 2006, pp. 135, 151).

From then on, the workers' response to deindustrialization transformed. Tenacious and stubborn forms of resistance across entire industrial basins, like those that existed around Saint-Etienne or, in the south of Puy-de-Dôme, around the Ducellier automotive equipment plants until the mid-1980s (Ponsard, 2019), were starting to disappear. Conflict, when it did occur, grew in intensity as its frequency diminished and often sought a more favorable social plan and therefore greater severance pay. In Creil (Oise), for example, workers from Chausson – another automotive equipment manufacturer – resorted to violence in 1995 during the third and final social plan, ransacking offices, destroying equipment, and occupying the prefecture (Linhart, Rist, and Durand, 2002, p. 34). Reactions of this kind were common throughout this period and occasionally took on astonishing forms, as when workers used their machinery and equipment to confront law enforcement, like the Carmaus miners who claimed to lay siege to Albi in 1991 during the "battle of Hermet" (Castellesi, 2021, p. 178).

Challenging and Politicizing Deindustrialization?

The managers who were on hand were found by the employees and bore the brunt of the workers' anger, becoming its targets. This led to the kidnapping of the company's directors and managers. This action has been part of the workers' repertoire since the strikes of 1936, if not earlier; as discussed previously, it underwent a resurgence in the spring of 1968 and continued in the years that followed. It was used once more in the early 2000s, but its intrinsic violence varied according to the threats or insults involved (Parsons, 2012; Hayes, 2012). Italian workers also resorted to this tactic at the Terni steel company, notably on two occasions, in 2004 and 2014 (Portelli, 2017, pp. 299–300, 427). This use of direct pressure on management to reconsider its decisions was accompanied by the recurrent use of environmental blackmail, whereby workers threaten to use the products they handle to pollute a site or to cause it severe damage: this type of action began in July 2000 in the Ardennes, when workers from an artificial silk company, Cellatex, threatened to spill thousands of liters of sulfuric acid into the Meuse River (Larose et al., 2001). The government's deep concern at the time, which helped employees obtain more favorable departure conditions, grew in popularity and other workers resorted to the same methods.

The spectacular and mostly masculine nature of these brutal reactions contrasts with the mostly feminine practice of writing about deindustrialization. Thus, the crisis was not merely about deindustrialization but also about the workers' movement: their inability to identify with the spokespeople involved forced militant workers to take up their pens. On occasion, associations made up of former employees would call upon the lettered to tell the story of the factory, the work, and the closure. Other times, writers would organize writing workshops for laid-off workers. At the time, the operation sought to help workers discuss their working lives, the closure and the pain it caused, thereby prolonging the mobilization by deploying new resources. For example, at the Levi's factory in La Bassée (Pas-de-Calais), which closed in March 1999, a writing workshop ran briefly in May and June 2000; it was attended by 25 female workers. But this type of project occasionally created tensions between artist-intellectuals and workers, who were locked into an irreducible social singularity, as seen in the efforts regarding the Moulinex factory closure in Caen in 2004 (Clarke, 2012; Vigna, 2016, p. 159). In addition, these labor writings on deindustrialization, which sought to preserve agency, however diminished, while breathing life into a class whose demise is constantly being trumpeted, primarily took place independently of any workers' movement. Indeed, workers' reactions to the closures are legion but also isolated and unable to coalesce in a way that reopens old social issues.

However, we cannot confine ourselves to acknowledging this powerlessness. Workers' protests against closures and deindustrialization failed to leverage any widespread challenge to the social and economic order, let alone revolution. They were not always as flamboyant, or heroic as other movements linked to miners, steelworkers, and other male bastions of heavy industry in France and Europe. But the fact remains that they did occur and the diversity of their forms and manifestations attests to the diversity of the labor world and also to the fact that this world was more than a passive victim throughout the process; it showed a real determination to limit, or at least tame, its impact. While the protests failed to prevent the closures, nor did they prevent the fragmentation and marginalization of the workers' group, they helped raise awareness of the resulting suffering and hardship while turning this suffering and hardship into an issue for public opinion and decision-makers alike. It is by no means certain that national and European decision-makers have taken stock of this suffering, nor that the answers they claimed to provide satisfied the workers' groups. The industrial drain continues to hit certain regions hard, regions in which economic activity has been in decline for almost 60 years, or two generations, at least. A political response that is equal to the challenge, one that includes an industrial component capable of offering stable and well-paying jobs, remains a long way off.

Finally, the British miners' strike is an event without equal in France's history of deindustrialization, where the conditions surrounding the politicization of closure-related conflicts took a different turn. The consequences of this absence may be twofold: without a traumatic reference point, deindustrialization clearly becomes a process that leaves no trace in people's memories, despite the pain that persists. One may go so far as to assume that this lack of memory is all the more gnawing because it prevents us from naming what happened. Undoubtedly, this absence also weighs on the left and the labor movement more broadly, like a significant event, both omnipresent and elusive, which must be considered, and which must be eradicated or *repaired*. In France, like in Belgium and Italy for different reasons, this gap continues to provide a breeding ground for the far right.

Notes

1 Some recent publications in the vast body of literature that address this conflict: Andrew, J.R. (1996). *Miners on Strike: Class Solidarity and Division in Britain*. Oxford: Oxford University Press; Cabadi, M. (2023). *Lesbiennes et gays au charbon. Solidarités avec les mineurs britanniques en grève, 1984–1985 [Lesbian and Gay Solidarity with Striking British Coal Miners, 1984–1985]*. Paris: EHESS, coll. Cas de figure; Curtis, B. (2013). *The South Wales Miners, 1964–1985*. Cardiff: University of Wales Press; Phillips, J. (2012). *Collieries, Communities and the Miners' Strike in Scotland*. Manchester: Manchester University Press.
2 See examples from two different national contexts: Vigna, X. (2012). *Histoire des ouvriers en France au XXe siècle [History of Workers in France in the 20th Century]*. Paris: Perrin; Cowie, J. (2010). *Stayin' Alive. The 1970s and the Last Days of the Working Class*. New York and London: The New Press.
3 For a comparative perspective, see Lutz, R. (2019). *Jenseits von Kohle und Stahl: Eine Gesellschaftsgeschichte Westeuropas nach dem Boom [Beyond Coal and Steel: A Social History of Post-Boom Western Europe]*. Berlin: Suhrkamp, pp. 147–152.
4 See Pigenet, M. and Tartakowsky, D. (dir.). (2014). *Histoire des mouvements sociaux en France: De 1814 à nos jours [History of Social Movements in France: From 1814 to the Present Day]*. Paris: La Découverte, particularly the chapter, Institutionalisation et mobilisation au temps de l'Etat social (années 1930-années 1970) [Institutionalization and Mobilization in the Social State Era (1930s–1970s)], pp. 337–354.
5 For more on these various movements, see Reid, D. (1986). *The Miners of Decazeville: A Genealogy of Deindustrialization*. Harvard University Press; Verschueren, N. (2018). Borinage 1959: Expressions culturelles d'une région en déclin industriel [Borinage 1959. Cultural Expressions of a Region in Industrial Decline]. *Cahiers Jaurès*, 230(4), pp. 109–128; Fontaine, M. (2025). *La société industrielle en question: Une histoire des mondes miniers (France, second XXe siècle) [Industrial Society in Question: A History of the Mining World (France, Latter 20th Century)]*. Paris: Gallimard.
6 For an account of this period, see Belleville, P. (1968). *Laminage continu. Crise d'une région, échec d'un régime [Continuous Lamination: A Regional Crisis, a Regime's Failure]*. Paris: Julliard. From a research perspective, see Raggi, P. (2019). *La désindustrialisation de la Lorraine du fer, 1963–2013 [The Deindustrialization of the Lorraine Iron Region, 1963–2013]*. Paris: Classiques Garnier.
7 Some of these films are available at the Fonds audiovisuel du Parti communiste français [French Communist Party audiovisual fund] website. https://www.cinearchives.org/

Reference List

Andolfatto, D. and Labbé, D. (2009). *Toujours moins ! Déclin du syndicalisme à la française*. Paris: Gallimard.
Andrew, J.R. (1996). *Miners on Strike: Class Solidarity and Division in Britain*. Oxford: Oxford University Press.

Artières, P. (2023). *La mine en procès. Fouquières-lès-Lens, 1970* [*The mine on trial, Fouquières-lès-Lens, 1970*]. Paris: Anamosa.

Barbichon, G. and Moscovici, S. (1962). Modernisation des mines, conversion des mineurs. Études sur les conséquences psychologiques et sociales de la modernisation dans les charbonnages du Centre-Midi. *Revue française du travail*, 3, pp. 3–201.

Beaud, S. and Pialoux, M. (1999). *Retour sur la condition ouvrière. Enquête aux usines Peugeot de Sochaux-Montbéliard*. Paris: Fayard.

Belleville, P. (1963, March 17). Lorraine: Tout le pays mosellan s'achemine vers la grève. *Tribune socialiste*.

Belleville, P. (1968). *Laminage continu. Crise d'une région, échec d'un régime*. Paris: Julliard.

Cabadi, M. (2023). *Lesbiennes et gays au charbon. Solidarités avec les mineurs britanniques en grève, 1984–1985* [*Lesbian and Gay Solidarity with Striking British Coal Miners, 1984–1985*]. Paris: EHESS, coll. Cas de figure.

Castellesi, R. (2019). 'Ils détruisent notre vie, ils cassent nos usines' Désindustrialisation et (dé)mobilisations ouvrières dans deux villes moyennes françaises, Romans et Autun (1949–2017). *20 & 21. Revue d'histoire*, 144(4), pp. 115–129.

Castellesi, R. (2021). *Les armes des faibles et la faiblesse des armes. Actions et réactions ouvrières en situation de désindustrialisation en France (1945–2012)*. History Thesis. Université de Bourgogne.

CGT. (1978). *Halte au massacre des industries! Nous voulons travailler*. Saint-Ouen: CGT.

CGT. (1981), *Chaix. La lutte par l'affiche*, Saint-Ouen: CGT.

CGT. (1984, December). *Quelle politique industrielle pour la France? Analyses et réflexions de la CGT*. Confederal Centre for Economic Studies.

Clarke, J. (2012). Social Exclusion, Creative Writing and Democracy: The Politics of a Socio-Literary Project in Caen. *Contemporary French Civilization*, 37(1), pp. 1–22.

Curtis, B. (2013). *The South Wales Miners, 1964–1985*. Cardiff: University of Wales Press.

Dard, O. (2006). Les institutions publiques françaises d'aménagement du territoire et la reconversion des bassins charbonniers. In Eck, J.-F., Freidemann, P. and Lauschke, K. (eds.) *La reconversion des bassins charbonniers. Une comparaison interrégionale entre la Ruhr et le Nord-Pas-de-Calais* [*The Reconversion of Coal Mines: An Interregional Comparison Between the Ruhr and Nord-Pas-de-Calais Regions*]. Revue du Nord, Hors-Série, coll. Histoire, 21. Lille: Université Charles de Gaulle, pp. 139–153.

Daumas, J.-C. (2017). Une France sans usines: Comment en est-on arrivé là? (1974–2012). In Daumas, J.-C., Kharaba, I. and Mioche, P. (eds.) *La désindustrialisation: Une fatalité?* Besançon: PU de Franche-Comté, pp. 17–42.

Eckert, H. (2006). *Avoir vingt ans à l'usine* [*Being 20 at the Factory*]. Paris: La Dispute.

Fontaine, M. (2014). *Liévin 74. Fin d'un monde ouvrier* [*Liévin 74. The End of a Labour World*]. Paris: Éditions de l'EHESS.

Fontaine, M. (2025). *La société industrielle en question. Une histoire des mondes miniers (France, second XXe siècle)* [*Industrial Society in Question: A History of the Mining World (France, Latter 20th Century)*]. Paris: Gallimard.

Galinier, P. and Jakubyszyn, C. (2001, March 6). Quand 'Chairman Kim', commandeur de la Légion d'honneur, faisait ses courses en France. *Le Monde*.

Gold, M. (2004). Worker Mobilization in the 1970s: Revisiting Work-Ins, Co-Operatives and Alternative Corporate Plans. *Historical Studies in Industrial Relations*, 18, pp. 65–106.

Hatzfeld, N. (2002). *Les gens d'usine. 50 ans d'histoire à Peugeot-Sochaux*. Paris: Éditions de l'Atelier.

Hayes, G. (2012). Bossnapping: Situating Repertoires of Industrial Action in National and Global Contexts. *Modern & Contemporary France*, 20(2), pp. 185–201.

Hayes, I. (2018). *Radio Lorraine cœur d'Acier 1978–1980. Les voix de la crise* [*Lorraine Heart of Steel 1978–1980. Voices from the Crisis*]. Paris: Presses de Science Po.

High, S. (2019). Donald Trump and the Rust Belt 5. *20 & 21. Revue d'histoire*, 144, pp. 35–51.

Lagroye, J. (2003). *La politisation* [*Politicization*]. Paris: Belin, coll. Socio-Histoires, pp. 365–366.

Larose, C. et al. (2001). *Cellatex, Quand l'acide a coulé*. Paris: Syllepses.

Linhart, D., Rist, B. and Durand, E. (2002). *Perte d'emploi, perte de soi* [*Loss of Work, Loss of Self*]. Toulouse: Eres.

Lutz, R. (2019). *Jenseits von Kohle und Stahl: Eine Gesellschaftsgeschichte Westeuropas nach dem Boom* [*Beyond Coal and Steel: A Social History of Post-Boom Western Europe*]. Berlin: Suhrkamp.

Margairaz, M. and Tartakowsky, D. (2020). *L'Etat détricoté. De la Résistance à la République en marche [The Unravelled State: From the Resistance to the Republic on the Move]*. Paris: Editions du Détour.

Maruani, M. and Meron, M. (2012). *Un siècle de travail des femmes en France, 1901–2011 [A Century of Women's Labour in France, 1901–2011]*. Paris: La Découverte.

Massé, P., Bloch-Lainé, F. and Masselin, P. (1963, March 22). *Rapport sur la situation des salaires du secteur nationalisé (Report on salaries within nationalized sectors)*. Report. https://openlibrary.org/works/OL1254075W/Rapport_sur_la_situation_des_salaires_du_secteur_nationalise%CC%81?edition=key%3A/books/OL6019850M&mode=all

Mazade, O. (2013, January). L'affaire Metaleurop: Une dénonciation impossible? *Terrains & Travaux*, pp. 23–40.

Michel, J. (1988). Les réactions syndicales face aux politiques charbonnières et à la fermeture des mines en Europe occidentale après 1945. *Revue belge d'histoire contemporaine*, XIX(1–2), pp. 131–146.

Parsons, N. (2012). Worker Reactions to Crisis: Explaining 'Bossnapping'. *French Politics, Culture & Society*, 30(1), pp. 111–130.

Perry, M. (2007). *Prisoners of Want: The Experience and Protest of the Unemployed in France, 1921–45*. Aldershot: Ashgate.

Phillips, J. (2006). The 1972 Miners' Strike: Popular Agency and Industrial Politics in Britain. *British Contemporary History*, 20, pp. 187–207.

Phillips, J. (2012). *Collieries, Communities and the Miners' Strike in Scotland*. Manchester: Manchester University Press.

Phillips, J. (2013). Deindustrialization and the Moral Economy of the Scottish Coalfields, 1947 to 1991. *International Labor and Working-Class History*, 84, pp. 99–115.

Pigenet, M. and Tartakowsky, D. (2014). *Histoire des mouvements sociaux en France: De 1814 à nos jours [History of social movements in France: From 1814 to the present day]*. Paris: La Découverte.

Ponsard, N. (2019). « Les militants dans la tourmente de « l'Affaire Ducellier » (1979–1985) » dans Béroud S., Bressol E., Pélisse J. and Pigenet M. (ed.), *La CGT, 1975–1995. Un syndicalisme à l'épreuve des crises*. Nancy: L'Arbre bleu.

Portelli, A. (2017). *La città dell'acciaio. Due secoli di storia operaia [The City of Steel: Two Centuries of Working-Class History]*. Roma: Donzelli.

Raggi, P. (2019). *La désindustrialisation de la Lorraine du fer, 1963–2013 [The Deindustrialization of the Lorraine Iron Region, 1963–2013]*. Paris: Classiques Garnier.

Reid, D. (1986). *The Miners of Decazeville: A Genealogy of Deindustrialization*. Harvard University Press.

Reid, D. (2018). *Opening the Gates. The Lip Affair 1968–1981*. London: Verso.

Rot, G. (2006). *Sociologie de l'atelier. Renault, le travail ouvrier et le sociologue*. Paris: Octarès éditions.

Sirot, S. (2011). *Le syndicalisme, la politique et la grève. France et Europe, XIXe-XXIe siècle*. Nancy: Arbre bleu.

Tilly, C. (1984). Les origines du répertoire d'action collective contemporaine en France et en Grande-Bretagne. *Vingtième Siècle. Revue d'histoire*, 4, pp. 89–108.

Tracol, M. (2019). Le gouvernement Mauroy face à la désindustrialisation: de la crise économique à la crise sociale et politique. *20 & 21. Revue d'histoire*, 144(4), pp. 65–79.

Verschueren, N. (2011). L'expression culturelle de la protestation dans un ancien bassin charbonnier. *Mouvements*, 65, pp. 68–78.

Verschueren, N. (2014). *Fermer les mines en construisant l'Europe. Une histoire sociale de l'intégration européenne*. Bruxelles: Peter Lang.

Vigna, X. (2004). Les ouvriers de Denain et Longwy face aux licenciements: 1978–1979. *Vingtième Siècle. Revue d'histoire*, 84, pp. 129–137.

Vigna, X. (2007). *L'insubordination ouvrière dans les années 68: Essai d'histoire politique des usines [Worker Insubordination in the Years Around 1968: An Essay on factory Political History]*. Rennes: Presses Universitaires de Rennes.

Vigna, X. (2016). *L'espoir et l'effroi. Luttes d'écriture et luttes de classes en France au XXe siècle [Hope and Terror: Writing Struggles and Classes Struggles in XXth France]*. Paris: La Découverte.

Wilson, G. (2002). "Our Chronic and Desperate Situation": Anthracite Communities and the Emergence of Redevelopment Policy in Pennsylvania and the United States, 1946–1965. *International Review of Social History*, 47, pp. 137–158.

11
ANTICIPATING JUST TRANSITIONS
Ecological Crisis and Future Deindustrialization

Alice Mah

Introduction

The ecological crisis has profound implications for the future of industrial capitalism, particularly for polluting, fossil fuel-intensive industries. Over the past 50 years, deindustrialization has been fueled by capital flight, as corporations move around the globe in search of cheaper labor and resources. It has been exacerbated by neoliberal policies of economic restructuring, which have weakened trade union movements around the world. Yet on a heating planet, the drivers of deindustrialization are shifting to include not only the imperatives of capitalist development but also the global race to reach net zero emissions. There is a new wave of deindustrialization that is unfolding and yet-to-come, precipitated by the ecological crisis.

Another term for this wave is 'just transition.' The concept of just transition has origins in the labor movement in the 1980s, based on the idea that planned transitions away from polluting industries need to offer social protections and new livelihoods for displaced workers and communities. In the context of climate change, the just transition has gained official policy recognition, particularly following the Katowice Climate Conference (COP24) in 2018 in Polish coal country, which was dubbed the "Just Transition COP" (Morena, Kraus, and Stevis, 2020). While the idea of just transition seeks to overcome conflicts between jobs and the environment, it remains a contested term for many workers and their communities. Most transitions from coal and other heavily polluting industries have been deeply unjust, resulting in job losses, urban decline, and profound uncertainty about the future.

This chapter argues that there are important lessons to be drawn from deindustrialization studies for anticipating just transitions which could help avoid repeating the mistakes of the past and offer insightful perspectives on alternative industrial futures. First, the chapter reflects on two contrasting predictions about future deindustrialization from the 1970s and their resonance today. Next, the chapter discusses two key lessons from deindustrialization studies for anticipating just transitions: first, exploring issues of loss in both climate and deindustrialization narratives, which cut across the jobs-versus-environment divide; and second, grappling with the dilemmas of toxic legacies. The conclusion discusses the implications of these lessons for anticipating just transitions.

DOI: 10.4324/9781003308324-16

Future Deindustrialization

Half a century ago, Daniel Bell's book *The Coming of Postindustrial Society* (1973) forecast the decline of manufacturing and the rise of the information economy. While Bell's thesis was influential, it was also widely criticized because the promise of post-industrial society never materialized. As the American scholars Bluestone and Harrison observed in 1982, the post-industrial economy resembled an hourglass, with a stark divide between high-paid and low-paid jobs and relatively few jobs in the middle. It remains full of precarious and insecure jobs. Despite the growth of the information economy over the past 50 years, deindustrialization has continued to devastate working-class communities around the world, with social, economic, and environmental impacts spanning generations. Moreover, the world still relies on manufacturing. The industrial heartlands have shifted within the global economy, as industrial capital moves in pursuit of cheaper resources and labor.

Bell's thesis conveyed an ideological discomfort with Western material dependence on industrial capitalism, with its associated working classes and pollution, and sought escape in the vision of an immaterial economy based on information rather than goods. His vision of a post-industrial society was steeped in assumptions about modernization and development, namely that societies would progress from a basis in industry to knowledge as they advanced. In the wake of factory closures in North America and Europe throughout the 1970s and 1980s, Bell's post-industrial society captured the imagination of many city planners and governments, who invested in the knowledge and service sector as manufacturing declined, a pattern that continues today. Yet it has led to sharpening inequalities, including the concentration of polluting industries in socially and economically disadvantaged communities and increasing precarity in both manufacturing and service jobs. As a former shipbuilder from Newcastle-upon-Tyne in the UK once told me, "We can't all sell each other baskets and jam" (Mah, 2012, p. 85). Nor has every deindustrialized city reinvented itself; many former industrial cities continue to have persistent levels of poverty and unemployment and lingering effects of toxic pollution (see Silver, 2015).

It is interesting to note the subtitle of Bell's book: 'A Venture in Social Forecasting.' The sociological ambition to engage in predictions of future outcomes seems outdated, part of a grand theorizing tradition no longer typical in the discipline. Another venture into social and economic forecasting, published just the year before, was *The Limits to Growth* (Meadows et al., 1972), which used modeling to predict the impacts of exponential growth in industrialization, population, food production, pollution, and resource use. The study warned that if present growth trends continued, we would reach and exceed the sustainable limits of the Earth within the next one hundred years.

In the context of ecological crisis, debates about the limits to growth have resurfaced over the past decade, with many scholars and activists challenging the pursuit of GDP-led growth, with calls for 'degrowth' or 'post-growth.' They argue that growth is unsustainable, running into economic limits of overcapacity and stagnation, as well as ecological limits that threaten the basis for life and well-being on Earth. Yet, for the most part, degrowth scholars focus on exploring post-capitalist alternatives on the periphery of industrial capitalism rather than engaging with questions of how to transform industrial capitalism.

Read together, there are striking parallels between these two forecasting ventures, despite their clear differences: both envision alternative industrial futures, one predicting the coming of post-industrial society and the other predicting the collapse of Earth systems due to exponential industrial growth. Furthermore, both advocate in effect for future deindustrialization, one as a positive outcome of an anticipated shift toward an information economy and the other as a normative position, as a way of avoiding social and ecological disaster. Both ventures were right, in some ways, in predicting future deindustrialization.

Fifty years on, the decline of global manufacturing as a share of total employment – or 'labor deindustrialization' – continues. Economic historian Aaron Benanav (2020) argues that global labor deindustrialization is linked to rising industrial overcapacity rather than to automation alone, which has led to a global slowdown of industrial output since the 1970s. As global industrial production has slowed down and stagnated, Benanov contends, the global labor population has grown, resulting in an overall trend of labor deindustrialization. In heavily polluting, fossil fuel-intensive industries, such as petrochemicals, labor deindustrialization is particularly pronounced (Feltrin, Mah, and Brown, 2022). It fosters the conditions for 'job blackmail' from employers who push workers to decide between their jobs and the environment. Indeed, in working-class communities that have already faced decades of labor deindustrialization, pollution, and job blackmail, calls for "just transitions" are often divisive (Lawhon and McCreary, 2020).

There is continuity between past and present debates about future deindustrialization, in the tensions between those who see future deindustrialization as positive and necessary, casting aside pollution and fossil-fuel dependence, and those who see it as negative and avoidable, resulting in the destruction of communities, jobs, and ways of life. Beyond the prognosis of future deindustrialization, though, there is another common theme that cuts across these divisions: loss.

Deindustrialization, Climate, and Loss

Loss is a key theme for many people living in deindustrialized communities and regions, of livelihoods, health, industries, meanings, and bonds, and ways of being in the world. Loss is also central for so many people who are grappling with the anxieties and displacements of the climate emergency. In debate about the 'jobs versus environmental' dilemma, the two worlds of industry and the environment are often pitted against one another, framed as incommensurable. This section elaborates possibilities for interconnection and resonance between these two worlds, through the shared theme of loss. First, it reflects on observations from a climate change cultural event held in the former motor city of Coventry as part of the City of Culture program in 2021. Then, it juxtaposes insights from two sets of literature on loss, one in relation to deindustrialization studies and another in relation to climate. By working through the recognition of loss across different scales and values, the section proposes a pragmatic approach toward addressing conflicts between jobs and the environment, opening up the discussion on anticipating just transitions.

November 2021, Coventry, UK. There is a largely invisible river that runs through the city of Coventry, underground, called the Sherbourne. Its presence is heard and noticed only in certain places, on the city's edge or near to drainpipes. Few residents know of its existence, how it rushes under the city streets, how it is the habitat for multiple species, how it receives old sofas and shopping trolleys, as a fly tipping hotspot, in the liminal place outside of civic sight. Another near-invisible thread runs through the city, that of the automobile industry. Once known as the UK's 'motor city,' there were many car factories woven throughout the city throughout the twentieth century: Jaguar, Daimler, Rover, and many other big names. Now, very few remain, and most have been converted to warehouses, shopping centers, and residential units, with not a trace of their former uses.

The Routledge Handbook of Deindustrialization Studies

For the past ten years, the Coventry Transport Museum has featured the same collection of bicycles and motorcars over the past century. There is one which I have seen countless times, a rolling video exhibition in a stationary made-in-Coventry black taxicab. Visitors enter the taxi as passengers, and the video is of a taxi driver inviting you for a ride through the city. The taxi driver takes you on a tour of the major car factory locations in the contemporary city, recalling how there used to be factories and social clubs in shopping and residential areas, accompanied by interviews with former male workers who discuss the good old times, of prosperity, camaraderie, and times of laughter.

It is here in the Coventry Transport Museum, that I participate in a workshop titled 'Talking about the Anthropocene,' featuring academics and sound artists who have been commissioned to make sound art for the Coventry City of Culture in 2021, including sounds of the Sherbourne River. The workshop coincides with the COP26 Climate Change Conference in Glasgow. I am aware of the irony of speaking at a public event about the 'Anthropocene' in a museum devoted to honoring the British motor car, to a half-empty room filled with academics, artists, and students, in a city marked by decades of industrial and urban decline. At the end of the workshop, we are invited to view a work of mobile art which is parked in the concrete square in front of the museum, by the artist Mike Stubbs, called 'Climate Emergency Services,' which will soon make the journey to COP26. This artwork captures the contradictions of the climate emergency and the age of the motor car more than any of the sound recordings or academic musings. 'Climate Emergency Services' is a customized vehicle, a van painted black with orange and yellow flames, in the style of souped-up racer cars. On the top of the van is a tank gun which pipes out birdsong. The juxtapositions of form and content in this artwork are jarring and suggest a painful journey.

Indeed, the pain and trauma of loss is a common theme to experiences of deindustrialization and of confronting the climate crisis. Elliott (2018, p. 301) articulates this connection poignantly, outlining the implications of the sociology of loss, which "examines what does, will, or must disappear rather that what can or should be sustained" in relation to the climate crisis through the themes of materiality, politics, knowledge, and practice. The loss of place is a particular point of commonality between deindustrialization studies and the social impacts of climate change, where loss of place is a result of social as well as ecological processes of displacement of people from their homes, livelihoods, communities, and lands (Elliott, 2018, p. 308). According to Elliott, paying attention to loss can highlight contradiction in terms of what can be lost or sustained, and through accepting that things might not be 'okay,' it can also enable us to imagine more deeply transformative visions.

Writing about industrial loss in coalfields and their communities' deindustrialization, Strangleman (2022, p. 15) makes the opposite point, noting that the story of industrial loss has sometimes "ironed out complexity and contradiction." The discrepancy between these findings may be accounted for in terms of the values and meanings of loss: whether loss is accepted or rejected, sudden or gradual, or just or unjust. For Elliott, there is a certain inevitability to loss in relation to climate change, and with it, an acceptance, while for Strangleman, industrial narratives of loss are painful and full of despair, but nonetheless they are instructive, and engaging with them can open up new possibilities for a low-carbon future. In other words, there is convergence between insights on the sociology of loss, particularly for engaging with the complicated relationship between toxic industrial pasts, presents, and futures.

Anticipating Just Transitions

The Dilemmas of Toxic Legacies

Over a decade ago, I published my first book, *Industrial Ruination, Community, and Place* (Mah, 2012), which examined industrial ruination as a lived process, marked by ambivalence and uncertainty, in three old industrial communities: Newcastle-upon-Tyne (shipbuilding, UK); Niagara Falls (chemicals, US and Canada), and Ivanovo (textiles, Russia). The concept of industrial ruination as a lived processes implies a sense of violence and injustice, through destruction, abandonment, and dislocation, of people, communities, and ways of life. Its manifestations are wide-ranging, spanning from job losses to toxic exposures to stigma associated with decline. Industrial ruination also evokes contradictory affects, of loss and mourning for the past, but also regret over the toxic harm in polluting industries, and over entangled histories of settler colonialism and imperialism (see High, 2018; Stoler, 2013). The findings of my work resonate with Sheryl Lee Linkon's (2018) concept of the 'half-life of deindustrialization,' the idea that deindustrialization, like radioactivity, has a half-life, with devastating and contradictory impacts that last for generations.

Looking back, I was interested in examining the opposite of Elliott's sociology of loss; in other words, on 'what can or should be sustained' rather than 'what does, will or must disappear.' However, my interest in this question wasn't due to industrial nostalgia. Instead, it was a question about collective heritage, history, and identity. In the face of industrial abandonment and dispossession, I wondered what knowledge, capacities, and resources in local industrial communities might be sustained. While attentive to structural barriers and ambivalent legacies of empire and colonialism, I focused on local narratives of resistance to top-down, one-size-fits-all models of capitalist development; strong place attachment to homes and communities; care, respect, and pride within former industrial communities; and humor and imagination about future constraints and possibilities.

In an edited volume on "toxic heritage," Kryder-Reid and May (2023) argue that there is an urgent societal need to grapple with hidden toxic histories, including the myriad impacts and harms of toxic heritage. As Kryder-Reid (2023) writes:

> Societies celebrate heroes and commemorate tragedies. But where in public memory is environmental harm? What if people thought about it not only as a science or policy problem, but also as a part of history? Would it make a difference if pollution, along with biodiversity loss and climate change, was seen as part of our shared heritage?

These are uncomfortable questions but important ones. They speak to a tension between preservation and destruction, or between sustainability and loss, in inherited material realities.

Of all the material forms of industrial ruination, toxic pollution is the most insidious. Sometimes, toxicity is evident in plumes of smoke and pools of sludge or in noxious smells and raging headaches, but often it is not sensed at all. Its harmful effects to health and the environment typically linger for generations, long after the factories and smokestacks have disappeared (Murphy, 2017; Boudia et al., 2021). In my research on the abandoned chemical industry in Niagara Falls, I explored the theme of toxic legacies, examining contaminated industrial sites as "unseen ruins" (Mah, 2012). Over the past decade, my research focus has shifted from the long-term social impacts of deindustrialization toward the environmental justice impacts of active industry, examining the global petrochemical industry as a toxic yet "essential" industry (Mah, 2023). Whether a dirty industry is declining or thriving, its toxicity endures as a form of industrial ruination.

173

On a planetary level, toxic industrial ruination is exemplified by the socially and environmentally damaging petrochemical industry. In 2022, scientists announced that chemical pollution had crossed a new planetary boundary, exceeding safe limits in rainwater and threatening the stability of Earth systems (Persson et al., 2022). Around the world, the harmful effects of petrochemical pollution are concentrated in low-income, working-class, and minoritized ethnic "fenceline" communities living adjacent to petrochemical industrial sites (Auyero and Swistun, 2009; Mah, 2023; Wiebe, 2016; Mah and Wang, 2019). The problem of toxic industrial ruination requires urgent public attention, but it is often neglected in political and academic debates, competing for attention amid overlapping social and ecological crises.

Although my explicit focus on ruination has changed over time, my interest in the theme of what should be sustained has endured, and this theme informs my recent work on environmental justice and green industrial transformations (Mah, 2023). Yet through reflecting on planetary ecological crises, I have also become preoccupied with the subject of 'what does, will or must disappear.' For, as painful as future deindustrialization may be, heavily polluting and fossil-fuel-based industries do, will, and must disappear.

This realization brings about new dilemmas and contradictions. Paprocki (2019) discusses the problem of 'anticipatory ruination,' where existing infrastructures and ecologies are destroyed as a way of preempting future environmental losses, often with uneven and unintended consequences. In a study of climate change mitigation discourses and practices in Khulna in coastal Bangladesh, Paprocki (2019) shows how anticipatory ruination occurred when rice agriculture was displaced by commercial shrimp cultivation in governmental efforts to adapt to the climate crisis, but the expansion of shrimp aquaculture wreaked havoc on local ecosystems, livelihoods, and communities.

The concept of anticipatory ruination leads me to the final theme in this chapter: anticipating just transitions, which has a more positive connotation, addressing questions of ethics, justice, and political agency. Whereas anticipatory ruination is a cynical descriptor for dispossession under the guise of environmental protection, anticipating just transitions is a call to imagine, plan, and 'design' just transitions, which could avoid repeating mistakes of the past while confronting dilemmas and structural inequalities and seeking sustainable as well as just pathways.

Discussion: Anticipating Just Transitions

In the global race to reach net zero emissions, decarbonization pressures *will* (very likely) result in future deindustrialization, not only directly in fossil-fuel industries but also in the top four 'hard-to-abate' industries: iron/steel, petrochemicals, cement, and aluminum, as well as in many other fossil-fuel-dependent industries. Further efforts to address the biodiversity crisis, chemical and plastic pollution, excessive waste, and other planetary ecological crises will also require dramatic reduction in polluting industries.

How is it possible to plan, anticipate, and achieve just and sustainable transitions in the most energy-intensive and difficult-to-decarbonize economic sectors? By bringing together debates about just transitions and deindustrialization studies, this chapter extends the temporal scope of consideration, to consider relationships between past, present, and possible future generations.

The concept of 'just transition' is widely used in climate policy and activism, but it remains a contested term. For many workers and residents living in deindustrialized communities, the just transition discourse falls short of offering a concrete alternative to fossil-fuel-based industries (Dobrusin, 2021; Lawhon and McCreary, 2020). Conversely, some scholars and activists argue that just transition policies are not radical enough because they align with "green growth" narratives of sustainable capitalist development and fail to address conflicts between sustainability and justice goals (Ciplet and Harrison, 2020; Paul and Gebrial, 2021).

Furthermore, the narrative of just transition has been used by different groups to advocate competing ideas of social and environmental justice. While environmental activists in Scotland have called for a "just transition" to accelerate the transition away from fossil fuels and petrochemicals, the coal industry in Poland has used the same concept to stall planned transitions away from coal (see Mah, 2023; Morena, Krause, and Stevis, 2020). To overcome these difficulties, Stevis and Felli (2020) make a case for a 'planetary just transition' that aims for greater inclusiveness and justice across different scales and temporalities.

Perhaps, the biggest problem with the just transition is the large gap between discourse and practice. In practice, the language just transition is most often invoked within local communities only once the job losses are on the table rather than as part of a wider discussion about collective histories or futures. This parallels debates about deindustrialization, which are often most heated in the immediate aftermath of factory closures. Both just transitions and deindustrialization take on a more reflective character when situated within the context of a wider history or pattern. Anticipating just transitions requires engaging with future-oriented thinking, of the kind that spans generations, drawing lessons from Bell's post-industrial society and the Club of Rome's report on the limits to growth, in terms of both what the authors got wrong and what they got right, factually as well as ethically and politically.

Methods of anticipating just transitions, which include envisioning 'designs for transitions,' occupy an uncomfortable space, of negotiating dilemmas and conflicts over the stakes of low-carbon transitions, situated within specific communities and places. Yet across competing visions of the just transition, there are growing multiscalar movements for social environmental justice, where alternative ecological visions and pathways are forging alliances and challenging long-dominant orthodoxies (see Mah, 2023). Damian White (2020, p. 20) optimistically points out that there are increasing convergences between "just transitions" and "designs for transitions," and "convergences between these currents might facilitate modes of anti-racist, feminist and ecosocialist design futuring that can get us to think beyond degrowth/Left ecomodern binaries and toward a design politics that can support a Green New Deal." Similarly, Escobar (2020, p. xii) argues that "Faced with crisis of our modes of existence in the world, we can credibly constitute the conjuncture as a struggle over a new reality, what might be called the pluriverse, and over the designs of the pluriverse."

Throughout history, many energy transitions have been deeply unjust, exacerbating existing social and economic inequalities (Newell, 2021). Indeed, as Yusoff (2018) and Lennon (2017) highlight in their research, the fossil fuel transition to coal was made possible by first using human labor as a form of energy under slavery. There are considerable risks that ongoing and future green industrial transitions will be too slow and ineffective and that they will continue to reinforce and reproduce inequalities. There are also more everyday lessons from deindustrialization studies for anticipating just transitions, both through an appreciation for the contradictions of loss and through reckoning with the implications of toxic heritage. This appreciation and reckoning with the complexities of lived experience through transition encourages a more nuanced approach to processes and struggles over just transitions and future deindustrialization.

The Routledge Handbook of Deindustrialization Studies

Reference List

Auyero, J. and Swistun, D.A. (2009). *Flammable: Environmental Suffering in an Argentine Shanty-town*. Oxford: Oxford University Press.

Bell, D. (1973). *The Coming of Post-Industrial Society: A Venture in Social Forecasting*. New York: Basic Books.

Benanav, A. (2020). *Automation and the Future of Work*. London: Verso Books.

Boudia, S., Creager, A.N.H., Frickel, S., Henry, E., Jas, N., Reinhardt, C. and Roberts, J.A. (2021). *Residues: Thinking Through Chemical Environments*. New Brunswick, NJ: Rutgers University Press.

Ciplet, D. and Harrison, J.L. (2020). Transition Tensions: Mapping Conflicts in Movements for a Just and Sustainable Transition. *Environmental Politics*, 23(3), pp. 435–456.

Dobrusin, B. (2021). A Just Transition for All? A Debate on the Limits and Potentials of a Just Transition in Canada. In Räthzel, N. and Stevis, D. (eds.) *The Palgrave Handbook of Environmental Labour Studies*. Cham: Palgrave Macmillan, pp. 295–316.

Elliott, R. (2018). The Sociology of Climate Change as a Sociology of Loss. *European Journal of Sociology/Archives Européennes de Sociologie*, 59(3), pp. 301–337.

Escobar, A. (2020). *Pluriversal Politics: The Real and the Possible*. Durham, NC: Duke University Press.

Feltrin, L., Mah, A. and Brown, D. (2022). Noxious Deindustrialization: Experiences of Precarity and Pollution in Scotland's Petrochemical Capital. *Environment and Planning C: Politics and Space*, 40(3), pp. 950–969.

High, S. (2018). *One Job Town: Work, Belonging, and Betrayal in Northern Ontario*. Toronto: University of Toronto Press.

Kryder-Reid, E. (2023, September 4). The importance of shining a light on hidden toxic histories. *The Conversation*.

Kryder-Reid, E. and May, S. (2023). Toxic Heritage: An Introduction. In Kryder-Reid, E. and May, S. (eds.) *Toxic Heritage: Legacies, Futures, and Environmental Injustice*. London: Routledge, pp. 1–6.

Lawhon, M. and McCreary, T. (2020). Beyond Jobs vs Environment: On the Potential of Universal Basic Income to Reconfigure Environmental Politics. *Antipode*, 52(2), pp. 452–474.

Lennon, M. (2017). Decolonizing Energy: Black Lives Matter and Technoscientific Expertise Amid Solar Transitions. *Energy Research & Social Science*, 30, pp. 18–27.

Linkon, S.L. (2018). *The Half-Life of Deindustrialization: Working-Class Writing About Economic Restructuring*. Ann Arbor: University of Michigan Press.

Mah, A. (2012). *Industrial Ruination, Community, and Place: Landscapes and Legacies of Urban Decline*. Toronto: University of Toronto Press.

Mah, A. (2023). *Petrochemical Planet: Multiscalar Battles of Industrial Transformation*. Durham, NC: Duke University Press.

Mah, A. and Wang, X. (2019). Accumulated Injuries of Environmental Injustice: Living and Working with Petrochemical Pollution in Nanjing, China. *Annals of the American Association of Geographers*, 109(6), pp. 1961–1977.

Meadows, D.H., Meadows, D.L., Randers, J. and Behrens, W.W. III (1972). *The Limits to Growth*. Club of Rome.

Morena, E., Krause, D. and Stevis, D. (2020). *Just Transitions: Social Justice in a Low-Carbon World*. London: Pluto Press.

Murphy, M. (2017). Alterlife and Decolonial Chemical Relations. *Cultural Anthropology*, 32(4), pp. 494–503.

Newell, P. (2021). *Power Shift: The Global Political Economy of Energy Transitions*. Cambridge: Cambridge University Press.

Paprocki, K. (2019). All That Is Solid Melts into the Bay: Anticipatory Ruination and Climate Change Adaptation. *Antipode*, 51(1), pp. 295–315.

Paul, H.K. and Gebrial, D. (eds.). (2021). *Perspectives on a Global Green New Deal*. London: Rosa-Luxemburg-Stiftung.

Persson, L. et al. (2022). Outside the Safe Operating Space of the Planetary Boundary for Novel Entities. *Environmental Science & Technology*, 56(3), pp. 1510–1521.

Silver, H. (2015). Editorial: The Urban Sociology of Detroit. *City & Community*, 14(2), pp. 97–101.

Stevis, D. and Felli, R. (2020). Planetary Just Transition? How Inclusive and How Just? *Earth System Governance*, p. 100065.

Stoler, A.L. (ed.). (2013). *Imperial Debris: On Ruins and Ruination*. Durham, NC: Duke University Press.

Strangleman, T. (2022). Contextualising the Coalfields: Mapping the Socio-Economic and Cultural Loss of the Coal Industry. In Bright, C. (ed.) *Education, Work and Social Change in Britain's Former Coalfield Communities: The Ghost of Coal*. Cham: Springer International Publishing.

White, D. (2020). Just Transitions/Design for Transitions: Preliminary Notes on a Design Politics for a Green New Deal. *Capitalism, Nature, Socialism*, 31(2), pp. 20–39.

Wiebe, S.M. (2016). *Everyday Exposure: Indigenous Mobilization and Environmental Justice in Canada's Chemical Valley*. Vancouver: UBC Press.

Yusoff, K. (2018). *A Billion Black Anthropocenes or None*. Minneapolis: University of Minnesota Press.

PART III

Communities, Identities, Affects

INTRODUCTION
Communities, Identities, Affects

Jackie Clarke

People and places have been at the heart of research in deindustrialization studies. While deindustrialization can be defined in economic terms as a decline in industrial employment, the phenomenon has increasingly come to be understood in terms of a broader set of associated social and cultural transformations. Central to the development of the field have been questions about the social implications of disinvestment, loss of industrial jobs, and the experience of living with industrial ruination. Industrial closures and mass redundancy plans represent a major rupture in working lives and destabilize work-based identities. As industrial workplaces have been shut down and the rhythms of industrial work have given way to those of a more service-based economy, so the networks and institutions of solidarity that had grown up in and around industrial workplaces were tested, eroded, or reconfigured. In some places once synonymous with industry, communities now grapple with a legacy of impoverishment, heightened racial inequalities, and/or social stigma; elsewhere, working-class populations have been displaced by gentrification. The effects of deindustrialization radiate through families and neighborhoods, and across generations, reshaping gender roles and understandings of class. The chapters gathered in this part of the handbook illustrate some of the principal ways in which scholars have explored these shifts through the lenses of community, identity, and affect.

One contribution of research on deindustrialization has been to bring into focus the continued significance of work and employment in the construction of social identities. While the study of labor had waned somewhat in Western Europe and North America by the 1990s, the emergence of deindustrialization as a significant object of historical and social scientific inquiry in the twenty-first century has generated something of a revival of interest. In particular, recent work on women whose jobs in manufacturing were threatened or lost has challenged a long-standing tendency to see women's paid work as secondary to their identities. Such studies highlight these workers' pride in their role as producers and their strong attachments to their products, their former workplaces, and the solidarities they forged there (Clarke, 2015; Gallot, 2015; Bonfiglioli, 2019; Bracke, 2019; Clark, 2022; Stride, 2019; Laframboise, 2023). Considerable attention has focused on the implications of job loss and employment transitions for working-class masculinities. Scholars have explored notably what it means for men employed in heavy industry to lose their jobs, often with no prospect of

DOI: 10.4324/9781003308324-18

similar (or similarly paid) work available, and how those brought up to see themselves as providers for their families have navigated a social world in which their job security, earning power, and sense of social value are radically compromised (Wight, 1993; Walkerdine and Jimenez, 2012; Kideckel, 2004). While working-class masculinity is often embodied in such studies, and in cultural representations of deindustrialization, by the figure of the white skilled man, some key contributions have also attended to the impact on migrant and racialized workers, often relegated to the most subordinate roles in industrial workplaces (Linkon, 2014; Sugrue, 1996; Gay, 2021; Laframboise, 2023).

If questions about work and the workplace have been central to the development of the field, the implications of deindustrialization have also been approached at a wider community level. Community is a term that is readily used in the English-language research on deindustrialization, though its cognates are less frequently used in studies in other languages, and the concept is not an uncontested one within the social sciences.[1] Its use here should not be taken to imply social homogeneity. Nor are communities understood by deindustrialization scholars as static. Rather, researchers have explored the impact of industrial closures and long-term industrial ruination on place-based attachments and social relations constructed within a workplace, neighborhood, or town (see Linkon and Russo, 2002; Cowie and Heathcott, 2003; Mah, 2012; High, MacKinnon, and Perchard, 2017). Place has loomed large in part because of the ways in which patterns of settlement were shaped by industrialization, resulting in populations that were often highly dependent on a single industry or company for employment. 'Pit village' or 'Steeltown' communities have certainly been mythologized and have become objects of nostalgia, but the very persistence of these myths points to the ways in which the meanings of place have been shaped by industrial history.

Likewise, communities can be understood as relations made over time through social and cultural practices. The forms of community life associated with industrial work differed across time and space. But in concentrated industrial settlements they were often structured in part by organizations such as trade unions and work-related social, cultural, or sports clubs (usually dominated by men), as well as by local festivities and less formal neighborly networks and practices sustained notably, as Valerie Walkerdine and Jimenez (2012) have highlighted, by women's unpaid affective labor. Such structures and practices could scarcely remain untouched by deindustrialization.

As these preliminary remarks make clear, deindustrialization studies has been particularly concerned with *working-class* communities and identities. These groups were profoundly affected by the transformations associated with economic restructuring, not least by changes in the labor market. As Jim Tomlinson has noted with reference to the UK, a key characteristic of the industrial economy, at least by the post-1945 period, was that it provided relatively well-paid jobs to workers with modest educational qualifications (Tomlinson, 2020, p. 201). This is not to say that all workers benefited equally. The idea that a working man should earn enough to support his family rested on the assumption that women's primary role was in the home, and as we have already noted, industrial workplaces were marked by significant race and gender hierarchies. Nonetheless, the availability of relatively well-paid industrial jobs, combined with the social protections of the welfare state, had allowed a significant section of the working class to access greater security and rising living standards in Western industrial democracies by the postwar period. The shift to a more service-based economy has seen the number of well-paid industrial jobs dwindle and has typically been characterized by a proliferation of low-paid insecure work (Tomlinson, 2016, pp. 90–92; Winant, 2019; Arquié and Grjebine, 2023, pp. 2–4).[2] In the former socialist states of Central and Eastern Europe, too,

Introduction

many look back on the socialist period as a time when the state and the factory or the mine provided relative security in comparison with the unfettered privatization, unemployment, and precarity that followed (see Bonfiglioli, 2025; Kideckel, 2008, 2004).

At the same time, deindustrialization has been accompanied by a shift in understandings of class and a profound transformation of the symbolic status of the working class. In Central and Eastern Europe, workers had been celebrated as the embodiment of socialist values. As David Kideckel (2004) observes of the miners in Romania's Jiu valley, "[d]uring socialism, the region was the mine, the mine the men, and the men socialist heroes" (p. 42). As Western European economies were rebuilt after the Second World War, industry had been widely seen as synonymous with national strength and industrial workers as having a patriotic mission. Organized workers were feted or feared, depending on one's political allegiances. Thus, French historian Xavier Vigna (2012) has defined the twentieth century as one in which the working classes occupied a central place in the political imaginary. In this period, the industrial worker was the paradigmatic embodiment of the working class. By the late twentieth-century, however, as heavy industry increasingly came to be seen as dirty and insufficiently modern, as industrial jobs were cut or production relocated to other parts of the world, as the industrial workforce shrank, and as neoliberal political ideologies came to the fore, the industrial worker was increasingly figured as a remnant of a social world that belonged in the past (Fontaine, 2014; Kideckel, 2004, p. 42; Bonfiglioli, 2020). Meanwhile, stigmatizing representations of working-class people as "chavs" or "welfare queens" became increasingly normalized (Tyler, 2008; Hancock, 2004).

Against this backdrop, a considerable body of work has now emerged that attends to the subjective and affective dimensions of deindustrialization – to its impact on the conditions in which a sense of self can be constructed, to the changing meanings and value attached to places, to the ways in which community and solidarity are enacted in struggles over deindustrialization or in its aftermath. A range of methods have been used to explore these themes, from ethnography and oral history to the study of working-class writing and other cultural representations.[3] Such methods allow researchers to access not only social practices but also processes of meaning-making 'from below.' As Steven High (2013) has put it: "writing about deindustrialization requires that we try to understand the world as the marginalized see it" (p. 141).

Oral history interviews offer participants an opportunity to relate and interpret aspects of their experience. They create an intersubjective space for storytelling and reflection on change over time, particularly where a life history approach is employed.[4] Oral historians turn to interviews not just to find out 'what happened' but also to explore how narrators make sense of their experience and the changes they have witnessed. Thus, for example, interviews with former workers have offered rich insights into the solidarities constructed in and around industrial workplaces, the sense of loss that often accompanies the end of this way of life, and the nature of struggles against deindustrialization (see High, 2003; Bonfiglioli, 2019; Clark, 2022). Such sources also reveal how subjects make use of the past, engaging in forms of reflective or critical nostalgia as a means of affirming devalued identities and solidarities (see Clarke, 2015; Strangleman, 1999).

While the oral history interview is an embodied encounter, and certainly one whose affective dimensions are rarely lost on those who participate in it, oral historians tend to pay particular attention to the analysis of speech and narrative. In contrast, a significant current of sociological research in deindustrialized communities in the UK has been informed by affect studies or what has been called the affective turn in the social sciences. One manifestation of this has been Geoff Bright's studies of 'social haunting' in former coalfield communities. Citing Avery Gordon, Bright (2021) describes social haunting as what happens when "disturbed feelings cannot be put away," when the social violence of the past resurfaces, revealing something that has been concealed (p. 214). Through participatory workshops labelled 'Ghost Labs,' Bright and his collaborators have used creative methods (song, film, comic books) and playful visual prompts to explore what Valerie Walkerdine has called 'communal being-ness.' One of the characteristics of this approach is its attention to the unconscious and unspoken and to affective atmospheres felt by the researchers (Bright and Ivinson, 2019).

This attention to affect is exemplified here by Walkerdine's chapter, which draws on her previous research in 'Steeltown,' south Wales, in the wake of the closure of the major steelworks on which the town depended. Walkerdine begins by cautioning against imagining deindustrialization as the rupture of a secure way of life. She reminds us that working-class communities in places like Steeltown had a long history of living with insecurity. Over time, she argues, they developed ways of being and 'affective practices' that allowed them to cope with a life of harsh working conditions, accidents, layoffs, and shifting market demands. A 'heavy industrial masculinity' was one response to these conditions. So too were close-knit relations among family and neighbors, whereby practical help would be provided when times were tough, often through women's unpaid caring labor. As plants were closed down, throwing large numbers of men out of work, these ways of communal being came under significant strain. Men who moved into low-status service jobs had to contend with a sense that such work was 'unmanly,' Walkerdine observes, while some young men continued to be brought up in the ideals of industrial masculinity in a context where such work was no longer available to them. At the same time, she argues, women's affective labor shored up men's sense of self, reinforcing the fantasy of the male breadwinner even as women took on greater responsibility for generating household income.

Recent studies have to some extent countered the emphasis on trauma and affective strain in Walkerdine's work. Scholars such as James Ferns (2019) or Jim Phillips, Valerie Wright, and Jim Tomlinson (2020) have highlighted stories of successful adaptation and resilience as workers from heavy industry transition into new sectors, while studies of young men in post-industrial areas have pointed to an evolution away from the norms of "hard man" masculinities (Roberts, 2018). However, as Walkerdine notes here, the diverging findings in the now-substantial British literature on men and masculinity in deindustrialized communities are at least in part a reflection of differing temporal and generational relationships to deindustrialization, as well as patterns of local economic development. While evidence gathered in the late twentieth century and early 2000s in closer temporal proximity to industrial closures is more likely to reveal signs of strain and a strong residual association between masculinity and manual labor, studies conducted from the second decade of the twenty-first century onward suggest greater openness to new forms of work and gender expression in the new generation. Nonetheless, Walkerdine contends, the affective histories of deindustrialized communities continue to echo into the present and can inform our understanding of political phenomena such as the vote for Brexit in many deprived deindustrialized areas in England and Wales.

As Christopher Lawson's chapter reminds us, ethnic diversity has been an important feature of the working classes in the US, the UK, and other former imperial states such as France. When we speak of industrial communities, we speak of communities shaped by histories of slavery, empire, and migration. On both sides of the Atlantic, racialized workers faced multiple forms of discrimination and structural inequality. With less access to formal

Introduction

qualifications, they tended to be hired to the least desirable, worst paid jobs in industry and were less likely to be union members than their white counterparts. These jobs bore the brunt of efforts to intensify production, as industries restructured and were also among the first to be cut as production sites were relocated or new technology introduced. Lawson charts the impact on Black and minority ethnic communities of successive waves of deindustrialization in the US and the UK, focusing particularly on the textile and automotive industries. In doing so, he highlights the lasting impact on urban communities from the 'motor city' of Detroit to the northern English textile town of Oldham, as deindustrialization accentuated racialized patterns of deprivation and residential segregation, fueling racial tensions and at times violent revolt.

Chiara Bonfiglioli's chapter reflects the significance of deindustrialization as a theme in the recent resurgence of scholarly interest class and labor relations in the socialist and post-socialist periods in Central and Eastern Europe. Focusing on the former Yugoslavia, she brings into view not just male-dominated 'heavy' industry but sectors such as textiles that employed women in significant numbers. As Bonfiglioli shows, the histories of deindustrialization, the transition away from socialism, and the break-up of the Yugoslav state in the 1990s are closely intertwined. The Yugoslav case is also of particular interest due to the distinctive model of workers' self-management that had been adopted there, fostering a sense of ownership among workers. Bonfiglioli highlights the brutal process of economic and social dispossession that followed in the post-Yugoslav era and the devaluation experienced by workers, especially women workers, as the old social model was dismantled. Drawing on oral histories, she identifies an 'industrial structure of feeling' in workers' memories that combines post-socialist and post-industrial nostalgia. "Yugoslav times," she argues (p. 218), "are often associated with Fordist modernity, productivity, and economic growth, with the socialist model functioning in ordinary citizens' memories not only as a model of normal life in a material sense but also as an ethical form of life." While such an outlook may be nostalgic, this was a nostalgia rooted, she argues (p. 224), in "lived experiences of solidarity, equality and job security that were lost with transition and deindustrialization."

Material, social, and symbolic changes of the kind analyzed by Walkerdine and Bonfiglioli, also reshaped understandings of place. Anoop Nayak's chapter discusses the production of place-based stigma in deindustrialized places and highlights forms of resistance enacted by local inhabitants in one such place, the English town of Middlesbrough. Drawing on Loïc Wacquant's work and on examples from the US, France, Canada, and Australia, as well as the UK, Nayak's account makes plain the class-based and racialized dynamics of territorial stigmatization. While much of the sociological work on this theme has centered on impoverished multi-ethnic, immigrant, Black, or Indigenous neighborhoods, Nayak shows how racialization combines with class to stigmatize poor white communities in deindustrialized areas. In the UK, a media genre of 'poverty porn,' exemplified by the 'reality' television series *Benefits Street*, has contributed significantly to this process. So too does a form of environmental stigma, which figures the population of deindustrialized areas such as Middlesbrough (once a major center of the iron and steel industry) as 'filthy whites.'

The widely used metaphor of the 'rust belt' illustrates all too clearly how the meanings of place are remade through deindustrialization. Nayak offers a novel way of countering this figuration of deindustrialized places as dead metal, reminding us that all matter is in constant motion. Drawing inspiration from the material and aesthetic properties of metal, he reframes Middlesbrough as a place of 'metallic vitalities,' where local people manage stigma by re-signifying place through activities such as protest and social media commentary.

The aestheticization of industrial ruins has been the object of some debate among scholars of deindustrialization.[5] For Steven High (2013), aestheticized responses to former industrial sites too often erase their history and politics or turn them into the commodity of "ruin porn." Nayak shows how an aesthetic and affective sense of place that is finely attuned to class politics can also illuminate and contribute to the rescripting of stigmatized post-industrial places.

Julia Wambach's chapter considers how, with the disappearance of industrial workplaces, alternative spaces emerge in which identities and emotions connected to industrial life can be reconstructed. While the regeneration of former industrial sites or neighborhoods as leisure spaces has often erased and neglected local working-class communities, leisure activities such as music and sport have also provided a means to express pride in place by constructing a sense of continuity with the industrial past. Thus, for example, Wambach shows how football clubs such as Racing Club de Lens and FC Schalke 04 from the former coalfields of northern France and the Ruhr in Germany, respectively, developed an increasingly strong club identification with the regional heritage of mining as their local mines closed. Wambach draws on a concept from the history of emotions to conceptualize this process as the creation of 'feeling communities.' These mediated communities reach beyond those who were directly involved in industry and tend to blur class identities, appealing to a set of masculine ideals associated with industry and a local identity as underdogs. As Wambach notes, there has to date been little interaction between the fields of deindustrialization studies and the history of emotions, despite the established interest in the affective dimensions of deindustrialization. Her chapter argues for a more productive dialogue between these two fields.

Handbooks like this one are usually published at a point when a field has reached a certain degree of maturity, a point where the contours of the field can be mapped and key findings reviewed. In this respect, the final contributor to this part of the handbook faced an unusual challenge: to scope an area of research that does not yet exist. As Liam Devitt observes, LGBTQ+ people are largely absent from our narratives of deindustrialization. Indeed, as scholars have examined the dismantling of industrial ways of life, they have attended particularly to the implications for normative forms of gender expression which served as a prop of social organization in industrial communities. In doing so, they have tended to exhibit what Devitt terms 'methodological straightness.' To carve out a space for a queer deindustrialization studies, Devitt turns to queer histories of labor, neoliberalism, and gentrification. Acknowledging some of the tensions that have existed between queer theory and theorizations of class, they point, nonetheless, to certain methodological affinities between queer studies and deindustrialization studies: both have been characterized by a desire to move beyond the traditional archive, to take autobiographical sources and material culture seriously, to construct what Cvetkovich (2003) calls an "archive of feelings." By mapping out this space for dialogue, Devitt lays the foundations for a more expansive understanding of deindustrial communities and their dynamics of gender, sexuality, and class.

Notes

1 On debates about the concept, see, for example, Walsh, J.C. and High, S. (1999). Rethinking the Concept of Community. *Histoire sociale/Social History*, 32(64), pp. 255–273; Blokland, T. (2001). Bricks, Mortar and Memories: Neighbourhoods and Networks in Collective Acts of Remembering. *International Journal of Urban and Regional Research*, 25(2), pp. 268–283. Beyond the English-speaking world, cognates for the term 'community' are sometimes considered more problematic and are less widely used in the scholarly literature. This is the case in French, for example,

Introduction

although related questions about social relations and social- and place-based identities are very much present in the literature. See, for example, Tornatore, J.-L. (2005). L'Invention de la Lorraine industrielle: Notes sur un processus en cours. *Ethnologie française*, 35(4), pp. 679–689; Castellesi, R. (2019). Ils détruisent notre vie. Ils cassent nos usine. *Désindustrialisation et (dé)mobilisations dans deux villes moyennes, Romans et Autun (1949–2017), Revue d'histoire*, 144, pp. 115–129.

2 Arquié, A. and Grjebine, T. (2023, March). Vingt ans de plans sociaux dans l'industrie: Quels enseignements pour la transition écologique? *La Lettre du CEPII*, 435, pp. 2–4.

3 For more on cultural representations, see Linkon, S.L. (2018). *The Half-Life of Deindustrialization: Working-Class Writing About Economic Restructuring*. Ann Arbor: University of Michigan Press, and the section of this handbook devoted to 'The Critical Cultural Work of Representations.'

4 There is an extensive literature on oral history theory. A useful starting point is Abrams, L. (2016). *Oral History Theory*. Abingdon: Routledge.

5 See the contributions to Strangleman, T., Rhodes, J. and Linkon, S. (eds.). (2013, Fall). Crumbling cultures: Deindustrialization, class and memory. *Special Issue of International Labor and Working-Class History*, 84.

Reference List

Abrams, L. (2016). *Oral History Theory*. Abingdon: Routledge.

Arquié, A. and Grjebine, T. (2023). Vingt ans de plans sociaux dans l'industrie: Quels enseignements pour la transition écologique? *La Lettre du CEPII*, 435, pp. 2–4.

Blokland, T. (2001). Bricks, Mortar and Memories: Neighbourhoods and Networks in Collective Acts of Remembering. *International Journal of Urban and Regional Research*, 25(2), pp. 268–283.

Bonfiglioli, C. (2019). *Women and Industry in the Balkans*. London: I.B. Tauris.

Bonfiglioli, C. (2020). Postsocialist Deindustrialisation and Its Gendered Structure of Feeling: The Devaluation of Women's Work in the Croatian Garment Industry. *Labor History*, 61(1), pp. 36–47.

Bonfiglioli, C. (2025). Class, Gender, and Industrial Structures of Feeling after Socialism: Post-industrial Lives in the Post-Yugoslav Space. In Strangleman, T. et al. (eds.) *Routledge International Handbook of Deindustrialization Studies*. Abingdon and New York: Routledge, pp. 218–231.

Bracke, M. (2019). Labour, Gender and Deindustrialisation: Women Workers at Fiat (Italy 1970s–1980s). *Contemporary European History*, 28(4), pp. 484–499.

Bright, G. (2021). Feeling, Reimagined in Common. Working with Social Haunting in the English coalfields. In Fazio, M., Launius, C. and Strangleman, T. (eds.) *Routledge International Handbook of Working-Class Studies*. London and New York: Routledge, p. 214.

Bright, G. and Ivinson, G. (2019). Washing Lines, Whinberries and Reworking 'Waste Ground': Women's Affective Practices and a Haunting within the Haunting of the UK Coalfields. *Journal of Working-Class Studies*, 4(2), pp. 25–39.

Castellesi, R. (2019). "Ils détruisent notre vie. Ils cassent nos usine." Désindustrialisation et (dé)mobilisations dans deux villes moyennes, Romans et Autun (1949–2017). *20&21. Revue d'histoire*, 144, pp. 115–129.

Clark, A. (2022). *Fighting Deindustrialisation: Scottish Women's Factory Occupations, 1980–1982*. Liverpool: Liverpool University Press.

Clarke, J. (2015). Closing Time: Deindustrialization and Nostalgia in Contemporary France. *History Workshop Journal*, 79(1), pp. 107–125.

Cowie, J. and Heathcott, J. (eds.). (2003). *Beyond the Ruins: The Meanings of Deindustrialization*. Ithaca, NY: Cornell University Press.

Cvetkovich, A. (2003). *An Archive of Feelings: Trauma, Sexuality and Lesbian Public Cultures*. Durham: Duke University Press.

Ferns, J. (2019). Workers' Identities in Transition: Deindustrialization and Scottish Steelworkers. *Journal of Working-Class Studies*, 4(2), pp. 55–78.

Fontaine, M. (2014). *Fin d'un monde ouvrier. Liévin 1974*. Paris: EHESS.

Gallot, F. (2015). *En Découdre: Comment les ouvrières ont révolutionné le travail et la société*. La Découverte.

Gay, V. (2021). *Pour la dignité: Ouvriers immigrés et conflits sociaux dans les années 1980*. Lyon: Presses universitaires de Lyon.

Hancock, A.-M. (2004). *The Politics of Disgust: The Public Identity of the Welfare Queen*. New York: New York University Press.

High, S. (2003). *Industrial Sunset: The Making of North America's Rust Belt, 1969–84*. Toronto: University of Toronto Press.

High, S. (2013, Fall). Beyond Aesthetics: Visibility and Invisibility in the Aftermath of Deindustrialization. *International Labor and Working-Class History*, 84, pp. 140–153.

High, S., MacKinnon, L. and Perchard, A. (eds.). (2017). *The Deindustrialized World: Confronting Ruination in Postindustrial Places*. Vancouver: UBC Press.

Kideckel, D. (2004). Miners and Wives in Romania's Jiu Valley: Perspectives on Postsocialist Class, Gender, and Social Change. *Identities*, 11(1), pp. 39–63.

Kideckel, D. (2008). *Getting By in Postsocialist Romania*. Bloomington: Indiana University Press.

Laframboise, L. (2023). 'La Grève de la fierté': Resisting Deindustrialization in Montréal's Garment Industry, 1977–1983. *Labour/Le Travail*, 91(1), pp. 57–88.

Linkon, S.L. (2014). Men Without Work: White Working-Class Masculinity in Deindustrialization Fiction. *Contemporary Literature*, 55(1), pp. 148–167.

Linkon, S.L. (2018). *The Half-Life of Deindustrialization: Working-Class Writing About Economic Restructuring*. Ann Arbor: University of Michigan Press.

Linkon, S.L. and Russo, J. (2002). *Steeltown USA: Work and Memory in Youngstown*. Lawrence: University of Kansas Press.

Mah, A. (2012). *Industrial Ruination, Community and Place: Landscapes and Legacies of Urban Decline*. Toronto: University of Toronto Press.

Phillips, J., Wright, V. and Tomlinson, J. (2020). Being a Clydesider in the Age of Deindustrialisation: Skilled Male Identity and Economic Restructuring in the West of Scotland since the 1960s. *Labor History*, 61(2), pp. 151–169.

Roberts, S. (2018). *Young Working-Class Men in Transition*. New York: Routledge.

Strangleman, T. (1999). The Nostalgia of Organisations and the Organisation of Nostalgia: Past and Present in the Contemporary Railway Industry. *Sociology*, 33(4), pp. 725–746.

Stride, R. (2019). Women, Work and Deindustrialization: The Case of James Templeton and Co., Glasgow, c1960–1981. *Scottish Labour History*, 54, pp. 154–180.

Sugrue, T. (1996). *The Origins of the Urban Crisis: Race and Inequality in Postwar Detroit*. Princeton: Princeton University Press.

Tomlinson, J. (2016). Deindustrialisation Not Decline: A New Metanarrative for Postwar British History. *Twentieth-Century British History*, 27(1), pp. 90–92.

Tomlinson, J. (2020). Deindustrialisation: Strengths and Weaknesses as a Key Concept for Understanding Post-War British History. *Urban History*, 47, p. 201.

Tornatore, J.-L. (2005). L'Invention de la Lorraine industrielle: Notes sur un processus en cours. *Ethnologie Française*, 35(4), pp. 679–689.

Tyler, I. (2008). Chav Mum, Chav Scum: Class Disgust in Contemporary Britain. *Feminist Media Studies*, 8(4), pp. 17–34.

Vigna, X. (2012). *Histoire des ouvriers en France au XXe siècle*. Paris: Perrin.

Walkerdine, V. and Jimenez, L. (2012). *Gender, Work and Community After Deindustrialization: A Psychosocial Approach*. Basingstoke: Palgrave.

Walsh, J.C. and High, S. (1999). Rethinking the Concept of Community. *Histoire sociale/Social History*, 32(64), pp. 255–273.

Wight, D. (1993). *Workers not Wasters: Masculine Respectability, Consumption and Employment in Central Scotland*. Edinburgh: Edinburgh University Press.

Winant, G. (2019). "Hard Times Make for Hard Arteries and Hard Livers": Deindustrialization, Biopolitics, and the Making of a New Working Class on Pittsburgh. *Journal of Social History*, 53(1), pp. 107–132.

12

COMMUNITY, AFFECT, AND DEINDUSTRIALIZATION

Valerie Walkerdine

Introduction

This chapter argues that to understand the full impact of deindustrialization we need to examine the affective aspects of that impact, often poorly understood because the effects are frequently subtle and complex. Drawing on generally available research coupled with my own particular research in one former UK industrial community, I seek to establish a means of engaging with the affective life of deindustrialized communities and to emphasize the cruciality of a long-term, cross-generational approach to the effects of deindustrialization.

The Formation of Industrial Communities

Industrialization began in the UK from the eighteenth century onward, which, as we know, was earlier than in many other countries. Primarily, this occurred because mercantile capitalism and slavery had made available financial resources allowing the emergence of an English bourgeoisie. This emerging enriched bourgeoisie were able to take advantage of natural resources: buying land, setting up mines, iron and steel works, and other forms of heavy industry, as well as buying into the inventions of steam power, engines, electricity, for example, (Lewis, 2002).

I mention this only to think about the issues that I discuss in this chapter: the creation of, and then the destruction via deindustrialization, of communities created around mines and factories. A central part of this was the creation of the category of the 'worker.' The worker is an element in the production of profit and the rate of profit across international trade. The worker should be understood as itself a production. Men and women had to be made into workers – to embody the category of worker to work according to those constraints through which profit was made. Workers had to embody work practices, recognizing also the consequences of worklessness even though the global trade in commodities and thus the rate of profit was insecure (e.g., the Workhouse in the UK; See Driver, 1989).

The fluctuation in demand and supply across international trade created the need for a workforce capable of accommodating themselves to fluctuations in the demand for labor produced by fluctuating rates of profit. Comprising primarily the dislocated rural poor, this

DOI: 10.4324/9781003308324-19

body of people had to be assembled into a disciplined industrial workforce. For instance, their relationship to work, time, and space had to be reconstituted to accommodate quite different forms of work and daily life (Adam, 1995).

While we know that industrialization meant that men, women, and children were all employed in heavy industry, in the period immediately prior to deindustrialization, the 'worker' was almost always covertly understood as male. I am arguing that industrialization as a process created the industrial worker as a series of embodied ways of being, as well as affective dispositions: the need to keep to industrial time, the need to display hardness and fortitude in the face of brutal and often dangerous physical work, the need to keep embodying the worker even in times of worklessness, as well as concurrent community dispositions involving the creation of a workforce living in close proximity to one another, working to a timetable often conveyed by bells, whistles, clocks, and living in circumstances often surrounded by the constant presence of factory housing and with objects such as winding gear or blast furnaces frequently located in the very center of their community. Such communities also often existed in quite isolated locations; locations chosen primarily because of their proximity to raw materials.

These difficult and dangerous work conditions, with accidents, layoffs, shifting demands for products etc. meant that the workers and the community in which they lived had to construct a means to contain continuity and ontological security, something which had to be achieved on both a personal and communal level.

I have emphasized this point as a prequel to understanding what happens when factories, works, and mines close. It is impossible to grasp the implications of deindustrialization without first understanding what the conditions of work and the affective practices of that work "created" as a means of coping with the conditions of work presented to them (Walkerdine, 2020).

All of these created the need to embody what I call 'heavy industrial masculinity.' We can understand this as a set of practices through which masculinity was performed and embodied, but we can also point to the fantasies through which such practices of masculinity were maintained. Indeed, those fantasies and practices were deliberately produced precisely both to produce a workforce capable of producing hard physical labor and for the community and the personal fortitude to withstand the conditions of that existence (Bederman, 1995).

My argument is that to understand the community and gendered effects of deindustrialization as well as its affects, we must understand what was there during the moment of heavy industry and how the loss of its presence was experienced.

The examples given in this chapter relate primarily to research undertaken in a former steel community in the south Wales Valleys, an area of steep-sided north–south valleys with poor transport links but plentiful raw materials – coal and iron. The transport links between Valleys communities were poor (Walkerdine and Jimenez, 2012). This research was conducted with former steelworkers and their families soon after the final closure (there had been three previous closures). The concepts used here were developed by working with interviews conducted in the community in which it was quite common for people to talk about how it was before the closure as compared with the present and what they missed – or did not miss. I aim here to set out the concepts developed during and after this research to stress the affective aspects of deindustrialization, which include rarely recognized aspects of gendered relationality as well as affective ties within the community itself.

The Organization of Time and Space

We exist in time, so that any understanding of place cannot simply be a slice through time (Massey, 2005). In other words, a community changes and morphs not only through time in its outward appearance but also through the character of its affective relations. I have called this phenomenon an affective history (Walkerdine, 2010, 2016a, 2016b). An affective history recognizes the affective work of shoring up continuity in a time of change and turbulence. We understand that the moment of industrialization itself is a rupture and one that changes the relation of people to the land, causes new settlements to be built, migrations to happen (in south Wales many workers came from Ireland), and new interpersonal relations and the organization of work, time, and family life. We are then faced with the threats to this informal community organization when confronted by the many changes and ruptures historically present within this period, roughly 1800 to 1980 in the UK.

In the south Wales case, there were several changes in ownership over the period of steel production as well as closures and reopenings, all derived from fluctuations in the price of commodities on global markets. Then, considering all that, the attempts to keep a community together as a sense of a communal being-ness (Studdert and Walkerdine, 2016; Studdert, 2006) is sorely threatened by the ongoing existence of industrialization itself. This is the historical landscape in which the final process of deindustrialization takes place. Not only is there an 'ultimate' closure imposed upon the entire 200-year lineage of industrialization, but this closure is final and total in the sense that it also becomes clear to the residents that no other industry is coming to fill the void. It is impossible therefore to underestimate the impact of this upon communities. Later in the chapter, I explore this in terms of the vote for Brexit in the UK, itself undoubtedly an effect of the turbulence and desolation caused by the finality attended upon this ending of industry. We would witness such effects across the deindustrialized world.

In short, we cannot think of deindustrialization simply as a trauma or rupture of a secure way of life. I am at pains to emphasize that the affective life of industrial communities was never easy and had always to adapt to the changing circumstances of industry, change that happened throughout industrial time. The issue then is how to think about this affective history.

Affective Life as Containment

There are many ways of understanding the affective life of a community facing constant threats. The one which made most sense to me when I was confronted with the reflections of community members on the time before and after closure was that it was the community itself that had to provide a set of practices of continuity in the face of 200 industrial years of vulnerability. However, it was also noted that this was not sufficient to withstand the effects of deindustrialization primarily because the affective practices (Walkerdine, 2020, pp. 18–22) that were developed were very dependent on ways of support which assumed the (fluctuating) presence of a central industry in the town. Thus, these practices, in a manner of speaking, mirrored the terms of existing industry. That is, the communities themselves had developed complex practices of support based upon an assumption that whatever state the industry was in at any particular time, nonetheless the community would always exist in one form or another, whether the times were 'bleak' or 'prosperous.' I will go on to explore this in due course. But, first of all, let me explore how we might think theoretically about the support for collective being.

> Nothing is secure. Nothing is secure at all. That's the sad thing about it. You can't relax. People are just stressed by the thought that I could be at work today and tomorrow it's closed, which they have in the Valleys. It's on the news. They've gone to work and the doors are locked.
>
> *(Walkerdine and Jimenez, 2012, p. 46)*

How do people survive and live with a continuing sense that nothing is secure? Countless people the world over live in this way. In recent history, in the global North we think of the effects of neoliberalism with the loss of the sense of regular and steady work for many as a new development, but the sense that nothing is secure is and always has been a way of life for many through historical time and across the world. Thus, we cannot think about this in terms of normality and pathology as if the sense of steadiness and continuity, of having enough, of not being threatened by cut-offs, layoffs, producing distress, and devastation were somehow pathological. Rather, it is important to recognize the need to create ways in which a sense of stability and support allows people to carry on and support each other.

In the research with the steel community, I turned to work on infancy which described ways in which caregivers' bodies themselves provided a sense of "holding" against a terrifying feeling of disintegration (Bick, 1968, pp. 484–486). I started to think about ways in which communities themselves might feel held together against the constant threat of the disintegration of community, and I turned to the work on the skin by Didier Anzieu (2014), which argued that the skin is not just a membrane that protects and holds together the physical body but has an affective role in providing a sense of being held together in relation to the threat of disintegration or falling apart. Anzieu argued that a group (in this case a community) also had an affective skin that allowed the sense of being held or belonging in the face of chronic insecurity. He called this a second or affective skin, which could, according to Willoughby (2004), hold the community together often in quite rigid ways to guard against survival anxieties. Rigidity, suggests Willoughby, can include the poor toleration of outsiders, which I will go on to document. This approach also suggested that we could understand the industry (factory, works, mine) as a psychic object, which means that it could be a rich source of the fantasy life of the community since it provided the central plank of the formation and continuity of the community.

When we consider that industry brought people together in close proximity to each other and with an industrial timetable of shared work, we also recognize the threats to security that were ever-present – the layoffs, closures etc. In Britain, where the Workhouse existed, in a time marked by a lack of welfare provision and the constant possibility of industrial accidents, it is no wonder that the people came together not only to fight for their rights through the creation of trade unions and collective bargaining but also to find ways of helping and supporting each other informally. This allowed them to withstand the ongoing hardships and provide constant support for each other in times of trouble. It produced a number of affective practices within our researched community.

I coined the term 'affective practice' based on the idea that affective life could be organized via social practices in the same way that Henriques et al. had argued that the discursive work of regulation and management was organized via discursive practices – that is, practices of governance through which the minutiae of everyday life was constantly surveilled

Community, Affect, and Deindustrialization

(Henriques et al., 1984). Of course, as we now understand, our affective life is also highly organized and governed, but here I am talking about the ways in which the community found practices to help and support each other within the confines of the regulation and constraints of their daily lives. For example, many people commented that it was important to keep difficulties within the family and not to share them (Bick, 1968). At first I thought of this as repressive, but it soon became clear from responses that this was not at all the case, that it functioned rather as a practice respectful of the fact that everyone had difficulties, and so it was important not to burden other people but to share things that strengthened the community rather than further place stress upon others. In relation to this, many participants described the community during the industrial era as a family. For them, this meant that in practical terms people supported each other as they would any members of a biological family. They did this by, for example, taking in and feeding other people's children and performing tasks to give practical help to each other. In addition, community members were discouraged from looking for work in other nearby communities on the grounds that each community had to look after its own. This worked well in a place in which so many people worked in the same industry, and so informal networks existed to introduce new potential employees to a workplace. This also had the effect of binding the locals closer together with a difficulty with outsiders.

Also, housing was usually terraced and so much could be shared; one example given was of having a wash day on which people put out their washing on the same day and talked to each other across the fences between gardens or yards (Walkerdine and Jimenez, 2012, p. 46). Time and space were punctuated by clocks, sounds such as hooters calling people to work and the sounds of workers walking together through the town to clock on or off.

To me, what becomes clear is that the development of shared affective practices was crucial to the possibility of going on being in industrial time. It does not mean that everything was good, ok, or even static, but rather it points to the simple presence of methods of sharing and coping passed down through generations. These aimed to offset as best they could the randomness of factory life. It is in this context that we can think about the changes to affective life produced by deindustrialization, but first I want to discuss how ideological tropes enter into the imagination and fantasy of community members and how these create ways in which certain tropes of masculinity and femininity are lived.

Creating the Male Manual Worker

Many men in the research discussed the fact that they disliked work in which they came home clean. If they got dirty at work, they felt like real men. Such men also had to signal their distance from femininity by being hard. When we explore this further we find that it is not simply the concern of some ageing male dinosaurs displaying toxic masculinity (Walkerdine, 2017). Rather, considerable ideological and discursive effort was put into creating the strong male manual worker, who could withstand difficult and often dangerous work conditions and understand them as evidence of successful masculinity. Bederman (1995) presents an analysis of the transformation of discourses of American manhood in the late nineteenth and early twentieth centuries, in which there was a call for the resurrection of savage qualities to stave off the repression of "masculine impulses". To become labor, a strong virile masculinity, closer to nature was to be honed – to be a man in the tradition of hard men. What we understand is that, in these circumstances, the valorization of what many now would regard as traditional and often toxic masculinity was a deliberate ideological, discursive, and affective production in which being strong, silent, dirty were markers of success in an industry in which physical weakness could create dangers for the worker and loss of profit if the masculine did not become effective labor. This also tended to result in the designation of femininity as other, bringing with it efforts not to be understood as feminine, including, for example, leaving all reading and writing to women. I had initially been surprised by how many older male workers could not read.

But just as this created the fantasy of the male manual worker, it also created that of the woman and the male child. Some older men really struggled after deindustrialization to even begin to take on household chores or know what to do with themselves, which is hardly surprising given all the effort to convince these men that they needed to be hard and not enter what was then considered the feminine domestic space. In addition, some men (and indeed women) passed on to young men the disdain historically developed for anything other than heavy industrial work, even though such work was no longer available. For example, some women industrial cleaners referred to a young man as "Mrs Mop," a pejorative term formerly used to describe women domestic cleaners (Walkerdine and Jimenez, 2012). Finally, some women also struggled: during the process of deindustrialization all attention was focused on the men being made redundant, and this meant that their wives and partners were suffering in silence, given the injunction not to bother other people. Some women were also trying to manage taking on the role of income provider while simultaneously maintaining to their men the fiction that the latter were still the breadwinners, even though, so to speak, unable to win any bread. Walkerdine and Jimenez argued that this created an unsustainable situation in which the present reality could not be easily confronted by the couple or family or indeed the community, as the women struggled to keep the fantasy of the male breadwinner in play, attempting to stave off unbearable pain and a sense of failure in the men. No support for any of this affective distress was available at the time of closure, as far as I know. This has serious consequences for the ways in which the transition to different gendered modes of employment was made.

Trauma

Should we describe what happened during deindustrialization as trauma? We can understand trauma as a blow and one that can have profound consequences for an engagement with time, body etc. – with profound affective and physical consequences. For example, a considerable amount of work exists that demonstrates that third-generation holocaust survivors suffer from difficulties with cortisol levels that indicate too easily raised stress levels (Yehuda et al., 1995, 1998, 2001). Thus, undoubtedly people and communities together can suffer from the effects of deindustrialization, and moreover, this can be communicated to and carried by subsequent generations. However, as far as I know, almost no research exists that addresses this issue. We can also ask if it is correct to call the suffering experienced and carried into the future 'trauma.' Kleinman et al. (1997) prefer the term social suffering, which has a different connotation in that it avoids medicalization. The claiming of suffering via a medicalized discourse tends both to individualize and to downplay the attribution of responsibility (Walkerdine and Jimenez, 2012, p. 82). Erikson (1994) argues that collective trauma can be experienced as 'a blow to the basic tissues of social life that damages the bonds attaching people together and impairs the prevailing sense of communality . . . a form of shock . . . , a gradual realization that the community no longer exists as an effective source of support' (p. 233). Erikson documents an example of the toxicity of a lake, meaning that the community can no longer support itself and has to move. What I am describing in relation to deindustrialization is not identical of course, but it does posit experiences in which a central part of the landscape (a mine, a foundry, a factory, e.g.) ceases to exist, meaning all the practices and ways of being together built around it are sorely tested. Thus, we can say that deindustrialization upsets the rhythms of community time and ruptures existing ways of being and relating.

Strangleman (2024) is critical of my use of the term trauma as applied to the difficulties about breadwinning referred to earlier (pp. 12, 22). His argument is that future generations have managed to move into different forms of employment and especially new practices of masculinity. However, we need to distinguish between the local effect at any given moment (e.g., the breadwinner), the effect on the next generation (e.g., the young men), and the sense of hope or hopelessness in a community. I am trying to understand what effect the 'blow' of deindustrialization has as it passes through biographical and historical time and across generations. Indeed, everyone has to move on, and things have to change. But while work has to be found, ways of living and being have to adapt to the changes, my interest here is in the often unnoticed ways in which something is carried across generations, even if it ceases to be understood as a direct effect of deindustrialization. In a recent article, I gave the example of a man who had moved as a child with his family on the £10 passage from postwar UK to Australia (Walkerdine, 2023a). As an adult, the man, now, comfortably off, always kept a fridge full of fizzy drinks – the very thing that could not be afforded when he was a child in the UK, a practice that spoke of the possibility of having enough. But we could argue that the need to fill the fridge with the drinks itself spoke to the possibility of an anxiety about not 'having enough' that had never gone away. Indeed, his children might also like the fridge full of drinks, but they would not necessarily any longer understand their significance. In this way, we can understand that affective histories create ways of being that pass certain affective dispositions down generations without subsequent generations understanding just why they feel a certain way (Walkerdine, 2016a, 2023a, 2023b). In relation to deindustrialization, we could think of people wanting to get away at all costs or not being able to leave, of never wanting to have anything to do with the work of previous generations, versus needing to keep a sense of industrial masculinity going, for example. There are many ways in which the past can transmit itself to future generations, but we should remember not necessarily to expect to find the obvious and think also of more subtle forms of affective history – what Revel calls micro-histories, the everyday forms of relating that make up the affective histories of industrialization and deindustrialization, taking us into its half-life, a toxic trace that exists in a subtle way for generations, differing by geography and circumstance into what we might call an affective ecology (Revel, 1996; Linkon, 2018).

The Next Generation

The work I carried out followed a closure that happened in 2003, and the fieldwork was conducted three years later in 2006–2007. This means that deindustrialization was raw at that point and people's feelings about the closure and the future were still settling. What about research that engages with subsequent generations in former industrial communities? We need to organize this work according to its date and location because what we begin to see is the changing 'half-life' as it exists across time and space.

In the UK, there were a number of studies that took place around 20 years ago with relatively close temporal proximity to deindustrialization in the areas in which they were undertaken. Nayak's research in the Northeast of England identified a group of working-class young men with a "prominent masculine legacy of manual labor [which] ran through their familial biographies" (Nayak, 2003a, p. 150; see also Nayak, 2003b). Also, they felt that school was of little importance for their future, which they saw as committed to skilled physical labor and 'hard graft.' Similarly, McDowell's (2003) research on young men in Sheffield and Cambridge also found a desire for semi- or unskilled manual work. Deindustrialization in Sheffield had taken place in the 1990s, whereas in Cambridge there was never any heavy industry. McDowell is at pains to note the labor market change and the desire of the young men to be the breadwinner. She moreover noted the impossibility of these occurring in what was fast becoming the new low-waged unskilled and insecure economy. In a similar vein, Nixon's (2006) research undertaken in Manchester in the early aughties found that the young men in the study, who had all experienced low attainment at school, unemployment, anti-authority positions, and a desire to undertake manual work, all ended up in low-paid insecure work. None expressed any desire to enter training or higher-paid new industries. Gater (2022) worked with a group of men in the Valleys who were in their thirties in the late 2010s, and they all preferred manual work outside.

I would argue therefore that in deindustrialized areas in the period after deindustrialization (often the 1980s, 1990s, and early 2000s in the UK), an affective legacy in at least a section of young men is a strong affective tie to manual work even though the work is different, of a lower status, and usually poorly paid and insecure. To understand this as a choice says something important about the need to feel connected to the masculinity of the industrial period and in that sense could potentially be understood as part of a desperate clinging together identified by Willoughby as an effect of community trauma.

Yet something was changing and later we see interesting shifts that suggest the openness to change. In work undertaken in the second decade of the twenty-first century and later in some locations, there has been a transformation of available work beyond the simply low-paid and insecure (though that is what underpins the economy). More importantly, we are temporally and historically further away from deindustrialization, and so it is likely that young people taking part in research at this period would have parents who were not employed in heavy industry (though their grandparents may have been). Thus, we might expect to see some changes. Of two studies that explore young masculinities in this period, though in very different locations, we see differing responses to a hugely different labor market in each place, but in both, given different circumstances, we witness more openness to other employment possibilities (Gater, 2022; Roberts, 2018).

Through this work, we learn of the geographical and temporal specificity of what happens. In some locations, alternative forms of work have come in, whereas in others, little has happened by way of new forms of employment, with former industrial communities existing in states of poverty and decline (see Emery, Powell, and Crookes, 2023). Roberts (2018) has explored the employment of young men in an area of Kent that formerly housed shipbuilding, mining, and milling. In this area, deindustrialization has witnessed regeneration, including a large increase in retail, wholesale, restaurants, and warehouses, so that now the area is ranked as in the least deprived third of the UK (Roberts, 2012). Having been one of the poorest areas of England, its proximity to London has meant improved transport links and a large investment (Roberts, 2018). What Roberts observed from his 7-year longitudinal study was that the young men had adapted to the new employment conditions and displayed forms of masculinity required within the new employment, what Roberts calls a form of inclusive masculinity more in tune with the emotional demands of retail work. Roberts claims that the differentiation in his findings can be explained through the contemporary nature of his research and participants' detachment from previous ways of being due to the decline in heavy industry and the coinciding rise in service sector work.

In contrast, Gater (2022), working in the south Wales Valleys, noted different kinds of changes. While there is little by way of well-paid work in the area, teenage boys have adapted a more hybrid form of masculinity in which they may well be influenced by the previous generation to aspire to work that is not related to manual labor (nursing, cooking, funeral parlor, paramedic, e.g.). This alongside changes in ways of relating to each other in which previously unthinkable practices such as young men hugging each other and crying in public have become commonplace, yet, at the same time the young men do not want to move away, and their poor educational attainment (many in offsite centers) means that the likelihood of their ever working in anything but low-paying work is very low. By contrast again, Nayak (2010), working in the Midlands, has noted both the possibilities of other kinds of work and a desperate kind of white youth racism that creates racial tension in communities that were formerly well mixed. He identifies a hardening of racist tropes in a kind of fantasy of dominant (white) masculinity with no work or future.

It would be possible to understand all of these developments as, in their different ways, an aspect of the affective half-life of deindustrialization, as I have sought to suggest. We cannot simply expect one response or for the affective legacy to be necessarily obvious – following or differing from previous generations, the creation of new patterns of relating and being together, the production of toxic separation and difference are all understandable within the framework I have set out in this chapter.

Politics (Brexit)

The political implications of deindustrialization are profound. In the UK, as elsewhere, the division of the population is well-known with inhabitants of former industrial communities often understood as conservative, racist, and longing for a return of empire. Likewise, in the US, they are characterized as racist and reactionary supporters of the Right. While the vote for Brexit in the UK can hardly be laid at the door of deindustrialized communities, the feeling of being unheard was very strong along with a distrust of the EU. In research carried out by David Studdert and myself, deindustrialized areas were and still are some of the most deprived in the UK (Walkerdine, 2018, 2020). There was a widespread vote for Brexit from inhabitants of deindustrialized areas of England and Wales which had not benefited from an influx of new forms of work.[1] In this research, undertaken in south Wales, concern was almost entirely about work. Indeed, it was about the possible return of industry once the European Union no longer had a say. In meetings that we conducted, examples were given of EU projects that had not benefited the area: two hospitals with less space than the one they replaced, a sculpture of a Welsh dragon and a bypass 20 years too late, for example. That money from the European Union could be used only for certain things, which did not involve the things that the town desperately needed, led many in the community to vote for Brexit in the hope that freedom from Brussels would release money to bring back industry to the town. This hope was based on a version of Lexit (Left Brexit) as championed by the politician Tony Benn in 1975 (Jacotine and Wellings, 2015). An in-depth interview with a low-waged Brexit supporter from the Valleys gave a number of examples of why Brexit was important, all to do with fairness, for example, fair pay and the end of modern slavery (Walkerdine, 2020, pp. 18–22). The participant pointed out the likelihood that my local car wash was staffed via modern slavery. But, most importantly, perhaps the clear message of the interview was that the middle-class minority refused to listen to what the working-class majority wanted. This majority wanted a say, a sense that they could influence policy to get the fair society with decent paying jobs. In other words, deindustrialization in those areas still left poor was being ignored by successive governments and by politicians and policymakers in general, who had their own ideas about what was best for such communities. This was amply demonstrated by the failure of local and national politicians to allow such people to lead them by understanding and responding to what they felt they needed (Walkerdine, 2020, pp. 18–22). Rather, politicians wanted the locals to support their agenda not to come up with one of their own. This feeling that the politicians and policymakers did not care was expressed in many sentiments from despair, to voting, to putting up alternative politicians.

We do not see here a reactionary demand for empire but a plea for decent waged work and the return of industry which would allow deindustrialized communities to return to their former status. As we know now, this is never likely to happen. Thus, it is incumbent upon us to ask about the consequences for the affective histories and social suffering of communities in which little well-paid work existed and in which every kind of shared practice is being challenged by the break-up of all patterns of mutuality (Studdert and Walkerdine, 2016). There is no doubt that there is a big investment in continuing this solidarity, but there are no mechanisms to support it, because it becomes harder and harder for people to work together. In south Wales, however, there were many indications that mutual local support in times of hardship was continuing as best it could. There was a really strong investment in exactly the mutuality that developed in the industrial era. There are many examples of this. In my own fieldwork in one Valleys community, people who had come to the community via a halfway house chose to stay even though the community was incredibly poor – they just felt accepted and welcomed. In another community, terrible flooding badly affected local homes. Many tradespeople offered their services free to bring carpets, electricity, general repairs, and the possibility of hope.

The Affective Life of Community After Deindustrialization

It seems clear that the affective practices developed during the industrial era still find their echoes in the present. However, we must understand the specificity and historicity of the conditions under which affects may be retained or changed. Not all deindustrialized locations are the same. The work of Roberts implies that those locations where significant investment in the area had occurred will produce new generations whose openness to different kinds of work and gender expression also promotes generational change. However, the generational continuity of certain affective practices is also evident. There is ample evidence of other affects, such as resentment, anger, hurt, and hostility, the sense of being ignored and with that also some determination to work together to have a say. There is very little in-depth work on the generational effects of industrial work and of deindustrialization and almost no attention paid to it (see Bithymitris, 2023). Nonetheless, we can extrapolate from other work on generational trauma and from the emerging field of epigenetic studies (Yehuda, 1995, 1998, 2001). Most work does not pay detailed attention to continuities and discontinuities in terms of affect. What work there is though does indicate that feelings held in common by communities offer hope, solidarity, and the desire for self-determination that is absolutely crucial for rebuilding. However, while politicians and policymakers want communities to help themselves in the absence of resources, there is no evidence that most communities are allowed the possibility of self-determination backed by money and resources. It is the strength of a community to be able to stand together and move forward together. More likely, splits within communities begin to emerge that produce more second-skin phenomena in which smaller groups within a community are set up against each other, for example, by race and ethnicity (Nayak, 2010), by class, by gender, and by political affiliation. Such splitting of groups one from another may be understood as produced by experiences of lack of safety or being in common.

The Sovereign Importance of Working in This Way on and After Deindustrialization

Affective practices, solidarity, and finding the ways that work for the meanings and affects held in common by the community (a relational approach) are important for rebuilding and developing the strength of the community. Yes, things are changing generationally in deindustrialized communities, but the effort taken in the name of profit to hone masculinities and femininities suitable for the new markets should not be forgotten, nor should it blind us to the complexities of the intergenerational effects of this history on individual and collective bodies in every possible sense. I will end this chapter with the example of a former mining community in which the largely female group was meeting as part of a research project (Ivinson and Bright, 2019). In the meeting, the participants appeared to hold others emotionally safe while recognizing how tough it has been on a personal level, while also seeming to look toward a way forward. Such was the effect of this on me, who observed the meeting as an artist commissioned to make an artwork, that I proposed an artwork as a series of photographs in which a group of women carried lights in the darkness, ushering in the possibility of light, and carrying that light forward into the next generation. I was worried that this would appear too abstract and 'arty farty,' but in fact it was very enthusiastically received. The group was very keen to tell me what it meant to them and the affects and history to which it bore witness.

Note

1 On the slightly different case of Scotland, see the chapter by Ewan Gibbs in this volume.

Reference List

Adam, B. (1995). *Timewatch: The Social Analysis of Time*. Cambridge: Polity.

Anzieu, D. (2014 [1989]) *The Skin Ego*. Trans. N. Segal. London: Routledge.

Bederman, G. (1995). *Manliness and Civilisation: A Cultural History of Gender and Race in the United States 1880–1917*. Chicago: University of Chicago Press.

Bick, E. (1968). The Experience of the Skin in Early Object Relations. *International Journal of Psychoanalysis*, 49, pp. 484–486.

Bithymitris, G. (2023). *Class, Trauma, Identity: Psychosocial Encounters*. London: Routledge.

Driver, F. (1989). The Historical Geography of the Workhouse System in England and Wales, 1834–1883. *Journal of Historical Geography*, 15(3), pp. 269–286.

Emery, J., Powell, R. and Crookes, L. (eds.). (2023). Class, Affect, Margins. *Special Issue of Sociological Review*, 71(2).

Erikson, K. (1994). *A New Species of Troubles: Explorations in Disasters, Trauma and Community*. New York: WW Norton.

Gater, R. (2022). 'Dirty, Dirty Job. Not Good for Your Health': Working-Class Men and Their Experiences and Relationships with Employment. In Simmons, R. and Simpson, K. (eds.) *Education,*

Work, Social Change in Britain's former Coalfield Communities. London: Palgrave Macmillan, pp. 107–126.

Henriques, J., Hollway, W., Urwin, C., Venn, C. and Walkerdine, V. (1984). *Changing the Subject: Psychology, Social Regulation and Subjectivity.* London: Routledge and Kegan Paul.

Ivinson, G. and Bright, N.G. (2019). Washing Lines, Whinberries and Reworking 'Waste Ground': Women's Affective Practices and a Haunting Within the Haunting of the UK Coalfields. *Journal of Working-Class Studies,* 4(2), pp. 125–139.

Jacotine, K. and Wellings, B. (2015). With or Without EU: Jeremy Corbyn and the Re-Emergence of Left-Wing Euroscepticism. *The Conversation* [online]. https://theconversation.com/with-or-without-eu-jeremy-corbyn-and-the-re-emergence-of-left-wing-euroscepticism-46626 (Accessed: 20 June 2024).

Kleinman, A., Das, V. and Lock, M. (eds.). (1997). *Social Suffering.* Berkeley, CA: University of California Press.

Lewis, B. (2002). *The Middlemost and the Milltowns: Bourgeois Culture and Politics in Early Industrial England.* Stamford: Stamford University Press.

Linkon, S.L. (2018). *The Half-life of Deindustrialization.* Ann Arbor: University of Michigan Press.

Massey, D. (2005). *For Space.* London: Sage.

McDowell, L. (2003). Masculine Identities and Low-Paid Work: Young Men in Urban Labour Markets. *International Journal of Urban and Regional Research,* 27(4), pp. 828–848.

Nayak, A. (2003a). 'Boyz to Men': Masculinities, Schooling and Labour Transitions in De-industrial Times. *Educational Review,* 55(2), pp. 147–159.

Nayak, A. (2003b). Last of the 'Real Geordies'? White Masculinities and the Subcultural Response to Deindustrialisation. *Environment and Planning D: Society and Space,* 21(1), pp. 7–25.

Nayak, A. (2006). Displaced Masculinities: Chavs, Youth and Class in the Post-Industrial City. *Sociology,* 40(5), pp. 813–831.

Nayak, A. (2010). Race, Affect, and Emotion: Young People, Racism, and Graffiti in the Postcolonial English Suburbs. *Environment and Planning A,* 42(10), pp. 2370–2392. https://doi.org/10.1068/a42177 (Accessed: 20 June 2024).

Nixon, D. (2006). 'I Just Like Working with My Hands': Employment Aspirations and the Meaning of Work for Low-Skilled Unemployed Men in Britain's Service Economy. *Journal of Education and Work,* 19(2), pp. 201–217.

Revel, J. (1996). Micro-Analyse et Construction du Social. In Revel, J. (ed.) *Jeux d'echelles. La micro-analyse à l'expérience.* Paris: Seuil, pp. 15–36.

Roberts, S. (2012). 'I Just Got on with It': The Educational Experiences of Ordinary, Yet Overlooked, Boys. *British Journal of Sociology of Education,* 33(2), pp. 203–221.

Roberts, S. (2018). *Young Working-Class Men in Transition.* New York: Routledge.

Strangleman, T. (2024). The World We Have Lost: Reflections on Varieties of Masculinity at Work. *International Labor and Working-Class History,* 105, pp. 9–25. doi:10.1017/S0147547923000315

Studdert, D. (2006). *Conceptualising Community: Beyond the State and the Individual.* Basingstoke: Palgrave Macmillan.

Studdert, D. and Walkerdine, V. (2016). *Rethinking Community Research.* Basingstoke: Springer.

Walkerdine, V. (2010). Communal Beingness and Affect: An Exploration of Trauma in an Ex-Industrial Community. *Body and Society,* 16(1), pp. 91–116.

Walkerdine, V. (2016a). Affective History, Working-Class Communities and Self-Determination. *Sociological Review,* 64(4), pp. 699–714.

Walkerdine, V. (2016b). Transmitting Class Across Generations. *Theory and Psychology,* 25(2). https://doi.org/10.1177/0959354315577856 (Accessed: 20 June 2024).

Walkerdine, V. (2017). Of Dinosaurs and Divas: Is Class Still Relevant to Feminist Research? *Subjectivity,* 10, pp. 1–12.

Walkerdine, V. (2018). 'No-One Listens to Us': Post-Truth, Affect and Brexit. *Qualitative Research in Psychology,* 17(1), pp. 143–158.

Walkerdine V. (2020). Chronicles of a Divided Land: Some Reflections on the 2019 General Election. In Cohen, P. (ed.) *Political Mindfulness Fresh Perspectives on Multiple Crises.* Compass Online, pp. 18–22.

Walkerdine V. (2023a). Afterword: Affective Histories and Class Transmission. *Sociological Review,* 71(2). https://doi.org/10.1177/00380261231152043 (Accessed: 20 June 2024).

Walkerdine, V. (2023b). 'I Just Wanna Be a Woman': Some Not So Simple Ways: Families, Femininity and/as Affective Entanglement. *Qualitative Research*, 28(10). https://doi.org/10.1177/10778004221098204 (Accessed: 20 June 2024).

Walkerdine, V. and Jimenez, L. (2012). *Gender, Work and Community After Deindustrialisation*. Basingstoke: Palgrave Springer.

Willoughby, R. (2004). Between the Basic Fault and the Second Skin. *International Journal of Psychoanalysis*, 85, pp. 179–196.

Yehuda, R. et al. (1995). Low Urinary Cortisol Excretion in Holocaust Survivors with Post-Traumatic Stress Disorder. *American Journal of Psychiatry*, 152, pp. 982–986.

Yehuda, R. et al. (1998). Phenomenology and Psychobiology in the Intergenerational Response to Trauma. In Danieli, Y. (ed.) *International Handbook of Multigenerational Legacies of Trauma*. New York: Plenum.

Yehuda, R. et al. (2001). Childhood Trauma and Risk for PTSD: Relationship to Intergenerational Effects of Trauma, Parental PTSD and Cortisol Excretion. *Development and Psychopathology*, 13(3), pp. 733–753.

13
DEINDUSTRIALIZATION AND RACIALIZED COMMUNITIES
A Historical Perspective

Christopher Lawson

Introduction

The October 25, 1980 edition of the *Oldham Weekly Chronicle* made for bleak reading. Multiple headlines announced the bad news. 'Another 170 Thrown out of Work' screamed one headline about the closure of the Dhobi Weatherlux factory, located in the old Vale Mill on Clegg Street, just south of the town center. Weatherlux produced waterproof clothing and was a supplier of major retailer Marks & Spencer (Bottomley, 1980). Another article in the same edition of the *Weekly Chronicle* covered a mock memorial service marking the closure of the Royd Mill in the Hollinwood neighborhood on the west side of Oldham (N.A., 1980). During the service, a wreath labeled 'Another mill dead, Mrs Thatcher' was laid in front of the mill by its former employees, and a photo of the wreath laying was included with the article. According to the foreman, Alex Thompson, "only about ten of the 232 redundant workers had found new jobs" (N.A., 1980). The *Chronicle* interviewed several of the newly redundant workers, including Nellie Warren from Glodwick, who had worked at the Royd Mill for 44 years. However, there was a noticeable omission from its coverage. Despite seven of the nine workers identifiable in the photo being South Asian, all of those interviewed by the *Chronicle* appear to have been white.

This glaring journalistic omission reflects a broader misrepresentation of who has been impacted by the process of deindustrialization – not just in Britain but across the global north – over the last 60 years. Deindustrialization has not only exposed and exacerbated preexisting inequalities in European and North American societies; it has also revealed how the memories and traumas of some are valued more than others when we tell the histories of the recent past.

In his reflection piece following the Working-Class Studies conference in Kent in September 2019, Steven High (2019) wrote that the focus of deindustrialization studies on predominately white communities reflected a "danger that we are contributing to the coding of the working-class as white." In Britain, continental Europe, and North America, the stereotypical industrial worker remains white, male, and steeped in local proletarian tradition.[1] However, this is misleading. The working classes in the Global North were never fully white or male and would become ever more diverse over the course of the twentieth century as

DOI: 10.4324/9781003308324-20

migrants came from around the world to work in factories, mills, and workshops, as well as in the caring services.[2] In the US, the racial diversity of the industrial working classes was in part the result of an internal process, as African Americans embarked on a Great Migration to northern cities like Detroit and Chicago.[3] Later, they would be joined by migrants from Asia and Latin America. In industrial centers of Western Europe, waves of migration from within and outside the continent produced a complex ethnic tapestry, and the postwar era brought significant migration from the far reaches of the declining European empires in Asia, Africa, and the Caribbean (Patel, 2021; Bennoune, 1975; Merrill, 2011).

In many cases, ethnic minority workers were faced with discrimination in the workforce and local housing market, living in crowded conditions and forced to take the most dangerous jobs without the full protection of trade unions (Sugrue, 1996). Then, as the process of deindustrialization took hold at different times in different places, the multi-ethnic working class of great industrial cities like Manchester, Detroit, and Montreal suffered a grinding economic decline and social dislocation that cut across racial, ethnic, and gender divisions.

The industrialization of Europe and North America was a global story: a story wrapped up in empire, slavery, and the exploitation of foreign peoples and resources on a grand scale.[4] Naturally then, the deindustrialization of countries like Britain and the US is also a global and imperial story. Deindustrialization is interconnected with the end of European empires and with the changing relationship with the Global North and Global South. The unwinding and afterlife of that imperial world, its interaction with distinctive local social and cultural formations, and the response of individuals, communities, and governments would fundamentally reshape the contours of contemporary societies on both sides of the Atlantic.

Diverse Industrial Workforces

The industrialization of the global north from the eighteenth century involved the forced or compelled movement of millions of people. Through the process characterized by Sven Beckert (2014) as "war capitalism," the great powers of Europe employed "slavery, colonial domination, militarized trade, and land expropriations" (Beckert, 2014, p. 60) to create an exploitative global economic system that fed its industries with critical raw materials and inputs. The most significant and most violent of these population movements was the trans-Atlantic slave trade, but there were also vast population movements within and between African and Asian colonies (see, e.g., Sturman, 2014). The restructuring of the Indian economy to meet the needs of the British state and British capital actually brought about an early form of deindustrialization.

Within the colonial metropoles, and in settler colonies like the US, labor was captured and mobilized to staff the factories, mills, and mines that created the wealth upon which the whole system was based. Initially, the populations which settled in the industrial cities of North America and Europe were largely of domestic or European origin. For example, before the 1890s, most northern American cities had minuscule African American populations (although New York City was somewhat of an exception), and the industrial working classes were largely made up of first- and second-generation European immigrants.[5] Black Americans remained predominately in the former slave states of the south, trapped in the exploitative system of sharecropping. However, this changed in the late nineteenth and early twentieth centuries, with the Great Migration of millions of Black Americans to northern cities looking to escape the segregationist South and find economic opportunities in the world's fastest growing industrial empire (Riis, 1957, pp. 110–111). Although these migrants did build new lives, find new jobs, and create a truly unique culture that has enriched American life for over a century, they found themselves at the bottom of the new structures of economic and social discrimination. They were often the last hired and the first fired, and they were placed in the least desirable positions. Until 1955, job listings in cities like Detroit could officially include discriminatory tags ("only open to whites" etc.) (Sugrue, 1996). Racial covenants restricted Black migrants from many all-white neighborhoods of northern industrial cities, forcing them to live in overcrowded and overpriced housing in specific inner-city areas (Wolfinger, 2007, pp. 181–182). As a result, the Black industrial working class was trapped in a very precarious position and was unavoidably exposed to any downturn or restructuring of the American economy.

Meanwhile, in Britain and Western Europe, the industrial working classes tended to be less racially diverse, as peasants streamed into the cities as the agricultural revolution changed the structure of rural economies. However, the Irish, and Jews escaping the pogroms of Eastern Europe, were a major part of the British industrial machine, and port cities like London and Liverpool were home to large communities of imperial subjects going back as early as the eighteenth century.[6]

In the twentieth century, the diversity of the European working classes would increase still further. The 'Windrush Generation' – so named after the ship that brought some of the first postwar West Indian migrants to the British metropole in 1948 – was a critical component of Britain's industrial recovery after the destruction of 1939–1945. France received considerable migration from its collapsing empire in Africa and Asia, especially following the bloody end to the Algerian conflict in the early 1960s.[7]

These migrations were driven by a combination of push and pull factors and were intimately connected to the changing nature of the relationship between Europe and its hinterlands. Velda Casey came to Oldham, near Manchester, from Barbados in 1962 because her brother had encouraged her to seek job opportunities there (Casey, 2016). However, she also came to overcome the colonial legacies of poverty. Like the vast majority of her fellow Barbadians, Casey's family were the descendants of slaves, forcibly taken across the Atlantic to produce the sugar that would feed Britain's industrial revolution, and that legacy of slavery and exploitation had resulted in poverty and limited opportunity on many Caribbean islands (see Thompson and Marshall, 2002; Brereton and Yelvington, 1999).

West Indians like Casey were joined in Oldham by an even larger community of Commonwealth citizens migrating from the South Asian subcontinent. Of particular note were the Mirpuris, from the Pakistani-controlled section of Kashmir, who began arriving in Oldham in the early 1960s after their farmlands and villages had been destroyed by a post-colonial development project, the Mangla Dam, over which they had no say ('Kashmir Cultural Day 2000', 2000). Between 50,000 and 100,000 people are estimated to have been displaced (Michel, 1967). Kashmir had been treated as a colonial hinterland by both the Britain and the post-independence Pakistani government, and the dam was part of a World Bank-financed post-colonial development project (Kalra, 2000, p. 54). The Mirpuris brought with them the scars of colonial exploitation – most had limited formal education and had little-to-no capital – they had used the displacement compensation to purchase their journeys to Britain. Upon arrival in cities like Oldham, Bradford, and Birmingham, they would form a critical piece of the British labor force, keeping the economy moving amid the challenges of massive war debts, high defense spending, and weakening trade conditions. They filled poorly paid and difficult roles like the overnight shifts at cotton textile mills and nursing shifts at psychiatric hospitals (Locke, 1976, preface, Chapter One). They lived in overcrowded conditions, sharing rooms in dilapidated inner-city housing to save money to send back home to family and relatives. They were driven by a "five-year plan" to get rich and then return home (Stacey, 2013, p. 44). However, by the late 1960s, the economic structure of Britain, and the Global North, was shifting rapidly beneath their feet. Deindustrialization would change the direction of their lives in distinct and profound ways.

When Deindustrialization Starts

The rise and fall of industries, with serious knock-on effects on the people who rely on those industries, has been a feature of global history for hundreds of years. Christopher Johnson's (1995) study of the decline of textile production in southern France over the nineteenth century is a useful reminder of this long history. European colonialism actually caused a form of deindustrialization in many parts of Asia and Africa. However, a strong case can be made for seeing the process that took place in the Global North during the twentieth century as qualitatively distinct. In their 1982 classic, Bluestone and Harrison established a working definition of deindustrialization: "a widespread, systematic disinvestment in the nation's basic productive capacity" (Bluestone and Harrison, 1982, p. 6). This process would irrevocably transform the economic and social structure of North American and European nations, with ethnic minority communities caught in the middle of the transformation.

One of the first prolonged processes of deindustrialization occurred in the British textile industry – in wool, linen, and cotton. These industries had faced significant growing international competition from the 1910s onward and significant tumult during the interwar period. In 1945, overall employment in cotton textiles was about half of its 1912 peak of 622,000 (N.A., 1967). Some other 'first industrial revolution' industries, such as coal mining also contracted significantly during the interwar period. However, the Second World War and the immediate postwar era brought a degree of stabilization and of full employment. This reprieve would not last long. The steel and textile industries began to rationalize on a large scale in the late 1950s, while the British coal industry experienced its greatest employment decline in the 1960s, during the tenure of the first Wilson (Labor) government (Ashworth, 1986).

The textile industries in the UK – including the linen industry in Northern Ireland – had majority female workforces whose work had long been undervalued by employers and politicians alike. In the 20 years following the end of the Second World War, wages in the textile industry fell by 30% relative to other industries (Devons, Crossley, and Maunder, 1968). The expansion of more 'modern' industries, such as electrical equipment, chemicals, automobiles, and other advanced machinery, provided alternative employment with better pay and conditions. Women in Oldham who did not want to work in the dusty mills could now find employment at electrical engineering and equipment firm Ferranti, which by the late 1960s was the second largest employer in the town. In 1900, nearly three-quarters of Oldham school leavers entered the mills; in 1950, that number was down to one-quarter (Law, 1999, p. 292).

With international competition growing and labor in relatively short supply, the British textile industry became more capital-intensive, and with new working practices came changes in the composition of the workforce. As it was increasingly important that equipment not be left idle, by the early 1960s many mills began operating 24 hours a day, with three fixed 8-hour shifts (N.A., 1957). At this time, it was still technically illegal for women to work overnight shifts, and mothers in particular had trouble accommodating to this new work discipline.[8] As a result, the mills looked even further afield for a "flexible workforce" that would be willing to take on the low-paying night shift jobs in a period of continuing low unemployment (Locke, 1976). In 1981, Mansoor Kazi, chairman of the Pakistani People's Association, estimated that 1,950 Pakistani Oldhamers worked in the textile industry, a number that probably represented an overall majority of adult men in the community (N.A., 1981b).

Immigrants faced racism in the hiring process, often obtaining only the most difficult and poorly paid jobs. Nevertheless, the mills were essential to provide them with an economic foundation, and job vacancies remained common even as overall employment in the industry continued to decline. Ernest Campbell from Jamaica said that, in the 1960s and early 1970s, "you could leave one job Tuesday morning and have another on Wednesday morning, . . . you were never out of a job in Oldham" (Campbell, 2017).[9] However, the economic crises of the early 1970s seriously damaged the ability of even this streamlined and technologically intensive version of the British textile industry to keep up with growing competition in the Global South. As a result, the days of plentiful employment were largely over by the second half of the 1970s, and between 1971 and 1991, 15,000 jobs in the Oldham textile industry disappeared, a drop of more than 80% (Kalra, 2000, p. 126).

The collapse of the cotton textile industry impacted every single Oldhamer. However, South Asian and West Indians faced a combination of overlapping challenges. First, there was the challenge of transferable skills. In 1983, 84% of unemployed men in Britain were classed as "manual workers," which is a category that included the majority of South Asians in Oldham (Burnett, 1994, p. 275). Coming from a peasant background, the Mirpuri community were especially likely to lack technical skills or accreditation (Kalra, 2000, pp. 53–54). In addition, by the early 1980s many of the first-generation migrants from Mirpur were in their late forties or fifties and thus faced the challenges of late career retraining and age discrimination (Kalra, 2000, p. 127).

Second, there was the impact of racial discrimination in the workplace – challenges that had always existed but were now amplified in both severity and impact as employment became scarce. In February 1976, young Asian and West Indian Oldhamers released a document titled "Life as We See It – In Black and White," which detailed various forms of discrimination at work, including cultural insensitivity and difficulty obtaining promotions because the foremen were overwhelmingly white (N.A., 1976). In 1979, Amalgamated Textile Workers' Union refused to support the largely South Asian workforce of the Maple Mill in Hathershaw in their complaints against intolerable working conditions. But the workers went ahead with the protests on their own and won (N.A., 1981b).

Third, there were challenges caused by the broader economic conditions. Ferranti and the engineering firms were also shedding thousands of jobs (N.A., 1981a). Mirpuris had traditionally been quite mobile in their job searches, and 66% of Mirpuris in Oldham had lived in another part of the UK before coming to the town (Locke, 1976, p. 7). During a local downturn in Birmingham in the late 1960s, Pakistani men had moved to Oxford for work (Shaw, 1988). However, by the early 1980s, this was no longer possible, as the generalized downturn in the British manufacturing sector meant that previously prosperous regions like the West Midlands were now also struggling.

Finally, there were challenges associated with the settlement pattern of Commonwealth citizens in industrial areas and the ways in which deindustrialization exacerbated spatial inequalities. Lacking resources and facing structural discrimination (including restrictions on access to council housing), Mirpuris arriving in Oldham had largely settled in the industrial working-class neighborhood of Glodwick, directly south of the town center. The traditional 'two-up two-down' row housing of the area was poorly maintained, and often lacked basic modern amenities, but it was affordable and close to various sources of industrial employment. Local council mortgage supports directed immigrants to Glodwick, and it quickly became the center of the Mirpuri community. Despite the limited resources of the new arrivals, the Mirpuris sought to gain a modicum of security through purchasing their homes, and at least 425 of the houses in the area were owned by South Asians by 1976 (Locke, 1976, p. 4).

However, as deindustrialization progressed, working-class South Asians living in neighborhoods like Glodwick became trapped in a deteriorating situation. Even as the local mills had closed in the 1960s and 1970s, Mirpuris in Glodwick had organized a mini-bus service to drop them off and pick them up from a number of mills in Shaw and Crompton (Locke, 1976, pp. 6–7). But with mill employment disappearing entirely, local residents were forced to take underpaid roles in service industries, call centers, and other employers widely scattered throughout the Greater Manchester region. Through the 1980s, bus services were privatized and reduced, and 43% of all households in the Oldham Borough did not have access to a car in 1992, one of the highest figures in the country. The figure was over 60% both in Glodwick and in the predominately British Bangladeshi ward of Coldhurst (N.A., 1991, p. 7).

Meanwhile, the social conditions in Glodwick began to change. Racial tension increased. Part of this was a reflection of the national political environment, which had been enflamed by the rhetoric of Enoch Powell and the rise of openly racist political organizations like the National Front, and which had seen the passage of increasingly harsh restrictions on Commonwealth migration.[10] However, it was also a result of an abandoned effort at housing redevelopment and the clumsy approach to community relations practiced by the local 'Community Development Project' (hereafter CDP).[11]

As part of the CDP, a study titled 'Housing Improvement and the Racial Conundrum' was conducted to gauge community support for clearance and rebuilding of housing in Glodwick (Barr, 1974, p. ii). In all, 76% of the non-Asian respondents made a "negative racial comment" without being prompted in any way to do so (Barr, 1974, p. 25). The report's author came up with the term 'racial negativism' to describe this general sense of tension and animosity. He noted that this 'negativism' was not simply evidence of some inveterate racism on the part of the white working-class residents but the result of years of misinformation and scapegoating on the part of the national media combined with a desire to blame someone for the town's economic and physical decline (Barr, 1974, p. 25).

As economic and social conditions in Glodwick deteriorated, those who could move elsewhere did so. This was not just the case for members of the white community but also for middle-class South Asians. Mashukul Hoque's grandfather was one of the first South Asians to settle in Glodwick, arriving there in 1951 or 1952 and saving up money with relatives to buy a house together in the neighborhood in 1959 for £300. However, he managed to transition from the mills to running a small grocery business, the proceeds of which allowed him and his family to escape to Manchester and eventually to the Cheshire stockbrokers' belt (Hoque, 2011–2012).

The story of Glodwick is a fairly extreme case – by the late twentieth century, Oldham was among the most deprived towns in England and one of the most segregated (Owen, 1994). However, all across the UK, similar neighborhoods could be found. Furthermore, the story of Glodwick is illustrative of a critical point – not only did deindustrialization impact racial minority communities, it intersected with other social, economic, and cultural transformations to produce particular patterns of segregation and deprivation that continue to mark British society.

A Second Deindustrial Revolution

By the 1970s, the process of deindustrialization had spread beyond 'first industrial revolution' industries like coal, steel, and textiles. In this process, the US was actually ahead of Britain and continental Europe.

In the immediate postwar era, the vast majority of the world's automobiles were made in the US – and most of these were made in a handful of intensely industrialized states in the upper Midwest, with the nerve center at Detroit, Michigan. However, the structure of the American auto industry began to shift soon after the end of the Second World War. The small, multistory factories built into the fabric of residential neighborhoods were on the way out. Some assembly lines became more automated, which required fewer workers. Capital was increasingly mobile, and many industries began to decentralize, partly to gain an edge over powerful unions.[12] Some factories left Michigan and other Midwestern states altogether, shifting production to states where there were fewer unions, and workers could be paid less.[13] As a result, despite this period being viewed as the apex of the American industrial golden age, Detroit lost 134,000 manufacturing jobs between 1947 and 1963, and workers faced regular bouts of unemployment during short-term downturns in the auto industry. In the immediate postwar era, African Americans made up 15% of the workforce in Detroit's auto industry (Sugrue, 1996, pp. 125–127). As mentioned earlier, discrimination in the workplace made African American employees particularly vulnerable, and these job losses blocked the economic mobility of working classes in the Motor City.

However, the job losses were only one half of the story. In some cases, the employment stayed in Michigan, but employers closed the old factories in the city and moved to larger, newer facilities in the suburbs to rationalize production. In 1957, for example, Ford opened a new assembly plan in Wixom, nearly 50 kilometers from downtown Detroit, while around the same time the older Packard Motor Car Co. factory in central Detroit was closed (Binelli, 2014). Similar patterns could be seen in Philadelphia, where inner city steel operations were closed, and a new US Steel plant was built near all-white Levittown (Conn, 2006, 134).

Inner-city factories like the Packard plant had been the economic foundation of Black communities in cities across the industrial heartland of the US, from Chicago to Detroit and Philadelphia. Because of redlining (discrimination in the availability of loans) and racial covenants, African Americans could not move to the suburbs, so moving to Wixom to work in the new Ford assembly plant was not an option. New highways disfigured previously prosperous inner-city areas, and white flight led to declines in tax receipts and services. The growth of other sectors, such as banking, financial services, pharmaceuticals, and health care, also occurred far away from majority Black inner-city communities. These jobs also required more education than manufacturing jobs, something that was increasingly inaccessible to unemployed or poorly employed Black people in the central city (Wolfinger, 2007). As the entire city faced a gut-wrenching process of deindustrialization and economic reconfiguration, many newly Black neighborhoods faced a slow decline into the poverty that their residents had hoped to escape (Carter, Schill, and Wachter, 1998).

As in Oldham, the divide was not only racial but also one of class. Black Detroit began to fragment as wealthier Blacks moved quickly out of areas that went into decline because of

Deindustrialization and Racialized Communities

job losses, with poor Blacks remaining trapped close to the downtown core. The departure from the inner city of wealthier, better-educated African Americans left many neighborhoods without social institutions and the structure necessary to advocate for economic and political change (Sugrue, 1996).[14]

In cities like Detroit, we can see the effect of the double disadvantage described by William Julius Wilson, who argued that there was a direct relationship between deindustrialization and the development of the modern American ghetto. At the intersection of race and class, working-class African Americans whose ancestors had travelled North to escape the horrors of sharecropping and segregation now faced mass unemployment and poverty as the American industrial empire unraveled (see Wilson, 1987).

Returning across the Atlantic, a similar process would begin somewhat later in Britain's 'motor city.' Coventry, in the West Midlands, was a great postwar success story, rising from the ashes of German bombing with wages well above the national average and massive in-migration as its factories turned out the cars, airplanes, and electrical equipment needed to drive a postwar society. As late as January 1974, in the middle of the Three-Day Week,[15] the unemployment rate in Coventry was still only 3%, below the national average of 3.6% (N.A., 1978–1984). However, the city was also uniquely vulnerable to the coming wave of industrial decline. In 1978, no similarly sized city in the whole country relied on manufacturing employment to the extent that Coventry did (Healey and Clark, 1984, p. 308). Furthermore, it was particularly reliant on the British auto industry, which had been poorly managed and faced a profound competitive challenge in the face of rising competition from Japan and continental Europe.

In 1976, Coventry was home to an estimated 26,300 Black and ethnic minority (BAME) residents or 7.9% of the civic population. Sixty-two percent of the BAME population was born in the "New Commonwealth,"[16] but the other 38% was British-born (N.A., c. 1978–1979, p. 3). The largest single community of ethnic minority Coventrians were Punjabi-speaking Sikhs. They were the first to come to the city in large numbers, and they had the most developed structure of community organizations. Most significantly, they had formed the first branch of the Indian Workers' Association (IWA) in the city in 1938 (Gill, 2013, p. 555).

The inner-city neighborhood of Hillfields was the entry point for successive waves of migrants to Coventry, just as Glodwick had been in Oldham, with a large housing stock of dilapidated terraced housing close to major industrial employment. By 1945, it was home to most of the city's small but growing South Asian community, and it was in desperate need of renovation and revitalization (CDP Reports and Papers, 1973).[17] At the same time, the industry that had been interspersed through inner city neighborhoods like Hillfields was moved to larger sites on the edge of the city. Triumph abandoned its inner-city location after one of its factories was destroyed in the Blitz, moving to an enlarged Standard factory at Canley, while Rootes moved to Ryton.[18] The similarities with Detroit are obvious, and Hillfields seemed almost destined for postwar problems.

By 1983, Coventry had lost an astounding 53,000 manufacturing jobs, including 21,000 at British Leyland and 7,000 at Chrysler/Peugeot, and official unemployment had climbed into the high teens (Healey and Clark, 1983, pp. 5–7). These job losses would once again have class and racial affects. According to a 1978 study by the Coventry Unemployed Workers' Centre, the unemployment rate for Black and ethnic minority Coventrians was running at almost twice the civic rate (N.A., c. 1978–1979, p. 4). Another study by the Unemployed Workers' Centre found that 23.2% of Asian youth were unemployed compared with 10% of white youth. Asian school leavers also took significantly longer to find a job and required

209

more interviews before landing a position. The report concluded "almost without exception, wherever blacks and whites compete, whites are given preference" (N.A., c. 1978–1979, p. 18).

Radhika Natarajan, Jordanna Bailkin, Kennetta Perry, and others have shown how Commonwealth citizens found themselves to be second-class citizens on arrival in the former colonial metropole, with unequal access to housing, welfare, and the law being the most obvious manifestations of this inequality (Bailkin, 2012; Perry, 2016; Shilliam, 2018; Virdee, 2014). But the differential impacts of deindustrialization that I have just described are another critical and often overlooked part of this story. Simply put, working-class ethnic minorities found themselves doubly disadvantaged at the intersection of the class and racial hierarchies of post-imperial, post-industrial British society. Just as in the American cities studied by William Julius Wilson, this double disadvantage often led to the segregation or ghettoization of a segment of the racialized population (Wilson, 1987). In Coventry, as in Oldham, a small but successful South Asian middle class was able to settle in more prosperous areas of the city, gaining a considerable presence in the civic community. Meanwhile, working-class ethnic minorities found themselves increasingly trapped in Hillfields and the adjacent neighborhoods of north Coventry, where declining property values and limited access to quality employment made socioeconomic progress nearly impossible and where the effects of the initial urban crisis would help create the subsequent crisis of later decades.

Although this chapter has focused largely on the Anglo American experience, ethnic minorities in continental Europe, Canada, and elsewhere have also experienced a particularly acute form of deindustrialization, where race, class, and decolonization have intersected to produce divided urban landscapes and profound social inequalities. Like the British colonial project in South Asia, the French colonization of North Africa in the nineteenth and twentieth centuries caused a collapse of traditional regional industries and the reallocation of land to French settlers. Facing considerable economic dislocation and the oppression of the imperial system, the peasant classes of Algeria and other North African colonies traveled into cities and eventually into the imperial metropole to sell their labor. As a result, by the mid-1950s, there were approximately 400,000 Algerians working in France (Bennoune, 1975). Because of legal restrictions on the employment of migrants, in addition to the structural barriers that also appeared in the British and American cases (including limited formal education of post-colonial migrants and informal discrimination), migrant workers in postwar France were concentrated in low-paid, precarious, and often dangerous roles and workplaces (Vigna, 2012, pp. 194–195). The auto industry employed thousands of workers of immigrant origin, notably from North Africa, and as this sector underwent multiple crises in the 1980s, foreign workers were among the worst affected by job cuts (Gay, 2021, p. 213). Although the deindustrialization of France was not as thorough or dramatic as that experienced on the other side of the channel, it also exposed tensions in the racially diverse and postcolonial society, ones that the French state was increasingly unwilling to confront or even acknowledge. Nowhere was this more apparent than in the former industrial suburbs around cities such as Paris and Lyon. As Loïc Wacquant notes in his classic study of "urban outcasts," the *banlieues* – a term that has now become synonymous with impoverished multi-ethnic neighborhoods around the periphery of French cities – were, like the ghettos of American cities, "territories ravaged by deindustrialization" (Wacquant, 2008, p. 147).

Deindustrialization is not only an urban phenomenon. As Steven High has pointed out, mill and mining towns in northern Ontario and Quebec were critical pieces of the Canadian and Quebecois settler-colonial projects. When the iron ore mine in Schefferville, Quebec closed in 1982 on the direction of future Prime Minister Brian Mulroney, the Naskapi and Innu who lived on the margins of the town were deeply affected. In a repeat of the *Oldham Weekly Chronicle* omission, dozens of other residents were quoted in the media in the days that followed the announcement, yet Indigenous people were almost never interviewed (High, 2023, p. 61).

Deindustrialization was also connected to two racialized social structures that have emerged in the last half century – the rise of the security state and the rise of the 'precariat.' As James Vernon has shown, airports like Heathrow were perfect microcosms of both structures. Heathrow was increasingly staffed by Black and South Asian Britons, most of whom were at the bottom of the employment hierarchy, in catering and cleaning, where they were treated poorly and had very low pay rates. Meanwhile, in the very same buildings, this labor force was subject to new, privatized forms of control and detention. About 20,000 Asian, African, and Middle Eastern migrants were detained at Heathrow Airport between 1971 and 1978, where security services were outsourced to Securicor (Vernon, 2021). Britain was the first country in the world with privatized airport security services. The security services increasingly used medical exams (including vaginal inspections) to determine the validity of Asian claims to settlement: according to Vernon, this "illustrates just how central Heathrow was to an immigration regime which sought to insulate Britain from its decolonizing Empire" (Vernon, 2021, pp. 237–238).

Conclusion

In his seminal work, Thomas Sugrue (1996) argues that the violent riots in Detroit during the summer of 1967 were not the cause or starting point of the great city's decline, as commonly understood, but rather the culmination and effect of over 20 years of deindustrialization, redlining, and deepening economic distress for working-class Black residents. What was to come in Detroit over the next 50 years – the collapse of the city's population, the virtual abandonment of civic infrastructure, and the racialized stigmatization of the city by Michigan state politicians – was simply the outworking of deindustrialization and its intersection with the preexisting divisions of American society.

Across the Atlantic, Oldham largely escaped the English 'race riots' of the 1980s, which exposed the racial discrimination that many Black Britons faced at the hands of the police but also reflected the impact of inner-city economic decline and high unemployment. Nevertheless, conflict simmered beneath the surface of the community, as what remained of the local textile industry drained away. Unemployment among South Asians remained twice as high as among white residents, and average pay was well below the national average. Far-right parties like National Front and the British National Party sought to exploit the division, while new government programmes, like the "New Deal for Communities" under New Labor, repeated some of the mistakes of the CDP and did not live up to their promises (see Hale, 2013).

Then, on 26 May 2001, the worst rioting Britain had seen in almost two decades began in Oldham. Two terrible days ensued, with dozens of injuries, destruction of property, and the firebombing of deputy Mayor Riaz Ahmad's house. Even more than in 1960s Detroit, it was clear that the violence on the streets of Glodwick and other nearby neighborhoods was a symptom, not a cause of the town's economic and social distress. Decades of deindustrialization, with neoliberalism and privatization layered on top of it, had broken down the concept of the "social" in British society, exposing the thinness of the promises of the postwar welfare state (Rose, 1996). Meanwhile, it also exposed the incomplete nature of the decolonization process. Here in the heart of the former imperial metropole, a metropole that had long since lost its privileged access to markets or competitive advantages, the racial hierarchies that had informed and justified the imperial project were still there. These racial hierarchies would then interact with the process of post-imperial economic restructuring, with terrible consequences for the social cohesion of communities such as Oldham.

Jim Tomlinson (2016) has described deindustrialization as the "meta-narrative" of postwar British history, connected as it is to many of the other great social transformations of postwar Britain, including the remaking of the labor force and the rise of the "caring services." The incredible blossoming in the study of its impact on communities and societies on both sides of the Atlantic is an unmitigated positive for the historical discipline.[19] Nevertheless, without a recognition of the diversity of those communities which it has impacted, we risk not only repeating the omission of the October 25, 1980 edition of the *Oldham Weekly Chronicle* but also missing one of the most critical connections of all – the interactions between deindustrialization and the end of empire. In a brilliant recent article on race in twentieth-century British history, Matera et al. (2023) ask whether the traditional histories of deindustrialization "fail us by reifying certain ways of seeing economic life – by reproducing the white male worker as the subject of history and, even, by reproducing the nation-state and the global north as the locus of historical activity?".

It is important that, when we write the histories of the post-industrial world, the voices of all communities are heard. These voices may tell us surprising things. Yes, of course, as described in the previous pages, deindustrialization has destroyed livelihoods, broken communities, exposed inequalities, and perpetuated discriminatory social structures. However, there are ambiguities. In Schefferville, the end of the mine opened up some opportunities, including revenue sharing, land rights, and Indigenous ownership of the railway (High, 2023, p. 75). As Sherry Lee Linkon (2018) points out in her powerful book, *The Half-Life of Deindustrialization*, many Black and Hispanic workers looked back on the postwar 'golden age' of the American industrial working class with ambivalence – even if they had been directly impacted by plant closures. For some, the present post-industrial reality brought more opportunity, safer work, and a chance to break out of social and employment structures that had always been under the control of wealthy white men. It is thus important that all voices are heard, that nothing is assumed, and that the true history of deindustrialization and its impact on the diverse communities of Europe and North America can be told in all of its richness and complexity.

Notes

1 In the British context specifically, the racialized nature of the 'traditional working class' is the subject of considerable sociological study. See, for example, Shilliam, R. (2018). *Race and the Undeserving Poor: From Abolition to Brexit*. Newcastle upon Tyne: Agenda Publishing; Virdee, S. (2014). *Racism, Class and the Racialized Outsider*. Basingstoke: Palgrave Macmillan.

2 See, for example, Patel, I.S. (2021). *We're Here Because You Were There: Immigration and the End of Empire*. London: Verso; Waldinger, R. (2001). *Strangers at the Gates: New Immigrants in Urban America*. Berkeley, CA: University of California Press.

3 For some of the most critical studies of this process and its place in modern American history, see Gregory, J. (2005). *The Southern Diaspora: How the Great Migrations of Black and White Southerners Transformed America*. Chapel Hill: University of North Carolina Press; Self, R. (2003). *American Babylon: Race and the Struggle for Postwar Oakland*. Princeton: Princeton University Press.

Deindustrialization and Racialized Communities

4 As vividly described by Beckert, S. (2014). *Empire of Cotton*. London: Macmillan. For the British story, see Barton, G.A. (2012). Towards a Global History of Britain. *Perspectives on History*, 50(7); Pocock, J.G.A. (1975). British History: A Plea for a New Subject. *Journal of Modern History*, 47(4), pp. 601–621; Sasson, T. et al. (2018). Britain and the World: A New Field? The Worlding of Britain. *Journal of British Studies*, 57, p. 689.

5 California is largely an exception to this story, which were home to large Asian (especially Chinese and Japanese) working-class communities facing considerable discrimination and economic exploitation. See, for example, Brooks, C. (2009). *Alien Neighbors, Foreign Friends: Asian Americans, Housing, and the Transformation of Urban California*. Chicago: University of Chicago Press; Lew-Williams, B. (2018). *The Chinese Must Go: Violence, Exclusion, and the Making of the Alien in America*. Cambridge, MA: Harvard University Press.

6 See, for example, Burton, A. (1998). *At the Heart of the Empire: Indians and the Colonial Encounter in Late-Victorian Britain*. Berkeley, CA: University of California Press; Saini, R. (2018). 'England Failed to Do Her Duty Towards Them': The India Office and Pauper Indians in the Metropole, 1857–1914. *Journal of Imperial and Commonwealth History*, 46(2), pp. 226–256.

7 See, for example, Shepard, T. (2006). *The Invention of Decolonization: The Algerian War and the Remaking of France*. Ithaca, NY: Cornell University Press; Alba, R. and Silberman, R. (2002). Decolonization Immigrations and the Social Origins of the Second Generation: The Case of North Africans in France. *International Migration Review*, 36(4), pp. 1169–1193.

8 This was the result of an 1844 labor law, which had largely brought night shifts at textile mills to an end. See Gurr, D. and Hunt, J. (1998). *The Cotton Mills of Oldham*. Oldham: Oldham Education & Leisure; Penn, R., Martin, A. and Scattergood, H. (1991). Gender Relations, Technology and Employment Change in the Contemporary Textile Industry. *Sociology*, 25(4), p. 583.

9 See also the significant number of job postings in local newspapers as late as the mid-1970s: N.A. (1973, July 19). '30m Profit Forecast for Courtaulds'. *Oldham Evening Chronicle*.

10 For a small sample of the excellent literature on the shifting boundaries of race and citizenship in postwar, decolonizing Britain, see Hansen, R. (2000). *Citizenship and Immigration in Postwar Britain*. Oxford: Oxford University Press; Schofield, C. (2013). *Enoch Powell and the Making of Postcolonial Britain*. Cambridge: Cambridge University Press; Schwarz, B. (2011). *The White Man's World: Memories of Empire*, Vol. I. Oxford: Oxford University Press.

11 For a complete history of the 'CDP' across Britain, see Loney, M. (1983). *Community Against Government: The British Community Development Project, 1968–78 – A Study of Government Incompetence*. London: Heinemann Educational Books, pp. 8–18.

12 The literature in this field is incredibly rich. See, for example, Cowie, J. (1999) *Capital Moves: RCA's Seventy-Year Quest for Cheap Labor*. Ithaca, NY: Cornell University Press; High, S. (2003). *Industrial Sunset: The Making of North America's Rust Belt, 1969–1984*. Toronto: University of Toronto Press; Stein, J. (2010). *Pivotal Decade: How the United States Traded Factories for Finance in the Seventies*. New Haven, CT: Yale University Press; Ullmann, J. (1988). *The Anatomy of Industrial Decline: Productivity, Investment, and Location in US Manufacturing*. New York: Quorum Books.

13 For a further exploration of this phenomenon, see Schulman, B. (1991). *From Cotton Belt to Sunbelt: Federal Policy, Economic Development and the Transformation of the South, 1938–1980*. New York: Oxford University Press.

14 For a further discussion of this phenomenon, see Hirsch, A. (1983). *Making the Second Ghetto: Race and Housing in Chicago, 1940–1960*. Chicago: University of Chicago Press; Kusmer, K.L. (1995). African Americans in the City Since World War II: From the Industrial to the Post-Industrial Era. *Journal of Urban History*, 21, pp. 458–504; Casey-Leininger, C.F. (1993). 'Making the Second Ghetto in Cincinnati: Avondale, 1925–1970'. In Taylor, H.L. Jr. (ed.) *Race and the City: Work, Community, and Protest in Cincinnati, 1820–1970*. Urbana, IL: University of Illinois Press, pp. 232–257.

15 A period from January to March 1974 when nonessential services and commercial enterprises had electricity supplies limited to three days a week as a way of rationing coal supplies during a strike by miners.

16 Imperial realms that gained their independence after 1945; previously the Commonwealth had largely referred to the white settler colonies such as Canada and Australia.

17 Also published in Lees, R. and Smith, G. (eds.). (1977) *Action-Research in Community Development*. London: Routledge.

18 Rootes would eventually be bought by Chrysler, while Triumph would be merged into British Leyland.
19 To highlight just a few of the excellent recent studies: MacKinnon, L. (2020). *Closing Sysco: Industrial Decline in Atlantic Canada's Steel City*. Toronto: University of Toronto Press; Strangleman, T. (2019). *Voices of Guinness: An Oral History of the Park Royal Brewery*. Oxford: Oxford University Press; Wetherell, S. (forthcoming 2025). *Liverpool and the Unmaking of Britain*. London: Bloomsbury.

Reference List

Alba, R. and Silberman, R. (2002). Decolonization Immigrations and the Social Origins of the Second Generation: The Case of North Africans in France. *International Migration Review*, 36(4), pp. 1169–1193.

Ashworth, W. (1986). *The History of the British Coal Industry, Vol. 5. 1946–1982: The Nationalized Industry*. Oxford: Oxford University Press.

Bailkin, J. (2012). *The Afterlife of Empire*. Berkeley, CA: University of California Press.

Barr, A. (1974). *Housing Improvement and the Racial Conundrum: A Report on Resident Attitudes to Housing Improvement in Glodwick, Oldham*. CDP/2/6, Oldham Local Studies and Archives (hereafter OLSA).

Barton, G.A. (2012). Towards a Global History of Britain. *Perspectives on History*, 50(7).

Beckert, S. (2014). *Empire of Cotton*. London: Macmillan.

Bennoune, M. (1975). Maghribin Workers in France. *MERIP Reports*, 34, pp. 1–30.

Binelli, M. (2014). *The Last Days of Detroit: Motor Cars, Motown and the Collapse of an Industrial Giant*. London: Vintage.

Bluestone, B. and Harrison, B. (1982). *Deindustrialization of America: Plant Closings, Community Abandonment and the Dismantling of Basic Industry*. New York: Basic Books.

Bottomley, F. (1980, October 25). Another 170 Thrown Out of Work: Unavoidable End of Weatherlux Famous Oldham Garment-Makers. *Oldham Weekly Chronicle*.

Brereton, B. and Yelvington, K. (eds.). (1999). *The Colonial Caribbean in Transition: Essays on Post-emancipation Social and Cultural History*. Gainesville, FL: University Press of Florida.

Brooks, C. (2009). *Alien Neighbors, Foreign Friends: Asian Americans, Housing, and the Transformation of Urban California*. Chicago: University of Chicago Press.

Burnett, J. (1994). *Idle Hands: The Experience of Unemployment, 1790–1990*. London: Routledge.

Burton, A. (1998). *At the Heart of the Empire: Indians and the Colonial Encounter in Late-Victorian Britain*. Berkeley, CA: University of California Press.

Campbell, E. (2017, February 8). *Interviewed: 'High Expectations' Oral History Project*. WIC/1/3, OLSA.

Carter, W., Schill, M. and Wachter, S. (1998). Polarisation, Public Housing and Racial Minorities in US Cities. *Urban Studies (Edinburgh, Scotland)*, 35, pp. 1889–1911.

Casey-Leininger, C.F. (1993). Making the Second Ghetto in Cincinnati: Avondale, 1925–1970. In Taylor, H.L. Jr. (ed.) *Race and the City: Work, Community, and Protest in Cincinnati, 1820–1970*. Urbana, IL: University of Illinois Press, pp. 232–257.

Casey, V. (2016, October 5). *Interviewed: High Expectations, An Oral History Project Undertaken by Oldham Anglo West Indian Over 50's Group*. WIC/1/4, OLSA.

Conn, S. (2006). *Metropolitan Philadelphia – Living with the Presence of the Past*. Philadelphia: University of Pennsylvania Press.

Cowie, J. (1999). *Capital Moves: RCA's Seventy-Year Quest for Cheap Labor*. Ithaca, NY: Cornell University Press.

Devons, E., Crossley, J.R. and Maunder, W.F. (1968). Wage Rate Indexes by Industry, 1948–1965. *Economica*, 35, pp. 392–423.

Gay, V. (2021). *Pour la Dignité: Ouvriers Immigrés et Conflits Sociaux dans les Années 1980*. Lyon: Presses universitaires de Lyon.

Gill, T. (2013). The Indian Workers' Association Coventry 1938–1990: Political and Social Action. *South Asian History and Culture*, 4(4), 554–573.

Gregory, J. (2005). *The Southern Diaspora: How the Great Migrations of Black and White Southerners Transformed America*. Chapel Hill, NC: University of North Carolina Press.

Deindustrialization and Racialized Communities

Gurr, D. and Hunt, J. (1998). *The Cotton Mills of Oldham*. Oldham: Oldham Education & Leisure.

Hale, S. (2013). *Blair's Community: Communitarian Thought and New Labour*. Manchester: Manchester University Press.

Hansen, R. (2000). *Citizenship and Immigration in Postwar Britain*. Oxford: Oxford University Press.

Healey, M. and Clark, D. (1983, October). *De-Industrialisation and Employment Decline in the West Midlands and Coventry*. Report. Coventry Polytechnic, 1134/2/1/1/27, Modern Records Centre, University of Warwick (hereafter MRC).

Healey, M. and Clark, D. (1984). Industrial Decline and Government Response in the West Midlands: The Case of Coventry. *Regional Studies*, 18(4), pp. 303–318.

High, S. (2003). *Industrial Sunset: The Making of North America's Rust Belt, 1969–1984*. Toronto: University of Toronto Press.

High, S. (2019, September 30). A New Era in Deindustrialization Studies? *Working-Class Perspectives* [Blog]. https://workingclassstudies.wordpress.com/2019/09/30/a-new-era-in-deindustrialization-studies/ (Accessed: 21 June 2024).

High, S. (2023). 'With Iron We Conquer': Deindustrialization, Settler Colonialism, and the Last Train Out of Schefferville, Quebec. *The Canadian Historical Review*, 104(1), pp. 50–75.

Hirsch, A. (1983). *Making the Second Ghetto: Race and Housing in Chicago, 1940–1960*. Chicago, IL: University of Chicago Press.

Hoque, M. (2011–2012). *Interviewed 2011–12 (Specific Date Unknown): Cotton, Curry and Commerce Oral History Recordings*. M185/11, OLSA.

Johnson, C. (1995). *The Life and Death of Industrial Languedoc 1700–1920*. Oxford: Oxford University Press.

Kalra, V. (2000). *From Textile Mills to Taxi Ranks: Experiences of Migration, Labour, and Social Change*. Aldershot, Hants: Ashgate.

Kusmer, K.L. (1995). African Americans in the City Since World War II: From the Industrial to the Post-Industrial Era. *Journal of Urban History*, 21, pp. 458–504.

Law, B. (1999). *Oldham, Brave Oldham: An Illustrated History of Oldham*. Oldham: Oldham Council.

Lew-Williams, B. (2018). *The Chinese Must Go: Violence, Exclusion, and the Making of the Alien in America*. Cambridge, MA: Harvard University Press.

Linkon, S.L. (2018). *The Half-Life of Deindustrialization: Working-Class Writing About Economic Restructuring*. Ann Arbor: University of Michigan Press.

Locke, A. (1976, March). *A Study of Mobility in a Pakistani Community*. CDP/4/5, OLSA.

Loney, M. (1983). *Community Against Government: The British Community Development Project, 1968–78 – A Study of Government Incompetence*. London: Heinemann Educational Books.

MacKinnon, L. (2020). *Closing Sysco: Industrial Decline in Atlantic Canada's Steel City*. Toronto: University of Toronto Press.

Matera, M., Natarajan, R., Perry, K.H., Schofield, C. and Waters, R. (2023). Marking Race: Empire, Social Democracy, Deindustrialization. *20th Century British History*, 34, pp. 552–579.

Merrill, H. (2011). Migration and Surplus Populations: Race and Deindustrialization in Northern Italy. *Antipode*, 43(5), pp. 1542–1572.

Michel, A. (1967). *The Indus Rivers: A Study of the Effects of Partition*. New Haven, CT: Yale University Press.

N.A. (1957). *UTFWA Plan for Cotton, 'Chapter Two – Production, Efficiency and Costs'*. TU2/9/6, OLSA.

N.A. (1967). *The Decline of the Cotton and Coal Mining Industries of Lancashire*. Manchester: Lancashire and Merseyside Industrial Development Association.

N.A. (1976, 19 February). Employers Under Fire. *The Guardian*, p. 5.

N.A. (c. 1978–1979). *A Racial Analysis of School-Leaving and Job-Finding in Coventry*. Unemployed Workers' Centre: General Correspondence, c. Jun 1978–Feb 1979. MSS.5/3/51, MRC.

N.A. (1978–1984). *Publications and Other Papers Mainly Concerning Economic Recession in Coventry*. 1978–1984, MSS.373/29, MRC.

N.A. (1980, 25 October). Wreath Marks Death of Mill. *Oldham Weekly Chronicle*.

N.A. (1981a, 29 January). Oldham Heads for 12.4pc Unemployed. *Oldham Evening Chronicle*.

N.A. (1981b, 5 May). Few Turn Out for March to Civic Centre over Jobless. *Oldham Evening Chronicle*.

N.A. (1991). *Oldham Borough Pakistani Community Profile (From the 1991 Census)*. L1470, OLSA.

Oldham Kashmir Cultural Day Steering Group. (2000). *Kashmir Cultural Day 2000 – Celebrating Diversity, Promoting Cohesion*. M166/21/10. OLSA.

Owen, D. (1994). Spatial Variations in Ethnic Minority Group Populations in Britain. *Population Trends*, 78, pp. 23–33.

Patel, I.S. (2021). *We're Here Because You Were There: Immigration and the End of Empire*. London: Verso.

Penn, R., Martin, A. and Scattergood, H. (1991). Gender Relations, Technology and Employment Change in the Contemporary Textile Industry. *Sociology*, 25(4), pp. 569–587.

Perry, K.H. (2016). *London Is the Place for Me: Black Britons, Citizenship, and the Politics of Race*. Oxford: Oxford University Press.

Pocock, J.G.A. (1975). British History: A Plea for a New Subject. *Journal of Modern History*, 47(4), pp. 601–621.

Riis, J. (1957 [1890]) *How the Other Half Lives: Studies Among the Tenements of New York*. New York: Sagamore Press.

Rose, N. (1996). The Death of the Social? Re-figuring the Territory of Government. *Economy and Society*, 25(3), pp. 327–356.

Saini, R. (2018). 'England Failed to Do Her Duty Towards Them': The India Office and Pauper Indians in the Metropole, 1857–1914. *Journal of Imperial and Commonwealth History*, 46(2), pp. 226–256.

Sasson, T. et al. (2018). Britain and the World: A New Field? The Worlding of Britain. *Journal of British Studies*, 57, pp. 677–708.

Schofield, C. (2013). *Enoch Powell and the Making of Postcolonial Britain*. Cambridge: Cambridge University Press.

Schulman, B. (1991). *From Cotton Belt to Sunbelt: Federal Policy, Economic Development and the Transformation of the South, 1938–1980*. New York: Oxford University Press.

Schwarz, B. (2011). *The White Man's World: Memories of Empire*, Vol. I. Oxford: Oxford University Press.

Self, R. (2003). *American Babylon: Race and the Struggle for Postwar Oakland*. Princeton: Princeton University Press.

Shaw, A. (1988). *A Pakistani Community in Britain*. Oxford: Basil Blackwell.

Shepard, T. (2006). *The Invention of Decolonization: The Algerian War and the Remaking of France*. Ithaca, NY: Cornell University Press.

Shilliam, R. (2018). *Race and the Undeserving Poor: From Abolition to Brexit*. Newcastle upon Tyne: Agenda Publishing.

Stacey, E. (2013). *Cotton, Curry, and Commerce: The History of Asian Businesses in Oldham*. Oldham: Oldham Council.

Stein, J. (2010). *Pivotal Decade: How the United States Traded Factories for Finance in the Seventies*. New Haven, CT: Yale University Press.

Strangleman, T. (2019). *Voices of Guinness: An Oral History of the Park Royal Brewery*. Oxford: Oxford University Press.

Sturman, R. (2014). Indian Indentured Labor and the History of International Rights Regimes. *The American Historical Review*, 119(5), 1439–1465.

Sugrue, T.J. (1996). *The Origins of the Urban Crisis: Race and Inequality in Postwar Detroit*. Princeton: Princeton University Press.

Thompson, A. and Marshall, W. (2002). *In the Shadow of the Plantation: Caribbean History and Legacy*. Kingston, Jamaica: Ian Randle Publishers.

Tomlinson, J. (2016). De-Industrialization Not Decline: A New Meta-Narrative for Post-war British History. *Twentieth-Century British History*, 27, pp. 76–99.

Ullmann, J. (1988). *The Anatomy of Industrial Decline: Productivity, Investment, and Location in US Manufacturing*. New York: Quorum Books.

Vernon, J. (2021). Heathrow and the Making of Neoliberal Britain. *Past & Present*, 252(1), pp. 213–247.

Vigna, X. (2012). *Histoire des ouvriers en France au XXe siècle*. Paris: Perrin.

Virdee, S. (2014). *Racism, Class and the Racialized Outsider*. Basingstoke: Palgrave Macmillan.

Waldinger, R. (2001). *Strangers at the Gates: New Immigrants in Urban America*. Berkeley, CA: University of California Press.

Wacquant, L. (2008). *Urban Outcasts: A Comparative Sociology of Advanced Marginality*. Cambridge: Polity.
Wetherell, S. (forthcoming 2025). *Liverpool and the Unmaking of Britain*. London: Bloomsbury.
Wilson, W.J. (1987). *The Truly Disadvantaged*. Chicago: University of Chicago Press.
Wolfinger, J. (2007). *Philadelphia Divided: Race and Politics in the City of Brotherly Love*. Chapel Hill, NC: University of North Carolina Press.

14

CLASS, GENDER, AND INDUSTRIAL STRUCTURES OF FEELING AFTER SOCIALISM

Post-Industrial Lives in the Post-Yugoslav Space

Chiara Bonfiglioli

Introduction

This chapter examines the class and gender implications of deindustrialization in a post-socialist context. It does so by providing an overview of recent scholarly works that address deindustrialization in the post-Yugoslav space, namely the successor states of what once was the Yugoslav Federation. After the Second World War, socialist Yugoslavia embarked upon an ambitious project of rapid industrialization, following the Soviet model. Its break from the Soviet bloc in 1948 led Yugoslav leaders to adopt a new form of market socialism integrated within the global market, based on workers' self-management and on the idea of the "withering away of the state" (Jović, 2009). Industrialization remained a key tenet of the self-managed Yugoslav model. Factories were envisaged as socially owned rather than state owned, and workers' participation to industrial production and profit redistribution was encouraged (Zukin, 1975). Due to the intimate linkage between socialist Yugoslavia and its industrialization project after the Second World War, and due to the simultaneous collapse of the federal state and of its industrial giants during the Yugoslav Wars (1991–1999) and their aftermath, the post-industrial character of many urban landscapes in the region cannot be disconnected from its post-Yugoslav element. Post-industrial, post-Yugoslav cities and towns are often in a state of utter decay and industrial ruination. Yugoslav times, conversely, are often associated with Fordist modernity, productivity, and economic growth, with the socialist model functioning in ordinary citizens' memories not only as a model of normal life in a material sense but also as an ethical form of life (Spasić, 2012; Greenberg, 2011).

In the last decade, there has been a renewed scholarly interest in class and labor relations during the period of state socialism and during post-socialist transformations, not only in the former Yugoslavia but in Central and Eastern Europe more widely (Archer, Duda, and Stubbs, 2021; Biti and Senjković, 2021; Ost, 2015; Siefert, 2020), also as a result of new social movements addressing issues of labor exploitation and precarity in post-socialism (Horvat and Štiks, 2015). The more specific theme of deindustrialization is also emerging as a way to counter the marginalization and dispossession experienced by working-class citizens and communities during factory closures. Women working in industry and their experiences

DOI: 10.4324/9781003308324-21

have been addressed for the first time in recent years, highlighting both the lower status of "women's factories" during socialism and the complete devaluation of women's industrial labor that followed the end of Yugoslavia (Bonfiglioli, 2019, 2020; Blagaić and Jambrešić Kirin, 2013; Vodopivec, 2010, 2020). Industrial workers' masculinities have also been investigated, from the glorification of heavy industry during socialist times to blue-collar workers' multifaceted responses to nationalism and neoliberalism (Matošević, 2019; Musić, 2021a; Archer and Musić, 2020). Anthropological and ethnographic studies on post-industrial heritage and communities are very prominent and seem to confirm Ognjen Kojanić's convincing argument that "the greatest contribution that the anthropology of post-socialism can offer to the anthropology of European peripheries is in the meticulous ethnographic attention paid to spaces and peoples that get marginalized as a consequence of political-economic processes and marginalizing discourses" (Kojanić, 2020, p. 57). In the next pages I will provide an overview of some recent studies on deindustrialization and post-industrial lives in the post-Yugoslav space, focusing mainly on workers' narratives and identities. Examples are drawn from a range of different industrial sectors, from the male-dominated steel, automotive, and shipyard industries to the feminized textile and fish canning industries.

Setting the Stage: Workers' Industrial Struggles in the Transition to Post-Socialism

After its break with the Soviet Union, Yugoslavia became well integrated in the world capitalist system through its original form of self-managed market socialism. From the 1970s onward, Yugoslavia participated in the global rearrangements in the capitalist system as a result of the interconnections and exchanges between Western and Eastern experts on the development of market economies (Bockman, 2011). In the field of textiles and garments, for instance, subcontracting for West Germany gradually increased over local production in the course of the 1970s and 1980s, making Yugoslav companies more and more dependent on Western orders (Musić, 2021b). After the death of its lifelong President Josip Broz Tito in 1980, Yugoslavia faced significant political and economic challenges, including a rising foreign debt. From 1987 onward, to repay IMF loans, Yugoslavia followed strict austerity measures, which were accompanied by a turn to neoliberalism in many Yugoslav factories.

In their in-depth research on the Borovo shoe and leather factory near Vukovar in Croatia, Sven Cvek, Jasna Račić, and Snježana Ivčić show that discourses about the post-industrial society were already permeating socialist Yugoslavia in the 1980s, justifying a shift in class relations with the purpose of disciplining workers. The working class was seen as resisting social change and economic restructuring. Workers also resisted nationalist discourses, and their inter-ethnic solidarity was still strong, until nationalist forces took over the unions and used them to strengthen ethnic divisions. In the late 1980s, Borovo employed up to 22,000 workers. The factory had greatly invested in "social standards," and while it was exposed to market trends, it also prioritized the social development of the community, namely housing, education, leisure, and culture (Perić, 2020). The resistance against neoliberal austerity measures put up by Borovo workers is exemplified by the march of 5,000 of them, both Croats and Serbs, to the capital of Yugoslavia, Belgrade, resulting in the occupation of the Federal Assembly in July 1988. Yugoslav-wide strikes involved over half a million employees in 1989, including Borovo employees (Cvek, Račić, and Ivčić, 2019).

Such demonstrative actions, however, could not prevent further austerity measures and the economic downfall that affected the region during the Yugoslav wars of the 1990s, when privatization, economic decline, inflation, and unemployment rose even further, leading to an overall destruction of jobs and of industrial development, a process that has been defined also as "de-development" (Meurs and Ranasinghe, 2003). The devastating economic and social impact of the post-socialist transformation has been documented for the entire Central and Eastern Europe, as well as the former Soviet Union (Ghodsee and Orenstein, 2021). When it comes to post-Yugoslav states, real gross industrial output fell sharply after 1989. It took almost two decades for post-Yugoslav states to reach their preexisting 1990 GDP level, and Bosnia-Herzegovina, Montenegro, and Serbia are still far from that target. Unemployment rates are among the highest in Europe, and social inequalities have risen sharply since the Yugoslav break-up (Stambolieva, 2016). In addition, the external debt of post-Yugoslav states is five times greater than that of Yugoslavia in 1990, and post-Yugoslav states' economies are highly dependent on loans and trade with core EU countries (Živković, 2015). The re-peripheralization of the region vis-à-vis of the European Union also led to a devaluation of local industrial production, especially for Slovenia and Croatia, which accessed the European Union in 2004 and 2013, respectively, and whose industrial production was highly prized in Yugoslav times.

Simultaneously, the remaining industrial production underwent a process of precarization, labor intensification, and increased exploitation. As Kideckel argues (2001, p. 115), the terms 'post-socialism' and 'transition' should not obscure the relevance of 'neo-capitalism' for East-Central Europe, namely of a "social system that reworks basic capitalist principles in new, even more inegalitarian ways than the Western model from which it derives." In this context, the working classes are placed at the bottom of the social scale, as "neo-capitalism manufactures social structures with which workers engage either as degraded suppliants or as alienated antagonists" (Kideckel, 2001, p. 115). This is especially the case in post-Yugoslav states, where the privatization process of former industrial complexes was intertwined with speculation, money laundry, and criminal networks connected to the neo-nationalist and postwar elites that gained power during the Yugoslav wars. Post-Yugoslav workers underwent a process of severe economic and social dispossession. They often worked without receiving wages, in the hope that the factory would recover, while new factory owners were able to engage in the "wild privatization" (Kurtović, 2020) or "systematic destruction" (Hodges, 2021) of formerly successful plants and could "strip assets, resell company plant, equipment and land, or take out loans against these, using the money to speculate in real estate transactions," until bankruptcy was declared, and workers were left empty-handed, while factory owners walked away with massive profits without being held accountable by the state (Živković, 2015). During these post-socialist transformations, many workers found that they could not claim back decades of social contributions, savings, or unpaid wages. Due to the bureaucratic and institutional chaos that followed the establishment of new nation-states, workers were also unable to access the legal and political resources to claim their legal dues. Disempowerment in relation to the privatization process, therefore, became a common phenomenon across the former Yugoslav space and across industrial sectors. Post-Yugoslav states ultimately joined the "race to the bottom" for production costs in the global capitalist economy, also offering, as in Serbia, subsidies to multinational companies for local investments, which tend to create a myriad of exploitative and precarious, low-paid jobs, with unionizing also being threatened (Reljanović, 2021).

Alongside economic and social dispossession, blue-collar workers in the post-Yugoslav region also experienced a sharp process of symbolic devaluation, after having been heralded as the self-managers of their respective factories during market socialism. When conducting my research on the textile industry in post-Yugoslav states, the sense of dignity interiorized by blue-collar workers during socialism contrasted with post-socialist values and practices, for instance the devaluation of manual workers which became rife after 1989, when factories closed one after the other. As trade unionists from the Varaždin area reported, in the 1990s, it was common to hear expressions like "every granny knows how to sew" or "You kick the bush and five seamstresses come out" to indicate the abundance of undervalued and easily replaceable middle-aged, female, low-educated textile workers. State celebrations such as International Women's Day, once an important landmark of industrial workers' structure of feeling during socialism, came to be seen as an uncomfortable remnant of a bygone totalitarian past. While during the socialist era members of management would distribute flowers to female workers, and women would have a small celebration in the factory, such celebrations became the object of ridicule, as revealed by a male narrator involved in the union:

> When after a couple of years, I bought flowers for all female union members, there were laughs among the management, and from our local simple people. [They would ask:] 'What stupidity are you doing?' They all forget that their pay comes from the work of those women. And even today there are smiles sometimes. I cannot name one company where the director would come and wish the people a happy 8th of March.

The same trade unionist added:

> I am not, how to say, Yugonostalgic, or socialist or anything else, but at that time you were happy to go to work. Because at that time you really could count on one hand the times when a supervisor, boss, director, technical director would call you 'cow,' 'goat,' and I am not mentioning the other insults.
>
> *(Bonfiglioli, 2019, pp. 120–121)*

This situation was a far cry from the former self-management system, in which workers had been formally the owners of their factories and able to make choices about profit redistribution. The limits of self-management have been debated at length by numerous authors, and current blue-collar narratives express overall disillusionment with the degree of decision-making that was possible during socialism. After privatization, the fact that some workers managed to remain shareholders of their factories after privatization did not always help, given that usually most shares would be concentrated in the hands of managers and investors. However, the 'feeling of ownership' linked to the self-management system allowed some workers to partially resist privatization and to establish their own self-managed companies in post-socialist times, as in the case of the DITA detergent factory in Tuzla, Bosnia-Herzegovina, the ITAS metal company in Ivanec, Croatia, and the pharmaceutical company Jugoremedija, in Zrenjanin, Serbia (Kurtović, 2020; Calori and Jurkat, 2018; Kojanić, 2023). The DITA workers' struggle, which included both male and female workers, was especially significant as it inspired a wider protest movement named the Bosnian Spring in 2014, as well as a subsequent graphic ethnography of their struggle (Gilbert, Kurtović, and Stapić, 2021). As Larisa Kurtović notes, the DITA workers' ability to restart production, and their refusal to let their factory succumb to ruination, is a strong reminder that researchers need to avoid seeing deindustrialization as an inevitable historical phenomenon. While these instances of self-organization and resistance are providing a horizon of hope for the involved

Workers' Industrial 'Structure of Feeling' and the Attachment to Factory Life

As Alice Mah has argued in her study of industrial ruination as a lived process in North America, the North of England, and post-Soviet Russia, "abandoned industrial sites remain connected with the urban fabric that surrounds them: with communities; with collective memory; and with people's health, livelihoods, and stories" (2012, p. 3). A growing historical and anthropological literature addresses industrial workers' memories in post-Yugoslav states and their experiences of post-socialist transformations and factory closures. Raymond Williams's (1977) concept of the "structure of feeling," revisited by scholars of deindustrialization to investigate the persistence of industrial modes of life after deindustrialization, is especially useful here (see Byrne, 2010). This industrial structure of feeling, rooted in the association between industrial work and the past socialist system that fostered industrial development, is strongly shared by several generations of industrial workers who came of age during the existence of Yugoslavia. Rory Archer and Goran Musić (2017) have written about industrial workplaces as 'socialist microcosms' during Yugoslav times, as factories provided workers with a variety of welfare benefits alongside stable employment. Housing, health care, childcare, and leisure opportunities were some of the benefits attached to industrial work, which greatly shaped workers' industrial structure of feeling and attachments to their factories as 'second homes.'

Factories were seen as centers of community life and as crucial means of livelihood, especially in towns that were mainly relying on industrial production and whose inhabitants' everyday routines revolved around the rhythms of big 'kombinats' or industrial plants. Sanja Potkonjak and Tea Škokić (2022) studied the impact left by the closure of the ironworks in the post-industrial town of Sisak, where the steel industry used to employ up to 14,000 workers. The closing of the plant led many younger citizens to migrate to the nearby capital city of Zagreb and created a generational gap and 'multiple temporalities' in relation to the town. While younger generations are attempting to build their own future either in Zagreb or in Sisak despite the end of industrial production, older generations mainly perceive the city as having 'no future' after the end of the ironworks. Former workers between the ages of 50 and 90 years old long for the industrial past that shaped their youth, as a narrator stated: "That was a giant, I thought it could not be destroyed. It would last forever, forever" (Potkonjak and Škokić, 2022, p. 87, our translation). The authors note that the crisis of the system coincided with the crisis of industrial workers who could not adjust to the values and rhythms of new times. The closing of the plant turned Sisak into a veritable ghost town. As a narrator retold, "It's not that the city fell into ruin, it was defeated. This is more than ruination. Ruination is an objective, economic category, but this is something on people's faces" (Potkonjak and Škokić, 2022, p. 91, our translation). Besides relocating to Zagreb, children and grandchildren of industrial workers are now migrating en masse to the West, with 'Europe' and Croatia's access to the European Union becoming a signifier of the job security and prosperity that was once possible in Yugoslavia.

"Once those smokestacks also fed my family," commented someone on Facebook under a newspaper article that described the demolition of the main smokestack in Sisak, damaged in the 2020 earthquake (Potkonjak and Škokić, 2022, p. 104, our translation).

Class, Gender, and Industrial Structures of Feeling

The representation of the ironworks as a 'mother' (*majka Željezara*) is symptomatic of the structure of feeling that the factory provided, rooted in a vision of hope for the future in its ability to feed its children and grandchildren.[1] This vision of the factory as provider and motor of industrial towns leads to consistent ambivalences in relation to the environmental pollution brought by industrial giants, in the past and in current times. Deana Jovanović (2018) has studied the re-industrialization of the copper mine in the Serbian town of Bor brought about by the Serbian state, and Bor inhabitants' perception of the omnipresent, toxic smoke, as necessary:

> She disliked 'the smoke,' just as everybody else did, but she believed, like many, that the smoke 'fed' the whole town. At that time, she would have given anything to get any kind of job at that company, even though it was heavily polluting the town in which her daughter was growing up.

Another narrator told Jovanović (2018), "Shush. While there is smoke, it's good." The copper smelter was seen as feeding the town and its inhabitants, even if it employed fewer people than during socialist times. Similarly, current environmental activism in Sisak neglects to acknowledge the polluting effects of the ironworks in socialist times (Potkonjak and Škokić, 2021). One exception when it comes to "smokestack nostalgia" is the case of Bakar, a small coastal town in Croatia, where the environmental damage produced by the coking plant during socialism is openly denounced by local citizens, and the demolition of the smokestack built in 1974 was celebrated as a new beginning in 1994 (Potkonjak and Alempijević, 2023).

At times, deindustrialization coexisted with labor intensification, as in the town of Štip in North Macedonia, where former textile giants Makedonka and Astibo (with over 6,000 and 3,000 workers respectively) had been replaced by a myriad of small private companies. In Štip, current workers directly compared their experience with that of their parents, who "came back from work smiling" and had access to a variety of institutional benefits. In the privatized textile industry, instead, workers were subjected to mobbing (a form of collective bullying), blackmailing, unpaid overtime, and a lack of flexibility around sick leave and holidays, which was especially taxing for women with family obligations. While during socialism the factory acted as a social buffer and provided its female workers with a certain flexibility when it came to combining productive and reproductive work, this was no longer the case in Macedonian private factories that had joined the "race to the bottom" for production costs that characterize the global garment industry (Bonfiglioli, 2015). One of my narrators, who used to work in the Makedonka factory as an accountant, was later forced to take up manual work to reach her pension age. After ten years of hard work, she was mortified when she was denied a production prize, because she had taken six months of unpaid leave to take care of her dying mother-in-law (Bonfiglioli, 2015, 2019). Former workers from the Makedonka cotton plant and Astibo fashion industry, as well as their children, longed for the times in which they felt respected as workers and duly compensated through a variety of benefits. Moreover, former workers also missed the cultural life that existed around the two factories during socialism, notably organized choirs, theatre performances, exhibitions, and literary clubs that existed in both factories, as a result of the democratization of culture during self-management (Vaseva, 2018).

Such attachments to factory life and to the golden era of industrial work are also present when factories remained open after deindustrialization, as in the case of Serbia, where workers engaged in different forms of 'mock-labor,' within nationalized factories that provide regular salaries for populist and clientelist purposes, as in the former Zastava car production company studied by Ivan Rajkovic in Kragujevac, Serbia. Workers had inherited the "industrialist ethos of work" from socialism but could not fulfil it in post-socialist times. They instead "killed time" in the semi-abandoned factory, while their boredom and dependency on the state salary led to widespread demoralization (Rajković, 2018).

Workers' post-socialist and post-industrial nostalgia, therefore, is rooted in lived experiences of solidarity, equality, and job security that were lost with transition and deindustrialization, as highlighted by the Transwork project (Transformations of work in post-transition Croatia, 2017–2021), which resulted in the collection of 132 thematically focused interviews conducted with workers of different ages and with different socioeconomic status in all parts of Croatia, from Pula, Rijeka, and Čakovec to Ilok and Dubrovnik, and which discussed the changes that took place in the workplace after the end of state socialism in 1990, after the global financial crisis of 2007/2008, and as a result of Croatia's accession to the European Union in 2013 (Biti and Senjković, 2021). In dialogue with the existing literature addressing deindustrialization in North America and Western Europe (Strangleman, 2017; High, MacKinnon, and Perchard, 2017), Reana Senjković highlights that similar feelings of longing and belonging are expressed by former industrial workers in the West: both 'Eastern' and 'Western' workers found a job easily, felt proud of their achievements in the workplace, were satisfied of their salaries, and worked for the same employer until their retirement. The concept of 'nostalgia,' however, is mainly used as a scholarly object when discussing workers' experiences of post-socialist countries, which hint at the stigmatization of any possible alternative system in the current neoliberal context, particularly the experiments in self-management carried out in Yugoslav times (Senjkovic, 2021). In the third and last section of this chapter, I will discuss the gendered impact of deindustrialization and factory closures on two feminized sectors, namely the textile industry and the fish canning industry, and on a male-dominated industry, shipbuilding.

Working-Class Femininities and Masculinities: Gendered Impacts of Deindustrialization

The devaluation of women's industrial labor in the post-Yugoslav region has been a scarcely researched subject until recent years, when several scholarly works started to investigate the impact of industrial collapse and ruination on different generations of women who came of age during socialist times, when women's equal participation in the industrialization effort came to be seen as the chief means to achieve women's emancipation in a socialist society. Dual workers' families were the norm among working-class citizens living in urban areas. Women's participation in the labor market in the former Yugoslavia greatly depended upon each republic's development, with Slovenia having the highest rates of education and employment and Kosovo the lowest. Women's employment rates reached a maximum average of 33–40% in the 1970s and 1980s, making Yugoslavia more similar to Western Europe than to East European socialist regimes. Despite the state's promise of socializing reproductive tasks, childcare provision remained extremely limited throughout the socialist era, especially in rural areas. Many women had to rely on grandmothers, other relatives, or neighbors to take care of their children while at work. Night shifts were also extremely problematic for female factory workers (Bonfiglioli, 2019). Nonetheless, the widespread character of industrialization meant that several generations of working-class and rural women joined the local factory, which was likely to be a 'woman's factory' if producing textiles or garments.

Class, Gender, and Industrial Structures of Feeling

The foundation of the Dalmatinka spinning mill and thread factory in the Dalmatian Hinterland, studied by curator and scholar Dragana Modrić, makes clear that such factories had an enormous impact when it came to the social and urban development of deprived areas, such as the town of Sinj and its surroundings (Modrić, 2018). Archival sources and interviews show that the first women who joined the night shifts in the factory were seen as "whores" and stigmatized by the local community, with older women crossing themselves when they saw a young female worker on a bike (Modrić, 2018). With time, however, families accepted that young women worked in the factory, bringing an additional salary home. To this day, such economic emancipation is remembered with gratitude by Dalmatinka pensioners, even by those who have no sympathy for the socialist system. Dalmatinka employed over 2,000 workers in its heydays and was once again perceived as 'the mother' of the town of Sinj:

> Dalmatinka was the mother of all the inhabitants of the city of Sinj and of its surroundings. She fed us, our children, our grandchildren, and we had a future. However, the war came and things did not stay like that. While we worked, there was welfare for all, possibilities, good wages, houses were built and the future of our children was built. . . . Now the factory is so abandoned, so pillaged, so destroyed, that it is terrible and ugly to tell our children and grandchildren that we once worked there.
>
> *(Bonfiglioli, 2019, p. 143)*

Interestingly, besides being a provider for all its inhabitants, the plant also served as a maternity ward for a short period during the Yugoslav wars, when the city was on the frontline. A female worker I met had given birth in the plant in the 1990s. The end of Dalmatinka as a community provider, coupled with women's devaluation as workers, became a source of shame – former workers felt ashamed to indicate that their beloved factory has turned into a wasteland.

Throughout the former Yugoslav region, it can be estimated that around 350,000 jobs in the textile industry were lost in the last 30 years.[2] Another very successful textile plant was the Slovenian *kombinat* named Mura, which employed up to 6,000 workers during socialist times and whose closure led to the loss of 2,635 jobs in 2009. As highlighted by Nina Vodopivec (2021a, 2021b), the affective and embodied experience of deindustrialization materializes in workers' using words such as "rubbish" and "garbage" to express their feelings of devaluation. In 2009, the factory under bankruptcy and restructuring was experienced as a toxic environment due to the lack of transparency and the individualization of workers' experiences of grief (Vodopivec, 2021a, 2021b). Vodopivec shows that workers are no longer represented as agents of social modernization but as a social problem, as they are unable to adapt to the new neoliberal context. In contrast, during socialism they had been praised for their diligence and encouraged to further self-sacrifice for the community – this was particularly true of female workers in labor-intensive industries such as textiles. This situation therefore led to a breakdown in trust and reciprocity and created a lack of discursive space to express such trauma, which resulted in physical and mental health issues, particularly for women who became unemployed.

Even if a number of Mura workers were dismissed with occupational illnesses, their survival strategies are embedded in the valorization and dignity of manual work experienced during socialist times: "People ask me: how did you survive? I survived, I managed. I am lucky to have such character and to have golden hands" (Vodopivec, 2021a, p. 183, our translation). The survival skills that former workers put in place during post-socialist transformations are indeed linked to their ability to use their "golden hands," as craft-makers, caretakers, smugglers, and other occupations in the informal sector. In the coastal city of Pula, the tourist sector, as well as the elderly care industry in neighboring Italy constituted the main outlet for unemployed women and women unable to survive on the meagre state pensions (Bonfiglioli, 2020).

Another female-dominated industry that was greatly affected by deindustrialization is the industry of fish canning in Slovenia and Croatia. As reconstructed by Ulf Brunnbauer, sardine canneries were introduced at the end of the nineteenth century in the Upper Adriatic, then under the Hapsburg Empire. The ports of Trieste and Rijeka were then connected to the major urban centers of the Empire such as Vienna, Prague, and Budapest by railway. The work was hard and poorly paid and mainly carried out by women. The predominance of the female workforce continued under socialism. The Mirna fish canning factory in Rovinj is still surviving after several waves of restructuring (Brunnbauer, 2021, 2023). This is not the case, however, for the Fabrika fish processing factory in Vela Luka, on the island of Korcula, or for the fish factory located in Banjole near Pula, which took various names such as Angelo Parodi, Učka, Istra, and Mirna from 1927 to 1990 (Vene and Borovičkić, 2018; Petrović, 2020).[3] Despite the hardships of the labor and phenomena such as underage work, the work in the fish industry is still remembered fondly by former workers, who "received a lot of recognition and felt acknowledged as a valuable part of society" (Brunnbauer and Hodges, 2019, p. 12). The welfare and leisure provided by the factory had a great impact on local livelihoods. Being part of these factories also meant emancipation and autonomy for workers coming from surrounding villages where patriarchal households and agricultural work made life even harder. As a narrator from the island of Lošinj retold to Tanja Petrović:

> I came from the countryside and was the ninth child in the family. When I was 12–13 years old, I had to wake up at 3 am or 4 am to go and look after the sheep. So, working in the factory was not that hard for me. At least I was on my own, I had my salary.
>
> *(Petrović, 2020, p. 37, our translation)*

Collective singing was also especially important to make work in the factory bearable and to establish a community among the fish workers, who were also often shunned due to their bad smell after spending the whole day cleaning fish. The odor of the canneries, as noted by Petrović, was used as one of the reasons to justify factory closures in view of expanding the tourist industry. The reliance on tourism as the main source of economic growth in coastal towns, and the representation of tourism as the future, means that the industrial heritage of the canning industry, as well as of the textile industry, is made invisible.

Tourism is presented as the future in the Croatian post-industrial town of Pula, where deindustrialization could be witnessed almost in real time in the past few years due to the collapse and bankruptcy of the Uljanik shipyard. The company had managed to survive with different degrees of state support until 2018, also thanks to the continuity in management in the transition to post-socialism, with former director Karlo Radolović being celebrated as a local hero.[4] This shipbuilding giant 'fed' the city of Pula. It provided a rare, secure wage for about 2,400 employees in its final phase (down from over 8,000 in the socialist era and over 3,000 in the late 1990s), as opposed to the fluctuating and seasonal earnings gained from tourism, and in contrast to many other firms in Croatia who stopped paying their employees on a regular basis. In socialist times, the firm subsidized a variety of public welfare organizations,

> from pension and health coverage, sports, and education, to voluntary fire fighters and the reconstruction of local roads. The shipyard also provided vital infrastructure for social life in the city of Pula, such as sports clubs and sport facilities, a punk and rock club, a pensioners' club, and so forth.
>
> *(Brunnbauer and Hodges, 2019, pp. 867–868)*

It also owned more than 2,700 apartments, making it a veritable motor of development for the city. Uljanik workers displayed the characteristics of blue-collar masculinity, with pride, mutual respect, and discipline being accompanied by risk-taking and alcohol consumption (Matošević, 2020). When workers experienced the latest and definitive crisis in 2018 and went on strike after wages were discontinued, feelings of suspicion, anxiety, fear, and paranoia were rife, especially in relation to current managers and politicians (Hodges, 2018). The end of the sounds of the shipyard was the most striking sign that industrial production in the city had stopped (Matošević, 2020).

In a radio-drama hosted by the local Radio Rojc, a female narrator said that her husband "had fallen into a depression" when he realized that the firm really was going to close, after working 25 years in the shipyard and thinking that he had a job for life. She was the one who tried to help him, as, she said, "during my working career I underwent many of these risings and fallings of companies." She started then doing all sorts of odd jobs to make ends meet while supporting her husband emotionally (Matošević, 2020, pp. 267–268, our translation). This narrative testifies to women's gendered labor of emotional care inside the home, which added to the pressure of making ends meet when their husbands became unemployed. Many working-class men in Pula worked in Uljanik, while their wives were often employed in feminized sectors, such as the Arena knitwear factory, definitively closed in 2014 (Bonfiglioli, 2020). Ironically, and somehow melancholically, a pub named 'Shipyard' is now successfully operating in the former premises of the Arena knitwear factory, which is overlooking the Pula harbor, even if Arena is permanently closed and even if the failed Uljanik shipyard is waiting for a new investor, with their former workers mostly surviving through tourism or emigration to the West.

Conclusions

Overall, this overview of post-industrial lives in post-Yugoslav states speaks to broader global debates on deindustrialization and the post-industrial society, bringing post-socialist experiences into view. The post-Fordist longing for a Fordist time in which job security and social protection were at least possible, if not widespread, seems to be a constant and so are feelings of symbolic and material devaluation and precarity in post-socialist, neoliberal times.[5] Another striking element is the persistence of working-class femininities and masculinities that were shaped by the self-management system in Yugoslavia, which fostered workers' attachments to local factories as microcosms of everyday life. The overlapping post-socialist and post-industrial transformations deeply affected older generations of former industrial workers who experienced the loss determined by factory closures as well as younger generations of current industrial workers who are still facing the intensification of working rhythms in greenfield industrial plants and private companies. While predominantly male-heavy industries such as steelmaking and shipbuilding had a higher status during socialism in contrast to feminized sectors such as textile production and fish canning, in the aftermath of deindustrialization and privatization, male and female workers' narratives appear to be very similar and largely shaped by class and generation alongside gender.[6] The anthropological and historical works reviewed in this chapter highlight the specific experiences of deindustrialization that characterize the post-Yugoslav region, with the simultaneous collapse of state socialism and of most industrial plants that used to 'feed families' still shaping former and current industrial workers' structure of feeling in post-Yugoslav states.

Notes

1 The same expression is used for the former ironworks in Zenica, Bosnia-Herzegovina.
2 Statistics and reports from late 1980s Yugoslavia list 474,000–487,000 workers in the industry, while current numbers in post-Yugoslav states amount to approximately 130,000 workers – not including the informal sector.
3 On the history of the fish canning factory Plavica on the island of Cres, see also: Kosmos, I. and Solis, I., 2023. *Plavica. Tvornica za preradu ribe/Fish factory, Cres* (exhibition catalogue, Croatian and English). Cres: Creski Muzej/ZRC SAZU.
4 For a history of the Uljanik shipyard, see Brunnbauer, U. and Hodges, A. (2019). The Long Hand of Workers' Ownership: Performing Transformation in the Uljanik Shipyard in Yugoslavia/Croatia, 1970–2018. *International Journal of Maritime History*, 31(4), pp. 860–878. https://doi.org/10.1177/0843871419874003; Petrungaro, S. (2019). Ethics of Work and Discipline in Transition: Uljanik in Late and Post-Socialism. *Review of Croatian History*, 15(1), pp. 191–213. https://doi.org/10.22586/review.v15i1.9803
5 On post-Fordist affect, see Muehlebach, A. and Shoshan, N. (2012). Introduction, Special Collection on Post-Fordist Affect. *Anthropological Quarterly*, 85(2), pp. 317–343. https://doi.org/10.1353/anq.2012.0030
6 Ethnic differences certainly play a role, too, in the deindustrialization process, especially in localities directly affected by the Yugoslav wars and ethnic cleansing. In these contexts, the end of industry is also associated with the end of the politics of "brotherhood and unity," namely solidarity and peaceful coexistence between ethnic groups, see Bonfiglioli, C. (2019). *Women and Industry in the Balkans*. London: I.B. Tauris, pp. 146–152.

Reference List

Archer, R., Duda, I. and Stubbs, P. (2021). *Social Inequalities and Discontent in Yugoslav Socialism*. Southeast European Studies. London: Routledge.

Archer, R. and Musić, G. (2017). Approaching the Socialist Factory and Its Workforce: Considerations from Fieldwork in (Former) Yugoslavia. *Labor History*, 58(1), pp. 44–66. https://doi.org/10.1080/0023656X.2017.1244331

Archer, R. and Musić, G. (2020). When Workers' Self-Management Met Neoliberalism: Positive Perceptions of Market Reforms Among Blue-Collar Workers in Late Yugoslav Socialism. In Burkhardt, J., Green, G.E. and Triebel, A. (eds.) *Labor in State-Socialist Europe, 1945–1989. Contributions to a History of Work*. Budapest, Hungary; New York, NY: Central European University Press, pp. 395–418.

Biti, O. and Senjković, R. (2021). *Transformacija Rada: Narativi, Prakse, Režimi*. Zagreb: Institut za etnologiju i folkloristiku.

Blagaić, M. and Jambrešić Kirin, R. (2013). The Ambivalence of Socialist Working Women's Heritage: A Case Study of the Jugoplastika Factory. *Narodna Umjetnost*, 50(1), pp. 40–73. https://doi.org/10.15176/VOL50NO102

Bockman, J. (2011). *Markets in the Name of Socialism: The Left-Wing Origins of Neoliberalism*. Stanford, CA: Stanford University Press.

Bonfiglioli, C. (2015). Gendered Citizenship in the Global European Periphery: Textile Workers in Post-Yugoslav States. *Women's Studies International Forum*, 49, pp. 57–65. https://doi.org/10.1016/j.wsif.2014.07.004

Bonfiglioli, C. (2019). *Women and Industry in the Balkans: The Rise and Fall of the Yugoslav Textile Sector*. London: I.B. Tauris.

Bonfiglioli, C. (2020). Post-Socialist Deindustrialisation and Its Gendered Structure of Feeling: The Devaluation of Women's Work in the Croatian Garment Industry. *Labor History*, 61(1), pp. 36–47. https://doi.org/10.1080/0023656X.2019.1681643

Brunnbauer, U. (2021). Oil Sardines, Labour and Ruptured Histories in the Upper Adriatic: The Mirna Cannery in Rovinj Since the Early Twentieth Century. *Journal of Mediterranean Studies*, 30(1), pp. 1–19. *Project MUSE*, https://muse.jhu.edu/article/852754

Brunnbauer, U. (2023). Congealed Labor, Preserved Fish: From the Adriatic Towards a Global History of the Canned Sardine. In *Frictions* (17.01.2023). https://doi.org/10.15457/frictions/0025

Brunnbauer, U. and Hodges, A. (2019). The Long Hand of Workers' Ownership: Performing Transformation in the Uljanik Shipyard in Yugoslavia/Croatia, 1970–2018. *International Journal of Maritime History*, 31(4), pp. 860–878. https://doi.org/10.1177/0843871419874003

Byrne, D. (2010). Industrial Culture in a Post-Industrial World: The Case of the North East of England. *City*, 6(3), pp. 279–289. https://doi.org/10.1080/1360481022000037733

Calori, A. and Jurkat, K. (2018). 'I'm Both a Worker and a Shareholder': Workers' Narratives and Property Transformations in Postsocialist Bosnia-Herzegovina and Serbia. *Comparative Southeast European Studies*, 65(4), pp. 654–768. https://doi.org/10.1515/soeu-2017-0043

Cvek, S., Račić, J. and Ivčić, S. (2019). *Borovo u Štrajku: Rad u Tranziciji 1987.-1991*. Zagreb: Baza za radničku inicijativu i demokratizaciju.

Ghodsee, K.R. and Orenstein, M.A. (2021). *Taking Stock of Shock: Social Consequences of the 1989 Revolutions*. New York, NY: Oxford University Press.

Gilbert, A., Kurtović, L. and Stapić, B. (2021, July–August). Reclaiming DITA. *Anthropology News*, 'Graphic Ethnography'. https://www.anthropology-news.org/articles/reclaiming-dita/ (Accessed: 21 June 2024).

Greenberg, J. (2011). On the Road to Normal: Negotiating Agency and State Sovereignty in Postsocialist Serbia. *American Anthropologist*, 113(1), pp. 88–100. https://doi.org/10.1111/j.1548-1433.2010.01308.x

Habinc, M. (2018). Second-Hand Clothes Shops in Slovenia: The Contemporary Situation in Its (A) Historical Perspective. *Studia Ethnologica Croatica*, 30, pp. 321–343. https://doi.org/10.17234/SEC.30.1

High, S.C., MacKinnon, L. and Perchard, A. (eds.). (2017). *The Deindustrialized World: Confronting Ruination in Postindustrial Places*. Vancouver; Toronto: UBC Press.

Hodges, A. (2018). *Worker Narratives of Blame and Responsibility During the 2018 Crisis: The Case of the Uljanik Shipyard, Croatia*. IOS Working Paper. https://doi.org/10.13140/RG.2.2.33717.93922

Hodges, A. (2021). Between Emic and Etic: 'Systematic' and 'Creative' Destruction During the Croatian Shipbuilding Crisis. *History in Flux*, 2(2), pp. 95–110. https://doi.org/10.32728/flux.2020.2.5

Horvat, S. and Štiks, I. (eds.). (2015). *Welcome to the Desert of Post-Socialism: Radical Politics after Yugoslavia*. Brooklyn, NY: Verso.

Jovanović, D. (2018). Prosperous Pollutants: Bargaining with Risks and Forging Hopes in an Industrial Town in Eastern Serbia. *Ethnos*, 83(3), pp. 489–504. https://doi.org/10.1080/00141844.2016.1169205

Jović, D. (2009). *Yugoslavia: A State that Withered Away*. West Lafayette, IN: Purdue University Press.

Kideckel, D.A. (2001). The Unmaking of an East-Central European Working Class. In Hann, C.M. (ed.) *Postsocialism: Ideals, Ideologies and Practices in Eurasia*. Abingdon, Oxon: Taylor and Francis, pp. 114–132.

Kojanić, O. (2020). Theory from the Peripheries: What Can the Anthropology of Postsocialism Offer to European Anthropology? *Anthropological Journal of European Cultures*, 29(2), pp. 49–66. https://doi.org/10.3167/ajec.2020.290204

Kojanić, O. (2023). Micron Engagements, Macro Histories: Machines and the Agency of Labor in a Worker-Owned Company. *History and Anthropology*. Advance online publication. https://doi.org/10.1080/02757206.2023.2172721

Kosmos, I. and Solis, I. (2023). *Tvornica za preradu ribe/Fish factory, Cres* (exhibition catalogue). Creski Muzej/ZRC SAZU.

Kurtović, L. (2020). When All That Is Solid Does Not Melt into Air: Labor, Politics and Materiality in a Bosnian Detergent Factory. *PoLAR: Political and Legal Anthropology Review*, 43(2), pp. 228–246. https://doi.org/10.1111/plar.12380

Mah, A. (2012). *Industrial Ruination, Community, and Place: Landscapes and Legacies of Urban Decline*. Toronto: University of Toronto Press.

Matošević, A. (2019). A Lot of Sweat, a Little Bit of Fun, and Not Entirely 'Hard Men': Worker's Masculinity in the Uljanik Shipyard. In Montgomery, D. (ed.) *Everyday Life in the Balkans*. Bloomington: Indiana University Press, pp. 179–188.

Matošević, A. (2020). Zvuk Deindustrijalizacije. Brodogradilište Uljanik i Soundscape Štrajka 2018. Godine. *Studia Ethnologica Croatica*, 32, pp. 259–282. https://doi.org/10.17234/SEC.32.12

Meurs, M. and Ranasinghe, R. (2003). De-Development in Post-Socialism: Conceptual and Measurement Issues. *Politics & Society*, 31(1), pp. 31–53. https://doi.org/10.1177/0032329202250159

Modrić, D. (2018). Kako (Je) Tvornica Mijenja(La) Grad: Primjer Tvornice Dalmatinka. *Narodna Umjetnost*, 55(2), pp. 129–146. https://doi.org/10.15176/vol55no206

Muehlebach, A. and Shoshan, N. (2012). Introduction. *Anthropological Quarterly*, 85(2), pp. 317–343. https://doi.org/10.1353/anq.2012.0030

Musić, G. (2021a). *Making and Breaking the Yugoslav Working Class: The Story of Two Self-Managed Factories*. Work and Labor: Transdisciplinary Studies for the 21st Century, Vol. II. Budapest; New York: CEU Press, Central European University Press.

Musić, G. (2021b). Outward Processing Production and the Yugoslav Self-Managed Textile Industry in the 1980s. In Komlosy, A. and Musić, G. (eds.) *Global Commodity Chains and Labor Relations*. Leiden: Brill, pp. 251–273.

Ost, D. (2015). Class After Communism: Introduction to the Special Issue. *East European Politics and Societies: And Cultures*, 29(3), pp. 543–564. https://doi.org/10.1177/0888325415602057

Perić, I. (2020, January 19). Moj san je da živim u Beogradu ili Borovu. *H-Alter*. https://arhiva.h-alter.org/vijesti/moj-san-je-da-zivim-u-beogradu-ili-borovu (Accessed: 21 June 2024).

Petrović, T. (2020). Fish Canning Industry and The Rhythm of Social Life in the Northeastern Adriatic. *Narodna Umjetnost*, 57(1), pp. 33–49. https://doi.org/10.15176/vol57no102

Petrungaro, S. (2019). Ethics of Work and Discipline in Transition: Uljanik in Late and Post-Socialism. *Review of Croatian History*, 15(1), pp. 191–213. https://doi.org/10.22586/review.v15i1.9803

Potkonjak, S. and Alempijević, N.Š. (2023). Rethinking the City in the Industrial Aftermath: Socio-Industrial Memory and Environmental Fallouts. *Narodna Umjetnost*, 60(1), pp 9–24. https://doi.org/10.15176/vol60no101

Potkonjak, S. and Škokić, T. (2013). 'In the World of Iron and Steel': On the Ethnography of Work, Unemployment and Hope. *Narodna Umjetnost*, 50(1), pp. 74–95. https://doi.org/10.15176/VOL50NO103

Potkonjak, S. and Škokić, T. (2021). A City Worth Fighting for: Accidental Environmentalism and Resistance in Post-Industrial Society. *Balkanologie*, 16(2). https://doi.org/10.4000/balkanologie.3535

Potkonjak, S. and Škokić, T. (2022). *Gdje Živi Tvornica? Etnografija Postindustrijskoga Grada*. Zagreb: Institut za etnologiju i folkloristiku.

Rajković, I. (2018). For an Anthropology of the Demoralized: State Pay, Mock-labour, and Unfreedom in a Serbian Firm. *Journal of the Royal Anthropological Institute*, 24(1), pp. 47–70. https://doi.org/10.1111/1467-9655.12751

Reljanović, M. (2021). Fleksibilizacija i prekarizacija na tržištu rada: redefinisanje radnih odnosa u postsocijalistickom svetu. In *Transformacija rada: narativi, prakse, režimi*. Zagreb: Institut za etnologiju i folkloristiku.

Senjkovic, R. (2021). Konfiscirana Sjecanja (Na Rad i Zaposlenost). In *Transformacija Rada: Narativi, Prakse, Režimi*. Zagreb: Institut za etnologiju i folkloristiku.

Siefert, M. (ed.). (2020). *Labor in State-Socialist Europe, 1945–1989: Contributions to a History of Work*. Work and Labor: Transdisciplinary Studies for the 21st Century, Vol. 1. Budapest, Hungary; New York, NY: Central European University Press.

Spasić, I. (2012). Yugoslavia as a Place for Living a Normal Life: Memories of Ordinary People in Serbia. *Sociologija*, 54(4), pp. 577–594. https://doi.org/10.2298/SOC1204577S

Class, Gender, and Industrial Structures of Feeling

Stambolieva, M. (2016). *Welfare State Transformation in the Yugoslav Successor States: From Social to Unequal.* Abingdon, Oxon: Routledge, an Imprint of Taylor & Francis Group.

Strangleman, T. (2017). Deindustrialisation and the Historical Sociological Imagination: Making Sense of Work and Industrial Change. *Sociology*, 51(2), pp. 466–482. https://doi.org/10.1177/0038038515622906

Vaseva, I. (2018). 'Red Is Our Flag That Proudly Flutters in the Wind': The Cultural Emancipation of Workers and the Labour Culture in 'Astibo' Fashion Industry in Štip in the 1960s until the 1980s. In *We Have Built Cities for You: On the Contradictions of Yugoslav Socialism.* Belgrade: Center CZKD-Center for Cultural Decontamination. https://www.czkd.org/meta-content/uploads/2018/06/Publikacija-We-Have-Built-Cities-for-You.pdf

Vene, L. and Borovičkić, M. (2018). Intangible Industrial Heritage of Vela Luka: Oral Histories of Fabrika, Ambalaža and Greben. *Studia Ethnologica Croatica*, 30, pp. 295–320. https://doi.org/10.17234/SEC.30.10

Vodopivec, N. (2010). Textile Workers in Slovenia: From Nimble Fingers to Tired Bodies. *Anthropology of East Europe Review*, 28(1), pp. 165–183. https://scholarworks.iu.edu/journals/index.php/aeer/article/view/659

Vodopivec, N. (2020). Our Factory: Textile Workers' Memories and Experiences in Slovenia. *Narodna Umjetnost*, 57(1), pp. 51–70. https://doi.org/10.15176/vol57no103

Vodopivec, N. (2021a). Interpretacije gubitka posla i propasti tvornice: primjer tekstilne tvornice Mura u Sloveniji. In *Transformacija rada: narativi, prakse, režimi.* Zagreb: Institut za etnologiju i folkloristiku, pp. 159–185.

Vodopivec, N. (2021b). *Tu se ne bo nikoli več šivalo: doživljanja izgube dela in propada tovarne.* Ljubljana: Inštitut za novejšo zgodovino.

Williams, R. (1977). *Marxism and Literature.* Oxford and New York: Oxford University Press.

Živković, A. (2015). From the Market . . . to the Market: The Debt Economy Under Yugoslavia. In Horvat, S. and Štiks, I. (eds.) *Welcome to the Desert of Post-Socialism: Radical Politics after Yugoslavia.* Brooklyn, NY: Verso.

Zukin, S. (1975). *Beyond Marx and Tito: Theory and Practice in Yugoslav Socialism.* Cambridge: MW Books.

15
METALLIC VITALITIES
Smog, Steel, and Stigma in a Deindustrial Town

Anoop Nayak

Introduction

As twilight descends a background hum reverberates, charging the atmosphere. A sharp hiss of gas and a fiery plume illuminates the shadowy blast furnace, momentarily revealing the tentacle pipework of a gigantic steel plant. In 2015, on the outskirts of Middlesbrough, the Redcar steelworks in Teesside, Northeast England, exhaled its final breath. This chromatic leviathan, once Europe's second largest steelworks, was finally laid to rest.

In an interview for the remake of his dystopian science fiction classic *Blade Runner* (1982), cinematic director Ridley Scott spoke about growing up in the region and the steelworks as visual inspiration for the film:

> There's a walk from Redcar into Hartlepool. I'd cross a bridge at night, and walk above the steel works. So that's probably where the opening of *Blade Runner* comes from. It always seemed to be gloomy and raining, and I'd just think, "God, this is beautiful." You can find beauty in everything, and so I think I found the beauty in that darkness.
> *(TeessideLive, 2017)*

Teesside, and its major town Middlesbrough, is arguably the most stigmatized place in the UK. This is evident in a plethora of reports on education and employment, health and longevity, pollution, drugs, alcohol, and early teenage pregnancy (Crowley and Cominetti, 2014; MacDonald, Shildrick, and Furlong, 2014; Plan International UK, 2016).

This chapter aims to explore not only the production of place-based stigma but also how these messages are received and occasionally overturned by residents and those familiar with the area. Through engaging the voices of locals, visitors, and the viewing public, the chapter demonstrates how critical respondents may temporarily shift, displace, and reconfigure stigma through a strategic 'rescripting' of place. Where much of the work on territorial stigma has focused upon the production and attribution of urban stigma, less is known about how people in low-income neighborhoods manage stigma and the extent to which they may resist or challenge it. In exploring these relations, like Scott, I also seek to illuminate shards of beauty and humanity amid Teesside's monochromatic, blasted landscapes.

DOI: 10.4324/9781003308324-22

To gain deeper insight into these processes, I examine the impact of two British television programs filmed in the region: a second series of the 'reality' TV show *Benefits Streets* and a live production of the property program *Location, Location, Location*. I contend that these shows perform as place-making devices that animate and amplify stigma through the production of media geographies that have material and affective consequences.

Before turning to Middlesbrough, Teesside, and the plight of the steelworks, I discuss a wider transnational literature on urban territorial stigma, engaging with accounts in different parts of Australia, Canada, Europe, and the US. The section signals the important insights crystallized primarily in the work of Löic Wacquant and colleagues, deepening this analysis in three ways (Wacquant, 2007, 2008; Wacquant, Slater, and Borges Pereira, 2014). First, at a *spatial-level* recasting the gaze from the racially marked multi-ethnic inner-city wards Wacquant and others explore to offer a consideration of 'left behind' post-industrial peripheries and polluted Rust Belt regions. Second, through a deeper *political engagement* that seeks to trace collective acts of resistance and resilience that work to refigure environmental stigma. Third, by taking a *vital materialist approach* to gain valuable insight into "territorial stigmatization in action" (Wacquant, Slater, and Borges Pereira, 2014, p. 1279) and the lively, eventful, scripting and rescripting of place.

The Spatiality of Stigma: Transnational Accounts

In his seminal compendium on stigma, the sociologist Erving Goffman classifies three forms of stigmata – "abominations of the body," "blemishes of individual character," and the "tribal stigma of race, nation, and religion" passed through generations. Goffman's account offers a bodily schematic of stigma, though he is at pains to point out that "a language of relationships, not attributes is really needed" (Goffman, 1963, pp. 13–14). In other words, much that is stigmatized in society has more to say about the prevailing social order than the stigmatized individual. Goffman's attention is drawn to how the stigmatized – the physically deformed, drug-users, or mentally impaired – manage stigma. Stigma is an affective category, animated through 'Othering' and displacement. For polite society it marks out that which is defiled, while for the recipients it is often a source of shame and oppression.

Goffman's pioneering approach has since been adapted and applied to understandings of social class disparagement and welfare in late-modern capitalism (McKenzie, 2015; Shildrick et al., 2012; Tyler, 2013). Furthermore, by locating stigma beyond the corporeal, through a broader 'spatial turn,' it can reveal how particular places might become repositories for wider social decline and moral depravity. Here, the spatial mapping of stigma is explicit in the work of Sibley, who remarks how "'spatial purification' is a key feature in the organization of social space," a means of mapping the pure and the defiled, hereby creating "geographies of exclusion," at the level of home, locality, and nation (Sibley, 1995, p. 77). These insights are profound and offer an important optic through which we can consider how stigma is lived not only across time but also across space. Critically, the geography of stigma comes to create the very conditions through which the contemporary ghetto, sink estate, banlieue, slum, or shantytown is drawn to compelling effect. Moreover, this can be traced in policy and discourse, coming to shape local and regional development initiatives, urban governance, regeneration, and gentrification strategies (Slater and Anderson, 2012; Holmes, 2022; Watt, 2020). These are the material effects of stigma.

The most influential writer on spatial stigma is the urban sociologist Löic Wacquant. His book *Urban Outcasts* (2008) has been pivotal in spearheading transnational research on what he terms "urban territorial stigma," defined as "a consequential and injurious form of action through collective representation fastened to place" (Wacquant, Slater, and Borges Pereira, 2014, p. 1278). Combining Goffman's concept of social stigma with Bourdieu's class theory of symbolic power and capital, Wacquant (2007, 2008) applies these ideas to understandings of spatial phenomena in the creation of the "ghetto." Here, he compares how residents in the impoverished districts of suburban Paris and inner-city Chicago each narrate their neighborhoods through tropes of race, poverty, crime, drugs, dirt, unemployment, and the morally defunct actions of residents, in what becomes a self-fulfilling prophecy of place. Wacquant exposes how residents in each locality accept the accounts of public officials, local press, and televisual media that declare their neighborhoods 'blemished places.' Invariably, residents blamed others in the community for decline, usually immigrants, troublesome neighbors, and local youth gangs. Reflecting on this tendency, Wacquant et al. document the complicit actions of residents in Paris and Chicago:

> In both places, residents loudly and harshly echoed urban denizens, public officials, and the commercial media in disparaging their own neighbourhoods as nests of social vitriol, vice, and violence. They likewise displaced the stain of dwelling in an area deemed a sociomoral purgatory onto others just like them, thereby validating it and further spreading its effects around them.
>
> *(Wacquant, Slater, and Borges Pereira, 2014, p. 1271)*

A defining feature of Wacquant's (2007, 2008) thesis then concerns how urban dwellers fulfill the dominant narrative of the neighborhood by conceding it to be a stigmatized place. In doing so, he contends, they "tend to validate, amplify and proliferate the discredit at its core" to such an extent they are implicated in "undercutting their capacity for collective action" (Wacquant, Slater, and Borges Pereira, 2014, p. 1275).

While political action may be stymied, recent ethnographies indicate that at least some urban residents are implicated in resisting territorial stigma and might challenge the normative depiction of their neighborhood as defiled territory, the consequence of social abjection. In focus group discussions with Black and Latinx youth in Camden, New Jersey, on the outskirts of Philadelphia, Cairns (2018) found Camden youth were aware of the negative representation surrounding their small town. In response, they drew upon a wider palette of place, acknowledging Camden's celebrated history, active community groups, and the success of local sports athletes. In doing so, youth engaged in the selective process of 'finding good in Camden,' dismantling social stereotypes and sketching a more even portrait of their town, replete with light and shade.

A striking example of the challenge to stigmatization is further found in research in Toronto's Regent Park – Canada's first and largest public housing estate. In the process of being demolished to make way for a mixed-use, mixed-income community, August discovered a compelling 'counternarrative' was in place where, paradoxically, residents pointed to the benefits of living in an area of 'concentrated poverty.' While recognizing social problems, "most people liked their homes; describing a convenient, service-rich, well-located neighborhood with a strong sense of community and an abundance of friendship and supportive social ties" (August, 2014, pp. 1317–1318). The lively downtown district was favorably compared with Toronto's bland suburbs, with residents placing a strong emphasis on social networks and belonging in the community; a theme found in other urban accounts of stigmatized neighborhoods, where what is a vilified place to many "outsiders" is home to those that are "insiders" (Cahill, 2007). The Aylesbury estate in Southeast London is emblematic. Notoriety meant Black cab taxi-drivers avoided the area, but as Watt identifies, "a remarkable degree of resident disregard, rejection, and active resistance of territorial stigmatization" existed (Watt, 2020, p. 28).

In a sophisticated study, exploring how residents living on a housing estate in Western Sydney respond to an Australian television comedy series about social housing, Arthurson, Darcy, and Rogers (2014) point to the diverse ways in which 'televised territorial stigma' is managed. The programme *Housos*, a contemporary satirical parody, "is a proxy for an 'underclass' that is explicitly spatialized through clearly recognizable signifiers," locating residents in specific urban environments. Arthurson, Darcy, and Rogers (2014) screened a first episode of the series to social housing tenants and community workers. They discovered, "tenants were not mere victims of territorial stigma"; instead, "[f]or some the homogeneity of disadvantage on estates underwrites community solidarity and can be a source of strength and pride" (Arthurson, Darcy, and Rogers, 2014, p. 1348), a theme echoed in McKenzie's (2015) research in the English working-class estate of St Ann's, Nottingham. Nevertheless, Arthurson et al. found most Western Sydney residents did recognize the typologies at play and viewed them as a point of dis-identification while attributing these characteristics to others on the housing estate, much in keeping with Wacquant's analysis. However, they further distinguish between the opinions held by tenants and those provided with social housing; the former viewing the latter as "welfare cheats" or "bludgers," living off taxpayer's money (Arthurson, Darcy, and Rogers, 2014). This at least suggests differing views according to the types of backgrounds and multiple identities inhabited by residents.

Wacquant identifies a host of renowned and notorious neighborhoods as ripe for the analysis of stigma, often where large-scale immigration, crime, and urban unrest occur. The colonial subjugation of racialized minorities as subhuman means black bodies historically carry with them a high propensity for stigma, which can be triggered through associations with crime, violence, drugs, and gangs; characteristics of Goffman's anatomy of stigma. Processes of racialization are prevalent where the symbolic architecture of race is central to the construction of the 'ghetto,' 'banlieue,' 'bairro,' or 'favela' as stigmatized terrain. In research with elderly white women in Buffalo, New York, Housel reports how out-migration and deindustrialization can corrode white privilege. As the Black demographic increased, services and government investment declined. For long-standing elderly white residents, the reduction in policing, higher crime rates, and falling house prices diminished aspects of white privilege as the locality gave way to racialized and spatialized stigma (Housel, 2009). In the run up to the Sydney Olympics, Shaw (2007) records how areas around "the Block" in Redfern, home to some of Australia's Aboriginal communities, were repeatedly stigmatized and subject to processes of white corporate gentrification.

Much of the work on spatial stigma concentrates on multi-ethnic housing estates, migrant diasporic quarters, Indigenous settlements, and predominantly Black and multicultural residential neighborhoods, such as New York's Lower East Side, St Paul's in Bristol, or poorer parts of South London (August, 2014; McKenzie, 2015; Shaw, 2007; Cahill, 2007; Slater and Anderson, 2012; Watt, 2020). It is then difficult to discern the 'blemish of place' from the blemish of race, where each is mutually reinforcing. A rare exposition is found in research exploring 25 low-income African American men and women who left the stigmatized urban neighborhoods of Chicago to move to Eastern Iowa for better opportunities. Participants claimed to experience "pervasive stigma that is associated not only with race and class, but also their former residence of Chicago." Some respondents cited "multiple instances where African Americans from other places were treated better than former Chicagoans," though the authors concede these views are subject to perception (Keene and Padilla, 2010, p. 1219).

Transnational literature on stigma is vital for understanding the connections between race and place as well as the forms of media scripting, policing, and government policy that collectively operate to stigmatize (and racialize) these locations. The study of Teesside as a peripheral post-industrial region offers sharper insight into spatial taint beyond the racialized 'ghetto,' reveals how processes of racialization combine with class to stigmatize poorer white communities in 'rust belt' regions, and demonstrates lively local resistance. The analysis here is underpinned by ethnographic and local historical research, as well as secondary data garnered from the national census, the Nomis database (UK Office of National Statistics, hereafter ONS), and current labor market survey statistics, all used to examine the 'scripting' and 'rescripting' of place. National and local print media is explored alongside social media sites, including a BBC website revealing how the public responded in the aftermath of a live screening of the popular Channel 4 property television show *Location, Location, Location*. Such national digital archives can generate "rich, thick description through grounded interpretations," as increasingly more people relay messages through blogs, tweets, internet forums, and social networking sites (Kozinets, Dolbec, and Early, 2014, p. 262). As Arthurson, Darcy, and Rogers (2014) suggest in their analysis of *Housos*, "media is a key medium through which distinctions of class and territorial stigma are shaped, imposed and reproduced."

Where *Housos* is a fictional comedy series, "which aims to reflect the multicultural nature of Australian society" (Arthurson, Darcy, and Rogers, 2014), this chapter explores the impact of the 'reality' television series *Benefits Street* and a screening of *Location Live* on Teesside residents. This is significant because unlike the more 'spectacular' urban sites Wacquant and others discuss, Middlesbrough is a deindustrialized locality with a predominantly white population of 82.4% (ONS Nomis, 2021). Moreover, the pseudo-documentary genre of *Benefits Street* and the live production of *Location* work to further substantiate the authenticity and credibility of these programs. Each program is replete with signifiers of class, *Benefits Street* utilizing material objects and symbols to connote life on the dole (Jensen, 2014), while *Location* invokes aspiration and class-based desires to move up or onto the property ladder. Significantly, these shows do not just represent place but produce it in dialogue with a wider circuit of culture. Furthermore, my interest in such media geographies extends beyond how place is constructed by public officials and media elites to consider how local people are active in contesting and 'rescripting' representations of place from the inside out; often in real time or in the near aftermath of events as they happen.

Contrary to Wacquant's thesis, the chapter discloses how people living in maligned neighborhoods may engage in small acts of haptic resistance, collective action, and sporadic protest. In the case of Middlesbrough, these activities occur alongside seismic global economic transformations. This is not to suggest then that place-based social class stigma can be instantly overturned and divorced from the negative attachments ascribed to localities and the people residing therein. Rather, it reveals how residents are knowledgeable architects of place – scripting and 'rescripting' it in everyday encounters. In exploring the eventfulness of place, we can further reveal how the markings of stigma can momentarily be erased, crossed-out, and collectively rescripted in a kaleidoscopic recalibration of location.

Middlesbrough: The Metallic Vitality of a Steel Town

The closure of the Redcar steelworks in 2015 brought an end to the 170-year-old history of steelmaking in Teesside. The plant serviced numerous workers in nearby towns and the surrounding commuter-belt villages, particularly those living in Middlesbrough, the nearest major agglomeration less than ten miles away. Middlesbrough and Teesside have a remarkable industrial past, specializing in the creation of iron and steel that were widely used for shipbuilding, cranes, bridges, and railroads. At the turn of the nineteenth century, Middlesbrough was producing around a third of the nation's iron. As a relative newcomer to production and extraction, the scripting of Middlesbrough saw it branded 'infant Hercules' by Prime Minister William Gladstone, on account of its mighty industrial prowess. It rapidly emerged from a rural hamlet of around 25 people to a global player in the manufacture of iron and steel, with a now buoyant population of 143,700 (ONS Nomis, 2021). The ironstone of Easton Hills, processed in Middlesbrough, meant local iron could be found in railways and bridges around the world, including Africa, India, and Australia's Sydney Harbour Bridge.

In *Vibrant Matter*, Jane Bennett seeks to explore the vital materiality of objects noting how, "the association of metal with passivity or a dead thingness persists" (Bennett, 2010, p. 55). Yet as an inorganic substance metal is made up of polycrystalline, where each crystal grows and presses against another, holding it in permanent tension. Iron ore is spawned through the elemental properties of the earth, being around 1.8 billion years old, before it is manufactured into contemporary steel. The blasting, hammering, smelting, bashing, bending, and fashioning of iron ore to make steel is part of the 'metallic vitality' Bennett writes of, where vibrating atoms indicate a molecular structure constantly in motion. Rethinking Middlesbrough not as 'dead space' but as resonating, vibrant matter composed of indivisible human and nonhuman relations, organic and nonorganic coproductions and constellations, is part of this lively materiality I seek to explicate via popular protest and place re-inscriptions.

It is evident that global and geological forces irretrievably shape Teesside. Where once it was exporting steel around the world, it later became reliant on foreign ownership. Becoming part of the British Steel Corporation in 1967, which became British Steel in 1988, it was held in high regard for quality manufacturing and continuous casting through innovative molding processes. In 1999, British Steel merged with the Dutch company Hoogevens to become Corus. By 2003, the company was floundering, declaring many of its Teesside operations, including the blast furnace, redundant. The Indian company Tata bought the works from Corus in 2007, but by 2009, with the global recession in full swing, there was a dramatic fall in the price of steel, and the plant was mothballed. Attempting to resuscitate the industry in 2010, Thai multinational steelmaking company Sahaviriya Steel Industries (SSI) took over but in the Autumn of 2015 fell into liquidation. The price of steel plate had dropped from £500 per ton to around half that amount. As the production costs of Redcar steel were £400 per ton, an industry and whole way of life stood to be extinguished. The 2,066 core workers directly employed by SSI at Redcar were made redundant, and it is estimated that this number rises to nearly 3,000 jobs when other workers in the supply chain are included. When the final furnace closed in 2016, it signaled the death of the steel industry and the decimation of skilled industrial work in the area.

Like a collapsing star the implosion of the steelworks followed the 'hollowing out' of Middlesbrough's vast petrochemical industries. Formed in 1927, Imperial Chemical Industries (ICI) specialized in synthetic ammonia for explosives and fertilizers used in the First World

War. In 1945, ICI at Billingham extended its operations to Wilton, developing into the largest chemical plant in the world, and by 1965 ICI employed 29, 000 workers in its Teesside plants (Shildrick et al., 2012). The later fragmentation of ICI into smaller manufacturing units, owned and operated by various multinational corporations in the 1990s, is indicative of a reversal in fortunes as new local-global relations assembled. AkzoNoble took over ICI in 2008, where after 80 years the chemical industry in Teesside came to an end. For MacDonald and Shildrick (2018), the scale and rapidity of Teesside's rise and subsequent decline are unique, even among Rust Belt cities in Europe and the US (MacDonald and Shildrick, 2018).

ONS Nomis (2021) official labor market statistics used throughout this section indicate that there are now no jobs in mining and quarrying, and only 4% of Middlesbrough's population are engaged in construction and manufacturing work, respectively. The number of people claiming out-of-work benefits is nearly twice (6.2%) that of the nation at large (3.6%). For those in full-time employment, their gross weekly income (£567.30) lags national averages (£642). Shildrick et al. (2012) characterize this as life in a 'low-pay, no-pay' economy, where poverty and insecurity are rife. What is evident is that the core of Middlesbrough's labor market – once forged in the white heat of blast furnaces, coke, chemicals, and steel plate – is diminished, fragmented, and no longer sustainable in its previous incarnation. Today, for those of working age the main form of employment is in health and social care, where over a quarter (27%) of Middlesbrough's active working population are to be found, double the percentage compared to Britain as a whole (13.7%). This mirrors Winant's account of Pittsburgh in the US Rust Belt region, where steel has been replaced by a fragmented health care sector, supported by a casualized workforce, working unpredictable hours on low pay (Winant, 2021).

Such seismic transformations impact most severely on future generations. Middlesbrough (21.6%) records over a third more workless households than in Britain (14%) as a whole, indicative of an uneven geography of poverty. Teesside's former strengths in steelmaking and petrochemical plant production may today be regarded as an ill-fated form of economic path dependency. However, this should not obscure how Middlesbrough was once the pinnacle of high modernity, with technical expertise in science and mechanical engineering, yet is paradoxically scripted as a decaying, 'left behind' place. The recent closure of the Redcar steelworks, coupled with the diminished petrochemical industries, has rendered the area to be tightly scripted as a redundant, deindustrial, blasted place – a smog-filled, toxic landscape.

Benefits Streets and the 'Boro: Politics and Protest

Series 2 of *Benefits Street* was filmed along Kingston Road on the Tilery Estate in Stockton-on-Tees, some six miles out from Middlesbrough. At the time of filming, the Work Foundation's Annual Population Survey 2012–2013 ranked the area as having the highest youth unemployment rate out of 53 British cities (Crowley and Cominetti, 2014). Only 22% of people own their own home, and life expectancy is 20 years below national averages. A BBC *Panorama* (2018) documentary subsequently declared Stockton-on-Tees, "England's most unequal town." Within this context, Love Productions, the creators of *Benefits Street*, decided to film the second instalment of the Channel 4 documentary in Stockton over four weeks, from 11 May 2015. *Benefits Street* has been singled out to be at the forefront of a genre of "austerity" or "poverty porn" (Allen, Tyler, and De Benedictis, 2014; Jensen, 2014), inciting moral judgment, class disgust, and no little academic scrutiny (Lawler, 2005; MacDonald, Shildrick, and Furlong, 2014; Tyler, 2008).

Metallic Vitalities

However, away from the cameras, not all residents subscribed to the denigrated representation of their neighborhood. Sue Griffiths (55 years), a mother of five, has lived on the estate for 30 years. She used to do bar work at a local racecourse until anxiety and depression led to a breakdown and life on benefits. Sue describes the strong community support received:

SUE: Everybody is there for each other. If you said to me – there's a million pounds – you wouldn't move me (*The Northern Echo*, 2015a).

Julie Young (53 years), who also appears on the show, has six children, and has lived on Kingston Road for 20 years:

JULIE: Tilery Estate is just marooned in the middle of nowhere, and you know what? They've put the best people – the salt of the earth – here. People with morals and ethics (*The Northern Echo*, 2015a).

Julie, a former Community Support Liaison Officer for the Council, worked until her son Reagan suffered a stroke at nine months old, leaving him severely brain damaged and physically impaired. Both Julie and Sue were working mothers until health-related circumstances intervened. It is also apparent they value friendship, support, and community on the Tilery Estate so do not necessarily subscribe to the neighborhood "lateral denigration and mutual distanciation" that Wacquant notes (2007, p. 68). As such, the stigmatized aspects of Teesside are challenged through ideas of kinship, care, and "thick" community relations (August, 2014). Here, "morals and ethics" are deemed more significant than wealth, where a refusal to move for "a million pounds" displaces stigma from low-income neighborhoods toward those invested in capital accumulation and urban gentrification.

Prior to Channel 4 filming *Benefits Street*, "Red Faction," a section of the Middlesbrough Football Club supporter's branch, displayed two striking banners at a football match. The first was directly aimed at Love Productions, a company largely owned by Rupert Murdoch and defiantly read, "Being Poor is Not Entertainment." The second was more concise, if less polite: "Fuck Benefits Street." The banners did not only communicate a message to the many thousands attending the match; rather, as a global televisual spectacle, football reaches a worldwide audience, with the "entertainment" banner appearing in the national press. Like handmade socialist banners of the past, paraded in marches during the 1984 miners' strikes, these messages draw on past radical action and speak back to power – this time inverting the gaze of the camera from the spectacle of poverty, unemployment, and individual fecklessness toward the production team and any impending media voyeurism.

Protest is vibrant matter. It emanates from the ties between Middlesbrough FC (popularly known as the 'Boro), the town and the nearby steelworks at Redcar. When SSI threatened the last steelworks in Redcar with closure, 'Boro players wore t-shirts inscribed with the slogan SOS, "Save Our Steel." Before another 'Boro match around 40 of the last remaining steelworkers were gamely applauded as they walked around the pitch prior to kickoff. The live wires of protest are further seen when steelworker families attended a torchlit vigil in September 2015 along the Majuba Road to save the Redcar plant. Bodies, lights, objects, noise, placards, symbols, and song charged the atmosphere, generating an affective mood of class solidarity. A petition created on the official Parliament petition page received over 23,242 signatures in support of saving Teesside steel industries, challenging assumptions of a wholly apathetic local working class. While none of this altered the plight of Redcar, such acts instigate a molecular politics that adds motion, dynamism, and vitality to events that may otherwise appear in stasis. These metallic vitalities coalesce and energize the town, club, supporters, and steelworkers.

The molecular politics reverberated in the aftermath of the closure, leading Middlesbrough Labour MP Andy McDonald to lambast the government, accusing it of "breathtaking industrial vandalism" (The Northern Echo, 2015b); a brutality Hudson, in his account of Teesside, unceremoniously depicts as *Wrecking a Region* (Hudson, 1989). The steelworkers' union, Community, were unable to halt closure; however, their claim that legal processes for redundancy were not followed was upheld by an employment judge, granting a pay out of £6.25 million that will result in a maximum of eight weeks' pay for workers. Middlesbrough FC developed a partnership package for ex-steelworkers (Middlesbrough, 2016) while 'Boro football supporters further demonstrated their support of former steelworkers, commemorating them in fitting style. In a final farewell, during a rare League Cup victory away at Old Trafford against Manchester United, around 10,000 fans held aloft their mobile phones, illuminating the night skies in an ambient show of solidarity with Redcar steelworkers, screened live around the world.

The atmosphere and auras stimulate a lively politics of resistance – a material assemblage that brings together work, football, steel, technology, human and nonhuman life-worlds. The placards, chants, light, and noise enact what Durkheim (1915) terms a "collective effervescence" that spills forth into action, when communities conjoin thought and practice. This collective effervescence is embodied through Red Faction's protest to a second series of *Benefits Street*, the presentation of signatures to Parliament in a bid to forestall plant closure, the creation of banners and folksong, the public commemoration of ex-steelworkers, partnership packages with the football club, and the legal entanglements leading to successful trade union court payouts.

Location Live: Locating and Relocating Stigma

The reputation of Middlesbrough as a "blemished place" (Wacquant, 2007) appeared to be sealed when in a live edition of the Channel 4 show, *Location, Location, Location* (2007), watched by three million viewers, presenters Kirstie Allsopp and Phil Spencer deemed the town to be the worst place to live in the country. Through a compilation of statistics comprising indices related to employment rates, the environment, crime, health and longevity, leisure, and lifestyle factors, the presenters delivered their verdict. Allsopp claimed Middlesbrough had "critical health levels, double the English average of drug abuse, 8% more smokers than the English average, and over a quarter of the inhabitants admitted to binge-drinking." Her colleague, Spencer echoed the inadequacies, adding, "90% of the residents never exercise and few eat healthily . . . robbery, burglary, sexual assault, violent crimes and car theft are all more than twice the UK average."

At the most intimate scale of the body, the comments articulate a corporeal disgust for lumpen, working-class bodies designated as lazy, unruly, and obese. These remarks closely follow Goffman's anatomy of stigma. That is, stigma is visibly embodied to the extent that "we believe the person with stigma is not quite human," and "on this assumption we exercise varieties of discrimination" (Goffman, 1963). However, these remarks also enact moral geographies of exclusion, performing as place-making statements. Allsop and Spencer's declaration of 'best and worst places to live' do not simply represent places, they define them. There is little doubt that such programs and headlines impact negatively upon property

Metallic Vitalities

prices, business investment, and engender territorial stigma. Through such spatial enactment stigma is rescaled, where geographies of exclusion become a means for mapping the pure and defiled areas of the nation (Sibley, 1995). Following *Location Live*, the cartography of stigma is seen where the national press ran with the headline, "Boro – the worst place to live in the UK" (Thornton, 2007).

Given this damning verdict, how might such compelling national representations be 'rescripted,' and is it even possible to dislodge the sticky signs of stigma surrounding places like Middlesbrough?

One of the mediums through which working-class people might 'speak back' to such class-laden typologies is through social media technologies. During the live screening of *Location*, viewers were invited to connect with the debate via texting and blogging. Shortly after Allsopp and Spencer poured scorn on Middlesbrough, viewers responded, challenging the perception that Middlesbrough was the worst place to live in the country.

> The stark contrast of sprawling industry and beautiful countryside make Middlesbrough a compelling place to live. Great nightlife too.
>
> *(Richard, Middlesbrough)*

> I am delighted that we are left to enjoy this area, the longer the area is perceived like this, the less knockers will want to visit. The Cleveland Hills, our coastline, our friendly and effacing people, our mighty River Tees, and our wonderful history sum up Middlesbrough beautifully.
>
> *(Harry)*

Such responses offer an alternative viewpoint on the town as a toxic post-industrial outpost, pointing instead to the accessible countryside, a vibrant nightlife, and the immediacy of the coastline. As such, people seek to redraw the town and "rescript" place through an alternative grammar, largely derived from a local, "insider" perspective that doesn't negate problems exist (Cairns, 2018), "when the work goes":

> It's a lovely place to live, [but] the steelworks closed. You see loads more people in the pub now. People who criticize us just don't get it; they don't understand what it's like when the work goes.
>
> *(Peter, Middlesbrough)*

For Sherry Lee Linkon (2018), the "half-life" of deindustrialization, a phrase derived from radioactive emissions, may not be as deathly as radioactive waste, but emanates a slow toxicity through, "high rates of various illnesses, as well as alcoholism, drug abuse, and suicide." Peter's remarks echo this analysis, where deindustrial trauma and loss are particularly scarring for young people. Recently, Middlesbrough was branded the "teenage pregnancy capital of England and Wales" based on ONS data revealing a 41.9% conception rate per 1,000 girls aged 15–17 years. In a report conducted by the charity Plan International UK (2016), in collaboration with the University of Hull, Middlesbrough was ranked as the "worst place to be a girl in England and Wales," a story that received national news coverage (Plan International UK, 2016). Responding to the report in an opinion piece for *The Guardian* (2016), Mieka Smiles, who lives in Middlesbrough with her husband and small daughter, remarked: "I do hope this sets sirens going in some government offices and gets them scrabbling to send help up the M1 [motorway] where it's most needed. But I doubt it will." "What I would humbly suggest," she continued, "is that pride in your town counts for a lot and shaming the 'worst place to be a girl' isn't exactly going to encourage or inspire anyone" (Smiles, 2016). Aware of Middlesbrough's stigmatized reputation, another forum respondent declared: "Not every young girl's ambition is to 'have lots of babies and get a free house'. . . Up the Boro!" (Marion, York). Such responses may indicate an awareness of stigma but not necessarily a compliance with it.

Environmental Stigma: Smog, Pollution, and 'Filthy Whites'

In 1996, the action group Air Quality Today leafleted thousands of Teesside households attempting to overturn engrained environmental stigma:

> Our biggest air quality problem on Teesside is one of perception. Some people think Teesside is a dirty, polluted place due to a history of dirty 'smokestack' industries and coal burning in homes. This may have been the case in the past, but these days it just ain't so! . . .
>
> If we have wrong perceptions of our area, WE CAN'T BE SURPRISED IF OTHERS DO AS WELL. A wrong perception could mean people do not invest in our area. This could mean jobs and prosperity going elsewhere.

This early bulletin allies to Wacquant's thesis that if the area is routinely stigmatized externally, the place risks internal amplification of this view. Clearly, environmental stigma lingers on, but what is the science regarding air quality today? If we turn to recent environmental assessments conducted by the World Health Organization it appears many of Britain's major cities including London, Leicester, York, Bristol, and Birmingham have worse air quality than Middlesbrough (WHO, 2018). What is not in doubt is that despite clean air reports, the town remains trapped in the ether of earlier industrial representations that exert the "socially noxious consequences" of stigmata (Wacquant, 2008, p. 68).

In a direct attempt to rescript place, some *Location Live* viewers referred to more recent environmental studies that contradict the long-standing myth that Middlesbrough is still a polluted, smog-filled town.

> I don't like the fact that the television show concentrates on only the bad points about my town, making it sound worse than it is. We breathe cleaner air than the Queen! And the regeneration projects are very well deserved. (Jonathan, BORO!).

> Originally a Smoggy myself, I hate to hear people only quoting the bad things about Middlesbrough, did you know that it has cleaner air than the city of Bath? (Marion, York).

Given that London has worse air quality than Middlesbrough, the claim, 'we breathe cleaner air than the Queen!' is not far-fetched.

Being a Smoggy is an industrial identity derived from the petrochemical plants of ICI, belching smokestack industries, and the early plant refineries of Dorman Long. Despite significant transformations to the environment, Teesside continues to exist in the popular

Metallic Vitalities

imagination as an archetypal "sulphurous zone" (Wacquant, 2008, p. 169). At a football match, away at neighbors Sunderland AFC, a somewhat unusual chant rang out from the terraces at the Stadium of Light:

What's it like to, what's it like to, what's it like to breathe fresh air? What's it like to breathe fresh air?

The hurling of environmental epitaphs, chained to a chemical smokestack past, is testimony to the circulation, 'stickiness,' and settlement of stigma.

To invert stigma and detoxify the contaminated Smoggy, some residents willingly affiliated with the term, embracing both pride in the industrial past and a neoliberal discourse of urban regeneration. As such, identifying as a Smoggy is a means of managing stigma; it is a defiled identity and figuratively polluted. Based on residence, Smoggies are deemed "filthy whites," tarnished by chemical pollutants, social welfare, and the specter of unemployment.

> The town is regenerating at a rapid rate, and I for one am proud to say I'm a Smoggie. We've got a whole new district being built – Middlehaven – which is set to rival many modern town centers with up to the minute first class facilities, hotels and shopping.
>
> *(Dawn)*

Making hygienic the defiled Smoggy through appeals to hyper-modernity is a means of refiguring the industrial past. Here regeneration as a form of urban renewal (Holmes, 2022) has the potential to cleanse Middlesbrough and its people from associations with poverty, grime, dirt, and pervasive industrial smog.

Where televisual media impose a fixed geography onto people and place, participants "spoke back" to the dominant gaze of *Location Live*, claiming the geodemographic survey was designed and "yet again, taken by southerners" who it is alleged, probably "didn't even visit our towns."

> Funnily enough I visited Middlesbrough for the first time ever last Saturday with my husband and 17-year-old son, to look at Teesside University and the town as well, where my son may spend the next three – four years. We were so impressed! . . . We saw plenty of regeneration, new modern buildings and fantastic facilities for the University and town. We saw big names in both financial and high street investors, and came away with nothing but a strong, positive outlook on Middlesbrough. This is a town that appears to be really going places.
>
> *(Teresa)*

Here, Teresa embraces the symbols of modernity through references to urban regeneration, financial investment, growth, and new buildings. This discourse of neoliberalism enables her to relocate Middlesbrough not as 'left behind' but an icon of economic transformation and modernity. The fact that many of the comments come from those who are not from Middlesbrough, but visit or frequent it, allows them to make independent assessments of the place. They dismantle stereotypes of childhood and youth, for example, the idea that Middlesbrough is replete with teenage mothers or inhospitable to students.

The Routledge Handbook of Deindustrialization Studies

In response to environmental stigma, other respondents drew upon the natural environment and 'thick' community relations.

Reading about my beloved hometown brings a tear to my eye. Where else in the country can you drive half an hour in one direction to some nice coastline, and half an hour in the other direction and be deep in the North Yorkshire Moors?

(Chris, Leighton Buzzard, formerly of Middlesbrough)

Well I'm from Nottingham, and live in Middlesbrough – but I lived in Bournemouth, Dorchester and Weymouth which are in supposedly "beautiful" Dorset. I would much prefer to live in Middlesbrough, more to do with friendly people.

(Newy)

Such attempts of stigma displacement were nearly given legal momentum following the live production of *Location* and the audience response, when then-Middlesbrough Mayor Ray Mallon reported the show to Ofcom for misrepresentation. Mallon cited footage of dilapidated houses in South Bank – which is not part of Middlesbrough – and the spurious allegation that 90% of residents do not exercise. Despite this challenge, Mallon's complaint against Channel 4 was not upheld on the grounds that the show is not a documentary but 'light entertainment.' Nevertheless, the sense of injustice, volume of complaints, and residential rescripting of place did have effects. Since the case, Allsopp went on record as saying she would never do a live show again admitting it was a mistake. No further live show of *Location* has followed.

Instead, when *Location* returned to Teesside in 2011 – "the worst place in the UK to live" – the presenters waxed lyrical about the charming nearby village of Yarm, the idyllic countryside and access to the coastline; leaving newspaper critics to reflect how *Location*, "comes back to Teesside and finds how nice it is after all" (Wainwright, 2011). Indeed, the documentary series, *The Mighty Redcar*, screened on the BBC in Autumn 2018 went as far as to offer an upbeat, hopeful portrait of young people in Teesside. TV critic Chitra Ramaswamy gave the programme a five-star rating, describing it as 'heart-warming':

The Mighty Redcar continues to be the antidote to *Benefits Street* . . . or any of the vile caricatures that make up the objectionable genre of poverty porn.

(Ramaswamy, 2018)

This contingent media 'rescripting' of Teesside offers a temporary circuit-breaker to the high-voltage current of stigmata.

Beyond the 'Blemish' of a Blasted Place

Middlesbrough is a laboratory for observing the stratospheric growth of industry, followed by seismic decline and deindustrialization (MacDonald and Shildrick, 2018). The geomorphology is of a 'blasted place' whose Jurassic landscape was excavated, drilled, and spliced open by nitroglycerine in the pursuit of base metal. Yet when it comes to the steelworks, as Marx famously remarked, "All that is solid, melts into air" (Marx, 1996). Successive industrial closures have seen Middlesbrough shift from being a site of über-modernity to a "left behind," contaminated, "sulphurous zone" (Wacquant, 2007). In this scripting, being a

Metallic Vitalities

young Smoggy is a tarnished, polluted identity, designated to those who are deemed 'filthy whites' on account of being thought to live in a noxious environment, subject to early teen pregnancy and tethered to a life on welfare benefits. They are cast as carriers of stigma and figures of defilement.

However, this study also demonstrates how abject subjects 'speak back' to the dominant regimes of representation that seek to define them. While residents did not entirely dismiss territorial stigma, they were effective in rearticulating it in the process of place reinscription. These acts include signaling the importance of close relationships between the town, its football supporters, and steelworkers; celebrating the rich industrial heritage of Teesside; inverting the gaze through the statement, 'Being Poor is Not Entertainment'; identifying advanced urban regeneration and regional development; using environmental data to challenge assumptions of pollution; acknowledging the magnificence of the coastline; or taking to social media and the streets to engage in petitions, protests, legal disputes, and other political activities in a lively, kinetic rescripting of place.

This vitality of working-class resistance is largely leeched out from Wacquant's thesis, resulting in a somewhat anemic analysis. Although the thick lines of stigma surrounding Middlesbrough are not easily erased, I have argued such struggles and tension enable the hidden, contested geographies of place to surface. They are vibrating matter. Teesside may indeed be cast as inert "dead space," but this ignores the pulsing "half-life" of deindustrialization (Linkon, 2018). Here, environmental stigma and social class disparagement are contested and resisted in the "management of spoiled identity" (Goffman, 1963). This sparky, "metallic vitality" (Bennett, 2010) composes an assemblage, where smog, steel, and stigma conjoin human and nonhuman matter to rescript place 'otherwise.' The examples witnessed in Middlesbrough of structured protest, haptic resistance, and molecular politics offer a love poem to the town's past, present, and future. Like local cinematic director Ridley Scott, many Teessiders illuminate hidden beauty in the very depths of deindustrial darkness.

Reference List

Allen, K.I., Tyler, I. and De Benedictis, S. (2014). Thinking with 'White Dee': The Gender Politics of 'Austerity Porn'. *Sociological Research Online*, 19(3). http://www.socresonline.org.uk/19/3/2. html (Accessed: 29 January 2019).

Arthurson, K., Darcy, M. and Rogers, D. (2014). Televised Territorial Stigma: How Housing Tenants Experience the Fictional Media Representation of Estates in Australia. *Environment and Planning A*, 46(6), pp. 1334–1350.

August, M. (2014). Challenging the Rhetoric of Stigmatization: The Benefits of Concentrated Poverty in Toronto's Regent Park. *Environment and Planning A*, 46(6), pp. 1317–1333.

Bennett, J. (2010). *Vibrant Matter: Towards a Political Ecology of Things*. Durham, NC: Duke University Press.

Cahill, C. (2007). Negotiating Grit and Glamour: Young Women of Colour and Gentrification. *City and Society*, 19(2), pp. 202–231.

Cairns, K. (2018). Youth, Temporality, and Territorial Stigma: Finding Good in Camden, New Jersey. *Antipode*, 50(5), pp. 1224–1243.

Crowley, L. and Cominetti, N. (2014). *The Geography of Youth Unemployment: A Route Map for Change*. The Work Foundation.

Durkheim, E. (1915). *The Elementary Forms of Religious Life*. Trans. J.W. Swain. London: Allen & Unwin.

Goffman, E. (1963). *Spoiled Identities: Notes on the Management of Stigma*. London: Penguin.

Holmes, H. (2022). 'Demarginalising' a Territorially Stigmatised Neighbourhood? The Relationship Between Governance Configurations and Trajectories of Urban Change. *Environment and Planning A: Economy and Space*, 54(6), pp. 1165–1183.

Housel, J. (2009). Geographies of Whiteness: The Active Construction of Racialized Privilege in Buffalo, New York. *Social and Cultural Geography*, 10(2), pp. 131–152.

Hudson, R. (1989). *Wrecking a Region: State Policies, Party Politics, and Regional Change in North East England*. London: Pion.

Keene, D.E. and Padilla, M.B. (2010). Race, Class, and the Stigma of Place: Moving to 'Opportunity' in Eastern Iowa. *Health and Place*, 16(6), pp. 1216–1223.

Kozinets, R.V., Dolbec, P.Y. and Earley, A. (2014). Netnographic Analysis: Understanding Culture Through Social Media Data. In Flick, U. (ed.) *Sage Handbook of Qualitative Data Analysis*. London: Sage, pp. 262–275.

Jensen, T. (2014). Welfare Commonsense, Poverty Porn, and Doxosophy. *Sociological Research Online*, 19(3). http://www.socresonline.org.uk/19/3/3.html (Accessed: 29 January 2019).

Lawler, S. (2005). Disgusted Subjects: The Making of Middle-Class Identities. *Sociological Review*, 53(3), pp. 429–446.

Linkon, S.L. (2018). *The Half-life of Deindustrialization: Working-Class Writing About Economic Restructuring*. Ann Arbor, MI: University of Michigan Press.

MacDonald, R. and Shildrick, T. (2018). Biography, History and Place: Understanding Youth Transitions in Teesside. In Irwin, S. and Nielson, A. (eds.) *Transitions to Adulthood Through Recession: Youth and Inequality in a European Comparative Perspective*. London: Taylor & Francis, pp. 74–96.

MacDonald, R., Shildrick, T. and Furlong, A. (2014). Benefits Street and the Myth of Workless Communities. *Sociological Research Online*, 19(3). http://www.socresonline.org.uk/19/3/1.html (Accessed: 29 January 2019).

Marx, K. (1996 [1848]). *The Communist Manifesto*. London: Pluto Press.

McKenzie, L. (2015). *Getting by: Estates, Class and Culture in Austerity Britain*. Bristol: Policy Press.

Middlesbrough, F.C. (2016, July 27). *Boro Launches Partnership Package to Help Former Steel Workers*. https://www.mfc.co.uk/news/boro-launches-partnership-package-to-help-former-steel-workers (Accessed: 29 January 2019).

The Northern Echo. (2015a, May 11). Benefits Street: Meet the residents of Kingston Road, Stockton.

The Northern Echo. (2015b, October 12). Middlesbrough MP Andy McDonald Issues Withering Attack on Government.

ONS Nomis. (2021). *Official Labour Market Statistics*. https://www.nomisweb.co.uk/reports/lmp/la/1946157060/printable.aspx

Plan International UK. (2016). *The State of Girl's Rights in the UK*. https://plan-uk.org/file/plan-international-ukthe-state-of-girls-rights-in-the-uk-2016pdf (Accessed: 29 January 2019).

Ramaswamy, C. (2018, September 13). The Mighty Redcar Review – Proper Heartwarming Film-Making. *The Guardian*.

Shaw, W. (2007). *Cities of Whiteness*. Malden: Wiley-Blackwell.

Shildrick, T., MacDonald, R., Webster, C. and Garthwaite, K. (2012). *Poverty and Insecurity: Life in Low-Pay, No-Pay Britain*. Bristol: Policy Press.

Sibley, D. (1995). *Geographies of Exclusion: Society and Difference in the West*. London: Routledge.

Slater, T. and Anderson, N. (2012). The Reputational Ghetto: Territorial Stigmatization in St Pauls, Bristol. *Transactions of the Institute of British Geographers*, 37(4), pp. 530–546.

Smiles, M. (2016, September 13). Calling Middlesbrough the Worst Place to Be a Girl Doesn't Help Us. *The Guardian*.

TeessideLive. (2017, May 9). *Trailer for Blade Runner 2049 Takes Us Back to a World Inspired by Teesside*. https://www.gazettelive.co.uk/news/teesside-news/trailer-blade-runner-2049-takes-13007760 (Accessed: 28 November 2018).

Thornton, L. (2007, October 15). Middlesborough Worst Place in UK. *The Mirror*. https://www.mirror.co.uk/news/uk-news/middlesbrough-worst-place-in-uk-513534 (Accessed: 12 May 2021).

Tyler, I. (2008). Chav Mum, Chav Scum: Class Disgust in Contemporary Britain. *Feminist Media Studies*, 8(4), pp. 17–34.

Tyler, I. (2013). *Revolting Subjects: Social Abjection and Resistance in Neoliberal Britain*. London: Zed Books.

Wacquant, L. (2007). Territorial Stigmatization in the Age of Advanced Marginality. *Thesis Eleven*, 91(1), pp. 66–77.

Wacquant, L. (2008). *Urban Outcasts: A Comparative Sociology of Advanced Marginality*. Cambridge: Polity.

Wacquant, L., Slater, T. and Borges Pereira, V. (2014). Territorial Stigmatization in Action. *Environment and Planning A*, 46(6), pp. 1270–1280.

Wainwright, M. (2011, September 19). Channel 4 and Middlesbrough Are Friends Again. *The Guardian*.

Watt, P. (2020). Territorial Stigmatization and Poor Housing at a London 'Sink Estate'. *Social Inclusion*, 8(1), pp. 21–33.

Winant, G. 2021. *The Next Shift: The Fall of Industry and the Rise of Health Care in Rust Belt America*. Cambridge, MA: Harvard University Press.

World Health Organization. (2018). *Global Ambient Air Quality Database (Update 2018)*. http://www.who.int/airpollution/data/cities/en/ (Accessed: 27 November 2018).

16

DEINDUSTRIALIZATION, LEISURE, AND FEELING COMMUNITIES

Julia Wambach

For the 2011 Superbowl, the American car manufacturer Chrysler made a commercial for its first new car after the financial crisis (2007–2009). The commercial titled *Born on Fire* was about Detroit, one of the iconic examples of the rise and fall of an industrial city built around the car manufacturers General Motors, Chrysler, and Ford. *Motown*, as Detroit was nicknamed, was once an affluent city, but global competition hit the city hard after the Second World War. Since then, Detroit has become iconic for deindustrialization and its consequences: urban decay, racial segregation, poverty, and violence, all of which eroded the social and material fabric of the city.

The commercial confronts this history of decay and tackles the negative image of the city. A male voiceover with a hoarse voice addresses the stereotypes of Detroit: "I got a question for you. What does this city know about luxury? What does a town that's been to hell and back know about the finer things in life?" The video shows images of gray factories and decaying houses. But then the voiceover and imagery flips: "Well, I'll tell ya. More than most." The commercial then describes the positive values of the city: Detroit is a city of hard work, conviction, and tradition. The clip ends with Detroit musician Eminem, who had driven the car during the clip and whose song *Lose Yourself* was used as background music. Eminem joins the local choir Selected of God on the stage of Detroit's famous Fox Theatre and says into the camera: "This is the Motor City. And this is what we do."

This commercial exemplifies the way in which deindustrialized cities and regions found a way to regain a "feeling community" around the emotion of pride (Pernau, 2017). The use of the word 'we' to create commonality and the focus on hard work are core pillars around which this sense of community is built. Those who watched the commercial at the time remember the emotional impact it had in a time of severe crisis. One user named Deetroiter commented on the commercial on YouTube:

Anyone who lived in the area when this came out can tell you, without a doubt, how uplifting the commercial was. Nobody expected it. Nobody knew it was coming. It just showed up on TV when the area and people were going through an incredibly trying time. Chrysler showed the rest of the world that while we were being beaten down and hurting, we would NEVER give up without a fight.[1]

DOI: 10.4324/9781003308324-23

Another person remembered

how poignant this commercial was at the time. The U.S. was trying so hard to recover from a horrible recession, everyone was broke, cities were crumbling, and people were legitimately scared for the future. I think everyone needed to see a bit of hope, and even just a new American car being sold gave some hope. The music from Eminem's song has that 'build-up' effect that evokes a feeling of getting ready for something to happen, like change. It was just a magnificent ad.[2]

Several people described how the ad gives them goosebumps whenever they watch it.[3]

The commercial captures a sense of community based on hard work in the car manufacturing business which resisted in a time of deindustrialization. But instead of showing the actual work in the factories, which were in decline, the commercial focuses on leisure and cultural production. Besides Eminem's song, the commercial shows a Detroit gospel choir, art (Diego Rivera's Detroit Industry Mural from the 1930s, and Detroit's Monument to Joe Lewis, an iron fist that recalls Detroit boxer Joe Lewis), and, first and foremost, sports. Figure skating Olympic medalist and Detroiter Meryl Davis appears in the commercial alongside American Football team the Detroit Lions in training.

In the following pages, I examine the role and fate of working-class communities during deindustrialization using examples in Europe, North America, and Australia. With a focus on leisure and cultural production, in particular music and sports, the chapter argues that the quest for community did not simply disappear when the industrial workplace – and with it a traditional locus of working-class solidarity – vanished. Instead, other places of working-class community became more important, for instance, the local soccer clubs. These places of working-class community reference the industrial labor of the past. Rather than opposing industry and leisure, these places however suggest a continuity between free time and cultural creativity and the vanished industrial work. Using a history of emotions approach, the chapter examines the feeling communities and local place identities around leisure, football clubs in particular, and their relationship with the declining industries that surround them from the 1960s until the end of the 2010s when the last mines in Western Europe closed.

The history of emotions concept has been largely neglected by deindustrialization studies so far even though emotions do play a major role in the phenomena that the field examines. For example, the emotion of nostalgia is very present in works on deindustrialization (see Strangleman, 2013; Berger, 2019; Clarke, 2015). To explicitly engage with emotions history however is beneficial for deindustrialization studies, as it allows us to study how emotions and feelings toward industrial work or deindustrialization change over time and the role emotions play in political actions (demonstrations, strikes, voting patterns, community formations, or dissolutions). Such an approach reflects the history of emotions' dictum: emotions have a history, and emotions make history.[4]

This chapter draws on Margrit Pernau's concept of 'feeling communities.' This concept builds on Barbara Rosenwein's 'emotional communities' and aims at understanding the role of feelings for individuals and collectives. Emotions, Pernau argues, "have a performative quality and can bring forth or strengthen the community towards which they are directed" (Pernau, 2017, p. 17). Pernau moreover underlines that feeling communities do not necessarily align with social communities, such as class. This is particularly important for deindustrial spaces, where clear-cut social categories of class blur with the loss of the workplace as class identities recompose and communities dislocate in the process of deindustrialization.

Displacing Feeling Communities?

Deindustrialization puts feeling communities at risk. The loss of the workplace dissolved regular meeting spots and routines. Sites of old factories and industrial wastelands, former places of feeling communities, have been repurposed and in some ways revitalized by turning them into leisure facilities focused on sports and entertainment. Working-class communities attached to their former workplaces, however, have often been dislocated by these leisure-focused projects, as they were geared toward tourists and high(er)-income clients.

A large debate in the research centers on whether and how locals took part or profited from these new leisure spaces. Detroit is just one example of these endeavors. Deborah Che has described how in the past 30 years the city turned its decaying downtown area into an entertainment district centered around two sports stadia to attract mega-events like the Super Bowl (Che, 2008, 2009). In Australia, Melbourne is another example of this trend, as Seamus O'Hanlon has pointed out. He explains how Melbourne's recent boom of international sporting and cultural festivals (the Australian Open in tennis, the Commonwealth games, a Formula One Grand Prix, the International Flower and Garden Show, and an arts and comedy festival) can be traced to developments in the early 1980s as part of the city's deliberate response to the consequences of deindustrialization, that is urban decay in Melbourne's inner city (O'Hanlon, 2009).

The argument for such developments is that they have the potential to generate substantial economic and social returns on local and regional government investment.[5] However, instead of recreating and involving local feeling communities in sports, the investment has tended to be geared toward attracting visitors, further investments, and changing the image of the cities (see O'Hanlon, 2009). In her study on casinos in Windsor, Ontario, Alissa Mazar (2020) has critically engaged with this myth that leisure industries such as casinos can provide decent, non-precarious jobs for those hit by deindustrialization. While there are some more positive accounts of urban regeneration, most of the literature suggests that these spaces become elite zones of middle-class consumption, displacing or excluding former feeling communities.[6]

One way to fight the displacement of feeling communities was music. Deindustrialization affected the production as well as the consumption of popular music as a leisure activity. Genres such as hardcore, house, punk, industrial, and heavy metal all share a common origin in deindustrialized, decaying cities of the 1980s, including Torino, Tampere, Manchester, and Düsseldorf (Bottà, 2020).

As historian of emotions Juliane Brauer has argued,

> Music can be an important resource and medium for processing one's experiences and mediating one's perception through emotions. In the same way, music can be a means through which emotions themselves are produced, modulated, and acted out. We can therefore say that music supports what is called "emotion work."
>
> *(Brauer, 2016, p. 7)*

While Eminem linked his persona to the story of white working-class loss of social status through deindustrialization in Detroit, a number of songs more explicitly reference the deindustrialization process and provide an emotional template for those who sing or listen to these songs.[7] In Bruce Springsteen's 1995 song *Youngstown*, he addresses the fate of a family in the former steel town in Ohio. Billy Joel's 1992 song *Allentown* on the frustration and hopelessness of the coal and steelworkers in Pennsylvania became an anthem for American blue-collar workers. In Germany, Herbert Grönemeyer's 1985 *Bochum* gave a voice and feeling of pride to the people of the post-industrial Ruhr valley. The song tackles the stereotypes outside of the region toward the gray post-industrial landscape: "Deep down in the west, where the sun is dusty, it is better, much better than one might think." *Bochum* became the hymn of the local football club Vfl Bochum. These songs are able appeal to and produce an array of feelings toward deindustrialization, such as nostalgia for the past, hopelessness, defeat but also hope and pride. Sung or heard together, they are able to produce a feeling community constructed around place, industry, and the experience of deindustrialization (Wallach, 2011).

Music has been used as a regeneration strategy in regions hit by deindustrialization as well as a tool for community formation. The music does not make negative feelings produced by deindustrialization more tolerable, Bottà argues, but those feelings are used for inspiration (Bottà, 2020). In the case of the Superbowl Commercial, Eminem's music arguably empowers its listeners to not give up on the fate of their city without fighting, as Deetroiter noted in the YouTube comment. In a similar spirit, Ray Hudson shows how the closing of a steel factory incited new creative regeneration strategies from activists who had fought against the factory's closing: instead of letting the communal effort fizzle out and produce recrimination, apathy, and resignation, the activists decided to reinvent the music tradition of the city by setting up a state-funded record company. Northern Recording focused on children and young adults, giving them the space to feel positive emotions, such as excitement, through music and potentially giving them job prospects in the music industry (Hudson, 1995).

This strategy has been used elsewhere. Popular music heritage in the deindustrializing cities of Wollongong in Australia, Detroit in the US, and Birmingham in the UK has also been used to enhance emotional well-being and civic pride in these places. While the top-down strategies for revitalization and community renewal discussed here further marginalize and displace communities affected by deindustrialization, popular music heritage strategies can lead to more culturally just outcomes while preserving a feeling community constructed around the former workplace. The collection, preservation and archiving, and curation of music shows that that their heritage is valued. Storytelling and heritage interpretations have further attracted those who would not enter a regular museum. And, most importantly, the visibility and valorization of music heritage provides brings people together, creating social ties and feeling community networks – emotional bonds – that were loosened or lost during deindustrialization processes (Cantillon, Baker, and Nowak, 2021).

This literature on music and deindustrialization shows that in contrast to the usual victimization and displacement of the communities affected by deindustrialization, some initiatives have served as a way to enhance creativity and empower people (Hamera, 2012; Jakubovic, 2020).

Sport, Deindustrialization, and Masculinity

Sports and sporting events provide a particularly apt arena in which emotions can be expressed, felt, managed, and used for a variety of purposes (Ahner, Jack, and Wambach, 2023). Notably, the communal aspect of sports, an activity where people come together and form groups – even rival groups – is important in deindustrialization processes. In a situation where old social ties and networks are being displaced and dissolved because of the loss of the workplace community, emotional spaces other than the workplace become more important. Sports is one of them and, because of its popularity, reaches even more people than music. As we will see, the work sport does is often infused by the industrial past, be it by its physicality, its ideal of masculinity, or insignia from the former workplace. We need to appreciate the relationship between sport, deindustrialization, and masculinity to understand the importance of sports clubs to recreate feeling communities in post-industrial times as discussed later.

Occupational health researchers have shown that deindustrialization has a direct impact on social but also physical environments (Rind, Jones, and Southall, 2014). Physical activity levels are particularly low in deindustrialized regions. In the early 2010s, Esther Rind and Andy Jones studied working men's clubs in Northeast England, that is, social clubs for recreation. Rind and Jones found out that the physical inactivity was due to the loss of the participants' occupational physical activity as the work disappeared. Furthermore, recreational facilities such as sports facilities and public green spaces, often owned and organized by the miners, have disappeared alongside the workplace. The loss of trust and community alongside the loss of the workplace have added to the loss of physical activity, since sports and other leisure activities were part of a communal lifestyle that no longer exists and was replaced by feelings of mistrust and fear of crime and personal safety (Rind and Jones, 2014, 2015).

To prevent the physical and emotional decline during deindustrialization, sport-for-development programs organized by nonprofit organizations, private corporations, and public actors have tried to use sports to tackle the consequences of deindustrialization. A publicly funded floor hockey program in Edmonton/Canada in the 2010s, for example, became an essential social hub for low-income and often homeless young men. The weekly hockey matches provided access to not only social services but also emotional values such as solidarity, hope, and love for marginalized individuals in precarious living and employment situations (Scherer, Koch, and Holt, 2016).

Sport provides a way to construct or reconstruct masculinity and male social and emotional bonds in times of deindustrialization, when loss of work dissolved the feeling community at the workplace and affected the self-image of men as hardworking breadwinners of the family. This is also true for those generations of young men who have not experienced the physically demanding jobs themselves but relate to the image of manhood through hard work that had to be sought elsewhere. An ethnographic study on hardcore gym culture in post-industrial South Devon and the Midlands in England argues that in the absence of meaningful employment in the regions studied, men transferred the physical work to their free time activities while doing sports. The gyms turned into "arenas of bodily labor" where men could display and work on their physical traits of masculinity infused by the heritage from earlier industrial times (Gibbs, Salinas, and Turnock, 2022, p. 233). At the same time, the men find a fraternal community at the gym, elders, and sparring partners whom they trust – just as they might have forged such relations at the industrial workplace.[8]

Sviatoslav Poliakov makes a similar argument about masculinity and sports in the context of post-Soviet deindustrialization. By studying a street workout community in Dagestan in the North Caucasus, Poliakov (2022) asserts that a "leisure career" in sports helps young underclass men to construct their masculinity in the absence of other career paths, such work or education. In post-industrial Wales, boys aged 13 or 14 ride, build, and fix their motorcycles for trail motorbiking in the surrounding hills, as Gabrielle Mary Ivinson has shown. This semi-clandestine leisure activity mimics the skills and experiences of industrial labor in the past, as it requires strength and skill and is carried out in dirty, dangerous environments. The joy it evokes in the boys adds to the establishment of the masculine identity and community infused by earlier industrial times (Ivinson, 2014).

In a similar vein, Anoop Nayak has shown that young white men can identify with an industrial work ethic even while being unemployed. In his study in the Northeast of England, he found that they did this through leisurely consumption, notably through embodied rituals of supporting their football club, drinking, and going out (Nayak, 2003, 2006, 2019). While the other examples cited here focus on participation in sporting activity, Nayak points to the significance of watching or supporting others who do sports, as an arena in which masculine identities and solidarities can be affirmed – all components of a feeling community inherited from the industrial past.

Sports and football clubs in particular are a locus where much of the feeling community lost through deindustrialization is assembled. Hooligans in the 1960s, 1970s, and 1980s and ultra-fan groups since the early 2000s have seldomly been associated with deindustrialization processes.[9] But the often violently expressed masculinity in these groups can be a consequence of and remedy for deindustrialization as Nicola Rehling has shown in a piece on hooligan films in Britain (Rehling, 2011). The release of emotions, the experience of emotional highs, and the pleasure of homosocial bonds are an important part of the process. The films show the fragmentation of working-class identities and communities and the search for masculinity, emotional community, and stability in the hooligan groups. Rehling shows that because of deindustrialization, the children of working-class parents were forced to work in white-collar jobs, as traditional working-class jobs were no longer available. Their social mobility thus adds to their uncomfortable search for a new (class) belonging – or to use the concept I have adopted here, they find a feeling community in hooligan and ultra-fan groups (Rehling, 2011).

The networks in those hooligan or ultra-fan groups expand beyond the stadium and the immediate purpose of supporting a sports club. The community formed by these closely tied networks consists of self-help, and sometimes this community was even one of shared economic interests, as Dinu Gutu has argued in the Romanian case. The ultra-fan groups which formed after the breakdown of communism used football as a pretext for meeting and shared leisure activities while in fact providing networks and economic exchanges. In a disintegrating post-communist but also post-industrial state, clientelist networks of survival could thus form in a seemingly leisure-based setting (Guțu, 2018).

In many deindustrialized places, watching a sports game was one of the few rituals and moments of mostly male sociability that survived after the workplace had ceased to exist. In a study on the British Midlands, Neil Stanley shows how leisure activities and football fandom, in particular, are related to the loss of the workplace. In the rituals around the weekly matches, the dissolving working-class communities could at least temporarily find a feeling community and recreate a sense of their past. "They [football teams] were perhaps one of the few functioning traces of a once vivid world," Stanley concluded (Stanley, 2017, p. 3). This process works particularly well if these teams identify with the industrial and working-class past.

(Post)industrial Sports Clubs

A number of sports clubs all over the globe pride themselves on the industrial past in their localities and thereby aim at taking over the feeling community inherited from work in the heavy industries. Post-industrial clubs seem to take up the image and community of working-class solidarities in the team of players, the fans, and the general image of the club.

These clubs all have a link to the now vanished industries. For example, the French club RC Lens was up to the 1970s financially supported by the local mining company (see Fontaine, 2010), players of the German club FC Schalke 04 of Gelsenkirchen were apprentices at the local mine (see Wambach, 2022), the American football club Pittsburgh Steelers honors with its name the steel industry of the city (see Beissel, Giardina, and Newman, 2014), and the British club West Ham United was founded by the Thames Ironworks and Shipbuilding Co. Ltd. Westham United's logo displays a hammer and its supporters continues to call themselves *the Hammers* or *the Irons* even though the company that founded the club for its workers had shut down by 1900.[10] Similarly, RC Lens's logo still shows a miner's lamp and Schalke's logo a stylized mining hammer. Schalke's players are called *Knappen*, miners, underlining its working-class origin and image.

Sport clubs play a significant role in refashioning place identity after the decline of industries.[11] As they have increasingly become brands in the period under discussion and hence increasingly mediatized entities, the media play a huge part in disseminating this refashioned place identity in times of deindustrialization. McGuirk and Rowe have shown this development in the case of Newcastle in New South Wales. The city was once known for its coal mining, shipbuilding, textile, and steel industries, until the 1980s when radical downsizing set in. The authors, two social and cultural geographers, studied post-match representations of the city and its rugby club in the 1997 Australian Rugby League Finale, which the local club Newcastle Knights won. Drawing on Stuart Hall's concept of resemanticization, they show how local and national media interpreted the club's victory as a turning point in the refashioning of the city. The players, who were said to represent the city and its inhabitants, incorporated the emotional values of the working class, such as a particularly masculine solidarity, spirit, and community. This was held to be the case even though the club refrained from involvement in any political action during deindustrialization. Furthermore, potentially troublesome events (violent strikes and class struggle) were neglected in the media coverage (McGuirk and Rowe, 2001).

Oftentimes, the attachment to the industrial past comes to the fore on specific dates when the industrial heritage is particularly remembered or its link with the club is deepened. These can be title wins, as in the case of the Newcastle Knights' Rugby Championship win. It could be the commemoration of an anniversary of the club, or the anniversary of a mining accident, such as the 2016 commemoration of a 1906 mine accident in Courrières in a ceremony held at the football stadium of RC Lens.[12]

Mourning of the industrial past is indeed a feeling expressed in sports stadia in deindustrialized regions. Take the case of Schalke 04, where the closing of the mines has been commemorated since the 2000s in special ceremonies at the stadium. These have taken place on the same day as a mine's closure, and (former) miners have been honored as special guests. The symbiotic relationship between Schalke 04 football club and the local mining community reached its apogee during the celebration of the closing of the last hard coal mine in Germany, Prosper Haniel, on December 19, 2018. The club, alongside its ultra-fans, celebrated the end of coal in the region with a sophisticated show in a candlelit stadium. The miners of Prosper Haniel were invited, the Ruhrkohle choir sang the *Steigerlied* (Overman's Song), and the players wore jerseys on which the names of closed mines figured instead of the sponsors (Wambach, 2022, p. 250).

Deindustrialization, Leisure and Feeling Communities

The clubs form a feeling community that takes up relics from the industrial past while replacing industry as a focal point for the expression of working-class masculinity. As Adam Beissel, Michael Giardina, and Joshua Newman observe, for example, the American football club Pittsburgh Steelers celebrates particularly physical and tough players, honoring "bygone industrial-era working-class masculinities at a moment when many of Pittsburgh's industrial pillars have been compromised (if not replaced) by the thrusts of new forms of capital production" (Beissel, Giardina, and Newman, 2014, p. 954). The Steelers (club and fans) thus form an imagined – and I would add emotional feeling – community – the so-called Steeler Nation which takes on the blue-collar civic identity marked by a hard-working hypermasculine ideal of the past. In this past developed "a masculine pride" in workers' "ability to face the gates of hell" which deindustrialization put under threat (Beissel, Giardina, and Newman, 2014, p. 956). The Steeler Nation also comprises the Pittsburgh diaspora, those who had worked in the city but had lost their jobs during deindustrialization and had to move elsewhere. The weekly visit to the stadium or the practice of gathering with friends and family to watch a broadcasted game could thus provide the "physical space for an embodied celebration of a working-class life and industrial manhood" (Beissel, Giardina, and Newman, 2014, p. 959). The Steelers performed "the toughest team in the toughest sport of the toughest city in the United States." Pittsburgh's most iconic players in the successful 2000s were players who incarnated physical violence (James Harrison), a masculine working-class identity that includes heavy drinking, a strong heterosexual masculinity, and white Rust Belt roots (Ben Roethlisberger), but in addition also progressive left-wing politics (Troy Polamalu). Similar dynamics are at play, when the players of the German club Schalke 04 from the former mining town Gelsenkirchen are called *Knappen* (miner) and were expected to represent the miners on the pitch by working honestly and playing physically (see Wambach, 2022).

While in the American case, sports teams were franchises that could simply be moved to another city, leaving their fans and the cities to themselves, the situation is different in Europe, for example, where sports clubs were closely tied to the locality and the community on site. In some European mining regions, local administrations recognized quite early in the process of declining industries the importance of the sports clubs for the emotional well-being and social cohesion of the locals. In such regions, which were often in the hands of socialists or social democrats, local politicians and administrations were the first to recognize the importance of sports clubs not just for attracting investors or tourists but first and foremost for their citizens. While many sports clubs and facilities had developed as a consequence of the mining industry, cities took over the responsibility for the infrastructure and invested in the stadia and clubs during deindustrialization. In Saint-Etienne, as Bruno Dumans (2011) has shown, the club was used to change the image of the city when the image of a *ville noire* was no longer attractive. Instead of representing a mining city in decay, the municipal administration and local businesses, such as the supermarket group Casino, invested in the Saint Etienne football club from the 1950s to turn it into the flagship of a new, modern city with which inhabitants could proudly identify. Since at least the 1970s, the club has been widely considered a central part of the city's *patrimoine* (heritage).

Saint Etienne served as a role model for other French cities, for example, for the Racing Club de Lens in the mining basin of Northern France. The socialist mayor André Delelis considered the club essential for the emotional social glue of the *Lensois*, and the city increasingly substituted the patronage of the mines (Fontaine, 2010, p. 217). While in the case of Saint Etienne, the city deliberately got rid of the industrial connotation of the club, the mining heritage survived in Lens and was given increased prominence. Fontaine points out that only since the end of the 1980s, when deindustrialization was complete (the last mine closed in 1986) has the mining heritage been brought to the fore as a marketing tool. In the process, the mining heritage was stripped of its conflictual past and reduced to stereotypes, expressed in the communal singing of Pierre Bachelet's 1982 nostalgic song _Les corons_ during half-time, for example. The song is focused on the private life of a mining family while excluding labor disputes notably in the process of deindustrialization. However, Fontaine also notices the emotional capacity of the club to create a community around the emotion of _fierté_ (pride). The pride referred not necessarily to being a son of a miner but to being part of an underdog community in the stadium and in the city of Lens in a deindustrialized region, which was often looked down upon – in particular by the capital, Paris (Fontaine, 2010, p. 257; Baudelle and Krauss, 2014).

In the case of the German club FC Schalke 04, a football club in the heart of the once industrial Ruhr valley, the club and the city administration were so deeply intertwined that the city treasurer was at one point convicted of fraud for having secretly embezzled tax revenue to support the club. Thirty years later, it was Gerhard Rehberg, former miner, social democratic mayor of one of Gelsenkirchen's boroughs, and chairman of the board of directors of Schalke 04, who initiated closer ties between the miners, mining heritage, and the club. Starting in the mid-1990s, he worked alongside Schalke's manager Rudi Assauer as one of the key figures behind Schalke's charitable programs to turn Schalke's headquarters into a "place to go for people with smaller and bigger problems" (Wambach, 2022, p. 268). In comparison to the English Premier League or the American Football League where clubs are owned by big investors, the German Bundesliga allows for a more participatory role of the fans in the club.[13] But even among German Bundesliga clubs, Schalke 04 stands out as one of the few clubs whose professional football team remains up to this day a nonprofit organization (_eingetragener Verein_) beneficial to society. This status, ferociously defended by the fans, the Schalke Ultras in particular, allows for a special role and mission during deindustrialization, that is providing a home and feeling community that got lost with the workplace (Wambach, 2022, p. 269).

However, rather like Racing Club de Lens, the club rediscovered its mining heritage relatively late during deindustrialization, seeing a need for solidarity and action to curb the effects of deindustrialization. From the mid-1990s, the club aimed at recreating and reinforcing the community threatened by the loss of a common workplace. They gave the miners a stage in the stadium where they could demonstrate against the closing of the mines, and when those mines were eventually shuttered, they invited miners to the stadium and celebrated them and the mining heritage of the region in speeches and communal singing of the _Overman's Song_, which became the club's anthem in the mid-1990s (Saupe, 2020). Furthermore, the club represented itself as a social hub for those in need by coordinating apprenticeship offers within the Schalke family and by teaming up with the municipal employment office. Since 2001, a not-for-profit foundation _Schalke Hilft_ (Schalke Helps) is involved in social projects in Gelsenkirchen and its immediate surroundings to alleviate poverty-related consequences of deindustrialization in the fields of education and equal opportunity.

The social engagement and mining image of the club was of course part of the image the club gave itself in a more and more professional football business (see Jonas, 2019). Schalke 04 has also been particularly successful since the mid-1990s, with the club winning the UEFA Cup in 1997 and the DFB Cup in 2001. Recent relegation to the second division has however impacted the availability of funding for the club's charitable interventions and its overall capacity to maintain the much-lauded Schalke family (see Wambach, 2022).

The success or misfortune of a club is often seen as key to the emotions attached to a place. In the aforementioned case of the Newcastle Knights, their championship win was seen as a way to uplift the region and its people from a state of decay. This is also true for RC Lens's championship win in 1998. In the German Ruhr valley, the double win of the UEFA Cup and the Champions League in 1997 by the local teams Schalke 04 and Borussia Dortmund served as a way to generate the formation of a place identity and an emotionally positive attachment to the Ruhr valley (Kisters, 2000).

But the development of a sports club and that of the city can also diverge, as in the case of a declining club and a city in transition after deindustrialization. In the case of Coventry, a British city in the West Midlands, Adrian Smith shows how the local rugby club, Coventry RFC, went bankrupt in the second half of the 1990s, while the city recovered from recession and deindustrialization by maintaining a manufacturing base and profiting from its geographical location and skilled labor to become a hub for distribution, financial services, and telecommunications (Smith, 1999). In contrast to other places, such as Lens or Gelsenkirchen, the city of Coventry did not financially help the club. The latter also lost spectators and fans to the high entrance fees. Other clubs in deindustrialized regions avoided rising ticket fees. Schalke 04, for instance, tried to price tickets cheaply with regard to the financial means of the fan base. In Coventry, the emotional attachment of a few diehard fans from the good old times when the city and the club were thriving (the last major final the club played was in 1974) did not suffice for the rugby club to survive in a professionalized and monetized sports business (Smith, 1999).

In a similar vein, Philipp C. Suchma describes how an unsuccessful sports team can even exacerbate the consequences of deindustrialization. Taking Cleveland as a case study, Suchma explores the decline of three professional sports franchises (baseball, football, and hockey) alongside the deindustrialization of the city between 1945 and 1978. The decline of sports from the "City of Champions" to the "Mistake on the Lake" mirrored the city image's decline from the "Best'Location in the Nation" to the "Mistake on the Lake," leaving its inhabitants shattered (Suchma, 2005).

The misfortune of a club, which aligns with the fate of the deindustrialized city or region, does not automatically mean that the community around the club dissolves. Many of the post-industrial working-class clubs play the role of underdogs and portray themselves as resisters in a monetized football business. Losing against bigger, more professional clubs only strengthens a close-knit community of club and fans who prefer honest, hardworking, decent players, and fans – again, values associated with the working-class past. For instance, when Schalke 04 failed to win the 2001 the Bundesliga championship at the very last moment, the fans dubbed the club "Meister der Herzen" (champion of the hearts) and celebrated its earnestness in comparison with the winner of the 2001 season, FC Bayern Munich, considered a club of the rich (Ulrich, 2013). The feeling of moral superiority is highest in times of unexpected triumphs.

Conclusion

During deindustrialization and the disappearance of work in the cities and regions affected, leisure takes on a new importance. The literature has been interested in questions of investments into leisure and sport facilities as a way to attract tourists and investors to decaying regions, but leisure practices and industries, in particular music and sports, also have an impact on the emotional infrastructure of those who live in deindustrialized regions. In this chapter, I have argued that music and sports provide arenas in which emotions engendered by deindustrialization can be expressed, felt, and used to create or recreate a community that had become fractured with the loss of the workplace.[14] As in the opening example of the Super Bowl commercial, the focus on leisure can help to change not just the outward image of deindustrialized places usually seen as gray, decaying, and backward places but to consider them as functioning feeling communities and homes of which people can be proud. To study community formation in leisure (not work) and the emotions it entails are key to writing a history of deindustrialization that does not focus on decay and negative stereotypes, but that gives way to a more positive narration of deindustrialized places all over the globe.

Notes

1 Deetroiter, comment on Chrysler. (2016). Imported From Detroit. *Campaign: Super Bowl Commercial with Eminem.* https://www.youtube.com/watch?v=mYsFUFgOEmM (Accessed 5 December 2024).

2 Drunkindonuts13, comment on Chrysler. (2016). Imported From Detroit. *Super Bowl Commercial with Eminem.* https://www.youtube.com/watch?v=mYsFUFgOEmM (Accessed 5 December 2024).

3 Srikantdafreak, Lightningblue648, and Pshailesh, comments on Chrysler. (2016). Imported From Detroit. *Super Bowl Commercial with Eminem.* https://www.youtube.com/watch?v=mYsFUFgO EmM (Accessed 5 December 2024).

The commercial also won several awards, both nationally and internationally, and received an Emmy Award for Outstanding Commercial and four Gold Lions at the International Festival of Creativity, Cannes, France in 2011.

4 See, for example, the introduction of Frevert, Ute. (2023). *The Power of Emotions: A History of Germany from 1900 to the Present.* Cambridge: Cambridge University Press, pp. 1–19 and the work of Ute Frevert's Center for the History of Emotions in Berlin.

5 Gratton, C., Shibli, S. and Coleman, R. (2005). Sport and Economic Regeneration in Cities. *Urban Studies*, 42(5/6), pp. 985–999. The authors focus on Sheffield in the UK.

6 One more positive account is Kohn, M. (2009). Dreamworlds of Deindustrialization. *Theory & Event*, 12(4). https://doi.org/10.1353/tae.0.0096

7 For emotional templates, see Brauer, J. (2022). Feeling Political by Collective Singing: Political Youth Organizations in Germany, 1920–1960. In Frevert, U. et al. (eds.) *Feeling Political: Emotions and Institutions since 1789.* Cham: Palgrave Macmillan, pp. 277–306.

8 On this aspect of the industrial workplace, see Strangleman, T. (2024). The World We Have Lost: Reflections on Varieties of Masculinity at Work. *International Labor and Working-Class History*, 105, pp. 9–25.

9 On hooliganism and ultra-fans, see, for example, Frosdick, S. and Marsh, P. (2013). *Football Hooliganism.* London: Willan. and Doidge, M., Kossakowski, R. and Mintert, S. (2020). *Ultras: The Passion and Performance of Contemporary Football Fandom.* Manchester: Manchester University Press.

10 For the History of West Ham United, see Korr, C.P. (1986). *West Ham United: The Making of a Football Club.* Urbana, IL: University of Illinois Press.

For an example of the construction of a mining identity of a football club, see also Arnal, T. (2013). Allez Racing: décryptage du processus d'affirmation et d'idéalisation d'une identité minière au sein d'un club de football amateur du bassin houiller aveyronnais (1951–1961). *Sciences sociales et sport*, 6(1), pp. 35–61.

11 On place-based identities and deindustrialization, see also Anoop Nayak's chapter in this volume.

12 See (2016, March 11) Catastrophe de Courrières: 110 ans après, les fans de Lens appelés à se marquer le visage pour se souvenir. *La Voix du Nord*, https://www.lavoixdunord.fr/art/sports/catastrophe-de-courrieres-110-ans-apres-les-fans-de-ia182b205n3378881 (Accessed 5 December 2024).

13 For a history of modern football, see McDougall, A. (2020). *Contested Fields: A Global History of Modern Football.* Toronto: University of Toronto Press.

14 See for the concept Seymour, M. (2022). *Emotional Arenas. Life, Love, and Death in 1870s Italy.* Oxford: Oxford University Press.

Reference List

(2016, March 11) Catastrophe de Courrières: 110 ans après, les fans de Lens appelés à se marquer le visage pour se souvenir. *La Voix du Nord.* https://www.lavoixdunord.fr/art/sports/catastrophe-de-courrieres-110-ans-apres-les-fans-de-ia182b205n3378881 (Accessed 5 December 2024).

Ahner, H., Jack, M. and Wambach, J. (2023, July 12). *Introduction to the Workshop Feeling Competitive – Sport as Affective Practice.* Berlin: Max Planck Institute for Human Development.

Arnal, T. (2013). Allez Racing: décryptage du processus d'affirmation et d'idéalisation d'une identité minière au sein d'un club de football amateur du bassin houiller aveyronnais (1951–1961). *Sciences sociales et sport,* 6(1), pp. 35–61. https://doi.org/10.3917/rsss.006.0035

Baudelle, G. and Krauss, G. (2014). The Governance Model of Two French National Museums of Fine Arts Relocated in the Province: Centre Pompidou Metz and Louvre-Lens. *Belgeo,* 1. https://doi.org/10.4000/belgeo.12765

Beissel, A.S., Giardina, M. and Newman, J.I. (2014). Men of Steel: Social Class, Masculinity, and Cultural Citizenship in Post-Industrial Pittsburgh. *Sport in Society,* 17(7), pp. 953–976. https://doi.org/10.1080/17430437.2013.806032

Berger, S. (2019). Industrial Heritage and the Ambiguities of Nostalgia for an Industrial Past in the Ruhr Valley, Germany. *Labor,* 16(1), pp. 37–64.

Bottà, G. (2020). *Deindustrialisation and Popular Music: Punk and 'Post-Punk' in Manchester, Düsseldorf, Torino and Tampere.* London: Routledge.

Brauer, J. (2016). How Can Music Be Torturous? Music in Nazi Concentration and Extermination Camps. *Music and Politics,* 10(1). https://doi.org/10.3998/mp.9460447.0010.103

Brauer, J. (2022). Feeling Political by Collective Singing: Political Youth Organizations in Germany, 1920–1960. In Frevert, U. et al. (eds.) *Feeling Political: Emotions and Institutions since 1789.* Cham: Springer, pp. 277–306.

Cantillon, Z., Baker, S. and Nowak, R. (2021). A Cultural Justice Approach to Popular Music Heritage in Deindustrialising Cities. *International Journal of Heritage Studies,* 27(1), pp. 73–89. https://doi.org/10.1080/13527258.2020.1768579

Che, D. (2008). Sports, Music, Entertainment and the Destination Branding of Post-Fordist Detroit. *Tourism Recreation Research,* 33(2), pp. 195–206. https://doi.org/10.1080/02508281.2008.11081305

Che, D. (2009). Techno: Music and Entrepreneurship in Post-Fordist Detroit. In Johansson, O. and Bell, T.L. (eds.) *Sound, Society and the Geography of Popular Music.* London: Routledge, pp. 261–81.

Chrysler. (2016). Imported from Detroit. *Campaign: Super Bowl Commercial with Eminem.* https://www.youtube.com/watch?v=mYsFUFgOEmM (Accessed: 5 December 2024).

Clarke, J. (2015). Closing Time: Deindustrialization and Nostalgia in Contemporary France. *History Workshop Journal,* 79(1), pp. 107–125.

Doidge, M., Kossakowski, R. and Mintert, S. (2020). *Ultras: The Passion and Performance of Contemporary Football Fandom.* Manchester: Manchester University Press.

Dumons, B. (2011). Le football dans la ville. Saint-Étienne au 20e siècle. *Vingtième Siècle. Revue d'histoire,* 111(3), pp. 11–21. https://doi.org/10.3917/vin.111.0011

Fontaine, M. (2010). *Le Racing club de Lens et les 'Gueules noires'.* Paris: Les Éditions de l'Atelier.

Frevert, U. (2023). *The Power of Emotions: A History of Germany from 1900 to the Present.* Cambridge: Cambridge University Press.

Frosdick, S. and Marsh, P. (2013). *Football Hooliganism.* London: Routledge.

Gibbs, N., Salinas, M. and Turnock, L. (2022). Post-Industrial Masculinities and Gym Culture: Graft, Craft, and Fraternity. *The British Journal of Sociology,* 73(1), pp. 220–236. https://doi.org/10.1111/1468-4446.12921

Gratton, C., Shibli, S. and Coleman, R. (2005). Sport and Economic Regeneration in Cities. *Urban Studies,* 42(5/6), pp. 985–999.

Guțu, D. (2018). World Going One Way, People Another: Ultras Football Gangs' Survival Networks and Clientelism in Post-Socialist Romania. *Soccer & Society*, 19(3), pp. 337–354. https://doi.org/10.1080/14660970.2017.1333677

Hamera, J. (2012). The Labors of Michael Jackson: Virtuosity, Deindustrialization, and Dancing Work. *PMLA*, 127(4), pp. 751–65. https://doi.org/10.1632/pmla.2012.127.4.751

Hudson, R. (1995). Making Music Work? Alternative Regeneration Strategies in a Deindustrialized Locality: The Case of Derwentside. *Transactions of the Institute of British Geographers*, 20(4), pp. 460–473. https://doi.org/10.2307/622976

Ivinson, G.M. (2014). Skills in Motion: Boys' Trail Motorbiking Activities as Transitions into Working-Class Masculinity in a Post-Industrial Locale. *Sport, Education and Society*, 19(5), pp. 605–620. https://doi.org/10.1080/13573322.2012.692669

Jakubovic, R. (2020). *Rust Belt Punk: An Autoethnographic Analysis of Punk Subculture in Youngstown, Ohio (1974–1979)*. PhD Dissertation, Union Institute & University. https://www.proquest.com/openview/7585d9a2ff38c25a650e4687abf0d4d4/1?pq-origsite=gscholar&cbl=18750&diss=y (Accessed: 13 September 2023).

Jonas, H. (2019). *Fussball in England und Deutschland von 1961 bis 2000: vom Verlierer der Wohlstandsgesellschaft zum Vorreiter der Globalisierung*. Göttingen: Vandenhoeck & Ruprecht.

Kisters, S. (2000). *Ruhrpott, Ruhrpott: Wie die Europapokaltriumphe von Schalke 04 und Borussia Dortmund Image und Identität des Ruhrgebiets veränderten*. Bochum: Deutsches Bergbau-Museum.

Kohn, M. (2009). Dreamworlds of Deindustrialization. *Theory & Event*, 12(4). https://doi.org/10.1353/tae.0.0096

Korr, C.P. (1986). *West Ham United: The Making of a Football Club*. Urbana, IL: University of Illinois Press.

Mazar, A. (2020). *Deindustrialization and Casinos: A Winning Hand?* London: Routledge. https://doi.org/10.4324/9781003028505

McDougall, A. (2020). *Contested Fields: A Global History of Modern Football*. Toronto: University of Toronto Press.

McGuirk, P. and Rowe, D. (2001). 'Defining Moments' and Refining Myths in the Making of Place Identity: The Newcastle Knights and the Australian Rugby League Grand Final. *Australian Geographical Studies*, 39(1), pp. 52–66. https://doi.org/10.1111/1467-8470.00129

Nayak, A. (2003). Last of the 'Real Geordies'? White Masculinities and the Subcultural Response to Deindustrialisation. *Environment and Planning D: Society and Space*, 21(1), pp. 7–25. https://doi.org/10.1068/d44j

Nayak, A. (2006). Displaced Masculinities: Chavs, Youth and Class in the Post-Industrial City. *Sociology*, 40(5), pp. 813–831. https://doi.org/10.1177/0038038506067508

Nayak, A. (2019). Re-Scripting Place: Managing Social Class Stigma in a Former Steel-Making Region. *Antipode*, 51(3), pp. 927–948. https://doi.org/10.1111/anti.12525

O'Hanlon, S. (2009). The Events City: Sport, Culture, and the Transformation of Inner Melbourne, 1977–2006. *Urban History Review/Revue d'histoire urbaine*, 37(2), pp. 30–39.

Pernau, M. (2017). Feeling Communities: Introduction. *The Indian Economic & Social History Review*, 54(1), pp. 1–20. https://doi.org/10.1177/0019464616683477

Poliakov, S. (2022). Masculinity Constructing among Street Workout Youth in Post-Soviet Dagestan. *Sport in Society*, 25(2), pp. 353–368. https://doi.org/10.1080/17430437.2020.1806824

Rehling, N. (2011). 'It's About Belonging': Masculinity, Collectivity, and Community in British Hooligan Films. *Journal of Popular Film and Television*, 39(4), pp. 162–173. https://doi.org/10.1080/01956051.2011.555252

Rind, E. and Jones, A. (2014). Declining Physical Activity and the Socio-Cultural Context of the Geography of Industrial Restructuring: A Novel Conceptual Framework. *Journal of Physical Activity and Health*, 11(4), pp. 683–692. https://doi.org/10.1123/jpah.2012-0173

Rind, E. and Jones, A. (2015). 'I Used to Be as Fit as a Linnet' – Beliefs, Attitudes, and Environmental Supportiveness for Physical Activity in Former Mining Areas in the North-East of England. *Social Science & Medicine*, 126, pp. 110–118. https://doi.org/10.1016/j.socscimed.2014.12.002

Rind, E., Jones, A. and Southall, H. (2014). How is Post-Industrial Decline Associated with the Geography of Physical Activity? Evidence from the Health Survey for England. *Social Science & Medicine*, 104, pp. 88–97. https://doi.org/10.1016/j.socscimed.2013.12.004\

Saupe, A. (2020). Kumpel, Kaue, Keilhaue. Historische Authentizität, Geschichtsmarketing und Erinnerungskultur. In Farrenkopf, M., Siemer, S. (eds.) *Perspektiven des Bergbauerbes im Museum. Vernetzung, Digitalisierung, Forschung*. Berlin/München/Boston: deGruyter, pp. 293–314.

Scherer, J., Koch, J. and Holt, N. (2016). The Uses of an Inner-City Sport-for-Development Program: Dispatches from the (Real) Creative Class. *Sociology of Sport Journal*, 33. https://doi.org/10.1123/ssj.2015-0145

Seymour, M. (2022). *Emotional Arenas. Life, Love, and Death in 1870s Italy*. Oxford: Oxford University Press.

Smith, A. (1999). An Oval Ball and a Broken City: Coventry, Its People and Its Rugby Team, 1995–98. *The International Journal of the History of Sport*, 16(3), pp. 147–157. https://doi.org/10.1080/09523369908714090

Stanley, N. (2017). *The Ruin of the Past: Deindustrialization, Working-Class Communities, and Football in the Midlands, UK 1945–1990*. PhD Dissertation, University of Western Ontario.

Strangleman, T. (2013). 'Smokestack Nostalgia', 'Ruin Porn' or Working-Class Obituary: The Role and Meaning of Deindustrial Representation. *International Labor and Working-Class History*, 84, pp. 23–37.

Strangleman, T. (2024). The World We Have Lost: Reflections on Varieties of Masculinity at Work. *International Labor and Working-Class History*, 105, pp. 9–25.

Suchma, P.C. (2005). *From the best of times to the worst of times: Professional sport and urban decline in a tale of two Clevelands, 1945–1978*. PhD Dissertation, Ohio State University. https://www.proquest.com/openview/4dc2fd29f042a203b61c8e13d41cdcb0/1?pq-origsite=gscholar&cbl=18750&diss=y (Accessed: 13 September 2023).

Ulrich, R. (2013, February 9). Tal der Tränen. *11 Freunde*. https://11freunde.de/artikel/tal-der-tränen/441959 (Accessed: 13 September 2023).

Wallach, J. (2011). Unleashed in the East: Metal Music, Masculinity, and 'Malayness' in Indonesia, Malaysia, and Singapore. In Wallach, J., Berger, H.M. and Greene, P.D. (eds.) *Metal Rules the Globe: Heavy Metal Music around the World*. Durham: Duke University Press, pp. 86–106. https://doi.org/10.1515/9780822392835-004

Wambach, J. (2022). Feeling Political Through a Football Club: FC Schalke 04, 1904–2020. In Frevert, U. et al. (eds.) *Feeling Political: Emotions and Institutions since 1789*. Cham: Springer, pp. 249–276. https://doi.org/10.1007/978-3-030-89858-8_9

17

"DAD, WHY DID YOU BRING ME TO A GAY STEEL MILL?"

Notes Toward a Queer Study of Deindustrialization

Liam Devitt

Introduction: "Dad, Why Did You Bring Me to a Gay Steel Mill?"

In "Homer's Phobia," a 1997 episode of television staple *The Simpsons*, Homer is afraid of the influence his new gay acquaintance John (voiced by none-other-than John Waters himself) may have on his family (Anderson, 1997). Particularly, Homer is worried that his son Bart, enticed by John's flamboyancy, may stray from heterosexuality. To prevent such a *disaster*, Homer takes Bart to a steel mill. Homer thinks that surely, the bastion of American working-class masculinity that is the steel industry will set Bart on the straight path. But, of course, this is a steel mill where all the workers are complete queens. In fact, the mill turns into a disco when the workers are on break. The reason the joke works is that industrial labor and queerness are seen as complete antitheses of each other. One is regimented, masculine, and honest, whereas the other may be informal, gender nonconforming, and deceitful. Thus, it is telling that much of the scholarship on deindustrialization does not examine queer people. As if queer people could not be the workers in these factories, mills, and mines, or if they could not be affected by the massive economic, social, and cultural shift of deindustrialization. Of course, queer people are everywhere – and as historian Anne Balay (2014) has examined in her work *Steel Closets,* they worked in the steel industry. As Moe tells Homer later in the episode: "Where have you been, Homer? Entire steel industry's gay. Eh, aerospace too, and the railroads! And you know what else? Broadway."

In this chapter, I will examine the connection between literatures on queer history, queer theory, and histories of deindustrialization. What insights can queer theory and history bring to studies of deindustrialization? What insights can a renewed focus on labor in the dein-dustrialized/ing moment bring queer studies?[1] Deindustrialization in North America and Western Europe roughly coincides with pivotal moments for LGBTQ communities, namely the rise and fall of gay liberation, the onset of the AIDS epidemic, and neoliberal restructur-ing.[2] In the 1980s and 1990s, LGBTQ people fought for their lives, just like industrial work-ers fought for their jobs. Scholars generally have examined little of this resonance, save for the Lesbians and Gays Support the Miners (LGSM) solidarity group during the 1984–1985 Miners' Strike in the UK.[3] Still, that great moment of solidarity is often portrayed as the urban queer reaching out to the downtrodden rural straight miner.

DOI: 10.4324/9781003308324-24

"Dad, Why Did You Bring Me to a Gay Steel Mill?"

What then of the queer worker? How might LGBTQ people have been affected by deindustrialization? How might it have affected the way they lived, worked, organized, and related to one another? This chapter is not going to answer those questions directly but rather examine the challenges that such lines of inquiry entail for queer historians and historians of deindustrialization. Indeed, I shamelessly adapt the subtitle of this chapter from feminist poet and scholar Adrienne Rich's germinal essay "Notes Towards a Politics of Location" (1986). It's in her spirit of fruitful provocation that I write this chapter.

In short, the aspiration of this chapter is to begin to clear a path for a queer study of deindustrialization, and perhaps most importantly, to entice scholars to travel along it.[4] My argument is this: deindustrialization, as a significant social, economic, and cultural shift, did not leave out queers. To better understand the queer and labor histories of the late twentieth century, historians must examine the effects of deindustrialization on queer communities.

First, I will examine the historiography of deindustrialization, illustrating the broad shift from immediate polemic response to attempts to make sense of the wider cultural impact of the process. I will pay close mind to who is made the focus of these studies and, crucially, whose lives are mourned. Second, I will examine queer theory and history and attempt to make a case for a renewed examination of deindustrialization and labor more broadly, when historians and theorists discuss queer and trans lives. Lastly, I will provide some avenues for further research and show how future scholars might bring renewed focus to queer lives during deindustrialization and its 'half-life.' Crucially, I want to provide an argument for a queer study of deindustrialization beyond the reasoning that queer people are marginalized within industrial labor and thus deserve to be represented in scholarship. I hope to go beyond that in arguing that a queer perspective in and of itself can shed new light on how deindustrialization's unfinished business continues to shape societies.

Deindustrialization – Who Is She?

Deindustrialization's aftermath and presence stretches beyond shuttered factories. Across North America and Western Europe, working-class communities, cultures, bodies, and politics have been irrevocably shaped by the deindustrialization that characterized much of the waning decades of the twentieth century. Plant closures and capital flight ripped apart single-industry towns while the deleterious aftereffects of the industry lingered in workers' bodies and the land. In many cases, the factory was the locus of the community, and with its removal, working-class communities and subjectivities are left adrift. Anglo-American academics initially positioned their work as a political response resisting deindustrialization, but from the 1990s on, the scholarly agenda shifted to simply try and make sense of the social and cultural fallout deindustrialization has wrought.[5] However, deindustrialization is not something confined to this period, or this so-called Western geography.[6]

Sherry Lee Linkon introduced the concept of deindustrialization's 'half-life,' comparing the lingering aftereffects of deindustrialization to the decay of radioactive material. Thus, the past is not simply confined to the past, and the violence of deindustrialization goes beyond the figures of the jobless steelworkers (Linkon, 2018, pp. 2–3). Deindustrialization lingers in later generations, and it continues to shape communities. Scholars of deindustrialization, often in a Thompsonian vein, seek to understand how this process affected workers' lives and identities from a place of respect and solidarity. As eminent scholars Jefferson Cowie and Joseph Heathcott write: "The point of departure for any discussion of deindustrialization must be respect for the despair and betrayal felt by workers as their mines, factories, and mills were padlocked, abandoned, turned into artsy shopping spaces, or even dynamited" (Cowie and Heathcott, 2003, p. 1). I suggest that we must push ourselves further still to better understand which workers are mourned, which workers are made visible in scholarship, and thus whose lives and labor are deemed valuable.

Deindustrialization studies, broadly speaking, has often focused on a mythologized white male and heterosexual proletarian – the no-nonsense steelworker or the hardworking miner. We see this view in the field's earliest works, especially those that home in on the recent aftermath of a particular wave of plant closure in a certain region or community.[7] The Rust Belt of the US looms large in particular. Further, many of the influential works in the field that interrogate gender focus in on industrial masculinities rather than the lived experiences of women or other genders.[8] In a similar vein, concerning race, there is a danger of what Gurminder Bhambra calls 'methodological whiteness.' Bhambra (2017) argues that in discussions of deindustrialization, "working-class" operates as a signifier that takes whiteness as implicit.[9] Similarly, we must resist a methodological straightness that takes heterosexuality and accompanying structures like the nuclear family as given.

While many of the works cited earlier are foundational to the field, and certainly the significance of deindustrialization to the future of this sort of hegemonic working-class masculinity is important, it is unwise to confine the social fallout of deindustrialization just to certain workers, when the reality is much broader. Recently, interventions from scholars focusing on experiences of women, racialized and immigrant workers have begun to complicate this picture, showing how the impact of deindustrialization stretches beyond the social world of certain white male workers.[10] As Alice Kessler-Harris (1993, p. 195) argued some 30 years ago of the future of US labor history, the male paradigm must be decentered, for otherwise the male workplace is framed as the ultimate progenitor of working-classness. She writes:

It is time for a new strategy – for a radical reconceptualization that takes on "the central organizing conception of labor history-class." It is time to see what happens when we pull class apart – to ask if it is possible to construct a discussion of the relation of production and the allocation of its product in a way that more fully encompasses the consciousness and identity of the people who participate in economic society. To do that we need to investigate the role of gender in shaping the ideas and actions of men and women and therefore in structuring the economic universe.

(Kessler-Harris, 1993, p. 193)

I propose a similar investigation along the lines of queerness and examine how sexuality shaped the social fallout of deindustrialization.

To begin, we must look at the nuclear family and the economic structures that reproduced it. Following the Second World War, much of the capitalist West underwent an economic boom. A driving force behind this boom was the implementation of industrial policy which prioritized mass production and mass consumption powered by industry. This industrial policy has come to be known by scholars as Fordism.[11] A key part of Fordism was the 'family wage.' A male breadwinner earned a so-called family wage – which, along with precarious gendered and racialized labor, was enough to keep reproducing a heterosexual nuclear family (Vosko, 2000, pp. 21–23). In essence, white families were able to subsist solely on a family wage because they were able to rely on un-or-poorly paid labor from racialized people and women to make up the difference. As Melinda Cooper writes: "As an instrument of redistribution, the standard Fordist wage actively policed the boundaries between women and men's work and white and Black men's labor, and in its social-insurance dimensions, it was inseparable from the imperative of sexual normativity" (Cooper, 2019, p. 23). In the US, for example, 'good jobs' in industry came with employer-sponsored health insurance.[12] With this, industrial production was not only embedded in a social order that reproduced heterosexuality as imperative, but it was an integral part of it. To access the full benefits of the postwar compromise, proximity to the heterosexual nuclear family was crucial. This process created a certain kind of industrial masculinity that, while hegemonic, was also quite precarious.

In *Exit Zero*, Christine Walley straddles the lines between history, autoethnography, and memoir as she chronicles her family's story of living through industrial and post-industrial Chicago. Her father, after the steel mill closes and he is left jobless, still clings to his steel-worker identity, even after he picks up precarious work as a security guard (Walley, 2013, p. 74). Walley notes that middle-class commentators are quick to pin an industrial masculinity as central to working-class communities. To Walley, this masculinity is instead contingent on a specific class position that was as exploited as it was hegemonic. She writes: "Deindustrialization had exposed the often-unsuspected fragility beneath the bravado of men like my father" (Walley, 2013, p. 76). The emasculated father, as Sherry Lee Linkon writes, is a common trope in literary representations of deindustrialized communities (Linkon, 2014, pp. 152–155). Fathers, now disconnected from their job, and thus the font of masculinity that they draw upon, are now left directionless. As Linkon continues, in many literary representations this emasculation has the effect of 'displacing' the futures of their sons now that the family tradition of working in the mine or factory is impossible to continue. But what of those whose futures were already displaced and were perhaps already disconnected from that type of masculinity?

I bring up the story of Walley's father not to create a strict oppositional dichotomy between such men and the queer people I seek to bring to the forefront. Rather, I wish to show a relationship. Deindustrialization is a process that interlocks with gender. It represented a shift away from Fordist capitalism and the family wage. In fact, Walley's father's new precarious employment as a security guard is illustrative of this wider structural shift. If this model regulated people, including queer people, into the nuclear family through work, what were the implications of its demise? Paradoxically, as I discuss in the next section, industrial production also provided the preconditions for queer identity and community. This contradiction, with the family wage both reproducing heterosexuality and providing the economic and social preconditions for other forms of sexual identity, crystallized a certain kind of industrial masculinity in tension with the nuclear family.

The (De)industrial Queer

Beyond the argument about queer representation, and the dangers of letting 'working-class' be coded as always already straight, there is a historical and empirical argument to be made as to the importance of industry and its decline to queer histories. Germinal texts in queer studies from John D'Emilio's 'Capitalism and Gay Identity' to George Chauncey's *Gay New York* and Leslie Feinberg's *Stone Butch Blues* all – in their own ways – underscore the importance of industrial capitalism to the emergence of gay community and identity as we know them in North America and Western Europe.[13] As D'Emilio argues, the increased dominance of wage-labor and the wave of urbanization in the nineteenth century allowed individuals to construct identities based on a personal life that existed outside the heterosexual family

(D'Emilio, 1993, p. 470). If one is earning a wage rather than being part of an interdependent family unit, one may have the freedom not only to engage in more sex outside the bounds of the family unit but also to form an identity around queer sex. This provides a valuable counterpoint to a more standard Foucauldian interpretation that places regulation from above front and center in the formation of modern sexuality, with a particular eye to the medical and juridical.[14] In D'Emilio's interpretation, there is both agency and regulation happening at the same time, specifically in the realm of social reproduction.[15]

Given these entangled histories of industrial capitalism and queer identity, why then, has deindustrialization not been treated with a similar level of significance by queer historians? Whether or not industrial labor in and of itself was a queer place, the economic and social transformation that deindustrialization brought about must be significant for queer people. One explanation for this absence is that queer theory often shifts away from class analysis, perhaps due to its emergence during the broader post-structuralist turn in humanities scholarship in the post-Cold War period. Indeed, class analysis alone will not get us to a full understanding of queer lives. Of course, the inverse is also true: without examining how labor and production shape social structure, how can we fully understand how sexuality and gender do? Granted, it is perhaps not surprising that queer studies have had other preoccupations. The agenda for the field has been shaped by flashpoint events like Stonewall, the rise and fall of gay liberation, increased visibility, the AIDS crisis, and some important political victories – and losses. In particular, the AIDS crisis shifted the focus of many queer activists from broad-based liberation to mere survival.[16] We might also hypothesize that because of the AIDS crisis, acts of solidarity between queers and those threatened by deindustrialization, like Lesbians and Gays Support the Miners, became more of an exception than the rule (Kelliher, 2021).

If we begin to place these events in conversation with the onset of deindustrialization, we can get a fuller picture of their significance. Particularly, we can get a better picture of how these events have shaped queer people's labor. While an in-depth analysis relating these events to broader histories of deindustrialization is a worthy endeavor, it is outside the scope of this chapter. Rather, in a spirit of trying to open up a space for future research, I will now follow these two lines of inquiry: the supposed incommensurability of Marxism and queer theory and the specter of deindustrialization in queer history.

Incommensurability

The lack of a conversation between the fields of deindustrialization studies and queer studies is illuminated by the debate about the compatibility of queer theory and Marxism.[17] Though class has always been central to deindustrialization studies, many of the field's eminent scholars, like Cowie (2019), Barry Bluestone and Bennett Harrison (1982) are far from being ardent Marxists. Despite that, the humanist Marxism of the British New Left, like the work of E. P. Thompson and Raymond Williams, has had an outsized influence on the field (Lawson, 2020, pp. 3–4). Compared to Marxism, queer theory might be seen as idealistic and un-materialistic. Early works of queer history, like those of D'Emilio, and Gary Kinsman (1987) in the Canadian context, are strongly influenced by Marxist critique, like the early gay liberation movement as a whole. But in the waning decades of the twentieth century, like many fields, queer studies turned to post-structuralism for theoretical backing, birthing what is now called queer theory. Thus, I counterpose Marxism and queer theory because they are respectively concerned with class and sexuality, the two ideas that scholars must reckon with in any queer study of deindustrialization. In teasing out how Marxism and queer theory do and do not agree, I hope to point to new directions for how class and sexuality may be approached in deindustrialization studies.

In stark contrast to Marxism, queer theory's aims are nebulous. As feminist theorist bell hooks speaks of queer, she means:

> queer not as being about who you're having sex with – that can be a dimension of it – but queer as being about the self that is at odds with everything around it and it has to invent and create and find a place to speak and to thrive and to live.[18]

Thus, the queer faces the material environment as an outside unto their self, and the task of the queer is to find a space within the hostile material to exist and to thrive. This seems at odds with a standard Marxist interpretation of material conditions and indeed resistance to oppression. Rather than the focus on a system, queer theory's focus is on a subject. Queer theory often purports to bring about a 'new world' but not in a capital-C Communist way. The task of queer theory, very broadly and perhaps uncharitably defined, is to reject and resist all it surrounds, with an eye to radical emancipation of queer subjects through subversive queer acts. This is the main cleavage often perceived between these two bodies of work: Marxism is about broad-based class liberation; queer theory is about individual, subjective resistance.

As Petrus Liu (2020) argues, queer theory and Marxism are not truly incommensurable in the sense of complete incompatibility, but rather they are dialectical. When we conceptualize the two frameworks as different ways of understanding society and its structure, rather than as ways to get at two different identities/positions (i.e., sexuality and class), we can have a "torturous conversation" between the two. Both bodies of work emphasize the material, albeit in different ways. Scholars can and should keep the two in dialogue. As both theories emerge out of the lived experiences of workers, queers, and working queers, and as scholars who should approach these lived experiences with respect, we have a duty to engage in Liu's 'torturous conversation.' Indeed, queer performance theorist Joshua Chambers-Letson writes of a "communism of incommensurability":

> In order to foster a world of boundless exchangeability, capitalism flattens difference into equivalence, making singularity into commensurability. In the place of capital's commons of equivalence, communism calls for a commons of incommensurability: a sphere of relation structured less by the flat social fictions of possession, equality, and equivalence, than by a mode of sharing out, just redistribution, and being together in racial and sexual particularity.
>
> *(Chambers-Letson, 2018, p. xx)*

This communism of incommensurability allows us to examine the deindustrial half-life with a queer lens. Rather than flattening out everything into a broad notion of 'community' or something like it, the effects of deindustrialization can be seen in their queer particularity, without losing sight of the basic social relations that shape these effects.

Specters of Queers Past

Where then might historians of queer labor take the field? The literature on queer labor history is small but mighty, with few works actively examining the significance of deindustrialization.

The work of historians Allan Bérubé and Miriam Frank, examining queer people in the labor movement in the postwar US offers crucial context. However, this scholarship – the work of Frank (2014) in particular – focuses on bargaining gains made by queer people and their unions – deindustrialization is mentioned only briefly. This is incredibly important history that must be told, but this narrative of queer labor justice must be contrasted with the simultaneous erosion in union power. One moment in queer labor history that is also very much about deindustrialization and has been comparatively well studied is the Lesbians and Gays Support the Miners (LGSM) solidarity group during the 1984–1985 Miners' Strike in the UK. LGSM was formed of like-minded gays and lesbians who raised money for striking miners from the gay community. This represented an until-then-unseen closeness and solidarity between a mainstream union and LGBT activists in Britain during the fight against the union-busting, austerity, and homophobia of the Thatcher government.[19] Anne Balay's work on queer workers in the steel industry also provides us with direction. Balay (2014) contrasts the simultaneous erosion of worker's conditions in the steel industry with the seeming upswing of LGBTQ rights in the 1990s and 2000s. When a homophobic hypermasculinity emerges in some steel communities, what implications does that have for queer workers and communities? We might think of Leslie Feinberg's (2014) *Stone Butch Blues,* where butch Jess takes a job at a cannery, gets involved in a union, but their machine is sabotaged by a coworker, leaving them injured and unemployed.

Within less-labor-focused queer studies, in a 2014 special issue of leading journal *GLQ* on the American Midwest, deindustrialization is rarely even mentioned, reduced to passing mentions of "working-class cultures" and "heartland" (Manalansan et al., 2014). Rather, the Midwest is examined as heteronormative middle America – and while the authors in this issue work to destabilize that inaccurate notion, the economic history that produced that heteronormative family structure is absented. More scholarship in queer history, theory, and studies must examine queer lives outside the metropole, and most certainly outside cities, and these scholars are a part of that necessary work. But deindustrialization needs to be in the picture.

This can be done by reading queer scholarship with an eye for deindustrialization. One window into this connection is through gentrification. As many scholars have shown—and we see in our daily lives, deindustrialization and gentrification are linked inextricably. For every factory that closes in a city, chances are it will be turned to luxury lofts, demolished to make way for blocky five-over-ones or turned into a "maker space."[20] Sarah Schulman's (2012) *Gentrification of the Mind,* her memoir of the AIDS epidemic, shows how the "literal gentrification of cities" and the shrinking of the queer political imagination relate. To Schulman, the vibrant queer political culture that birthed ACT UP, an activist group fighting for justice during the AIDS crisis, is no more because the material conditions that made such resistance happen have shifted so greatly. High rents bar working queers who wish to migrate to the metropole for community, safety, and crucially, safer work. As Schulman laments, cities are often left with a preponderance of corporate queers with Ivy League degrees, leaving working-class queers and a radical queer politics sidelined in favor of a narrow liberal outlook. As Jin Haritaworn writes, as gentrification takes hold and certain environments are regenerated for certain queers, we must ask:

> [What] else is going on, and who else is on the scene as certain queer bodies become a lovely sight in the shadow of racialized Others; as transgender bodies, whose dehumanization rarely gains the status of injustice, gain visibility as colourful subjects in

revitalized areas that have let go of people of colour; and as assimilated rights-bearing subjects re/turn towards murderous times and places with queer nostalgia. It further involves asking who or what becomes legible as gay, queer or trans, and who gets run over on the intersections.

(Haritaworn, 2015, pp. 3–4)

To take Haritaworn's insights over to deindustrialization, we must not let a queer study of deindustrialization be an ironic manufactory of white queer nostalgia for an industrial past previously thought to be straight. If we are to examine queer lives, it must not be to cast them as a valorized figure in contrast to the specter of the racialized Other that haunts many deindustrialized areas, as seen clearly in both Brexit and the Trump campaign. We cannot 'salvage' the white gay steelworker of Youngstown to further cast shadow upon racialized others. In short, this queer study of deindustrialization I propose must not succumb to reactionary fears. It must be one that is not only intersectional in method but also oriented to justice for deindustrialized areas that goes beyond good and bad memories but to a fair future.

Deindustrialization's role in the shifting queer political imaginary affects scholars who study at the nexus I describe in this chapter in two ways. First, this is the world we live and work in and the political imaginary of younger scholars in particular, who have never lived under the conditions of Fordism. Second, because queer histories generally focus on metropolitan urban environments which have weathered deindustrialization better, deindustrialization's role is generally subsumed into neoliberalism or gentrification. To look at this from a cultural perspective, if it were not for deindustrialization, the Detroit Black queer ball culture that Marlon M. Bailey (2013) examines so generously in *Butch Queens Up in Pumps* would not have existed in such ways. Nor would Detroit techno. Examining queer and trans working-class lives with an eye to deindustrialization can help disturb the idea that queers must flee the always already hostile periphery to the welcoming metropole – clearly demarcating where queer life (especially queer political life) is and is not.

Traces of Queer Lives in Deindustrialization

Throughout this chapter, I have been critical of existing scholarship in deindustrialization studies. At the same time, my critique is rooted in the field's foundational commitment to the people and communities affected by deindustrialization. If we are to do right by them and to tell their stories, we must make sure that the tapestry of deindustrialization's story that we weave not only includes queer lives but shows how significant deindustrialization was for queer history. Therein lie the directions for further research. Queer and deindustrialization histories share similar resonances, along both methodological and thematic lines, including a heavy use of oral history and an impulse to honor and cultivate the stories of those on the margins. Another resonance that future scholars can explore is that of trauma, and the ephemeral traces that it can leave, whether we speak of the trauma of deindustrialization or violence against queer and trans people. How might these violences be remembered and their traces explored? How might scholars examine this in a way that is regenerative rather than voyeuristic?

As Steven High (2013) has noted, so much of deindustrialization scholarship has focused on loss and in particular, the loss of a working-class identity and indeed way of life. Likewise, queer history and theory has examined trauma through crisis, especially with regard to the AIDS crisis. Neither of these respective emphases is either surprising or unwarranted.

Much has been lost, whether the livelihoods in a mill town or the far, far too many lost to AIDS. What can this emphasis on trauma do for a queer study of deindustrialization? Conversely, what may it obscure? Both fields rely on both the ephemeral and the material to construct feelings of loss. For example, the 'structure of feeling' of deindustrialization is constituted by both the material conditions of the past and present (e.g., plant closure) and the ephemeral traces of what once was. With this, historians must contend with the inherent methodological difficulty in balancing both the material effects of deindustrialization on a base level and the ephemeral traces it leaves on places, bodies, and cultures that may not be necessarily accessible in the traditional archive. The challenge becomes more complex only when we try to get at the *queer* history.

As queer contrasts to Williams's 'structures of feeling,' Jose Esteban Muñoz's 'Ephemera as Evidence' and Ann Cvetkovich's 'archive of feelings' may help us get at queer histories of deindustrialization. Muñoz, a scholar of performance, argues that ephemeral traces of queer acts serve as valuable evidence for scholars, despite outdated notions of academic "rigor" that exclude queer lives from what is deemed good scholarship (Muñoz, 1996, pp. 6–7). He suggests that scholars move beyond a traditional archive, as it is unable to fully capture queer life, instead asking scholars to examine performance, art, and other nontraditional sources. Muñoz links Williams's structure of feelings to the queer ephemeral he describes. To him, queerness is itself a structure of feeling – a public culture built upon traces of queer acts. With this, looking at the constellation of sources he terms the ephemeral is not completely discon- nected from the material but is something that rather refashions it (Muñoz, 1996, p. 10). Essentially, Muñoz is making the case for a queer history and queer studies that goes beyond the traditional archive, rejecting methodological straightness in favor of methods that favor the ephemeral, the experimental, and the minoritarian. For the study I propose in this chap- ter, such an approach is fundamental for scholars of deindustrialization seeking to look at queer life. A focus on the queer ephemeral is not in any way something that is incompatible with the study of deindustrialization – something that is so grounded in material conditions and social relations shifting so rapidly – but rather something that colors in that existing evidence. An expansive focus of what could be considered evidence allows scholars to get at histories of sexuality, feelings, and indeed labor.

But where are we to find these traces? Muñoz, by his own admission, is making more of an argument as to what using queer performance as evidence *could* do methodologically rather than where such traces ought to be found and what they could say (Muñoz, 1996, p. 6). To think practically, scholars could incorporate more discussion of queer cultural production, material cultures, and autobiography. Those working with oral history can incorporate col- laborative mapping, photo elicitation, on-site interviews, and other methods that can take something otherwise hard to incorporate, like the façade of a warehouse, into something contextualized within a life story. Further, we can take an approach to 'life story' in our interview guides that does not unconsciously 'straighten' queer life by forcing it into a linear childhood-marriage-work-family-to-present narrative that privileges heteronormative life.

Ann Cvetkovich's notion of the 'archive of feelings' is valuable in helping us contextual- ize and interpret queer sources. Cvetkovich's work focuses on trauma in lesbian cultures and how it is and is not recorded. Trauma, like queer life, rarely leaves concrete records, thus, a new archive is needed. To Cvetkovich, the archive of feelings is more of a method than an actual brick-and-mortar repository of documents – it is reading cultural texts with an eye to memory, feeling, and emotion. As Cvetkovich writes: "the archive of feelings is both mate- rial and immaterial, at once incorporating objects that might not ordinarily be considered archival, and at the same time resisting documentation because sex and feelings are too personal or ephemeral to leave records" (Cvetkovich, 2003, p. 244). Here we might find resonance with Linkon's 'half-life.' The archive of feelings can provide a generative understanding of past damage and trauma that is a refusal to, in Linkon's words, 'get over it,' mixing a hope for change and regeneration with the very real trauma and mourning. The task of future scholars should be not only to record damage or rescue those voices from the "enormous condescension of posterity" but to go beyond damage and locate desire and regeneration (Thompson, 1977, p. 13).

Conclusion: Regeneration

The 2000 film *Billy Elliot* (Daldry, 2000) and its subsequent musical adaptation of the same name tell the story of Billy, a queer-coded boy learning to dance ballet in the North of England amid the 1984–1985 Miners' Strike. His father and brother are striking miners themselves and are initially hostile to Billy's dancing – relating it to femininity and, of course, homosexuality. However, this queer child quickly becomes the community's last hope as the strike drags on and the miners' fortunes grow dimmer. The community bands together to send Billy to audition for a prestigious ballet school in London, which Billy gets into. But, of course, the miners lost the strike. *Billy Elliot* is the perfect neoliberal tale of the deindustrial queer. There is nothing left for Billy in County Durham, the best he can do for his community is not only leave but perform a sort of gendered labor at odds with the masculine industrial labor of his family. But what of stories of deindustrialization that do not conform to an understanding of deindustrialization as loss without limit or an understanding of resource communities as always already homophobic and the metropole as always already welcoming?

This question is in part what this chapter has broached. Throughout this chapter, I have made two main, interrelated arguments for a queer study of deindustrialization. First, that queer people have not been adequately represented in histories of deindustrialization, as the field has generally been bound by a methodological straightness, contributing to a coding of the working class as always already straight. Second, I have argued that there is something particularly valuable for scholars in adopting a queer perspective on deindustrialization. With the critical use of queer theory, the relationship between sexuality, gender, class, and work can be explored more fulsomely, as can questions of memory and trauma. To back up these arguments and provide new directions for further study, I have discussed methodological resonances between the two fields, paying specific attention to ideas of public feelings, memory, oral history, and trauma.

I will conclude with a short discussion of regenerating both queer histories in deindustrialized places. Unangax̂ scholar Eve Tuck, in her essay 'Suspending Damage: A Letter to Communities,' urges scholars to take a pause on research that centers only damage to vulnerable communities and to instead center desire. Tuck acknowledges that the focus on damage on the part of researchers has been in part to catalog damage so redress can be sought. While this is a good intention, she argues that damage-centered research has reproduced a notion that the subjects of the research are always already ruined, traumatized, and irreparably damaged (Tuck, 2009, pp. 412–413). While Tuck is mostly speaking to her expertise in Indigenous studies, we can take her insights and apply them to the study I propose in this chapter. Whether we speak of the crises of AIDS or deindustrialization, much has been written – and indeed felt – about mourning. One of the questions I have posed in this chapter is 'who gets to be mourned?' However, scholars must also ask: what can be regenerated? How can communities affected by these crises like AIDS or deindustrialization or the interlocking systems of oppression like capitalism and heteropatriarchy regenerate themselves? We must be careful not to easily accept a queer regeneration along the lines that Jin Haritaworn diagnoses, in which certain respectable (white and bourgeois) queers arise from places once deemed degenerate – like a silk flower somehow blooming from the grounds of an abandoned textile factory (Haritaworn, 2015, pp. 4–7). Such a regeneration is inequitable on the face of it. We must not only examine the past of the deindustrial queer and continue to weave the complex and multivocal tapestry that we might have but also look to the future and to ways of living in kinder relations.

Notes

1 I use queer studies here to refer to a transdisciplinary study of queer lives, of which queer theory and history are a part. I use this term to keep the use of queer theory relegated to the specific post-structuralist school of thought that emerged in the 1990s, with key thinkers being Judith Butler, Eve Sedgwick, Michael Warner, Lauren Berlant, and Jack Halberstam, among others.

2 For an analysis of the connection between neoliberalism and the AIDS crisis, see McCaskell, T. (2016). *Queer Progress: From Homophobia to Homonationalism.* Toronto: Between the Lines.

3 For more on LGSM and LGBTQ-trade union links in Britain, see Kelliher, D. (2021). *Making Cultures of Solidarity: London and the 1984–5 Miners' Strike.* London and New York: Routledge; Robinson, L. (2013). *Gay Men and the Left in Post-War Britain: How the Personal Got Political.* Manchester: Manchester University Press; Purton, P. (2019). *Champions of Equality: Trade Unions and LGBT Rights in Britain.* London: Lawrence & Wishart.

4 I choose my words carefully here. I am not proposing a 'queering' of deindustrialization or arguing that deindustrialization itself is a queer process of some sort. My focus here is on how deindustrialization impacts and has impacted queer communities rather than potential queer particularities of the process.

5 For a good historiographical overview of these changes, see Lawson, C. (2020). Making Sense of the Ruins: The Historiography of Deindustrialisation and Its Continued Relevance in Neoliberal Times. *History Compass,* 18(8). https://doi.org/10.1111/hic3.12619

6 I am focusing on the wave of deindustrialization starting in the 1970s with the onset of the neoliberal transition in North America and Western Europe – the imperial core, if you will. Following the collapse of the Eastern Bloc and USSR, there has been significant deindustrialization in these regions. And, of course, deindustrialization somewhere often means industrialization elsewhere – often the Global South. I situate this chapter's geographical focus within North America and Western Europe, with an even stronger focus on the Anglophone world. For empire and deindustrialization, see Sarkar, P. (1992). De-Industrialisation Through Colonial Trade. *Journal of Contemporary Asia,* 22(3). http://www.jstor.org.lib-ezproxy.concordia.ca/stable/4409201; Roy, T. (2000). De-Industrialisation: Alternative View. *Economic and Political Weekly,* 35(17). http://www.jstor.org.lib-ezproxy.concordia.ca/stable/4409201

7 For examples of earlier works in the field that have a strong focus on the way certain workers were affected by plant closure, see Dudley, K.M. (1994). *The End of The Line: Lost Jobs, New Lives in Postindustrial America. Morality and Society.* Chicago: University of Chicago Press; Pappas, G. (1989). *The Magic City: Unemployment in a Working-Class Community.* Ithaca, NY: Cornell University Press.

8 For interrogations of gender and industrial masculinity, see McIvor, A. (2013). *Working Lives: Work in Britain since 1945.* Basingstoke: Palgrave Macmillan; Walkerdine, V. and Jimenez, L. (2012). *Gender, Work and Community After De-Industrialisation.* London: Palgrave Macmillan.

9 For a discussion of this issue deeper in the British context, see Matera, M. et al. (2023). Introduction: Marking Race in Twentieth Century British History. *Twentieth Century British History,* 34(3). https://doi.org/10.1093/tcbh/hwad036

10 For new analyses that push the field of deindustrialization studies into new directions regarding race and gender, see Bonfiglioli, C. (2019). *Women and Industry in the Balkans: The Rise and Fall of the Yugoslav Textile Sector.* London: I.B. Taurus; Hackworth, J. (2019). *Manufacturing*

Decline. New York: Columbia University Press; Clarke, J. (2015). Closing Time: Deindustrialization and Nostalgia in Contemporary France. *History Workshop Journal*, 79. http://www.jstor.org.lib-ezproxy.concordia.ca/stable/43917311; Kalra, V. (2000). *From Textile Mills to Taxi Ranks: Experiences of Migration, Labour and Social Change*. New York: Routledge.

11 For the initial coinage of the phrase, see Gramsci, A. (1999). Americanism and Fordism. In *Selections from the Prison Notebooks*. London: ElecBook.

12 For more on this dynamic, along with how a transition to pink-collar health care work occurred in the US Rust Belt following plant closure, see Winant, G. (2021). *The Next Shift: The Fall of Industry and the Rise of Health Care in Rust Belt America*. Cambridge, MA: Harvard University Press.

13 To be clear, I am referring to a gay community in the way that 'homosexual,' 'gay,' 'lesbian,' and other words exist as identity signifiers in a broadly Western and contemporary context. Neither I nor D'Emilio are suggesting that same-gender attraction or sex did not happen before industrial capitalism. D'Emilio, J. (1993). Capitalism and Gay Identity. In Abelove, H., Barale, M.A. and Halperin, D.M. (eds.) *The Lesbian and Gay Studies Reader*. London and New York: Routledge; Chauncey, G. (1994). *Gay New York: Gender, Urban Culture, and the Makings of the Gay Male World, 1890–1940*. New York: Basic Books.

14 See Part Four of Foucault, M. (1990). *The History of Sexuality*. Vol. 1. New York: Vintage.

15 Further, D'Emilio's analysis is very much confined to a US-centric milieu in which the climax of queer history is Stonewall, from which all other homosexuality springs, which is generally considered to be a parochial interpretation of queer history. For a critical discussion of the global resonances (and lack thereof) of Stonewall, see Arondekar, A. (2020). The Sex of History, or Object/Matters. *History Workshop Journal*, 89. https://doi.org/10.1093/HWJ/DBZ053. For an examination of 'queer work' focusing on service labor and cruise ships in the postwar era, see Bérubé, A. (2011). 'Queer Work' and Labor History. In D'Emilio, J. and Freedman, E.B. (eds.) *My Desire for History: Essays in Gay, Community, and Labor History*. Chapel Hill: University of North Carolina Press.

16 For an overview of how the AIDS crisis and neoliberal governance impacted LGBTQ activism and institutions in the US, ultimately resulting in a large degree of non-profitization, see Beam, M. (2018). *Gay, Inc: The Nonprofitization of Queer Politics*. University of Minnesota Press.

17 For an introduction to debate of incommensurability of queer theory and Marxism, see Eng, D.L. and Puar, J.K. (2020). Introduction: Left of Queer. *Social Text*, 38(4). https://doi.org/10.1215/01642472-8680414. For further discussion, see Lewis, H. (2022). *The Politics of Everybody: Feminism, Queer Theory, and Marxism at the Intersection*, 2nd ed. London: Zed Books.

18 This is far from the only or definitive definition of queerness but simply a popular one: hooks, b. (2014). *Are You Still a Slave? Liberating the Black Female Body*. Eugene Lang College. For the challenges of defining queerness and queer theory, see Berlant, L. and Warner, M. (1995). What Does Queer Theory Teach Us about X? *PMLA*, 110(3). http://www.jstor.org.lib-ezproxy.concordia.ca/stable/462930

19 For more on the LGSM, see Robinson, L. (2013). *Gay Men and the Left in Britain: How the Personal Got Political*. Manchester: Manchester University Press; Kelliher, D. (2021). *Making Cultures of Solidarity: London and the 1984–5 Miners' Strike*. London and New York: Routledge.

20 In North America, 'five-over-one' apartment buildings (five floors of residential on top of one floor of retail) are increasingly popular new construction in gentrifying areas, promising increased density, quality of life, and a solution to the housing crisis. For popular critiques of the architectural style and its myriad failures, see Wagner, K. (2023, March 31). Single-Stair Layouts Are Not Going to Fix the Housing Crisis. *The Nation*. https://www.thenation.com/article/society/single-stair-building-codes-housing/; Kodé, A. (2023, January 20). America, the Bland. *New York Times*. https://www.nytimes.com/2023/01/20/realestate/housing-developments-city-architecture.html.

Reference List

Arondekar, Anjali. (2020). The Sex of History, or Object/Matters. *History Workshop Journal*, 89, pp. 207–13. https://doi.org/10.1093/HWJ/DBZ053

Anderson, M. (dir.). (1997). *The Simpsons*, Season 8, episode 15, "Homer's Phobia." Aired 16 February 1997.

Bailey, Marlon M. (2013). *Butch Queens up in Pumps: Gender, Performance, and Ballroom Culture in Detroit*. University of Michigan Press. https://doi.org/10.3998/mpub.799908

Balay, Anne. (2014). *Steel Closets: Voices of Gay, Lesbian, and Transgender Steelworkers*. Chapel Hill: University of North Carolina Press.

Beam, Myrl. (2018). *Gay, Inc: The Nonprofitization of Queer Politics*. University of Minnesota Press. http://www.jstor.org.lib-ezproxy.concordia.ca/stable/10.5749/j.ctv3dnp0n

Berlant, Lauren and Warner, Michael. (1995). What Does Queer Theory Teach Us About X? *PMLA*, 110(3), pp. 343–349. http://www.jstor.org.lib-ezproxy.concordia.ca/stable/462930

Bérubé, Allan. (2011). 'Queer Work' and Labor History. In D'Emilio, John and Freedman, Estelle B. (eds.) *My Desire for History: Essays in Gay, Community, and Labor History*. Chapel Hill: University of North Carolina Press, pp. 259–269.

Bhambra, Gurminder K. (2017). Brexit, Trump, and 'Methodological Whiteness': On the Misrecognition of Race and Class. *The British Journal of Sociology*, 68(S1), pp. S214–S32. https://doi.org/https://doi.org/10.1111/1468-4446.12317

Bluestone, Barry and Harrison, Bennett. (1982). *The Deindustrialization of America: Plant Closings, Community Abandonment and the Dismantling of Basic Industry*. New York: Basic Books.

Bonfiglioli, Chiara. (2019). *Women and Industry in the Balkans: The Rise and Fall of the Yugoslav Textile Sector*. London: I.B. Taurus.

Chambers-Letson, Joshua. (2018). *After the Party: A Manifesto for Queer of Color Life*. New York: NYU Press.

Chauncey, George. (1994). *Gay New York: Gender, Urban Culture, and the Makings of the Gay Male World, 1890–1940*. New York: Basic Books.

Clarke, Jackie. (2015). Closing Time: Deindustrialization and Nostalgia in Contemporary France. *History Workshop Journal*, 79, pp. 107–125. http://www.jstor.org.lib-ezproxy.concordia.ca/stable/43917311

Cooper, Melinda. (2019). *Family Values: Between Neoliberalism and the New Social Conservatism*. New York: Zone Books.

Cowie, Jefferson. (2019). *Capital Moves: RCA's Seventy-Year Quest for Cheap Labor*. Ithaca, NY: Cornell University Press.

Cowie, Jefferson and Joseph Heathcott. (2003). *Beyond the Ruins: The Meanings of Deindustrialization*. Ithaca, NY: Cornell University Press.

Cvetkovich, Ann. (2003). *An Archive of Feelings: Trauma, Sexuality and Lesbian Public Cultures*. Durham: Duke University Press.

Daldry, Stephen. (2000). *Billy Elliot. 110 Minutes*. United Kingdom: Universal.

D'Emilio, John. (1993). Capitalism and Gay Identity. In Abelove, Henry, Barale, Michèle Aina and Halperin, David M. (eds.) *The Lesbian and Gay Studies Reader*. London and New York: Routledge, 467–476.

Eng, David L. and Puar, Jasbir K. (2020). Introduction: Left of Queer. *Social Text*, 38(4), pp. 1–24. https://doi.org/10.1215/01642472-8680414

Feinberg, Leslie. (2014). *Stone Butch Blues*. 20th Anniversary ed. Leslie Feinberg, 1993.

Foucault, Michel. (1990). *The History of Sexuality*. Translated by Robert Hurley. Vol. 1. New York: Vintage, 1978.

Frank, Miriam. (2014). *Out in the Union: A Labor History of Queer America*. Philadelphia, PA: Temple University Press.

Gramsci, Antonio. (1999). Americanism and Fordism. In *Selections from the Prison Notebooks*. London: ElecBook, 561–563.

Hackworth, Jason. (2019). *Manufacturing Decline*. New York: Columbia University Press. https://doi.org/10.7312/hack19372

Haritaworn, Jin. (2015). *Queer Lovers and Hateful Others: Regenerating Violent Times and Places*. London: Pluto Press.

High, Steven. (2013). 'The Wounds of Class': A Historiographical Reflection on the Study of Deindustrialization, 1973–2013. *History Compass*, 11(11), pp. 994–1007.

hooks, bell. (2014, May 6). *Are You Still a Slave? Liberating the Black Female Body*. Eugene Lang College.

Kalra, Virinda. (2000). *From Textile Mills to Taxi Ranks: Experiences of Migration, Labour and Social Change*. New York: Routledge.

Kelliher, Diarmaid. (2021). *Making Cultures of Solidarity: London and the 1984–5 Miners' Strike*. London and New York: Routledge.

Kessler-Harris, Alice. (1993). Treating the Male as 'Other': Redefining the Parameters of Labor History. *Labor History*, 34(2–3), pp. 190–204. https://doi.org/10.1080/00236569300890121

Kinsman, Gary. (1987). *The Regulation of Desire: Sexuality in Canada*. 1st ed. Montreal: Black Rose Books.

Kodé, Anna. (2023, January 20). America, the Bland. *New York Times*. https://www.nytimes.com/2023/01/20/realestate/housing-developments-city-architecture.html

Lawson, Christopher. (2020). Making Sense of the Ruins: The Historiography of Deindustrialisation and Its Continued Relevance in Neoliberal Times. *History Compass*, 18(8). https://doi.org/https://doi.org/10.1111/hic3.12619

Lewis, Holly. (2022). *The Politics of Everybody: Feminism, Queer Theory, and Marxism at the Intersection*. 2nd ed. London: Zed Books.

Linkon, Sherry Lee. (2014). Men without Work: White Working-Class Masculinity in Deindustrialization Fiction. *Contemporary Literature*, 55(1), 148–167. http://www.jstor.org.lib-ezproxy.concordia.ca/stable/43297950.

Liu, Petrus. (2020). Queer Theory and the Specter of Materialism. *Social Text*, 38(4), pp. 25–47. https://doi.org/10.1215/01642472-8680426

Manalansan, Martin F., IV, Nadeau, Chantal, Rodríguez, Richard T. and Somerville, Siobhan B. (2014). Queering the Middle: Race, Region, and a Queer Midwest. *GLQ: A Journal of Lesbian and Gay Studies*, 20(1–2), pp. 1–12. https://doi.org/10.1215/10642684-2370270

Matera, Marc, Natarajan, Radhika, Perry, Kennetta Hammond, Schofield, Camilla and Waters, Rob. (2023). Introduction: Marking Race in Twentieth Century British History. *Twentieth Century British History*, 34(3), pp. 407–414. https://doi.org/10.1093/tcbh/hwad036

McCaskell, Tim. (2016). *Queer Progress: From Homophobia to Homonationalism*. Toronto: Between the Lines.

McIvor, Arthur. (2013). *Working Lives: Work in Britain since 1945*. Basingstoke: Palgrave Macmillan.

Muñoz, José Esteban. (1996). Ephemera as Evidence: Introductory Notes to Queer Acts. *Women & Performance*, 8(2), pp. 5–16. https://doi.org/10.1080/07407709608571228

Purton, Peter. (2019). *Champions of Equality: Trade Unions and LGBT Rights in Britain*. London: Lawrence & Wishart.

Rich, Adrienne. (1986). Notes Towards a Politics of Location. In *Blood, Bread and Poetry: Selected Prose 1979–1985*. New York: Norton, 210–231.

Robinson, Lucy. (2013). *Gay Men and the Left in Post-War Britain: How the Personal Got Political*. Manchester: Manchester University Press.

Schulman, Sarah. (2012). *The Gentrification of the Mind: Witness to a Lost Imagination*. Berkeley, CA: University of California Press.

Thompson, E.P. (1977). *The Making of the English Working Class*. Harmondsworth: Penguin, 1963.

Tuck, Eve. (2009). Suspending Damage: A Letter to Communities. *Harvard Educational Review*, 79(3), pp. 409–427.

Vosko, Leah. (2000). *Temporary Work: The Gendered Rise of a Precarious Employment Relationship*. Toronto: University of Toronto Press.

Wagner, Kate. (2023, March 31). Single-Stair Layouts Are Not Going to Fix the Housing Crisis. *The Nation*. https://www.thenation.com/article/society/single-stair-building-codes-housing/

Walkerdine, Valerie and Jimenez, Luis. (2012). *Gender, Work and Community after De-Industrialisation*. London: Palgrave Macmillan.

Walley, Christine. (2013). *Exit Zero: Family and Class in Postindustrial Chicago*. Chicago: University of Chicago Press.

Winant, Gabriel. (2021). *The Next Shift: The Fall of Industry and the Rise of Health Care in Rust Belt America*. Cambridge, MA: Harvard University Press.

PART IV

The Critical Cultural Work of Representations

INTRODUCTION
The Critical Cultural Work of Representations

Sherry Lee Linkon

Introduction

'Representations' is a capacious term. As an action, representation emphasizes the process of making meaning; as an object, it encompasses a vast range of texts through which meaning is constructed and circulates. Nearly every chapter of this volume presents analysis based, at least in part, on representations of some kind, and academic writing itself is a representation. Still, as the chapters in this part demonstrate, critical readings of a wide range of representations can provide fresh insights into the significance of and responses to deindustrialization. These chapters also suggest the value of approaching representations, especially artistic and creative texts, through a more critical lens.

Within deindustrialization studies, we most often foreground documentary representations, especially photographs and interviews that focus on the conditions of industrial and deindustrial labor or on how workers, their families, and residents of deindustrialized communities describe their lives. We know that these forms are not objective or transparent. Alessandro Portelli argued that oral histories are inherently subjective, revealing not what happened to people but "what they wanted to do, what they believed they were doing, and what they now think they did" (Portelli, 1991, p. 67). Photographers, too, make choices about focus and framing, sometimes quite deliberately and sometimes without conscious intent, and professional, artistic, and household photographs all reflect how their creators see things. Subjectivity allows access to the perspectives of participants in history and culture, enabling us to understand the meaning and human consequences of economic change. Indeed, part of what we value in representations is that they give us access not so much to what happened to people but, as Herbert Gutman famously suggested, to what they did with what was done to them (Gutman, 1987, pp. 326–328).

Perception, memory, response, and affect have become ever more central concerns of deindustrialization studies as the events and shifts we study recede in time. Over the years, we may lose access to primary sources and to people with firsthand experience. Equally important, as I have argued, deindustrialization continues to influence social actors and communities across time, but its meanings change. The children and grandchildren of displaced workers see the past differently from those who experienced plant closings first hand, and,

DOI: 10.4324/9781003308324-26

like all representations, their stories, songs, and images reflect their perspectives and position-alities (Linkon, 2018). Portelli's argument about what oral histories reveal applies equally to the artist designing a commemorative sculpture, the poet imagining how residents saw "no trespassing" signs outside the mill where their fathers worked, or the choreographer staging a dance performance inside an abandoned factory.[1] At the same time, the subjectiv-ity of these artists differs from that of former coal miners or shoemakers. Their connection with deindustrialization is more distant and retrospective, and their work is shaped by their aesthetic frameworks, tools, and purposes. Such representations offer nuanced, constructed responses to the economic, social, and political shifts associated with deindustrialization. Further, because these representations reach audiences far beyond the archive, heritage site, or academic book or article, they also help us understand how ideas about work, place, and capitalism circulate. If we are interested in the half-life of deindustrialization, and especially if we are interested in the influence of economic change on politics and culture, creative representations are crucial sources.

While deindustrialization studies scholars have not ignored these representations, we have also not engaged with them as fully as we could. In part, this is a matter of disciplinary con-ventions. Historians and social scientists dominate this field, and the questions and methods that shape their work prioritize content over aesthetics or form. If our intention is to explain what happened, we might well write about what a photograph shows without considering how and why it was created or how the framing, focus, or angle of vision influence how we think about the content. We quote passages from a novel to show that people remember industrial work in conflicted ways, but we rarely consider either the larger storyline or how the author's choices about language, narrative perspective, or detail construct the feeling that the passage conveys. Questions about *how* a representation works or *why* it looks or sounds a particular way or *who* it reached and what they did with it can seem to distract from the story of what really happened or the material and political conditions a text reflects. And this focus on content over form is reasonable given the concerns that motivate much of our research.

Yet what really happened is as much a matter of culture and perception as it is of social structures and practices. Our understanding of deindustrialization would be enriched by connecting with scholarship that delves critically into how representations construct, nego-tiate, and critique economic change and our discourses about it. The contributors to this part interrogate the contexts in which representations are produced, the varied ways they circulate, and how audiences use and respond to them. Their work demonstrates what rep-resentations can offer but also the kinds of questions we can bring to them. When a literary scholar like Peter Thompson, an art historian like Dora Apel, or a musicologist like Giacoma Bottà analyzes representations, they consider not only the ideas and attitudes embedded in those texts but also the forces that shaped the texts and how stylistic, spatial, formal, and other choices communicate and influence cultural ideas through those texts. When historians like Piyusha Chatterjee or Helen Wagner draw on these approaches, they demonstrate how critical analysis of representations can deepen our understanding of how ideas develop and are reinforced. They show how representations can be at once objects of debate and also sites of resistance and critique.

As this part illustrates, critical work *about* representations – especially work focused on creative representations rather than documentary sources – demonstrates both *what* repre-sentations reveal and *how* they operate, and together these chapters show how different ways of working with representations can complement each other. These chapters also model criti-cal strategies for analyzing representations in relation to their rhetorical situations and their

Introduction

creators' and audiences' positionalities as well as their form, content, and style. These pieces make clear that research focused on creative representations shares many of the concerns and critical perspectives of more documentary analysis and can contribute important insights to this field.

Construction Sites

Deindustrialization involves objective economic actions and material, social, and political effects, but it is also, as performance studies scholar Judith Hamera writes in *Unfinished Business: Michael Jackson, Detroit, and the Figural Economy of American Deindustrialization*, "a representational and rhetorical shorthand" (Hamera, 2017, p. 9). The meanings attached to that shorthand are rooted in, transmitted by, and revised through representations. The stories people tell may emerge from the experience of deindustrialization, but they also produce and intervene in the social meanings of deindustrialization. That process is, as Stuart Hall explains, embedded in a system of discourse that "limits and restricts" how we speak and act (Hall, 1997, p. 3). Representations are created within structures of power, but they also construct meanings that may resist or critique those structures. As Hamera argues in describing the "figural economy" of performance, representations reflect structural changes, but they can also "congeal into public spectacles, circulate through a wide variety of media, and offer 'lessons'. . . about normative and aberrant relations to capital in transitional times" (Hamera, 2017, p. 4). Representations are developed by social actors, guided by their intentions and interests, built from existing materials, and both follow and reimagine familiar patterns. Like the construction of a building, representations usually involve multiple players – cultural workers but also funders, builders, promoters, and users. We can most fully understand representations when we consider the circumstances of their production and consumption as well as the content they present.

The chapters in this part all consider how the economic, social, and political conditions of particular locations shape the style and content of representations but also the rhetorical situations in which they were created, their paths of circulation, and audiences' responses to them. Helen Wagner traces how photo books and regional image campaigns "congealed" into a discourse of the Ruhr as a site of industrial heritage and deindustrial decline, but she also shows that those images presented conflicting claims about the region's identity and became the subjects of public debate. Peter Thompson locates Kate Beaton's graphic memoir *Ducks* in relation to the author's life trajectory and in the broader context of workers leaving Cape Breton when coal mines closed to work in the oil and gas fields of Alberta. The memoir uses narrative and images to articulate affective tensions as well as social and political conflicts about work, place, power, and the environment. In her analysis of photographs and public art in Detroit, Dora Apel compares three approaches to art that enact quite different relationships with local power structures and communities. The contrasts among these projects demonstrate how the conditions in which representations are constructed and displayed yield projects that facilitate or obstruct the Black residents' ability to be present in, make use of, and intervene in public space. Apel's work illustrates how, as Hamera has written, creative representations can draw our attention to "race and racial hierarchies as defining elements of the deindustrial" (Hamera, 2017, p. 5). Piyusha Chatterjee extends our attention to social hierarchies by focusing on gender and place in her analysis of three film representations of women textile workers in South Asia. While the films dramatize and document the experiences of women workers in a particular industry and region, Chatterjee suggests, they also highlight the theme of loss in their struggles, enabling audiences to understand the violence of capitalism as an interrelated and global issue. Giacomo Bottà draws our attention to circulation in his analysis of punk music, tracking how the genre emerged in major cities as economic restructuring was taking shape and was then adopted by musicians in deindustrializing places. Punk was often associated with deindustrialized cities, but its reach and meanings extended far beyond them. Ultimately, Bottà suggests, punk enables deindustrialization to take on new and contested meanings for diverse audiences. Together, these chapters emphasize how representations reflect the intentions and perspectives of their creators and their sponsors, the social and political conditions of their production, and the responses of their audiences. They demonstrate ways of reading representations that engage fully with their complexity and recognize their role in defining and redefining the meanings of work and deindustrialization.

These chapters also remind us that genres construct and disseminate meanings differently. Consider how a song differs from an oral history. An oral history is created because an interviewer wants to learn about the perspectives of participants in significant events, and informants may also have an interest in explaining their version of history. Similarly, a songwriter might want to share their vision, but they also hope to connect with other musicians and listeners, to experiment with musical styles, or to gain visibility and earn a living. These different purposes shape the content and form of their representations. The two forms also circulate in distinct ways. Oral histories may be archived, published, or incorporated into cultural heritage exhibits, and audiences come to them with some intentionality, through searching online, visiting a museum, or reading a book. Listeners encounter songs in varied ways, sometimes purposefully but often not, and music becomes part of their everyday lives, a resource for enjoyment and for establishing social identities and bonds. Bottà argues that the multidimensionality of music makes it an especially useful source for understanding how the meaning of and responses to deindustrialization are transformed as they travel, while oral historians might counter that interviews provide focused and specific attention to workers' experiences. As scholars, we could approach any genre of source in this way, noting not only its provenance but also the affordances and constraints of its form, its creators' subjectivity and intentionality, and the ways it circulates and is used. As the chapters in this part demonstrate, such questions can yield rich and complex readings that help us understand what deindustrialization means in cultural, social, and political terms.

Memory Work

Deindustrialization studies is almost by definition preoccupied with the past, and representations have been central to our efforts to preserve and to analyze memory. While we often prioritize documentary, primary materials in those efforts, when they are not available, scholars have turned to novels and other creative, secondary representations, as Marion Fontaine noted in her keynote at the 2023 conference of "Deindustrialization and the Politics of Our Time" (Fontaine, 2023). Like the carefully designed exhibits of a museum, the carefully constructed narratives of novels or films take audiences into the past, through the lens of the present. Three key differences deserve our attention. First, unlike heritage sites which clearly prioritize their interest in preserving memory, creative representations are not produced primarily to inform or engage audiences with the past. While writers and artists often conduct research to ensure that their representations reflect the conditions of the past, they generally prioritize aesthetic and affective qualities over historical accuracy or analysis, and many value invention as a tool for facilitating insight and emotional responses. Second, unlike museum exhibits or historical sites, these representations are often portable and designed to be accessed and used in multiple ways – in print and digital publication and posted or broadcast widely. Audiences encounter them in varied settings, and they come to them with different purposes – and sometimes with no purpose at all. Unlike the visitors to a heritage site, readers may pick up a novel or decide to stream a film without even realizing that it addresses industrial labor or economic change. Creative representations may thus operate as accidental heritage, and in the process, they extend the memory work of deindustrialization studies to broad and diverse audiences. Third, creative representations of deindustrialization are often created by people who did not live through it but are nonetheless inspired by it. They may have inherited memories from family and community narratives, the deindustrialized landscape, heritage sites, and even scholarly work, and they continue the chain of memory transmission, adding their own interpretations through the literature, film, music, and art that they create.

As several chapters here suggest, the process of preserving and transmitting memory through representations helps us understand how ways of remembering are influenced by the conditions of the present, including conflicts over identities and power. In his chapter, for example, Peter Thompson considers how representations created by younger workers and residents draw on other people's memories but also highlights tensions around how people remember differently. In *Ducks*, he argues, Beaton shows how workers carried memories of Cape Breton with them to the oil fields of northern Alberta, maintaining a sense of connection and identity rooted in the past, but the nature of those memories could be a source of conflict across generations. In the memoir, Kate explains that she learned the region's history from heritage sites like the Glace Bay Miners' museum, while an older colleague has more direct memories and finds her distance from the past of their home community frustrating. As Thompson argues, this divide reflects Beaton's secondary relationship with industrial history but also the contemporary conditions that drive her move to Alberta, especially the need to earn money to pay off student loans incurred in her effort to prepare for some kind of post-industrial life for herself. As Thompson's analysis shows, representations draw on and produce memory, but they also make visible conflicts over memory.

Helen Wagner makes a similar point in tracing debates about how representations define the meaning of the past as part of the identity of the Ruhr. She notes a critique often lobbed at deindustrialized communities (and at scholars who focus their attention on the losses of deindustrialization): that holding on to the past forestalls changes that could foster a brighter post-industrial future. She traces how conflicts and debates among residents, companies, and regional leaders over how to represent the past played out in photo collections, commentaries, and advertisements that articulated the identity of the Ruhr in competing ways. Wagner's analysis reminds us that representations do not just reflect disputes about memory. They contribute to them. Further, she argues that defining the Ruhr around the memory of its former industries 'economizes' the region's industrial past, construing memory as a core resource for attracting state and private funding as well as tourism.

As Hamera argues, representations can be especially helpful in resisting what Micaela di Leonardo calls the "folk model" of deindustrialization that focuses on displaced workers, most of them white and male (Hamera, 2017, p. 114). Creative materials may be especially effective in bringing attention to workers who do not fit that stereotype as well as to those whose relationship with deindustrialization is not primarily rooted in their own labor. Apel demonstrates this in her analysis of art in Detroit, arguing that representations can highlight conflicts over whose version of place and the past is recognized in public memory. Apel contrasts photographic portraits of Black workers and residents with the more familiar – and often depopulated – images of that city's deteriorating factories and schools, and she identifies such images as examples of "activist memory that rewrites the narrative of Detroit as ruined and unpeopled." She also examines how conflicts over public art play out in contexts of both neighborhood decline and gentrification, making visible the distinct histories and perspectives of the city's Black working class. Across these examples, Apel suggests, Black spatial politics play out in relation to capitalism as well as memory, reminding us – like Thompson and Wagner – that even as representations articulate and preserve memory, that process is embedded in economic relations and social conflicts.

Traveling and Transforming

While representations are often site- or time-specific, rooted in and focused on a specific place or moment, they travel in multiple ways. They can take us into the minds and experiences of varied social actors, providing access to the perspectives of people with whom we cannot speak directly. They enable us to envision places and experiences that would otherwise be beyond our reach. They can also facilitate comparative analysis and scholarly collaborations that could yield more ambitious, complex, global insights about deindustrialization. These qualities also enable representations to carry ideas about deindustrialization to audiences who are not directly affected by it, and in the process, they can generate new insights into the significance and meaning of economic change.

Chatterjee's analysis of films about textile workers illustrates how representations travel across space, taking global audiences into factories and homes in South Asia. This is true for scholars but also for the broader audiences that these films reach. Chatterjee emphasizes how the films translate large-scale sociopolitical concepts into scenes of everyday life, making global patterns of exploitation and resistance visible in concrete, human terms. This may be especially important for forms of representation, like films and music, that are easily distributed and consumed globally. The independent and documentary films that Chatterjee describes targeted North American and European audiences for whom they seem intended to prompt empathy and possibly outrage. Like Tillie Olsen's well-known 1930s poem "I want you women up north to know" (Olsen, 2007), the films do not just reveal the working conditions and lives of the people who make the clothing purchased in wealthy regions. They challenge viewers to recognize their complicity in a system of class exploitation. These films thus enable the meaning of work and of deindustrialization to travel from the Global South to the Global North, from industrial growth to deindustrialization, from documentation to entertainment to political critique.

For scholars interested in the ongoing influences of economic change, representations are essential sources for tracing how ideas about deindustrialization travel across space and time. They may be created by people with direct connections with deindustrialization but also by those with much more distant ties. They can thus help us see how the cultural ripples of economic restructuring spread within but also far beyond deindustrialized places. Bottà offers the most forceful argument for this quality of representations, tracing how punk music traveled from large economic capitals like London or New York to industrial cities like Manchester or Torino, so that a genre that did not originate with deindustrialization came to be associated with it. Even more important, he argues that the music also carried ideas about and responses to economic restructuring to audiences elsewhere, articulating an attitude of

Introduction

resistance rooted in but not constrained to deindustrialization. Further, he suggests, punk provided a cultural release valve for the pain of deindustrialization, enabling audiences to imagine new identities and meanings. Punk music, he suggests, transcended time and space, and it facilitated transformational meaning-making for its audiences.

Representations may also enable a wider scope for deindustrialization studies as a field. While our central concerns have been the causes, experiences, and consequences of deindustrialization, when we expand our view to encompass research focused on creative representations, we see how the idea of deindustrialization has itself expanded, including in some scholarly approaches that are not represented in this part. As noted earlier, Hamera's study of Detroit offers an especially provocative and useful example of how analysis of the "figural economy" of deindustrialization can help us "conceptualize and imagine" the cultural significance of the shift from an industrial economy to an economy of "financialization" (Hamera, 2017, p. 3). Other scholars approach narratives of contemporary work as reflective of deindustrialization, using the concept without engaging directly with either shutdowns or deindustrialized regions. In his 2017 book *The Work of Art in the Age of Deindustrialization*, Jasper Bernes argues that economic restructuring provides a framework for understanding changing conditions for and ideas about the making of poetry and visual arts (Bernes, 2017). These analyses often resist valorizing industrial labor and its memory. In an article about television shows representing the gig economy and tipwork, for example, Annie McClanahan cautions against "recurring fantasies of how great things were under the wage," though she acknowledges the cultural power of the ideal of stable, secure, meaningful employment. It is difficult to represent the precarity of contemporary work, she notes, "without seeming to imply that being forced to rely on a wage for one's survival constitutes stability or security" (McClanahan, 2019). Hamera writes that the "cruel optimism" of public discourse "arises from rhetoric glamorizing contemporary contingent labor as flexible and entrepreneurial," but she also challenges the "attachment to the Fordist labor-management compact made retrospectively more appealing in light of its retraction" (Hamera, 2017, p. 4). Although we might want to debate the uses of deindustrialization in these analyses, pushing for fuller engagement with the history of industrial labor as well as its long-term effects, we should welcome scholarship that recognizes the centrality of deindustrialization in contemporary culture and politics. Together with studies like Sonali Perera's *No Country: Working-Class Writing in the Age of Globalization* and Joseph Entin's *Living Labor: Fiction, Film, and Precarious Work* (Perera, 2014; Entin, 2023), these projects suggest the value of expanding critical discussions of the half-life of deindustrialization into deeper analysis of representations. Such work reveals how the meaning of deindustrialization is being transformed as creative representations – and critical analysis of them – travel across time, space, and disciplines.

Conclusion

Scholarly analyses of representations of deindustrialization invite us to think critically about how representations of work and its loss are changing and how the conditions of contemporary capitalism and globalization are influencing representations. The chapters in this part illustrate the value of treating literature, film, art, and music as significant sources of insight into deindustrialization, and they demonstrate strategies for reading representations critically. They reveal just some of the many ways deindustrialization scholars can use representations, whether as sources for insight into work and its loss, as in Chatterjee's use of film to analyze gender and power in the lives of South Asian women in the textile industry, or as responses

The Routledge Handbook of Deindustrialization Studies

to and interventions in the meanings of deindustrialization, as in Wagner's discussion of debates over the identity of the Ruhr or Apel's tracing of Black spatial agency in Detroit. They highlight how representations reveal but also enact the conflicts, social and political but also internal and affective, that economic change generates. Together, they also constitute an argument for representations as sources for understanding how the meanings of work, community, place, and capitalism continue to be influenced by the memory of industrial work and ideas about the causes, effects, and continuing significance of deindustrialization.

Note

1 I have specific cases in mind here: Greg Moring's design for a set of gates depicting steelworkers in action for Youngstown State University (see Gwin, Harold. Elm Street Gates Will Tell Story at YSU. https://vindyarchives.com/news/2009/apr/01/gates-at-ysu-to-tell-story/), Nowak, Mark. (2004). *Shut Up Shut Down*. Minneapolis: Coffee House Press, and Michele Dunleavy's *Steel Valley Rhythms* dance project (micheledunleavy.com).

Reference List

Bernes, Jasper. (2017). *The Work of Art in the Age of Deindustrialization*. Palo Alto: Stanford University Press.

Dunleavy, Michele. *Steel Valley Rhythms*. http:micheledunleavy.com (Accessed: 15 June 2024).

Entin, Joseph B. (2023). *Living Labor: Fiction, Film, and Precarious Work*. Ann Arbor: University of Michigan Press. https://doi.org/10.3998/mpub.11738099

Fontaine, Marion. (2023, June). The Un-Making of the French Working Class? Nation and History of Deindustrialization. Paper presented at the Deindustrialization and the Politics of Today Conference, Sydney, Nova Scotia.

Gutman, H. (1987). Labor History and the Sartre Question. In *Power & Culture: Essays on the American Working Class*. New York: Pantheon Books, pp. 326–328.

Gwin, Harold. 2009. Elm Street Gates will Tell Story at YSU. *The Vindicator Archives*. https://vindyarchives.com/news/2009/apr/01/gates-at-ysu-to-tell-story/

Hall, Stuart. (1997). *Representation: Cultural Representations and Signifying Practices*. London: Sage.

Hamera, Judith. (2017). *Unfinished Business: Michael Jackson, Detroit, and the Figural Economy of American Deindustrialization*. New York, NY: Oxford University Press.

Linkon, Sherry Lee. (2018). *The Half-Life of Deindustrialization: Working-Class Writing About Economic Restructuring*. Ann Arbor: University of Michigan Press.

McClanahan, Annie. (2019). TV and Tipworkification. *Post45*, p. 1. https://post45.org/2019/01/tv-and-tipworkification/

Nowak, Mark. (2004). *Shut Up Shut Down: Poems*. Minneapolis: Coffee House Press.

Olsen, Tillie. (2007). I Want You Women Up North to Know. *New Labor Forum*, 16(2), pp. 135–137. https://doi.org/10.1080/10957960701279439

Perera, Sonali. (2014). *No Country: Working-Class Writing in the Age of Globalization*. New York: Columbia University Press.

Portelli, A. (1991). What Makes Oral History Different? In Robert, P. and Alistair, T, (eds.) *The Oral History Reader*. New York: Routledge, pp. 63–74.

18

BLACK SPATIAL AGENCY AND CULTURAL JUSTICE

Race, Ruins, and Gentrification in Detroit

Dora Apel

Introduction

The experience of deindustrialization is publicly understood primarily through representation, but different kinds of representation offer different political perspectives. What – and who – is included or excluded? How is meaning produced? For what audience? At stake are ongoing social and cultural policies and prevailing myths about deindustrialization's effects on the lives that are most affected – the poor, Black, and minority populations that bear the brunt of deindustrialization with its attendant economic decline and environmental degradation. Nowhere is this more starkly evident in the US than in the majority-Black and working-class city of Detroit, still known as the Motor City though largely abandoned by the auto companies. Here the relationship of race to place and space is central to the impact as well as the representation of deindustrialization. In this chapter, I focus on three representational approaches to life in Detroit that either recognize and advocate for Black spatial agency while resisting racialized marginalization, or that repress and occlude Black spatial agency, especially in the wake of gentrification.

The first approach is community art projects that attempt to intervene creatively at a local level in the developing life of impoverished and marginalized neighborhoods and to counter market-driven agendas for artmaking. The second approach, with an opposing aim, is the corporate attempt to instrumentalize and control public art as well as public space to create an upscale and sanitized perception of the city that makes the central business district of downtown Detroit more appealing to affluent white people, in particular, while largely disappearing, ignoring, or suppressing the rest of the majority-Black and working-class city. The third approach engages in a form of social and cultural justice by representing the ongoing life and cultural heritage of the city's Black population through photography, complicating the misleading narrative of an empty and decaying city produced by the depopulated ruin imagery that has evoked widespread cultural fascination over the last two decades. The photographic works in this approach facilitate a cultural justice dialogue that remembers a richly creative history as well as a legacy of poverty and neglect while the community art of the first approach serves as a form of grassroots activism for community engagement, creative growth, and social justice. The approach of corporate-sponsored art, however, employs the

DOI: 10.4324/9781003308324-27

The Routledge Handbook of Deindustrialization Studies

privatization of public space as a tool for exclusion and the manipulation of perception for commercial gain.

In different ways and for opposing purposes, these three forms of representation intervene in the ongoing life of the city and actively engage in constructing new social and cultural meaning by making the Black spatial agency of city residents either visible or invisible, with spatial agency understood as "the ability to use, make or regulate a public space," including for purposes of political visibility (Montgomery, 2016, p. 777). Community art and the photography of Black life are designed to encourage and support Black spatial agency while the corporate approach is meant to suppress it. Together, these representational perspectives reproduce the contested racial history of Detroit, where a long-standing cultural heritage is often forgotten, marginalized, or repressed. Though Black lives are largely missing from the ruin images of recent years, the majority of photographers and artists discussed here seek to open a larger space for critical and oppositional artistic practices. These examples of critical practice act as case models for thinking about how visual representation functions more broadly in deindustrialized cities around the world and how representation may be used to either help remember what has been suppressed, or, conversely, instrumentalized to deepen the already existing racialized poverty and oppression that is central to capitalism and to strategies of urban financial 'revitalization.'

Memory Activism

Combined with segregation, housing discrimination, and urban renewal, deindustrialization has produced a racialization of poverty in a city that once served as the global center of the auto industry. So we begin with a dispute over a visual display at an industrial ruin that was meant to protest the empty promise of capitalist prosperity for all. In 2013, the year an emergency manager appointed by the Michigan governor took the city of Detroit into bankruptcy, a political controversy erupted over placards at the Packard Plant that spelled out the Nazi slogan 'Arbeit macht frei.' Famously created on a gate at Auschwitz, the placards were placed in the windows of the plant's production line bridge spanning East Grand Boulevard (Figure 18.1).

The Packard Plant was the first modern automobile factory and is now the largest and most iconic industrial ruin in the nation. Designed by Albert Kahn and built by the Packard brothers in 1903, it includes 47 buildings spread over more than 40 acres on Detroit's east side. When the city suffered four recessions in the 1950s, the turning point for Detroit's economy, auto manufacturers and dealers began to reduce their workforces, close plants, and relocate to other parts of the country that were white and nonunion. As an independent producer, Packard was unable to compete with the Big Three auto companies of Ford, General Motors, and Chrysler and closed its doors in 1956. Yet it remains a well-known ruin repeatedly photographed in its various phases of ongoing decay and for many years served as a haven for small businesses, graffiti artists, urban explorers, paintball battles, techno parties, raves, fashion and wedding shoots, auto scrappers, and the homeless.

When the posters of *Arbeit macht frei* appeared, complaints of racism and antisemitism were immediately raised by Jewish community groups, prompting community volunteers to hastily remove the placards. But there may be a better way to understand the point of reproducing this slogan in the context of the abandoned Packard Plant. The assertion that 'work sets you free' metaphorically likens the tens of thousands of Detroit's laid-off auto workers to the destroyed lives of the Jews under Nazi rule. Both were treated as expendable

Figure 18.1 Packard Plant with placards spelling *Arbeit macht Frei* on the production line bridge, 2013. (Photo courtesy: James Fassinger)

human populations, an ugly truth disguised with a high-flown phrase. Of course the abandonment of the workers in Detroit is not the same as the genocide of the Jews, but figuring the destructive effects of one in terms of the catastrophe of the other underscores not only the tragic conditions that industrial abandonment has wrought upon generations but also the disillusionment that has come with it – the death of the American Dream and the belief that hard work will bring about wealth and well-being. In this sense, the placards may be seen as a form of memory activism, an ironic protest and gesture of resistance that keeps alive the memory of corporate and state abandonment and the resulting devastation of the majority-Black and working-class population in the city.

In 2019, the landmark production line bridge collapsed and seemed to further signal the unstoppable downward spiral of progress brought about by deindustrialization since the industrial heyday of the 1940s. Considered a period of prosperity because of wartime production, the 1940s was also a period rife with racial tensions leading to 'hate strikes' and the eruption of riots in 1943, in which the overwhelming majority of more than 400 people killed or injured by the police were Black. The effects of industrial disinvestment last for decades, especially in those cities where industry once dominated, destabilizing communities through the loss of jobs, homes, and health care. Reductions in the tax base in turn lead to cuts in public services; crime increases; as does suicide, drug and alcohol abuse, family violence, and depression. Landscapes decay and cultural resources decline, as does faith in government. Deunionized workers who find new jobs do so at far lower wages, contributing to an almost inescapable cycle of continuing decline (see Russo and Linkon, n.d.; Linkon, 2018). In Detroit, whites were able to leave the city for home mortgages in the suburbs starting in the 1950s, but Black people were prevented from doing so by the discriminatory practice of redlining by the federal Home Owners Loan Corporation, which drew boundaries around neighborhoods based on residents' race and deprived them of private and government loans, resources, and services. This turned Detroit into a Black ghetto and effectively racialized poverty.

Photographs of industrial ruins such as those of the Packard Plant and the protest placards mounted there evoke the destructiveness of capitalist deindustrialization in ways that might otherwise remain invisible or forgotten. Such images convey the halt in progress that ruins represent and the failure of capitalism's dependence on perpetual economic growth.[1]

Community Arts Projects

The Detroit art scene began booming when land and buildings could be acquired cheaply by artists hoping to pioneer a new way of life based on creative communities, ecological green space, or no-profit public missions. The move by many artists into Detroit also represents, at least in part, a desire to reject the symbolic order and promote community solidarity and creative freedom. Though unable to solve egregious problems such as high unemployment, crumbling infrastructure, or access to health care and higher education, community art projects nonetheless help produce strengthened communities by focusing on inclusion, embracing local histories, and offering opportunities for spatial agency that affirm the identities and utilize the resources of the neighborhood.

While artists engaged in community arts projects hope to create value determined by standards other than the capitalist market, their work, as Julia Yezbick shows, is almost inevitably instrumentalized by the city to market the city and raise property values (Yezbick, 2020). When it does not conform to the needs of corporate entities or the state, however, the unsanctioned work of artists may be criminalized and demolished, as was demonstrated by city actions against Detroit's most famous street project, the Heidelberg Project created by Tyree Guyton.

Begun in 1986, Guyton's project reclaimed abandoned houses on Heidelberg Street, where Guyton grew up, just north of the culturally rich Black neighborhood known as Black Bottom. Guyton created massive installations by painting and decorating abandoned houses, covering the Dotty Wotty House with polka dots (Figure 18.2), festooning the Party Animal House with stuffed animals, or covering the House of Soul with hundreds of vinyl record albums. Guyton made use of thousands of other discarded objects in outdoor installations. The Heidelberg Project became a commentary on Detroit's abandonment by the auto companies and the state and drew widespread global attention, becoming a major city landmark that attracted, according to the guest book, at least 150,000 visitors from 144 countries every year. This made the Heidelberg Project the third-most-visited cultural attraction in Detroit and infused thousands of dollars into the local economy by visitors to the city.

But complaints from neighbors, who considered Guyton's work a form of glorified blight, evoked the sympathy of city officials who were apparently embarrassed by the way the project called attention, however creatively, to declining neighborhoods with no obvious benefit to real estate market values. Twice, in 1991 and 1999, Detroit mayors Coleman Young and Dennis Archer, respectively, sent in bulldozers to tear down large parts of the project. From 2013 to 2015, arsonists set 12 fires and burned down five buildings in the Heidelberg Project (all unsolved), while efforts to rebuild have been twice thwarted when the project was

Figure 18.2 Tyree Guyton, The Dotty Wotty House, The Heidelberg Project. (Photo courtesy: Gregory Wittkopp)

denied community partnership with the Detroit Land Bank Association. The Land Bank Association refused to sell Guyton and Jenenne Whitfield, his wife and CEO of the Heidelberg Project, the 40 vacant lots surrounding the project for Heidelberg 3.0, a reimagined project that would include an artists' village, with live-work studios, an arts academy, and businesses that cater to them. This refusal occurred despite the fact that Guyton and the Heidelberg Project have achieved world renown and were the subject of the HBO documentary *Come Unto Me: The Faces of Tyree Guyton*, directed by Nicole Cattell in 1999; were featured on the Vision TV documentary *Urban Shrines*, produced by Toronto-based Markham Street Films in 2005; and were included in the French documentary *Detroit: The Cycles of the Mental Machine* in 2007, providing evidence of hope, determination, and creativity in the face of official resistance.

Nonetheless, in 2017, Guyton and Whitfield partnered with two artists/gallery owners to purchase two buildings in the McDougall-Hunt neighborhood, two blocks from the Heidelberg Project, and moved their headquarters to McDougall Street. In 2018, the Heidelberg Project launched the Heidelberg Arts Leadership Academy, a free in-school or after-school arts education program for students in grades four through twelve. They also established an Ambassador-in-Residence Program to help create community projects and a Curator-in-Residence Program. But, by 2023, financial hardships caused the project to scale back, lay off its staff members, and put its headquarters up for sale (Gross, 2018; Jones and

Carr, 2023; See also The Heidelberg Project, n.d.). The project remains an outdoor museum and still has plans for future growth. Despite its current struggles, by forging social ties and creative community networks over its nearly 40-year history, Guyton and Whitfield have helped others to effect the transformation of traumatic conditions into opportunities for Black spatial agency and creative growth.

Another famous community arts project was produced by Power House Productions, founded in 2009 and run by Gina Reichert and Mitch Cope to help promote creative neighborhood stabilization while rejecting a dependence on market values but with a different result. In Banglatown, a neighborhood straddling the border between Detroit and Hamtramck and home to many Bangladeshis, older East Europeans, Blacks, and young whites, Cope and Reichert, funded by numerous public and private grants, bought and sold over 40 properties and worked to help secure them against decay and drug dealers. Power House Productions created the Play House, the Sound House, the Squash House, the Power House, the Jar House, and a skate and sculpture park, among other projects. Some of these houses acted as residences for visiting artists, while others became art projects produced by artists working in association with the nonprofit and now serving the local community. The Squash House, for example, turned a fire-damaged home into a squash court and a squash garden; the Play House became a space for performance such as theater, dance, and puppet shows as well as for music and language classes; the Sound House is an experimental sound studio where invited artists use the house as a studio space in exchange for public presentations of their work.[2]

The first house was the Power House, a former foreclosed drug house that Cope and Reichert purchased from the bank in 2008 after living in the neighborhood for several years. They envisioned establishing it as an artist residency/community arts center/meeting house, which ultimately led to the idea of acquiring and revitalizing surrounding foreclosed houses. The Power House produced its own electricity from solar and wind power, asserting a form of self-reliance and sustainability that speaks to its moniker as a 'power house.'

Though it was not their goal, by adapting houses for reuse, Cope and Reichert de facto helped raise property values in the local housing market, which allowed the city to present Power House Productions as an example of revitalization. The original Heidelberg project, on the other hand, despite its ability to draw immense numbers of visitors, was regarded by the city as mere spectacle that did not raise property values or support the local housing market, and this led the city to adopt a hostile stance (Yezbick, 2020, p. 333). Yet both projects engage local residents, especially young people, and empower their ability to make, use, or regulate public space.

Gentrification and Perception

Since Detroit declared bankruptcy in 2013 – regarded as the nadir of its decline – gentrifying neoliberal capitalists have sought to create their own narrative of the city, counterposing images of upscale renewal and revival to those of stark collapse. To help counter the view of Detroit as a postapocalyptic landscape, multibillionaire real estate developer Dan Gilbert helped promote a different image of the city through commissioned murals, leading some observers to proclaim that Detroit, "driven by art (not automobiles). . . is staging an impressive comeback" (The Toronto Star, cited in Brown, 2017). Employing a strategy of market-driven 'placemaking,' Gilbert attempted to rebrand Detroit by using art, among other things, to shape and control perceptions of city space as safe, sanitized, and welcoming to white shoppers and gentrifiers in particular as well as Black middle and upper classes. Unlike community gardens in low-income neighborhoods or neighborhood parks, however, the goal of market-driven placemaking is to revive street life to increase commerce and rents.

Gilbert is the owner of Quicken Loans, the largest online mortgage lender in the US and a subsidiary of Rock Ventures, the parent company of all Gilbert's holdings. Quicken Loans was ranked fifth by the *Detroit News* as a foreclosure-inducing mortgage lender in Detroit over the previous decade, and therefore a very likely contributor to the blight in which 200,000 households were displaced across the state (Baker, 2019; Cohen, 2015). Gilbert denied responsibility for contributing to the foreclosure crisis, which neoliberals like to blame on the victims or on other causes. He has bought up more than a hundred properties in downtown Detroit with the idea of luring businesses, entrepreneurs, consumers, and suburbanites to the central business district. With investments in a midtown sports arena and properties surrounding it by the late Mike Illitch, the billionaire founder of Little Caesar's Pizza, the downtown and midtown real estate development along a slice of Woodward Avenue totals 7.2 miles.[3]

Following Detroit's declared bankruptcy, and despite Gilbert's role in predatory lending, his Rock Ventures partnered with other stakeholders to create two planning documents outlining a vision for the city: *A Plan for Our Time* and *A Placemaking Vision for Downtown Detroit*. Both emphasize the need to change the perception of the city. In *A Plan For Our Time*, the authors state, "reality, of course, is very important. However, *perception* – and perhaps more to the point, an understanding of existing perceptions together with conscious acts taken to change them in support of the vision – is *exceedingly important*" (author's emphasis).

To accomplish this change in perception from a bankrupt Black city to a thriving and street-friendly urban oasis, the document suggests the aesthetic strategy of incorporating art into the streetscape. Over 45 artists were invited to paint large-scale murals in the Eastern Market district, which a casino in the central business district owned by Dan Gilbert helped sponsor. Gilbert's real estate company Bedrock Detroit, in consultation with the Library Street Collective, an art gallery housed in a Gilbert building, also commissioned 27 artists (mostly international with a handful of local artists) to paint murals on Z Lot, a parking garage on Library Street. In addition, Gilbert commissioned a six-story mural by street artist HENSE, as well as two 18-story murals, one by Shepard Fairey and one by How & Nosm on the Compuware Building, now known as One Campus Martius, which houses Gilbert's Quicken Loans headquarters (Figure 18.3).

The twin brothers known in the graffiti world as How & Nosm (Raoul and Davide Perre) created a mural called Balancing Act, using their signature colors of blacks, reds, and grays to create intricate patterns and shapes, in this case, a kind of totem balancing on one foot, meant to represent the 'balancing act' of poor and working-class Detroiters. Street artist Shepard Fairey, most famous for his iconic 'Hope' posters for Barack Obama's first presidential bid, produced a decorative black, red, and cream-colored stencil-like design with wavy lotus leaves that offers an elegant showcase for his signature likeness of the head of the French wrestler Andre the Giant, displayed inside a five-point star at the center of the mural.

Yet even as these murals associated with street culture went up, actual street culture was suppressed. As Alesia Montgomery notes, market-driven placemaking "subordinates the black urban poor, even as it incorporates their street cultures" (Montgomery, 2016, p. 1). Indeed, gentrification usually leads to increased racist state repression, encouraging police forces to 'crack down on crime' as a front for social cleansing that leads to the mass

Figure 18.3 Shepard Fairey mural on the right, 2015; How & Nosm on the left, 2016 on One Campus Martius. (Photo courtesy: Sal Rodriguez)

incarceration of Black people, the poor, and other oppressed minorities. Gilbert installed hundreds of surveillance cameras all over the downtown central business district, not only to keep down crime but to ward off and punish unsanctioned street art.[4] His use of surveillance cameras and policing of street art must be understood as attempts to elide the Blackness and urban poverty of the city through the private regulation of public space and control of Black spatial agency. In 2015, the City of Detroit also gave Gilbert the right to limit the legal rights of the public to choose when and how they appear downtown. This occurred after security guards at Campus Martius and the Detroit riverfront prevented marches by an antiwar group and the gathering of petition signatures by an anti-foreclosure group in 2013 and 2014 (Montgomery, 2016, pp. 787–788).

The case of Shepard Fairey offers the most glaring example of the attempt to manage and control unsanctioned street art. While working on his commissioned mural for Gilbert's Quicken Loan headquarters, Fairey also tagged nine buildings around the city with his well-known Andre the Giant images. He told the *Detroit Free Press* at the time, "I still do stuff on the street without permission. I'll be doing stuff on the street when I'm in Detroit" (Bethencourt and Stryker, 2015). But his noncommissioned paste-ups led to the issuing of two felony warrants for tags on city property with a possible $10,000 fine and up to five years in jail.[5] Fairey turned himself in at the Los Angeles International Airport and returned to Detroit to be arraigned. The case was eventually dismissed; although the City of Detroit appealed, the Michigan appeals court refused to reinstate vandalism charges.

In his efforts to control street art, Gilbert supports the prosecution of graffiti artists as vandals even as he attempts to harness the 'street cred' of such artists to burnish his corporate image and market the city to future businesses and suburban shoppers.

Yet the vision for Detroit's 'renewal' that Gilbert was pivotal in establishing does not include most of the city but is concentrated on the roughly seven-square-mile real estate empire owned by himself and the Illitch family, an area primarily populated by college-educated millennials. Thus, in a city of 139 square miles, where more than 30% of the majority-Black population lives below the poverty line, it is only the small central business district that is being "revitalized."[6]

Gentrification involves more than the purchase of abandoned buildings and the privatization of public space; it also comes at a cost to the local population in terms of displacement and dislocated community. For example, in 2014, about 20 tenants, most of them young artists and musicians, were evicted from their apartments on Griswold Street about a year after more than one hundred of their neighbors across the street in a subsidized apartment building for seniors and disabled people were evicted.[7] They were all victims of the 'development' plans for the city, which evicted low-income residents to make way for upscale housing and entertainment. The two buildings are in Capitol Park, one of the areas targeted by capitalists associated with Dan Gilbert, who himself owns at least six properties in the area.

Gentrification should come with anti-displacement and rent control protections for lower-income renters and other vulnerable groups. But displacement of lower-income people by an influx of the middle class or affluent who are lured by the restoration and upgrading of run-down urban areas is the very definition of gentrification. Rising rents and living costs reduce affordable housing and prevent displaced residents from benefiting from the economic growth and greater availability of services that come with investment. Displaced residents also suffer because of the disruption of community ties.

While ruin tourists and urban explorers may enjoy ruins, the affluent suburban whites whom real estate developers such as Gilbert seek to attract tend to be leery of even entering an overwhelmingly Black and poor city like Detroit. But they are drawn by the perception of a thriving bastion of middle-class commerce, arts, and entertainment, which requires that the majority-Black population be generally screened from view – thus proving that perception of the city may indeed be more important than reality in its ability to elide the ongoing effects of deindustrialization and urban decline.[8] Ironically, however, the two 18-story murals commissioned by Gilbert for the north side of the One Campus Martius building, murals meant to be emblematic of cultural renewal and creativity by street artists, are now permanently blocked from view by new construction that expands the corporate footprint of Gilbert's property.

Gentrification produces a narrative of renewal that actively forgets and obliterates the past. Since 2014, for example, Black Detroiters have been described by city officials in explicitly anti-Black terms as undeserving of access to potable water despite the hardship and health hazards this produces and in the face of international condemnation (Apel, 2018). As Jessi Quizar writes,

> The sense that Black people are undeserving recipients of public resources that is particularly visible in water discourse has also arguably bolstered a much wider wave of neoliberal reforms to the Detroit economy – millions of dollars in tax abatements to benefit a largely White business expansion, for instance, while the majority-Black and

working-class neighborhoods of the city are often denied even the most basic of public spending – things like electricity for street lights and asphalt for road repair.

(Quizar, 2020, p. 442)

If we understand gentrification as the appropriation of land by the wealthy, facilitated by the state, entailing displacement and exclusion by race and class, we must also reject the myth of redevelopment as social progress.[9] In part, this myth is propagated by commissioned murals, a good example of how the financial sector takes control of public space by offering displays of authorized street art even as it sets about repressing street culture.

Photography and Cultural Justice

The best-known images of Detroit's ruination are the depopulated images produced by photographers such as Andrew Moore (*Detroit Disassembled*), the French team of Yves Marchand and Romain Meffre (*The Ruins of Detroit*), and Camilo Jose Vergara (most recently, *Detroit Is No Dry Bones: The Eternal City of the Industrial Age*).[10] I have argued that such images tend to have contradictory effects and are too often dismissed as mere 'ruin porn.' They speak to our fears of civilizational decline while helping to soothe those anxieties from a safe distance. Portraying "beauty in decay," they domesticate the sense of brokenness, fragmentation, and violence at the core of ruination through the mental mastery of the pictured catastrophe and the aesthetic pleasure it produces in what may be called the deindustrial sublime.[11] Yet the same images also evoke the disastrous failure of neoliberal capitalism and invite consideration of how such a dismal future might be averted. Ruin images can thus play an activist role in representing the inability of capitalism to adequately support its working-class populations and the racialized poverty and loss of agency that have resulted.

A number of photographers, however, have sought to counter the notion of a city already empty and abandoned by turning their camera lenses toward ongoing life in the city, including residential areas near sites of industrial ruin, abandoned houses, or other rundown spaces where people still live and work. Complicating the picture of Detroit by showing its people in all their modes of endurance and survival, their work constitutes a form of activist memory focused on social justice that helps to change our understanding of the past, present, and, potentially, the future.[12]

Dave Jordano, who grew up in Detroit and whose father worked all his life for General Motors, has made many return trips to the city from his home in Chicago to demonstrate that "Detroit is not the city of death and decay" represented in the media and to show the human consequences of living in a post-industrial city. His book *Detroit – Unbroken Down* portrays many of the city's residents, including single portraits, mixed race families, and community groups, along with commentaries on their strategies for survival and their creativity. Though such images may lack the frisson of postapocalyptic decay, they make visible the ongoing life and effects of Black spatial agency in the city.

In *Michael, Poletown, Detroit, 2011*, for example, Jordano pictures a smiling man with dreadlocks, rolled up jeans, and no feet sitting on his stoop (Figure 18.4).

Writes Jordano,

A well-known and popular character in the downtown area affectionately known as Dreadlock Mike, he lost his feet after he jumped out of the second floor window of a burning building. He recently moved with his girlfriend and three others into a small

Figure 18.4 Dave Jordano, *Michael, Poletown, Detroit, 2011*. (Photo courtesy: Dave Jordano)

run down house just east of Eastern Market. He often wheel-chaired over to the I-75 and Mack Avenue freeway entrance or to Comerica Ballpark during home games and waited, but never asked for donations. Sadly, Michael and a friend were killed by a hit and run driver one evening in August of 2013 while crossing the street returning from a Detroit Tigers ball game.

(Jordano, 2015, p. 148)[13]

Despite the harsh conditions of his life, Michael meets the gaze of the photographer serenely, showing us the face of resilience, a willingness to defy the odds with the support of his community. The contradiction between harsh conditions and resilience speaks to a wellspring of communal strength and creativity. At the same time, a poor and disabled Black man living in a run-down house with four others and killed by an anonymous driver seems like a metaphor for the poor Black population of Detroit itself, its determined ability to endure despite its long-standing abandonment by an indifferent state that leaves it to its own devices no matter the consequences.

Spatial agency in Detroit can also take desperate forms driven by necessity, and Jordano does not shy away from their representation. In *Woman Sleeping in a Parking Lot, Eastside, Detroit*, Jordano's image of a sleeping woman on the grassy edge of a large, nearly empty parking lot evokes the housing crisis in Detroit (Figure 18.5). Wearing gold pants, she is barefoot as she lies on her stomach in the sun atop a blanket, with her worldly belongings gathered into a few bags and stored in a shopping cart that stands nearby. According to

Figure 18.5 Dave Jordano, *Woman Sleeping in a Parking Lot, Eastside, Detroit, 2010.* (Photo courtesy: Dave Jordano)

Homeless Action Network of Detroit, more than 20,000 people were unhoused in Detroit, Highland Park, and Hamtramck in 2010, when Jordano took this photo. By 2021, that number dropped to about 5,700, with most finding shelter in emergency shelters or transitional housing. Due to poverty, unemployment, and a lack of resources, the homeless are overwhelmingly Black and include veterans and students, often suffering from chronic health conditions, mental illness, drug addiction, domestic violence and abuse or a combination of these factors. The homeless were especially susceptible to the coronavirus pandemic.

The photo reminds us of the resilient yet bare survival of thousands in the impoverished conditions inherent to a racist, sexist, and class-based economic system. While the better-known images of depopulated ruins evoke a romantic nostalgia for the past, an imagined glimpse into a ruined future, or a rumination on the dialectic of nature and culture, Jordano's images instead gaze unflinchingly into the present, offering a more granular understanding of the racialized effects of deindustrialization, including both the perseverance and the limits of Black and minority spatial agency.[14]

Determined to represent aspects of Black urban experience beyond poverty and decline, photographers Isaac Diggs and Edward Hillel set about documenting Black spaces in Detroit where legendary music from the blues to Motown to techno was produced and where electronic musicians continue to work today. In *Electronic Landscapes: Music, Space, and Resistance*, Diggs and Hillel photograph the ongoing uses of historical sites and Black

Black Spatial Agency and Cultural Justice

spaces, suggesting that the psychological safety provided for Black producers by Black spaces is critical for the creative revitalization of our deindustrialized cities. Seeking out Detroit's techno, house, and hip-hop musicians in their home studios and renovated buildings, and focusing on the links between race, space, and cultural production, they also produce a form of activist memory that rewrites the narrative of Detroit as ruined and unpeopled (see Apel, 2021, pp. 100–103). In what scholars in critical heritage studies have called cultural justice, the preservation and representation of artistic, cultural, and musical heritages in the wake of deindustrialization can play a critical role in urban revitalization, especially if such heritage is mobilized to capture the cultural identities, practices, and values of communities that have been marginalized or effaced (Cantillon, Baker, and Nowak, 2021).

Diggs and Hillel's photo of Sterling Toles, a hip-hop artist, producer, and educator, shows him working on his computer before a large textile image of Black youths (Figure 18.6). In a recorded interview with Toles at his loft apartment in May 2018, Toles observes, "There is an immense density of emotion that can happen in a space that is perceivably destitute. To me, we condense the externals to expand the internal. . . . And we're not making music for you, we're making music to heal. We are trying to transform trauma here" (Toles, 2021). The transformation of trauma must be seen as central to the politics of memory, resistance, and cultural justice. Toles's practice helps forge social ties and community networks in a form of cultural justice and rejuvenation for overlooked communities of Black musicians who have experienced poverty and trauma while promoting imagination and healing. Diggs and

Figure 18.6 Isaac Diggs & Edward Hillel, *Sterling Toles #2*, 2017. (Photo courtesy: Diggs & Hillel)

Hillel's photos in turn document those activist efforts and contribute to Black spatial agency and cultural justice.

Diggs and Hillel's photo of the United Sound Systems Recording Studios, Detroit's first independent recording studio operating since 1939, documents the site where many well-known recordings were made, from John Lee Hooker, Charlie Parker, and Miles Davis to Bob Seger and Parliament (Figure 18.7). The lone empty chair in the large empty space surrounded by a red curtain below the hovering lights evokes the endurance of Black space and music, as if sound might still be lingering in the air. When the building was threatened with destruction by a proposed highway expansion, it conjured memories of the past when Detroit's highway planners, while careful not to disrupt white middle-class residential neighborhoods, felt no compunction about destroying Black neighborhoods, especially those closest to downtown (Harvey, 2012).[15] In response to the threat of destruction, the Detroit Sound Conservancy, founded by Carleton Gholz, helped lead a fight to preserve the renowned site and United Sound Systems was declared a local historic district by the city in 2015. The Michigan Department of Transportation purchased the site in 2019 with plans to move it to an adjacent area and eventually sell it (Apel, 2015). Though still a story of displacement for a highway, this victory in preservation is another form of cultural justice, especially after the bulldozing of Paradise Valley and Black Bottom, both neighborhoods famous for their contributions to American music, including blues, big band, and jazz, in the name of 'urban renewal' in the 1960s.

Figure 18.7 Isaac Diggs & Edward Hillel, *United Sound Systems Recording Studios*. (Photo courtesy: Diggs & Hillel)

Black Spatial Agency and Cultural Justice

Motown greats such as Aretha Franklin, Isaac Hayes, Marvin Gaye, and Smokey Robinson and the Miracles also figured among United Sound Systems recording artists. Motown, the American record label founded by Berry Gordy in Detroit in 1959, famously helped shape the sounds of a generation and helped achieve the racial integration of popular music. By documenting and commemorating music's past and present, including its built heritage, Diggs and Hillel's photographic project preserves cultural heritage, affirms a positive cultural identity, and restores spatial agency for the majority Black residents of the city beyond deindustrial decline and corporate gentrification.

Both Dave Jordano and Diggs and Hillel focus on the evolving relationship between ruination and the creative life and history of the city, seeking to intervene in the flow of negative affect created by representations of Detroit's industrial abandonment and decay by presenting images that portray a storied heritage and that multiply connections between economic decline and ongoing life in the city. As a form of activist memory that preserves connections to the artistic life and history of a marginalized population, their works create a more complex understanding of Black cultural contributions that enrich perceptions of Detroit as the images themselves become part of its ongoing life.[16] As Dave Jordano asserts,

> All photographers have a point of view and mine embraced the idea of revealing a more human kind of connection to the city. It was important to me that this work be viewed as a testament to the perseverance of those who have continually struggled to get by and that their lives mattered. It's not all just about emptiness and abandonment.
>
> (Jordano, 2015, p. 23)

Indeed, the city's declining population still stands above 600,000 people, which may come as a surprise to those whose view of Detroit has been shaped primarily by images of empty industrial landscapes and abandoned houses.

Conclusion

Political protests such as the placards at the Packard Plant, activist photography, and artistic community endeavors such as the Heidelberg Project and Power House Productions infuse the city with their own kind of vitality and social justice ethos, validate community memory and history, and become part of the creative and cultural life of the city, complicating the narrative of decay and decline by mobilizing neighborhoods, cohorts, and supporters. However, we must be cautious about romanticizing, as John Patrick Leary observes, "isolated acts of resistance without acknowledging the massive political and social forces aligned against the real transformation, and not just stubborn survival, of the city" (Leary, 2011). Though these acts of resistance are vital for preserving cultural heritage and supporting the ongoing creativity and spatial agency of majority-Black and working-class people in the city, privatized placemaking subverts the ability of low-income and marginalized groups to help shape, use, and benefit from a revitalized downtown business core. Until the economic and social transformation of society makes it possible to support the entire population and provide equality and opportunity for all, ongoing economic struggle for the many and prosperity for the few will remain the order of the day. Nonetheless, these photographic and community projects represent forms of memory activism and cultural justice that are crucial to any kind of city revitalization because they connect our understanding of the past to our experience of the present and our vision for an emancipatory future.

The Routledge Handbook of Deindustrialization Studies

Notes

1 The text on the Packard Plant is revised and excerpted from Apel, D. (2015). *Beautiful Terrible Ruins: Detroit and the Anxiety of Decline*. New Brunswick: Rutgers University Press, pp. 85–86.

2 See 'The Community Houses of Power House Productions', *Forecast*, n.d., written by staff of Public Art Review, viewed 15 June 2024, https://forecastpublicart.org. Also see the Power House Productions Facebook page and website at http://www.powerhouseproductions.org

3 On the capitalist cycle of investment and disinvestment, see Tache, J. (2022, January 6). *Understanding and Fighting Gentrification: A Revolutionary Orientation*. Liberation School. https://www.liberationschool.org/gentrification-a-revolutionary-understanding (Viewed: 15 June 2024).

4 When three teenage white girls from Grosse Pointe Woods spray-painted 'Izzy,' 'bitch,' 'fuck,' and 'Welcome to Detroit' on the alley side of a Gilbert-owned building, Gilbert went to extraordinary lengths to have them identified and punished, sending surveillance photos of the event to all 12,500 of his employees, asking them to post the photos on their social media and offering to cover the cost of repainting the interior and exterior of their home as a reward for information leading to the identification of the perpetrators, in effect turning his employees into his own private police force. The teenage girls, whom Gilbert called 'degenerates,' were quickly identified and received a sentence of 60 hours of community service.

5 There are over a thousand publicly accessible art murals on the exterior walls of buildings in Detroit. A hundred of these murals were commissioned by the city through its City Walls program, launched in 2017, but the overwhelming majority are street art made by artists reclaiming empty spaces, proclaiming their resistance to the narrative of decay that helped spawn the photography genre of 'ruin porn' and often celebrating Black and Brown communities. The murals are frequently produced with the permission of local business and property owners; indeed, they are welcomed by them and have become a tourist attraction.

6 Under steady criticism for his inability or unwillingness to transform Detroit in a way that includes the majority-Black and working-class population (and after suffering a severe stroke in 2020), Dan Gilbert responded with increased outreach through philanthropic projects. In 2021, Gilbert, with his wife Jennifer, announced a $500 million investment in metro Detroit over ten years, with the first $15 million to be put toward paying off property tax debt of low-income homeowners who qualify for the initiative. At the same time, Gilbert, who has been the recipient of numerous tax breaks, in 2022 received a $60 million tax break for yet another building project. See Newman, E. (2022, July 26). $60 Million Tax Break for Dan Gilbert's Hudson Site Project Approved by Detroit City Council. *WDET*. https://wdet.org/2022/07/26/60-million-tax-break-for-dan-gilberts-hudsons-site-project-approved-by-detroit-city-council (Viewed: 15 June 2024).

7 For more on the effect of gentrification on senior access to housing, see Perry, T. et al. (2021). Advocating for the Preservation of Senior Housing: A Coalition at Work Amid Gentrification in Detroit, Michigan. *Housing Policy Debate*, 31(2), pp. 254–273. https://doi.org/10.1080/10511482.2020.1806899

8 On the rhetoric of settler-colonialism used to lure white "urban pioneers," see Quizar, J. (2019). Land of Opportunity: Anti-Black and Settler Logics in the Gentrification of Detroit. *American Indian Culture and Research Journal*, 49(2). https://doi.org/10.17953/aicrj.43.2.quizar

9 For a global view of gentrification, see Lees, L., Shin, H.B. and López-Morales, E. (2016). *Planetary Gentrification*. Cambridge: Polity Press.

10 For discussions of works by these photographers, see Apel, D. (2015). *Beautiful Terrible Ruins: Detroit and the Anxiety of Decline*. New Brunswick: Rutgers University Press; and Apel, D. (2017). Detroit is No Dry Bones. *Michigan Historical Review*, 43(2), pp. 106–108.

11 On the deindustrial sublime, see Apel, D. (2015). Introduction. In *Beautiful Terrible Ruins: Detroit and the Anxiety of Decline*. New Brunswick: Rutgers University Press. Using Erich Fromm's concept of transcendence, Chris Vanderwees similarly argues that such photographs evoke the human need to exceed the limits of existence by experiencing catastrophe in mediation. See Vanderwees, Chris. (2017). Erich Fromm's Psychoanalysis of Transcendence and the Photography of Detroit's Ruins. In Graybow, S. (ed.) *Progressive Psychoanalysis: Essays on Psychoanalysis as a Social Justice Movement*. Newcastle: Cambridge Scholars Publishing, pp. 42–66.

12 For more on industrial ruination as a lived process, see Mah, A. (2012). *Industrial Ruination, Community and Place: Landscapes and Legacies of Urban Decline*. Toronto: University of Toronto Press.

13 This ongoing series may be seen on Jordano's website at davejordano.com, which also includes *A Detroit Nocturne, Marijuana Dispensaries*, and *Early Detroit Work* among other projects.
14 Jordano's work has been exhibited nationally and internationally in museums and galleries. In 2015, Jordano was awarded the Canadian AIMIA AGO prize for photography, and his work is held in several permanent collections, including the Museum of Fine Arts, Boston, the Museum of Fine Arts, Houston, the Detroit Institute of Arts, the Cleveland Museum of Art, the Library of Congress, Washington DC, and the Mary and Leigh Block Museum of Art at Northwestern University in Evanston, Illinois.
15 David Harvey observes,

> The reengineering of inner cities in the United States in the wake of urban uprisings in the 1960s just happened to create major physical highway barriers – moats, in effect – between the citadels of high value downtown property and impoverished inner-city neighborhoods.
>
> Harvey, D. (2012). *Rebel Cities: From the Right to the City to the Urban Revolution.* London: Verso, p. 117

16 Other works that offer more complex portraits of the city include the video *Four Stories* (2003–2004), featuring ethnically diverse teens from Detroit's now-closed Chadsey High School, produced by Dawoud Bey; *Beyond Borders: Latino Immigrants and Southwest Detroit* (2010), presenting the lovingly decorated religious shrines in the yards of the Latinx community along with portraits of Latinx immigrants by Carlos Diaz, and photographs of neighbors, alternative urban lifestyles, and street culture from *Your Town Tomorrow* (2010) by Corine Vermeulen.

Reference List

Apel, Dora. (2015). *Beautiful Terrible Ruins: Detroit and the Anxiety of Decline.* New Brunswick: Rutgers University Press.

Apel, Dora. (2018). Thirsty Cities: Who Owns the Right to Water? In Lindner, Christoph and Meissner, Miriam (eds.) *The Routledge Companion to Urban Imaginaries.* New York: Routledge, pp. 25–40.

Apel, Dora. (2021). Against the Ruins: Music and Black Space in Detroit. In Diggs, Isaac and Hillel, Edward (eds.) *Electronic Landscapes: Music, Black Space and Resistance in Detroit.* New York: KGP. https://www.krisgravesprojects.com/book/electroniclandscapes

Baker, Rachel. (2019). Towards a Politics of Accountability: Feminist Ethics of Care and Whiteness in Detroit's Foreclosure Crisis. *Radical Housing Journal.* https://www.academia.edu/38815903/Toward_a_politics_of_accountability_Feminist_ethics_of_care_and_whiteness_in_Detroits_foreclosure_crisis?email_work_card=view-paper

Bethencourt, Daniel and Stryker, Mark. (2015, June 26). Shepard Fairey Charges: Fine Line between Art, Crime? *Detroit Free Press.* https://www.freep.com/story/news/local/michigan/detroit/2015/06/25/shepard-fairey-arrest-warrant-mixed-/29295239

Brown, Brian. (2017, September). Re-Picturing the 'Post-Fordist' Motor City: Commissioned Street Art in Downtown Detroit. *Architecture_Media_Politics_Society*, 12(1). https://www.scienceopen.com/hosted-document?doi=10.14324/111.444.amps.2017v12i1.001

Cantillon, Zelmarie, Baker, Sarah and Nowak, Raphaël. (2021). A Cultural Justice Approach to Popular Music Heritage in Deindustrialising Cities. *International Journal of Heritage Studies*, 27(1), pp. 73–89. https://doi.org/10.1080/13527258.2020.1768579

Cohen, Rick. (2015, July 6). Dan Gilbert Still Fighting Charges that Quicken Was Subprime Lender in Detroit. *Nonprofit Quarterly.* https://nonprofitquarterly.org/dan-gilbert-still-fighting-charges-that-quicken-was-subprime-lender-in-detroit

Gross, Allie. (2018, September 21). Heidelberg Project is Coming Home, with New HQ in Neighborhood. *Detroit Free Press.* https://www.freep.com/story/news/local/michigan/detroit/2018/09/21/detroit-heidelberg-project/1346622002

Harvey, David. (2012). *Rebel Cities: From the Right to the City to the Urban Revolution.* London: Verso.

The Heidelberg Project website https://www.heidelberg.org

Jones, W. and Carr, B. (2023, September 26). Heidelberg Project in Detroit Scaling Back Due to Financial Hardship. *Click On Detroit.* http://www.clickondetroit.com

Jordano, Dave. (2015). *Detroit – Unbroken Down*. Brooklyn: Powerhouse Books.

Leary, John Patrick. (2011, January). Detroitism. *Guernica*. https://www.guernicamag.com/leary_1_15_11

Linkon, S.L. (2018). *The Half-Life of Deindustrialization: Working-Class Writing about Economic Restructuring*. Ann Arbor, MI: University of Michigan Press.

Mah, Alice. (2012). *Industrial Ruination, Community and Place: Landscapes and Legacies of Urban Decline*. Toronto: University of Toronto Press.

Montgomery, Alesia. (2016, July). Reappearance of the Public: Placemaking, Minoritization and Resistance in Detroit. *International Journal of Urban and Regional Research*, 40(4), pp. 776–799.

Quizar, Jessi. (2020). A Bucket in the River: Race and Public Discourse on Water Shutoffs in Detroit. *Social Identities*, 26(4), pp. 429–445.

Russo, John and Linkon, Sherry Lee. (n.d.). *The Social Costs of Deindustrialization*. Center for Working Class Studies, Youngstown State University. https://ysu.edu/center-working-class-studies/social-costs-deindustrialization

Tache, Joe. (2022, January 6). *Understanding and Fighting Gentrification: A Revolutionary Orientation*. Liberation School. https://www.liberationschool.org/gentrification-a-revolutionary-understanding

Toles, Sterling. (2021). Interview. In Diggs, Isaac and Hillel, Edward (eds.) *Electronic Landscapes: Music, Black Space and Resistance in Detroit*. New York: KGP, May 2018. https://www.krisgravesprojects.com/book/electroniclandscapes

Vanderwees, Chris. (2017). Erich Fromm's Psychoanalysis of Transcendence and the Photography of Detroit's Ruins. In Graybow, Scott (ed.) *Progressive Psychoanalysis: Essays on Psychoanalysis as a Social Justice Movement*. Newcastle: Cambridge Scholars Publishing, pp. 42–66.

Yezbick, Julia. (2020). Domesticating Detroit: Art Houses, Blight, and the Image of Care. *City & Society*, 32(2), pp. 316–344.

19

UNCOVERING THE DISCOVERY OF THE RUHR

Representations of Deindustrialization in Germany's Former Industrial Heartland

Helen Wagner

When German Nobel Prize-winning author, Heinrich Böll, teamed up with German photographer, Chargesheimer, to publish a book on the Ruhr in 1958, he opened with a rather astonishing observation: "The Ruhr has not yet been discovered" (Böll and Chargesheimer, 1958, p. 5). This statement, which would eventually become the probably most famous of all first sentences in books written about the Ruhr, may have come as a surprise to its contemporary readers. For the Ruhr was not only the biggest industrial area in Europe, but it had also repeatedly been at the center of national and international political turmoil in the first half of the twentieth century (Scharrenburg, 2017; Thiemeyer, 2016). Furthermore, an established tradition of literary and photographic representations of the Ruhr dated back to the Interwar Period (Grütter, 2014).[1] However, it was not the region's industrial or political significance that Böll considered undiscovered. Rather, it was the people and the landscape they were living in. To him, the people were virtually covered up by the well-known figures of the region's economic magnitude:

> One in four large cities has its place there, one in eight Germans its home. In a hundred years, the population has increased fifteen fold, while in Germany it has barely tripled. But even numbers remain only mysticism or conceptual barbed wire, as long as the object which they are supposed to explain remains unknown: 6,000,000 people, 120,000,000 tons of coal, 10,000,000 tons of steel – reality is hidden behind zeros, the province in which the people live and the coal is mined, the steel is produced, is relegated to a misty distance. The Ruhr has not yet been discovered.
>
> *(Böll and Chargesheimer, 1958, p. 5)[2]*

With their book, Böll and Chargesheimer wanted to depict the region with a raw and yet empathic focus on the industrial landscape as a space for everyday life and hard work (Schneider, 2007, pp. 273–274). To them, the industrial landscape appeared as a space in which cities merged into one another with almost no green or white but with soot blackening the walls and the sky. They depicted a landscape that was characterized not only by plants, noise, and industrial smells but foremost by hard-working people, whom they perceived as honest and down to earth.

DOI: 10.4324/9781003308324-28

The book has drawn the attention of historical research in several dimensions. First, Böll and Chargesheimer unknowingly portrayed the Ruhr on the eve of deindustrialization, traveling it in 1957 and publishing their account of the region under the title 'Im Ruhrgebiet' [Inside the Ruhr] in the following year. With the beginning of the coal crisis just around the corner, they portrayed the Ruhr during a time that would eventually become its history's turning point, as the director of the regional Ruhr Museum, Heinrich Theodor Grütter, pointed out in an exhibition dedicated to the book in 2014 (Grütter, 2014, p. 286). Second, the book sparked outrage from local politicians over the supposedly negative portrayal of the region, which they thought was misleading and damaging to its image, its cities, and its inhabitants (Grebe, 2014). The dawn of the coal crisis cast a different light on the controversy, revealing that the book was offering not only a view of the region in the present but also a glimpse of its potential future. This future potential would be measured not only in economic development but also in how the region was perceived from the inside and from the outside. The "very soon legendary photo book" not only triggered a heated debate about the appropriateness of the region's portrayal, but it also initiated "a swelling tide of photo books about the Ruhr, which has not subsided to this day" (Grütter and Grebe, 2014a, p. 16, 2014b, pp. 9–10). In a 2014 exhibition, the Ruhr Museum counted 62 photo books that followed Bölls and Chargesheimers's *Im Ruhrgebiet* between 1958 and 2014. While some documented a certain perspective on the region, like the outsider view of Böll and Chargesheimer 'discovering' the Ruhr as a seemingly terra incognita, others produced specific images, often directly countering negative perceptions of the Ruhr as an economically and culturally poor industrial landscape.

While images shape the perception of urban spaces in general, the Ruhr has a specific tradition of visual, especially photographic, representations that shape how people from inside and outside look at the region. Together with literary representations, photographic accounts of the region drew the attention of historical and literary scholars since the 1980s, when the social history of the working class was gaining attention in universities, research institutions, and museums (Eskildsen, 1981; Borsdorf and Eskildsen, 1987; Barbian, 1997; Hallenberger, 2000). Nevertheless, for a long time representations were seen as merely an add-on to the history of deindustrialization that was understood primarily as an economic process that had social consequences and also a "cultural side" (Rüsen, 2000, p. 175). In this chapter, I argue, that we should understand the economic, social, and cultural changes as constitutive elements of deindustrialization. Literary and visual representations are valuable sources for analyzing the meanings of deindustrialization, as a growing body of research has shown (Barbian, 2007; Linkon, 2013; Linkon, 2018; Caspers et al., 2019). In case of the Ruhr, these sources are especially crucial to understand the ongoing debate about the region's relation to its own past. There has been increasing criticism that the Ruhr is stuck in its own past and that the strong focus on its industrial heritage would block its way into a post-industrial future (RAG-Stiftung, 2016; Herbert, 2018; Muschick, 2021). Some have argued that the region's dedication to industrial heritage was a way of culturally compensating for feelings of loss due to deindustrialization (Grütter, 2007, 2017). I would instead argue that the strong presence of the region's past is much more a result of the economization of the industrial past as a resource in the competition for state funding and private investments. Furthermore, I argue that the way the region's past was used to create a future also means that the emphasis on industrial heritage is becoming more problematic in the present (Wagner, 2022).

In this chapter, I look at representations of deindustrialization at the intersection of photography and image politics. Image politics purposefully influence how a region is perceived, drawing on existing images including visual representations. I will focus on how image campaigns depicted the Ruhr and what they tell us about its contested identity. Although the Ruhr was Europe's biggest industrial area and a motor of German industrialization, its identity as an industrial space was constantly up for debate. In the first half of the twentieth century, the region was seen not only as an industrial giant but also as an industrial Moloch with conflicting patterns of fascination and disapproval for the cultural and social dimensions of industrial modernity. Since the late 1950s, deindustrialization has added another layer to the discussion as the Ruhr came to be perceived as a space of ongoing social and economic crisis and struggles with environmental issues like polluted air and soil. This debate not only affected the cultural response to industrialization and deindustrialization processes, but it also influenced its economic and social development, as the region's image shaped the way politicians, investors, and residents thought about funding the regional economy and about investing and living in the Ruhr. The perception of the Ruhr was heavily influenced by literary and visual representations of the region, which were taken up by image politics that built on existing images as much as to counter them.

Most photo books published in the 1920s and 1930s, especially those published during the Nazi-dictatorship from 1933 to1945, tried to paint a positive picture of the Ruhr as a prospering industrial area that still left room for rural idyll (Schneider, 2007, p. 272). When Böll and Chargesheimer published what they considered an authentic representation of the industrial landscape and its inhabitants, causing outrage among local politicians and institutions over the seemingly defaming book, the *Siedlungsverband Ruhrkohlenbezirk* (SVR) published its own photo book in return. The SVR, a regional association responsible for, among other things, planning and publicity, published a photo book called *Ruhrgebiet. Porträt ohne Pathos* [The Ruhr. Portrait without pathos] to paint a more positive and – in the eyes of local representatives – more appropriate picture than Böll and Chargesheimer (Siedlungsverband Ruhrkohlenbezirk, 1959). In this book, the region's heavy industry was either left out of the photos or shown in dramatic forms that added an emotional dimension to the image of an industrial giant, contrary to the book's title. Overall, the book depicted an industrial landscape untouched by crisis, even though the process of economic decline had already begun.

In 1959, the year the SVR published its book, the first big coal mine shut down due to the coal crisis. Within ten years, the number of operating mines in the Ruhr had shrunk from 142 to only 57 (Goch, 2002, p. 162). German media depicted the Ruhr as a region fighting an ongoing battle with economic and social decline, facing the "the worst structural crisis of the century in the heartland of German industry," leaving behind the "largest mine-graveyard throughout Europe."[3] In the 1970s and 1980s, the Ruhr struggled not only with the consequences of the first and second coal crises but also with the consequences of the oil and steel crises. At the time, those creating representations of the Ruhr had to consider not whether they should paint an aesthetic picture of the industrial landscape but rather how to depict the consequences of deindustrialization.

Facing a seemingly constant state of economic crises, the Ruhr had to consider not only what its future would look like but also whether it would have a future at all. Unlike other regions, the Ruhr was never defined by natural, political, or administrative criteria; its identity as a region was based entirely on the rapid growth of the coal and steel industries in the late nineteenth century. The decline of these key industries in the second half of the twentieth century therefore raised the question of whether the Ruhr would continue to exist as a unified region in the future. We can see this in efforts by many of the region's cities to distance themselves from the Ruhr. In the 1950s and 1960s, slogans such as "Essen is quite different" tried to distinguish cities from the expectations of what a city in Germany's industrial heartland would be like (Fleiß, 2010). From the perspective of the SVR, the Ruhr's regional association, this was a dangerous development. The association's head of PR wanted to end the cities' demarcation attempts and laid out a strategy for a major shift in regional image politics. In the early 1970s, the SVR started a new image campaign to promote the Ruhr as an attractive and productive industrial area and to cast off the image of a region in crisis. Most importantly, the campaign presented the Ruhr as a coherent space to prevent it from dissolving into separate cities with different, competing images.

SVR's head of PR, Dietrich Springorum, had big plans for his new strategy. In cooperation with a futurology scientist and journalist, the SVR planned to host a world exhibition in the Ruhr in 1970, parallel to the world expo in Osaka, Japan. Under the title 'The Ruhr on its way into the year 2000,' the Ruhr-Expo was supposed to honor the fiftieth anniversary of the foundation of the SVR. The goal was to create a common vision for the region's future and to "show that we will not waste any more time crying for lost glory."[4] After initial excitement, the project failed due to high costs and competition between the cities of the Ruhr. Eventually, it was realized as a much smaller exhibition that traveled throughout Germany, France, Italy, and Great Britain. The exhibition, "Das Ruhrgebiet – heute schon Zukunft" [The Ruhr – future already] (Siedlungsverband Ruhrgebiet, 1973), combined photos of the industrial landscape and the region's opportunities for leisure and cultural activities with maps and charts showing the region's economic structure to depict the exhibition and its catalog the Ruhr's future as one that could be designed and managed, not a scenario of uncontrollable crisis and disaster. It was supposed to show the effects of large-scale structural reform programs and thorough regional planning using factual but also optimistic language. Texts, images, maps, and statistics aimed at presenting the region as a space shaped by systematic and scientific planning.

The exhibition was part of a bigger PR-strategy titled 'The Ruhr – Heading for a New Future.' In contrast to the efforts of single cities trying to distance themselves from the region's negative image, the head of PR in the SVR wanted to address those stereotypes confidently. In 1974, he designed a campaign using drawings by a popular German cartoonist that turned the negative stereotypes about the Ruhr as a dusty and ugly industrial landscape into something funny, reinterpreting the region's image rather than suppressing it. Posters and advertisements using these images were meant to offer an ironic take on common negative stereotypes of the region. In Springorum's view, this was a more promising strategy than trying to normalize the Ruhr's image by pretending it was like any other place in Germany. However, Springorum's irony did not win over the cities' political leaders. Representatives of Duisburg, Essen, Bochum, and Dortmund feared the campaign would do even more harm to the region's image, as historian Uta C. Schmidt has shown in her research on Springorum's strategy (Schmidt, 2006). Due to the political outcry, the campaign was stopped immediately. In the following years, however, the perception of the Ruhr as a crisis-ridden region with a low life value strengthened, mainly due to media attention that followed the pattern of "outside observers, especially the media, [defining] deindustrialized communities as places of failure" (Russo and Linkon, 2003, p. 202).

From the inside, there was a growing interest in the transformation of the Ruhr, partly driven by a socially critical perspective on the consequences of deindustrialization. Highly influential was the photography program of the Folkwang School, a local arts college that from 1972 to 2007 was partly integrated in the University of Essen.[5] After the department of design and its photography program became part of the University of Essen in 1972, cooperation developed between photography and social history research. Among other things, this resulted in exhibitions in local museums in the 1980s (Eskildsen, 1981; Borsdorf and Eskildsen, 1987).

A first exhibition and accompanying photo book in 1981 show how the social documentary approach of the Folkwang photography program produced a socially critical image of the Ruhr in the late 1970s and 1980s. This "democratization of the image of the Ruhr" (Grütter, 2014, p. 286) reflects increasing cooperation between professional and nonprofessional photographers. In preparation for the exhibition, an open call invited clubs and individuals to contribute photos on 'Living and Working.' Most of the photos displayed and subsequently published in the catalog showed black-and-white scenes of heavy industrial work, run-down industrial wastelands, workers' housing estates, and pictures of everyday family and school life, clubs, and neighborhood festivals. They also showed graffiti with racial slurs and 'no-future' slogans. The photo book did not aestheticize representations of the Ruhr; it offered subjective documentation of life in the region. The title, *Wie lebt man im Ruhrgebiet? Bewohner fotografierten, Bilder von Amateuren und Profis* [How to live in the Ruhr? Residents photographed. Pictures of amateurs and professionals], marked the book as an interior view of the region, documented by residents who, as if in passing, photographed their everyday lives. Both the title and the visual language of the book served as strategies of authentication, claiming the authority of locals to depict their experiences of everyday life in the Ruhr. The book thus focused on the perspectives of the region's inhabitants, whose photographic practices oscillated between stubborn appropriation and reproduction of internalized visual norms and clichés. Projects like this complemented the social history research, which also focused on the past everyday life of the Ruhr's inhabitants using the then-new method of oral history (Niethammer, 1983a, 1983b; Niethammer and Plato, 1985).

The strong research focus on the region's industrial history resulted in a growing commitment to document the ongoing process of deindustrialization. A very influential example for this is an exhibition of the predecessor of today's Ruhr Museum, which in the 1980s was called Ruhrlandmusuem. In 1985, the museum instructed ten photographers to document the Ruhr's transformation and displayed the results in an exhibition called "Endlich so wie überall? Bilder und Texte aus dem Ruhrgebiet" [Like any other place after all? Images and texts from the Ruhr] – a title that became a dictum of the discussion about the Ruhr's deindustrialization process (Borsdorf and Eskildsen, 1987). The photos were published along with essays by influential social historians of the region and literary texts. The texts addressed the Ruhr as an industrial landscape and problematized the attribution of 'home' to the region from various perspectives, whether from the perspective of migrants, against the background of a lack of individual future prospects, or the aesthetic quality of the landscape. Other than images of 'Jobs' and 'Leisure Time,' the photographs were taken in black and white. Centering the question of regional specificity, the pictures showed the Ruhr as a unique industrial landscape but also as an urban space like any other. The book referenced established motifs such as industrial backdrops in contrast to rural scenes or the typical architecture of collieries and workers' settlements, but it also depicted an interchangeable urban space by displaying images of everyday life, of work and leisure that refrained from conventional motifs such as pigeon breeding or coal-dust-smeared miners. The titular question 'Like any other place after all?' brought out the tension between normalization and regional specificity. The project was part of a larger initiative of the Ruhrlandmuseum to create a photographic archive of the region that should include historic pictures as well as document the deindustrialization

The Routledge Handbook of Deindustrialization Studies

process. The project was intended as a counterpoint to regional image politics, as historian Lutz Niethammer made clear in his 1987 essay:

> These pictures by a new generation of photographic intellectuals from the Ruhr, contribute to the active creation of an identity from below and from inside for the elsewhere propagated image of the driving force of Germany, so that it does not degenerate into make-up.
>
> *(Niethammer, 1987, p. 9)*[6]

He criticized the region's image politics as degenerating into make-up, referring to the latest PR strategy of the Ruhr's regional association, which had been reformed and renamed into *Kommunalverband Ruhrgebiet (KVR)* in 1979.

While the need to deconstruct the negative image of the Ruhr as a region of failure had grown more and more important, it was not until the mid-1980s that the regional association of the Ruhr mounted a major national image campaign. After the failure of the ironic cartoon campaign ten years earlier, this effort aimed to suppress the negative clichés by normalizing the region's image. The campaign depicted the Ruhr as an economically powerful and as an aesthetically and culturally attractive region. These motifs, which appeared in newspaper ads and billboards all over Germany, were presented through large-format photographs with an accompanying text box and the campaign slogan: "Das Rurhgebiet – ein starkes Stück Deutschland" [The Ruhr – A driving force of Germany][7] – the slogan Lutz Niethammer mocked in his essay about the photo project.

The first images, published in 1985, set the tone of the campaign that ran until 1995. It showed an idyllic scenery with cows lying in green grass in front of calm water and trees in the background (Figure 19.1). Taking the position of an imaginary visitor, the text underneath the picture asked, where the Ruhr can be found. The poster answered in a text box, stating that the Ruhr is by no means the gray industrial landscape one might expect but full of flourishing green nature reflecting determined efforts to conserve nature and re-naturalize old industrial sites. As this ad shows, the campaign sought to deconstruct the area's negative image as an ugly industrial landscape with no nature and no quality of life for its inhabitants. To accomplish this, the ads contrasted the rural idyll with other images showing the region's possibilities for leisure activities. The campaign also compared the urbanity of the region to international metropoles. For example, a 1986 image showed a coffee house scene, suggesting that one could find the culture of Vienna in the Ruhr, as the ad's text claimed.

The strategy also aimed to visually normalize the Ruhr to break down common clichés about everyday life in the region. For example, a poster from 1988 showed a radiant young woman hanging up equally radiant white laundry, countering the image of laundry blackened from the soot of endlessly smoking factory chimneys. The blue sky over the Ruhr – an image that Willy Brandt made popular during the national elections of 1961 – was no longer presented as a vision of the future but as a long-realized present. Here, the campaign did not present the consequences of deindustrialization as failure but as an improvement of living conditions. Accordingly, another poster from 1991 showed a little boy lying on a hay bale and enjoying the fresh air in the Ruhr, suggesting that air pollution no longer endangered residents, especially children.

However, the campaign did present the Ruhr not only as an attractive place to live but also as an attractive place for investment and for companies to settle down. This meant

Figure 19.1 KVR-campaign motif, 1985, Kommunalverband Ruhrgebiet, ed. Das Ruhrgebiet. Ein starkes Stück Deutschland: 10 Jahre Werbung für eine unerschöpfliche Region. Essen, Düsseldorf: Pomp, 1996, p. 10.

retaining the image of the Ruhr as an industrial center while also highlighting changed forms of industry and new types of work. The ads emphasize the region's potential in educating young people for modern technology jobs and as a producer of new technology at the same time. In 1987, ads featured images of robotic research at a university in highlighting and the revolution of telecommunication by local companies. The campaign also presented new industrial sectors replacing coal mining and steel production. For example, a photo from 1988 showed a winding tower reflected in the polished engine hood of a newly fabricated Opel-car (Figure 19.2).

The winding tower served as a symbol of the past contrasting with the Opel car factory a new and prosperous industrial branch situated at a former coal mining site. The short text in the ad references 'future' three times – virtually demanding it for a region that seemed to have lost its future with the end of the classic industrial era. As a major car producer, Opel was meant to prove that the future of the region could still be designed through planning and structural reform programs funding new industrial branches to replace coalmines and steel plants – a belief that was threatened by the end of the economic boom in the Western industrial world (Doering-Manteuffel and Raphael, 2010; Hartog, 2015).[8] The sunrise symbolized the positive change brought about by the economic reforms and the change from a past based on mining to a new but different industrial future. As a whole, the campaign did not make many references to the region's past, except for one 1987 ad that referenced important moments or events in the preindustrial past of the Ruhr but leaving out its more recent industrial history.

Figure 19.2 KVR-campaign motif, 1988, Kommunalverband Ruhrgebiet, ed. Das Ruhrgebiet. Ein starkes Stück Deutschland: 10 Jahre Werbung für eine unerschöpfliche Region. Essen, Düsseldorf: Pomp, 1996, p. 64.

This changed completely with the follow-up campaign "Der Pott kocht" [The pot is boiling] launched in 1998 (Kommunalverband Ruhrgebiet and Springer&Jacoby, 2000). Here, the reference to the region's industrial past was key.

The campaign responded to criticism that the earlier efforts depicted a Ruhr that was far from reality and driven by a negative image and a lack of confidence. The new campaign presented the region as unique and special for its industrial past, a development pushed by the efforts of the International Building Exhibition (IBA) Emscher Park, which began in 1989 and ran until 1999 (Reicher, Niemann, and Uttke, 2011). During that time many material relics of the region's industrial past were turned into monuments and spaces for cultural events. The motifs of the new KVR campaign prominently featured these new industrial heritage sites. Now, it was the conductor who directed the rhythm in a steel mill featured in a 1998 ad (Figure 19.3). Another ad claimed that a DJ playing in a vivid nightclub situated in the pithead buildings of a former mine was the son and grandson of coal miners. The ad-text suggested that he continued the family tradition of working nightshifts in a mine performing a new type of labor, thus profiting from the transformation of deindustrialized sites into cultural spaces (Figure 19.4). These images highlighted the many cultural events in the region, presenting the Ruhr not as trying to catch up with other metropoles but as having its own unique urban culture.

The campaign staged the uniqueness of the area by actively reframing its existing image. In a way, this campaign picked up where the cartoon campaign left off in the 1970s, redefining

Uncovering the Discovery of the Ruhr

Figure 19.3 KVR-campaign motif, 1998 Kommunalverband Ruhrgebiet, and Springer&Jacoby, eds. Ein Starkes Stück Selbstbewusstsein: Der Pott Kocht. Bottrop, Essen: Pomp, 2000, p. 46.

Figure 19.4 KVR-campaign motif, 1998, Kommunalverband Ruhrgebiet, and Springer&Jacoby, eds. Ein Starkes Stück Selbstbewusstsein: Der Pott Kocht. Bottrop, Essen: Pomp, 2000, p. 42.

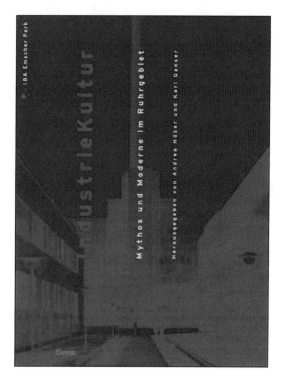

Figure 19.5 Final publication of the IBA Emscher Park, 1999, Andrea Höber and Karl Ganser, eds., IndustrieKultur: Mythos Und Moderne Im Ruhrgebiet (Essen: Klartext, 1999).

terms with negative connotations, like 'Pott,' a name for the area used in the campaign's main slogan in more positive ways. This reinterpretation was based on casting the industrial past as a source of pride that distinguished the Ruhr throughout Germany and the Western industrial world. The campaign also suggested that the region should be proud to be finding new ways to build on its industrial past – a way that was mainly shaped by the IBA Emscher Park.

The building exhibition functioned as a large-scale reform program, especially for the northern part of the Ruhr. It presented itself as a "Werkstatt für die Zukunft alter Industriegebiete" [workshop for the future of old industrial regions] (Minister für Stadtentwicklung, Wohnen und Verkehr des Landes Nordrhein-Westfalen, 1988), thus claiming to design new ideas of the future not only for the Ruhr but for Western industrial society in general. To this end, it pursued projects not only in landscape design and housing construction but also in public history. Integrating public history into the building exhibition was not meant to intensify the examination of the region's industrial past for its own sake or to strengthen a critical awareness of history. Rather, the director of the IBA Emscher Park, Karl Ganser, called for a targeted transfiguration of the industrial past, which was to be narrated as a unique selling point of the Ruhr. In his eyes, the missing perspective for the future of the region had to be created by a new image strategy that, contrary to the previous strategy, emphasized the uniqueness of the Ruhr by positively reinterpreting the industrial past. He offered a motto for this new strategy: "Proud of yesterday – courageous for tomorrow" [Stolz auf gestern – Mutig für morgen] (Archiv im Haus der Geschichte des Ruhrgebiets

Figure 19.6 Ruhr.2010-campaign motif, 2010, Julia Frohne et al. (ed.): Ruhr: Vom Mythos Zur Marke, Marketing und PR für die Kulturhauptstadt Europas RUHR, 2010 (Essen: Klartext, 2010), p. 15.

(AHGR) Bochum, 1996). The pride in yesterday was based on a mythologization of the industrial past, which is why Ganser explicitly called for a transfiguration of the coal and steel industry. He pleaded for the creation of strong images of the material relics of the industrial past. The aesthetics of industrial design were put into focus and enhanced using artistic lighting or visual effects, as can be seen for example on the cover of the IBA's final publication called "Industriekultur. Mythos und Moderne im Ruhrgebiet" [Industrial Culture. Myth and Modernity in the Ruhr] (Höber and Ganser, 1999) (Figure 19.5).

The industrial past thus served as a resource for marketing a new form of tourism centered on industrial heritage as well as in the cultural and creative sector. This development peaked in the region's 2004 application for the title of the European Capital of Culture in 2010, which served a double purpose. It was meant both to improve the Ruhr's image to the outside world and to create a sense of identity for those within the region. To do this, deindustrialization had to be presented as a success story. Following the strategy of the International Building Exhibition, the narrative did not focus on classic economic reform programs as the settlement of new service or production branches, but rather on the cultural sector as the driving force for managing the process of deindustrialization. This is captured in the motto of the application for the title of Capital of Culture: "Change through Culture – Culture through Change" [Wandel durch Kultur – Kultur durch Wandel] (Pleitgen, 2010).

At the same time, the European Capital of Culture offered an opportunity to present the Ruhr as a coherent space like no image campaign before, expressed in the new label of 'European Metropolis Ruhr' chosen for the application. The spatial designation 'Ruhrgebiet,' on the other hand, was to be relegated to the background, as one of two managing directors of the 'Ruhr.2010' campaign emphasized: "Ruhrgebiet smelled very much of the past, evoked images of dying mining, the steel industry going out of business, washed-up cities and a poisoned landscape. We wanted to tackle this image" (Pleitgen, 2010).[9] The image posters for the Capital of Culture illustrated this approach to industrial heritage as a means of shaping the future.

For example, a poster showing a new building at the World Heritage Site Zeche Zollverein included a quotation from Swiss writer Adolf Muschg, who had been a member of the national jury for the title of European Capital of Culture. In his reflection on the jury's decision in favor of the Ruhr, he wrote that the "former coal-mining area no longer breathed dust, but future" (Figure 19.6) (Muschg, 2005). Half a century after Heinrich Böll and Chargesheimer claimed that the Ruhr had not yet been discovered, the world was invited to discover yet another Ruhr that had nothing to do with the old images of a dirty and failing industrial region but that was presented as ready for a post-industrial future.

However, just as Böll wrote on the eve of deindustrialization, one could say the region still somehow seems "relegated to a misty distance."[10] Now, representations of the Ruhr that focus on its industrial heritage hide what went lost in the process of turning the past into a resource for the future. The urge to use the past merely as a resource to create a future-oriented identity for the region led to the creation of shortened and smoothed narratives. Problematic parts of the region's history, such as the suffering that came with hard industrial work, class struggle, or racism against labor migrants, were left out to produce a narrative that would serve as a marketing instrument for the Ruhr. Representations of the past were oriented at their utilization potential as an image resource for the future. A critical historiography of deindustrialization processes should try to deconstruct this market-oriented utilization of the past and could thus bring more clarity and differentiation into the current discussion about the risks of the past hindering the future.

Ultimately, such research could help deindustrialization studies, as it considers how communities have made sense of deindustrialization processes, which is essential to the understanding of current debates about how feelings of neglect in the working class might give rise to populist movements. While a simple causal connection between more economically challenged parts of the Ruhr and electoral success of Germany's far right-wing party fails to provide a sufficient answer to a very complex problem, a closer look at how the far right reaches out to the communities of deindustrialized spaces might help. In the Ruhr, right-wing extremists increasingly use nostalgic images of the industrial past for their political campaigns, as Stefan Berger has pointed out (Berger, 2021). The success of this usage of the past by the far right of the present can be understood only if we take a broader look at how the past was integrated in the collective identity and memory of the communities in question. Therefore, analyzing representations of deindustrialization in the Ruhr from a critical perspective sheds an important light on a region that often serves as a point of reference in transnational comparisons of deindustrialization processes.

Notes

1 Cf. Grütter, H.T. (2014). Böll/Chargesheimer und die Folgen. Das Bild des Ruhrgebiets im Strukturwandel. In Grütter, H.T. and Grebe, S. (eds.) *Chargesheimer*. Köln: Buchhandlung Walter König, pp. 284–297.

2 Jede vierte Großstadt hat dort ihren Platz, jeder achte Bundesdeutsche seine Heimat; in hundert Jahren ist die Bevölkerungszahl ums Fünfzehnfache gestiegen, während sie in Deutschland kaum ums Dreifache stieg. Doch bleiben auch Zahlen nur Mystik oder begrifflicher Stacheldraht, solange der Gegenstand, den sie erklären sollen, unbekannt bleibt: 6.000.000 Menschen, 120.000.000 Tonnen Kohle, 10.000.000 Tonnen Stahl – da wird die Wirklichkeit hinter Nullen versteckt, wird die Provinz, in der die Menschen leben, die Kohlen gefördert werden, der Stahl erzeugt wird, in nebelhafte Ferne gerückt. Entdeckt ist das Ruhrgebiet noch nicht.
  Böll, H. and Chargesheimer. (1958). *Im Ruhrgebiet*. Frankfurt am Main: Büchergilde Gutenberg, p. 5 (translation by the author).
3 "Im Herzen der deutschen Industrie wütet die ärgste Strukturkrise des Jahrhunderts. . . . Zwischen Rhein und Ruhr liegt der größte Zechen-Friedhof Europas", N.N. (1967, April 9). Kumpel Antons Ende: SPIEGEL-Report über die Krise an der Ruhr. *Der Spiegel* (translation by the author).
4 "nach außen demonstrieren, daß wir keine Zeit mehr damit verlieren, vergangener Herrlichkeit nachzujammern", N.N. (1969, April 9). 'Ruhr-Expo 70' Hat Sich Etabliert: Im Schatten Einer Alten Zeche Wird Für Die Zukunft Geplant. *Ruhr Nachrichten* (translation by the author).
5 On the history of universities in the Ruhr, see, for example, Celebi, T.J. (2013). Zwei Namen, Zwei Traditionen Und Eine Universität: Gemeinsam Auf Dem Weg. *Duisburger Jahrbuch 2014*; Celebi, T.J. (2015). Universität als Steuerungsinstrument: Die Ruhr-Universität Zwischen Gesellschaftspolitik, Hochschul- Und Landesplanung. In Hoppe-Sailer, R., Jöchner, C. and Schmitz, F. (eds.) *Ruhr-Universität Bochum: Architekturvision Der Nachkriegsmoderne*. Berlin: Mann, pp. 21–30; Claßen, L. (2003). Hochschulen Und Fachhochschulen Im Ruhrgebiet. In Lange, S. (ed.) *Metropolregion Ruhr: Perspektiven Für Das 21. Jahrhundert*. 1st edn. Oldenburg: Verl. Kommunikation & Wirtschaft, pp. 37–43.
6 [Dadurch konnten diese Bilder einer neuen Generation fotografischer Intellektueller aus dem Revier dazu beitragen, daß der andernorts betriebenen Imagebildung für das starke Stück Deutschland durch eine aktive Identitätsbildung von unten und innen Leben eingehaucht wird, damit sie nicht zur Maskenbildnerei verkommt.] Niethammer, L. (1987). Neue Aspekte der Ruhr Kultur: Zu einer Sammlung aktueller Fotodokumentationen aus dem Ruhrgebiet. In Borsdorf, U. and Eskildsen, U. (eds.) *Endlich so wie überall? Bilder und Texte aus dem Ruhrgebiet*. Essen: Kulturstiftung Ruhr, p. 9 (translation by the author).
7 [Das Ruhrgebiet – ein starkes Stück Deutschland], Kommunalverband Ruhrgebiet (ed.). (1996). *Das Ruhrgebiet. Ein starkes Stück Deutschland: 10 Jahre Werbung für eine unerschöpfliche Region*. Essen, Düsseldorf: Pomp.
8 The Opel factory was eventually shut down in 2014 and is therefore a well-known example for the shortcomings of a classic approach to economic reforms in the Ruhr.
9 [Ruhrgebiet roch sehr nach Vergangenheit, rief Bilder von sterbendem Bergbau, verlöschender Stahlindustrie, abgewrackten Städten und vergifteter Landschaft hervor. Gegen dieses Image wollten wir angehen.] (translation by the author).
10 See note 2.

Reference List

Barbian, J.-P. (1997). Die Entdeckung des Ruhrgebiets: Facetten eines unvollendeten Gesamtkunstwerks. In Barbian, J.-P. and Heid, L. (eds.) *Die Entdeckung des Ruhrgebiets: Das Ruhrgebiet in Nordrhein-Westfalen 1946–1996*. Essen: Klartext, pp. 9–22.

Barbian, J.-P. (2007). "Schau in den Ofen, da glüht die Kraft": Der Widerschein des Ruhrgebiets in der deutschen Literatur des 20. Jahrhunderts. In Ditt, K. and Tenfelde, K. (eds.) *Das Ruhrgebiet in Rheinland und Westfalen: Koexistenz und Konkurrenz des Raumbewusstseins im 19. und 20. Jahrhundert*. Paderborn: Ferdinand Schöningh, pp. 289–311.

Berger, S. (2021). Vom Nutzen und Nachteil der Nostalgie: Das Kulturerbe der Deindustrialisierung im globalen Vergleich. *Zeithistorische Forschungen*, 18(1), pp. 93–121. https://doi.org/10.14765/ZZF.DOK-2299

Böll, H. and Chargesheimer. (1958). *Im Ruhrgebiet*. Frankfurt am Main: Büchergilde Gutenberg.

Borsdorf, U. and Eskildsen, U. (eds.). (1987). *Endlich so wie überall? Bilder und Texte aus dem Ruhrgebiet*. Schriftenreihe der Kulturstiftung Ruhr 3. Essen: Kulturstiftung Ruhr.

Caspers, B., Hallenberger, D., Jung, W. and Parr, R. (2019). *Ruhrgebietsliteratur seit 1960: Eine Geschichte nach Knotenpunkten.* Berlin: J.B. Metzler. https://doi.org/10.1007/978-3-476-04868-4

Celebi, T.J. (2013). Zwei Namen, zwei Traditionen und eine Universität: Gemeinsam auf dem Weg. *Duisburger Jahrbuch 2014*, pp. 46–51.

Celebi, T.J. (2015). Universität als Steuerungsinstrument: Die Ruhr-Universität zwischen Gesellschaftspolitik, Hochschul- und Landesplanung. In Hoppe-Sailer, R., Jöchner, C. and Schmitz, F. (eds.) *Ruhr-Universität Bochum: Architekturvision der Nachkriegsmoderne.* Berlin: Mann, pp. 21–30.

Claßen, L. (2003). Hochschulen und Fachhochschulen im Ruhrgebiet. In Lange, S. (ed.) *Metropolregion Ruhr: Perspektiven für das 21. Jahrhundert.* 1. Ausg, Edition Städte – Kreise – Regionen. Oldenburg: Verl. Kommunikation & Wirtschaft, pp. 37–43.

Doering-Manteuffel, A. and Raphael, L. (2010). *Nach dem Boom: Perspektiven auf die Zeitgeschichte seit 1970.* 2nd edn. Göttingen: Vandenhoeck & Ruprecht.

Eskildsen, U. (ed.). (1981). *Wie lebt man im Ruhrgebiet: Bewohner fotografierten, Bilder von Amateuren und Profis.* Essen: Museum Folkwang.

Fleiß, D. (2010). *Auf dem Weg zum "starken Stück Deutschland": Image- und Identitätsbildung im Ruhrgebiet in Zeiten von Kohle- und Stahlkrise.* Duisburg: Univ.-Verl. Rhein-Ruhr.

Goch, S. (2002). *Eine Region im Kampf mit dem Strukturwandel: Bewältigung von Strukturwandel und Strukturpolitik im Ruhrgebiet.* Essen: Klartext.

Grebe, S. (2014). "Dabei habe ich die härtesten Photos gar nicht veröffentlicht!": Neue Fotografien Chargesheimers aus dem Ruhrgebiet 1957. In Grütter, H.T. and Grebe, S. (eds.) *Chargesheimer.* pp. 14–28.

Grütter, H.T. (2007). Klio an der Ruhr: Geschichtskultur im Ruhrgebiet. In Borsdorf, U., Grütter, H.T. and Nellen, D. (eds.) *Zukunft war immer: Zur Geschichte der Metropole Ruhr.* Essen, pp. 234–245.

Grütter, H.T. (2014). Böll/Chargesheimer und die Folgen: Das Bild des Ruhrgebiets im Strukturwandel. In Grütter, H.T. and Grebe, S. (eds.) *Chargesheimer.* pp. 284–297.

Grütter, H.T. (2017). Klio an Ruhr und Emscher: Geschichtskultur im Ruhrgebiet. *Forum Geschichtskultur Ruhr*, 7(2), pp. 15–24.

Grütter, H.T. and Grebe, S. (eds.). (2014a). *Chargesheimer: Die Entdeckung des Ruhrgebiets.* Köln: Buchhandlung Walter König; Katalog zur Ausstellung im Ruhr-Museum vom 26. May 2014–18 January 2015.

Grütter, H.T. and Grebe, S. (2014b). Vorwort. In Grütter, H.T. and Grebe, S. (eds.) *Chargesheimer,* pp. 9–10.

Hallenberger, D. (2000). *Industrie und Heimat: Eine Literaturgeschichte des Ruhrgebiets.* 1. Aufl. Essen: Klartext.

Hartog, F. (2015 [orig. 2003]) *Regimes of Historicity: Presentism and Experiences of Time.* European Perspectives.

Herbert, U. (2018, December 21). Schön war es nirgends und nie. *Frankfurter Allgemeine Zeitung.*

Höber, A. and Ganser, K. (eds.). (1999). *Industriekultur: Mythos und Moderne im Ruhrgebiet.* Essen: Klartext.

Kommunalverband Ruhrgebiet (ed.). (1996). *Das Ruhrgebiet. Ein starkes Stück Deutschland: 10 Jahre Werbung für eine unerschöpfliche Region.* Essen, Düsseldorf: Pomp.

Kommunalverband Ruhrgebiet and Springer&Jacoby (eds.). (2000). *Ein starkes Stück Selbstbewusstsein: Der Pott kocht.* Bottrop, Essen: Pomp.

Linkon, S.L. (2013). Narrating Past and Future: Deindustrialized Landscapes as Resources. *International Labor and Working-Class History*, 84, pp. 38–54. https://doi.org/10.1017/S0147547913000240

Linkon, S.L. (2018). *The Half-Life of Deindustrialization: Working-Class Writing about Economic Restructuring.* Class Culture. Ann Arbor: University of Michigan Press.

Minister für Stadtentwicklung, Wohnen und Verkehr des Landes Nordrhein-Westfalen. (1988). *Internationale Bauausstellung Emscher Park: Werkstatt für die Zukunft alter Industriegebiete. Memorandum zu Inhalt und Organisation.* Düsseldorf: Boss-Druck.

Muschg, A. (2005, March 17). Natürlich waren wir bestechlich: Die Jury ist sich einig: Nur Essen oder Görlitz kann Europas Kulturhauptstadt 2010 sein. Warum? Bekenntnisse des Jurors. *Die Zeit*, p. 12.

Muschick, S. (2021, May 4). Auch die Vergangenheit kann Zukunft verhindern. *Frankfurter Allgemeine Zeitung.*

N.N. (1967, April 9). Kumpel Antons Ende: SPIEGEL-Report über die Krise an der Ruhr. *Der Spiegel.*

Uncovering the Discovery of the Ruhr

N.N. (1969, April 9). "Ruhr-Expo 70" hat sich etabliert: Im Schatten einer alten Zeche wird für die Zukunft geplant. *Ruhr Nachrichten.*

Niethammer, L. (ed.). (1983a). *Die Jahre weiß man nicht, wo man die heute hinsetzen soll: Faschismuserfahrungen im Ruhrgebiet. Lebensgeschichte und Sozialkultur im Ruhrgebiet 1930–1960*, Vol. 1. Berlin u.a.: Dietz.

Niethammer, L. (ed.). (1983b). Hinterher merkt man, daß es richtig war, daß es schiefgegangen ist: Nachkriegserfahrungen im Ruhrgebiet. *Lebensgeschichte und Sozialkultur im Ruhrgebiet 1930–1960*, Vol. 2. Berlin, Bonn: Dietz.

Niethammer, L. (1987). Neue Aspekte der Ruhr Kultur: Zu einer Sammlung aktueller Fotodokumentationen aus dem Ruhrgebiet. In Borsdorf, U. and Eskildsen, U. (eds.) *Endlich so wie überall? Bilder und Texte aus dem Ruhrgebiet.* Schriftenreihe der Kulturstiftung Ruhr 3. Essen: Kulturstiftung Ruhr, pp. 6–9.

Niethammer, L. and von Plato, A. (eds.). (1985). Wir kriegen jetzt andere Zeiten': Auf der Suche nach der Erfahrung des Volkes in nachfaschistischen Ländern. *Lebensgeschichte und Sozialkultur im Ruhrgebiet 1930–1960*, Vol. 3. Berlin, Bonn: Dietz.

Pleitgen, F. (2010). Ruhr: Vom Mythos zum Marke. In Frohne, J. et al. (eds.) *Ruhr: Vom Mythos zur Marke.* Essen: Klartext, pp. 6–8.

RAG-Stiftung (ed.). (2016). *Das Schicksalsjahrzehnt: Zukunftsstudie RAG-Stiftung.* With the assistance of S. Manz and H.-T. Köster. Essen; Impulse für die Zukunft des Ruhrgebiets und zusätzlicher Blick auf das Saarland.

Reicher, C., Niemann, L. and Uttke, A. (eds.). (2011). *Internationale Bauausstellung Emscher Park: Impulse: Lokal, Regional, National, International.* 1. Aufl. Essen: Klartext-Verl.

Rüsen, J. (2000). Die Zukunft der Vergangenheit. In Jordan, S. (ed.) *Zukunft der Geschichte: Historisches Denken an der Schwelle zum 21. Jahrhundert.* Berlin: Trafo, pp. 175–182.

Russo, J. and Linkon, S.L. (2003). Collateral Damage: Deindustrialization and the Uses of Youngstown. In Cowie, J., Heathcott, J. and Bluestone, B. (eds.) *Beyond the Ruins: The Meanings of Deindustrialization.* Ithaca, NY and London: ILR Press Cornell University Press, pp. 201–218.

Scharrenburg, O. (2017). Die Ruhrbesetzung. In Krull, L. (ed.) *Westfälische Erinnerungsorte: Beiträge zum kollektiven Gedächtnis einer Region.* Forschungen zur Regionalgeschichte. pp. 115–125.

Schmidt, U.C. (2006). "Lasst uns den Kohlenpott umfunktionieren!": Repräsentationspolitik der Stadtlandschaft Ruhrgebiet. In Saldern, A. von (ed.) *Stadt und Kommunikation in bundesrepublikanischen Umbruchszeiten.* Beiträge zur Kommunikationsgeschichte Bd. 17. Stuttgart: Steiner, pp. 257–282.

Schneider, S. (2007). "Solche Darstellungen akzeptieren wir nicht!": Zur Rezeption des Bildbands "Im Ruhrgebiet" von Heinrich Böll und Chargesheimer. In Grütter, H.T. and Grebe, S. (eds.) *Chargesheimer.* pp. 270–283.

Siedlungsverband Ruhrgebiet (ed.). (1973). *Ruhrgebiet: Pläne, Programme, Projekte.* Essen: SVR.

Siedlungsverband Ruhrkohlenbezirk (ed.). (1959). *Ruhrgebiet: Porträt ohne Pathos.* Stuttgart, Berlin: Europa Contact Ges. f. Intereurop. Beziehungen.

Thiemeyer, G. (2016). *Die Geschichte der Bundesrepublik Deutschland: Zwischen Westbindung und europäischer Hegemonie.* Stuttgart: Kohlhammer Verlag.

Wagner, H. (2022). *Vergangenheit als Zukunft? Geschichtskultur und Strukturwandel im Ruhrgebiet.* Beiträge zur Geschichtskultur Band 45. Köln: Böhlau.

20
MAKING THE HUMAN WRECKAGE VISIBLE
Deindustrialization in Kate Beaton's *Ducks*

Peter Thompson

Introduction

Kate Beaton's 2022 graphic memoir, *Ducks: Two Years in the Oil Sands*, is set in the period just before she became famous for her *Hark! A Vagrant* comics series and for children's books *The Princess and the Pony* (2015) and *King Baby* (2016). The very personal narrative of *Ducks* reflects a much larger social phenomenon that is more than a century old: people moving from the economically depressed East Coast of Canada to other places – historically Boston and Toronto – but much more commonly over the past two decades to participate in massive resource extraction projects in Alberta. Beaton's[1] story is familiar for many who graduated high school in Atlantic Canada in the late 1990s and early 2000s. After finishing an undergraduate degree in history at Mount Allison University, Beaton finds no job prospects in the small town where she grew up (Mabou, Cape Breton), so she decides to spend two years in the oil patch in Fort McMurray, Alberta to make enough money to pay off her loans before finding a job in her field.

Reviewers and readers have found much to praise in *Ducks*, especially Beaton's visually striking and immersive style that brings the audience into the oil sands, a distant and vaguely understood part of the country, despite its importance as a resource base. *Ducks* explores the dangers and tensions of a hypermasculine industry and a setting in which men outnumber women by fifty to one – themes reinforced by two graphic scenes in which Katie is the victim of sexual violence. The narrative also explores the environmental implications of Canada's oil sands; its title references the death of hundreds of ducks which landed in a toxic tailing pond at the Syncrude site in 2008.

Representations of the social and economic fallout of mine and factory closures add much to the study of deindustrialization. This is especially true in a place like industrial Cape Breton, where this narrative of decline is so engrained in perceptions of the region. Representations can capture the ambivalent response of communities to the collapse of industry; more importantly, they can contribute significantly to struggles over collective memory that accompany such shifts by highlighting their cultural impact and by provoking debate over competing versions of the past. Like other graphic memoirs, *Ducks* exploits the tension between looking and reading, pushing the narrative forward through sparse conversations between Katie and

DOI: 10.4324/9781003308324-29

the people around her and through shocking images of the oil sands. Beaton uses maps to draw attention to the distinction between Cape Breton and Alberta, and she moves among several narrative perspectives, sometimes inserting herself as an observer of historical events that she explains to the audience. And like other graphic memoirists, she makes deliberate decisions to leave out certain events from the narrative sequence, making them even more powerful when they happen "off-screen" (Kyler, 2010; Pedri, 2015; Olsza, 2019).

In what follows, I want to focus on Beaton's depiction of the tension between two seemingly very different economic scenarios: the perpetually deindustrializing region of Cape Breton and the rapidly booming area of Northern Alberta. Through her focus on the movement of people between these two places, Beaton shows how deindustrialization on the East Coast facilitates intense development in Alberta. In her narrative, the collapse of Atlantic Canada's fishery, coal mines, and steel industry reshapes her home region at the same time as it pushes the gendered, environmental, and social impacts of extractive capitalism elsewhere.

Representing Deindustrialization in Cape Breton

The reviews for *Ducks*, found everywhere from *the New York Times* to *the Guardian*, have been overwhelmingly positive. Many focus on the memoir's complex treatment of nostalgia; Beaton's sharp exploration of overlapping systems of exploitation; her depiction of sexual violence; and her skill in composition, pacing, and tone. In *the New Yorker*, Sam Thielman suggests that "if there is a predominating visual influence in *Ducks*, it is the work of the proletarian Ashington Group, who painted the collieries and barracks where they labored and lived" (Thielman, 2022). Many reviews focus on the visual style, noting, for example, that "Beaton's figures are rendered in scrunchy, expressive lines, a little less cartoonish than the figures of *Hark! A Vagrant*, but vividly expressive" (Grady, 2022). Others emphasize the economic and cultural analysis that plays out in the book. Reviewers respond at once to Beaton's nuanced exposé of the cultural and environmental impact of the oil sands and to the dynamics of her community's experience of deindustrialization, a process that lands so many of her friends in alienating and dangerous jobs far from home.

The Athabasca region that Beaton documents was, between 2005 and 2008, one of the most rapidly industrializing places in the world.[2] In his 2017 book, *The Patch: The People, Pipelines, and Politics of the Oil Sands*, Chris Turner asserts that "There's likely never been a boom like the one that convulsed Fort McMurray circa 2007," noting that "even Dawson City didn't have multiple $5-billion industrial expansion projects simultaneously on the go" (Turner, 2017). Like Beaton, Turner contextualizes the frantic and contradictory nature of life in the oil sands during this period. Also, he draws inspiration from the 2008 incident in which 1,611 ducks accidentally flew into a tailings pond, at once bringing attention locally to the environmental impacts of the oil sands and making this corner of Canada the focus of international news. He writes:

> As a central character in the broader narrative of the global energy industry in the age of climate change, the story of the oil patch that arose over the last fifty years in Alberta's oil sands – *the Patch*, for short – began with those slain ducks. The birds and the tailings pond became a proxy for a wider polluted world in conflict, and in short order the whole industry became the embodiment of climate change itself, the poster child for the whole sinful age of fossil fuels, the face of an invisible global catastrophe.
>
> *(Turner, 2017, p. xxiii)*

As the cover image of Katie standing on a large tractor looking back at the rolling hills of Cape Breton suggests, though, *Ducks* has two primary settings, Alberta and Cape Breton, which are defined in opposition to one another but are also interconnected. At the same time as Fort McMurray is in the midst of this unstoppable boom, with even local restaurants flying in prospective employees and offering high salaries (Turner, 2017, p. 6), Cape Breton is experiencing a multi-decade decline as mines and steel mills closed (see MacKinnon, 2020). *Ducks* provides insight into the complex connections between deindustrialization in one part of Canada (the East Coast) and industrial development in another (Alberta), making clear that these two processes are intimately linked. This makes her memoir much more than one individual's story about work and the loss of home but a broader meditation on the capricious nature of resource development and the far reach of its costs.

In his 2012 article, "Oil and World Literature," Graeme Macdonald suggests that "All modern writing is premised on both the promise and the hidden costs and benefits of hydrocarbon culture" (Macdonald, 2012, p. 31) and that the movement of oil and the literature that it inspires forces us to see the relationship between places such as Washington and Riyadh, or between Fort McMurray and Mabou. While Beaton's memoir can be placed within a growing body of literary and artistic work that explores the environmental and social impacts of the oil sands, *Ducks* is also a narrative distillation of Jefferson Cowie and Joseph Heathcott's observation that

> what we call deindustrialization may best be understood with hindsight as one episode in a long series of transformations within capitalism . . . the industrial age is alive and well, even if the locations have changed {and yet] the painful realities of job loss appear very different on the ground to workers and their families.
>
> *(Cowie and Heathcott, 2003, pp. 3–4)*

Ducks also captures the importance of memory in representations of deindustrialization: one of the book's main motifs is the memory of home for workers displaced from Cape Breton, but Beaton's home region itself is defined by the place of resource extraction in its cultural memory.

The field of deindustrialization studies has increasingly turned to cultural representations to understand the social transformations inherent in industrial closures and the economic shifts that emerge from them.[3] Like Judith Hamera, this chapter considers deindustrialization as "uneven, locally inflected, multifaceted, and still in process: both a change in the dominant mode of production and a 'struggle over meaning and collective memory'" (Hamera, 2017). Deindustrialization studies provides a number of important insights for understanding *Ducks* and the contest over meaning that plays out in its pages, and in turn, *Ducks* extends insights into the collective struggle over memory and meaning that is at the heart of deindustrialization studies. In her work on Niagara Falls, Alice Mah suggests that the experience of workers and community members in places impacted simultaneously by factory closures and the environmental residue left behind by closed industries is marked by what she calls "ambivalent nostalgia" (Mah, 2012), the combination of a longing for the stability and cultural meaning inherent in industrial work and the recognition of the harmful impacts of these activities. Julie Burrell's work on depictions of the post-industrial working class in African American women's theatre provides a framework for understanding conflicting regional identity markers: just as the Rust Belt represents "an abandoned landscape of decay" (Burrell, 2021, p. 59) but also a space of cultural revival and a crucial political battleground, Beaton's Cape Breton is at once beautiful, remote, economically depressed, and mythologized.

Beaton uses the visual style of the graphic novel to great effect. Her cartoonish depictions of environmental and sexual violence explore these dynamics in ambivalent ways that complement and upend photographic and literary treatments of the same phenomena. The memoir brings together the full weight of Nova Scotian literature's nostalgic impulse, the homesickness of the outmigration narrative, and the environmental ramifications of the oil sands. At the same time, Beaton explores the specific circumstances of deindustrialization on the East Coast and its impact on her life both financially and culturally. As part of a generation that experiences a kind of 'echo' of deindustrialization, Beaton is immersed in the cultural history of extraction and manufacturing in Cape Breton even as she knows that these activities and the social stability they provided are unavailable to her.

Cape Breton and Alberta

As I write this chapter in a coffee shop in downtown Ottawa, a group at the table beside me is talking about where they grew up. When one tells his colleagues that he is from Cape Breton, it sets off a familiar sequence: "Oh, it's so beautiful," "The people in Cape Breton are so nice," "Do you miss home?" This prompts a succinct explanation from the displaced Cape Bretoner: "I moved here for work twenty-five years ago, but no matter how long I've lived in Ontario, I always miss home." Many writers have suggested that this nostalgia for a real or imagined home place has always defined Nova Scotian culture (Davies, 1991; Delisle, 2013; Bryant, 2017; Marr, 2022). These scholars chart the importance of the home place in Atlantic Canadian literature while also acknowledging how the concept reinforces regressive ideas about gender, sexuality, and settler colonialism. The experience of leaving the region for economic reasons is a key trope in the literature and popular culture of Atlantic Canada.[4]

This underlines a key relationship between the region and the oil sands: cascading waves of deindustrialization in Atlantic Canada have led to people leaving in huge numbers for the oil patch, especially during the boom years of the early 2000s. Beaton's memoir makes clear that itinerant workers come to the oil patch from many places and that the experiences of racialized workers in Fort McMurray are even more difficult than what she faced, but she focuses on how the pattern of movement between Cape Breton (and other parts of Atlantic Canada) and the oil sands disrupts workers' connection with home and perpetuates their exploitation (Neis et al., 2022; Mazer, 2022).

Ducks explores nostalgia and the broader sense of disruption that are so central to Nova Scotian literature and popular culture. For Beaton, this phenomenon is marked by a tension between economic concerns and cultural connections to home. *Ducks* is populated by men (and a few women) from Cape Breton who have moved to the oil sands to find work after losing their jobs either as miners or in the fishery or, like Katie, after finding that they have no prospects on the East Coast. In the first panels of the memoir, Katie tells the reader that "Cape Breton used to export fish, coal, and steel; but in 2005, its main export is people," who have "gone to be cheap labor where booming industries demanded it" (Beaton, 2022, p. 10). She also notes that Cape Breton culture is defined in large part by two "diametrically opposed experiences: a deep love for home, and the knowledge of how frequently we have to leave it to find work somewhere else" (Beaton, 2022, p. 11). *Ducks* explores the economic and especially the cultural impacts of deindustrialization and Cape Breton's status as a 'have-not' region of Canada. Beaton recalls that since her childhood, the media, her teachers, her parents, literature, and music all reinforced the idea that there are no opportunities in Cape Breton. More importantly, seeing local industries close taught the people Katie grew up with that "any job is a good job . . . even a bad job is a good job" (Beaton, 2022, p. 12). A 20-page section toward the end of *Ducks* focuses squarely on this proposition and the consequences of accepting it: as the ducks land on the tailings pond, Katie notices that she and her coworkers have strange rashes and persistent coughs, and two men die on or near the site (one of a heart attack and another in a car crash).

The mantra "any job is a good job" puts Katie and the rest of this pool of cheap labor at risk, but it also animates their sense of alienation as the memory of the East Coast lingers over their time in Alberta. Older men from Newfoundland call Katie 'my ducky,' a regional phrase, and they listen to the Newfoundland Radio Hour in their trucks on break. Katie constantly runs into cousins and other relatives on site, and her friend Doug says that "Everyone's cousin is here" (Beaton, 2022, p. 152).

The yearning for home expressed in *Ducks* results in a visual and narrative dichotomy between rural Cape Breton and the oil sands sites. Beaton contrasts the rolling hills and gentle coastline of Cape Breton with the almost alien-like desecration of the oil sands. As seen in Figures 20.1 and 20.2, the first images in the sections introducing Cape Breton and Syncrude Mildred Lake (Katie's first posting in the oil sands) present nearly identical aerial views looking over the horizon, as if they were photographs taken from a plane or a drone. The Cape Breton image features the small village of Mabou with its small houses nestled into a tree-lined landscape with hills, the harbor in the background, the Mabou River running through, and St. Mary's Catholic Church as its focal point. It looks like it could come from a brochure advertising an excursion on the Ceilidh Trail. In the following section, the aerial view using identical framing focuses on the vast Syncrude site, but here houses are replaced by holding tanks, the church by a smokestack, and the hills by layers of earth uncovered through strip-mining.

On the surface, the contrast between the idyllic landscape of Cape Breton and the deracinated oil sands reflects workers' sense that their 'real life' is elsewhere (I'll talk about this in more detail later). This implies that Fort McMurray is a kind of 'non-place,' a transitory space with resources to be extracted and little else. But even as the memoir focuses on the displaced and solitary workers who are separated from 'home,' *Ducks* stresses that Fort McMurray has many young families who live there full-time, a detail that is jarring for readers who have not visited the region. In this sense, *Ducks* is designed to shock the reader: Beaton juxtaposes scenes set in rural Cape Breton and urban Victoria with images of extreme environmental degradation in northern Alberta. By bringing readers to this distant place that they may never visit, Beaton evokes a visceral reaction, inviting us to think about our own complicity in the development of the oil sands and its environmental and social impacts.

This project of making the oil sands visible is complemented by Beaton's exploration of the history of deindustrialization on the East Coast. Beaton connects the loss of jobs in factories and mines in Cape Breton over the past five decades to the movement of workers from the East Coast to Alberta. Consider, for example, a debate some of the workers have about young men who come to Alberta from Newfoundland, make obscene amounts of money, and then live beyond their means. An older worker chastises a young man, telling him that he's "only digging a hole," to which he replies, "Yeah, a hole that's full of oil for a hundred more years." The older worker responds that "The Grand Banks were full too" (Beaton, 2022, p. 112). For the workers who populate *Ducks*, industrial and extractive projects are inherently transient and need to be treated accordingly. When Katie asks her older friend

324

Making the Human Wreckage Visible

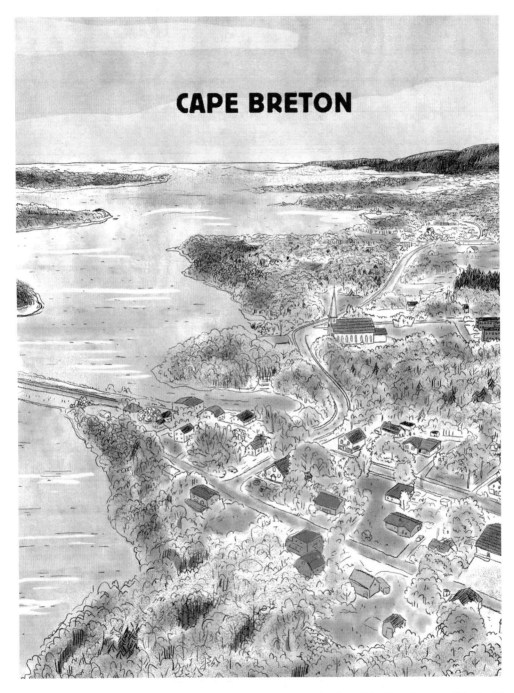

Figures 20.1 and 20.2 From *Ducks: Two Years in the Oil Sands*. Copyright Kate Beaton. (Used with permission from Drawn & Quarterly)

Figures 20.1 and 20.2 (Continued)

Making the Human Wreckage Visible

Doug what he did in Cape Breton, he responds, "I did it all. I did everything. . . . Coal, fishing, steel. But that's all gone, isn't it" (Beaton, 2022, p. 225). Katie's relationship with these industries is different, because she never harbored any illusions that well-paying work would be available to her in Cape Breton. She left the island in search of a career instead of to salvage one.

Beaton explores the idea that industrial development tricks us into thinking that its factories and coal mines are permanent features of the landscape and social fabric. Her characters experience firsthand that there is no fall of "*the* industrial era"; instead, they see that the collapse of Cape Breton's mines and factories is actually just a shift of industrial capacity and investment elsewhere (Bluestone and Harrison, 1982, p. 6). In *Ducks*, material reminders of this fall, such as shuttered factories and displaced workers, provide evidence of the fleeting nature of an economic system premised on yanking as many resources from the ground and ocean as we can as quickly as we can. The characters in *Ducks* internalize this message: having seen what happened to the coal and fishing industries in Cape Breton, Katie and the others are trying to get as much money from working in the oil sands while it lasts – while still lamenting the fall of the extractive economy on the East Coast and the way in which this process severs their ties to home.

The conversations between Doug and Katie reveal much about this tension. When they discuss the history of mining on the island, Katie tells Doug that she knows very little about that history, noting that she remembers a few details about it from a visit to the Cape Breton Miner's Museum as a child. She recalls being very sad for the pit ponies, but Doug gets frustrated that she knows so little about the mines: "What did you ever know about them, and what did you lose when they closed?" (Beaton, 2022, p. 292). The generational divide between Doug and Katie is essential for the narrative, as it drives home the doubly alienated position Katie occupies with respect to Cape Breton's industrial history. For her, coal mining is just a set of images and identity-markers, and so the transition from the industrial era to the post-industrial era is abstract. Mostly, it means that she needs to move elsewhere to pay off her student loans. For Doug, though, the closure of the mines represents not just an economic loss but perhaps even more importantly a cultural one. In this sense, *Ducks* depicts the alienation and ironic distance that come from growing up in a place like post-industrial Cape Breton. Katie has no nostalgia for the mines themselves. She encounters symbols of industrial life through popular culture (the pit ponies or the Men of the Deeps (Beaton, 2022, p. 291)), yet she is deeply aware of the material impacts of these economic shifts. Beaton depicts her experience of coal mining as not that much different than the experience of a tourist or a viewer of television shows about Cape Breton. For Katie, much more than for Doug, Cape Breton's industrial history represents a past that was not a tangible part of her life, even though she is clearly shaped by this economic shift.

Student Loans

Reviews of the memoir rightly focus on Beaton's depiction of labor and the environmental destruction of the oil sands, but her portrait of deindustrialized Cape Breton also shows how the exploitative conditions of outmigration and work in the oil sands are compounded by the student loan system. Beaton's narrative reveals how student loans create a kind of underclass with few options but to take the first job that comes along. Beaton grew up in a large family with meagre resources, and she was able to go to university by taking out sizable student loans. After graduation, however, she cannot find secure work in her field, and she needs to travel to the oil sands to perform alienating and sometimes dangerous work to pay off her loans. This necessity links the limited choices available to Katie with those of her fellow workers: both the former miners and fishermen and recent history graduates are drawn into the destructive work of the oil sands to stay afloat.

Katie's class position is complicated because she grew up working class (as she stresses throughout the narrative) and went to university to pursue her interest in history, a move that ironically results in her working in the oil sands. As a warehouse worker, Katie earns less than the men who do skilled and manual labor, but the narrative is marked by a persistent sense of status confusion. For example, Katie is promoted over her friend and fellow Cape Bretoner, and some of the workers are ridiculed for their inability to read. The narrative's crisp exploration of class and gender and the way dispossession on the East Coast underwrites dangerous and exploitative work in Alberta is heightened by these contradictions. The lives of Katie and Doug and their fellow workers are overdetermined by interwoven structural forces like the student loan system and deindustrialization. When Katie does finally get a job in her field (at the Maritime Museum of British Columbia in Victoria), the loans catch up with her, and she returns to work in the oil sands. Thus, while the narrative mainly focuses on Katie's individual circumstances and experiences, it also makes clear that those personal choices are always influenced by larger economic and social forces.

"People Kid Themselves If They Think the Only Life They're Living is Somewhere Else"

One of the keys to understanding *Ducks* is the tension among competing visions of the oil sands: the Athabasca region is at once an economic engine, an environmental catastrophe, a hypermasculine boomtown, a home for young families, a symbol of Canadian prosperity, and a testament to the country's broken relationship with Indigenous communities. In contrast, for those in Nova Scotia, the oil sands area is a distant and vague mishmash of all of these things but also a symbol of opportunity. Toward the end of the memoir, Beaton highlights this idea when Katie comes home and overhears a conversation between her father and his friend, Lauchie, who is getting ready to move to Alberta. Lauchie boasts to Katie's father about how "there's something for everyone out there" (Beaton, 2022, p. 427). When he hears that Katie had worked in the oil sands, he cuts her off before she can tell him what it is actually like, once again insisting "Oh, you wouldn't believe the things they have, Neil!" (Beaton, 2022, p. 427). It is no accident that this appears at the end of the narrative. Katie's frustration with Lauchie's self-assured (but incorrect) knowledge about the oil sands (which mirrors that of other outsiders, including a *Globe and Mail* reporter who contacts Katie about her experiences) clearly fuels her desire to illustrate the realities of the place through this book.

To this end, *Ducks* parlays its sense of transience and its exploration of (often inaccurate) assumptions about the oil sands into a broader philosophical meditation on the concept of 'real life' and the place of work in defining one's identity and purpose. For Beaton, the concept of home is clearly tied to space and to cultural anchors like family, speech patterns, and music, but the place of work in that mix is unresolved. For most Canadians, the reality of the oil sands is so far-removed that people do not see what actually happens there. For Katie, though, Fort McMurray is a place where she effectively puts her life on hold for work. She sees the period she spends there as a suspension of time: she will work there for two or three years (or however long it takes for her to pay off her student loans) and then return to

Making the Human Wreckage Visible

the real and very different trajectory of her life. In this sense, *Ducks* asserts that the concept of itinerant work itself is paradoxical. Katie and her coworkers are suspended in a seemingly permanent state of temporary work, calling attention to the idea that all extractive projects are inherently unstable and precarious.

This is even more profound for the workers who have spent years in the oil sands, for whom there is no clear end date for their time there. In the same exchange cited earlier, Katie asks Ambrose if he was a fisherman "before" to which he responds, "I'm still a fisherman. I'm just here" (Beaton, 2022, p. 113). A few pages later, he chides Katie, "You know, we're all in two places here . . . people kid themselves if they think the only life they're living is somewhere else" (Beaton, 2022, p. 133). The nature of the work in the oil sands upends normal patterns of family and professional life: men travel to the camps for two weeks at a time, leaving their wives and families behind in places like Newfoundland and Cape Breton. They live in dormitories, and as *Ducks* suggests, also in a kind of suspended animation during the time they are on the site but then are equally disruptive when they return home.[5] In a broader sense, the oil sands, as depicted by Beaton, represent a bargain in which one's previous professional, social, and familial identity is placed on hold – not discarded, as Ambrose's comment makes clear, but paused. This exchange also shows that the development of the oil sands relies on the collapse of the resource economy on the East Coast even as sustaining the post-industrial economy in Atlantic Canada relies on the destruction of the environment and the alienation, sexual violence, and exploitation that Beaton documents in *Ducks*.

This comes up explicitly later in the memoir in another conversation between Katie and Doug. Katie asks why Doug thinks so many people from the East Coast are here. He is surprised by the question and responds matter-of-factly that people came to the oil sands simply because that is where the jobs are. Doug's pragmatism fails to satisfy Katie, though, and she asks him a series of more existential questions, such as "Do you think this place makes people better or worse?" noting that "camp's not a normal place, is it?" As she puts it, "Nobody likes it here. Everyone wishes they were somewhere else" (Beaton, 2022, pp. 224–225). Without saying it out loud, Katie and Doug land on a profound observation about life in the oil sands and in extractive capitalism more generally: the alienation they feel in the camps mirrors the dislocation that led them there in the first place. They are simply encountering it in a different environment. While *Ducks* explores the disconnect between Fort McMurray and Cape Breton, Beaton also makes clear that the distinction between these two regions is arbitrary. Both are products of the same economic and political structure.

Beaton's exploration of 'real life' versus 'camp life' brings together several strands of the narrative, especially in her depiction of gendered violence and harassment. As one of the only women on the sites where she works, Katie is subject to catcalls, stares, and unwanted attention from her male coworkers. Her bosses essentially tell her that she needs to be tough and that this is a man's world, making the two graphic incidents in which she is raped especially jarring. Beaton connects the hypermasculine and violent space of the camps not just to the gender imbalance but to this sense of being away from real life and the idea that ethics are almost paused in the oil sands. Katie asks another coworker if people are different at home than when they are at the camp. People "do things here that they wouldn't do at home," she comments, and then asks, "But is that who they really are? Or are they who they are at home?" He sarcastically dismisses these questions, but later Katie and her sister Becky discuss what it would be like if their own father had taken a job out West to support their family. She asks "Do you wonder if he'd be like those guys, because that's what it makes you? That's what it turns them into" (Beaton, 2022, p. 316). Beaton implies that the distance between home and the camp distorts the behavior and perceptions of the workers in the oil sands. In the end, though, these questions remain unanswered. Beaton is not interested in trashing the oil sands so much as exploring their complex dynamics. In *Ducks*, workers' emotional attachments to home and dismissive attitudes to Fort McMurray play out in contradictory ways. The hypermasculine setting of the camp takes its toll on the male workers as well as on the few women, as men are judged on their willingness to sacrifice their bodies for the job. Ultimately, *Ducks* portrays a world in which sexual violence, environmental calamity, homelessness, drug abuse, bodily injury, and the alienation of workers get pushed to the margins of Canadian society. Beaton's narrative and visual techniques draw attention to these issues and make the audience examine their own complicity in such systems.

Belonging, Ownership, and Settler Colonialism

Composed in the spirit of making visible the things that Canadian society wishes to push to the margin or ignore, *Ducks* is partially inspired by Beaton's coming to terms with the oil sands' destruction of Indigenous communities. The still unfolding "colonial story in the Athabasca region" is a particularly ugly site of "continuing encounter between Indigenous and non-Indigenous peoples" (Joly, 2017, p. 12), as the Canadian state facilitates the extraction of oil by large corporations using exceptionally destructive practices, including open-pit mining on a massive scale, at the expense of Indigenous communities (Baker, 2021; Todd, 2022; Murphy, 2017; Schindler, 2014; Schmidt, 2020). As Zoe Todd has written, Alberta

> is built on the occupied territories of diverse Indigenous nations and confederacies whose histories, philosophies, and survivance (Vizenor, 2010) encompass and co-constitute the lands the nation state traverses – including territories storied, governed, and claimed by Dene, Cree, Blackfoot, Stoney Nakoda, Nakota Sioux, Tsuu'tina, Saulteaux, and Metis peoples.
>
> *(Todd, 2022, p. 2, citing Vizenor, 2010)*

The story of the oil sands is thus a story structured by settler colonialism.

In the afterward, Beaton writes that she did not learn about the history of dispossession of Indigenous people in school and came to it later in life. She points out that "The oil sands operate on stolen lands. Their pollution, work camps, and ever-growing settler populations continue to have serious social, economic, cultural, environmental, and health consequences for the Indigenous communities in the region" (Beaton, 2022, p. 434). She recreates a YouTube clip in which Celina Harpe, a Cree elder from Fort McKay, details the impacts of the oil sands on the Athabasca River and on people in her community who are dying of cancer. Beaton explores the complex layers of complicity here, too, writing, "But this is us too. We're not the president of Shell, but we're here" (Beaton, 2022, p. 361). In the same way as the memoir visualizes the environmental impact of the oil sands, the lives of the people who work in them, and the broken sense of home created by the boom and bust cycle of deindustrialization and resource extraction, *Ducks* connects the fuel that we rely on with the dispossession of Indigenous peoples in the Athabasca region.

It is necessary, however, to consider how this aspect of the narrative also ties together Alberta and Cape Breton. Although the memoir explicitly addresses the role of Canada's settler society in its destruction of the Athabasca region, the question of belonging in and ownership over the space of Cape Breton is left unanswered. In a scene at the end of the memoir,

330

Making the Human Wreckage Visible

Katie is hiking along the coast and happens to walk on a neighbor's property. She apologizes, sparking a conversation about 'his' land. The man tells her that even though Cape Breton is "a piece of nothing," he is saving this land for his son in case he ever moves back to the East Coast from wherever he is currently living (Beaton, 2022, p. 427). Beaton once again gives voice to the ambivalent sense of nostalgia experienced by Cape Bretoners and the sadness of this man's family at the loss (even temporary) of their son. Beaton explores the concept of home, the disruption created by outmigration, and the destructive impacts of mining in Alberta at the same time as she leaves questions about Cape Breton's settler history and her family and community's rootedness to that landscape largely unexamined.

Conclusion

Ducks focuses on the relationship between two peripheral regions in Canada: Cape Breton and the Athabasca oil sands. By tracking Kate Beaton's movement between these two spaces, the memoir provides insight into shifts in Canada's industrial capacity. The narrative demonstrates that cycles of industrial development and deindustrialization often involve moving the violence and exploitation inherent in extractive projects to the margins. In *Ducks*, the promise of money and employment is contrasted with the persistence of homelessness, displacement, alienation, environmental destruction, sexual violence, and drug abuse in the oil sands. As much as it is a story about personal loss – of home, of culture, of the environment – *Ducks* always turns our attention to the structural forces that govern Canada's extractive economy and how they impact at an individual level. The narrative stresses that we are all complicit in the development of the oil sands. Beaton explicitly connects, in ways that few authors have, the beauty of Cape Breton with the destruction of the oil sands. For Beaton, we cannot have one without the other, and the preservation of the landscape she holds so close depends on the desecration of the Athabasca region. *Ducks* demonstrates that cultural representations offer profound insights into the phenomenon of deindustrialization. There are, of course, many historical studies that examine the fall of industry in Cape Breton and the movement of people from that region to the oil sands. The graphic memoir allows Beaton to explore the effects of these shifts on herself and members of her community in visceral ways that more traditional scholarly methods may not capture. In particular, the graphic memoir provokes the reader to consider their own complicity in perpetuating an economic model that discards communities and destroys the environment. The graphic memoir also allows Beaton to reveal the ambivalence that she and her fellow workers feel about the closure of dangerous mines and the costs of working in the oil sands.

Beaton points out that as the Cape Breton landscape recovers and its economy tanks, the Athabasca landscape is being destroyed and the economy booms – partially on the backs of workers whose livelihoods were destroyed on the East Coast. In other words, the increase in development in the oil sands is not a discrete event from the decrease in development on the East Coast; in fact, it is the same event and both the activity itself (the literal extraction of oil from the ground) and the social fabric that sustains it (including the sense of nostalgia for home) are interconnected. Thus, industrial development in places like Fort McMurray relies on disinvestment from industrial activity in places like Cape Breton. Canada has a series of terms for eliding this connection (have vs have not, home vs away, Western alienation vs Eastern decline), but Beaton's graphic memoir makes us rethink this. The sense of living in a kind of suspended reality is driven by the structural economic forces that determine life in the oil sands and the vision of resource extraction that Beaton uncovers in the narrative is one where the gutting of Cape Breton and the far-off and ongoing destruction of the Athabasca region are deeply intertwined. The triumph of *Ducks* is that its deeply visual style and the personal nature of the story itself – a story, it should be said, that consciously makes the people who work in these industries visible and multidimensional – brings the push-pull nature of deindustrialization into focus.

Notes

1 Following the text itself, I refer to the author of *Ducks* as 'Kate Beaton' and the main character of *Ducks* as 'Katie.'

2 There is a growing body of literature on poetry, documentary, art, and other forms of literature that respond to Canada's oil sands. See, among many other examples, Braunecker, Melanie. (2020). *A Greed to Which We Agreed? Representations of the Oil Industry in Canadian Petro-Literature*. PhD Diss., University of Graz; McCurdy, Patrick. (2022). Excavating CBC's Docudrama The Tar Sands. *Imaginations: Journal of Cross-Cultural Image Studies*, 13(1), pp. 81–106; Takach, Geo. (2017). *Tar Wars: Oil, Environment, and Alberta's Image*. Edmonton: University of Alberta Press. Crucially, we can also think about *Ducks* alongside the tradition of worker-written literature. Consider, for example, Melanie Unrau's 2019 PhD thesis, where she argues that "oil workers have intimate knowledge of the ecological harm and physical danger of oil work [and this poetry expresses] the relationship between fossil fuel consumption, greenhouse gas emissions, and global warming." Unrau, Melanie. (2019). *'Tend the Rusted Steel Like a Shepherd': Petropoetics of Oil Work in Canada*. PhD Diss., University of Manitoba.

3 See, among other examples, Souther, Mark. (2017). *Believing in Cleveland: Managing Decline in "The Best Location in the Nation"*. Philadelphia: Temple University Press; Beck, John. (2021). *Landscape as Weapon: Cultures of Exhaustion and Refusal*. London: Reaktion Books; Fraser, Emma. (2016). Awakening in Ruins: The Virtual Spectacle of the End of the City in Video Games. *Journal of Gaming and Virtual Worlds*, 8(2), pp. 177–196; Rhodes, James. (2019). Rust Belt Chic: Deindustrialization, Places and Urban Authenticity. *Journal of Urban Cultural Studies*, 6(2–3), pp. 265–286; Thompson, Peter. (2019). *Nights Below Foord Street: Literature and Popular Culture in Postindustrial Nova Scotia*. Montreal: McGill-Queen's University Press; Linkon, Sherry Lee. (2018). *The Half-Life of Deindustrialization: Working-Class Writing about Economic Restructuring*. Ann Arbor: University of Michigan Press; Apel, Dora. (2015). *Beautiful Terrible Ruins: Detroit and the Anxiety of Decline*. New Brunswick: Rutgers University Press; Bottá, Giacomo. (2020). *Deindustrialisation and Popular Music: Punk and 'Post-Punk' in Manchester, Düsseldorf, Torino, and Tampere*. London: Rowman and Littlefield; Micu, Andreea. (2018). Photographing the End of the World: Capitalist Temporality, Crisis, and the Performativity of Visual Objects. *Performance Philosophy*, 4(1), pp. 39–52; Rosa, Brian. (2022). Deindustrialization Without End: Smokestacks as Postindustrial Monuments. *Geohumanities*, 0(0), pp. 1–26; Bernes, Jasper. (207). *The Work of Art in the Age of Deindustrialization*. Stanford: Stanford University Press.

4 There are many examples of this, and Beaton depicts a number of them in *Ducks*, including the music of Ron Hynes and Lennie Gallant.

5 This comes up in another argument between Katie and Ambrose, where he tells her that "not every family can handle it" and that the time workers spend at home is also "chaos" (Beaton, 2022, p. 231).

Reference List

Apel, Dora. (2015). *Beautiful Terrible Ruins: Detroit and the Anxiety of Decline*. New Brunswick: Rutgers University Press.

Baker, J.M. (2021). "Do Berries Listen? Berries as Indicators, Ancestors, and Agents in Canada's Oil Sands Region." *Ethos*, 86(2), pp. 273–294.

Beaton, Kate. (2015). *The Princess and the Pony*. New York: Arthur A. Levine Books.

Beaton, Kate. (2016). *King Baby*. New York: Arthur A. Levine Books.

Beaton, Kate. (2022). *Ducks: Two Years in the Oil Sands*. Montreal: Drawn and Quarterly.

Beck, John. (2021). *Landscape as Weapon: Cultures of Exhaustion and Refusal.* London: Reaktion Books.

Bernes, Jasper. (2017). *The Work of Art in the Age of Deindustrialization.* Stanford: Stanford University Press.

Bluestone, Barry and Harrison, Bennett. (1982). *The Deindustrialization of America: Plant Closings, Community Abandonment, and the Dismantling of Basic Industry.* New York: Basic Books.

Bottá, Giacomo. (2020). *Deindustrialisation and Popular Music: Punk and 'Post-Punk' in Manchester, Düsseldorf, Torino, and Tampere.* London: Rowman and Littlefield.

Braunecker, Melanie. (2020). *A Greed to Which We Agreed? Representations of the Oil Industry in Canadian Petro-Literature.* Ph.D. Diss., University of Graz.

Bryant, Rachel. (2017). *The Homing Place: Indigenous and Settler Legacies of the Atlantic.* Waterloo: Wilfrid Laurier University Press.

Burrell, Julie. (2021). Postindustrial Futurities in Contemporary Black Feminist Theater. *Frontiers: A Journal of Women's Studies*, 42(1), pp. 58–91.

Cowie, Jefferson, and Heathcott, Joseph. (2003). *Beyond the Ruins: The Meanings of Deindustrialization.* Ithaca, NY: ILR Press.

Davies, Gwendolyn. (1991). *Studies in Maritime Literary History, 1760–1930.* Fredericton: Acadiensis Press.

Delisle, Jennifer Bowering. (2013). *The Newfoundland Diaspora: Mapping the Literature of Outmigration.* Waterloo: Wilfrid Laurier University Press.

Fraser, Emma. (2016). Awakening in Ruins: The Virtual Spectacle of the End of the City in Video Games. *Journal of Gaming and Virtual Worlds* 8(2): 177–196.

Grady, Constance. (2022, September 15). In Ducks, Kate Beaton of Hark! A Vagrant Goes Bleak and Desolate. *Vox.* www.vox.com/culture/23351672/ducks-two-years-in-the-oil-sands-kate-beaton-review (Accessed: 18 June 2024).

Hamera, Judith. (2017). *Unfinished Business: Michael Jackson, Detroit, and the Figural Economy of American Deindustrialization.* New York: Oxford University Press.

Joly, Tara. (2017). *Making Productive Land: Utility, Encounter, and Oil Sands Reclamation in Northeastern Alberta, Canada.* Ph.D. Diss., University of Aberdeen.

Kyler, Carolyn. (2010). Mapping a Life: Reading and Looking at Contemporary Graphic Memoir. *The CEA Critic*, 72(3), pp. 2–20.

Linkon, Sherry Lee. (2018). *The Half-Life of Deindustrialization: Working-Class Writing about Economic Restructuring.* Ann Arbor: University of Michigan Press.

Macdonald, Graeme. (2012). Oil and World Literature. *American Book Review*, 33(3), pp. 7–31.

MacKinnon, Lachlan. (2020). *Closing Sysco: Industrial Decline in Atlantic Canada's Steel City.* Toronto: University of Toronto Press.

Mah, Alice. (2012). *Industrial Ruination, Community, and Place: Landscapes and Legacies of Urban Decline.* Toronto: University of Toronto Press.

Marr, Gemma. (2022). *The Backwoods, the Bucolic and the In-Between: Navigating Desire in Atlantic Canadian Literature.* Ph.D. Diss., Carleton University.

Mazer, Katie. (2022). Dump Truck Destiny: Alberta Oil, 'East Coast' Workers, and Attachment to Extraction. *Antipode: A Radical Journal of Geography*, 54(6), pp. 1923–1943.

McCurdy, Patrick. (2022). Excavating CBC's Docudrama The Tar Sands. *Imaginations: Journal of Cross-Cultural Image Studies*, 13(1), pp. 81–106.

Micu, Andreea. (2018). Photographing the End of the World: Capitalist Temporality, Crisis, and the Performativity of Visual Objects. *Performance Philosophy*, 4(1), pp. 39–52.

Murphy, Melanie. (2017). Afterlife and Decolonial Chemical Relations. *Cultural Anthropology*, 32(4), pp. 494–503.

Neis, Barbara et al. (2022). *Families, Mobility, and Work.* St. John's: Memorial University Press.

Olsza, Malgorzata. (2019). Photography as a Mirror in Alison Bechdel's Graphic Memoir Are You My Mother? A Comic Drama. *Image and Narrative*, 20(3), pp. 38–50.

Pedri, Nancy. (2015). What's the Matter of Seeing in Graphic Memoir? *South Central Review*, 32(3), pp. 8–29.

Rhodes, James. (2019). Rust Belt Chic: Deindustrialization, Places and Urban Authenticity. *Journal of Urban Cultural Studies*, 6(2–3), pp. 265–286.

Rosa, Brian. (2022). Deindustrialization Without End: Smokestacks as Postindustrial Monuments. *Geohumanities*, 9(2), pp. 1–26.

Schindler, David. (2014). Unravelling the Complexity of Pollution by the Oil Sands Industry. *Proceedings of the National Academy of Sciences*, 111(9), pp. 3209–3210.

Schmidt, Jeremy. (2020). Settler Geology: Earth's Deep History and the Governance of in situ Oil Spills in Alberta. *Political Geography*, 78, pp. 102–132.

Souther, Mark. (2017). *Believing in Cleveland: Managing Decline in "The Best Location in the Nation"*. Philadelphia: Temple University Press.

Takach, Geo. (2017). *Tar Wars: Oil, Environment, and Alberta's Image*. Edmonton: The University of Alberta Press.

Thielman, Sam. (2022, September 23). How Kate Beaton Paid off her Student Loans. *The New Yorker*. https://www.newyorker.com/books/page-turner/how-kate-beaton-paid-off-her-student-loans (Accessed: 18 June, 2024).

Thompson, Peter. (2019). *Nights Below Foord Street: Literature and Popular Culture in Postindustrial Nova Scotia*. Montreal: McGill-Queen's University Press.

Todd, Zoe. (2022). Fossil Fuels and Fossil Kin: An Environmental Kin Study of Weaponized Fossil Kin and Alberta's So-Called 'Energy Resources Heritage'. *Antipode: A Radical Journal of Geography*, 0(0), pp. 1–25.

Turner, Chris. (2017). *The Patch: The People, Pipelines, and Politics of the Oil Sands*. Toronto: Simon and Schuster.

Unrau, Melanie. (2019). 'Tend the Rusted Steel Like a Shepherd': Petropoetics of Oil Work in Canada. Ph.D. Diss., University of Manitoba.

Vizenor, Gerald. (2010). *Manifest Manners: Narratives on Postindian Survivance*. Lincoln: University of Nebraska Press.

21

THE SOUND OF DEINDUSTRIALIZATION

Giacomo Bottà

Introduction

British band Leatherface first recorded 'Dead Industrial Atmosphere' as the last track on their LP *Mush*, released in the UK in 1991. The raunchy punk rock of the band from Sunderland had evolved at that point into a melodic and melancholic sound, accompanying the emotion-led lyrics of singer Frankie Stubbs. References to William Blake's 'dark satanic mills' and to air that smells of 'religion and Vauxies beer' exemplify the complex atmosphere. The reference to a Sunderland brewery briefly identifies the band's hometown, though the song feels more like a sonic manifesto about the atmosphere of desperation than a representation of a specific place or industrial experience.

Almost 30 years later, in April 2019, the visual artist, photographer, and filmmaker Andy Martin filmed Stubbs performing an acoustic version of "Dead Industrial Atmosphere" in the "dry dock of the last standing shipyard (formerly Doxford's) on Sunderland's River Wear" (Type, 2019). Stubbs sits with an acoustic guitar in hand, a bottle of red wine in the chair next to him, surrounded by a rusty harbor waiting to be dismantled to make space for a double carriageway. The scene looks like it must smell of bad beer, rust, and guano. But while we can identify the specific location, Stubbs could easily be sitting in a similar space in Antwerp, Pori, or Rotterdam, and the setting would evoke a familiar dead industrial atmosphere with the same material, olfactory, and affective dimensions.

The song echoes of the idea of an urban atmosphere that, as Matthew Gandy (2017) writes, combines the "layers of gases enveloping the planet" and "the prevailing mood of a place, situation, or cultural representation such as the feeling evoked by a film or a novel" (Gandy, 2017, p. 355). Gandy reconstructs a genealogy of 'atmosphere,' from the first aerial views of cities from airplanes to its use in describing affect within the 'new phenomenology' to politics to late capitalism's urban microclimates. Across these ontological realms, we see the indeterminacy and malleability of the concept of atmosphere and its connections with subjectivity. The dead industrial atmosphere of Stubb's song is not limited to Sunderland; it describes deindustrialization itself. Deindustrialization is a *Strukturwandel*, a structural economic change in the realm of production that affected and is still affecting identities, places, and communities around the world (Cowie and Heathcott, 2003; Linkon, 2018). It is part

DOI: 10.4324/9781003308324-30

of a polycrisis (Tooze, 2022) involving multiple global negative phenomena, from economic recession to the oil crisis, from the implementation of neoliberalism to robotization, which intertwine and amplify each other.

In this chapter, I argue that music offers the ideal source to investigate deindustrialization, exactly because of its ways of representing. Unlike visual or narrative representations, like photography or fiction, music doesn't only memorialize individual stories or narrate specific cities shrinking, factories closing, and communities imploding. Music can deploy visual and narrative dimensions and their tropes, but it also extends into affective and performative dimensions. Its role in representing deindustrialization is at once more elusive but also, I would argue, more important.

As a ubiquitous presence in people's everyday lives, music provides a means to escape from the depressive conditions of a shrinking city. Deindustrialization music functions as a mediator of a temporary condition and indicates a 'way out' toward a possible post-industrial society and condition. Music works in this way because, while it is created within a particular creative industry, it is consumed by audiences in varied platforms and ways, and it can facilitate both individual and collective pleasure and contribute to community building (Bennett, 2001; Frith, 1996). In this chapter, I examine how communities hit by deindustrialization across the world have created cultural networks of resilience and built pedagogical instruments for their transmission across spatial and temporal divides. Through music, they established cultural valves to release pain, sadness, grief, and rage while also at times celebrating a lost identity. I will show how music under the polycrisis of deindustrialization became a "vanishing mediator" (Jameson, 1973, p. 52) that could go beyond the industrial city and its imaginary and begin to envision identities and meanings for a possible post-industrial society.

I draw here on almost two decades of building and analyzing an archive of interviews with musicians and other cultural producers and artefacts such as albums, tapes, magazines, posters, and fanzines, mostly but not exclusively to the European landscape. As I have discussed elsewhere (Bottà, 2009; Bottà, 2020), popular music operates in three dimensions. First, through lyrics, popular music constructs a *textscape* that speaks to listeners and spells out ideas, dreams, expectations, and desires in direct and powerful ways. Second, popular music has a strong visual component, anchoring sounds to faces, bodies, clothes, times, and places through images on record covers, photo shootings, videos, and music-related merchandise. Finally, of course, music is made up of sounds produced by real or virtual electric instruments and by the human voice. I argue that while consumers perceive the meanings represented in these dimensions of popular music, deconstructing them enables us to understand the internal logic of music as representation and its interactions with certain imaginaries.

Industrial Sounds

Deindustrialization represents a long fade out of the history of industrial work and cities. Therefore, if we want to understand how deindustrialization sounds, we must understand the idiosyncratic and 'very material' relation between music, industry, and place. We can trace musicians' fascination with industrial production and its associated sounds to the attempt to reproduce industrial noises from the beginning of the twentieth century, ranging from Russian avant-garde to German serial music and Italian futurism. In 1913, Italian futurism painter Luigi Russolo published *L'arte dei Rumori* (The Art of Noise) (Russolo, 1967), an art manifesto in favor of noise. He described the articulation and classification of noises as a revolution in music inspired by modern life in big cities and by human progress. He wrote that industrial and especially warfare noises could lead to new music, and he attempted to systematically identify, classify, and reproduce these sounds. He also built new instruments (*intonarumori*) and wrote scores for that purpose (Maina, 2011).

A decade later, industrial noise became even more prominent in the Soviet avant-garde. Communist filmmakers, visual artists, novelists, and composers saw the factory as the space where workers were emancipating and where socialism arising. On the fifth anniversary of the Russian revolution in 1922, in Baku, composer Arseny Avraamov performed the *Symphony of Factory Siren*, conducting the whole city as an orchestra. In 1926–1927, Alexander Mosolov's *The Iron Foundry*, the first movement of a lost ballet suite titled *Stal* (steel), used orchestral sounds produced with metal sheets. He also emphasized repetition as a significant feature of the industrial soundscape. These examples played out in classical music performed in symphony halls, operas, and theatres, despite initial audience perplexities (Belgiojoso, 2014).

Popular music engaged with industrialization in a more thematic way, starting with the Anglo-Saxon tradition of songs written and performed by workers during the eighteenth century and the first industrial revolution. Singers often put new lyrics to old rural melodies, creating songs about the industrial worker's condition, memorializing strikes and accidents, or simply helping with repetitive work at the assembly line, on merchant ships, and in mines (Mac Coll, 1954). During the 1960s so-called folk revival (Brocken, 2003; Mitchell, 2007), these songs circulated in vinyl anthologies such as *The Iron Muse: A Panorama of Industrial Folk Music* (Topic Records, 1963), and some were recorded by individual artists, as in Pete Seeger's *American Industrial Ballads* (Folkway Records 1956).

But popular music also incorporated industrial sounds, especially as the blues mutated thanks to great migration from the American South to big industrial cities like Chicago and Detroit (Goven, 2005, pp. 62–69). In the so-called Chicago blues, for instance, original blues from the Delta of Mississippi, which used acoustic guitars and pianos, turned electric, consolidating a core musical formation of guitar, bass, and drums that remains the basis of contemporary rock music. Artists such as Muddy Waters, Jody Williams, Bo Didley, and Hubert Sumlin cranked up the sound of electric guitar with valve amplifiers and used the slide technique to bring in feedback, distortion, and noise. Several of these musicians also worked in factories, and the influence of heavy, noisy, and repetitive machinery emerged in their sound (Smith, 1999).

In Detroit, we find a further connection between music and industry: the first example of 'industrial city entrepreneurship' that created, developed, serialized, and distributed its own music. Berry Gordy Jr. founded the Tamla/Motown record label in 1958 after having worked on Ford assembly line (Quispel, 2005). The production of Motown music paralleled the automobile assembly process, with recording studios assembling hits for the pop charts. Motown exploited this industrial branding starting with its name, short for Motor Town, the nickname of Detroit. Some Motown songs also included literal sounds of the industry. Ivy Joe Hunter allegedly played metal bars and tire chains to fortify the beat in Martha and the Vandellas' hits "Dancing in the Streets" and "Nowhere to Run" (Williams, 2022).

This synergy among industrial production, cities, and sounds peaked with the German band Kraftwerk starting in the 1970s. Famous for hit singles like 'The Robots,' 'Autobahn,' and 'The Model,' the band from Düsseldorf combined art music with Black influences, noise with place marketing. Started by Ralf Hütter and the late Florian Schneider (born Schneider-Esleben) and consolidated into a quartet with Wolfgang Flür and Karl Barthos, the band is still active today, though Hütter is the only original member. Defining its work as a *Gesamtkunstwerk* (total work of art), Kraftwerk now performs mostly in museums like MoMa and Tate Art.

Kraftwerk also exemplifies how music can transcend place. Its members have referred to the band's music as *industrielle Volksmusik* (Schütte, 2020). Possibly translated as 'industrial folk music,' the term juxtaposes 'industrial,' therefore modern, delocalized, gray, and noisy, with 'Volksmusik,' a genre dominated by idyllic references to a rural past. However, this idiosyncratic phrase also constitutes a powerful statement of intent. It implies that the synergy between the industrial city and industrial music could be as just as natural as the one between *Volksmusik* and rural pastures. Kraftwerk built on industrial sounds from across the twentieth century: noise and repetition, Soviet avant-garde and Italian futurism, simple folk melodies, and Black music. Also, it looks forward toward future genres, including the techno, electro, and house music that arose in Black communities in industrial Detroit and Chicago and with industrial and heavy metal bands such as Nine Inch Nails, Die Krupps, Nitzer Ebb, and Rammstein. In the process, the music represents a range of places as well as times.

Across these examples of 'industrial city music,' several elements stand out. The first is noise. Since the industrial revolution, noise has become a major preoccupation in industrial cities, which have attempted to tame it, although this has long proved difficult. Machinery along with traffic and political turmoil have long been central to the soundscape of industrial cities. In *Le Bruit* (Botte and Chocholle, 1984), Botte and Chocholle identify specific features of noise, including intermittence, erraticness, and randomness as well as complexity, brevity, and modulation, and they note that these can be perceived as disagreeable for some. This, they suggest, shows that noise is subjective and therefore has a cultural and aesthetic dimension.

Noise and repetition are often seen as signifiers of performers' industrial city origins. They become part of narratives that purport to explain the music. For instance, an article about Black Sabbath's drummer starts like this:

> When Bill Ward was a young kid growing up in post-war Birmingham, he used to walk past the factories where they stamped the edges of sheets of metal and make up rhymes and rhythms in his head. Back then he never dreamed, of course, that the noises he was imagining would eventually lead him into a career as a successful musician and one of the founding fathers of an entire genre.
>
> *(Everley, 2022, p. 40)*

This trope is somehow always connected to childhood and to the past, where the creative potential of industrial noise enters the artist's consciousness as a sort of epiphany. The idea of an organic connection between place and sound persists, even as some artists articulate a more conflicted version of the story. Reflecting on this trope, Cabaret Voltaire's Richard Kirk offers a different view of the influence of industrial noise:

> I think there's a myth about Sheffield that we were trying to replicate the sound of factories. I lived in the East End of Sheffield and from where I was you could see right down into the valley which was full of all these big fucking black buildings churning out Christ knows what. You could hear the stuff going on at night – but there was never any notion in Cabaret Voltaire of trying to make the noise of the factory. Why would you want to do that? You want to move away from that, escape into some alternative reality. It was grim, Sheffield, but it was the boredom it created that prompted us

to start the band. There were very few clubs, very little music apart from Tony Christie or whatever, so we decided to invent some.

(Quoted in Stubbs, 2021)

This ambivalence toward industrial noise as creative engine doesn't mean we should disregard the industrial soundscape, whether as a catalyst or as something to escape.

In the visual dimension, red brick has long been a strong signifier of industrial background, going back at least to Charles Dickens's description in *Hard Times* of the fictional Northern city of Coketown: "a town of red brick, or of brick that would have been red if the smoke and ashes had allowed it" (Dickens, 1894, p. 367). Red bricks were the most common building material, left bare in most factories and other industrial buildings, and bands around the world have used the red brick wall as background for promotional photos to amplify their authenticity and connection to 'the street.'

Another significant feature of music in industrial cities is displacement. We often associate displacement with deindustrialization, forgetting that industrial cities were often built upon a mass or individual migration from the countryside, other countries, or even other parts of a city. Industrial migration helped create the Chicago blues, for instance, and it brought several musicians of Irish descent into the Manchester scene of the 1970s. In addition, because industrial cities tend to resemble one another, place attachment is always somewhat artificial. Industrial music often connects not with a specific place but rather with a transnational community or subaltern scene.

A fourth feature of industrial city music is the connection with work. As an ideological and logistical element, work becomes a theme and a resource for industrial city bands, setting them apart from other musicians while also enabling them to develop musical ideas and distribute them across the world autonomously. The industrial city has also facilitated the development of music production tied to specific imaginaries of work, like Motown. Moreover, work also provides a narrative that establishes the identity and significance of certain bands and individual artists.

Deindustrializing Music

Like many aspects of industrial cities, music changes with the economic restructuring of deindustrialization. Starting in the 1970s, factory and mine closings undermined the structural organization of industrial cities and affected communities and individual lives in serious and sometimes tragic ways, effects that are still unfolding (Linkon, 2018). Deindustrialization generated a variety of local musical responses that amplified a shared sense of doom and destruction and sometimes anticipated real material developments. Equally important, much like deindustrialization itself, this music quickly circulated around the world. Deindustrialization music was not, then, simply a response to local experiences of shutdowns. Rather, it articulated and at times mediated a way out of the polycrisis of economic change.

Across several decades, from the end of the 1960s toward the 1990s to today, and in various countries as deindustrialization spread, punk has been an especially significant genre of deindustrialization music. Starting in the 1970s, punk articulated the restlessness and lack of future perspective embedded in deindustrialization. Worley defines punk in political terms, emphasizing its oppositional stance, its disregard for authority, its embrace of its own marginalization, and its do-it-yourself attitude (Worley, 2017, pp. 10–11). As Stacy Thompson shows, punk established itself through networked scenes and communities, and it resisted commodification and the music industry (Thomson, 2004, pp. 3–4). Initially linked to cultural capitals like New York City and London, rather than key sites of deindustrialization, punk applied a "semiotic guerrilla warfare" (Hebdige, 1979, p. 105) to familiar images, making the banal everyday both menacing and attractive. Punk adopted an irregular and improvised attitude of provocation to dramatize British decline (Hebdige, 1979, p. 87). Dramatizing implies performance as well as a critical and sometimes political perspective. We see this in the social realism of The Clash and the Jam, and in more surrealistic music from Sex Pistols, Siouxie and the Banshees, and Raincoats. These bands addressed the boredom and uncertain future brought on by the economic crisis, but they also articulated and responded to the crisis. That enabled them to find a way out through creative industries of the cultural capitals of London and New York, including not only the music industry but also the artistic world of fashion designers, photographers, filmmakers, visual artists, and fans who 'went punk' and consolidated its success.

Punk quickly spread to industrial cities thanks to the media attention and moral panic it generated. It offered a straightforward way for disillusioned youth to participate, and they brought a sudden and interesting mutation toward industrial city themes and sounds. This occurred at a moment when many young people were working toward industrial careers as students in polytechnics, as blue-collar apprentices, and as office workers but were also already conscious that their socioeconomic reality was coming to an end. Less involved in the cultural center's art world, young bands from industrial cities were establishing their own sonic and visual dimensions and addressing change in new ways. They were also beginning to dissociate music from the industrial imaginary. The synergy of industrial city music was transforming into an eccentric cycle, where crisis and creative endeavors feed into each other.

For example, Manchester-based The Fall's song 'Industrial Estate' talks about industrial settings right in the moment they were imploding. Other bands used industrial imaginaries for logos, record covers, and photo shootings. Pere Ubu from Cleveland experimented with noises in their debut LP *The Modern Dance* (1978), providing a mold for others across the world (Coney, 2018). In interviews, Pere Ubu members referred to Cleveland and its deindustrializing landscape as their main inspiration, as singer David Thomas puts it:

> We were savages living in the ruins of a great civilization of Rockefellers and Carnegies. Growing up, we owned downtown. Nobody wanted it. We roamed the streets like they were ours. The Flats was a place of deep mystery. It was our modern art museum. We would drive through the steel mills and within 20 yards of open blast furnaces. We weren't duplicating those sounds. Those sounds were showing us the way to change the narrative vehicle of modern music.
>
> *(Quoted in Stewart, 2017)*

Interestingly, Thomas's explanation resonated with Kirk's point about Sheffield: the band wasn't imitating the sounds of industry. Instead, the setting and imaginary pointed to creative change. If music and the industrial city had built a cohesive and cyclical set-up during the whole industrial era, during deindustrialization this ceased to work. The result was music that was less tied to deindustrializing places and a topographic displacement and more associated with a deindustrializing atmosphere that extended across the whole world. Issues that appeared to be local acquired more global and sinister connotations. Industrial city music's displacement expanded to a disjunction between place and music.

The Sound of Deindustrialization

The sound of hardcore punk echoes some elements mentioned earlier. It is characterized by speed, shouted texts, repetitive distorted guitar riffs, and political do-it-yourself attitude. Its imaginary is less locality-centered, with bands such as Discharge and Crass in England, Declino and Negazione in Italy, Slime and Razzia in Germany, and Black Flag and Dead Kennedys in the US all presenting continuous expressions of doom. Moreover, this attitude reflects the polycrisis, connecting with Cold War escalation and nuclear fear as well as the disentrancement of deindustrialization.

As this suggests, deindustrialization extended beyond specific locations to this global dark atmosphere, so it was not anchored in specific locations of musical production. If early "London" punk was "dramatizing" a crisis, hardcore punk is a structure of feeling and articulating economic change (Williams, 1977). Desperation, sadness, and anger in hardcore punk cover the whole affective range. It is far too abrasive and militant to memorialize; it is forever linked to a marginal condition, just like the deindustrialization process itself.

Take for instance 'Omicida 357 Magnum' from the 1984 released split cassette *Mucchio Selvaggio* by Negazione from one-company-town Turin (Italy). The song opens with an uncanny and atonal guitar riff juxtaposed with the singer's declaiming voice, stating the exact location of a road rage incident that ended with a gun murder and the victim's and perpetrator's names. The text seems to be lifted straight out of a newspaper. Once bass and drums enter, the song accelerates swiftly, followed by a mid-tempo passage before another acceleration. The lyrics become more expressionist, delivering an urban true crime snapshot. As the song fades out, the singer mutters "Primo Gennaio 1984 a Torino" (January 1, 1984, in Turin). Despite this specificity, the song does not fetishize Turin itself. What makes the song memorable is that the event could have happened in New York City, Antwerp, or any other city. Mental health issues, suicides, political unrest, and stress build musical tropes whose common denominator is placeless deindustrialization and a broader critique of the social effects of economic change.

Post-punk further develops this deindustrializing atmosphere. "Post-punk" has been applied to a variety of musical expressions, ranging from 1970s ska revival to guitar-based experimentalism, from punk-funk to early electro experiment, from industrial music to proto-garage (Reynolds, 2006). In post-punk, the sonic palette of the basic rock instrumentation is expanded through panning and echo effects, in a way like dub, while the guitar uses funky riffs, and the bass draws inventive and complex lines. This sonic expansion articulates similarly messy and shrinking urban and industrial settings, where voids began to be amplified and the noise/silence dichotomy became more unpredictable.

While punk has a clear Anglo-Saxon origin, post-punk is more complex, as we see in its reliance on Black influences from funk and dub. Post-punk's seminal bands come from different countries and sing in various national languages. German Fehlfarben, Italian CCCP – Fedeli alla Linea, and Belgian TC Matic all worked with dissonance, noise, and space, once again amplifying an affective response to the *Strukturwandel*, though in a less furious and more cerebral way than in hardcore punk. Moreover, post-punk works with space by adopting pauses and moments of silence as narrative element, as if songs would be imploding. For example, Fehlfarben's 'Militürk' (from *Monarchie un Alltag*, 1980) starts with a repetitive echoed drumbeat accompanied by a vaguely Middle East synth noise; the bass enters after 30 seconds and the sharp guitar riff after 45 seconds. The voice delivers the iconic German lyrics about kebab dreams in Berlin one minute after the beginning of the song. There is not a rush to immediately deliver a compact wall of sound but more an attempt to deconstruct it through subtraction and layering. This song, also recorded as 'Kebap Träume' by

D.A.F., another band from Düsseldorf, delivers an impressionist take on Berlin and on Turkish immigration, ending with controversial statements such as "Germany, everything is over" and "we are the Turks of tomorrow," as if directly lifted from the populist yellow press. It addresses the inexorable decline of West Berlin, where immigration, the political climate, and deindustrialization together created a social setting that fueled racism and social segregation. To make a comparison with industrial city music, Motown and its Hitsville recording studio layered tracks carefully to achieve an iconic and exhilarating wall of sound that hinted at economic upswing, widening purchasing power, and progress in civil rights (Smith, 1999). Post-punk is the opposite, the sonic equivalent of the disassembling and disposal of an obsolete machine in front of our eyes.

Music, Deindustrialization, and the Built Environment

Even if deindustrialization music seems to transcend geographical location, it fetishizes the industrial built environment and celebrates its ubiquity. Industrial cities were marked by compartmentalized divisions of social class and facilitated the accumulation of capital by the owning class (Engels, 1969), a pattern that was replicated across nations and territories, so that similar kinds of structures and materials appeared in different places. Similarities continued with deindustrialization, which disrupted these cities and made portions of the built environment vacant and obsolete. Vital elements of a music ecosystem such as rehearsal spaces and small performance venues took over former warehouses and vacant factory spaces.

For instance, Joy Division rehearsed in T. J. Davidson's Rehearsal Studio, in a former warehouse in Manchester Knott Mill. In 1979, Kevin Cummins photographed the band rehearsing there in a room with bare walls, a wooden floor of long boards, and a number of big windows that let in as much natural light as possible – all elements designed for production or warehousing (Cummins, 2021). Moreover, the band doesn't pose in the usual rock and roll vernacular manner, standing in line by a wall, facing the camera in a menacing way or performing energetically live in front of an enthusiastic audience. Instead, they look defiantly into the lens and seem focused on rehearsing, not performing. They wear austere office clothes, and even their posture, whether sitting down or standing, seems somehow bureaucratic. The image suggests that this is a band at work in the 'industrial world.' As was common in the music press of that era, the pictures are shot in black and white, therefore somehow made timeless. The setting, the band's appearance, and the black and white tone suggest a sense of timelessness, as if the band had always belonged in this warehouse. Together with the band's music, this use of the built environment implies a strong connection with industrial work and thus an authentic link with deindustrialization.

Further, at least in the beginning, the deteriorated and empty built environment was viable as it was, the rustier the better, and most importantly, it was available for little or no cost everywhere. Deindustrialization was spreading in cities all over the world, and empty warehouses provided an extensive and readily recognizable material and mediated trope for deindustrialization music. Moreover, alternative uses of the deindustrialized built environment reflected the politics of hardcore punk, as industrial wastelands became sites of squatting and experimental housing solutions, alternative cultural production and consumption, egalitarianism, extreme left-wing and anarchist ideologies, animal liberation, and other do-it-yourself actions.

This political 'imaginary of deindustrialization' survives at the margins even today, however the post-industrial dimension of punk also led to a commodification of the decaying industrial atmosphere. Eager buyers saw charm and potential in spaces that seemed to offer an authentic urban experience. The historical patina of these sites made them ripe for gentrification, and developers turned them into gyms, theatres, restaurants, galleries, and luxury housing. This phenomenon puts 'deindustrialization music' under a different light: was it participating into the commodification of decay or was it simply a 'vanishing mediator' acting between two realities and disappearing in the making? This can be addressed only by looking into the way music under deindustrialization has been heritagized.

Deindustrialization Music and Heritage

Deindustrialization has a complex relation to memorialization. Industrial parks and heritage sites have become common features of national and supranational history building, as in the case of the *European Route of Industrial Heritage*. However, often these sites highlight their aesthetic value, detached from the often-tragic history of their dismissal and non-use, as if they were not the result of deindustrialization, but simply built for their touristic and contemplative function, as ready-made ruins. We can see a similar erasure of connections in some of the music of deindustrialization. Some bands and genres arising during deindustrialization have acquired new meanings along the years, while others have reemerged from oblivion thanks to generational turns, and others will be forever forgotten. The relationship between bands and specific cities is not straightforward, as some bands have been used for purposes of local promotion and neoliberal profit-making.

For example, Joy Division's iconic cover of the *Unknown Pleasure* LP has been available on T-shirts sold in fast fashion shops, adapted into merchandise (Greenwood, 2013), and featured in memes stating that "if you see this shirt, the rent in your neighborhood will go up," hinting at the subcultural capital associated with the band. Three of the original band members have penned autobiographies (Hook, 2012; Sumner, 2015; Morris, 2020), and *Control*, a biopic directed by Anton Corbijn, appeared in 2007. The band was nominated for the Rock and Roll Hall of Fame in 2023. Bass player Peter Hook has been touring for years, presenting Joy Division's albums in their entirety with a band of musicians, some of whom are younger than the songs they perform, while the other surviving members still play together under the name New Order.

Joy Division's music achieved a cultural status, and their memorialization impacted Manchester and not the other way around. Apart from a couple of iconic shots on a bridge in Hulme and the warehouse images in their rehearsal space, the band preferred to adopt a stern 1930s-inspired imaginary associated with continental Europe and Germany in particular (Bottà, 2018), while their music reflected on existential bleakness and the human condition. But Manchester still claims them as part of the city's heritage. The band's lyrics don't reference the city, nor do their images or their sound involve explicit connections, but a dedicated *Manchester Music Tour* features some of Joy Division's local landmarks. This is true of other bands as well, which have been embedded into canons of local heroes to be celebrated and exploited as part of the post-industrial heritage tourism in cities (Bottà, 2021).

While bands ranging from Editors to IDLES today reproduce post-punk's abrasive sound and exploit a deindustrialization imaginary, they do not trace their images or their sounds to particular places. Rather, they articulate the historical and socioeconomic conditions of distress and hopelessness that transcend place.

Music from industrial cities is today often repackaged, cleaned, digitized, and curated to promote urban real estate and the gentrification of post-industrial core areas. It is still possible to shoot a video like Martha and the Vandellas dancing in the paint shop of a *Ford* factory (Smith, 1999), but its meaning will be forever different, forever tied to what some call heritage and someone else memory. The Manchester club *The Hacienda FAC 51* closed following bankruptcy and a campaign to demonize club culture in post-Thatcherite England, but it now houses a complex of expensive apartments with the same name as the nightclub. Such projects heritagize deindustrialization music as part of local branding as cities attempt to present themselves as 'post-industrial.' What we see in such efforts is the extraction of value from the industrial city in a sort of second cycle of exploitation.

Conclusions

The music of deindustrializing cities functions as what Fredric Jameson calls a "vanishing mediator" (Jameson, 1973). Jameson introduced the term in his discussion of Max Weber's *The Protestant Ethic and the Spirit of Capitalism* (first published in German 1905). In the transition between the precapitalist and capitalist eras, Jameson writes, Protestantism acted as a bridge, and it emerged radically changed, deprived of its initial function, vanished. Similarly, the music of deindustrializing cities created a bridge, a transition. It translated meanings and practices from the industrial city, based on production, to the post-industrial city, based on consumption. Music has anticipated and facilitated this passage, having characteristics of both these worlds. Punk and post-punk are not dead, but their social function has changed radically: from being subordinate and critical, but also communitarian and celebratory, they have become another product co-opted in the commodification of space.

However, this is not the whole story of what music offers. It has static functions, like giving us pleasure, and it also has dynamic ones, capable of reflecting the complex conditions and articulations of culture, economy, politics, and society. We see both in stories about the return of several crisis music practices in recent years – 1990s raves, 1970s free festivals, 1980s post-punk, even 1930s *Sprachgesang*. These stories are often accompanied by photos of students throwing their heads back while dancing under a railway bridge. They remind us that the aesthetic of crisis can be beautiful and compelling. We should all try to dance under a railway bridge at least once in our lifetimes. But while it may never again feel like it did in 1981, music's revolutionary potential for individuals and social change cannot be diminished. Deindustrialization music teaches us that cultural production, the search for alternatives, and human endeavors can lead to potential resolutions and steps forward, even in the face of a polycrisis.

Deindustrialization studies often focus on loss, starting with the demise of industrial production and the associated organization of work and on its consequences for the working class. While varied representations offer sources and frameworks for examining the losses of the past and struggles to construct a different future, music articulates the affective atmosphere of deindustrialization in especially powerful ways. Also, it helps us imagine and engage affectively and creatively with socioeconomic change. Music can not only reflect the lives of dispossessed people. It can empower them.

Reference List

Belgiojoso, Ricciarda. (2014). *Constructing Urban Space with Sounds and Music*. Farnham: Ashgate.
Bennett, Andy. (2001). *Cultures of Popular Music*. New York: Open University Press.

Bottà, Giacomo. (2009). The City That Was Creative and Did Not Know: Manchester and Popular Music 1976–97. *European Journal of Cultural Studies*, 12(3), pp. 349–365.

Bottà, Giacomo. (2018). Trying to Find a Clue, Trying to Find a Way to Get Out! The European Imaginary of Joy Division. In Power, M. (ed.) *Heart and Soul: Critical Essays on Joy Division*. London: Rowman & Littlefield.

Bottà, Giacomo. (2020). *Deindustrialisation and Popular Music: Punk and 'Post-Punk' in Manchester, Düsseldorf, Torino and Tampere*. London: Rowman and Littlefield International.

Bottà, Giacomo. (2021). The Sound of Düsseldorf City Walk: Authenticity in Real-life and Virtual Implementations of Music Heritage Tourism. *Popular Music History*, 14(1).

Botte, Marie-Claire and Chocholle, René. (1984). *Le Bruit*. Paris: Presses universitaires de France.

Brocken, Michael. (2003). *The British Folk Revival 1944–2002*. London: Routledge.

Coney, Brian. (2018, January 22). *40 Years On: Pere Ubu's The Modern Dance Revisited*. www.thequietus.com (Accessed: 7 March 2018).

Cowie, Jefferson, and Heathcott, Joseph. (2003). *Beyond the Ruins: The Meanings of Deindustrialization*. Ithaca, NY and London: Cornell University Press.

Cummins, Kevin. (2021). *Joy Division: Juvenes*. London: Cassell.

Dickens, Charles. (1894). *Hard Times*. London: Chapman and Hall.

Engels, Fredrick. (1969). *The Condition of the Working Class in England*. Moscow: Panther Press.

Everley, Dave. (2022, June 30). Fell on Black Days. *Classic Rock*.

Frith, Simon. (1996). *Performing Rites*. Oxford: Oxford University Press.

Gandy, Matthew. (2017). Urban Atmospheres. *Cultural Geographies*, 24(3), pp. 353–374.

Goven, Jennifer. (2005). From the Delta to Chicago: Muddy Water's Downhome Blues and the Shaping of African-American Identity in Post World War II Chicago. *Mc Nair Scholars Journal*, 8(1), pp. 62–69.

Greenwood, Travis Rand. (2013, May 21). 14 Pop Culture Spoofs Inspired By Joy Division's 'Unknown Pleasure'. *BuzzFeed*.

Hebdige, Dick. (1979). *Subculture: The Meaning of Style*. London: Routledge.

Hook, Peter. (2012). *Unknown Pleasures: Inside Joy Division*. London: Simon & Schuster.

Jameson, Frederic. (1973). The Vanishing Mediator: Narrative Structure in Max Weber. *New German Critique*, 1, pp. 52–89.

Linkon, Sherry Lee. (2018). *The Half-Life of Deindustrialization: Working-Class Writing about Economic Restructuring*. Ann Arbor: University of Michigan Press.

Mac Coll, Ewan (ed.). (1954). *The Shuttle and Cage: Industrial Folk Ballads*. London: Workers Music Association.

Maina, Claudia. (2011). The 'Scoppiatore'. The Intonarumori by Luigi Russolo. *Digimag*, 65.

Mitchell, Gillian. (2007). *The North American Folk Music Revival: Nation and Identity in the United States and Canada 1945–1980*. Aldershot: Ashgate.

Morris, Stephen. (2020). *Record Play Pause: Confessions of a Post-Punk Percussionist: The Joy Division Years*. London: Constable.

Quispel, Chris. (2005). Detroit, City of Cars, City of Music. *Built Environment*, 31(3), pp. 226–236.

Reynolds, Simon. (2006). *Rip It Up and Start Again. Postpunk 1978–1984*. London: Penguin.

Russolo, Luigi. (1967). *The Art of Noise*. New York: Something Else Press.

Schütte, Uwe. (2020). *Kraftwerk. Future Music from Germany*. London: Penguin.

Smith, Suzanne E. (1999). *Dancing in the Street: Motown and the Cultural Politics of Detroit*. Cambridge, MA: Harvard University Press.

Stewart, Dillon. (2017, November 22). Pere Ubu's David Thomas Returns Home. *Cleveland Magazine*. https://clevelandmagazine.com/entertainment/music/articles/pere-ubu's-david-thomas-returns-home (Accessed: 2 July 2024).

Stubbs, David. (2021, September 22). Inscriber of the Future: Remembering Richard H. Kirk. *The Quietus*. https://thequietus.com/news/remember-them/richard-h-kirk-obituary-cabaret-voltaire/ (Accessed: 2 July 2024).

Sumner, Bernard. (2015). *Chapter and Verse: New Order, Joy Division and Me*. New York City: Thomas Dunne.

Thomson, Stacy. (2004). *Punk Productions: Unfinished Business*. Albany: State University of New York Press.

The Routledge Handbook of Deindustrialization Studies

Tooze, Adam. (2022, June 24). *Defining Polycrisis – From Crisis Picture to Crisis Matrix. Chartbook Newsletter.* https://adamtooze.com/2022/06/24/chartbook-130-defining-polycrisis-from-crisis-pictures-to-the-crisis-matrix/ (Accessed: 2 July 2024).

Type, Martin. (2019). Frankie Stubbs – Dead Industrial Atmosphere (Live at Pallion Shipyard). *Martin Type.* www.martintype.co.uk (Accessed: 20 October 2022).

Williams, Raymond. (1977). *Marxism and Literature.* Oxford: Oxford University Press.

Williams, Richard. (2022, October 17). Ivy Joe Hunter Obituary. *The Guardian.*

Worley, Matthew. (2017). *No Future: Punk, Politics and British Youth Culture, 1976–1984.* Cambridge: Cambridge University Press.

22
GARMENT WORKERS THROUGH THE LENS OF LOSS
The Long Shadow of Deindustrialization in South Asian Films

Piyusha Chatterjee

Introduction

Terese Agnew's *Portrait of a Textile Worker* is of a woman working on a sewing machine, her eyes looking down at her hands gently guiding the fabric in front of her. She is wearing a *dupatta* modestly over both shoulders. The sparse jewelry – a ring and a pair of earrings – indicates only a lack of abject poverty. Behind her, another woman at another machine is looking up, her eyes focused on something else in the room. One can imagine the stitches falling at a regular rhythm and the hum of the machines enveloping the women in the room. The portrait is inspired by a photograph taken undercover by American labor activist Charles Kernaghan at a factory in Bangladesh, which Agnew recreated from thousands of clothing labels that people cut from their garments and sent to Agnew. As Agnew writes, "the repetition of thousands of other people cutting their labels . . . amplifies the presence of the woman we finally see" (Agnew, 2005). It reminds us of the labor of Third World or Global South women in the production of garments bought and sold around the world every day.

Anti-sweatshop campaigns, including those run by Kernaghan himself (Risen, 2022), draw on such affective and effective portraits to garner support for ethical production and procurement practices in the garment industry. Such images, however, fail to convey the complex experiences produced by the different local histories inflected with class and caste politics, patriarchal social norms, and capitalist forces (Kibria, 1995). Films enable diverse and distant audiences, consumers of fast fashion, activist groups, and Western publics to see this industry through a different lens. They nudge us to look beyond representations of garment workers from the Global South as either "passive victim(s) of global capital" (Kabeer, 2015, p. 11) or cheap labor that stole jobs from deindustrializing countries in the West. In films, we see these workers as women (and men) with needs, desires, motivations, and agency, as participants and not just victims in the transnational flow of capital and commodities. In this chapter, I will examine three films that, in different ways, make visible the emotional, affective, and lived experiences of women entangled in the supply chains of garment production. While they reflect three distinct genres – a Bollywood drama, an independent film, and a documentary, all three films show us how garment workers struggle against or negotiate with broader economic, political, and cultural forces in a globalized economy.

DOI: 10.4324/9781003308324-31

By offering a window into these women's lives, the films invite Western and metropolitan audiences to recognize these workers as agentive subjects, on and off the factory floor.

It may seem odd here to examine images of active workers in a region that has seen phenomenal and impressive economic growth over the last few decades,[1] but this success occurred during a period when developed countries of the West were deindustrializing, and the two processes are intertwined. Since the 1980s, many companies, especially garment retailers and fashion brands, chose to move or outsource their manufacturing production to the Global South. As Doreen Massey puts it, "production really is a social process" (Massey, 1995, p. 15). While decisions about the location – and relocation – of production reflect sociocultural and political factors and local historical and material conditions, those moves also affect workers' experiences. Many scholars in deindustrialization studies have examined the social cost of factory closures and offshoring decisions on working-class communities, cities, and neighborhoods, but we do not always consider the social costs for those on the other side of these moves.

As I will show in this chapter, the relocation of production that is a central effect of deindustrialization should not be read in terms of 'us vs. them' narratives. Stories of struggle, loss, and victory shown in these films complicate our conversations about economic restructuring and deindustrialization, which have often ignored the workers on the far side of the global supply chain. The films enable us to see the full social process of economic change. They show women performing different kinds of labor connected to the garment industry – factory work, home-based work, domestic and reproductive labor, and entrepreneurial and activist work for themselves and their communities. Attending to these stories illuminates the complexity of women's experiences and busts some myths around women from South Asia. In the process, it forces us to view deindustrialization through a wider lens.

Deindustrialization and the Theme of Loss

Loss has been a central theme in deindustrialization studies, usually focused on losses suffered by workers and working class communities because of factory closures in the industrialized West (High, 2021). Reframing deindustrialization as a problem that pits "corporate capital against local community" (High, 2023, p. 46), scholars have taken up the "toxic sociocultural, environmental, health, and political aftermath" (Berger and High, 2019, p. 1) of factory closures and documented their effects on individual lives that are reduced to data sets elsewhere. The list of social costs is long: job losses, deteriorating communities, crises of identity, the lack of stable income, physical and mental harm, deskilling, the loss of homes due to evictions and gentrification, the ruination of industrial landscapes, and revitalization, redevelopment, and renewal programs that erase working-class history and a sense of place.[2]

The list makes clear that the transformation is as much a cultural process as it is economic, and both unfold slowly. Sherry Lee Linkon (2018) describes the lingering sense of loss in working-class lives and communities as a "half-life." Memories of embodied harm and the struggle to adapt to the demands of economic restructuring ensure that industrial life and work remain present long after closures. Tim Strangleman (2017, p. 479) describes a process of "continuities and more subtle change" – the slowly fading but still palpable past in the present. Alice Mah (2012, p. 8) describes the still unfolding "tensions, contradictions, and contingencies within the lived experiences of people who occupy" deindustrialized landscapes as "ruination."

While the idea of loss is strong and rarely articulated positively, Mah (2009, p. 301) also notes that those who have lived through deindustrialization find community, social bonding, and belonging in place through this shared sense of loss – experiences and memories colored by hurt, injury, pain, and devastation. Loss is, therefore, a critical emotion and experience for those undergoing this transformation. It shapes their identities, worldviews, and choices, and it is passed on as an intergenerational memory. Disentangling the different threads of this emotional experience helps us recognize how deindustrialization can feel like a change that is "at once too diffuse and too localized to be noticed" (High, 2021, p. 98). Yet the experience of economic change is never just local, and even when deindustrialization scholars frame discussions of loss in terms of the processes of global capitalism, they rarely acknowledge the emotional dimension through a global lens.

In the second half of the twentieth century, South Asia witnessed rapid economic growth in part due to the rise of export-oriented garment manufacturing in these countries. While the economic success of India is often ascribed to the information technology sector, garment manufacturing also fueled this growth.[3] In Bangladesh, following the failure of the jute industry, ready-made garment manufacturing sector became the primary growth driver in the 1980s and currently comprises 75% of the country's export trade (Rahman, 2014). Pakistan has seen less growth in the textile sector, but that sector climbed from 30% to 61% of the country's export trade by 2010 (Khaliji et al., 2013).

This growth story is frequently framed as a spectacular achievement, yet it did not generate development, reduce poverty, or empower the poor, women, and waged laborers (Nayyar, 1998; Nanda, 2009; McCartney, 2014; See also Rahman, 2014). Deindustrialization of the West and (re)industrialization of the developing countries do not mean a direct transfer of wealth from one region to the other (Schindler et al., 2020). The Global South witnessed a concentration of labor-intensive production activities, but Global North countries remain sites of top-level management, design, and research and development for transnational corporations. Many factors contribute to this spatial division of labor, including social relations of production shaped over time by local historical conditions and relationships embedded with power hierarchies (Massey, 1995). Developing countries show uneven patterns of growth and decline, as Andy Pike (2022, p. 3; c.f. Rodrik, 2016) notes, experiencing "differentiated pathways and geographies and institutions" of deindustrialization. India, for example, has maintained or increased manufacturing activities even as it has undergone deindustrialization in some cities and sectors and witnessed a widening wealth gap. Shriya Anand and Aditi Dey (2022) describe this as "industrial destabilization" marked by noticeable local and regional patterns of deindustrialization and reindustrialization.

The implications of deindustrialization on the Global South may have remained underexamined so far, but more critical attention to this region could bridge and blur the North/South divide and help us better understand capitalism's global reach. Instead of searching for symmetrical developments across differentiated geographies or looking for evidence that deindustrialization in Global South regions is similar to what happened in the Global North, we need to pay attention to thematic arcs that enable us to see clearly the experiences of the Global South. The three films examined in this chapter show us how the themes of loss and labor struggle play out in South Asia and may complement and complicate the narratives deindustrialization studies has developed based on examples from the North.

The Eternal Optimism of Brand India

In the late 1990s, the song "Made in India" by Indi-pop artist Alisha Chinai became a raging success. It expressed a woman's desire for a soulmate who was made in India. In a society where women exercise "few choices when it comes to labor, production, and reproduction of social norms and family relations" (Kumar and Curtin, 2002, p. 358), the song spoke of female longing and an Indian identity that was not in opposition to but in conversation with the West. Like the woman in the song, the heroine of *Sui Dhaaga: Made in India* by Sharat Katariya (2018), a Hindi language drama released in 2018, dares to dream and yet remains true to her traditional values. She is the quintessential Bollywood stay-at-home woman, "productive, uncomplaining, kind, pragmatic and equally at home with Indian tradition and colonial (and postcolonial) modernity" (Mehta, 2011, p. 11).

Sui Dhaaga repackages the nostalgia for small town life experienced by migrants in metropolitan cities (Kumar, 2013), but unlike films such as *Gangs of Wasseypur*, which fixate on violence, illegality, illicit behavior, crime, and raw sexuality to represent life in rural India, Katariya emphasizes the theme of economic and infrastructural challenges. In the backdrop is the history of a *mohalla* — a community of craftworkers engaged in textile and garment production who have lost their traditional occupations of weaving, dyeing, tailoring, and related jobs to industrialized garment manufacturing. Relocation of manufacturing to the Global South regions was accompanied by the disappearance of traditional occupations in the textile and garment industry. The films show this loss as an intergenerational and communal experience in the neighborhood.

The central male character, Mauji (played by Varun Dhawan), is an expert tailor but works as a shop assistant for a sewing machine seller in the city. The wounds of economic and cultural loss in his family are so deep, we're told, that no one dares mention tailoring as a profession. Mauji is also not our usual overbearing and masculine Bollywood hero but a man caught between an abusive employer and a family that does not consider his job good enough. The plot moves forward when the female protagonist, Mauji's stay-at-home, uncomplaining wife Mamta (played by Anushka Sharma), voices her longing for a life of dignity and self-reliance. This expression of female desire counters Mauji's repeated assurance that all's well (*sab badiya hai*). Mamta clearly leads the changes in their lives, but she is also careful not to overstep her boundaries as a woman and daughter-in-law of the household. To mask her strength, she lets her husband take the credit for her ideas. But she is tempted to abandon her husband and family for a job in garment manufacturing in the city. This temptation presents itself in the form of a Bollywood stereotype – the anti-heroine, a westernized woman and a business owner who, as Ravinder Kaur (2003, p. 201) puts it, represents the "celluloid occident that delimits traditional boundaries". But Mamta refuses to leave her family. Instead, she takes on the challenge of designing clothes as part of a competition for seed funding to start a company. In the process, she encourages the community to return to their traditional occupations and establishes a cooperative of artisans. This makes her the heroine of the film. The loss that had pervaded the film is overcome by reinventing tradition to meet market demands.

Sui Dhaaga contributes toward a repackaging of India into a brand, as in campaigns like 'India Shining' and 'Make-in-India' that successive political regimes used to pitch India for the international market. Aimed at redefining the nation as a manufacturing powerhouse, these campaigns present a "new economic imaginary . . . (and) a commitment to a new and liberal economic model" (Wyatt, 2005, p. 467). *Sui Dhaaga* is just one Bollywood film that contributes to this effort (Mehta, 2011, p. 1). We can see this in the film's ending, when the cooperative, led by Mamta and Mauji, wins the design competition, which provides seed funding they use to start a clothing line called 'Mad-in-India' (sic). The happy ending embraces neoliberal market values of creativity, risk-taking, and entrepreneurialism as a way out of poverty.

Deblina Dey (2018, p. 61) argues that *Sui Dhaaga* "fails to do justice to its own mission" of critiquing capitalism, but that is not its aim. Rather, the film works to build consensus for a nation eager to develop an intimacy with global capitalism. Though it begins by narrating the failures of a developmental state in rural India, it ultimately pins hope on capitalism and neoliberalism to address the problems left behind by the previous economic and political order. The story unites an idyllic small-town neighborhood and erases tensions around caste, religion, and gender through song and dance. It smooths over real-world challenges, particularly problems rooted in the transformation of labor processes in the garment sector, by valorizing innovation, entrepreneurialism, and reinvention of tradition in marketable forms.

That said, the film also presents a nuanced understanding of women's lives in small towns and their challenges in/upon entering the labor market. Unlike the 'angry young man' figure portrayed by Amitabh Bachchan in films from the 1970s and the 1980s, Bollywood has never had a parallel female figure who expresses the angst of women from poor and working-class backgrounds (Manzar and Aravind, 2019). The treatment of Mamta's character in *Sui Dhaaga* is refreshing for two reasons. First, it is a layered representation of a new-age Bollywood heroine who "does not hesitate to scheme and connive to meet her ends" (Kishore, 2019, p. 146) and meets the challenges presented by patriarchy and capitalism with wit and guile. Second, it is uncommon to have women from small-town India occupy screen space in a somewhat liberating and empowering role. In the film, Mamta finds a way to engage with capitalism and participate in the global exchange of commodities by negotiating with a patriarchal family structure. That her persona never fully emerges free from patriarchal constraints is because of Bollywood films' "unquestioned acceptance of patriarchy" (Mehta, 2011, p. 9).

The Working Women in Dhaka

If *Sui Dhaaga* fails to portray the real-life challenges of working in the textile and garment industry in South Asia, Rubaiyat Hossain tackles the subject head-on in *Made-in-Bangladesh*. The film presents the real-life story of a young woman who fights a gritty battle against her employer, the state, and the society to unionize workers in her factory. Like the American biopic *Norma Rae* that explores the life of Crystal Lee, a textile worker and union organizer from North Carolina (see Toplin, 1995), *Made-in-Bangladesh* (2019) (released as *Shimu* in Bengali) is inspired by the true story of a garment worker and union activist in Bangladesh (Vitali, 2020; *The Business Standard*, 2022). The plot revolves around protagonist Shimu, played by Rikita Nandini, who works in a garment manufacturing unit in Dhaka, and follows her on and off the factory floor. If the script bears resemblances to the Hollywood film, it also fills a void. Few cultural representations focus on women workers from the Global South or their contributions to working-class struggles.

One of the factors that led companies to relocate garment manufacturing to Bangladesh was the availability of a "feminized labor," workforce comprised of cheap, disposable and predominantly women workers (Fudge, 1991). In a country where few women held paid employment before the 1980s (Rahman, 2014), women today comprise over 80% of the workforce in the ready-made garment sector in Bangladesh (Rahman and Islam, 2013, p. 41). Most are migrants from rural areas who move to Dhaka in search of employment. Despite the size of the female workforce and its significance of the garment sector to the economy, less than 1% of the unionized workers in the industry are women (Rahman, 2014, p. 64). Women's participation in unions is significantly impacted by Bangladeshi patriarchal and religious norms that force women to be obedient workers and allow them less control over their work lives. As Jennifer Bair (2010) argues, gender differences have played a key role in producing and sustaining this cheap labor market.

With the entry of women in the labor market, however, some patriarchal gender norms have relaxed, especially in urban-industrial areas, and this has produced complex new social realities (Rock, 2003). The working conditions and wages are dismal, but the urban setting and steady income allow these working women more freedom to move around the city and some flexibility to negotiate patriarchal codes of conduct, providing them some degree of empowerment and control over their own lives (Mamun and Hoque, 2022). Shimu and her friends work outside home, including night shifts. In one of the scenes, they are shown walking back home from the factory at daybreak. As the film shows, they enjoy certain sexual freedoms and exercise more choice over their lives than women cloistered in the domestic sphere. On the dark side, as is evident from the film's storyline, these women face multiple forms of abuse and violence at home and in the factory (Islam, 2016; Naved et al., 2018).

Hossain's film is a sensitive portrayal of this reality. In an interview before the film's release, she said the film was as much about the struggle against patriarchy as it was about fighting capitalism and big corporations that are exploiting women (Hurtes, 2018). The growth of Bangladesh's garment export rests on the back of women like Shimu who shoulder an unfair share of the workload. They are underpaid and work in unsafe and unhealthy conditions. They also have primary responsibility for all the unpaid work in the domestic sphere. In the film, Shimu shoulders the responsibility of being the breadwinner of the family and performs all the domestic unpaid labor at home. She is subjected to verbal and physical violence by her partner when the factory owner threatens her with consequences for trying to unionize workers. Women's empowerment often requires a negotiation with patriarchal social norms outside the workplace, and it is determined by a complex set of additional factors such as age, marital status, and level of autonomy within cultural traditions (Kibria, 1995).

The theme of loss reverberates in this film slightly differently than in *Sui Dhaaga*, and it is not underpinned by nostalgia. The storyline shows what happens after a factory fire kills one worker, forcing the owner to halt production and resulting in loss of income for workers. Fear of job loss looms large when women workers start organizing themselves. Other forms of loss also cast subtle shadows. Stepping outside the boundaries set by a patriarchal society and engaging in actions, such as unionizing, that are considered to be in the male domain sometimes brings loss of reputation and loss of freedom to work outside home. Conversations between Shimu and her friends in the film make it clear that the working conditions in the factory are not ideal, but their lives could be worse. References to domestic workers and sex workers convey the limits of possibility for women from poor and rural backgrounds.

Several scenes offer political commentary on the exploitative practices in garment supply chains. In one scene, Shimu makes a clandestine recording of an exchange between the factory owner and a buyer. However, to understand the conversation, which transpires in English but impacts her and other workers in the factory, she has to ask the social worker. Through such scenes, the film challenges viewers to recognize power asymmetries in the global supply chain of garment production.

Such a balanced portrayal casts garment workers neither as mere victims of capitalism nor solely as the beneficiaries of rosy growth. It offers a tough and complicated dose of reality. The film goes beyond depicting violence on women and holds out hope through examples of collective action and an indomitable spirit to fight back. *Made-in-Bangladesh* presents the voices of textile workers from South Asia in a narrative that is both well-rounded and grounded in experience. In a review of the film published in *Agitate!*, Elora Halim Chowdhury (n.d.) describes the film as a bold and rare portrayal of "multi-dimensional lives of female labor in Bangladesh – in joy, sorrow, love and struggle." Apart from the fact that the film begins with the loss of life of a worker in a fire, it also reminds about the threat of job loss that looms large over garment workers' lives and the loss of dignity and of reputation faced by them.

'Mother Courage'[4] of Karachi

Discount Workers by Ammar Aziz and Christopher Patz (2020) bridges the two ends of the garment supply chain over another kind of loss associated with the growth of the South Asian garment industry. The film documents the legal battles and nightmares of the survivors and the families of victims of a denim factory fire in Pakistan, and shines a light on questions of responsibility and reparations for the harm caused to them by the fast fashion industry. As it follows the fight for justice, it also presents a meticulous documentation of the labor involved in this work and shows how the lives of family members of workers in garment factories are entangled and impacted by the gaps and anomalies in the production network. The effect of poor working conditions, violation of safety protocols by factory owners, and a lack of will on the part of the state to regulate corporations are felt far beyond the workers' bodies and cause irreparable damages to their lives. The injustices and struggles reverberate through families and generations.

The camera in the film follows Saeeda Khatoon, chairperson of the Baldia Factory Fire Affectees' Association, as she seeks justice for the death of her son and other workers in a 2012 fire that killed over 250 workers (BBC News, 2012). When Saeeda lost her son in the factory fire, she also lost her only source of economic and social support. She used to depend on her son's income from the garment factory. The fire was ruled a case of arson and the result of a political rivalry between two local parties (BBC News, 2020). The factory was owned by garment supplier and local business owner Ali Enterprises. When one of its major clients, the German company KiK, agreed to pay US$5.15 million in damages to those affected by fire, the association argued that this was not enough to compensate for the irreparable losses and permanent damages caused to the victims and their families. It also asked KiK to take responsibility for the safety violations in the factory. In addition, the association sought action against RINA, the Italian auditing agency that had issued a certificate of compliance to the factory days before the incident (case report, European Center for Constitutional and Human Rights, 2019; Hasan, 2012).[5]

Discount Workers presents Saeeda's efforts to mobilize the community into action to seek justice and fight for change. The documentary makes visible the uphill task that workers in the Global South face in negotiating their rights against transnational corporations and systems that inherently favor the rich. Multiple levels of subcontracting in the supply chain means that workers are located at huge distances and caught in asymmetrical power relationships with multinational companies at the top of these buyer-driven supply chains (Hale and Wills, 2005). Laws and regulations related to labor, environment, and workplace safety standards are "most closely aligned to the interests and imaginaries of international and local elites, with adverse implications for developing countries, their firms and their workers" (Munir et al., 2017). As the documentary shows, when workplace tragedies strike, workers are left with no income and very little financial and other aid to compensate for the real losses suffered and to rebuild their lives.

The film makes this argument through Saeeda's journey from the narrow lanes of Karachi to the streets of Germany, where the association that she represents was fighting to bring KiK to court. Clad in a *burqa* and headscarf with a backpack over one shoulder, she appears an unstoppable force. Her persona challenges representations that construct Muslim women from developing countries as docile, oppressed, and in need of rescue by the West (Mishra, 2007; See also Abu-Lughod, 2002). As the film progresses, Saeeda emerges as an incredibly strong person who cares deeply about people and the cause, is never afraid to speak her truth, and even admonishes others for their lack of zeal.

Marilyn Waring (1999, p. xxvi) notes that "we still won't recognize the bulk of the work that women do in an unpaid capacity". But Saeeda's story makes that unpaid labor visible when she talks about cooking and caring for her 18-year-old son who died in the fire. As an activist and a campaigner for justice, she also took on other forms of economically non-productive care work. Like her, many families had lost children, spouses, or parents in the fire, many of whom were their family's sole breadwinners. The magnitude of this loss was overlooked in compensations and systemic failure to bring the auditing agency and the clients of Ali Enterprises to own responsibility.

Aziz and Patz find innovative ways to help us see the odds stacked against workers and the systemic and structural failures that lie behind their challenges – inadequacies of the state or of the infrastructure, poverty, linguistic barriers, and absence of empathy. They make stylistic choices to capture the power imbalances, such as when the screen turns dark during a conversation because of power outage, a subtle indicator of infrastructural challenges. As they follow Saeeda going door to door seeking support and information for the campaign, many stories of inequalities emerge. Families recount how their compensation claims hinged on providing evidence that those who died held jobs at the factory or were at work the night of the fire. Except for an occasional grainy cellphone video or rudimentary photo identity card, there was often very little photographic or documentary evidence to go with. Alongside drawing on footage of real-life events in the courts, in front of news media, and members of the public, the film uses interviews with Saeeda and other families to piece together these challenges.

Saeeda died of cancer in 2022 (Ashraf, 2023), two years after the film's release. The film immortalizes what has been noted otherwise in the media about changes in her persona in her journey from being a stay-at-home mother to an activist, which earned her the epithet "Mother Courage" (Sahoutara, 2020). The film documents her act of claiming public space locally and internationally for activism. As she moves between public and private spheres in the film, from court rooms to family meetings in the homes of victims, she challenges the place traditionally assigned to Muslim women behind *purdah*. She defies the notion of stay-at-home women as apolitical beings when the camera documents her presence in the labor court in Pakistan, in protest demonstrations on the streets of Karachi, and in Germany speaking to the media and the public to generate awareness about the cause. When she takes on the role of a representative for men, women, and children of the workers' community in Baldia, she contests the oft-circulated images of women from South Asia as helpless victims. Similar to Shimu's character in *Made-in-Bangladesh*, her story contributes toward expanding representations of working-class women from South Asia and shifts the narrative about Global South workers and their families – from being victims of capital to subjects negotiating and participating in shaping global capitalism from below.

Conclusion

Borrowing Lauren Laframboise's 2023 proposition to treat deindustrialization as a framework that helps make visible the concrete effects of wider and invisible structural forces on laboring lives, the chapter turns to these films as a way to grasp the experiences of labor in the Global South, particularly South Asia. Deindustrialization is neither as widespread nor as systematically produced in the region, yet a sense of loss is ever-present among workers. One must only look as far as the multiple incidents of fires and building collapses in garment factories in the region to realize the loss suffered by workers and their families. If the slow violence of deindustrialization has been tearing apart working-class communities in developed countries (High, 2021), capital mobility and a global reorganization of production through just-in-time or lean manufacturing practices have inflicted other forms of loss in South Asia (Jha and Chakraborty, 2014). The films help make these experiences more accessible and generate further conversations, both in Western nations and within South Asia.

Some of the challenges of engaging with Global South experiences of labor are around translation and accessibility. Local contexts and socially embedded experiences can be difficult to comprehend for an international public located at vast spatial, linguistic, and cultural distance. Women's lives and labor are sometimes even more difficult to grasp due to patriarchal social norms that create challenging circumstances around them having a voice and bringing their own experiences to the foreground. Films, with their audiovisual textuality and mediative ability, can help bridge this distance in a way that neither academic writing nor oral histories can achieve. The films examined in this chapter not only represent workers from South Asia in the cultural domain, they also help translate their experiences to varied local, national, and international audiences. Reading the three films together makes the complexities of the experiences of economic restructuring among workers in South Asia more visible. That the stories they tell also depend on the filmmakers' own positionalities further brings out the underlying cultural politics of economic restructuring. The contrasting worldviews *vis-à-vis* labor issues in the Global South help articulate the local politics that shapes and underpins the experiences of this transformation.

Notes

1 For an overview of the region's economic history since the 1950s, see Roy, Tirthankar. (2017). *The Economy of South Asia: From 1950 to the Present.* Cham: Palgrave Macmillan, e-book.

2 See the works of Linkon, Sherry Lee. (2018). *The Half-Life of Deindustrialization: Working-Class Writing about Economic Restructuring.* Ann Arbor: University of Michigan Press. https://doi.org/10.3998/mpub.8432351 (Accessed: 2 October 2023); Strangleman, Tim. (2013, Fall). "Smokestack Nostalgia," "Ruin Porn" or Working-Class Obituary: The Role and Meaning of Deindustrial Representation. *International Labor and Working-Class History*, (84), pp. 23–37. https://doi.org/10.1017/S0147547913000239. Also see MacKinnon, Lachlan. (2019). Post-industrial Memoryscapes: Combatting working-class erasure in North America and Europe. In De Nardi, Sarah, Orange, Hilary, High, Steven and Koskinen-Koivisto, Eerika (eds.). *The Routledge Handbook of Memory and Place.* London: Routledge, pp. 175–184; High, Steven. (2013). Beyond Aesthetics: Visibility and Invisibility in the Aftermath of Deindustrialization. *International Labor and Working-Class History*, 84, pp. 140–153. https://doi.org/10.1017/S0147547913000276; Mah, Alice. (2012). *Industrial Ruination, Community, and Place: Landscapes and Legacies of Urban Decline.* Toronto: University of Toronto Press, 2012. For an overview of the literature on the experiences of deindustrialization by the working classes, see High, Steven. (2013). "The Wounds of Class": A Historiographical Reflection on the Study of Deindustrialization, 1973–2013. *History Compass*, 11(11), pp. 994–1007.

3 See Table 1: Share of readymade garments in India's exports 1960–1961 to 2000–2001 in Mezzadri, Alessandra. (2012). Reflections on Globalisation and Labour Standards in the Indian Garment Industry: Codes of Conduct Versus "Codes of Practice" Imposed by the Firm. *Global Labour Journal*, 3(1), pp. 40–62. https://doi.org/10.15173/glj.v3i1.1112; Also see Table 1: Trends in US apparel imports by region and country in Gereffi, Gary. (1999). International Trade and Industrial Upgrading in the Apparel Commodity Chain. *Journal of International Economics*, 48(1), pp. 37–70. https://doi.org/10.1016/S0022-1996(98)00075-0.

4 Sahoutara, Naeem (2020, October 11). Mother Courage. *Dawn.com*. https://www.dawn.com/news/1584293 (Accessed: 2 October 2023).

5 Pakistan-based filmmaker Ammar Aziz, who co-directed *Discount Workers* with Christopher Patz, noted in an email to the author of the chapter that the German clothing brand's name is an acronym of 'Kunde ist König' which literally translates to 'customer is king.'. . . The film doesn't incorporate any interviews with Saeeda (or anyone else for that matter). We decided to have primarily an observational approach, in which through their interactions (and actions) we have tried to tell the story, rather than them talking to the camera, etc.

Reference List

Abu-Lughod, L. (2002). Do Muslim Women Really Need Saving? Anthropological Reflections on Cultural Relativism and Its Others. *American Anthropologist*, 104(3), pp. 783–790.

Agnew, T. (2005). *Portrait of a Textile Worker*. http://tardart.com/html/ptw.php (Accessed: 29 August 2023).

Anand, S. and Dey, A. (2022). Industrial Destabilisation: The Case of Rajajinagar, Bangalore. *Urban Studies*, 59(13), pp. 2660–2678. https://doi.org/10.1177/00420980211044005.

Ashraf, Z. (2023). Remembering Saeeda Baji and Her Struggle for Justice in Baldia Factory Fire Case. *The News*. https://www.thenews.com.pk/print/1026162-remembering-saeeda-baji-and-her-struggle-for-justice-in-baldia-factory-fire-case (Accessed: 23 August 2023).

Aziz, A. and Patz, C. (Directors). (2020). *Discount Workers*. Kloos & Co. Medien GmbH.

Bair, J. (2010). On Difference and Capital: Gender and the Globalization of Production. *Signs: Journal of Women in Culture and Society*, 36(1), pp. 203–226.

BBC News. (2012). *Death Toll from Karachi Factory Fire Soars*. https://www.bbc.co.uk/news/world-asia-19566851 (Accessed: 1 October 2023).

BBC News. (2020). *Pakistan Fire: Two to Hang for Karachi Garment Factory Inferno*. https://www.bbc.co.uk/news/world-asia-54250075 (Accessed: 3 October 2023).

Berger, S. and High, S. (2019). (De-)Industrial Heritage: An Introduction. *Labor*, 16(1), pp. 1–27. https://doi.org/10.1215/15476715-7269281.

Case Report. (2019). *European Center for Constitutional and Human Rights*. https://www.ecchr.eu/fileadmin/Fallbeschreibungen/CaseReport_KiK_Pakistan_August2019.pdf (Accessed: 1 October 2023).

Chowdhury, E.H. (n.d.). Shimu – Made In Bangladesh: A Story of Women's Struggle. *Agitate!*. https://agitatejournal.org/shimu-made-in-bangladesh-a-story-of-womens-struggles/ (Accessed: 13 September 2023).

Dey, D. (2018). Stitching and Unstitching Labour with Sui Dhaaga. *Economic and Political Weekly*, 53(43), p. 61.

Fudge, J. (1991). Reconceiving Employment Standards Legislation: Labour Law's Little Sister and the Feminization of Labour. *Journal of Law and Social Policy*, 7, pp. 73–89.

Gereffi, G. (1999). International Trade and Industrial Upgrading in the Apparel Commodity Chain. *Journal of International Economics*, 48(1), pp. 37–70. https://doi.org/10.1016/S0022-1996(98)00075-0.

Hale, A. and Wills, J. (2005). Introduction to *Threads of Labour Garment Industry Supply Chains from the Workers' Perspective*. Malden: Blackwell.

Hasan, S.S. (2012). Deadly Karachi Blaze Was 'Waiting to Happen'. *BBC News*. Retrieved from https://www.bbc.co.uk/news/world-asia-19577450 (Accessed: 3 October 2023).

High, S. (2013). "The Wounds of Class": A Historiographical Reflection on the Study of Deindustrialization, 1973–2013. *History Compass*, 11(11), pp. 994–1007.

High, S. (2013). Beyond Aesthetics: Visibility and Invisibility in the Aftermath of Deindustrialization. *International Labor and Working-Class History*, 84, pp. 140–153. https://doi.org/10.1017/S0147547913000276.

High, S. (2021). The "Normalized Quiet of Unseen Power": Recognizing the Structural Violence of Deindustrialization as Loss. *Urban History Review*, 48(2), pp. 97–115. https://muse.jhu.edu/article/791422.

High, S. (2023). The Radical Origins of the Deindustrialization Thesis: From Dependency to Capital Flight and Community Abandonment. *Labour/Le Travail*, 91, pp. 31–56. muse.jhu.edu/article/895667.

Hossain, R. (Director). (2019). *Made-in-Bangladesh*. Khona Talkies, Beofilm, Les Films de l'Après-Midi, Midas Filmes, Cinema Cocoon.

Hurtes, S. (2018). *Interview with Rubaiyat Hossain: 'I Believe in a Feminist Intervention in Cinema'*. https://rm.coe.int/interview-rubaiyat-hossain/16808ae844 (Accessed: 25 February 2023).

Islam, S. (2016). Feminization of Employment and Gender Inequality of Bangladesh Labor Market: The Case of Garment Industries. *Developing Country Studies*, 6(2), pp. 157–168.

Jha, P. and Chakraborty, A. (2014). Post-Fordism, Global Production Networks and Implications for Labour: Some Case Studies from National Capital Region, India. *Institute for Studies in Industrial Development Working Paper* no. 172. https://isid.org.in/wp-content/uploads/2022/09/WP172.pdf (Accessed: 18 January 2023).

Kabeer, N. (2015). Women Workers and the Politics of Claims-Making in a Globalizing Economy. *United Nations Research Institute for Social Development Working Paper* 2015–13. https://www.unrisd.org/ (Accessed: 23 August 2023).

Katariya, S. (Director). (2018). *Sui Dhaaga: Made in India*. Yash Raj Films.

Kaur, R. (2002). Viewing the West through Bollywood: A Celluloid Occident in the Making. *Contemporary South Asia*, 11(2), pp. 199–209. https://doi.org/10.1080/0958493022000030168.

Khaliji, B.A., Jaffari, S.I.-A., Shahzad, A. and Mehtab, M. (2013). Role of Textile Sector in Domestic Resources Development. *Business Management Dynamics*, 2(10), pp. 14–27.

Kibria, N. (1995). Culture, Social Class, And Income Control in the Lives of Women Garment Workers in Bangladesh. *Gender & Society*, 9(3), pp. 289–309.

Kishore, V. (2019). Bollywood Vamps and Vixens: Representations of the Negative Women Characters in Bollywood Films. In Hedenborg-White, M. and Sandhoff, B. (eds.) *Transgressive Womanhood: Investigating Vamps, Witches, Whores, Serial Killers and Monsters*. BRILL, pp. 141–151.

Kumar, A. (2013). Provincialising Bollywood? Cultural Economy of North-Indian Small-town Nostalgia in the Indian Multiplex. *South Asian Popular Culture*, 11(1), pp. 61–74. https://doi.org/10.1080/14746689.2013.764642.

Kumar, S. and Curtin, M. (2002). "Made in India": In between Music Television and Patriarchy. *Television & New Media*, 3(4), pp. 345–366. https://doi.org/10.1177/152747602237279.

Laframboise, L. (2023). The Politics of Deindustrialization in Canada. *Active History*. https://activehistory.ca/blog/2023/06/09/the-politics-of-deindustrialization-in-canada/ (Accessed: 1 September 2023).

Linkon, S.L. (2018). *The Half-Life of Deindustrialization: Working-Class Writing about Economic Restructuring*. Ann Arbor: University of Michigan Press.

MacKinnon, L. (2019). Post-industrial Memoryscapes: Combatting Working-class Erasure in North America and Europe. In De Nardi, S., Orange, H., High, S. and Koskinen-Koivisto, E. (eds.) *The Routledge Handbook of Memory and Place*. London: Routledge, pp. 175–184.

Mah, A. (2009). Devastation but also Home: Place Attachment in Areas of Industrial Decline. *Home Cultures*, 6(3), pp. 287–310. https://doi.org/10.2752/174063109X12462745321462.

Mah, A. (2012). *Industrial Ruination, Community, and Place: Landscapes and Legacies of Urban Decline*. Toronto: University of Toronto Press.

Mamun, M.A.A. and Hoque, M.M. (2022). The Impact of Paid Employment on Women's Empowerment: A Case Study of Female Garment Workers in Bangladesh. *World Development Sustainability*, 1, pp. 1–11. https://doi.org/10.1016/j.wds.2022.100026.

Manzar, B., & Aravind, A. (2019). (Re) Thinking Women in Cinema: The Changing Narrative Structure in Bollywood. *South Asian Popular Culture*, 17(1), pp. 1–13. https://doi.org/10.1080/14746689.2018.1585601.

Massey, D. (1995). *Spatial Divisions of Labour: Social Structures and the Geography of Production*. 2nd edn. London: Macmillan.

McCartney, M. (2014). The Political Economy of Industrial Policy: A Comparative Study of the Textiles Industry in Pakistan. *The Lahore Journal of Economics*, 19, pp. 105–134.

Mehta, R.B. (2011). Bollywood, Nation, Globalization: An Incomplete Introduction. In Mehta, R.B. and Pandharipande, R.V. (eds.) *Bollywood and Globalization: Indian Popular Cinema, Nation, and Diaspora*. London and New York: Anthem, pp. 1–14.

Mezzadri, A. (2012). Reflections on Globalisation and Labour Standards in the Indian Garment Industry: Codes of Conduct Versus 'Codes of Practice' Imposed by the Firm. *Global Labour Journal*, 3(1), pp. 40–62. https://doi.org/10.15173/glj.v3i1.1112.

Mishra, S. (2007). 'Saving' Muslim Women and Fighting Muslim Men: Analysis of Representations in the New York Times. *Global Media Journal*, 6(11).

Munir, K., Ayaz, M., Levy, D.L. and Willmott, H. (2017). The Role of Intermediaries in Governance of Global Production Networks: Restructuring Work Relations in Pakistan's Apparel Industry. *Human Relations*, 71(4), pp. 560–583.

Nanda, N. (2009). The Indian Growth Story. *Journal of Asian and African Studies*, 44(6), pp. 740–765.

Naved, R., Rahman, T., Willan, S., Jewkes, R. and Gibbs, A. (2018). Female Garment Workers' Experiences of Violence in Their Homes and Workplaces in Bangladesh: A Qualitative Study. *Social Science & Medicine*, 196, pp. 150–157. https://doi.org/10.1016/j.socscimed.2017.11.040.

Nayyar, D. (1998). Economic Development and Political Democracy: Interaction of Economics and Politics in Independent India. *Economic and Political Weekly*, 33(49), pp. 3121–3131.

Pike, A. (2022). Coping with Deindustrialization in the Global North and South. *International Journal of Urban Sciences*, 26(1), pp. 1–22. https://doi.org/10.1080/12265934.2020.1730225.

Rahman, R.I. and Islam, R. (2013). Female Labour Force Participation in Bangladesh: Trends, Drivers and Barriers. *ILO Asia-Pacific Working Paper Series*. https://www.ilo.org/wcmsp5/groups/public/-asia/-ro-bangkok/-sro-new_delhi/documents/publication/wcms_250112.pdf (Accessed: 26 July 2022).

Rahman, S. (2014). *Broken Promises of Globalization: The Case of the Bangladesh Garment Industry*. Plymouth: Lexington Books.

Risen, C. (2022). Charles Kernaghan, Scourge of Sweatshops, Is Dead at 74. *New York Times*. https://www.nytimes.com/2022/06/14/us/charles-kernaghan-dead.html (Accessed: 29 August 2023).

Rock, M. (2003). Labour Conditions in the Export-oriented Garment Industry in Bangladesh. *South Asia: Journal of South Asian Studies*, 26(3), pp. 391–407. https://doi.org/10.1080/008564003 2000178943.

Rodrik, D. (2016). Premature Deindustrialization. *Journal of Economic Growth*, 21, pp. 1–33. https://doi.org/10.1007/s10887-015-9122-3.

Roy, T. (2017). *The Economy of South Asia: From 1950 to the Present*. Cham: Palgrave Macmillan.

Sahoutara, N. (2020). Mother Courage. *Dawn.com*. https://www.dawn.com/news/1584293 (Accessed: 2 October 2023).

Schindler, S., Gillespie, T., Banks, N., Bayırbağ, M.K., Burte, H., Kanai, J.M. and Sami, N. (2020). Deindustrialization in Cities of the Global South. *Area Development and Policy*, 5(3), pp. 283–304. https://doi.org/10.1080/23792949.2020.1725393.

Strangleman, T. (2013). "Smokestack Nostalgia," "Ruin Porn" or Working-Class Obituary: The Role and Meaning of Deindustrial Representation. *International Labor and Working-Class History*, (84), pp. 23–37. https://doi.org/10.1017/S0147547913000239.

Strangleman, T. (2017). Deindustrialisation and the Historical Sociological Imagination: Making Sense of Work and Industrial Change. *Sociology*, 51(2), pp. 466–482.

The Business Standard. (2022). *'Shimu (Made in Bangladesh)' to Hit Theatres This Weekend*. https://www.tbsnews.net/splash/shimu-made-bangladesh-hit-theatres-weekend-381841 (Accessed: 28 September 2023).

Toplin, R. (1995). Norma Rae: Unionism in an Age of Feminism. *Labor History*, 36(2), pp. 282–298. https://doi.org/10.1080/00236569512331385472.

Vitali, V. (2020). Interview with Rubaiyat Hossain. *BioScope*, 11(1), pp. 92–95.

Waring, M. (1999). Introduction to the Second Edition in *Counting for Nothing: What Men Value and What Women are Worth*. 2nd edn. Toronto and Buffalo: University of Toronto Press.

Wyatt, A. (2005). Building the Temples of Postmodern India: Economic Constructions of National Identity. *Contemporary South Asia*, 14(4), pp. 465–480. https://doi.org/10.1080/09584930600839180.

PART V

Memories, Memorialization, and the Heritage of Deindustrialization

INTRODUCTION

Memories, Memorialization, and the Heritage of Deindustrialization

Stefan Berger

Narrativizations of Industrial Heritage-Making in Place and Time

The heritage of deindustrialization is inextricably linked to memories of an industrial past and of deindustrialization itself. What is being preserved of an industrial era, when the industry, or large parts of it, is gone, depends on three factors: first, how successful the economic transition has been from the industrial era to a post-industrial or re-/neo-industrial era; second, how strong the political will has been to mark the industrial era and its lifeworlds as anchor point of local/regional identification;[1] and third, how diverse cultural and scientific actors have framed the evolving heritage discourse in a way that is speaking to both the present and future of deindustrializing places, often in contested ways (Berger, 2020a). Deindustrialization undoubtedly means ruination (Edensor, 2005), but how the ruins are being dealt with differs substantially from place to place. And it is not only the question what is preserved but also how it is preserved. All this depends on the dominant heritage discourse in any given deindustrializing place. Key heritage actors serve as memory activists developing specific forms of memorialization of an industrial past. They narrativize the heritage in concrete ways to give meaning to it. At the same time, memory activists make use of that heritage so as to aid the transitioning of the affected place to a thriving future (Berger, 2023). Industrial heritage, thus, in manifold and often contradictory ways, represents what Sherry Lee Linkon (2018) has so memorably termed 'the half-life of deindustrialization,' that is, a presence of a past that is in some places more past than in others but that everywhere is haunting the everyday of these places and the people living in them.

Who are the key heritage actors and memory activists that we encounter in the making of industrial heritage in different parts of the world? Prominent among them are intellectuals, artists, architects, filmmakers, writers, preservationists, academics, museum directors, and other representatives of the cultural sphere, but we also meet here representatives of the government and administration of affected cities and regions, political parties, trade unions, social movements, and industrial companies. In other words, it is often a broad panoply of people coming from very different walks of life who play a role in how the industrial heritage discourses develop at any given moment in time. Heritage actors as memory activists can be individuals, but they can also be institutions and organizations. In the field of industrial

DOI: 10.4324/9781003308324-33

heritage, museums, monuments, associations promoting industrial heritage, preservationist organizations, universities, employers' federations, and a whole range of other institutions come to mind. In the international field, The International Committee for the Conservation of Industrial Heritage (TICCIH) has been, since 1973, following the first international conference for the conservation of the industrial heritage in Ironbridge, England, a forum for all aspects of the preservation and interpretation of industrial heritage (Douet, 2013).[2] And within the Association of Critical Heritage Studies (ACHS), industrial heritage has played a prominent role as an object of analysis ever since it was founded in the early 2010s.[3] Furthermore, the Working-Class Studies Association (WCSA) has, since its inception in 2004, time and again shown a keen interest in the heritage of the working class as an integral part of industrial heritage.[4]

Critical heritage studies have developed the notion of an "authorized heritage discourse" (Smith, 2006) that is dominant and associated with the state as well as powerful elites in any given society. Yet it is never the only show in town. Several other oppositional heritage discourses can work against this 'authorized' one seeking to challenge it from below. Oppositional heritage discourses are often associated with a range of civil society actors, among which social movements are particularly prominent. Such a binary and dichotomous construction of heritage discourses is, on the one hand, helpful in highlighting power structures that are invariably linked to questions which heritage is preserved and endowed with which messages. On the other hand, scholars should be wary of constructing this notion in too binary a way, as there are many overlaps between heritage discourses from above and from below. The border between 'authorized' and 'non-authorized' is often fuzzy. Looking at concrete cases of the production of industrial heritage, we find a sheer endless variety of changing and reconstituted alliances between different heritage actors coming from diverse ways of life, 'above' and 'below.' There are several cases of industrial heritage-making, where representatives of a powerful authorized heritage discourse work hand in hand with civil society actors and social movements. Any comparison of these processes in different locations will have to pay attention to the specifics of such alliances in each and every individual case.

A specific place of heritage-making hence has to be the starting point of any analysis of the multiple meanings of industrial heritage. That place can be a factory, a neighborhood surrounding a factory, a factory town, an industrial city, or metropolis, or, indeed, a polycentric industrial region. In other words, the size of the space that is being examined can differ quite substantially, but it is always intensely local/regional. Space can best be understood as a construction, which takes place as a process over time, has fuzzy borders, and incorporates multiple forms of identification. Social inequalities are always produced and reproduced in those particular spaces (Massey, 1984). Furthermore, that local/regional space that is the focus of most examinations of heritage-making stands in constant exchanges with wider spaces that impact on what is going on locally/regionally. There are regions surrounding these places which impact on local conditions, for example, the federal states within larger nation-states, the nation-states themselves, and transnational entities, in Europe especially the European Union, which develop their own ideas and policies regarding industrial heritage (Berger, 2020b, pp. 297–301). The European Route of Industrial Heritage (ERIH) has its origins in an intensely regional experience, the Route of Industrial Heritage of the Ruhr region in Germany. Expanding this concept of an industrial heritage route from the Ruhr to Europe with the help of European institutions was one way of emphasizing something that Europe had in common. None of the many European routes that exist in Europe today are so widespread and cover such a large terrain of Europe as ERIH. It has several hundred members,

Introduction

often prominent institutions, from 27 European countries covering thousands of industrial heritage sites.[5]

The chapter by Christa Reicher and Liliana Iuga pays due attention to the interlinking of these different local, regional, national, and transnational/transregional spaces in the formulation of industrial heritage strategies. Dealing with postmining landscapes in the Ruhr (Germany), Belval (Luxembourg), and Nord-Pas-de-Calais (France), they underline how important the support of political, economic, social, and cultural elites has been in these three deindustrializing areas, when it came to developing some form of urban planning that would integrate the industrial pasts of these places into visions of a re-/neo-industrialized and/or post-industrial future. In the Ruhr, major projects involving a great deal of urban planning, including the International Building Exhibition (IBA) Emscher Park in the 1990s and the follow-up project of the creation of a landscape park around the Emscher River in the north of the Ruhr, have become paradigmatic examples with huge international repercussions of how concepts of industrial heritage could be utilized by urban planners to make the immediate surroundings of post-industrial places more livable. Transregional transfers have been hugely influential in the making of heritage landscapes. Reicher and Iuga show how ideas and practices developed in the Ruhr in the 1990s inspired Luxemburgish and French attempts to preserve their coal and steel heritage.

Enriching places of former industry with culture and science was one option. Hence, Reicher and Iuga analyze the spreading of museums, cultural centers, creative quarters, and universities around former industrial plants. Cultural institutions have been of the utmost importance in moving former places of industry to becoming places of culture (Berger, 2020a, pp. 16–22). Another option was the renaturation of former industrial sites. The concept of 'industrial nature' (Industrienatur) originated in the Ruhr, where landscape parks were created around former mining and steelworks sites. From there the concept spread to other places in Europe and the wider world. The protection and enhancement of the biodiversity of these post-industrial sites was a deliberate strategy for the "greening" of formerly industrial regions (Angelo, 2021; Eiringhaus, 2018). 'Industrial nature' was one way of thinking post-industrial structural change together with the making of attractive landscapes in which people want to live.

The renaturation of former industrial landscapes went hand in hand with their revitalization: the IBA Emscher park had set standards during the 1990s that were copied ten years later by the IBA in Lusatia in Eastern Germany. Improving the livability of former industrial regions renaturation also promoted tourism, including ecotourism through the construction of thematic trails and joining the European Route of Industrial Heritage. However, this merger of landscapes of industrial heritage with environmental concerns has by no means been universal. Especially in Britain, the industrial heritage landscapes of Manchester, Glasgow, and South Wales are rarely linked in any meaningful ways to environmental concerns, but we also find little reference to the environment at industrial heritage sites in the Nord-Pas-de-Calais, Asturias, and Sesto San Giovannni. Outside of Europe, from Australia to China, the environmental discourse at industrial heritage sites remains also weak. Do we have here, one is inclined to ask, somewhat of a German exceptionalism in the strong linkages between German industrial heritage sites and a problematization of the environmental costs of industrialization? (Berger, 2020b, p. 296).

Incorporating the legacies of the industrial past into strategies of city- and region-scape-making was always done by urban planners with one eye toward making those 'scapes' more attractive for future investments into the cities and regions that were transformed.

365

Planners and architects, Reicher and Iuga remind us, provided the concrete frameworks for adding value to post-industrial sites. An embedded capitalism (Polanyi, 1944), they argue, has been beneficial for setting up public-private partnerships in the promotion of industrial heritage landscapes. Within capitalist economies, the support of capital and state institutions for those landscapes has been a crucial resource and precondition for their realization. Adding value to places with an industrial past was a deliberate strategy of capital to commodify and touristy that past (Boltanski and Esquerre, 2020; Xie, 2015). Such touristification did not necessarily serve the people most affected by deindustrialization, and it also rarely furthered a deeper understanding of both the industrial pasts and the deindustrialization processes. Instead, it aestheticized industrial sites presenting them in their 'Sunday best' and hiding the grime, sweat, and hard work as well as the exploitation that once went on at these sites. The aesthetic glow of industrial heritage can be deliberately misleading as ideology legitimating diverse forms of capitalism. In a more direct capitalist sense, profits can be drawn from industrial pasts through industrial heritage tourism. Nevertheless, the economic motives for industrial heritage-making went hand in hand, in a great number of possible combinations, with motives more related to questions of identification and community-building. There are, indeed, cases where the two can be entirely disentangled, but, more often than not, they appear side by side impacting on each other in more or less complex ways.

Like all contributions in this part of the handbook, Reicher and Iuga emphasize that industrial heritage is not a thing of the past, contained in its pastness. Instead, it is very much a construction of the past in the present with the intention of molding a particular future. As such, it is often contested between different memory activists constructing sometimes diametrically opposed visions of the future on the basis of different representations of the past. Achim Landwehr's notion of "pluritemporality" might be useful here in understanding not just the importance of specific places but also the crucial significance of specific layers of time that do not evolve consecutively but are always present at one and the same time (Landwehr, 2020; see also Lorenz and Bevernage, 2013). Time, in other words, is not ordered like pearls on a string, moving from one point in the past to the present and further to the future. Rather, past, present, and future are present at any one given moment in time, and it is precisely the interaction between these layers of time which give time its specific meaning. Translated to the field of industrial heritage, this means that we might frequently encounter at industrial heritage sites understandings of linear time. A company was founded in w, developed between w and x, and closed its gates in y. It was transformed into a heritage site in z and since then has developed in certain ways. However, the time of industrial heritage is always the present time, in which the past is constructed in ways that have their origins in the positionality of the constructor who does the constructing with a view to how that past can be made meaningful for the future. Hence, past, present, and future are all present at one and the same time in the moment of the construction of time.

Understanding the specificities of place and the interrelationship of different layers of time is thus crucial for comprehending diverse regimes of industrial heritage, both tangible and intangible (Smith and Akagawa, 2009). Of course, industrial heritage often means large structures, like blast-iron furnaces, mineshafts, textile mills, and factory buildings being preserved and transformed into different forms of reuse: museums, cultural centers, blocks of flats, office space, and others. But industrial heritage also means the musical heritage of working-class cultures, their food preferences, their forms of sociability, their pastimes, their ways of speaking (often in the form of socio-dialects), and many other things that are not so much located in a thing but are rooted in ideas and practices. Both the tangible and intangible forms of industrial heritage are being preserved to tell a particular narrative about the industrial past.

These narratives are tied to specific interests of diverse groups in society. As these groups do not have the same interests, heritage narratives become contested. They are at their most powerful when they become hegemonic and command overwhelming support from the vast majority of heritage and memory activists in a particular place. The Ruhr region in Germany has arguably constructed the richest industrial heritage landscape in the world precisely because its memoryscape[6] has been so unified (Berger, 2019, 2025). We have here the extraordinary case that virtually all-important memory activists, from above and below, are united in presenting a very uniform master narrative[7] about the region's industrial past and its 'structural change' (Strukturwandel). This master narrative is aligned to the development of the Ruhr as a region still holding onto a substantial industrial sector while successfully developing other parts of the regional economy, such as services, health industries, logistics, and trade. This unity derives from the strong corporatist mindset that characterizes Rhenish capitalism in Germany and makes employers, trade unionists, and representatives of the state look for compromises that would benefit all of their interests. This "conflict partnership" (Müller-Jentsch, 1999) also worked in relation to the construction of industrial heritage landscapes and their associated memoryscapes. The key realms of memory in the Ruhr are all associated with its industrial past. There is, in effect, no memory of the Ruhr region as Ruhr region outside of its industrial past and its deindustrialization since the 1960s (Berger et al., 2019).

Comparative Perspectives on the Ambivalences of Nostalgic Memory in the Making of Industrial Heritage

On a scale of industrial heritage production from 0 to 10, the Ruhr would score full points. Other places have produced impressive landscapes of industrial heritage, and we have many studies on industrial heritage sites, but they focus overwhelmingly on individual cases. The only journal exclusively dedicated to the study of industrial heritage, the German-language *Industriekultur*, has published many excellent volumes detailing thousands of individual case studies of industrial heritage-making.[8] Only more recently do we see attempts to compare, either within one and the same country,[9] across countries involving parts of entire continents,[10] and even globally dealing with different parts of the world (Mah, 2012; Berger and Pickering, 2018). The latter studies are mostly glocal in character in that they choose to compare specific localities in very different parts of the world. The industrial heritage strand within the Deindustrialization and the Politics of Our Time (DéPoT) project will further encourage such glocal comparisons.[11]

Juliane Tomann in her chapter gives us a comparative glimpse of the development of industrial heritage in post-communist countries of East-Central and Southeastern Europe. As she emphasizes, under Communism industrial heritage was often preserved to memorialize an idealized working class which had allegedly become the dominant class with the establishment of Communist regimes after the Second World War. Hence, industrial heritage legitimated the Communist dictatorships and glorified the role of Communist Parties in improving the lives of ordinary workers (Lehmann, 2022). However, these attempts at preserving the industrial heritage were limited by a severe lack of financial resources. After the fall of Communism, the neoliberal transformation of post-communist countries witnessed rapid deindustrialization that left behind manifold forms of ruination (Ther, 2016). Industrial heritage was not regarded as important, partly because it was associated with the hated Communist regimes that had been toppled and partly because the neoliberal future-orientation did have no place for the industrial past to become meaningful for its visions of a post-industrial future. It became part of a toxic heritage that hardly anyone wanted to touch in the first ten years following the collapse of Communism in Eastern Europe. Yet thereafter Tomann analyses an albeit limited rediscovery of industrial heritage across a range of different countries, including Poland, the Czech Republic, Hungary, and the Western Balkans. She cites many examples of the revitalization, revalorization, musealization, and touristification of industrial heritage in all of these countries telling a story from neglect to nostalgia.

Nostalgia has become a much-debated concept in deindustrialization studies. It is now widely seen as an important resource strengthening progressive social movements in their attempts to construct a future for regions affected by deindustrialization. Forms of nostalgic memory thus can provide opportunities for those most affected by deindustrialization, that is, the workers. Svetlana Boym's (2001) 'reflective nostalgia,' Alaistair Bonnett's (2010) 'radical nostalgia,' and Laurajane Smith's and Gary Campbell's (2017) 'progressive nostalgia' are some prominent attempts to create conceptual tools with which the emotions of nostalgia can be aligned to deindustrialization and industrial heritage in ways that would foster the carrying over of the values and norms of solidaristic working-class communities from industrial pasts into post-industrial presents. Tim Strangleman (2013) has rightly warned about nostalgia being a politically polyvalent sentiment that can be used by the political left and the political right. It can serve a depoliticized voyeurism just as much as a politically empowering search for a more socially just future.

In some places, like in the Ruhr in Germany, the impressive landscape of industrial heritage is tied politically to a social democratic project. Social Democrats encouraged the development of such a heritage landscape with a view to signaling their intention to protect the ordinary people ('der kleine Mann' in German) from the vagaries of deindustrialization. In time, other political parties, notably the Christian Democrats with their strong social wing, have bought into this heritage narrative, making it stronger. In the Ruhr, industrial heritage honored the worker through preserving the places associated with their work. Social and Christian Democratic municipal governments in line with Social Democratic- and Christian Democratic-led state governments in North-Rhine Westfalia provided much of the finances that made the creation of this unique heritage landscape in the Ruhr region possible (Berger, 2025). However, both left-wing and right-wing populisms have also used industrial heritage politically to support their messages that 'the system' had betrayed the people and that the latter would find their true champions only in populist parties. The popularity of Donald Trump in the deindustrialized mid-West of the US or the success of Brexit in Britain rests to some degree on such messages to people who have suffered under neoliberal processes of deindustrialization (Berger, Fontaine, Pattison, and Rhodes, 2025). In Germany, the rise of the Alternative for Germany (AfD) in places like the Ruhr and in deindustrialized regions of East Germany also partly rests on its message of support for workers allegedly left to their own devices by the mainstream political parties (Berger, 2022a).

The memories of an industrial past and the nostalgia for it are indeed politically ambivalent. They can serve a politics of despair, but they can also encourage a politics of hope. Studies on industrial heritage can benefit from paying attention to what Ann Rigney has called the "memory-activism nexus" (Rigney, 2018).[12] Which urban social movements were empowered by industrial heritage to put forward 'memories of hope' for those most affected

Introduction

by deindustrialization? How does industrial heritage have to look in specific places and at specific times to fulfil such a function? Heritage activism and memory activism have played a vital role in constructing heritage landscapes, and such activism was, more often than not, politically motivated. Urban regeneration in deindustrializing cities and regions is connected to such activism which was particularly successful when it could forge lasting alliances with powerful elites in society, politics, and the economy. But it could also struggle against those elites and create an oppositional politics fighting against neoliberal panaceas for industrial closures. A comparative and transregional approach to the study of industrial heritage would be particularly helpful in analyzing which conditions were most helpful in furthering the agendas of social movements pursuing a "memory of hope" vis-à-vis deindustrialization processes (Baumeister, Bonomo, and Schott, 2017).

In Tomann's chapter nostalgia in post-communist countries was connected, above all, to a 'memory of despair' and to feelings of loss: loss of a strong workplace community, loss of being valued as a worker and treated with respect and dignity by their social superiors, loss of high wages and summer holiday provisions as well as childcare through the companies, and loss of good health care provisions. Such a longing for what was good in the past goes hand in hand with feelings of degradation and humiliation in the present. Tomann argues that this might be different for different groups of workers. Middle managers, engineers, and higher paid employees were far less inclined to wallow in nostalgic remembrances and instead stressed the inevitability of the transformation thereby repeating its neoliberal master narrative. Ordinary workers, by contrast, were far more nostalgic about the old times, even if these feelings went hand in hand with the full recognition of the negative elements of Communism, such as corruption, shortages of goods, and authoritarian forms of government.

Nevertheless, through nostalgic forms of memory, workers in East-Central Europe and the Western Balkans were defending their past values and past 'structures of feeling,' as they had been lived in the everyday and bringing them into the present.[13] This was far more difficult, where neoliberalism was strong and the memory of the working class was subsumed under the memory of the opposition to Communism, as was the case with the memory of Solidarność in Poland. Despite the fact that the actual conversion of derelict industrial areas in post-communist countries was often financially and politically difficult, some industrial heritage preservation did take place and we learn much from Tomann's chapter on places like Vítkovice, Katowice, Ostrava, and Borsod. Here, industrial heritage initiatives could be successful, only if they took a highly commodified and commercialized approach to preserving industrial pasts that were in line with neoliberal thinking (Pehe and Wawrzyniak, 2024).

However, some element of industrial heritage-making was intimately connected to the construction of identifications, especially through museums. Thus, the Silesian Museum in Katowice, for example, attempts to underpin strong regional Silesian identifications, partly through the promotion of industrial heritage. It could be said that it was taking a leaf out of the book of industrial heritage-making in the Ruhr, where the forging of a strong regional identification was the paramount objective of an industrial heritage landscape signaling the togetherness of an industrial region as a region. In fact, many advisers on industrial heritage, from museum directors to preservationists, traveled from the Ruhr to Silesia to advise on the making of industrial heritage landscapes. These translocal connections were particularly sensitive, Tomann argues, as industrial heritage in Silesia could easily be constructed as a 'foreign,' that is, German, heritage. After all, the region had been part of the German Reich for much of its nineteenth- and first half of the twentieth-century history, that is, during the

The Routledge Handbook of Deindustrialization Studies

time of high industrialization. This has drawn Silesian industrial heritage into the contested memory wars surrounding Poland's present-day identifications (Harper, 2018).

Otherwise, Tomann's case studies for East-Central Europe and the Western Balkans highlight the linkages between the time layers of past, present, and future. Industrial heritage became, like in Western Europe, analyzed by Reicher and Iuga, a resource for future regional development. However, it remained far more politically contested than in the West. Especially the memory and museum landscapes in Poland were highly politicized. Directors of museums and memory institutes have been routinely replaced with every change of government. As the example of the Polish textile town of Łódź shows, heritage landscapes could also be used for harmonizing social relations of the past and presenting a rather one-sided picture of universalist tolerance, innovative entrepreneurship, and technological achievement in the service of the revitalization of the former textile town.

Reading the chapter by Reicher/Iuga on Western Europe alongside the chapter by Tomann on East-Central and Southeastern Europe, readers will be struck by some crucial differences, notably timing. Whereas deindustrialization processes in Western Europe started in the 1950s and 1960s, in post-communist states they began in earnest only from the 1990s onward. Furthermore, there are crucial differences in terms of state responses, trade union involvement, corporatist versus neoliberal responses, and the valuation of the remnants of an industrial past. However, there are also striking similarities in terms of the commodification, commercialization, and touristification of industrial heritage, and across Europe, east and west, the promotion of industrial heritage has been bound up with issues of regional identification.

Such a profound link between industrial heritage and regional identification has produced in many parts of the world sentiments of regional belonging, something expressed in German in the concept of "Heimat" (Applegate, 1990). Thus, for example, the Ruhr area has become a 'Heimat' for many of its inhabitants through their strong identification with the industrial past of 'their region.' Such a sense of 'Heimat' is based on strong emotional bonds with a particular place. It is a strength in terms of the willingness of people to defend that place and the values that it represents against all political moves to destroy it. It is also a strength in providing strong bonds between people feeling the same attachment to place. However, 'Heimat' sentiments can also suggest commonalities where there are clear differences of interest. It can paper over those differences and become an ideology in the interest of elites to hide forms of social inequality and lack of solidarity between different social groups. As such, it is, like "nation," a janus-faced concept that can be liberating and oppressive at the same time (Berger, 2022b).

Decolonial, Gender, Class, Race, Ethnic, and Religious Perspectives on Industrial Heritage

If we move from the Global North to the Global South, as we do with Marion Steiner's chapter in this part of the book, all of the European conceptualizations of industrial heritage become problematic. Steiner provides a range of post- and decolonial perspectives on industrial heritage questioning the usefulness of adopting Western concepts in the Global South. Whereas the Western narratives often celebrate the idea of progress through industry, technical innovation, economic growth, and an overall superiority of the West vis-à-vis the rest, industrial heritage in the Global South, Steiner argues, should lead to sustained reflections about how Western colonialism and imperialism thwarted local development paths.

Introduction

The West did not bring modernity and progress. Its promises regarding the development of allegedly 'underdeveloped countries' rang hollow. Instead, the West was the harbinger of exploitation, extractivism, and the violent enforcement of a Western model not in tune with local developments (Arregui, Mackenthun, and Wodianka, 2018).

Steiner's chapter draws attention to what she calls 'heritage imperialism,' that is, the simple fact that countries in the Global North have more money and resources to preserve their heritage than countries in the Global South. And it is not just a question of money: the countries in the Global North have been able to set the conceptual framework for defining industrial heritage in such a way as to give the heritage of the Global North the upper hand in comparison with the Global South. It was always earlier, more innovative, and more authentic. Heritage-making is thus connected to power relationships. It is about what and who gets omitted from our understanding of heritage and how an industrial past is remembered. Steiner emphasizes how in the Global South it was especially Indigenous people who were marginalized and impoverished by processes of industrialization pushed by colonizing forces. Industrial heritage in the Global South has often been 'toxic heritage,' quite literally in the case of Bhopal in India, a case extensively discussed by Steiner, but also in a more metaphorical sense elsewhere, where industry was the source of much suffering and exploitation of local people. The latter, of course, could and did include non-Indigenous parts of the population, and there are commonalities between exploitation processes in the Global North and the Global South. The big divide, however, lies in the impact of colonialism and imperialism, where the countries in the Global North are responsible for stymying independent local developments in the Global South and, at times, in the Global North itself, as was the case with the Sámi territories across northern Europe or the Indigenous populations in cases of settler colonialism (Rhodes, Price, and Walker, 2021).

Steiner not only highlights the destructive energies of Western concepts of industrial heritage. She also shows how the principles derived from these concepts that guide our understanding of heritage, such as authenticity and integrity, are in dire need of revision if the aim is to move to a truly global understanding of industrial heritage. This means reforming global institutions such as TICCIH and ICOMOS. The first step toward such ambitions is understanding heritage as a social construction, formed by the West, and a political battlefield for the promotion of healthier, more sustainable, and fairer environments for the great majority of the people living on this planet. This necessitates a deeper understanding of the glocal nature of industrial heritage. Specific local places in the Global North, such as Berlin in Germany, were intimately connected to specific local places in the Global South, such as Valparaiso in Chile, in often exploitative power relationships benefiting one-sidedly the countries in the Global North and their few collaborators in the Global South (Steiner, 2019).

Although Steiner's decolonial perspective relies on a division between the Global North and the Global South that is inspired by Immanuel Wallerstein's world-systems theory (Wallerstein, 2004), she also concedes that the perspective on what is north and south is highly context-dependent. In a study of industrial heritage within one country, for example, Sweden, Sweden's north can be constructed as being part of the Global South. This insistence that 'global north' and 'global south' are no absolute categories but fluid and situation-specific adds an important dimension to any comparative framework for the study of industrial heritage.

Steiner's chapter links decolonial perspectives on industrial heritage to the use of ethnographic research methods and an understanding of research as being 'action centered.'

In other words, the researchers interested in working on industrial heritage have to immerse themselves into the field and train themselves in particular in the gift of 'active listening.' Oral history approaches are central to this kind of research, as they have been in research on deindustrialization more generally (Portelli, 2005). Steiner also picks up the theme of nostalgia arguing in favor of heritage activists developing understandings of a "progressive nostalgia" (Smith and Campbell, 2017) that would allow for a construction of the future of deindustrializing places in line with demands for global solidarity and social justice.

Steiner highlights the ongoing discrimination of women both in industrial history and in current heritage practices. She organizes her chapter around the heritage work of five women who have had a difficult time in pursuing their careers in academia facing much discrimination and prejudice because of their vision of an alternative industrial heritage more in line with decolonial perspectives. These visions are questioning a male Western understanding of heritage based on superlatives and competition between different sites. Instead, Steiner sketches a specifically female non-Western vision of industrial heritage based on understandings of community, solidarity, and a fairer deal between the nations of the Global North and the Global South. Thus, she connects decolonial perspectives to gender perspectives on industrial heritage.

Gender is also the central theme of Lucy Taksa's chapter that is focused on the global railway heritage. As railways have been the precondition for industrial development almost everywhere in the world, their heritage is forming a truly global landscape. Despite a great diversity of local contexts, Taksa finds remarkable similarities between many initiatives that are often rooted in a strong emotional link between railways and the people. She demonstrates that the discourses surrounding this heritage are based overwhelmingly on the development of technology and hardware. By contrast, the people who worked on the railways and the communities they formed are at best a secondary interest at many railway heritage sites. Where they talk about railway workers, the hegemonic masculinities that were established during the foundational age of the railways have been reproduced in railway heritage initiatives. The connections between an object fetishism and the masculine connotations inherent in technological developments are strong. Railway heritage sites thus tend to ignore the change in gender norms that have accompanied the development of Western societies throughout the twentieth century and especially since the 1970s. The increasing feminization of the railway workforce is largely written out of the memory landscapes provided by railway heritage, and the complex gender relationships on the railways do not form an important part of what is commemorated at former railway sites. Working with Judith Butler's concept of the "performativity" of gender (Butler, 1990), Taksa traces how railway heritage has sustained traditional understandings of patriarchal family relations. Gendered cultures of work and the messiness of gender relations are widely ignored, and traditional gender roles reinforced – something Taksa demonstrates, among other things, with the popular *Thomas the Tank Engine* stories.

The Nizhny Tagil charter on industrial heritage of 2003[14] underlined how industrial heritage is linked to forms of identification. However, Taksa's chapter is a reminder that gender identifications or at least gender awareness are often ignored in industrial heritage initiatives. Laurajane Smith's chapter asks similar questions to those of Taksa in relation to class. She argues that deindustrialization did not only bring a displacement of working-class communities but that subsequent industrial heritage initiatives often erased the memory of those communities. Instead, middle-class values have underpinned industrial heritage initiatives. They have reinforced neoliberal constructions of past, present, and future in the dominant

Introduction

narratives of the industrial heritage discourse as it prevails in England, the US, and Australia, the three countries that are at the center of attention in Smith's chapter. However, she also posits that an alternative heritage discourse from below can reassert working-class community pride and advance a critical form of heritage that normatively sides with the values of social solidarity and social justice (Shackel and Palus, 2006; Smith, Shackel, and Campbell, 2011; Berger, 2020b, pp. 289–295).

Her chapter in the handbook is based on a long-term project of hers, comparing visitor reactions to exhibitions and displays of working-class memories of deindustrialization (Smith, 2021). Thus, she shifts the focus of attention from the production of industrial heritage initiatives to the reception of those initiatives, something that is done far too little in the study of industrial heritage. Focusing on labor history museums and heritage sites, Smith, like Taksa, works with Butler's concept of 'performativity' and asks how the performance of visiting these sites is shaping and legitimating particular understandings of labor and working-class pasts. She found that visitors often had a strong personal, familial connection to labor and working-class history betraying a mixture of loss, lament, pride, and empathy with the stories told at the sites. She demonstrates how visitors can use the working-class heritage to boost their self-esteem and encourage them in their struggles against present-day economic and social injustices. It also allows them to insert the story of working-class people into the national narratives of their respective nation-states from which they are routinely excluded.[15] Smith argues for the need to engage with the emotional side of working-class heritage and foster expressions of grief and loss that can be used in present-day struggles for greater social justice. Forms of "progressive nostalgia" can be made productive in this process (Smith and Campbell, 2017).

The chapters on the links between industrial heritage and gender/class identifications could well have been augmented by chapters on race, ethnicity, and religion – identifications that were often vital in industrial regions and that have been dealt with very differently in the making of industrial heritage and its representations. The legacy of slavery meant that many industrial places from Detroit to Sao Paulo and from the Midlands to Paris had a large Black working-class population. Their experiences and lifeworlds intermingled with issues of class and gender producing intersectional forms of identification (Crenshaw, 2014). Furthermore, many industrial heartlands attracted migrant labor that developed strong ethnic group identifications intersecting with their class and gender identifications. If industrial heritage has sidelined labor and working-class memories, it ignored Black and migrant memories of both industrialization and deindustrialization even more. Where those memories are present it is due largely to sustained memory and heritage activism from Black and migrant groups to insert their heritage into the dominant forms of industrial heritage-making (Dellios, 2022; Triece, 2016).

Where the working class was strongly Christian in orientation, class, gender, racial, and ethnic identifications mingled with religious ones. Of all the Christian denominations it was Catholicism that developed the strongest ties with working-class communities. A sizable Catholic labor movement, including Catholic trade unions and political parties with a strong labor wing, is remembered at labor heritage sites, although it is rarely at the center of attention. The dominant narratives of scientific progress, economic power, and technological advances put not just a Socialist but also a Christian labor heritage into the shadows (Heerma van Voss, Pasture, and de Maeyer, 2005). Very little is known about how other religions, such as Islam, Hinduism, or Buddhism, and their relationships with the subaltern are represented at industrial heritage sites, in particular in the Global South.

Toward a Global Comparative Typology of Industrial Heritage-Making

All chapters in this part are transregional and comparative, calling for more comparisons of industrial heritage landscapes. We have already observed the general trend in the field to upscale our study of industrial heritage and deindustrialization: from the local to the regional, national, and transnational/-regional. This is a welcome development, as comparisons promise to shed new light on individual cases by allowing a sharper look at what was specific and what was general about their development. However, comparisons should not be set up in a rigid way with the definition of two or more units of comparison that are strictly bordered and delineated from each other. Instead, any comparison must take into account that, more often than not, heritage-makers and memory activists from different cases were in touch with each other, learnt from each other, and adapted strategies, ideas, and practices from each other. In this sense, the study of transregional interlinkages needs to precede any comparison (Berger, 2020c).

This is very clear with Reicher's and Iuga's analysis of postmining landscapes in Germany, Luxembourg, and France. Tomann argues that more comparative work is needed on community memory of post-communist Europe, as this would, in her view, lead to a better understanding of heritage actors and memory activists in their conceptualizations of industrial heritage. Steiner calls for more comparisons and glocal studies into the interlinkages of industrial heritage initiatives between the Global North and the Global South. Taksa underlines the need for more global comparisons into the refusal of a truly global railway heritage to make gender a meaningful concept of analysis. Smith's comparison of the reception of labor heritage sites in the Anglophone world is a masterpiece of sustained comparison and would benefit from being extended to other language worlds.

A more transregional and comparative study of industrial heritage and its reflections on the memory of both industrialization and deindustrialization needs to think hard on the impact of language on different understandings of heritage (Braber, 2018). Thinking about the languages in which heritage and memory making are formulated starts with the very concept of 'heritage.' This English word contains the notion that one individual/generation/ cohort inherits something from the previous one and needs to decide what to do with it: to disregard it or to develop it, to loathe it or to cherish it. It needs decisions on how it should be developed, but the notion that there is something inheritable between generations is taken for granted in this concept. In French, 'patrimoine' is a concept not only far more gendered than heritage, also it refers, in its basic meaning, to individuals and their net assets, that is, their financial estates. There is therefore already a valuation inherent in 'patrimoine' that naturalizes that 'patrimony' and makes it difficult to question it. The German 'Industriekultur' does not have references to inheritance and assets at all, except that the concept of 'culture' in German is highly loaded with something to be cherished and nurtured. It is a strongly middle-class concept associated with the self-perfection of individuals through culture (Bildung). Extending this bourgeois concept to the industrial world is tantamount to a reevaluation of the worth of industry. Popularized in the 1960s and 1970s, it was part and parcel of an attempt to integrate the industrial world and its inhabitants, above all the workers, into a bourgeois understanding of 'Kultur' from which they had traditionally been excluded. This brief discussion of how difficult straightforward translations of 'patrimoine' and 'Kultur' as 'heritage' are, already indicates how many linguistic traps lie in wait for those scholars keen on comparing across language boundaries. Berger, Dicks, and Fontaine (2020) have disentangled the diverse meanings inherent in 'community,' 'Gemeinschaft,' and

Introduction

'communauté' in English, German, and French – another example of how important attention to language is in cross-language comparisons of industrial heritage. And it is, of course, necessary to be aware also of the possible different conceptual meanings of the same word in one language across different countries in which (allegedly) the same language is spoken: the inflections of concepts such as 'community' were, after all, not the same in the US, Britain, and Australia.

Discussions of the need to properly historize[16] different linguistic concepts could be extended considerably,[17] but let me just give one more example: the concept of 'deindustrialization' used in the English-speaking world refers to something disappearing, namely industry. As a concept it already emphasizes loss and destruction. Also, it signals inevitability as though we are dealing with processes that are determined by the power of capital to shift whole industries from one place to another. Very different connotations are inherent in the concept of 'Strukturwandel' used in the German-speaking world. Here, structures are changing, and there is no reference to something disappearing. Change replaces loss. What is changing can be very different: factories might be replaced by other factories from the same branch of industry, that is, structural change can signal reindustrialization. Particular branches of industry could also be replaced by other branches of industries, in which case we would be talking about processes of neo-industrialization. Or we could see a change from industry to services and the emergence of post-industrial service-sector economies. However, it is often stressed in the German-speaking literature that there is no direct replacement of industry with services, as in most cases, the services that are emerging are closely tied to older industries that may have weakened but are still there and that, furthermore, many services are organized themselves in an industry-like way (Lehner and Noll, 2016, pp. 25, 27). Hence, the differentiation between industry and services is far more porous than imagined in the fantasies of Fourastiere (1949), Bell (1976), and others who wrote about the emergence of post-industrial societies in the Global North. Overall, the languages of 'deindustrialization' and 'Strukturwandel' signify very different understandings of what was going on in processes of industrial closure.

The comparisons of industrial heritage landscapes so far indicate a strong relationship between the development of these landscapes and the unfolding of the deindustrialization process itself. I have tried elsewhere to develop a global typology of how industrialization and deindustrialization are remembered, how such memories are related to nostalgia, and how nostalgic forms of remembering are related to three specific memory regimes and three types of political responses to deindustrialization (Berger, 2021). The latter are, first, market-radical neoliberal political strategies that leave deindustrialization processes to the markets and do not intervene in them. Second, statist strategies see an interventionist state seeking to guide processes of deindustrialization. Third, corporatist strategies involve negotiated forms of deindustrialization between the state, trade unions, and employers (Berger, MacKinnon, Raggi, and Wilson, 2025). The three regimes of memory are antagonistic, cosmopolitan, and agonistic forms of memory that narrate both the industrial past and deindustrialization in different ways.[18]

Antagonistic memory is one that orders the world into 'enemies' and 'friends,' 'in-groups' and 'out-groups.' It speaks only to the 'in-group' and constructs an 'other' as 'enemy' that needs to be destroyed. It is mono-perspectival and works through mobilizing passions of belonging to the 'in-group.' Neoliberal, market-radical concepts of deindustrialization often work with antagonistic forms of memory seeking to eradicate the memory of alleged enemies, that is, trade unions, the labor movement, and the working class. Its heritage strategy is one of silencing the memory of these groups identified as 'enemies.' Hence, they engage in either very little heritage work, or their heritage work stresses the technological progress of a bygone age that is safely moored in the past and has, at best, antiquarian value.

Opposition against such neoliberal antagonistic memory regimes comes from groups close to the labor movement and the working class who construct agonistic forms of memory as counter-memory. It mobilizes the passions of social justice and solidarity arguing for a radical historization of the industrial past and the processes of deindustrialization. Not based on simple binaries of 'enemies' and 'friends,' its multi-perspectivity points to the political aspects of heritage-making and memory work within democratic political frameworks. Agonistic memory posits an ongoing political task to endow heritage and memory with the meanings that would foster solidaristic communities in the present. Its politicization of industrial heritage relies on an understanding of an open-ended political process based on conflicting interests that are mediated in a democratic political sphere.

Such agonistic forms of memory are different from but closely related to cosmopolitan forms of memory that are prominent in state-led and corporatist forms of deindustrialization.[19] They value embedded forms of capitalism and stress that any processes of deindustrialization have to be managed with the working-class communities affected by deindustrialization uppermost in mind. They therefore plan for structural change and provide perspectives of employment and a positive future for working-class communities affected by deindustrialization. They encourage a multi-perspectival dialogue between different social actors in the pursuit of a consensus between them that might benefit all – the interests of capital, labor, and the state. Once this consensus has been reached, however, cosmopolitan memory also works in binary ways, excluding those standing outside of this consensus, neoliberal market radicals on the one hand and anti-capitalist fundamentalists on the other.

Hence, in contrast to cosmopolitan forms of memory, agonism is characterized by a more open-ended understanding of memory processes that are more radically multi-perspectival and avoid exclusions. However, it remains a central conundrum in agonistic approaches what to do with actors who do not accept that all political memory contests need to take place within a democratically constituted forum, where all memory perspectives can be heard and negotiated in an adversarial way that falls short of constructing 'enemies' that need to be destroyed. Would not those undemocratic memory activists still have to be excluded from the forum, as they threaten the democratic memory contest itself? In other words, can agonism really exist without any exclusionary practices?

Based on my admittedly very sketchy attempt to come up with a typology of industrial heritage-making that relates the deindustrialization processes to types of memory and types of nostalgia (Berger, 2021), we would arrive at the following differentiation: much of the English-speaking world in the Global North (including Australia) would follow the market-radical antagonistic/agonistic pathway to industrial memory regimes and heritage landscapes, whereas many of the continental Western European countries that have corporatist and statist traditions would follow cosmopolitan memory regimes with some doses of agonism inserted into them. The post-communist world of Eastern Europe seems to be shifting from an initial marked-radical antagonism with hardly any agonistic elements to more cosmopolitan forms of memory – not the least under the impact of the strong exchanges with Western Europe inside the European Union. In the Global South, decolonial perspectives provide an agonistic challenge to the dominant understandings of industrial heritage in the Global North. The memory regimes of deindustrialization in the Global South differ widely between market-radical, statist, and corporatist forms, depending on where you

Introduction

look at certain moments in time. Hence, different countries from the Global South align to diverse forms of industrial memory landscapes while through their decolonial perspectives forming a type of their own. Undoubtedly, this very rough first attempt at a global typology of industrial heritage regimes and their relations to processes of memory formation and processes of deindustrialization will have to be refined in the years to come. It is meant as an encouragement to other scholars to continue thinking globally on the constitution of heritage landscapes and their relationship to processes of deindustrialization. The comparative and transregional reflections on these heritage landscapes in the chapters of this part of the book should be read as another step in this direction.

Notes

1 I prefer the concept of "identification" (Hall, 1996) to concepts of identity, as they are less essentialist and more self-aware of the constructed nature of all identity-formation. 'Identification' allows change over time and interrelations with other 'identifications.' It is not as absolute and rigid a concept as that of 'identity' (see Berger, 2022c; on identity see also Lorenz, 2024).
2 https://ticcih.org/ (Accessed: 2 June 2024).
3 https://www.criticalheritagestudies.org/history/ (Accessed: 2 June 2024). On the concept of 'critical heritage,' see Smith, 2006.
4 https://workingclassassn.org/ (Accessed: 7 June 2024).
5 https://www.erih.net/about-erih/ (Accessed: 2 June 2024).
6 I take the notion of a 'memoryscape' from the work of Dai Smith on the way in which the landscape of the South Wales coalfield has been remembered. See Smith (1993).
7 On the concept of 'master narrative,' see Thijs (2008).
8 https://industrie-kultur.de/ (Accessed: 7 June 2024).
9 It is interesting that there are few systematic comparisons of the emergence of industrial heritage landscapes and their meanings on a national level. At best we have systematic inventories, but even these more often than not remain on a regional level. For a first systematic attempt to compare the deindustrialization of industrial regions and their accompanying memoryscapes in the form of industrial heritage landscapes in different parts of Germany (see Berger, Goch, and Kellershohn, 2025).
10 High (2003) was a pioneering comparative study of deindustrialization in the US and Canada. See also more specifically on the memory of deindustrialization High and Lewis (2007). For Europe see Storm (2014) and Jaramillo and Tomann (2021), Voigt (2021) and Raphael (2023).
11 https://deindustrialization.org/ (Accessed: 3 June 2024); on the concept of the 'glocal,' see Beyer (2021).
12 See also Ann Rigney's ERC project on 'memories of hope' titled 'Remembering Activism': https://rememberingactivism.eu/ (Accessed: 24 May 2024). It has produced a string of its own publications, for example, Rigney and Smits (2023), and it has inspired many others, including myself, to follow in her footsteps. See Berger, Scalmer, and Wicke (2021) and Berger and Koller (2024).
13 The 'structures of feeling' idea goes back to Williams (1961), who used it to refer to the collective dynamic in which communities develop their own self-understandings which, in specific historical situations, can become counter-hegemonic.
14 https://ticcih.org/about/charter/ (Accessed: 8 June 2024).
15 In my own study on national historical narratives in Europe, I have argued that narratives of class have been merged in multiple ways with narratives of nation. Exclusion was only one, albeit prominent, possibility among a variety of different alignments between the two. See Berger with Conrad (2015).
16 Since the mid-1990s, I have used the term 'historism' and 'historist' rather than 'historicism' and 'historicist' in the English language, so as to avoid confusion between two very different concepts. Whereas 'historism' is associated, above all, with the work of Leopold von Ranke and is an evolutionary concept that understands all political and social order as historically developed and grown, 'historicism' refers to theories that posit history following predetermined laws toward a particular end, as they were analyzed by Karl Popper. The German language uses two different terms for these entirely different concepts: 'Historimus' and 'Historizismus.' I have argued that the English

The Routledge Handbook of Deindustrialization Studies

language would benefit from introducing this distinction and no longer conflating the two concepts by using the same term for both.

17 This is, of course, a major concern among historians studying the history of concepts. See Berger (2022c, pp. 179–202).

18 On theories of agonistic memory that can, in my view, be usefully applied to deindustrialization studies, see Cento Bull and Hansen (2016) and Colom, Cento Bull, and Hansen (2021).

19 Among theorists of agonistic memory, this question of how close agonistic and cosmopolitan memory are is a highly contested one. For my own position in this debate, see Kansteiner and Berger (2021).

Reference List

Angelo, H. (2021). *How Green Became Good. Urbanized Nature and the Making of Cities and Citizens.* Chicago: University of Chicago Press.

Applegate, C. (1990). *A Nation of Provincials. The German Idea of Heimat.* Berkeley, CA: University of California Press.

Arregui, A., Mackenthun, G. and Wodianka, S. (eds.). (2018). *DEcolonial Heritage: Natures, Cultures, and the Asymmetries of Memory.* Münster: Waxmann.

Baumeister, M., Bonomo, B. and Schott, D. (eds.). (2017). *Cities Contested: Urban Politics, Heritage and Social Movements in Italy and West Germany in the 1970s.* Frankfurt/Main: Campus.

Bell, D. (1976). *The Coming of Postindustrial Society.* New York: Basic Books.

Berger, S. with Conrad, C. (2015). *The Past as History. National Identity and Historical Consciousness in Modern Europe.* Basingstoke: Palgrave MacMillan.

Berger, S. (2019). Industrial Heritage and the Ambiguities of Nostalgia for an Industrial Past in the Ruhr Valley, Germany. *Labor. Studies in Working-Class History,* 16(1), pp. 37–64.

Berger, S. (2020a). Preconditions for the Making of an Industrial Past: Comparative Perspectives. In Berger, S. (ed.) *Constructing Industrial Pasts. Heritage, Historical Culture and Identity in Regions Undergoing Structural Economic Transformation.* Oxford: Berghahn Books, pp. 1–26.

Berger, S. (2020b). Narrativizations of an Industrial Past: Labour, the Environment and the Construction of Space in Comparative Perspective. In Berger, S. (ed.) *Constructing Industrial Pasts. Heritage, Historical Culture and Identity in Regions Undergoing Structural Economic Transformation.* Oxford: Berghahn Books, pp. 288–305.

Berger, S. (2020c). Comparative and Transnational History. In Berger, S., Feldner, H. and Passmore, K. (eds.) *Writing History. Theory and Practice.* 3rd edn. London: Bloomsbury, pp. 292–316.

Berger, S. (2021). Vom Nutzen und Nachteil der Nostalgie. Das Kulturerbe der Deindustrialisierung im globalen Vergleich. *Zeithistorische Forschungen,* 18(1), pp. 93–121.

Berger, S. (2022a). The Alternative für Deutschland (AfD) and its Appeal to Workers – with Special Reference to the Ruhr Region of Germany. *Totalitarianism and Democracy,* 19(1), pp. 47–70.

Berger, S. (2022b). Heimat im Ruhrgebiet. Eine historische Perspektive. In Hombach, B. and Richter, F. (eds.) *Auf Streife durchs Revier. Kriminalität im Ruhrgebiet und gesellschaftliche Folgen.* Essen: tectum.

Berger, S. (2022c). *History and Identity: How Historical Theory Shapes Historical Practice.* Cambridge: Cambridge University Press.

Berger, S. (2023). Deindustrialised Spaces. In Gutman, Y. and Wüstenberg, J. (eds.) *The Routledge Handbook of Memory Activism.* London: Routledge, pp. 253–258.

Berger, S. (2025, forthcoming). Die Moderne wird Geschichte: die Industriekulturalisierung des Ruhrgebiets. In Berger, S. and Kellershohn, J. (eds.) *Geschichte des Ruhrgebiets,* Vol. 3. Cologne: Böhlau.

Berger, S., Borsdorf, U., Claßen, L., Grütter, H.T. and Nellen, D. (eds.). (2019). *Zeit-Räume Ruhr. Erinnerungsorte des Ruhrgebiets.* Essen: Klartext.

Berger, S., Dicks, B. and Fontaine, M. (2020). Community': A Useful Concept in Heritage Studies? *International Journal of Heritage Studies,* 26(4), pp. 325–351.

Berger, S., Fontaine, M., Pattison, J. and Rhodes, J. (2025, forthcoming) Deindustrialization and Populist Politics in North America and Western Europe. In High, S. and Berger, S. (eds.) *The Politics of Industrial Closure.* Toronto: University of Toronto Press.

Berger, S., Goch, S. and Kellershohn, J. (eds.). (2025, forthcoming) *Der Strukturwandel von Industrieregionen in Deutschland. Eine Bestandsaufnahme.* Magdeburg: Landeszentrale für politische Bildung.

Introduction

Berger, S. and Koller, C. (eds.). (2024). *Memory and Social Movements in Modern and Contemporary History. Remembering Past Struggles and Resourcing Protest.* Basingstoke: Palgrave MacMillan.

Berger, S., MacKinnon, L., Raggi, P. and Wilson, G. (2025, forthcoming) Traditions of State Management of Industrial Decline in Europe and North America. In High, S. and Berger, S. (eds.) *The Politics of Industrial Closure.* Toronto: University of Toronto Press.

Berger, S. and Pickering, P. (2018). Regions of Heavy Industry and Their Heritage – Between Identity Politics and 'Touristification: Where to Next? In Wicke, C., Berger, S. and Golombek, J. (eds.) *Industrial Heritage and Regional Identities.* London: Routledge, pp. 214–236.

Berger, S. and Scalmer, S. and Wicke, C. (eds.). (2021). *Remembering Social Movements. Activism and Memory.* London: Routledge.

Beyer, P. (ed.). (2021). *Globalization/Glocalization: Developments in Theory and Applications.* Leiden: Brill.

Boltanski, L. and Esquerre, A. (2020). *Enrichment: A Critique of Commodities.* London: Polity.

Bonnett, A. (2010). *Left in the Past. Radicalism and the Politics of Nostalgia.* New York: Continuum.

Boym, S. (2001). *The Future of Nostalgia.* New York: Basic Books.

Braber, N. (2018). Pit Talk in the East Midlands. In Braber, N. and Jansen, S. (eds.) *Sociolinguistics in England.* Basingstoke: Palgrave MacMillan, pp. 243–274.

Butler, J. (1990). *Gender Trouble: Feminism and the Subversion of Identity.* London: Routledge.

Cento Bull, A. and Hansen, H.L. (2016). On Agonistic Memory. *Memory Studies,* 9(4), pp. 390–404.

Cento Bull, A., Hansen, H.L. and Colom-González, F. (2021). Agonistic Memory Revisited. In Berger, S. and Kansteiner, W. (eds.) *The Agonistic Memory of War in Twentieth-Century Europe.* Basingstoke: Palgrave Macmillan, pp. 13–38.

Crenshaw, K. (2014). *On Intersectionality. Essential Writings.* New York: The New Press.

Dellios, A. (2022). *Heritage Making and Migrant Subjects in the Deindustrializing Region of the Latrobe Valley.* Cambridge: Cambridge University Press.

Douet, J. (ed.). (2013). *Industrial Heritage Re-Tooled: The TICCIH Guide to Industrial Heritage Conservation.* London: Routledge.

Edensor, T. (2005). *Industrial Ruins. Space, Aesthetics and Materiality.* Oxford: Berg.

Eiringhaus, P. (2018). *Industrie wird Natur. Postindustrielle Repräsentationen von Region und Umwelt im Ruhrgebiet.* Essen: Klartext.

Fourastié, J. (1949). *Le Grand Expoire de XXe Siècle. Progrès Techniques, Progrès Économique, Progrès Sociale.* Paris: Presses Universitaires de France.

Hall, S. (1996). Introduction: Who Needs Identity? In Hall, S. and du Gay, P. (eds.) *Questions of Cultural Identity.* London: Sage, pp. 1–17.

Harper, J. (2018). *Poland's Memory Wars. Essays on Illiberalism.* Budapest: Central European University Press.

Heerma van Voss, L., Pasture, P. and de Maeyer, J. (eds.). (2005). *Between Cross and Class. Comparative Histories of Christian Labour in Europe, 1840–2000.* Berne: Peter Lang.

High, S. (2003). *Industrial Sunset. The Making of North America's Rustbelt, 1969–1983.* Toronto: University of Toronto Press.

High, S. and Lewis, D.W. (2007). *Corporate Wasteland. The Landscape and Memory of Deindustrialization.* Toronto: Between the Lines.

Jaramillo, G. and Tomann, J. (eds.). (2021). *Transcending the Nostalgic: Deindustrialized Landscapes across Europe.* Oxford: Berghahn Books.

Kansteiner, W. and Berger, S. (2021). Agonism and Memory. In Berger, S. and Kansteiner, W. (eds.) *Agonistic Memory and the Legacy of 20th Century Wars in Europe.* Basingstoke: Palgrave MacMillan, pp. 203–246.

Landwehr, A. (2020). *Diesseits der Geschichte. Für eine andere Historiographie.* Göttingen: Wallstein.

Lehmann, N-H. (2022). Socialism and the Rise of Industrial Heritage: The Preservation of Industrial Monuments in the German Democratic Republic. In Gantner, E.B., Geering, C. and Vickers, P. (eds.) *Heritage under Socialism. Preservation in Eastern and Central Europe.* Oxford: Berghahn Books, chapter eight.

Lehner, F. and Noll, H-P. (2016). *Ruhr Zukunftsprojekt. Von der eingebildeten zur wirklichen Metropole.* Essen: Klartext.

Linkon, S.L. (2018). *The Half-Life of Deindustrialization. Working-Class Writing about Economic Restructuring.* Ann Arbor: University of Michigan Press.

Lorenz, C. (2024) Who are We? Reflections on Collective Identities. *Moving the Social. Journal of Social History and the History of Social Movements*, 73.

Lorenz, C. and Bevernage, B. (eds.). (2013). *Breaking Up Time. Negotiating the Borders Between Present, Past and Future*. Göttingen: Vandenhoeck & Ruprecht.

Mah, A. (2012). *Industrial Ruination, Community and Place. Landscapes and Legacies of Urban Decline*. Toronto: University of Toronto Press.

Massey, D. (1984). *Spatial Divisions of Labor. Social Structures and the Geography or Production*. New York: Methuen.

Müller-Jentsch, W. (ed.). (1999). *Konfliktpartnerschaft. Akteure und Institutionen industrieller Beziehungen*. Munich: Hampp.

Pehe, V. and Wawrzyniak, J. (eds.). (2024). *Remembering the Neoliberal Turn. Economic Change and Collective Memory in Eastern Europe after 1989*. London: Routledge.

Polanyi, K. (1944). *The Great Transformation. The Political and Economic Origins of Our Time*. New York: Farrar & Rinehart.

Portelli, A. (2005). This Mill Won't Run No More': Oral History and Deindustrialization. In Russo, J. and Linkon, S.L. (eds.) *New Working-Class Studies*. Ithaca, NY: Cornell University Press, pp. 54–72.

Raphael, L. (2023). *Beyond Coal and Steel. A Social History of Western Europe after the Boom*. Cambridge: Polity.

Rhodes II, M.A., Price, W.R. and Walker, A. (eds.). (2021). *Geographies of Post-Industrial Place, Memory and Heritage*. London: Routledge.

Rigney, A. (2018). Remembering Hope: Transnational Activism Beyond the Traumatic. *Memory Studies*, 11(3), pp. 368–380.

Rigney, A. and Smits, T. (eds.). (2023). *The Visual Memory of Protest*. Amsterdam: Amsterdam University Press.

Shackel, P.A. and Palus, M. (2006). Remembering an Industrial Landscape. *International Journal of Historical Archaeology*, 10(1), pp. 49–71.

Smith, D. (1993). *Aneurin Bevan and the World of South Wales*. Cardiff: University of Wales Press.

Smith, L. (2006). *Uses of Heritage*. London: Routledge.

Smith, L. (2021). *Emotional Heritage. Visitor Engagement at Museums and Heritage Sites*. London: Routledge.

Smith, L. and Akagawa, N. (eds.). (2009). *Intangible Heritage*. London: Routledge.

Smith, L. and Campbell, G. (2017). Nostalgia for the Future'. Memory, Nostalgia and the Politics of Class. *International Journal of Heritage Studies*, 23(7), pp. 612–627.

Smith, L., Shackel, P.A. and Campbell, G. (eds.). (2011). *Heritage, Labour and the Working Classes*. London: Routledge.

Steiner, M. (2019). *Die chilenische Steckdose. Kleine Weltgeschichte der deutschen Elektrifizierung von Valparaíso und Santiago de Chile, 1880–1920*. Weimar: Bauhaus-Universität Weimar. https://doi.org/10.25643/bauhaus-universitaet.3925

Storm, A. (2014). *Post-Industrial Landscape Scars*. London: Palgrave Macmillan.

Strangleman, Tim. (2013). Smokestack Nostalgia. 'Ruin Porn' or Working-Class Obituary: The Role and Meaning of Deindustrial Representation. *International Labor and Working-Class History*, 84, pp. 23–37.

Ther, Philipp (2016). *Europe since 1989. A History*. Princeton, NJ: Princeton University Press.

Thijs, K. (2008). The Metaphor of the Master: 'Narrative Hierarchy' in National Historical Cultures. In Berger, S. and Lorenz, C. (eds.) *The Contested Nation. Ethnicity, Class, Religion and Gender in National Histories*. Basingstoke: Palgrave Macmillan, pp. 60–74.

Triece, M.E. and Lewis, D.W. (2016). *Urban Renewal and Resistance: Race, Space and the City in the Late Twentieth to Early Twenty-First Centuries*. Lanham: Lexington Books.

Voigt, S. (eds.). (2021). *Since the Boom. Continuity and Change in the Western Industrialized World after 1970*. Toronto: University of Toronto Press.

Wallerstein, I. (2004). *World-Systems Analysis. An Introduction*. Durham, NC: Duke University Press.

Williams, R. (1961). *The Long Revolution*. London: Chatto & Windus.

Xie, F. (2015). *Industrial Heritage Tourism*. Bristol: Channel View Publications.

23

INDUSTRIAL MEMORY LANDSCAPES IN URBAN PLANNING PROCESSES

Comparative Perspectives from Germany, Luxembourg, and France

Christa Reicher and Liliana Iuga

Introduction

Today, post-industrial structural change with its complex consequences for society represents a global phenomenon. A significant case study in this context is the post-mining transformations, which represent a long-standing, multifaceted, and spatially differentiated aspect of European spatial development. Understanding these complex transformation processes and exploring effective strategies for conceiving, designing, and building sustainable post-mining regions that preserve their industrial memory landscapes remains a topical challenge for spatial planning and research in Europe.

Industrial decline and deindustrialization have been differently experienced and managed in various socioeconomic and political contexts, not always addressing the issue of whether industrial heritage should also be preserved and integrated into the future of the region. In many cases, the closing of industrial production units has been predominantly viewed from an economic standpoint, with little regard for preserving the physical remnants or the community's collective memory. This resulted in the "production of spaces of ruination," which were either demolished at a later point and replaced by new construction or simply abandoned in the absence of redevelopment proposals (Edensor, 2014). In other cases, activists (often architects, artists, and intellectuals with little or no institutional support) struggled to save from demolition at least fragments of the materials fabric by having the most important buildings listed as part of national legislation. In this way, they hoped to transform the question of the mining legacy into a "matter of concern" for residents and public authorities (Păun Constantinescu et al., 2017). When more consensus for preservation could be reached among public and private actors, key buildings and technical equipment were conserved and refurbished, transforming them into integral components of open-air museums. To enhance the appeal of such initiatives, new architectural structures would be introduced, creating differentiated spaces for the creative development of a various museal concept displaying specific cultural and educational features. While these endeavors added value for the local community and created pockets of tourist interest, they frequently remained isolated initiatives,

DOI: 10.4324/9781003308324-34

lacking integration into broader regional planning strategies and the overall revitalization of the area. An alternative perspective, exemplified by the case studies discussed in this chapter, illustrates how a collaborative effort involving politicians, planners, and intellectuals can yield solutions for the structural transition toward a post-industrial future.

In this chapter, we look at three case studies from Germany, Luxemburg, and France to emphasize the importance of planning and culture for the sustainable redevelopment of post-mining regions. First, in thinking about the agents of transformation, we highlight the agency of planners and architects, together with political decision-makers and local communities, in contributing to the transformation of these areas. In discussions about the agents of change in deindustrialization contexts, the role of planners and planning is often overlooked, not least because in many cases, for various political and economic reasons, the opportunity of revitalization seems simply out of reach. Typically, the recognized agents of change are states, regional and local governments, grassroots activists, business, and trade unions (Berger, 2020, p. 1). Second, we have selected three case studies to showcase distinct approaches to preserving and harmonizing the built and natural environment, with a deliberate focus on safeguarding and enhancing the site's distinctive characteristics. The Ruhr region stands as an example for thinking large-scale and creating new concepts for the integrated preservation of built and natural landscapes. In Belval, Luxembourg, a former industrial site was redeveloped as a cultural, residential, and business district, with the preserved industrial structures, particularly two blast furnaces, serving as prominent features in the urban design proposal. In Nord-Pas de Calais, France's largest mining area, efforts were made to inscribe the Mining Basin on the UNESCO World Heritage List and provide an institutional framework facilitating the cooperation between various stakeholders in territorial planning. These efforts were doubled by punctual interventions of renovating industrial architecture and establishing flagship cultural attractions in cities such as Lens and Lille.

The chapter will address several questions: what role do culture and memory play in developing concepts of urban and regional planning? How can post-industrial structural change contribute to the transformation of a region in an attractive future location? Which framework conditions contribute to an added value for urban and regional development? Which findings from the case studies analyzed in this chapter could be transferable?

Industriekultur in Urban Planning Processes

In the last decades, culture has become an increasingly important factor for the economic development of cities and regions in Europe, playing a central role in future-oriented urban development strategies (Kunzmann, 2002, p. 186). This reflects broader structural changes within economy itself, with a reorientation from manufacturing toward services and the production of knowledge and culture. In this context, heritage becomes a resource for urban regeneration and regional transformation (Madgin, 2009; Breitbart, 2013).

Culture is considered a driver of spatial development for several reasons. First, culture creates identity and a specific attachment to the place. Second, culture creates image, having become an indispensable element in contemporary place-marketing strategies. However, cultural offerings can develop their desired effect only if the spatial environment has the corresponding urban development and landscape qualities. Third, culture creates employment opportunities. The cultural industry is now seen as a field of action for economic development.

Industrial Memory Landscapes in Urban Planning Processes

The termination of industrial activities can lead to the abandonment of the place and the loss of historical industrial fabric. What kind of usage concepts can be proposed afterwards? What kind of narratives about the past should they communicate and in which form? How can they make the past legible in a spatial and social context? Architects and planners provide some answers to these questions in the framework of 'industrial culture.'

Particularly well-known in the German context, the term 'industrial culture' (*Industriekultur*) has traditionally denoted the physical remnants of former industrial locations, encompassing both the constructed environment and the surrounding landscape. The recent focus on the integration of intangible aspects not only in the analysis of this past but also in strategies of redevelopment has prompted a redefinition of the concept in terms of establishing connections between past, present, and future (Harfst et al., 2018, pp. 1–9).

Bole has defined industrial culture as "a dynamic phenomenon in which past and present industrial production is embedded in the human physical environment, social structures, cognitive abilities, and institutions that might influence the future development choices of (post)industrial communities" (Bole, 2021, p. 10). The resulting structural heterogeneity highlights the need for a comprehensive, integrated approach in preserving and managing industrial landscapes, considering the interplay of technical, economic, societal, social, and cultural aspects. Policymakers and academics advocated for industrial culture as a means to bring new opportunities in regions and cities struggling with deindustrialization and shrinkage (Bole, 2021, p. 13). This is precisely where planning can make an impact by proposing sustainable, transformative, and future-oriented solutions. Regions where these solutions have already been successfully implemented, leading to positive socioeconomic change, provide valuable learning examples in this regard. Although responding to global dynamics, local action has been decisive in identifying strategies for addressing decay (Fernández Agueda, 2014).

The last 50 years have witnessed significant shifts in the conceptualization of the heritage field, as well as in the strategies for preserving historical industrial infrastructure. Important discussions on developing comprehensive preservation concepts for industrial heritage took place in Germany in the mid-1980s, with a focus on examples such as the Zollverein mine in Essen and the Völklinger Hütte in Saarland. As proposed in this contribution, the German example has served as an inspiration for other contexts, facilitating post-industrial redevelopment at the Belval site in Luxembourg and in the Nord-Pas de Calais region of France.

The discussions regarding the transformation of abandoned manufacturing structures and industrial landscapes contributed to debates on historic preservation, signalizing a rupture with the traditional understanding of conservation and proposing instead a more future-oriented perspective that is increasingly gaining ground. This paradigm shift has, in turn, resulted in the acknowledgment of World Heritage status in two of the case studies discussed in this chapter, in the Ruhr and Nord-Pas de Calais regions. Interdisciplinary teams of planners, economists, cultural scientists, and other experts deal with questions such as these: can large-scale industrial facilities be meaningfully embedded in the present and future of a city? What solutions are available for their further use, and how can they be maintained technically and financially within a sustainable framework? Can architectural and urban development quality be maintained given changing requirements for technical and energy standards?

Important insights and answers to the questions outlined here were obtained through experimental, short-term uses, thus 'avoiding' lengthy planning and approval processes to test the acceptance and suitability of possible solutions. However, this strategy does not exclude the need to implement medium- and long-term conservation measures. Currently, we are experiencing a change of trends in culture and in certain areas of the economy, that is, media, design, creative industries, leading to a growing demand for a "rough atmosphere in industrial buildings that are considered chic" (Buschmann, 2006).

The Case Studies

The case studies discussed in this chapter refer to the largest mining regions in Germany, France, and Luxembourg, which have often been studied in comparison due to their similarities and functional connections throughout history. This contribution analyses some of the lessons learned from (Western) European experiences in this regard by discussing approaches for the 'design and re-making' of post-mining regions. In this framework, the planners' approach constitutes one important element, as demonstrated by regional and strategic planning initiatives like the International Building Exhibition (IBA), an urban and regional development format which took place in the Ruhr region from 1989 to 1999, which has increased the livability of the region and created the spatial framework for broader socioeconomic development plans. Yet the success is not unconditioned nor unquestioned.

Ruhrgebiet Industrial Cultural Landscape (Germany)

Historical Context and Developments

From the nineteenth century onward, the Ruhr region, delimited by the Rhine River on the west, the river Lippe to the north, and the Ruhr in the south, experienced significant change due to industrialization based on access to high-quality coal. As a result, medieval towns such as Duisburg and Dortmund turned into industrial cities and former rural villages such as Bottrop into towns of 50,000 residents and more. Several waves of (international) immigration led to significant population growth in the area, as this expanding industry offered well-paid employment. By 1900, Germany was the third largest coal producer in the world after the US and Great Britain. Further expansion of coal mining in the first half of the twentieth century was accompanied by the establishment of other industrial branches, such as chemical, military, and electrical industries.

Although the coal industry in the Ruhr region experienced its last peak in 1956, when almost 500,000 employees worked in mining, the industry was declining. The 1958 coal crisis was triggered by an increasing replacement of coal with natural gas and oil, signaling the beginning of the post-mining era. It led to a first round of closures of mines and job cuts and "[b]y 1976 the number of mines had fallen from 148 to 35; production had halved, and the workforce had dropped to 150,000" (Hoppe, 2010, p. 28). The full extent of the crisis was strongly felt following the world economic recession of 1974/1975, when the growing availability of cheaper steel from Asia and the popularity of alternative materials (e.g., plastics) in certain manufacturing sectors led to job cuts in this sector as well. As a result, a *sectoral decline and structural change* (Eltges, 2008, p. 535) in both coal mining *and* the steel industry had begun. The Ruhr region, the former German industrial heartland, began the transition from an industrial to the service and ultimately knowledge economy with consequences for the demographic, urban, and environmental development in the region.

Nowadays, with five million residents, the Ruhr region is (still) one of the five largest agglomerations in Europe, in a polycentric setting consisting of 53 cities and municipalities stretching over an area of approximately 4,500 square kilometers. The region has no single dominant core city; rather, three of the largest cities (Dortmund, Essen, and Duisburg) have very similar population levels, each with around half a million inhabitants.

The diversity of demographic and socioeconomic conditions on the ground is considerable: 'shrinking,' 'waiting' and 'growing' represent some of the adjectives used to describe a variety of transformation processes that can be observed. The numerous abandoned buildings in the region still tell stories of a past of prosperity in a landscape upon which long-term continuous industrial exploitation has produced severe environmental damage including air and water pollution. The poor environmental conditions, in particular, have contributed to a negative public image that has characterized the region for decades.

Industriekultur as Post-Industrial Heritage: Planning Challenges and Opportunities

The region's spatial structure is defined by comparatively constant but relatively low-density urban development of city districts and neighborhoods interlinked by open spaces with various uses. In terms of planning, this creates challenges but also brings opportunities for development. On the one hand, there are no recognizable or distinct city boundaries that separate municipalities from each other. On the other hand, one can identify many internal edges, where built, residential areas border natural open spaces and provide access to leisure opportunities such as walking and cycling in seminatural spaces.

The mining industrial heritage and its transformation into industrial culture is the central collective experience of this region. At the beginning of the International Building Exhibition (Internationale Bauausstellung – IBA) Emscher Park, the Ruhr area presented itself as a densely populated urban landscape. It was rich in open spaces, but these were cut up by motorways, expressways, waterways, railway lines, and power lines. In addition, many areas were contaminated due to former industrial use.

The IBA was initiated by the state of North Rhine-Westphalia as a structural policy program to create a comprehensive strategy of revitalization, guided by the motto "change without growth." This initiative introduced innovative landscape planning and architectural concepts, promoting 'industrial culture' as a core element of regional identity. Established in 1989, the IBA operated for ten years, functioning as a facilitator of planning processes without directly implementing projects. It rather aimed to stimulate and support different stakeholders in developing such initiatives under the umbrella of a coherent concept. Under Karl Ganser's leadership, the IBA launched public calls for project proposals, ranging from the Emscher Landscape Park to new residential developments and the conservation of industrial landmarks. Funding for these projects was provided 40% from private investors and 60% from federal and EU funds. In 1996, the IBA Emscher Park represented Germany at the Venice Architecture Biennale under the theme "Change without Growth," which led to increasing international recognition of its innovative approach (Reicher et al., 2008, pp. 8–10).

With the decision of the state government of North Rhine-Westphalia to organize an International Building Exhibition on a regional scale in the Ruhr region for the first time, not only has the awareness of regional cooperation changed, but planning processes started to be guided by other laws. From that point on, the decisive planning basis for individual municipalities was no longer a comprehensive master plan envisioning spatial development but integrative cooperation on pioneering projects that transcended municipal boundaries. This change in planning and implementation processes was made possible by the distinctive agency of the IBA company, which was able to implement ambitious projects more independently and quicker. To guarantee the quality of the projects, international planning and architecture competitions were organized. With their special expertise and international vision, the prize-winners were able to implement projects in the Ruhr region with a claim to sustainability (although the term was not yet established, this understanding set the course). Overall, the IBA presented itself as a means of "integrated regional development" in which the ecological and cultural renewal of the region was regarded as a necessary condition for economic development.

The IBA brought about a mental shift in dealing with the post-industrial landscape. There was a consensus among the actors involved that the urban landscape should become more valuable in the minds of planners and decision-makers (Reicher et al., 2008, p. 16). The focus shifted from individual stakeholders preserving their autonomy of action to the necessity of collaborating and developing future-oriented concepts. The IBA undertook a comprehensive reevaluation of the urban landscape of the Ruhr area, and in doing so it made full use of its potential. It brought about a fundamental and strategic change in the way we deal with urban nature, from a 'residual landscape,' to appreciation and a process of reshaping it into a new urban cultural landscape. In spatial terms, it was about discovering qualities, integrating brownfield sites, overcoming barriers, and connecting previously isolated landscape areas through high ecological functionality and authentic design. New alliances between industry, culture, and nature were created in the IBA era and still shape the characteristics of the urban landscape today. In many places, the ways in which nature has reclaimed industrial sites has become a much appreciated ecological and aesthetic characteristic.

Currently, the identity of the Ruhr area is strongly defined by these developments, in particular by the ways in which concepts such as *Industriekultur* and *Industrienatur* have been applied. This perception is linked to a fundamental learning process experienced by the region: the obsolete architectures of the industrial age, together with the 'ruined' landscapes, have now become urban and landscape aesthetic achievements, iconic developments of the post-industrial Ruhr area.

The Emscher Landscape Park – Approaches to Restructuring and Redevelopment

The Emscher Landscape Park, developed under the motto "Workshop for the Future of Old Industrial Regions" in an area which span along the river Emscher between Duisburg and Bergkamen, having an east–west extension of about 70 kilometers and a north–south extension of 15 kilometers, is the central concern and the unifying theme of this building exhibition. It was intended to give the Emscher region more attractiveness and at the same time more urban planning order (IBA Emscher Park project catalog, 1999).

Blast furnaces, machine halls, winding towers, collieries, gasometers, and coking plants are among the most characteristic architectural remnants of the industrial era. With the beginning of the mining crisis and the progressive structural change, these buildings lost their use and raised the question of how to deal with the material remains of this complex legacy. The goal of the IBA was to treat this industrial heritage respectfully and, by creatively repurposing them with cultural uses, strengthen the regional character. A first example that drew international attention include the areal of the former Zeche Zollverein (Figure 23.1) – which was awarded UNESCO World Heritage status in 2001, 15 years after the mine's closure. It has now become a vibrant site for culture, gastronomy, and art (Figure 23.2).[1] Another example is the Duisburg Landscape Park, which was turned into an ecological park with outdoor

Industrial Memory Landscapes in Urban Planning Processes

Figure 23.1 Zollverein: UNESCO World Heritage Site. (Photo: Fabio Bayro Kaiser)

Figure 23.2 Zollverein as tourist destination. (Photo: Fabio Bayro Kaiser)

climbing, a diving center, meeting hall, and a stage amid the ruins of the former cookery. On weekend nights, a lightshow illuminates the buildings (Hemmings and Kagel, 2010).

Among the over 100 projects on industrial heritage and its reuse, many focused on improving the quality of the environment, such as the ecological reconstruction of the Emscher system and the creation of the Emscher Landscape Park. In sum, with the International Building Exhibition (IBA) Emscher Park, the Emscher region, and indeed the Ruhr region as a whole made significant advances toward a more sustainable development. The transformation process has developed an extensive media appeal especially with the aforementioned projects focusing on an interplay of elements from industrial culture, art, and ecological restoration. The International Building Exhibition, which took place over a decade from 1989 to 1999 and showcased its outcomes on an international platform to a diverse audience of stakeholders and planners, has profoundly transformed the local, national, and international perception of the region. The region's negative image has been left behind, becoming an area that now attracts international attention in the context of a new 'Industrial Revolution' and tourism.

Moreover, the IBA Emscher Park has strengthened cooperation between cities, particularly among the institutions and departments responsible for planning processes. This cooperation was driven partly by financial funding opportunities and requirements and partly by the recognized need for reforms within individual city administrations. Effective project implementation necessitates interdisciplinary collaboration from the planning authority to the cultural department, from the building inspectorate to the green space department and across city boundaries.

The long-term impact of the IBA Emscher Park includes follow-up accomplishments such as the designation of the European Capital of Culture RUHR 2010, an urban regional contract, the ruhrcities project, the award of Green Capital of Europe 2017, and the International Garden Exhibition Ruhr (IGA) 2027. The metamorphosis of the Ruhr Metropolitan area into a sustainable and polycentric urban region was already in progress at the beginning of the new millennium. However, it became evident that to sustain and further advance this transformation, new impulses and innovative ideas were needed.

Cité des Science Belval (Luxembourg): From Iron and Steel Works to University Location

Esch-sur-Alzette, with a population of 35,000 residents, is the second largest city in Luxembourg. It has experienced a sustained population growth since 1991 to a large extent due to the redevelopment project in Belval, where the University of Luxembourg has also established headquarters. The town emerged as the primary center of the mining area in Luxembourg in the 1870s. The exploitation of minette deposits in the southern region, along the border with France, triggered a substantial development after 1880. Luxembourg's iron industry evolved in a functional connection with the Ruhr region – initially serving as a raw material provider for Germany's most important mining area before 1900. Around the turn of the century, this development continued through the establishment of new industrial capacities by companies from Aachen region, Aachener Hütten-Aktien-Verein, and Gelsenkirchener Bergwerks AG (GBAG). The influx of immigrant workers insured the continuous development of the site. The 1920s represented a peak of production capacities, with 47 blast furnaces in operation. The Belval site with its iron production facilities and the associated processes is one of these highlights of this rich history, especially because the blast furnaces are in a close functional and architectural connection and are clear testimonies of the historical production processes (see Buschmann, n.d.).

Although the steelworks in Esch/Belval were completely refurbished and modernized for a higher production capacity from 1965 to 1979, the industrial decline could not be avoided. This became particularly visible in 1997, when one of the three remaining blast furnaces in Belval was sold to a Chinese company and effectively dismantled and reconstructed in China.[2]

An important political decision, that of supporting the reconversion of the site, promoted a partnership between the Luxembourg government and the ARBED steel group. This collaboration resulted in the establishment of AGORA, a development company founded in 2000. This public-private partnership aimed to create a new district on the decommissioned industrial site. Ultimately, it is due to this independent institution that planning processes could be connected to international discourses and practices, leading to the establishment of a coherent planning concept. A new master plan was to be developed based on an urban development competition, with the aim of building a new city for 7,000 residents, as well as creating work and research positions for 25,000 people. The framework conditions for the development of Belval were negotiated by politicians, planning authorities, and the stakeholders of the development company AGORA and ultimately set out in an agreement on the further planning process.

The competition was won in 2002 by a multidisciplinary team in cooperation with the Dutch planning office Jo Coenen and the landscape designers of Buro Lubber of 's-Hertogenbosch. The master plan proposed the transformation of Belval from a monocentric city to a City of Science ("Cité des Sciences"), in which various institutions of higher education and innovative research centers would be located alongside offices for public administration and business (Figure 23.4). The site would also accommodate two new residential complexes, with adequate recreational and educational facilities. Essentially, the plan proposed to implement a sustainable transition from brownfield site to a mixed-use residential, research, and 'office town' while integrating green areas, modern transport infrastructure, and the old and new architecture into a coherent concept.

When the question increasingly arose as to how and with what effort it might be possible to integrate existing industrial buildings into the new master plan, the responsible stakeholders made use of the experts who had already gained experience in dealing with the industrial heritage in the Ruhr region. The personal and institutional transfer of know-how ultimately led to potentials being filtered out of the supposedly unsolvable problems of the existing industrial buildings and ways of preserving them being developed.

The success story of the urban redevelopment scheme implemented in Belval was promoted through equally successful marketing campaigns. Over the past two decades, the completion of each new construction phase has been marked by cultural events and public unveilings. Equally celebrated has been the inauguration of landmark buildings, such as Rockhal, Luxembourg's largest concert hall, which opened for the public in 2005. Gradually, the architectural programs envisioned as part of the redevelopment scheme were completed and inaugurated: office and business centers, a multifunctional plaza, research centers of the university that pioneer innovative, transdisciplinary programs, and the two residential districts. Although not initially envisioned, the preservation of the two remaining blast furnaces, symbolically called "cathedrals" of the new era (Wiseler, n.d.), became a focal point of the redevelopment plan, as the structures were placed under monument protection (Figure 23.3). Furthermore, a program for protecting the biodiversity of the area was launched in 2016.[3]

Figure 23.3 Blast furnace A and City of Science Belval. (Photo: Henri Goergen)

A key aspect of this success lies in the approach to the preserved industrial structures, which were considered as 'truly integrated heritage.' In other words, they were not preserved as artifacts in open-air museums but were incorporated into the overall urban design scheme.[4] The history of the steelworks, with its infrastructure and the communities of workers, was strategically included into strategies for self-representation. The local mining history is recalled and celebrated through exhibitions, festivals, and museum displays. Mining museums were established as early as the 1970s and continued with a stronger impetus in the 1990s, being integrated into a comprehensive touristic strategy of the region.[5] The blast furnace system in Esch/Belval benefited from conservation works and started to receive visitors in 2014. The future-oriented focus of the site is visible including in the methodologies for historical research and dissemination, which privilege digitization.[6]

However, the decision-making process behind the acclaimed success story of Belval's redevelopment faced scrutiny for adhering to business-oriented models. Scholars observing the decision-making process and the dynamics among the diverse stakeholders involved in the redevelopment contended that Belval could have benefited from more substantial local participation and more adaptive and flexible projects. Instead, the implementation of the master plan unfolded as a top-down approach, prioritizing particular categories of stakeholders. The promise of a mixed-use environment was arguably just partially fulfilled, with office spaces receiving preferential treatment over other intended uses (Becker et al., 2019).

Meanwhile, the process of promoting the city and its new image continued in 2022 in the context of European Capital of Culture, which was awarded to the Esch region as a whole, being shared among 19 municipalities in this border region shared by France and

Figure 23.4 Luxembourg Learning Centre/University Library Belval. (Photo: Jean Goedert)

Luxemburg. This created the opportunity for staging a wide range of creative events, during which the industrial past and its physical remains was reread and reinterpreted in artistic performances.[7]

Nord-Pas de Calais Mining Basin (France): UNESCO World Heritage List and Beyond

The Nord-Pas de Calais Mining Basin, located in the northernmost part of France, extends to the south of Lille, and encompasses a broad, 12-kilometer wide and 120-kilometer-long area from east to west. Over the course of three centuries, the coal mining industry, initiated in 1720, has significantly influenced the region's topography, leaving behind lasting relics such as winding towers, transportation infrastructure, coal pits, mining towns, but also slag heaps, a characteristic landscape resulting from the intensive mining activity. The peak of coal mining exploitation occurred in 1930, when the region produced 35 million tons of coal, constituting 64% of France's total coal production at that time. The availability of jobs in the area drew in a considerable influx of foreign laborers, with a notable presence of Polish, Moroccan, and Algerian workers. Although in the aftermath of the Second World War, the region played a key role in the postwar reconstruction efforts, soon the industrial sector began to experience a gradual decline due to diminishing demand and underlying structural challenges. By the 1980s, unemployment had become a widespread concern, with the last pit being closed in 1990 (Horn, n.d.).

The Nord-Pas de Calais region has been subject to comparative analysis with the Ruhr agglomeration, particularly because both areas underwent similar structural transformations from the 1960s to the 1990s and had to deal with significantly altered and polluted landscape and fragmented urban structures (Eck, Friedemann, and Lauschke, 2006; Lusso, 2013). However, it should be noted that the profiles of these two regions differed significantly. During the 1980s, the Nord-Pas de Calais Mining Basin had a population of 1.2 million, much less than Ruhr's 5.4 million inhabitants. Furthermore, the Nord-Pas de Calais Mining Basin consisted of smaller- and medium-sized towns, whereas the Ruhr is an urban agglomeration including cities of around 400,000–500,000 inhabitants (Eck, 2006, p. 11).

As described by Marion Fontaine (Fontaine, 2020, p. 190), the initial response to the closure of the mines was far from considering valorizing the mining history or preserving its physical remnants. Following the initial shock, mining communities sought individual strategies to adapt to the new circumstances. Preservation was largely absent from the official agendas; on the contrary, authorities thought about ways of eradicating the remnants of the past and promoting reindustrialization in the region. Above all, they felt compelled to erase the Nord's negative reputation through the construction of new housing, highways, and shopping malls.

Even in this context, various heritage-led interventions were undertaken to repurpose the sites. As early as the 1980s, several collieries were transformed into mining museums, complemented by tourist, cultural, and educational facilities. These endeavors served a dual objective: on the one hand, preserving the industrial heritage of the past and on the other hand, establishing contemporary community spaces representing key points for the revitalization of the area. Alongside the restored historical industrial structures, modern architecture emerged, while open areas were converted into public parks or venues for hosting events and open-air exhibitions (Langer, 2019, pp. 1–9).

These initiatives marked a clear turn in the state's strategy to counterbalance social and economic decline in the north by encouraging the development of service and cultural economy. Besides preserving industrial spaces, it also supported the creation of cultural institutions and organizations that would keep alive the collective memory of local mining communities through its embedment into artistic performances. In this way, the immaterial heritage of local communities became part of new cultures of display and representation (Rautenberg, 2012). Although the success of these initiatives has been contested, being criticized mostly for presenting overly positive narratives that disregarded, in fact, the miners' agency (Fontaine, 2020, p. 194), they contributed quite effectively to the broader process of creating a new image for the region. Given the current demographic changes, meaning an influx of inhabitants who have not experienced the glorified period of industrialization, nor its painful decline, it can be assumed that in the future, the strategies of creating and representing the identity of the region will become more flexible and integrative.

In parallel, the complex issue of land degradation was addressed through actions aimed at the ecological restoration of the area and the redevelopment of slag heaps. Public entities and private organizations collaborated in this endeavor, resulting in the establishment of pedestrian and biking paths and their integration into projects for sustainable tourism, combining natural, built, and cultural attractions (Lemoine, 2016).

Industrial Memory Landscapes in Urban Planning Processes

To coordinate the urban, socioeconomic, and ecological restructuring of the region, the Mission Bassin Minier was established in 2000 through the collaboration of state, regional, and local decision-makers. This initiative assembled a multidisciplinary team entrusted with mediating the relationships among various stakeholders, including local communities and the broader public (Patou, 2023). Under the coordination of Mission Bassin Minier, the complex heritage of the region was inscribed on the UNESCO World Heritage List in 2012 as a 'developing and vibrant cultural landscape.' This recognition acknowledged the Nord-Pas de Calais Mining Basin as a particularly well-maintained cultural landscape characterized by its enduring coherence and homogeneity, a testament to a remarkable industrial development extending over three centuries (ICOMOS, n.d.). The inventory carried out between 2000 and 2009 resulted in the nomination of 109 separate sites, including a large array of objects, from pits and coal transport infrastructure to mining villages with their cultural and educational facilities. Beyond the immediate goal of securing international recognition as an exceptional heritage site, this effort also led to the establishment of an institutional framework for future collaboration and fostered the adoption of conservation measures at the regional and municipal level. The outstanding universal value of the site was identified in the "very complete material testimonies of technical, industrial, architectural, urban and social orders," which implied, beyond the technical structures and characteristic landscapes, also a call for remembering the social and political developments in the area, including worker solidarity, the spread of trade unionism, and the dissemination of socialist ideas (ICOMOS, n.d.).[8]

Not least, new cultural infrastructure played a key role in the revitalization and rebranding of the major cities within the region. In 2004, Lille became the European Capital of Culture, marking a significant milestone in increasing the city's prestige and that of its metropolitan area, encompassing around three million residents (Paris and Baert, 2011). In 2012, the Louvres-Lens Museum opened in a newly designed, minimalist star architecture building designed by Japanese architecture studio SANAA (Cominelli and Jacquot, 2020). The initiative was part of a joint public-private strategy for urban regeneration; as expressed by Louvre officials, it represented a commitment to the social and economic revitalization of the region though high culture (Louvre, 2023). A piece of statement architecture, the building was meant to integrate well within the site, being surrounded by a park designed by French landscape architect Catherine Mosbach. Rather than as a mere preservation of the site, the park was conceived as a creative reinterpretation of the mining heritage through landscape design. Materials reclaimed from the mining site were repurposed in an open, performative process, which also allows them to be transformed with the passage of time (Santiago, 2015, p. 50).

In the context of the Louvre's arrival in Lens, another urban planning initiative was launched under the name Une Fabrique de la Ville. Led by urban planner Jean-Louis Subileau and architect and planner Guillaume Hebert and drawing inspiration from the IBA Emscher Park, Une Fabrique de la Ville supports local communities in developing a territorial strategy by providing technical expertise and fostering institutional cooperation among various stakeholders.[9]

Although producing a significant impact in transforming the region's image and economy, cultural initiatives are just one ingredient that cannot fully solve the complexity of political, social, and economic problems. Despite the intention to connect with grassroots initiatives, the mobilization to safeguard heritage seems to have been predominantly technocratic and institutional, leaving residents unsure about their role in the process (Mortelette, 2020). As elsewhere, popular discontent and feelings of abandonment are exploited by extremist parties, making the Nord-Pas de Calais one of the strongholds of Front National (Fontaine, 2020, p. 185). Moreover, in what concerns the heritage infrastructure, there is a need to address the issue of securing sustainable funding for its ongoing maintenance and conservation.

Conclusion

Each of the case studies discussed in this chapter demonstrates a different approach to the issue of creating heritage-sensitive post-industrial transformation. Certainly, local planning traditions, socioeconomic and political contexts, as well as the constellations of actors involved, with their agendas and interests, are context-specific and bear a significant weight on the solutions for transformation. However, despite individual shortcomings, each of these cases has been considered internationally as examples of good practice through the collaboration of public and private entities and the implementation of pioneering solutions. Furthermore, these regions have gained insights from each other's experiences. Both Belval and Nord-Pas de Calais have learned from the experience of dealing with derelict industrial buildings in the Ruhr region. In turn, the Ruhr region has drawn on the strategy of Nord-Pas de Calais in its attempt to make the industrial cultural landscape a UNESCO World Heritage Site. In all three case studies, more or less independent forms of organization and institutions have been established to initiate, coordinate, and mediate the process of implementing industrial heritage projects. The international exchange of experience – from technical know-how in dealing with the preservation of a blast furnace to innovative planning concepts – was an important condition for successful action in dealing with industrial heritage. Consequently, in all three case studies, the industrial past has been retained as a legible layer in the redevelopment of the location. The built and repurposed historical elements have become carriers of identity and, in combination with new uses and new architecture, have preserved local specificity. The legacy of the coal and steel industries, when incorporated into current urban development plans or contemporary architecture, enriches locations by infusing them with historical depth. This depth is particularly meaningful in an era characterized by increasing digitalization and homogenization, which tend to create uniformity.

As this chapter has shown, each context comes with its challenges and provides a new set of experiences but also a set of tools that can be tested in other settings. Building on the existing infrastructure and accumulated experience, the transformation of former industrial regions is still ongoing, being faced with new challenges, such as demographic and climate change, the stability of democratic structures, energy transition, and sustainability.

Notes

1 https://www.nrw-tourism.com/a-zollverein-coal-mine (Accessed: 12 May 2023).
2 *The Story behind Belval*. www.agora.lu/belval?/lang=en (Accessed: 11 November 2023).
3 *When Belval became an Integral Part of a UNESCO Biosphere Reserve*. https://www.agora.lu/belval-integral-part-of-a-unesco-biosphere-reserve/?lang=en (Accessed: 22 October 2023).
4 *Belval: Contemporary Urban Planning Promotes Heritage and Reinvents It*. https://www.agora.lu/belval-contemporary-urban-planning-promotes-heritage-and-reinvents-it/?lang=en (Accessed: 11 November 2023).
5 Fondation Bassin Minier. *Legacy of the Past. Industrial Tourism in Southern Luxembourg*. https://fondationbassinminier.lu/wp-content/uploads/2021/09/Spurensuche_3_EN_V2_RZ_20210903_Web.pdf (Accessed: 6 November 2023).
6 See, for example, the official webpage of the Luxembourg Centre for Contemporary and Digital History (C^2DH). https://www.c2dh.uni.lu/ (Accessed: 6 November 2023).

7 *ESCH2022, European Capital of Culture.* https://esch2022.lu/en/ (Accessed: 6 November 2023).

8 https://whc.unesco.org/en/list/1360/documents/ (Accessed: 9 December 2024)

9 *Association Euralens.* https://unefabriquedelaville.fr/2019/09/24/euralens-2/ (Accessed: 16 May 2024).

Reference List

Becker, Tom, Hesse, Markus and Leick, Anick. (2019). The 'Science City' in Belval – Planning a Large-Scale Urban Development Project in a Small Country. In Darchen, Sébastien and Searle, Glen (eds.) *Global Planning Innovations for Urban Sustainability.* London and New York: Routledge, Taylor & Francis Group, pp. 180–196.

Berger, Stefan (ed.). (2020). *Constructing Industrial Pasts: Heritage, Historical Culture, and Identity in Regions Undergoing Structural Economic Transformation.* New York: Berghahn.

Berger, Stefan and Wicke, Christian. (2017). Introduction. *The Public Historian*, 39(4), pp. 10–20. https://doi.org/10.1525/tph.2017.39.4.10.

Bole, David. (2021). 'What Is Industrial Culture Anyway?' Theoretical Framing of the Concept in Economic Geography. *Geography Compass*, 15(11), p. e12595. https://doi.org/10.1111/gec3.12595.

Breitbart, Myrna Margulies. (2013). *Creative Economies in Post-Industrial Cities: Manufacturing a (Different) Scene.* Re-Materialising Cultural Geography. London: Routledge, Taylor & Francis Group.

Buschmann, W. (n.d.). *Das Hochofenwerk Belval.* Rheinische Industriekultur. Luxemburg, Eisen- und Stahlwerk Belval. http://www.rheinische-industriekultur.de/objekte/xLuxemburg_Belval/Belval.html

Buschmann, W. (2006). Industrielle Flächendenkmäler. In Wiemer, Karl Peter (ed.) *Dem Erbe verpflichtet. 100 Jahre Kulturlandschaftspflege im Rheinland. Festschrift zum 100-jährigen Bestehen des Rheinischen Vereins für Denkmalpflege und Landschaftsschutz.* Münster: Rheinischer Verein für Denkmalpflege und Landschaftsschutz, pp. 207–244.

Cominelli, Francesca and Jacquot, Sébastien. (2020). Star Architecture Landing in UNESCO Sites: Local Frictions and Regulations. In Alaily-Mattar, Nadia, Ponzini, Davide and Thierstein, Alain (eds.) *About Star Architecture.* Cham: Springer International Publishing, pp. 247–266. https://doi.org/10.1007/978-3-030-23925-1_15.

Darchen, Sébastien and Searle, Glen (eds.). (2019). *Global Planning Innovations for Urban Sustainability.* London and New York: Routledge, Taylor & Francis Group.

Eck, Jean-François, Friedemann, Peter and Lauschke, Karl (eds.). (2006). *La Reconversion des Bassins Charbonniers: Une Comparaison Interrégionale entre La Ruhr et Le Nord/Pas-de-Calais; Actes du Colloque International Villeneuve-d'Ascq et Roubaix, 13–15 Novembre 2003.* Lille: Ed. Revue du Nord.

Edensor, Tim. (2014). *Industrial Ruins: Space, Aesthetics and Materiality.* London: Bloomsbury Publishing.

Eltges, M. (2008). Das Ruhrgebiet – eine regionalwirtschaftliche Analyse. *Informationen zur Raumentwicklung*, No. 9(10), pp. 535–548.

Fernández Agueda, Beatriz. (2014). Urban Restructuring in Former Industrial Cities: Urban Planning Strategies. *Territoire en movement. Revue de géographie et aménagement*, pp. 23–24. http://journals.openedition.org/tem/2527. https://doi.org/10.4000/tem.2527

Fontaine, Marion. (2020). Between Dream and Nightmare: Political Conventions of the Industrial Past in the North of France. In Berger, Stefan (ed.) *Constructing Industrial Pasts: Heritage, Historical Culture and Identity in Regions Undergoing Structural Economic Transformation.* New York: Berghahn, pp. 184–198.

Goedert, J., Lorang, A. and Paglianrini, L. (2023). *Paysages du Fer: Mutations du bassin luxembourgeois-lorrain de la minette du XVIIIe au XXIe siècle.* Luxembourg: Editions Klopp.

Gruehn, D. (2017). Regional Planning and Projects in the Ruhr Region (Germany). In Yokohari, Makoto, Murakami, Akinobu, Hara, Yuji and Tsuchiya, Kazuaki (eds.) *Sustainable Landscape Planning in Selected Urban Regions.* Science for Sustainable Societies. Tokyo: Springer Japan, pp. 215–225.

Harfst, Jörn, Wust, Andreas and Nadler, Robert. (2018). Conceptualizing Industrial Culture. *GeoScape*, 12(1), pp. 1–9. https://doi.org/10.2478/geosc-2018-0001.

Hemmings, Sarah and Kagel, Martin. (2010). Memory Gardens: Aesthetic Education and Political Emancipation in the 'Landschaftspark Duisburg-Nord'. *German Studies Review*, 33(2), pp. 243–261.

Hoppe, W. (2010). *Das Ruhrgebiet im Strukturwandel.* Diercke spezial. Braunschweig: Verlag Westermann.

Horn, C. (n.d.). *Das Bergbaurevier Nord-Pas-de-Calais – Frankreich.* http://urbanplanet.info/urbanism/das-bergbaurevier-nord-pas-de-calais/

ICOMOS. (n.d.). *UNESCO World Heritage Convention. Nord-Pas de Calais Mining Basin.* 2012 Advisory Body Evaluation (ICOMOS). https://whc.unesco.org/en/list/1360/documents/ (Accessed: 9 December 2024).

Jonas, M. (2014). The Dortmund Case – On the Enactment of an Urban Economic Imaginary. *International Journal of Urban and Regional Research*, 38, pp. 2123–2140.

Kiese, M. (2019). Strukturwandel 2.0: Das Ruhrgebiet auf dem Weg zur Wissensökonomie. *Standort. Zeitschrift für Angewandte Geografie*, 43(2), pp. 69–75.

Krehl, Angelika and Siedentop, S. (2019). Toward a Typology of Urban Centres and Subcenters – evidence from German City Regions. *Urban Geography*, 40(1), pp. 58–82. https://doi.org/10.1080/02723638.2018.1500245

Kunzmann, R. Klaus. (2002). Kultur, Wirtschaft und Raumentwicklung. *Informationen zur Raumentwicklung*, Heft 4/5, pp. 185–197.

Langer, Piotr. (2019). 'Post-Mining Reality' in Western Europe: Selected Collieries in Belgium and France Following Discontinuation of Coal Mining. *IOP Conference Series: Materials Science and Engineering*, 471, p. 112003. https://doi.org/10.1088/1757-899X/471/11/112003.

Leick, Annick, Hesse, Markus and Becker, Tom. (2020). From the 'Project within the Project' to the 'City within the City'? Governance and Management Problems in Large Urban Development Projects Using the Example of the Science City Belval, Luxembourg. *Raumforschung Und Raumordnung | Spatial Research and Planning*, 78(3), pp. 249–265. https://doi.org/10.2478/rara-2020-0009.

Lemoine, G. (2016). Brownfield Restoration as a Smart Economic Growth Option for Promoting Ecotourism, Biodiversity, and Leisure. In *Bioremediation and Bioeconomy*. Elsevier, pp. 361–388. https://doi.org/10.1016/B978-0-12-802830-8.00015-0.

Louvre. (2023). The Louvre-Lens. https://www.louvre.fr/en/the-louvre-in-france-and-around-the-world/the-louvre-lens (Accessed: 9 December 2024).

Lusso, Bruno. (2013). Patrimonialisation et greffes culturelles sur des friches issues de l'industrie minière. *EchoGéo*, 26. http://journals.openedition.org/echogeo/13645. https://doi.org/10.4000/echogeo.13645

Madgin, Rebecca. (2009). *Heritage, Culture and Conservation: Managing the Urban Renaissance.* Saarbrücken: VDM Verlag.

Margulies Breitbart, Myrna. (2013). *Creative Economies in Post-Industrial Cities: Manufacturing a (Different) Scene.* London: Routledge, Taylor & Francis Group.

Metropole RUHR Business. (2018). *Gewerbliches Flächenmanagement Ruhr, Phase IV, Zwischenbericht.*

Mortelette, Camille. (2020). La patrimonialisation de l'héritage minier dans le Nord-Pas-de-Calais: un outil efficace de réconciliation de la population locale avec son passé? *Les Cahiers de la recherche architecturale urbaine et paysagère*, (7), pp. 1–23. https://doi.org/10.4000/craup.3828

Paris, Didier and Baert, Thierry. (2011). Lille 2004 and the Role of Culture in the Regeneration of Lille Métropole. *Town Planning Review*, 82(1), pp. 29–44. https://doi.org/10.3828/tpr.2011.7.

Patou, Marie. (2023). Gros plan sur la Mission Bassin Minier Nord – Pas-de-Calais. *e-Phaïstos*, 11(2). http://journals.openedition.org/ephaistos/11540. https://doi.org/10.4000/ephaistos.11540

Păun Constantinescu, Ilinca, Dascălu, Dragoş and Sucală, Cristina. (2017). An Activist Perspective on Industrial Heritage in Petrila, a Romanian Mining City. *The Public Historian*, 39(4), pp. 114–141. https://doi.org/10.1525/tph.2017.39.4.114.

Polivka, Jan, Reicher, Christa and Zöpel, Christoph. (2017). Zukunftswege der Agglomeration Ruhr. In *Raumstrategien Ruhr 2035+. Konzepte zur Entwicklung der Agglomeration Ruhr*. Dortmund: Ketteler Verlag, pp. 227–261.

Rautenberg, Michel. (2012). Industrial Heritage, Regeneration of Cities and Public Policies in the 1990s: Elements of a French/British Comparison. *International Journal of Heritage Studies*, 18(5), pp. 513–525. https://doi.org/10.1080/13527258.2011.637945.

Reicher, C. et al. (2008). *International Building Exhibition Emscher Park. The projects 10 years later.* Essen: Klartext Verlag.

Reicher, C., Kunzmann, K., Polívka, J., Roost, F., Utku, Y. And Wegener, M. (2011). *Schichten einer Region – Kartenstücke zur räumlichen Struktur des Ruhrgebiets.* Berlin: Jovis.

RVR (Regionalverband Ruhr). (2017). *Regionalstatistik Ruhr: Hochschulen.*

Urban Transition Alliance. (2018). *InnovationCity Ruhr | Model City Bottrop A Blueprint for a Futureproof City – Case Study by WBCSD and ICM.* https://urbantransitions.org/wp-content/uploads/2017/01/InnovationCity-Ruhr_20181127.pdf (Accessed: 5 December 2018).

Vega Santiago, Zeltia. (2015). A Collection of Stories: Euralens Centralité and the Louvre-Lens Museum Park. *Journal of Landscape Architecture*, 10(2), pp. 44–57. https://doi.org/10.1080/18 626033.2015.1058571.

Wiseler, Alain. (n.d.). *Konversion des Hochofens Belval.* https://www.rheinische-industriekultur.com/seiten/objekte/orte/xLuxemburg/Objekte/-belval.html

Yokohari, Makoto, Murakami, Akinobu, Hara, Yuji and Tsuchiya, Kazuaki (eds.). (2017). *Sustainable Landscape Planning in Selected Urban Regions.* Science for Sustainable Societies. Tokyo: Springer Japan. https://doi.org/10.1007/978-4-431-56445-4.

24

MEMORIALIZATION OF INDUSTRIAL PASTS IN POST-SOCIALIST COUNTRIES

Juliane Tomann

Introduction

In early January 2023, several German newspapers reported that the east German region Lusatia was set to become the European Capital of Culture within the next 10 to 15 years (DPA, 2023; Metzner, 2023). At first glance, this might seem like a far-fetched claim made by regional politicians to help change the image of a deindustrializing area, which has been undergoing extensive economic restructuring and renaturation of its post open-cast lignite mining landscapes since the demise of the German Democratic Republic (GDR) in 1989. Yet Lusatia would fit the mold of other post-industrial places that have held the title – in the western part of Germany, Essen (together with the Ruhr region) became the European Capital of Culture in 2010; and the former industrial hotspot Chemnitz – also located in the post-socialist part of Eastern Germany – will follow suit and hold the European title in 2025. While the designation for Essen and the Ruhr region has further promoted the successful integration of its industrial past into present cultural developments and fostered its image as a renowned international blueprint for industrial heritage, Chemnitz plans to take a more subtle approach toward its long-standing industrial history and aims to reinterpret its historically successful entrepreneurial spirit by linking it with innovative perspectives on (industrial) work today (Stadt Chemnitz, 2019). In Lusatia's case, the newspapers quote politicians who refer to its "wonderful cultural landscape," shaped among other factors by its industrial past and evolving heritage sites. To be sure, holding the prestigious title would help to further advance the cultural landscape of the deindustrializing region. But how would the focus on cultural developments impact ways of dealing with the multiple legacies of lignite mining in the emerging heritage sites? Will the vestiges of an industrial past, which are closely related to the memory of the GDR and its socialist past, be critically addressed and put into historical context? Or will the former sites of industrial labor be turned into commercialized, aestheticized stages that function merely as a backdrop for entertainment and cultural events?

For now, the answers to these questions remain to be seen. However, the designation of former industrial hotspots like Chemnitz and (perhaps later on Lusatia) as European Capitals of Culture are indicative of the changing perception and meaning of the industrial past in Eastern Germany along with other post-socialist countries. This chapter aims to explain these

DOI: 10.4324/9781003308324-35

shifts in dealing with the industrial past in post-socialist countries; its goal is to investigate how industrial memories did or did not emerge, materialize, and change since 1989. To do so, it will first focus on the specifics and variations of the far-reaching transformation processes which followed the breakdown of the socialist systems during the 1990s as they have deeply impacted the emergence of industrial memories and heritage. These multiple transformations after 1989 created a climate of political change, economic decline, and social instability in which the material remains of closed-down industrial sites often fell into oblivion or were dismantled. The remnants of the industrial era were perceived as deeply intertwined with the just overcome and now "unwanted" socialist era; the inheritance of industrial pasts was thus seen as "toxic in both physical and social sense" (Mérai and Kulikov, 2021, p. 5). However, the recent developments in Chemnitz and Lusatia reveal that industrial pasts are being rediscovered not merely as a negative burden of the past but as a positive resource for (re)creating a sense of origin and tradition for the present and for looking toward the future. Most importantly socialist industrialization gets – at least in some cases – inscribed and integrated into *longue durée* regional narratives which emphasize a long-term industrial development (Handro, 2022).

In a second step, the chapter will focus on selected case studies to explain mnemonic practices, such as nostalgic recollections of industrial work, as well as material-based modes of dealing with industrial pasts. The chapter provides examples of revitalization or revalorization of post-industrial brownfield areas along with cases where the industrial era is musealized or integrated in the touristification of a place. These cases imply that dealing with the industrial past is characterized by more factors than the region's post-socialist trajectory. In some places, like Upper Silesia in Poland, the industrial past is perceived as difficult because industrialization is connected to the time when the region was part of Prussia; it can thus be considered a foreign legacy with all the difficult connotations attached. A closer look at these case studies further reveals that European initiatives have most recently become influential for industrial memory making in the region.

Furthermore, the chapter addresses the fact that processes of memorializing industrial pasts have not started from scratch after 1989 and outlines efforts to commemorate or memorialize industrialization and industrial work during the socialist period. Despite the general trend that industrial pasts fell into oblivion in the initial years of transformation, these initiatives and their outcomes impacted and influenced modes of remembering and representing industrial pasts after 1989.

Stretching from Albania to Estonia and from Eastern Germany to Russia, the post-socialist region covers a wide geographical area. Engaging with the development of the whole region exceeds the scope of this chapter. Despite the aforementioned overarching trajectories of transformation in the region, the political, economic, social, and cultural developments in its different countries varied to large extents. Thus, the memorialization of industrial pasts took different paths and shapes and was driven by distinct actors with diverse and sometimes ambivalent outcomes. Taking stock of these various phenomena and finding common denominators within this fragmented and heterogeneous field is thus a challenging endeavor. To provide an overview and point out similarities and differences within modes and practices of industrial memory making, the focus of this chapter will be limited to Central-Eastern Europe with some examples from Southeastern Europe. The chapter provides spotlights on exemplary cases stemming predominantly from the neighboring countries Poland, the Czech Republic, and Eastern Germany, with supplementary examples from Hungary and the Western Balkans. The selection of cases mirrors the state of research on industrial memory in this region which is at this point mainly focused on urban environments and less on suburban or agricultural settings. The chosen examples will occur in different parts of the chapter so that they create recurrent themes throughout the text.[1]

Complex Transformations

The end of the superpower rivalry of the Cold War and the breakdown of the Soviet Union spurred hopes for a more democratic future all over the former Eastern bloc. What started out as the celebrated and glorious overturning of an unwanted system with triumphant leaders coming from the West promising prosperity, liberty, and political freedom soon turned out to be a highly complex and ambiguous endeavor: while the initial years after 1989 might have been "a mixture of euphoria and heightened expectations," that original glory quickly became contested (Ghodsee and Orenstein, 2021, p. 2). Right-leaning politicians began to contest the origins of the newly established democracies and saw the break with the old system as too weak, advocating for more lustration; voices from the Left pointed out the damaging costs of economic restructuring for societies' social fabric (Borodziej, Holubec, and von Puttkamer, 2020; Hilmar, 2020). The introduction of economic reforms and the conversion from planned to market economy led to a significant recession, a substantial decline in production, and accelerating unemployment rates, accompanied by a concurrent collapse of the socialist welfare system. Most of the economies in the newly established democracies recovered by the end of the 1990s, but the economic reforms brought about a loss of social and economic security and purchasing power for the population (Ghodsee and Orenstein, 2021; Ther, 2010).

These snapshots provide just a small glimpse of what happened in the region in question in the aftermath of 1989, while the full picture was much more complex and diverse in different countries and subregions. Attempts to capture and describe this complexity were varied: the special case of the GDR in its reunification with the FRG brought about special terms like "Wende" (change) or "Beitritt" (accession) (Kollmorgen, 2010).[2] Some of the terms in use were infused with expectations and wished-for outcomes, like democratic transition and transformation period as well as post-socialism or post-communism to name just the most widespread variations (Kopeček and Wciślik, 2015). Initially used to describe the fall of the dictatorships in Latin America and in Southern Europe by political scientists during the late 1970s and 1980s, the term transition was applied to the region. It signaled advocation for a universalist approach to transferring established Western success models onto an anticipated tabula rasa found after the collapse of socialism – an approach with substantial normative charge and inherent bias. Highlighting the shortcomings of this universalist approach, the term transformation stresses the unexpected ambiguities and contradictions of the reform processes. The emerging paradigm of transformation emphasizes that the legacies of socialism have to be taken into account on the way to liberal democracy and market economy, acknowledging the embeddedness of local institutions and anticipating the possibility of reconfigurations, modifications, and readjustments to democracy and capitalism by local elites (Stykow, 2013; Hachmeister et al., 2023, p. 17).

From this perspective, the transformations in Central-Eastern and Southeastern Europe after 1989 were more compressed, multi-layered, and in the end "more chaotic" than comparable developments in other regions (Werftenkollektiv, 2022, p. 10). Removing dictatorships in Southern Europe in the 1970s had first and foremost a political dimension and was focused on introducing a democratic system (Portugal, Spain, Greece). Economic restructuring in response to the steel and coal crisis in Western Europe and West Germany was mostly focused on providing economic and, to some extent, social solutions to bolster its effects. In Central-Eastern and Southeastern Europe, these challenges had to be addressed simultaneously and the systemic change of the political system from dictatorship to liberal democracy was coupled with reforming and restructuring the economies (Offe, 1996; Kopeček and Wciślik, 2015). Transforming state-owned businesses meant finding new property models including practices of privatization, industrial reorganization, and a change from Fordism, which is mainly associated with industrial production, to post-Fordism subsequently causing large-scale deindustrialization (Pike, 2009, p. 54). In addition to this double "dilemma of simultaneity" (Offe, 1996, p. 35), in some cases nation-state building was at stake as in the aftermath of the breakup of the Czechoslovak Socialist Republic into two separate states in 1992. The transformations in the region were therefore not a belated structural change or a catch-up development related to Southern or Western Europe but – due to how deeply and broadly the changes occurred and affected society – a phenomenon of "its own quality" (Werftenkollektiv, 2022, p. 10).[3]

At this point, scholarly debates about how to understand the transformation period in Central-Eastern and Southeastern Europe have mostly been influenced by political scientists, sociologists, and anthropologists. A critical historical account of the transformation is still in its infancy, and the debate about how to historicize the period after 1989 is "fragmentary" (Filipkowski and Gulińska-Jurgiel, 2021). One of the arguments put forward by historians is that the transformation had a fundamentally neoliberal character. Philipp Ther maintains that the "neoliberal transformation" was supposed to introduce radical reforms to unleash and set free the imagined power of free markets while the idea of freedom was focused predominantly on the economy, which ultimately meant subordinating and subjecting the political sphere to economic thinking (Ther, 2022, p. 21). For neoliberal thinkers like Milton Friedman and other proponents of the Chicago School, the former socialist countries provided ideal testing grounds for introducing radical economic reforms which were too risky and complicated to introduce elsewhere (Ther, 2022, p. 21). Scholars describe the region as a "laboratory" (Kopeček and Wciślik, 2015, p. 12; Wawrzyniak and Pehe, 2023, p. 1) for testing and applying neoliberal practices and implementing measures in the spirit of the Washington Consensus. Based on the Washington Consensus, influential international organizations such as the International Monetary Fund and the World Bank in collaboration with international advisors and local experts implemented a pattern for reforming the socialist economies and linking them with the global market. This pattern was based on the idea that foreign aid and the reduction of international debt would be granted but tied to the introduction of fiscal discipline, measures for reducing inflation, a liberalization of trade, and the opening of domestic markets to foreign goods (Wawrzyniak and Pehe, 2023, p. 3). Wawrzyniak and Pehe conclude that "mass privatization of state-owned-enterprises sped up by the liberalization of inward foreign direct investment, was among the defining processes of the 1990s." As a result, the privatization of state-owned enterprises led to "abrupt deindustrialization, decomposition and the symbolic devaluation of the working class" (Wawrzyniak and Pehe, 2023, p. 3). In line with other scholars, Wawrzyniak and Pehe maintain that economic restructuring subsequently turned into a "normative project with a 'liberal pedagogy' that aimed to create ideal liberal subjects . . . and an 'entrepreneurial' or 'neoliberal' self" (Wawrzyniak and Pehe, 2023, p. 3).

Taking into account the characteristics of the transition helps in understanding why the socialist era and its industrial remains – which were strongly associated with it – were understood as an "unwanted past" in the aftermath of 1989 (Czepczyński and Soovāli-Sepping,

The Routledge Handbook of Deindustrialization Studies

2015; Tursie, 2015; Balockaite, 2012). As a consequence, the industrial past only gradually began to be integrated into general tendencies in memorialization after 1989, which were initially deeply concerned with regained national independence and identities, the reconstruction of regional identities, and aspects of dissonant heritage, understood as layers of the past which had been silenced in socialist times (Murzyn, 2008).

A Matter of Timing: Preservation of Industrial Sites Before 1989

The preservation of industrial pasts and forms of industrial heritage as a response to deindustrialization from the 1970s onward was not limited to Western Europe. Scholars recently claim that a "parallel development of the notion of industrial heritage in socialist and nonsocialist countries" can be observed (Geering and Vickers, 2021, p. 7; Lehmann, 2021, p. 195). It is thus important to take into account efforts to preserve and commemorate industrial pasts before 1989 to understand their effects and influence on the post-1989 situation.

The example of the Czech city of Ostrava, located at the Czech-Polish border, illustrates early efforts to preserve sites of industrial production and the everyday lifeworld of its workers. The larger Ostrava-Karviná region has a long history as a mining district, and the city of Ostrava became an important industrial center thanks to the combination of black coal and heavy industry (Jordánová, 2016, p. 3; Pokludová, 2022). Coal deposits were discovered in the second half of the eighteenth century, and ironworks were founded in the neighboring village of Vítkovice in 1828 when the region belonged to the Habsburg empire. The economic development of the city further relied on its connection to the Vienna-Cracow railway which opened in 1847 (Sucháček, 2019). Following the economic takeoff, Ostrava urbanized quickly and developed into a multi-ethnic and multi-confessional place as well as a cultural and political center for the region (Pokludová, 2022). In the aftermath of the Second World War, the city was turned into the "steel heart of Czechoslovakia." Within the planned economy, the focus was shifted more exclusively toward heavy industry, chemical industry, and machinery (Pokludová and Popelka, 2022, pp. 161, 168).

Attempts to pay tribute to the importance of the industrial development of the region and to memorialize it date back to the beginning of the twentieth century, when for instance in 1902 the mayor of the city planned an industrial and trade museum, which was supposed to capture the mining and industrial development of the town and the region for the future. The outbreak of the First World War and the political situation of the interwar years put an end to this initiative as well as to other attempts to collect remnants of industrial production and mining lifeworlds (Pokludová and Popelka, 2022, p. 170). When in the 1960s some of the technologically outdated mines began to close down, Czechoslovak preservation experts asserted the significance of their value for the industrial development of the region and wanted to preserve them. However, their efforts to put them under heritage protection were not successful, and the symbols of the beginning of industrialization vanished from the city center of Ostrava (Pokludová and Popelka 2022, p. 171). In the late 1980s, mining engineers successfully demanded the protection of the history of mining activities in the city. A contract between the National Committee of the City of Ostrava and the general directorate of the Ostrava-Karviná mines from September 2, 1988, paved the way to opening the Mining Museum on Ostrava's oldest mining site "Anselm" in 1993, which is now called "Landek Park" (Pokludová and Popelka, 2022, pp. 171f.). It is advertised today as the "largest mining museum" in the Czech Republic and a place where visitors can discover the "secrets of authentic mining environment" in "extensive underground paths" (Dolní Vítkovice, n.d.).

Industrial Pasts in Post-Socialist Countries

Similar efforts to preserve traces of early industrialization were made in the Hungarian Borsod Industrial Area, located in the Northeast of the country near the Slovakian border. Between 1952 and 1983, several museums opened, and preservation projects were realized which presented the history of iron and steel works as well as remnants of ore and mineral mining (Németh, 2018, p. 103). Györgyi Németh points out that most of these projects had been designed to support the implementation of a communist ideology by demonstrating evidence for technological development and progress in a region where accelerated industrialization took place following the communist takeover in 1948 (Németh, 2018, p. 105). Despite this ideological background, some of the preserved objects became "cherished monument[s]" where iron workers expressed their professional and regional identity during the socialist era (Németh, 2018, p. 105). In the aftermath of 1989 and the onset of a fundamental deindustrialization, remnants of the industrial past of the region seem to have turned into a burden: the long-standing coal mining and iron production tradition was replaced by a focus on medieval history, and industrial heritage vanished from the regional landscape (Németh, 2018, p. 107).

A closer look at preservation strategies in the German Democratic Republic (GDR) provides further insightful examples in which mining and industrial production sites had been preserved for ideological reasons under a socialist regime before 1989. The preservation of technical monuments in the GDR was part of the politics of history of the leading socialist party SED and can be traced back to the 1950s. A significant change occurred in the 1970s: In 1974, amendments to the constitution of the GDR were made, including the abandonment of the idea of a German reunification, which might lead to the principle of a coexistence of two German states. This new status quo had significant impacts on the politics of history. "Progressive" traditions as well as historical monuments were supposed to highlight the independent historical development of the German Democratic Republic, yielding the creation of a distinct socialist identity for its citizens (Campbell, 2005, p. 3). In this redefined ideological context, the preservation of historical monuments took on a crucial role: it had to support the development of a sense of belonging for GDR citizens which was rooted in the achievements of the socialist state and the role of the working-class movement (Kruner, 2020, p. 299; Handro, 2022).

When less efficient and outdated industrial complexes were closed, protectionists were able to remodel some into educational sites, aiming to improve the technological understanding of the GDR citizens (Kruner, 2020, p. 303; Lehmann, 2021, p. 196). The Mining Museum in Oelsnitz/Ore Mountains is one of the examples of these developments: due to a decrease in coal resources, the GDR government decided to shut down the coal mining site in 1967, effective in 1976. By 1986, the most iconic aboveground facilities were turned into a mining museum, which was supposed to legitimize a Marxist theory of history by materially representing the history of productive forces and by paying tribute to the activities of the working class and the industry's impact on the landscape (Kruner, 2020, p. 306f; Lehmann, 2021, p. 205). The museum is still open today and is currently being renovated and restructured (Bergbaumuseum Oelsnitz, 2023).

While this and the other aforementioned examples from the museum sector signal a continuity of preservation efforts before and after 1989, it should be noted that especially in the GDR, most preservation efforts were carried out as collaborations between state institutions and mass cultural organizations. Voluntary work on the conservation of industrial monuments was coordinated by the Gesellschaft für Denkmalpflege (Association for Preservation) as a part of the Kulturbund der DDR (Cultural Association of the GDR), the mass cultural organization of the GDR. The involvement of a wide range of volunteers has been described as successful and efficient but also difficult, as the agendas of the scientific institutions of monument preservation and the volunteers on site often differed (Lehmann, 2021, p. 207). With the dissolution of the Kulturbund over the course of German reunification in early 1990, the activities and voluntary work on the conservation of industrial monuments that it oversaw came to an end.

Intangible and Tangible Heritage of Industrial Pasts in the Aftermath of 1989

From Neglect to Nostalgia: Memories of Socialist Industrial Work

Nostalgia and its various regional adaptations like "Ostalgie" in East Germany are a vivid social and cultural phenomenon, which is often linked to memories of socialist industrial labor within small working groups or brigades. Nostalgia is a complex and multi-layered term that covers a range of different meanings (Smith and Campbell, 2017). Its first known use was by Swiss medical student Johannes Hofer in his 1688 dissertation. He used the term to describe "a feeling of loss and longing stemming from a spatial detachment, not unlike homesickness, but more profound and with severe symptoms" (Boele, Noordenbos, and Robbe, 2019, p. 3). Today, the word is mostly used in connection with past times (and to a lesser extent to spaces) and is no longer a pathological symptom. Instead, it's understood as an ontological condition that is strongly connected to "temporal longing and estrangement" (Stătică, 2021, p. 651), a feeling of loss in the present responding to something that is 'missing' from the past. While the present is perceived as insufficient by the nostalgic individual for a variety of reasons – be it for a missing sense of identity, community, agency, or a longing for certain objects or relationships – the past is invoked in a positive way (Tannock, 1995, p. 454; Wawrzyniak, 2021).

In the political and social climate of the multiple layers of transformation from socialism toward liberal democracy and a capitalist economy in Central-Eastern and Southeastern Europe, nostalgia's inherent positive approach toward the socialist past is often met with a critical attitude labeling the nostalgic individuals' feelings as "regressive or delusional" (Tannock, 1995, p. 455). Post-socialist nostalgia has thus become a buzzword to describe as well as criticize the "irrational" attitudes of those who feel left behind, are lost in the processes of transformations, and not capable of coping with the severe ongoing social and economic changes (Velikonja, 2009; Petrović, 2014, p. 92). David A. Kideckel has described the nostalgia of former miners after the termination of coal mining in the Romanian Jiu Valley as a form of "angry nostalgia" for the past, which he defines as counterproductive in the process of developing new or alternative outlooks for the region (Kideckel, 2020, p. 229). The discourse on nostalgia is, however, not limited to the region under scrutiny but discussed in the wider field of deindustrialization studies. Jefferson Cowie and Joseph Heathcott coined the term "smokestack nostalgia" and used it to warn of the dangers of sentimentalizing, uncritical attitudes toward industrial pasts (Cowie and Heathcott, 2003; Jaramillo and Tomann, 2021).

The segment of nostalgia for industrial work during socialism articulated by former industrial workers seems to be especially controversial as it undermines the "triumphalist discourses" of overcoming the socialist economic system and the subsequent mainstream neoliberal narratives (Petrović, 2017, p. 15). A number of studies have engaged with the phenomenon of industrial (and post-socialist) nostalgia in the region, focusing on nostalgia as a mnemonic practice, which is not limited to glorifying a lost past. Instead, these analyses rest on the conviction that nostalgia reveals the shortcomings and pitfalls of the political, economic, and social transformations that former workers face in the present. How is socialist industrial work remembered in the context of the "neoliberal" present – a present characterized by industrial reorganization including privatization and downsizing of industries which has left former industrial workplaces in deterioration, workers laid-off, and in some regions a shrinking standard of security in health care and living standards?

Analyzing the memories of workers from a cable factory in Serbia that was (due to its size and debt) not immediately privatized after socialism disintegrated, Tanja Petrović notices that the employees remember working under socialism in a nostalgic and positive way as a time of modernization that the company brought to the formerly agricultural region. Furthermore, they associate industrial work during the Yugoslav period with being treated with dignity and respect and emphasize the benefits connected to the socialist organization of work, such as high salaries, solid health insurance, and the possibility of going on summer holidays. The nostalgic and positive view of the past is rooted in the sharp contrast they experience in the present, characterized by feelings of "personal degradation and humiliation," a situation where the workers who formerly perceived themselves as "actors of modernization" feel "deprived of social agency" (Petrović, 2017, p. 21). Petrović interprets the nostalgic industrial labor memory of the workers not as a passive lament for better times but as "affective, passionate, sensory," not only as a critique of the present but as a "mobilizing, legitimizing, and even an emancipatory" element with the potential to intervene in the present (Petrović, p. 26; Todorova, 2014, p. 7; Berger, 2020, p. 2). With its affective potential for the present, the bottom-up memory of industrial work from the Yugoslav period contradicts the emergence of industrial heritage with its top-down processes of aestheticization, musealization, and – as Petrović argues – pacification and fossilization of industrial pasts. Thus, nostalgic narratives also function as a reminder that socialist industrialization and modernization are integral parts of European contemporary history and challenge normative views on post-socialist Europe (Petrović, 2017, p. 25; Petrović, 2014, p. 97).

The emancipatory potential of nostalgia to challenge and counter the dominant discourses of the present is stressed by other scholars, too (Boele, Noordenbos, and Robbe, 2019, p. 5; "progressive nostalgia" Smith and Campbell, 2017, p. 624; Todorova, 2010; "reflective nostalgia" Boym, 2001). For the Polish case, Joanna Wawrzyniak emphasizes the critical potential of nostalgic recollections of socialist industrial workers because of their inherent potential to show "what went wrong with transformation" and enrich the discourse about the ambiguities of both the past and the present (Wawrzyniak, 2021, p. 89). The findings of a large-scale oral history project conducted with employees from several big firms located throughout the country between 2010 and 2018 revealed two main narrative strands on how the economic transition after 1989 is remembered. The first narrative focused on the future, discrediting the socialist economic system and stressing the necessity to reorganize production and work, a process which the interviewees described as inevitable, without alternative. The study found that this viewpoint tended to be expressed by higher-ranking or better-qualified employees like managers, executives, or engineers and echoes the mainstream neoliberal narratives of the 1990s. The second narrative was classified as past-related and contained nostalgic expressions for elements of work in the socialist era, such as a feeling of loss regarding forms of sociability, community values like mutual help and group solidarity, and class agency (Wawrzyniak, 2021, p. 85; also Todorova, 2010, p. 7).

The study argues in the same vein as Frances Pine, who found that a positive recollection of the socialist past does not imply negating its bad elements like "corruption, shortages, queuing and intrusions of the state" but choosing to emphasize other aspects like "economic security, full employment, universal healthcare and education" (quoted in Todorova, 2010, p. 5). Wawrzyniak notes, however, that the critical and reflective potential of those nostalgic recollections of industrial work in socialist times has not been able to develop its impact to defend past values that remain important for the present. In the Polish case, the post-socialist industrial nostalgic narratives were suppressed by two factors: the neoliberal public discourse of the 1990s which "injected into society a powerful, dominant narrative that was not supportive of any positive memories of socialist industrialism" (Wawrzyniak, 2021, p. 89). Second, the politics-driven heritage sector is not supportive of nostalgic recollections of socialist work either. Instead, it condemns positive memories of everyday socialist life, emphasizing the role of the anti-socialist opposition and Solidarity movement's role in the democratization of the country and pushing aside the importance of everyday life. In conclusion, the nostalgic memories under scrutiny remain personal recollections of industrial socialism rather than contributing to a critical or reflective potential (Wawrzyniak, 2021, p. 92).

From Brownfields to Cultural Centers? Conversion of Derelict Industrial Areas

As a result of accelerated deindustrialization after 1989, defunct industrial and related subsidiary structures either fell into dereliction or have become subject to conversion (Pike, 2009, p. 54; Jigoria-Oprea and Popa, 2017, p. 2724). In places where structural and functional processes of conversion, regeneration, reuse, or redevelopment have been delayed or unsuccessful, abandoned former industrial sites turned into brownfields.[4] Due to the complexity accompanying brownfield areas involving economic, political, social, environmental, and legal aspects, attempts to convert them are difficult and brownfields remain a challenging phenomenon in most post-socialist states (Martinat et al., 2016; Jigoria-Oprea and Popa, 2017, p. 2724). Case studies on Pančevo (Serbia), Reșița, and Lugoj (Romania) illustrate the problems of urban restructuring processes which might lead to the formation of urban industrial ruins (Jigoria-Oprea and Popa, 2017; Jucu and Voiculescu, 2020). How such "new-ruins" impact processes of memorialization of industrial pasts and what practices of (informal) use evolve around these structures is a topic for future, more in-depth research (Kisiel, 2021, p. 21).

The region also features important sites where the conversion of brownfields led to the emergence of new industrial heritage sites. One of the most recent examples is the Lower Area of Vítkovice, a part of the municipality of Ostrava in the Czech Republic. The Vítkovice Steelworks were heavily developed as a part of the government's focus on heavy industries as a driver of national economic stability as well as the basis for weapon production in the Soviet Bloc (Pokludova, 2022). Up until 1989, facilities and factories in Ostrava and its vicinity mined 86% of Czechoslovak coal and provided 82% of coke production as well as 70% of steel production (Sucháček, 2019).

However, symptoms of economic stagnation were already palpable in the Vítkovice Steelworks in the 1980s, and attempts to stabilize and optimize coal mining and production only delayed its decline (Pokludova, 2022). After 1989, the enterprise was privatized, and the production of coal and steel was mostly closed down in 1998. The termination of iron smelting and the coking plant turned the area into the largest brownfield in Ostrava, eventually

Industrial Pasts in Post-Socialist Countries

covering more than 180 hectares (Jordánová, 2016, p. 5).[5] Due to the close proximity of the steelworks to Ostrava's city center, the question of how to deal with the huge area was pressing, yet the issue was discussed ambiguously. The Vítkovice Company, as the owner of a still functioning part of the complex, considered its derelict part a ruin while preservationists advocated for its historical values (Hurníková, 2017, pp. 44f., 52). Attempts to preserve elements of the site as cultural heritage had been in place since 1993, but it wasn't until 2002 that the complex was listed as a national cultural heritage site for its representation of the complete technological flow from the extraction of coal to coke and ending with steel (Sucháček, 2019, p. 10). Several objects have been preserved and adapted in use: In 2012, the original historical energy distribution station was converted into an interactive museum focused on technology ("Small World of Technology"). It was accompanied by a newly built facility ("The Big World of Technology") with further exhibitions on civilization and nature. Furthermore, the former gas container ("Gong") was preserved and rebuilt into a large multifunctional congress center with gallery spaces. Finally, in 2015, the blast furnace No. 1 was turned into a new landmark ("Bolt Tower") by adding a superstructure to its top which serves as an elevated viewpoint (Hurníková, 2017, p. 33).

Today, Lower Vítkovice is considered a successful culturally led regeneration project and the third most visited tourist attraction in the Czech Republic (Sucháček, 2019, p. 12). The project ran in different stages starting in 2006 and transformed the former industrial site into a cultural, educational, and recreational facility, hosting music festivals, scientific symposia, and theatre performances while the industrial character of the site and its buildings is still intact, incorporating the past into the present use (Jordánová, 2016, p. 6). Yet the successful project reveals the more general tensions involved in converting and reusing industrial areas, namely the tension between the need to preserve the rawness of the hard physical work that characterizes the site's past and the adaptations necessary to contextualize, narrate, or explain its past to the public at the risk of sanitizing and wiping out its integral parts (Jordánová, 2016, p. 6).

The conversion of Lower Vítkovice partly overlaps with Ostrava's application process for the title European Capital of Culture, which started in 2009. Ostrava did not win the title, but the two-year preparation process contributed to the development of various projects connected to rethinking the city's identity (Duží and Jakubínský, 2013, p. 61). Furthermore, scholars argue that the success of the project is linked to the dedicated engagement of the private owner who founded an NGO, which makes it possible to draw on private-public partnerships as well as EU funds: "The owner of Vítkovice has a strong reputation, and his life is connected with Ostrava city" (Duží and Jakubínský, 2013, p. 63).

Around 100 kilometers north of Ostrava, the site of a former coal mine in the Polish city of Katowice underwent a similar conversion process to Lower Vítkovice, though its functional adaptation and redevelopment follows a slightly different pattern. Katowice and the agglomeration including Bytom, Gliwice, and Zabrze in the Polish voivodeship Silesia have a comparably long and intense history of coal mining and (heavy) industrial production to Ostrava. Situated on the eastern fringe of Prussia, Katowice developed especially rapidly and implemented a specific urban and architectural development plan after town rights were granted in 1856. It became part of the Second Polish Republic in the aftermath of the First World War in 1922, which promoted the city's integration and further development due to its economic value but also because of its vicinity to the newly drawn German-Polish border.

After the Second World War, Katowice became the backbone of heavy industry and coal mining in the socialist Polish People's Republic and faced similar challenges of restructuring, privatization, and downsizing to other industrial centers after 1989. Despite this general trend, Katowice managed the transition to market economy comparably well, for instance, by establishing a special economic zone and successfully attracting new international investors. Economic restructuring was bolstered by urban recreation plans and by attempts to reinvent the city's image, shifting it from a dark and gray industrial place to a sustainable, future-oriented one (Tomann, 2017). The city's industrial past was thus not perceived as an asset in this process during the first years of economic reconstruction, though this attitude has changed since the turn of the millennium (Murzyn-Kupisz and Gwosdz, 2011, p. 123). The construction of the biggest shopping center in the region (Silesia City Center), which opened in 2005, is a case in point. The retail area is situated on a former mine where most of the remnants of mining activities were demolished, but some traces of the past were kept: the engine house, a boiler house, and the 30-meter-high tower of the former "Jerzy" mine were integrated into the commercial retail landscape (Murzyn-Kupisz and Gwosdz, 2011, p. 123). The website of the shopping mall honors the history of its location in a detailed way: it includes a range of archival images and emphasizes that the shopping center is the first revitalization project on a former mining area in the region and is dedicated to "promot[ing] the Silesian culture and traditions" (Silesia City Center, n.d.).

These attempts to salvage references to the industrial past were, however, not primarily aimed at the creation of industrial heritage but occurred rather as the side product of a commodified approach to the past. While the shopping center is located on the fringes of the city, another defunct coal mine in the very center of Katowice underwent functional and structural conversion, too. Designed to fill the urban void in the heart of the city center, the Katowice "strefa kultury" ("Culture Zone") was by far the largest regeneration project financed by public funds in a post-industrial setting in Poland and aimed at brownfield regeneration via cultural flagship projects (Sobala-Gwosdz and Gwosdz, 2017, p. 28). The Culture Zone emerged on the site of the former mine "Katowice," which was closed down in 1999 and covered approximately 20 hectares in the northern part of the city center in close vicinity to Katowice's urban and visual landmark "Spodek" ("The Saucer," a multipurpose sports and entertainment hall with its typical bend roof concrete construction from the socialist period). The core objects of the Culture Zone were planned and realized between 1999 and 2015, preceding processes of clarification of landownership and linking the area to the existing infrastructure. The project consists of three main flagship projects which are supposed to bring education, high culture, exhibition, and recreational space to the city center: the relocation of the Silesian Museum, a new headquarters for the National Polish Radio Symphony Orchestra (NOSPR), and the International Congress Centre (MCK), which is the most recent element of the project and was finished in 2015. The award-winning architectural project of the Silesian Museum combines newly erected facilities with the preservation of existing nineteenth- and twentieth-century mining structures. Its main exhibition halls are located underground – a facet that can be interpreted as "hidden architecture" (Kiciński, 2011 in Sobala-Gwosdz and Gwosdz, 2017, p. 31) or as a symbolic reference to the former use of the site as a coal mine (Tomann, 2016). The headquarters of the Symphony Orchestra is newly constructed, yet its elevation with red brick and red-painted window niches contains references to the local miner communities' traditions. The International Congress Center also connects to coal mining heritage with its black facades and a "black garden" on its south side (Sobala-Gwosdz and Gwosdz, 2017, p. 33). The implementation of these flagship cultural projects has changed the urban structure of Katowice's city center to a large extent, increasing the value and attractiveness of the whole area, which results in perceivable "direct and indirect economic and social effects" for the area (Sobala-Gwosdz and Gwosdz, 2017, p. 37). Critics of the project point out that it works as a "monofunctional 'festive space'" that forms an enclave within the city center and lacks a fluid connection to the existing urban structure (Sobala-Gwosdz and Gwosdz, 2017, p. 37).

The Hungarian Borsod Industrial Area has a similarly long and intense coal mining and iron making history to the examples from Poland and the Czech Republic, mentioned earlier. The area has seen numerous attempts to reuse derelict mining and production facilities during socialist times (see section "A Matter of Timing"). Yet in the aftermath of 1989, industrial sites have been left in decay with only a small number of production facilities being reused or converted. Györgyi Németh argues that the flagship city of accelerated socialist industrialization in the region, Miskolc, has recently tried to replace and renew its image as a steel city by putting its medieval past at the center of its attempts at rebranding itself. The restored medieval castle Diósgyőr was turned into a key touristic site that is supposed to function as "a proud symbol of the whole city" while its industrial past seems to be perceived as a burden and evokes negative connotations. The remains of heavy industry are "scarcely considered to be valuable industrial heritage." Despite small groups of actors who try to invent new cultural formats to reuse former production sites, the city of Miskolc has not integrated former industrial sites into its latest urban development plans (Németh, 2018, pp. 106f.).

Between Renaturation and Revitalization: Post-Industrial Landscapes

As in other regions, brownfields are not an exclusively urban issue for CEE and SEE. They also occur as rural post-industrial spaces, for instance, in the aftermath of extensive agricultural exploitation or as the outcome of open pit mining of coal or ores. After the industrial activities have ended, the abandoned post-industrial rural places often undergo spontaneous processes of natural and vegetative transformation resulting in new "industrial nature" or "new wilderness" (Cilek, 2002 and Lipsky, 2011 cited in Kolejka et al., 2017, p. 224). One example of the emergence of post-industrial landscapes was described by Kolejka et al. for the Austrian-Czech border region (Kolejka et al., 2017). Another peculiar example can be found in the Lusatia region in East Germany in the former GDR.

After 1949, Lusatia had been turned into the industrial powerhouse of the GDR by extensive lignite mining, its most visible image being the enormous, model-socialist lignite processing plant "Kombinat Schwarze Pumpe" (combine black pump). After the German reunification, 80% of its production sites had been declared inefficient and closed down (Barndt, 2010, p. 283). To mitigate the consequences of the deindustrialization that followed, large-scale landscape projects and local development programs were implemented, one of them being the Internationale Bauausstellung (International Architecture Exhibition, IBA) "Fürst Pückler Land." Relating to the model project IBA "Emscher Park" (1989–1999), which had a significant impact on the post-industrial transformation of the West German Ruhr Region, the program was supposed to convert the devastated Lusatian post-mining landscape. While in the Emscher area a large park was erected, in Lusatia, among other projects, nine gigantic holes left by lignite mining were flooded, which led to the subsequent production of a vast lake district between 2000 and 2010. As the creation of this partly man-made, partly naturally evolving new lake district and the emergence of new recreational leisure spaces was planned to take years, the IBA program also featured temporary exhibitions about the cultural and industrial history of the region. Implemented to help stimulate discussions about the regional and cultural identity of deindustrializing Lusatia, the exhibitions were aimed at providing space to navigate and negotiate the temporality of "instant rupture" and "loss, shock, and change" that occurred in the aftermath of the demise of the GDR and the subsequent deindustrialization of the region (Barndt, 2010, p. 283). A similar approach to revitalizing a large former lignite mining district was taken in the southern area of Leipzig and resulted in the creation of the so-called "Leipziger Neuseenland" (New Lake District) as a recreational space and tourist destination between 1999 and 2006 (Pérez-Sindín, 2021). Such large-scale revitalization and landscape transformation projects are discussed from a variety of angles, including their positive impacts on the economic and socio-structural development of the area, the post-closure environmental hazards they bring with them, and questions of green gentrification (Pérez-Sindín, 2021). Further, such landscape transformation projects pose questions regarding processes of memorialization of industrial pasts: How can the tension between the past and the creation of a new and livable environment with the inherent simultaneous extensive erasure and submergence of any traces of its former use be resolved?

IBA leadership in Lusatia claimed that the "visible artificiality of the lakes will bear witness to the region's industrial past" (quote in Barndt, 2010, p. 283). Yet with the transforming landscape which used to be related predominantly to labor and is now turned into recreational spaces, "the inhabitants of Lusatia – and, by extension, interested tourists – are asked to take leave from a past and an identity bound to the labor of mining" (Barndt, 2010). In the future, a denser net of cultural institutions aimed at preserving and interpreting the history of the region, like the visitor center of the "Lausitzer Seenland" (Lusatia Lake District), might help to counterbalance this tension.

Exhibiting the Industrial Past

The conversion of brownfields is often connected to the construction of exhibition spaces or museums, as exemplified in the case of Katowice. With the reopening of the Silesian Museum on the premises of a former coal mine, a permanent exhibition was installed displaying an extensive history of Upper Silesia for the first time in Poland. Thus, despite its authentic premises, the museum is not an "industrial" one solely devoted to portraying the industrial past of the region. Rather its objective is to illustrate how the "unique identity of the region" developed, with industrialization being depicted as one element in this genesis (exhibition text quoted in Tomann, 2016). The extremely detailed display testifies to the region's search for its own identity, not only in a post-industrial and post-socialist setting but especially as a process of coming to terms with its history as a border region deeply influenced by Germans, Poles, and the local Upper Silesian population including national antagonisms and religious diversity. Initial plans to highlight the industrialization of the region as its pivotal turning point illustrated by a life-sized model of a steam engine at the beginning of the exhibition were toppled, the museum director fired, and the exhibition concept fundamentally changed in 2013. The accompanying public and political debate culminated in the question of whether an emphasis on industrialization would undermine the region's framing as a Polish one and open the opportunity for a pro-German interpretation of the Upper Silesian past (Tomann, 2016; 2017). Despite these amendments, the museum remained a bone of contestation and the right wing PiS government replaced its director again in 2021 (Wawrzyniak, 2021, pp. 90f.; Jedlecki, 2021).

The Europejskie Centrum Solidarności (European Solidarity Centre), which was established on the site of the former Gdańsk Shipyard in northern Poland in 2014, is another example that illustrates the difficulties of memorializing the history of industrial lifeworlds. The newly erected facility is situated right next to Gate Nr. 2, the site where Lech Wałęsa led striking workers in August 1980, a successful protest causing the establishment of the first independent trade union in socialist Eastern Europe (Peters, 2015). The site focuses on the history of the Solidarity trade union and highlights Poland's achievements in its national struggle for liberation in 1989, meaning that a critical reflection of the industrial past, especially on the socialist industrial lifeworlds of the site, remains in the background.

While these examples are related to heavy industry, the Polish city of Łódź's main industrial sector relied on light and textile production. The city's history is deeply intertwined with industrialization in this sector as well as international trade in the nineteenth and twentieth centuries, and it maintained its image as a workers' city during state socialism. As other post-socialist places, it has been trying to reshape its image and rebuild its identity after 1989 by reestablishing connections with European history while simultaneously obscuring and snipping out the socialist past (Young and Kaczmarek, 1999; 2008). For purposes of place promotion, Łódź created its own version of a "Golden Age" around an imagined nineteenth-century tradition of harmonious multiculturalism, industrial dynamism, and the rebirth of a pre-socialist entrepreneurial spirit (Young and Kaczmarek, 2008, p. 61). Rek-Woźniak and Woźniak (2020) have shown that the museum narratives in Łódź aim at creating a vision of industrial history inspired by entrepreneurial spirit and free from industrial or ethnic conflicts. Industrial history is narrated from the top-down perspective of entrepreneurs and founding figures like Ludwik Geyer, while the working class is not represented as a social group. They are depicted without agency and put in the passive position of "beneficiaries of industrial paternalism" (Rek-Woźniak and Woźniak, 2020, p. 16). Portraying the history of Łódź without paying much attention to the lower working classes also entails the marginalization of socioeconomic conflicts, inequalities, and trauma within the development of the industrial town.

Industrial Pasts and Tourism

The aim of redeveloping and converting industrial facilities is often to improve living conditions and standards for a region's inhabitants. As the examples mentioned earlier demonstrate, the conversion of industrial facilities for touristic purposes has become a popular practice for boosting the attractiveness of post-industrial regions and cities in Central-Eastern and Southeastern Europe. With increasing numbers of "industrial tourists" in Poland, the destinations have started to create various forms of promoting industrial heritage, including thematic trails, forms of ecotourism (for instance, linking post-mining landscapes with built and immaterial heritage in eco-parks in former mining areas), and guided tours (Jędrysiak, 2011; Józwiak and Sieg, 2021; for Slovakia see Ilkovicová and Ilkovic, 2022).

Touristic development of post-industrial sites also has a strong European element. Networking initiatives such as ERIH (European Route of Industrial Heritage) promote industrial heritage sites across countries with a common corporate design and online presence, thus strengthening the attractiveness of touristic sites related to industrial history. Behind the common marketing approaches lies a European narrative of industrial development as an important factor of European identity. The ERIH website claims, "nothing has left its mark [on Europe's past] as clearly as the two centuries following the beginning of the Industrial Revolution" (ERIH, n.d.). In a 2017 publication, Tanja Petrović lamented the absence of most Central-Eastern and Southeastern European countries from ERIH's website (Petrović, 2017, p. 25). Since then, the number of museums, technical monuments, and other relics related to the industrial past in Central-Eastern and Southeastern Europe represented in ERIH's website has been on the rise, and the popularity of industrial heritage is increasing in the region. The socialist industrial past is increasingly becoming touristified as well. The case of the Polish model-socialist town Nowa Huta is a case in point. Built in the east of Cracow as a residential settlement along with the Lenin steel mill in the 1950s, the dissonant and formerly unwanted socialist heritage was turned into a tourist product by companies like "The Crazy Guides." Offering playful "Communist Tours" with performative elements of time travelling through the town in vintage cars and vintage dining experiences, the tours act as a "catalyst for change" in the interpretation of the socialist past for both tourists and residents (Banaszkiewicz, 2016, p. 2). How this effect relates to relicts and remains which are connected more closely to socialist industrial production is a subject for future research.

What's Next? Perspectives for Future Research

This chapter started out with a strong focus on the simultaneity and multiplicity of the transformations that occurred in Central-Eastern and Southeastern Europe in the aftermath of 1989. It outlined how the change to a market economy and the accompanying deindustrialization had an initial impact on how industrial pasts were remembered in post-socialist countries. The strong connection between state socialism and the modernization and industrialization projects implemented in many places after 1945 turned this segment of the industrial past into an unwanted feature, one to be overcome together with socialism in the turbulent times of transformation. The chapter then highlighted the shifts in this perception over time from cultural oblivion toward the multiple ways of memorializing industrial pasts. Personal, nostalgic recollections of socialist work which have an inherent affective potential to undermine and challenge the understandings of the transformations as a success story are one example. Despite initial neglect, successful large-scale conversion projects of former industrial sites have been implemented in the region, which illustrates the potential of industrial heritage to become a resource for future regional development. This entanglement between processes of memorialization and the commodification and marketing of the industrial past is an aspect which needs to be studied in more detail in future research.

It is not only the socialist industrial past that has been and still is an ambiguous element of memory culture in the region. The examples in this chapter also illustrate that the interpretation of pre-socialist industrial pasts can become a conflicting narrative. The case of the Polish region Upper Silesia shows that – despite the fact that industrialization is a key feature in its development – as part of the German history of the region it is interpreted as a foreign legacy. European perspectives on the industrial development of the nineteenth and early twentieth century – as offered by the ERIH initiative – propose a more integrated approach. It thus seems important to broaden the study of industrial memory making by including the question of how European aspects shape and influence the emergence of industrial heritage. Additionally, it is essential to incorporate initiatives to preserve industrial remains and relicts during the socialist period into the analytical framework. Some of these institutions are still intact and enable us to trace the development of industrial heritage over time.

Industrial Pasts in Post-Socialist Countries

The overview further indicates that research on industrial memory and heritage in Central-Eastern and Southeastern Europe is still an emerging academic field: while literature on the transformation phase in political science and anthropology is rich, interdisciplinary approaches on memory and heritage of industrial pasts in the region are only beginning to gain scholarly attention. To accelerate and broaden research in this area, I would like to point out a few desiderata and possible future research directions. The examples of Katowice (Poland), Ostrava (Czech Republic), and Miskolc (Hungary) show the differences in the emergence, preservation, uses, and functions of industrial heritage after 1989. This diverging development is interesting because the cities shared comparable processes of accelerated industrialization and were – due to their status as important industrial centers – partner cities during state socialism and have preserved partnership until today. Connecting case studies on cities with similar developments in the industrial sector before 1989 in a comparative approach would help shed further light on the political, social, and cultural conditions that foster or hamper the emergence of industrial heritage in the aftermath of 1989. A comparative approach would also be insightful for shedding light on the history of industrial heritage production during the socialist time before 1989. This chapter discussed that with examples from the GDR and Czechoslovakia, where preservation of industrial monuments and industrial heritage took place under state socialism in manifold ways. A broader sample of cases from different socialist countries would help to specify the political and social contexts of such practices and put them in a broader context of the history of preservation of industrialization before 1989. Additionally, the (dis)continuities of such memory practices in the newly emerging political, social, and economic realities after 1989 need to be studied in more detail. What attempts at saving material relics and remains of industrial culture along with written documentations of decommissioning plants can be observed in the initial years of the transformations? How did communal memory initiatives evolve in the process of deindustrialization, and how did they try to gain commemorative agency (Wurzbacher, 2023)? A point of departure for investigating these aspects could be the initiative of workers, engineers, or managers which focused on the preservation of their own working environment as well as their achievements after their plants were shut down in the direct aftermath of 1989. Such processes of self-historization took place in several plants in Eastern Germany, one of them being the Industriemuseum Brandenburg a.d. Havel (Industrial Museum in Brandenburg upon Havel). The soon-to-be-redundant workers of the decommissioning steelworks and the rolling mill had the unique chance to document the workflow, the working culture, and everyday life of the workers along with details from the material culture in the unique moment right before the plant was shut down, financed by short-term job-creation means. This subjective collection of material remains, together with interviews with the workers, created the basis for establishing the museum. Studying the accompanying conflicts and controversies – which occurred around the question of whether the preservation of technical equipment like a huge oven and other technical devices would obstruct the creation of new workplaces – would provide new insights into the development of industrial heritage after 1989 (Industriemuseum Brandenburg, n.d.; Krohn, 2023).

The aspect of (dis)continuities in practices of memorialization is closely linked to another field of inquiry which focuses more closely on actors and agents of industrial memory in the making. How do the agendas of urban and other civil society activists change the emergence and interpretation of industrial heritage? Can such community-based actors "from below" – who are predominantly not policymakers or heritage experts – successfully put forward different layers of memory and modify approaches toward industrial heritage? How

413

does the generational or gender aspect pan out in this constellation? These suggestions are by no means exhaustive, yet they might serve as points of departure for fostering a deeper understanding of how industrial heritage emerges and is being used in post-socialist countries.

Notes

1 I would like to thank Marcus Böick, Magdalena Banaszkiewicz, Joanna Wawrzyniak, and Györgyi Németh for their critical reading of the text.
2 Most recently, historian Ilko-Sascha Kowalczuk has used the term "Übernahme" (takeover) to describe the reunification of Germany (Kowalczuk, 2019). For an overview of the specificities of the transformation in East Germany, see Marcus Böick: "Die Erforschung der Transformation Ostdeutschlands seit 1989/90 Ansätze, Voraussetzungen, Wandel Version: 1.0," in Docupedia-Zeitgeschichte, 18 October 2022 (Böick, 2022). http://dx.doi.org/10.14765/zzf.dok-2424
3 In recent attempts to historicize the events in 1989/1990, historical scholarship draws attention to the fact that these years are not to be perceived as a "zero hour" yet had a longer pre-history in the region as well as a global context (Ther, 2016; Mark et al., 2019). Scholars further draw attention to the decline of industrial production during late socialism, eventually accelerated by the political transformation (Peters, 2021).
4 The definition of brownfield varies as the term covers areas of diverse scales, related not only to industrial elements but also to the agricultural, military, or residential realm. Thus, brownfields occur not only in urban environments but also in rural areas.

> A brownfield site is any land or premises which has been previously used or developed and is not currently fully in use, although it may be partially occupied or utilized. It may also be vacant, derelict, or contaminated. Therefore, a brownfield site is not available for immediate use without intervention.
>
> *(Alker et al., 2000, quoted in Duží and Jakubínský, 2013, p. 55)*

Brownfields are distinguished from blackfields, understood as polluted areas with high-level contamination causing environmental and health risks (Duží and Jakubínský, 2013, p. 56).
5 "Black Meadow" and "Nová Karolina" are two other major brownfield areas in Ostrava's city center which are currently part of urban development and revitalization projects.

Reference List

Balockaite, R. (2012). Coping with the Unwanted Past in Planned Socialist Towns: Visaginas, Tychy, and Nowa Huta. *Slovo*, 24(1), pp. 41–57.

Banaszkiewicz, M. (2016). A Dissonant Heritage Site Revisited – The Case of Nowa Huta in Krakow. *Journal of Tourism and Cultural Change*, 15(2), pp. 185–197. https://doi.org/10.1080/147668 25.2016.1260137

Barndt, K. (2010). Memory Traces of an Abandoned Set of Futures: Industrial Ruins in the Postindustrial Landscapes of Germany. In Hell, J. and Schönle, A. (eds.) *Ruins of Modernity*. Durham: Duke University Press, pp. 270–293.

Bergbaumuseum Oelsnitz. (2023). *Glück auf!* https://www.bergbaumuseum-oelsnitz.de/

Berger, S. (2020). Introduction: Preconditions for the Making of an Industrial Past. Comparative Perspectives. In Berger, S. (ed.) *Constructing Industrial Pasts. Heritage, Historical Culture, and Identity in Regions Undergoing Structural Economic Transformation*. New York and Oxford: Berghahn, pp. 1–26.

Boele, O., Noordenbos, B. and Robbe, K. (2019). Introduction: The Many Practices of Post-Soviet Nostalgia: Affect, Appropriation, Contestation. In Boele, O., Noordenbos, B. and Robbe, K. (eds.) *Post-Soviet Nostalgia Confronting the Empire's Legacies*. New York: Routledge, pp. 1–17.

Böick, M. (2022). Die Erforschung der Transformation Ostdeutschlands seit 1989/90 Ansätze, Voraussetzungen, Wandel Version: 1.0. *Docupedia-Zeitgeschichte*. https://doi.org/10.14765/zzf. dok-2424

Borodziej, W., von Puttkamer, J. and Holubec, S. (2020). Introduction. In von Puttkamer, J., Borodziej, W. and Holubec, S. (eds.) *From Revolution to Uncertainty. The Year 1990 in Central and Eastern Europe*. Oxon and New York: Routledge, pp. 1–10.

Boym, S. (2001). *The Future of Nostalgia*. New York: Basic Books.

Campbell, B.W. (2005). *Resurrected from the Ruins, Turning to the Past: Historic Preservation in the SBZ/GDR 1945–1990*. PhD Dissertation. University of Rochester.

Cowie, J. and Heathcott, J. (2003). *Beyond the Ruins. The Meanings of Deindustrialization*. Ithaca, NY: Cornell University Press.

Czepczyński, M. and Sooväli-Sepping, H. (2015). From Sacrum to Profanum: Reinterpretation of Communist Places of Power in Baltic Cities. *Journal of Baltic Studies*, 47(2), pp. 239–255. https://doi.org/10.1080/01629778.2015.1102154

Dolní Vítkovice. (n.d.). *Mining Museum in Landek Park*. https://www.dolnivitkovice.cz/en/landek-park/

dpa Berlin/Brandenburg. (2023, January 11). Lausitz soll Europas Kulturhauptstadt werden. *Zeit Online*. https://www.zeit.de/news/2023-01/11/lausitz-soll-europas-kulturhauptstadt-werden?utm_referrer=https%3A%2F%2Fwww.google.com%2F

Duží, B. and Jakubínský, J. (2013). Brownfield Dilemmas in the Transformation of Post-Communist Cities: A Case Study of Ostrava, Czech Republic. *Human Geographies – Journal of Studies and Research in Human Geography*, 7(2), pp. 53–64.

European Route of Industrial Heritage. (n.d.). ERIH, the European Route of Industrial Heritage, Your Guide to Europe's Industrial Heritage. https://www.erih.net/

Filipkowski, P. and Gulińska-Jurgiel, P. (2021). Einleitung. Multiple Zugänge zur Transformation. In Filipkowski, P. and Gulińska-Jurgiel, P. (eds.) *Historisierung der Transformation (Historie. Jahrbuch des Zentrums für Historische Forschung Berlin der Polnischen Akademie der Wissenschaften)*. Berlin: Zentrums für Historische Forschung der Polnischen Akademie der Wissenschaften, pp. 9–16.

Geering, C. and Vickers, P. (2021). Heritage Under Socialism: Trajectories of Preserving the Tangible Past in Postwar Eastern and Central Europe. In Gantner, E., Geering, C. and Vickers, P. (eds.) *Heritage Under Socialism. Preservation in Eastern and Central Europe, 1945–1991*. New York and Oxford: Berghahn, pp. 1–34.

Ghodsee, K. and Orenstein, M.A. (2021). *Taking Stock of Shock. Social Consequences of the 1989 Revolutions*. New York: Oxford University Press.

Hachmeister, M., Hock, B., Jacobs, T. and Wurzbacher, O. (2023). Multiple Transformations: An Introduction. *Journal of Contemporary Central and Eastern Europe*, 31(1), pp. 15–26.

Handro, S. (2022). Discarded and Forgotten? The Legacy of GDR Industrial Culture. *Public History Weekly*, 10(4). https://doi.org/10.1515/phw-2022-19818

Hilmar, T. (2020). "Economic Memories" of the Aftermath of the 1989 Revolutions in East Germany and the Czech Republic. *East European Politics and Societies and Cultures*, 35(1), pp. 89–112.

Hurníková, V. (2017). *Iconic Industry. The Making of Meaning in the Lower Area of Vítkovice*. MA Thesis. University of Oslo.

Ilkovicová, L. and Ilkovic, J. (2022). Mining Educational Trail in Slovakia. *Land*, 11(6). https://doi.org/10.3390/land11060936

Industriemuseum Brandenburg. (n.d.). *Industriemuseum Brandenburg an der Havel*. https://www.industriemuseum-brandenburg.de/

Jaramillo, G.S. and Tomann, J. (eds.). (2021). *Transcending the Nostalgic. Landscapes of Postindustrial Europe Beyond Representation*. New York and Oxford: Berghahn.

Jedlecki, P. (2021, March 10). Nowa dyrektor Muzeum Śląskiego bez doświadczenia i konkursu. "To najgorsza wiadomość z możliwych". *Gazeta Wyborcza*. https://katowice.wyborcza.pl/katowice/7,3 5063,26868215,nowa-dyrektor-muzeum-slaskiego-bez-doswiadczenia-i-konkursu.html

Jędrysiak, T. (2011). Turystyka kulturowa w obiektach poprzemysłowych – zagadnienia ogólne. *Turystyka Kulturowa*, 6, pp. 7–35.

Jigoria-Oprea, L. and Popa, N. (2017). Industrial Brownfields: An Unsolved Problem in Post-Socialist Cities. A Comparison between Two Mono Industrial Cities: Reşiţa (Romania) and Pančevo (Serbia). *Urban Studies*, 54(12), pp. 2719–2738. https://doi.org/10.1177/0042098016655057

Jordánová, K. (2016). The Industrial Heritage of Ostrava – Authenticity at the Crossroads. *The Friends of Czech Heritage Newsletter*, 15, pp. 4–7.

Józwiak, M. and Sieg, P. (2021). Tourism Development in Post-Industrial Facilities as a Regional Business Model. *Sustainability*, 13(4). https://doi.org/10.3390/su13042028

Jucu, I.S. and Voiculescu, S. (2020). Abandoned Places and Urban Marginalized Sites in Lugoj Municipality, Three Decades After Romania's State-Socialist Collapse. *Sustainability*, 12(18). https://doi.org/10.3390/su12187627

Kideckel, D.A. (2020). The Coal-Environment Nexus: How Nostalgic Identity Burdens Heritage in Romania's Jiu Valley. In Berger, S. (ed.) *Constructing Industrial Pasts: Heritage, Historical Culture and Identity in Regions Undergoing Structural Economic*. New York and Oxford: Berghahn, pp. 228–241.

Kisiel, P. (2021). When We Say Post-Industrial – We Mean Ruins. *Heritage & Society*, 14(1), pp. 20–45. https://doi.org/10.1080/2159032X.2021.2022070

Kolejka, J., Klimánek, M., Hradek, M.M. and Kirchner, K. (2017). Czech Post-Industrial Landscapes in the Border Zone with Austria. Identification, Typology and Value. *Mitteilungen der Österreichischen Geographischen Gesellschaft*, 159, pp. 221–242. https://doi.org/10.23781/moegg159-221

Kollmorgen, R. (2010). Diskurse der deutschen Einheit. *Aus Politik und Zeitgeschichte*, 30–31, pp. 6–13.

Kopeček, M. and Wciślik, P. (2015). Introduction: Towards an Intellectual History of Post-Socialism. In Kopeček, M. and Wciślik, P. (eds.) *Thinking through Transition: Liberal Democracy, Authoritarian Pasts, and Intellectual History in East Central Europe After 1989*. Budapest and New York: Central European University Press, pp. 1–39.

Kowalczuk, I.-S. (2019). *Die Übernahme. Wie Ostdeutschland Teil der Bundesrepublik wurde*. München: C.H. Beck.

Krohn, M. (2023). Wandel statt Totalverlust. Arbeitsbiographische Transformationserfahrungen in Brandenburg an der Havel im Kontext der Ausstellung "VEB Zukunft GmbH" (2021/22). In Weiß, P.U., Zündorf, I. and Schmidtmann, F. (eds.) *Umstrittene Umbrüche. Das Ende der SED-Diktatur und die Transformationszeit in Brandenburg*. Berlin: Metropol, pp. 285–301.

Kruner, K. (2020). Der Authentizitätsbegriff in der Technischen Denkmalpflege der Deutschen Demokratischen Republik. In Farrenkopf, M. and Meyer, T. (eds.) *Authentizität und industriekulturelles Erbe. Zugänge und Beispiele*. Berlin and Boston: DeGruyter, pp. 293–309.

Lehmann, N.-H. (2021). Socialism and the Rise of Industrial Heritage: The Preservation of Industrial Monuments in the German Democratic Republic. In Gantner, E., Geering, C. and Vickers, P. (eds.) *Heritage Under Socialism. Preservation in Eastern and Central Europe, 1945–1991*. New York and Oxford: Berghahn, pp. 195–216.

Mark, J., Iacob, B.C., Rupprecht, T. and Spaskovska, L. (2019). *1989: A Global History of Eastern Europe*. Cambridge: Cambridge University Press.

Martinat, S., Dvorak, P., Frantal, B., Klusacek, P., Kunc, J., Navratil, J., Osman, R., Tureckova, K. and Reed, M. (2016). Sustainable Urban Development in a City Affected by Heavy Industry and Mining? Case Study of Brownfields in Karvina, Czech Republic. *Journal of Cleaner Production*, 118, pp. 78–87. https://doi.org/10.1016/j.jclepro.2016.01.029

Mérai, D. and Kulikov, V. (2021). From Burden to Resource: Uses of Industrial Heritage in East-Central Europe. In Mérai, D. et al. (eds.) *From Burden to Resource: Uses of Industrial Heritage in East-Central Europe*. Budapest: Archaeolingua, pp. 5–13.

Metzner, T. (2023, January 12). Lausitz als Kulturhauptstadt Europas?: Brandenburgs Kulturministerin gibt Anstoß für Bewerbung. *Tagesspiegel*. https://www.tagesspiegel.de/potsdam/brandenburg/lausitz-als-kulturhauptstadt-europas-brandenburgs-kulturministerin-gibt-anstoss-fur-bewerbung-9165912.html

Murzyn, M.A. (2008). Heritage Transformation in Central and Eastern Europe. In Howard, P. and Graham, B. (eds.) *The Routledge Research Companion to Heritage and Identity*. London: Routledge, pp. 315–346.

Murzyn-Kupisz, M.A. and Gwosdz, K. (2011). The Changing Identity of the Central European City: The Case of Katowice. *Journal of Historical Geography*, 37, pp. 113–126.

Németh, G. (2018). Contested Heritage and Regional Identity in the Borsod Industrial Area, Hungary. In Wicke, C., Berger, S. and Golombek, J. (eds.) *Industrial Heritage and Regional Identities*. Oxon and New York: Routledge, pp. 95–119.

Offe, C. (1996). *The Varieties of Transition: The East European and East German Experience*. Cambridge: Polity Press.

Pérez-Sindín, X.S. (2021). More-Than-Representational Postmining Landscapes in the Former Coal Regions of Eastern Germany: Between Economic Revitalization and Risk Society. In Jaramillo, G.S. and Tomann, J. (eds.) *Transcending the Nostalgic: Landscapes of Postindustrial Europe beyond Representation*. New York and Oxford: Berghahn, pp. 64–89.

Peters, F. (2015). Solidarność Yesterday – Solidarity Today? The European Solidarity Center in Gdańsk Endeavors to Combine the Past with the Present. *Cultures of History Forum*. https://doi.org/10.25626/0041

Peters, F. (2021). Polens spät- und postsozialistische Transformation als Abschied von der industriellen Moderne. In Filipkowski, P. and Gulińska-Jurgiel, P. (eds.) *Historisierung der Transformation (Historie. Jahrbuch des Zentrums für Historische Forschung Berlin der Polnischen Akademie der Wissenschaften)*. Berlin: Zentrum für Historische Forschung der Polnischen Akademie der Wissenschaften, pp. 43–70.

Petrović, T. (2014). Mourning the Lost Modernity: Industrial Labor, Europe, and (post)Yugoslav Post-Socialism. In Petrović, T. (ed.) *Mirroring Europe. Ideas of Europe and Europeanization in Balkan Societies*. Leiden: Brill, pp. 89–113.

Petrović, T. (2017). Nostalgia for Industrial Labor in Socialist Yugoslavia. Or Why the Post-Socialist Affect Matters. In Slavković, M. and Đorgović, M. (eds.) *Nostalgia on the Move*. Belgrade: Pozitiv Print, pp. 14–29.

Pike, A. (2009). De-Industrialization. In Thrift, N. (ed.) *International Encyclopedia of Human Geography*. Oxford: Elsevier, pp. 51–59.

Pokludová, A. (2022). Industrie- und/oder Kulturzentrum mit überregionaler Bedeutung? Mährisch Ostrau und Umgebung im 19. und 20. Jahrhundert. In Berger, S. et al. (eds.) *Kulturelle Langzeitfolgen industriellen Strukturwandels Ruhrgebiet – Tschechien – Slowakei*. Leipzig: Leipziger Universitätsverlag, pp. 213–236.

Pokludová, A. and Popelka, P. (2022). From the "Steel Heart of Czechoslovakia" to Post-Industrial Space: Boom, Crisis and the Cultural Heritage of the Ostrava-Karviná Mining District. In Bluma, L., Farrenkopf, M. and Meyer, T. (eds.) *Boom – Crisis – Heritage. King Coal and the Energy Revolutions After 1945*. Berlin and Boston: DeGruyter, pp. 161–178.

Rek-Woźniak, M. and Woźniak, W. (2020). Working-Class and Memory Policy in Post-Industrial Cities: Łódź, Poland, and Tampere, Finland, Compared. *International Labor and Working-Class History*, 98, pp. 5–21.

Silesia City Center. (n.d.). *Silesia Dzisiaj*. http://www.silesiacitycenter.com.pl/historia#silesia-dzisiaj

Smith, L. and Campbell, G. (2017). "Nostalgia for the Future": Memory, Nostalgia and the Politics of Class. *International Journal of Heritage Studies*, 23(7), pp. 612–627.

Sobala-Gwosdz, A. and Gwosdz, K. (2017). "Katowice effect"? Regeneration of the Site of the Former Katowice Coal Mine through Prestige Cultural Projects. *Urban Development Issues*, 56(4), pp. 27–40. https://doi.org/10.2478/udi-2018-0010

Stadt Chemnitz. (2019). *Bid Book*. https://chemnitz2025.de/fileadmin/khs/03_INFORMIEREN/Bidbook/BidBook-deutsch.pdf

Stătică, I. (2021). Overlapping Nostalgias: Negotiating Space and Labor in the (Post)Communist City of Bucharest. *Space and Culture*, 24(4), pp. 650–663.

Stykow, P. (2013). Postsozialismus, Version: 1.0. *Docupedia-Zeitgeschichte*. https://doi.org/10.14765/zzf.dok.2.250.v1

Sucháček, J. (2019). The Benefit of Failure: On the Development of Ostrava's Culture. *Sustainability*, 11(9). https://doi.org/10.3390/su11092592

Tannock, S. (1995). Nostalgia Critique. *Cultural Studies*, 9(3), pp. 453–464.

Ther, P. (2010). 1989 – eine verhandelte Revolution, Version: 1.0. *Docupedia-Zeitgeschichte*. https://doi.org/10.14765/zzf.dok.2.604.v1

Ther, P. (2016). *Die neue Ordnung auf dem alten Kontinent. Eine Geschichte des neoliberalen Europas*. Berlin: Suhrkamp.

Ther, P. (2022). Kotransformation – Reichweite und Grenzen eines Konzepts. In Böick, M., Goschler, C. and Jessen, R. (eds.) *Jahrbuch Deutsche Einheit 2022*. Berlin: Ch. Links.

Todorova, M. (2010). Introduction: From Utopia to Propaganda and Back. In Todorova, M. and Gille, Z. (eds.) *Post-Communist Nostalgia*. New York and Oxford: Berghahn, pp. 1–14.

Todorova, M. (2014). Introduction: Similar Trajectories, Different Memories. In Todorova, M., Dimou, A. and Troebst, S. (eds.) *Remembering Communism: Private and Public Recollections of Lived Experience in Southeast Europe*. Budapest: CEU Press, pp. 1–26.

Tomann, J. (2016). "The Light of History": The First Permanent Exhibition on Upper Silesian History in Poland Avoids Sensitive Issues and Focuses on Ostensible Consensus. *Cultures of History Forum*. https://doi.org/10.25626/0048

Tomann, J. (2017). *Geschichtskultur im Strukturwandel. Öffentliche Geschichte in Katowice nach 1989*. Berlin: De Gruyter Oldenbourg.

Turşie, C. (2015). The Unwanted Past and Urban Regeneration of Communist Heritage Cities. Case Study: European Capitals of Culture (ECoC). Riga, Pilsen and Wroclaw. *Journal of Education Culture and Society*, 6(2), pp. 122–138. https://doi.org/10.15503/jecs20152.122.138

Velikonja, M. (2009). Lost in Transition: Nostalgia for Socialism in Post-Socialist Countries. *East European Politics and Societies*, 23(4), pp. 535–551. https://doi.org/10.1177/0888325409345140

Wawrzyniak, J. (2021). "Hard Times but Our Own". Post-Socialist Nostalgia and the Transformation of Industrial Life in Poland. *Zeithistorische Forschungen/Studies in Contemporary History*, 18(1), pp. 73–92.

Wawrzyniak, J. and Pehe, V. (2023). Neoliberalism, Eastern Europe and Collective Memory: Setting the Framework. In Pehe, V. and Wawrzyniak, J. (eds.) *Remembering the Neoliberal Turn. Economic Change and Collective Memory in Eastern Europe After 1989*. London and New York: Routledge, pp. 1–18.

Werftenkollektiv, Ther, P., Brunnbauer, U., Filipkowski, P., Hodges, A., Petrungaro, S. and Wegenschimmel, P. (2022). *In den Stürmen der Transformation. Zwei Werften zwischen Sozialismus und EU*. Berlin: Suhrkamp.

Wurzbacher, O. (2023). From Collective to Association? Figurations of Remembering and Former State-Owned Enterprises in Post-1989 Eastern Germany. *Journal of Contemporary Central and Eastern Europe*, 31(1), pp. 67–81.

Young, C. and Kaczmarek, S. (1999). Changing the Perception of the Post-Socialist City: Place Promotion and Imagery in Łódź, Poland. *The Geographical Journal*, 165(2), pp. 183–191.

Young, C. and Kaczmarek, S. (2008). The Socialist Past and Postsocialist Urban Identity in Central and Eastern Europe: The Case of Łódź, Poland. *European Urban and Regional Studies*, 15(1), pp. 53–70.

25
THE MEMORIALIZATION OF CLASS IN INDUSTRIAL HERITAGE INITIATIVES

Laurajane Smith

Introduction

The memorialization of industries following deindustrialization has become commonplace. As Stanton observes in her review of the history of such memorialization, the conventions of considering industrial heritage tend to reflect "solidly middle-class visions," often in the interests of supporting neoliberal economies (Stanton, 2019). The gentrification of industrial and working-class neighborhoods has frequently been facilitated by the conservation and repurposing of industrial buildings, working, as Coffee argues, to redefine the rights of working-class people to inner cities (Coffee, 2024). Deindustrialization's devastating economic and social impact is often reinforced as working communities become physically or emotionally displaced from their intangible and material heritage. The importance of heritage projects "from below" and their consequence for community solidarity, well-being and self-esteem are well documented in the heritage literature as attempts to reassert community pride in the face of economic marginalization and national historical forgetting.[1] The focus of this chapter, however, is to examine how visitors interact with exhibitions and displays of working-class memorialization and to understand the memory and identity work that they do and how this is informed by issues of class.

People like to visit places where they will see people like themselves in the exhibition and among other visitors. This deceptively simple observation is one of the core findings of work done with museum visitors over the last two decades[2] – museums, as sites of heritage-making, work to include and exclude people from their narratives simultaneously. An illustration of this is museum visiting being a predominantly middle-class activity despite social inclusion policies and curatorial activism inspired by the New Museology. Museums have their own set of "feeling rules" (Williams, 1977; Hochschild, 1979) and unspoken acceptable 'rules' of acting, behaving or simply 'being' in a museum, which frames visiting as a social and socializing activity. The cultural capital "accumulated" by visiting is well documented in the museum studies literature, as is the tendency for museums, particularly museums that tell national and nationalizing histories, to attract a profile of visitors that fits neatly in the white middle and elite social classes (see, e.g., Merriman, 1991; Black, 2012; Bounia et al., 2012; Kinsley, 2016). This process equally discourages those whose identity does not fit comfortably into this class and ethnic profile (Hall, 1999; Bennett et al., 2010).

DOI: 10.4324/9781003308324-36

However, much of this research has been undertaken across national institutions. The socializing practices of visiting museums telling the histories and stories of socially and politically marginalized groups have been less well studied. This chapter considers the feeling rules and 'cultural capital' of a small sample of labor history museums and heritage sites in England, the US, and Australia. In the first instance, it draws on the overall results of a study of 4,502 visitors to museums and heritage sites (Smith, 2021). The chapter draws on this data to discuss visitors' memory and identity work at such sites. Also, it provides a comparative context for the social and political work visiting working-class museums does. I argue that visitors' performances of meaning-making are expressive of disparities in experiences of social privilege and disadvantage. Understanding how visitors mediate experiences of social privilege and disadvantage is vital to inform critical museological and interpretive strategies that address class identity and experience.

The Performativity of Visiting

As numerous scholars have argued, visiting a museum is an expression of cultural capital, social positioning, and attainment (see, e.g., Bourdieu, 2012; Merriman, 1991; Hanquinet, 2016; Bennett, 1995). As such, visiting in Western contexts recruits a particular social profile – tertiary educated, white, and middle-class (Black, 2012, pp. 21–25). Thus, it is unsurprising that many museums, especially national institutions, have been criticized for maintaining the social and political status quo and speaking selectively to particular historical and contemporary social experiences and understandings. Concerns about the lack of diversity in the overall profile of museum visitors have led to social inclusion policies to encourage the development of more inclusive visitor profiles (Sandell, 2003; Smith and Waterton, 2009; Chynoweth et al., 2020). Additionally, curatorial and other professional practices have attempted to engage in progressive interventions in the heritage work of museums to diversify their impact and appeal (see, e.g., Sandell and Nightingale, 2012; Janes and Sandell, 2019; Chynoweth et al., 2020).

Nonetheless, the visitor profile has tended not to change (Selwood, 2006; Bennett et al., 2010; Black, 2012; Smith, 2021). Arguments ranging from entry costs being too high and institutional and professional inertia constraining real change may partly account for this failure (Selwood, 2006; Kidd, 2011; Janes, 2016). However, so many museums, particularly those telling national and nationalizing histories and speaking mainly to a select audience, recursively reinforce exclusionary practices. That is, museums and other sites of heritage-making do not educate or inform their visitors. Instead, visitors and heritage and museum professionals work collectively (sometimes in concert and sometimes in discord) to create and recreate heritage narratives and the social and political values that underpin them. What is rehearsed in the practice of visiting are narratives that reflect and speak to particular audiences; in short, visitors recreate heritage meanings that speak to themselves and people like themselves.

The stories of how working-class people have "fought for fair wages; humane hours of work and leisure time; the right to join a union; safe, sanitary, and democratic workplaces" (Forrant and Trasciatti, 2022, p. 1), among other achievements, tend to be misrecognized or actively forgotten in broader national histories and narratives. Unsurprisingly, national museums in Western contexts tend to be dominated by white, middle-class visitors while excluding, among many others, working-class visitors (Kallio and Mansfield, 2013; Bennett et al., 2010; Smith, 2021). Over the last few decades, however, there has been a significant growth in labor museums and other commemorative sites by and for working-class communities (Stanton, 2019; Dicks, 2008; Linkon, 2018; WorkLab: The International Association of Labour Museums, n.d.). How visitors use heritage and the social and political meanings they construct is under-researched, and how working-class/labor heritage sites are used by visitors is often actively misunderstood (For exceptions to this, see Dicks, 2000; Dicks, 2008; Bagnall, 2003). This partly stems from a misunderstanding of heritage as intimately linked to mawkish nostalgia and a hesitation by intellectuals to engage with the emotionality of heritage and, in particular, expressions of grief and loss.

Heritage is a process of utilizing the past to make meaning in and for the present to address social problems and navigate social change. Heritage cannot usefully be reduced to what museums collect or to sites and places. These things may be redefined as the cultural tools utilized in remembering and commemorating (Smith, 2006). In remembering, forgetting, and commemorating social values and narratives about belonging, a sense of place, identity, and well-being are constructed for use in the present and to inform aspirations for reimagined futures (Smith, 2006; Macdonald, 2013; Harrison et al., 2020). This definition of heritage is important because heritage, conceptualized as a practice, takes on performative functions. Drawing on Butler's (Butler, 1990) definition of performativity, heritage practices perform or re/create particular understandings of the past that inform, legitimize, or challenge the meanings and understandings assigned to contemporary experiences. Heritage meanings and narratives, and the social and political values they legitimize, are continually remade not simply through the practices of museum collecting and exhibiting but also through visiting.

Ethnographic research with working-class communities and workplace collectives in Western contexts has not only documented the growth of labor heritage museums and sites but has also illustrated the role this plays in asserting the legitimacy of working-class histories and the importance of such heritage to community self-esteem (Dicks, 2000; Reeves et al., 2011; Eklund et al., 2021; Dellios, 2022; Shackel, 2018; Strangleman, 2013; Taksa, 2019; Berger, 2020; Forrant and Trasciatti, 2022). As many of these studies demonstrate, investments by communities in commemorating their histories are an interlinked expression of self-esteem and a claim for wider societal recognition or acknowledgment, the aims of which are often to seek redress for ongoing economic and social injustice.

Working-class communities increasingly struggle with representation as established left-leaning political parties move to court middle-class votes, and trade unions remain politically marginalized (Smith and Campbell, 2011). Claims for recognition, however, are often misrecognized or go unnoticed. Labor museums and heritage sites tend not to attract visitors from the middle or elite classes. This is not simply a failure of potential audiences to engage with the histories of these sites, and their messages about the legacies of class injustice, but a performative expression of a lack of social recognition. Moreover, social commentators have a pronounced tendency to misunderstand and thus misrecognize the purpose and values of the memorialization of working-class history and heritage.

Misrecognition takes two forms. One stems from arguments Alistair Bonnet makes about the inability of the left to engage with emotions associated with the past and, in particular, expressions of nostalgia (Bonnett, 2010). Traditionally, the left has been forward-looking and action-focused, embodying Joe Hill's call to 'don't mourn organize.' As Mansfield and Trustam observe, there is a significant hesitation in engaging with mourning and grief, which could include anger, in the processes of working-class memorialization, yet as they note, these emotions are essential for coming to terms with loss (Mansfield and Trustram, 2013, p. 453).

Acknowledging and addressing loss is often vital for moving toward future aspirations and goals. However, nostalgia has often been dismissed as self-indulgently backward-looking (see Lowenthal, 2015; Hewison, 1987), inevitably politically conservative, and integral to facilitating right-wing populism (Kaya, 2020; Gest et al., 2018; Wodak, 2020). These assumptions tend to encourage the dismissal of working-class memorialization as overtly emotional, inherently reactionary, and fueling right-wing populist movements.

As many have now argued, nostalgia does not have a singular expression, can be critically reflective and future-orientated, and may have either politically progressive or conservative consequences (Boym, 2002; Bonnett, 2010; Smith and Campbell, 2017a). This does not mean that all working-class memorializations work to advance politically progressive claims for recognition (see Hochschild, 2018; Westmont, 2024; Bevernage et al., 2024); the romanticization of working-class memorialization practices is also a form of misrecognition of community agency. Working-class communities make their own political choices, but the recognition of that is often hindered by a hesitation to acknowledge the importance of grief and anger and how the mediation of loss works to affirm political choices and aspirations for the future. The study, outlined later, aimed to understand the repertoires people used to facilitate the memory and identity work they undertook while visiting the labor museums and sites identified later (see also Table 25.1).

Research undertaken at 45 different genres of museums and heritage sites in England, the US, and Australia in which interviews (consisting of both closed and open-ended questions) were conducted with 4,502 visitors argues that there are quite distinct heritage performances that visitors undertake (Smith, 2021). Quantitative and qualitative data analyses were conducted to define overall patterns in visitor responses and provide depth and nuance to those patterns. Details of the analysis can be found in Smith (2021); however, for this chapter, it is helpful to note that the 45 sites were divided into institutions representing national and nationalizing histories and sites representing contested and/or marginalized history. The former group was represented by, among others, genres of sites that commemorated: histories of war, frontier expansion in the case of the latter two countries, exhibitions of national symbols such as the Smithsonian American History Museum's *The Star-Spangled Banner*, and stately homes/presidential plantations. Dissonant sites were grouped into genres representing working-class history, immigration history, Indigenous culture and colonial history, and exhibitions and sites that examined the histories and/or legacies of enslavement and the slave trade. Labor history sites that explicitly discussed organized labor and

Table 25.1 Heritage sites and numbers of interviews

Labor History Sites	N=
National Coal Mining Museum in Wakefield	85
North of England Open Air Museum, Beamish	128
Tolpuddle Martyrs Museum	60
Mt Kembla Heritage Centre	38
Museum of Australian Democracy at Eureka	86
Museum of Work & Culture, Rhode Island	18
The Youngstown Historical Center of Industry and Labor, Ohio	22
Rivers of Steel, Pittsburgh	20
Total interviews	**457**

deindustrialization were selected. Class issues are relevant to other museums, particularly immigration and civil rights museums, but the 'labor genre' identifies museums and sites explicitly organized around labor and de/industrialization. It must be stressed that comparisons across the sites in the three countries could not be classified as 'like with like.'

Nonetheless, identical core interview questions asked across the sites attempted to get a sense of how visitors used particular sites and genres of site. Each question was coded, and descriptive statistics and cross-tabulations of variables that included visitor demographics, the genre of site, and country of origin, among other variables, were generated using SPSS to identify patterns in the data. The data coding was based on themes in visitor responses and incorporated consideration of a visitor's "register of engagement" or RoE (Smith, 2021, p. 74). That is, the emotional intensity and valence of the response, coupled with the intensity of engagement with the exhibition/interpretive content, as much as the meanings the visitor consequently constructed, informed the coding process. 'Intensity' was a relative measure across the extensive database of interviews.

In summary, the investigation's overall results revealed some differences in visitor responses between the three countries. A core theme from the research, as with research at other studies at labor history sites, was a strong sense from visitors of their frustration and loss that labor history had been misrecognized or forgotten in national narratives and history-making. In discussing this issue, domestic visitors in the US were more prone to talk about 'patriotism' and what this forgetting and misrecognition meant to their sense of patriotic investment in national identity. In Australia and Britain, this sense of exclusion was talked about in terms of national identity rather than patriotism. At the same time, in the US, visitors were more likely to explicitly link their understanding of heritage to family than domestic visitors in England and Australia. However, these differences were less pronounced than those between national and dissonant sites and between the different genres of sites in each of these two categories (Smith, 2021, p. 141). Visitor demographics, mainly concerning whether or not a visitor identified as belonging to a social or politically dominant or nondominant ethnic identity[3] or whether or not they possessed a tertiary qualification, also influenced visitor responses. These results argued that several visitor heritage performances could be identified.

Two performances, in particular, were identified that underwrote and informed a further set of four heritage performances. The first and most prevalent of these, which dominated at national institutions, was defined as a 'performance of privilege.' Domestic visitors within each country and from dominant ethnic identities tended, on the RoE, to be cognitively uncritical and emotionally invested in reinforcing their prior knowledge, values, and beliefs. These performances tended to produce politically conservative readings of history and supported contemporary conservative social and political values aimed at maintaining the status quo. These performances were occasionally conscious and self-critical but were often unconscious and taken for granted, although they were vigorously defended when challenged by curatorial interventions.

Conversely, domestic visitors from nondominant ethnic backgrounds and, to a less sharply defined extent, those from dominant ethnic backgrounds but with low educational attainment tended to be more emotionally and intellectually engaged in self-conscious heritage work. This latter performance was, in short, generally undertaken in the context of marginalization and misrecognition. It tended to be most prevalent at sites of dissonant and contested histories, including sites of working-class labor history, resulting in politically progressive heritage-making. This is not to say that *all* visitors from particular backgrounds and social experiences engaged in these performances, only that visitors of certain backgrounds were overrepresented.

Visitors at labor history sites tended to almost exclusively identify as being from dominant ethnic backgrounds but, relative to other sites, attracted a higher frequency of visitors without tertiary qualifications who were engaged in "lower supervisory-routine"[4] occupations than at all other genres of sites. Indeed, at museums of labor history, the second performance in relation to educational attainment became most pronounced. At other dissonant sites, such as those addressing immigration or the histories and legacies of enslavement, the latter performance was more closely associated with self-defined ethnic identity. Those who identified as international tourists occupied the middle space between these two performances. Tourists were defined as nonresidents of the country where the site they were interviewed was located. This group, often less invested in the national narratives represented by the sites they visited, tended to be a little more critically engaged than domestic visitors from dominant ethnic backgrounds.

Based on either experiences of privilege or marginalization, these two performances underwrote and informed a further four performances: reinforcement, intergenerational communication, recognition, and misrecognition. The most frequent of these was reinforcement; when informed by experiences of social or political privilege, this took the form of the assertion of a visitor's entrance narrative and the values underpinning that narrative. When informed by the performance of social exclusion, reinforcement centered on far more self-conscious affirmations that the social experiences and identities of the visitor mattered: in short, it generated self-conscious expressions of self-esteem and moral self-worth. Intergenerational communication similarly facilitated the transmission of inherited privilege or self-conscious and reflective engagement with familial social or political values. Intergenerational communication occurred in several variants, the most relevant to labor history sites being those in which older family members passed on familial or social histories and values to younger family members. Visitors also sought to make emotional links to absent, often deceased, older family members such as parents or grandparents. Performances of recognition were antithetical to performances of privilege that lacked self-awareness and reflection, while such performances overwhelmingly underwrote performances of misrecognition.[5] The research also suggested that learning was not something with which visitors were engaged. Although changes of view and self-reflection did occur, this was relatively rare and did not necessarily preclude the embodiment of a visitor's assertion of the meaning a site had to them. Personal meanings were often expressed regardless of the meaning a site or exhibition was defined as having by curatorial or other heritage professionals.

In the context of the wider study's overall findings, the chapter examines what visitors were doing at labor history museums. It identifies the memory and identity work in which visitors were engaged. That is, it identifies the heritage-making performances and the socializing work the visitors performed at these sites. The 'cultural capital' of visiting museums, as traditionally defined by Bourdieu, was not in evidence as it was at national museums. However, a form of capital that expressed and affirmed self-esteem and regard for class and familial identity and experience was nonetheless performed at these sites. As Sayer argues, self-esteem and the development of moral self-worth in the context of class marginalization are powerful assertions that have material consequences in struggles for social and economic justice (Sayer, 2005). As various ethnographic observations of working-class communities have identified, the ability to affirm and assert individual and group self-worth is critical (e.g., Dicks, 2000; Cashman, 2006; High and Lewis, 2007; Smith and Campbell, 2011; Bonnett and Alexander, 2012; Strangleman, 2013; Loveday, 2014; De Nardi et al., 2019; Forrant and Trasciatti, 2022). They can be vital platforms from which communities and labor organizations can mount claims to redistribute resources while negotiating the social and economic changes brought about by deindustrialization.

Museums and Heritage Sites of Working-Class Histories – Visitor Profiles and Responses

The underlying performance of social exclusion, which at labor sites tended to correlate to relatively low educational attainment and lower-supervisory-routine occupations, informed the four other heritage-making performances. The two most frequent performances at labor sites were those of an affirming reinforcement of self and group identity and the social values that defined those identities and that of intergenerational communication. While the other two performances did occur, they were relatively uncommon compared to other museums. This section will go through the core interview questions (For interview questions, see Smith, 2021, pp. 99–100), discussing any cross-tabulations defined as statistically significant[6] to clarify the factors underpinning these performances.

Interview Population

The labor museums and heritage sites included in this study are listed in Table 25.1, alongside the number of interviews undertaken. Interviews were generally undertaken over four to five days, and differences in visitor numbers are due to the uneven number of visitors attracted to different sites. Visitor numbers were meagre in the US, reflecting low visitor attendance at the selected museums, while there were higher numbers of visitors at labor history museums in England. The results are influenced by the dominance of data from England (60% of interviews), identified later; however, this is suggestive and implies that labor heritage sites are more frequently and routinely visited in England than in Australia and the US. This may well be a factor in the sites chosen in each country. Still, it may also reflect the differential degree to which class as a social organizing factor is explicitly acknowledged in the three countries and is worth further research. Indeed, museums and sites in Australia and the US with comparable visitor numbers to those in England were not identified. It is also noted that the time between interviews in England (2004) and those in the US and Australia (2010–2013) is substantive. These issues introduce limitations to the study, and the reader is asked to be mindful of these; no claim is made of like-to-like comparisons. Nonetheless, meaningful patterns and observations about how visitors used these sites are derived from the data that confirm ethnographic work with working-class communities about the importance and role of self-esteem and intergenerational communication (Smith, 2021; Smith et al., 2011; Linkon, 2018; De Nardi et al., 2019). The findings also point to themes for further in-depth research.

Of those interviewed at labor history sites, 49% were male and 51% female; in the overall study, females represented 54% of visitors, with males only being in the majority at sites of war commemoration, where they represented 54% of visitors. Gender as a variable had little influence on visitor use of sites. However, men were the majority at English labor museums, representing 51% of visitors. Labor history sites had a slightly older profile than other museums, with 32% of visitors aged 44 and under and 68% aged 45 or over. In the overall study, those 45 or over amounted to 58% of visitors, with older visitors being more frequent at labor history museums and at museums of frontier history and stately homes/presidential plantations. Age was a significant factor in the intensity of memory and identity work and types of performances undertaken at sites, particularly at labor museums.

Visitors were asked to self-identify and describe their ethnic background or affiliation; 91% at labor museums identified as affiliated with a dominant ethnic identity, which visitors often defined as White British, Caucasian American, or Ango-Australian. A further 3% (15 people) identified as affiliated with nondominant ethnic identities, and 6% were international tourists. Of the 15 people from nondominant backgrounds, 11 were interviewed at Australian sites. The relative lack of ethnic diversity at labor sites may speak to ethnic divisions and racial politics within working-class communities and requires further research.

Visitors with university education accounted for 57% of those interviewed in the wider study; however, this fell at labor sites to 42%. In defining occupations, the study used the 'standard occupational classification' (SOC 2000) from the UK, as it was used during the initial interviews in that country. For ease of analysis, this was then grouped into professional, managerial, intermediate, and own account occupations, accounting for 72% of visitors in the overall study. Those in lower supervisory, semi-routine, and routine occupations accounted for 15% (while a highly mixed group of students, unemployed and retired, who declined to nominate their previous employment accounted for 13%). At labor sites, while visitors holding occupations from the first group were still dominant at 67%, the second group of occupations rose to 23% (with 10% from the mixed 'unemployed' group). Although not explicitly asked, it often emerged during the interviews that those visitors with university degrees and/ or who had occupations in the first group frequently identified as having parents or grandparents who identified as working-class.

First-time visitors account for 65% of those interviewed at labor sites, 35% were returning visitors, while 55% had traveled from a home address rather than a holiday or business address. These were similar frequencies to the overall study; however, returning visitors and those traveling from home were more frequent at the English labor sites and, in all three countries, were more likely not to hold university qualifications (28% of returning visitors had been to university versus 40% who had not).

Reasons for Visiting

Each person interviewed was presented with a list of reasons for visiting and was asked to select a statement "that most closely matched their reason" for their visit to the site that day.[7] Of those selected, 18% chose an educational reason (combined 'education' and 'to find out about'), while 21% chose recreation, and a further 29% collectively chose 'to think about' or 'to explore or remember what it means to be.' The selection of 'education' is below that of the overall sample (31%), while 'to think about' was selected by 9% and explore/remember was chosen by only 4% in the overall sample, the latter being a particular feature of labor sites. This is linked to responses to other questions that emphasized feelings of empathy and strong personal and familial links that, in turn, underpinned performances of intergenerational communication and affirming reinforcement.

Definitions of Heritage

Visitors were each asked to define 'what the word heritage meant' to them. The responses to this question were influenced by country of origin, with Americans more frequently referencing family links and both Americans and Australians making emotive links to cultural background and identity. At the same time, English visitors tended to offer definitions framed by the authorized heritage discourse (AHD) or intangibility more frequently (Smith and Campbell, 2017b; Smith, 2021, p. 117). Definitions offered at labor sites followed similar frequencies to the overall study results except in one respect. The definition of heritage as 'intangible,' which referenced things such as tradition and workplace memories and skills, among other things, was predominant at the English labor history sites. This variable, otherwise absent or infrequent at different site genres, also occurs more frequently at labor sites in Australia and the US. The tendency of visitors at labor sites to reference intangible factors such as tradition, workplace knowledge and skills, or family is important, as these definitions framed the performative work undertaken at these sites, which were often informed by self-aware reminiscing and empathy.

Connection to Heritage

Three questions aimed to reveal how visitors characterized the history and heritage represented by the site or museum they were visiting and to see if they had any connection to that history or heritage. The overall study found that on the RoE, strongly expressed personal connections made at sites tended to underpin politically progressive affirmations that reinforced personal, familial or class identity, and engendered self-esteem. Two early questions in the schedule asked, 'whose history or heritage are you visiting here?' and 'are you part of the history represented here?' In contrast, a third penultimate question asked if any aspect of the museum or site being visited spoke to or was linked to the visitor's identity.

In response to the first of these questions, 56% of visitors said that the history or heritage they were visiting belonged to working-class history, frequently accentuating a sense of pride. An additional 20% identified that they were visiting their familial heritage, with return visitors more frequently nominating this response (27% of those visitors versus 16% of first-time visitors). A strong sense of personal connection to the sites visited was evident in the 63% who considered themselves part of the history represented by the site and the 70% who made links between personal identity and the site, with returning visitors more likely to make those links through familial or personal connections. A strong sense of connection recorded at labor sites tended to be more frequent compared to the overall sample, where 57% and 51%, respectively, saw themselves as part of the history or drew links to their identity.

How Does it Make You Feel?

Visitors expressed a range of emotions generated by being at the sites. A particular feature of labor sites was what Smith and Campbell identify as a progressive form of nostalgia linked to social memory and remembering (Smith and Campbell, 2017a). Although expressed by 14% of visitors to labor sites, this variable tended to differentiate this genre from other genres in the overall study. It was also more frequently expressed by returning rather than first-time visitors (24% vs 9% respectively), by those who had not been to university (20% vs 6% of tertiary educated), and by older visitors (18% vs 4% of those 44 and younger). Other features of the response to this question were feelings of pride (9%) and historic gratitude for working-class achievements (21%), the latter slightly more frequently expressed by those without tertiary qualifications (22% vs 19%). This feeling of historic gratitude was also a feature in the genre that represented frontier history in Australia and the US and tended to be connected to the labor history of agricultural workers represented by stockmen and cowboys and is almost absent in other genres (including war commemoration sites).[8] The tendency to identify nostalgia as significant for fueling right-wing populist positions further marginalizes the memorialization of labor and working-class histories. Historical gratitude and pride in the past may also interlink with or be variants of a broader sense of nostalgia. The qualitative data shows that historical gratitude, pride, and more general forms of nostalgia could and did support either left- or right-wing readings of labor history, and these emotions did not inevitably lead to specific ideological positions by themselves. However, failures to acknowledge or misrecognize pride and gratitude in memorializing the working-class past undermines more comprehensive social understandings of contemporary identities based on class and the experiences of deindustrialization. Misunderstanding the emotionality of the labor past in the present works to reduce the social acceptance of pride in class achievements. Compare this to the feeling rules at many sites of national heritage-making, where patriotic/nationalistic pride in national achievements tended to be seen as legitimately affirming (Smith, 2021, p. 172).

What Experiences Do You Value on Visiting This Place?

Wanting to experience or make imaginative and empathetic connections with people in the past or present was the most frequently valued experience at labor sites (25%). It distinguished this genre from other genres in the study. The next most frequent response was to nominate an educational experience (17%), and a further 15% selected the experience of undertaking memory and identity work – affirming their sense of class, familial, and/or gender identities through reminiscing and other forms of remembering.

Those visitors who emphasized empathetic experiences and talked about the memory and identity work they were doing tended not to hold university degrees (29% and 21%, respectively vs 20% and 9% of those with university degrees); to be older (27% and 20% vs 21% and 6%); and to be returning visitors (29% and 19% vs 23% 14%). Those in lower-supervisory-routine positions engaged more frequently in self-conscious memory and identity work (28% vs 14%). Both returning visitors and those who had traveled from a home address strongly emphasized a sense of 'physically being in place' at the museum or site. This emphasis on physicality found synergy with Samuel's notion of heritage places as "theatres of memory," the sense of simply being in place adding to the strength of feeling and occasion of the memory work visitors were undertaking (Smith, 2006, p. 305). Those with degrees, and particularly if they were 44 or under and first-time visitors, tended to emphasize either educational or recreational experiences or nominated they had come to see a particular artifact – variables on the RoE that were identified as passive engagement.

What Does Being Here Mean to You?

'Being at' labor sites were marked by making strong and predominantly personal or familial active connections (38%). Again, this was a particular feature of both this genre and immigration museums that set them apart from other genres. Strongly made personal connections were most frequently made by older visitors (37% vs 25%), those in lower-supervisory-routine occupations (40% vs 34%), returning visitors (47% vs 27%), and those without tertiary qualifications (41% vs 33%).

Commemoration, much of it active, was also expressed as important to 18% of visitors, while 11% and 16% nominated recreation or education, respectively, the latter two being more frequently expressed by younger visitors. First-time visitors, those in professional occupations and with university degrees, stressed 'education.' As noted in the wider study, 'education' as a reason for this and preceding questions was often either a relatively passive form of engagement on the RoE or suggested visitor discomfort – that is, offering the potential educational role of the museum as a polite form of "The content of the interpretive material discomforts me" (Smith, 2021, p. 294).

Are There Any Messages About the Heritage or History of Australia/America/England That You Take Away From This Place?

The emotional repertoires engendered through visitors' connections and the imaginative empathy valued at labor sites correspond to a relatively low no-message response (16%). In the overall sample, 30% of visitors nominated that they took no message from their visit, and while this is a complicated response and could often indicate low visitor engagement, dissonance over curatorial messages or simply that attaining 'a message' was not the purpose of the visit, the relatively low frequency at labor sites suggests an overall active engagement of most visitors.

When messages were taken away, they tended to rest on simple reflections about how hard life was or still is (21%) and or were more profound reflections of historical gratitude based on an enabling sense of humility (13%). A further 13% also engaged in critical reflection on modern issues. This variable was found infrequently in all other genres except for the enslavement legacy sites and immigration sites.

Those with tertiary education, occupying professional positions or first-time visitors, tended to fall into two groups in response to this question. Those who engaged, within the relative RoE across the study, passively with the site they were visiting tended to take away 'no message' or they engaged deeply on the RoE and were critically engaged and using the site to reflect on modern issues. The former group tended to express some dissonance and discomfort with the sites they visited, while the latter group frequently engaged in a performance of intergenerational communication that worked to make emotional and reflective links to absent or deceased parents or grandparents, their lives, and industrial achievements. Older visitors also more frequently undertook critical reflections (15% vs 9%).

Returning visitors, those in lower-supervisory-routine occupations, those without university degrees, and/or those who had traveled from a home address tended to express historical gratitude and to reflect on and measure the difference in living standards between the past and present. Returning visitors and those who had traveled from a home address were also more frequently likely to note that the site affirmed their own identity. Older visitors expressed more historical gratitude than younger visitors (13% vs 9%).

What Meaning, If Any, Does an Exhibition Like This Have for Contemporary Australia/America/England?

A quarter to a third of visitors at most genres in the study identified sites as aides to national memory. At the same time, only 19% did so at labor sites (the only other exceptions were sites discussing the legacies and histories of enslavement). As aides to memory, labor sites were instead characterized as aides to personal memory (17%) or as aides to 'group memory,' specifically class memory (16%), characterizations relatively infrequent at other site genres. A further 29% of visitors identified the contemporary meaning of labor sites as educational, a relatively high response compared to different site genres, with the overall frequency being only 17%. This emphasis on education, particularly concerning this question (and in comparison to the following and previous questions), is interesting. The high education response here does not reflect people identifying that they have had an educational experience or expressing polite discomfort. Instead, it strongly reflects that these sites were educational for younger generations and groups to which the visitors did not belong. That is, they were defined as being an educational resource for other people. This reflects and underpins the strong intergenerational communication that many visitors at these sites undertake with their children or grandchildren. However, it also reflects a significant sense of loss of community following deindustrialization. It expresses a lament that while working-class history was not part of national remembering, it should be.

Those who had been to university (24% vs 14%) were far more likely to see the site they were visiting as an aide to national memory, and in doing so, they often depersonalized their visit. Those who had not been to university far more frequently (37% vs 18%) defined the meaning of the site as 'educational' – that is, lamenting its lack of national acknowledgment and registering hope that children and those from non-working-class backgrounds would learn from the site. Similarly, return visitors nominated the site's educational values. Still, they were also more frequently nominating the site as a personal or class memory aid. In contrast, first-time visitors tended to identify the site's meaning as a depersonalized aide to national memory.

Is There Anything You've Seen/Read/Heard Today That Has Changed Your Views About the Past or the Present?

This question attempted to gauge the extent to which visitors had changed their view and the degree to which their understanding of the history or heritage on display had deepened. Overall, 80% of visitors said either no or that their views had been reinforced, and at labor sites, 78% reported no change. Younger visitors were far more likely to change their views than those aged 45 and over (32% vs 17%). While this is good news for those visitors who, in response to the previous question, expressed hope that younger people would learn something from the site, it also, as argued concerning the wider study, illustrates the extent to which "educational/learning" discourses about visiting is problematic (Smith, 2021, p. 137). The learning discourse tends to stress that learning is done when people are presented with information and contexts where they are invited to 'learn.' However, as Biesta (2013) argues, learning occurs only when people have the desire and a purpose for acquiring new information or skills. At the labor sites, those engaged in learning were very often those who were already politically and socially receptive to the messages offered at the sites (Pekarik and Schreiber, 2012). But, more importantly, they tended to be engaged in heritage performances of intergenerational communication in which older family members accompanying younger visitors passed on social or familial histories. That is, the sites facilitated learning opportunities that, on the whole, were realized through the agencies of their visitors.

Discussion: Overall Patterns of Memorialization and Remembrance

Labor museums and sites are marked by strong familial and personal connections that underwrite performances of intergenerational communication and overt and self-conscious forms of remembering and identity-making, wherein sites were used as aides to class and familial memory. In opposition to other genres of dissonant sites and national museums, labor sites tended to actively measure social changes across time and express various forms of historical gratitude that often incorporated a sense of loss or 'progressive nostalgia' for the past. This nostalgia was not expressed as a desire to return to the past but acknowledged that the past was more difficult and fraught than the present. Acknowledgment was also offered for the gains that previous generations had made in workplace reform or celebrated the work and skills of labor and their contributions to contemporary living standards – which did not receive adequate national recognition. To redress this lack of recognition, visitors frequently nominated the importance of the educational possibilities of museum and heritage visiting for younger generations.

The connections made by visitors were expressive of a practice of visiting informed by social and political exclusion, itself reinforced by experiences of deindustrialization. This influenced performances of intergenerational heritage-making and affirmative assertions of community, individual, or familial self-esteem.

Strong personal and empathetic links to the sites were more frequently made by those over 45 and/or who did not hold university qualifications, lived locally, and/or were repeat visitors. As the qualitative analysis of the interviews illustrates (Smith and Campbell, 2017a; Smith, 2020, 2021), this profile tends to equate with those visitors using local heritage resources to assert an affirming performance that reinforces their sense of group and individual identity. Museums and heritage sites were used to self-affirm and were not used by this group to 'learn' about a past that such visitors were closely linked to and had experienced. Museums were arenas where visitors rehearsed, legitimized, and expressed feelings that their social experiences mattered. This expression has consequences, not simply for individual and group well-being, but politically, as affirmations of moral self-worth are used as platforms in wider struggles for social justice.

Those 44 and under, those with university degrees, and/or first-time visitors, and/or visitors from holiday addresses were likelier to see the sites as offering an educational experience and making fewer personal links. On the RoE, these factors are less actively used and engaged with this heritage than those represented by other groups. However, deeper engagement from this group could and did occur, especially as evidenced by the messages generated from their visit that reflected on past and present social issues. Deeper qualitative examinations of the interviews reveal that members of this profile, particularly when only one generation or a university degree away from familial experiences of working-class histories, tended to use the sites to make intergenerational links (Smith, 2021, pp. 240–258). These performances could be facilitated by older family members or were used to understand, remember, and emotionally connect with absent older family members. Embedded in this form of remembrance was often recognition of class mobility and associated gratitude alongside an enabling humbleness to previous generations. It would also include an inevitable reinforcement of familial transmitted social and political values such as those associated with community pride and organized labor.

The memory and identity work that visitors to labor heritage undertake supports observations made in the broader ethnographic work about the value and meaning of working-class heritage and the role of that heritage in the present (see Dicks, 2000; Eklund et al., 2021; Dellios, 2022; Shackel, 2018; Taksa, 2019; Berger, 2020; Forrant and Trasciatti, 2022). In particular, the findings reinforce the importance of intergenerational communications, as Dicks has emphasized, to working-class heritage while also reiterating the degree to which older generations, at least, use heritage to seek not only societal but intergenerational acknowledgment and respect. This highlights the degree to which the affective force of loss and the need for acknowledgment of loss and the achievements of organized labor documented in much of the ethnographic work are played out in the ways older visitors engage with and use labor heritage.

A complex interplay of emotions of loss, lament, pride, and empathetic gratitude occurred at the labor sites in this study as people made a range of personal and intergenerational connections to place or family histories and heritage. The forms of 'cultural capital' thus constructed and embodied by the visit are entirely different to those expressed at national and nationalizing museums. Museums of working-class history speak to their audiences who work to perform heritage-making that addresses their community and individual needs and aspirations. People visit museums and heritage to see people 'like themselves'; in the context of national institutions, this tends to reinforce social privilege and the status quo; at sites of working-class heritage, the generation of recognition of group identity and moral self-worth works to build an emotional and political resource from which to question and challenge the social status quo.

Conclusion

The ability to feel pride in past achievements speaks to the development of contemporary moral self-worth, which is important in class marginalization, deindustrialization, and the loss of work. These powerful assertions have material consequences in informing the judgments and ideological positions individuals and communities choose to affirm in struggles for social and economic justice (Sayer, 2005). Emotions such as pride, gratitude, and nostalgia do not have discrete or singular expressions but rather are bounded and managed by different rules of feeling in different social contexts. As I have argued elsewhere, visitors will tend to uncritically reassert and emotionally affirm the social status quo in sites of national heritage-making (Smith, 2021, 2022). The feeling rules at sites of national heritage-making legitimize the affective repertoires on display, so much so that visitors' emotions in these contexts are so naturalized that they will often go unnoticed or unremarked. In sites of dissonance, including labor heritage sites, the emotional repertoires on display have different feeling rules that make sense to the communities who visit, manage, and are represented by such sites. Those rules and the affective repertoires they legitimize may seem incomprehensible to those outside the relevant community, but the need to recognize and understand them is worth acknowledging. The emotional repertoires and affective intensities of the memorialization practices of visitors to labor heritage needs further examination for understanding the contemporary ideological choices communities and individuals make. This is especially the case as heritage performances undertaken in the context of social marginalization are often more considered and self-conscious than the memorialization practices framed by and then work to uphold social inclusion and privilege.

Notes

1 See, for example, chapters in Robinson, I. (ed.). (2012). *Heritage from Below*. London: Routledge; Smith, L., Shackel, P.A. and Campbell, G. (eds.). (2011). *Heritage Labour and the Working Classes*. London: Routledge; Berger, S. (ed.). (2020). *Constructing Industrial Pasts*. Oxford: Berghahn Books; Dicks, B. (2000). *Heritage, Place and Community*. Cardiff: University of Wales Press; High, S.C. and Lewis, D.W. (2007). *Corporate Wasteland: The Landscape and Memory of Deindustrialization*. Ithaca,

NY: ILR Press; Linkon, S.L. (2018). *The Half-Life of Deindustrialisation*. Ann Arbor: University of Michigan Press; Shackel, P.A. (2018). *Remembering Lattimer*. Champaign: University of Illinois Press; Shackel, P.A. (2023). *The Ruined Anthracite*. Champaign: University of Illinois Press, among many others.

2 Smith, L. (2012). *Emotional Heritage*. London: Routledge; Smith, L. (2006). *Uses of Heritage*. London: Routledge; for earlier work, see also Merriman, N. (1991). *Beyond the Glass Case*. Leicester: Leicester University Press.

3 Interviewees were asked to describe in their own words their ethnic or background or affiliation. For ease of analysis, these were then grouped into politically dominant or nondominant categories.

4 The British 'standard occupational classification (SOC 2000)' was used to classify and code occupations. See Office for National Statistics. (2019). *SOC 2000 and NS-SEC on the LFS*. https://webarchive.nationalarchives.gov.uk/20160108030321/www.ons.gov.uk/ons/guide-method/method-quality/specifi c/labour-market/soc-2000-and-ns-sec-on-the-lfs/index.html (Accessed 21 December 2019). For ease of analysis, these were then grouped into two groups.

5 For more specifics on these performances, see Smith, L. (2012). *Emotional Heritage*. London: Routledge.

6 'Statistically significant' refers to results that are unlikely (at a certain level of probability) to have occurred by chance. Tests used included Chi-square, Fisher's Exact Test, and Monte-Carlo re-samplings.

7 The cards proffered listed the reasons in order as recreation; education; taking the children; did not come specifically to see site or exhibition name, just in the area; to find about topic of exhibition/interpretation; to explore what it means to be Australian/American/British; followed, where relevant, by one or two reasons specific to the exhibition or site; other.

8 At war commemoration sites, gratitude was frequently expressed as a message that was taken away from a site rather than something that was embodied or felt.

Reference List

Bagnall, G. (2003). Performance and Performativity at Heritage Sites. *Museum and Society*, 1(2), pp. 87–103.

Bennett, T. (1995). *The Birth of the Museum: History, Theory, Politics*. London: Routledge.

Bennett, T., Savage, S., Silva, E., Warde, A., Gayo-Cal, M. and Wright, D. (2010). *Culture, Class, Distinction*. London: Routledge.

Berger, S. (ed.). (2020). *Industrial Heritage, Culture and Regional Identity in Regions/Cities Undergoing Structural Transformation*. Oxford: Berghahn Books.

Bevernage, B., Mestdah, E., Ramahlo, W.S.C. and Verberg, M.-G. (eds.). (2024). *Claiming the People's Past: Populist Engagements with History and the Challenges to Historical Thinking*. Cambridge: Cambridge University Press.

Biesta, G. (2013). Interrupting the Politics of Learning. *Power and Education*, 5(1), pp. 4–15.

Black, G. (2012). *Transforming Museums in the Twenty-First Century*. London: Routledge.

Bonnett, A. (2010). *Left in the Past: Radicalism and the Politics of Nostalgia*. Bloomsbury Publishing USA.

Bonnett, A. and Alexander, C. (2012). Mobile Nostalgias: Connecting Visions of the Urban Past, Present and Future Amongst Ex-Residents. *Transactions of the Institute of British Geographers*, 38, pp. 391–402.

Bounia, A., Nikiforidou, A., Nikonanou, N. and Matossian, A.D. (2012). *Voices from the Museum: Survey Research in Europe's National Museums, EuNaMus Report No. 5*. Linköping: Linköping University Electronic Press.

Bourdieu, P. (2012). *The Logic of Practice*. Stanford: Stanford University Press.

Boym, S. (2002). *The Future of Nostalgia*. Basic Books.

Butler, J. (1990). Gender Trouble, Feminist Theory, and Psychoanalytic Discourse. In Nicholson, L. (ed.) *Feministm/Postmodernism*. London: Routledge.

Cashman, R. (2006). Critical Nostalgia and Material Culture in Northern Ireland. *Journal of American Folklore*, 119, pp. 137–160.

Chynoweth, A., Lynch, B., Petersen, K. and Smed, S. (eds.). (2020). *Museums and Social Change: Challenging the Unhelpful Museum*. London: Routledge.

Coffee, K. (2024, forthcoming). The Gentrification of Working-Class Heritage in Lowell, Massachusetts. In Bozoğlu, G., Campbell, G., Smith, L. and Whitehead, C. (eds.) *Routledge International Handbook of Heritage and Politics*. London: Routledge.

De Nardi, S., Organge, H., High, S. and Koskinen-Koivisto, E. (eds.). (2019). *The Routledge Handbook of Memory and Place*. London: Routledge.

Dellios, A. (2022). *Heritage Making and Migrant Subjects in the Deindustrialising Region of the Latrobe Valley*. Cambridge: Cambridge University Press.

Dicks, B. (2000). *Heritage, Place and Community*. Cardiff: University of Wales Press.

Dicks, B. (2008). Performing the Hidden Injuries of Class in Coal-Mining Heritage. *Sociology*, 42(3), pp. 436–452.

Eklund, E., Holm, A. and Reeves, K. (2021). Industrial Heritage Agents, Actors and Outcomes: Regional Case Studies from Broken Hill and the Latrobe Valley. *Journal of Australian Studies*, 45(4), pp. 524–542.

Forrant, R. and Trasciatti, M.A. (eds.). (2022). *Where are the Workers? Labor's Stories at Museums and Historic Sites*. Urbana, IL: University of Illinois Press.

Gest, J., Reny, T. and Mayer, J. (2018). Roots of the Radical Right: Nostalgic Deprivation in the United States and Britain. *Comparative Political Studies*, 51(13), pp. 1694–1719.

Hall, S. (1999). Whose Heritage? Un-Settling 'The Heritage', Re-Imaging the Post-Nation. *Third Text*, 13, pp. 3–13.

Hanquinet, L. (2016). Place and Cultural Capital: Art Museum Visitors Across Space. *Museum & Society*, 14(1), pp. 65–81.

Harrison, R., DeSilvey, C., Holtorf, C., Macdonald, S., Bartolini, N., Breithoff, E., Fredheim, H., Lyons, A., May, S., Morgan, J. and Penrose, S. (2020). *Heritage Futures: Comparative Approaches to Natural and Cultural Heritage Practices*. London: UCL Press.

Hewison, R. (1987). *The Heritage Industry. Britain in a Climate of Decline*. London: Methuen.

High, S.C. and Lewis, D.W. (2007). *Corporate Wasteland: The Landscape and Memory of Deindustrialization*. Ithaca, NY: ILR Press.

Hochschild, A.R. (1979). Emotion Work, Feeling Rules, and Social Structure. *American Journal of Sociology*, 85(3), pp. 551–575.

Hochschild, A.R. (2018). *Strangers in Their Own Land: Anger and Mourning on the American Right*. New York: The New Press.

Janes, R.R. (2016). Museums and the Responsibility Gap. In Gosselin, V. and Livingstone, P. (eds.) *Museums and the Past: Constructing Historical Consciousness*. Vancouver: UBC Press.

Janes, R.R. and Sandell, R. (eds.). (2019). *Museum Activism*. London: Routledge.

Kallio, K. and Mansfield, N. (2013). Labour and Landscape. *International Journal of Heritage Studies*, 19(5), pp. 401–407.

Kaya, A. (2020). *Populism and Heritage in Europe: Lost in Diversity and Unity*. London: Routledge.

Kidd, J. (2011). Challenging History: Reviewing Debate within the Heritage Sector on the 'Challenge' of History. *Museum & Society*, 9(3), pp. 244–248.

Kinsley, R.P. (2016). Inclusion in Museums: A Matter of Social Justice. *Museum Management and Curatorship*, 31(5), pp. 474–490.

Linkon, S.L. (2018). *The Half-life of Deindustrialization: Working-Class Writing About Economic Restructuring*. Ann Arbor: University of Michigan Press.

Loveday, V. (2014). "Flat Capping It": Memory, Nostalgia and Value in Retroactive Male Working-Class Identification. *European Journal of Cultural Studies*, 17(6), pp. 721–735.

Lowenthal, D. (2015). *The Past is a Foreign Country-Revisited*. Cambridge: Cambridge University Press.

Macdonald, S. (2013). *Memorylands: Heritage and Identity in Europe Today*. London: Routledge.

Mansfield, N. and Trustram, M. (2013). Remembering the Buildings of the British Labour Movement: An Act of Mourning. *International Journal of Heritage Studies*, 19(5), pp. 439–456.

Merriman, N. (1991). *Beyond the Glass Case: The Past, the Heritage and the Public*. Leicester: Leicester University Press.

Pekarik, A.J. and Schreiber, J.B. (2012). The Power of Expectation. *Curator: The Museums Journal*, 55(4), pp. 487–496.

Reeves, K., Eklund, E., Reeves, A., Scates, B. and Peel, V. (2011). Broken Hill: Rethinking the Significance of the Material Culture and Intangible Heritage of the Australian Labour Movement. *International Journal of Heritage Studies*, 17(4), pp. 301–317.

Robertson, I. (ed.). (2012). *Heritage from Below*. London: Routledge.

Sandell, R. (2003). Social Inclusion, the Museum and the Dynamics of Sectorial Change. *Museum & Society*, 1(1), pp. 45–62.

Sandell, R. and Nightingale, E. (eds.). (2012). *Museums, Equality and Social Justice*. London: Routledge.

Sayer, A. (2005). Class, Moral Worth and Recognition. *Sociology*, 39(5), pp. 947–963.

Selwood, S. (2006). Unreliable Evidence: The Rhetoric of Data Collection in the Culture Sector. In Mirza, M. (ed.) *Culture Vultures: Is UK Arts Policy Damaging the Arts*. London: Policy Exchange.

Shackel, P.A. (2018). *Remembering Lattimer: Labor, Migration, and Race in Pennsylvania Anthracite Country*. Champaign: University of Illinois Press.

Shackel, P.A. (2023). *The Ruined Anthracite: Historical Trauma in Coal-Mining Communities*. Champaign: University of Illinois Press.

Smith, L. (2006). *Uses of Heritage*. London: Routledge.

Smith, L. (2020). Industrial Heritage and the Remaking of Class Identity – Are We All Middle Class Now? In Berger, S. (ed.) *Industrial Heritage, Culture and Regional Identity in Regions/Cities Undergoing Structural Transformation*. Oxford: Berghahn Books.

Smith, L. (2021). *Emotional Heritage: Visitor Engagement at Museums and Heritage Sites*. London: Routledge.

Smith, L. (2022). Heritage, the Power of the Past, and the Politics of (Mis)Recognition. *Journal for the Theory of Social Behaviour*, 54(4), pp. 623–642.

Smith, L. and Campbell, G. (2011). Don't Mourn Organise: Heritage Recognition and Memory in Castleford, West Yorkshire. In Smith, L., Shackel, P.A. and Campbell, G. (eds.) *Heritage, Labour, and the Working Classes*. London: Routledge.

Smith, L. and Campbell, G. (2017a). "Nostalgia for the Future": Memory, Nostalgia and the Politics of Class. *International Journal of Heritage Studies*, 23(7), pp. 612–627.

Smith, L. and Campbell, G. (2017b). The Tautology of 'Intangible Values' and the Misrecognition of Intangible Cultural Heritage. *Heritage & Society*, 10(1), pp. 26–44.

Smith, L., Shackel, P.A. and Campbell, G. (eds.). (2011). *Heritage, Labour, and the Working Classes*. London: Routledge.

Smith, L. and Waterton, E. (2009). *Heritage, Communities and Archaeology*. London: Duckworth.

Stanton, C. (2019). Displaying the Industrial: Toward a Genealogy of Heritage Labor. *Labor: Studies in Working-Class History*, 16(1), pp. 151–170.

Strangleman, T. (2013). Smokestack Nostalgia, Ruin Porn or Working-Class Obituary: The Role and Meaning of Deindustrial Representation. *International Labor and Working-Class History*, 84, pp. 23–37.

Taksa, L. (2019). Remembering and Incorporating Migrant Workers in Australian Industrial Heritage. *Labor*, 16(1), pp. 81–105.

Westmont, C.V. (2024, forthcoming). Trumpian Populism and Coal Mining Heritage in Northeastern Pennsylvania. In Bozoğlu, G., Campbell, G., Smith, L. and Whitehead, C. (eds.) *Routledge International Handbook of Heritage and Politics*. London: Routledge.

Williams, R. (1977). Structures of Feeling. *Marxism and Literature*, 1, pp. 128–135.

Wodak, R. (2020). Final Commentary: Learning from the Past(s)? Contesting Hegemonic Memories. In De Cesari, C. and Kaya, A. (eds.) *European Memory in Populism: Representations of Self and Other*. London: Routledge, pp. 276–293.

WorkLab: The International Association of Labour Museums. (n.d.). Home page, https://worklab.info/

26
UNCOVERING GENDER TRACKS

Erasure and Railway Industrial Heritage Initiatives Across the World

Lucy Taksa

Introduction

On July 17, 2003, the Nizhny Tagil Charter for Industrial Heritage "was passed by the assembled delegates at the triennial National Assembly of" the International Committee For The Conservation Of Industrial Heritage (TICCIH) Congress held in Moscow. The TICCIH is the world organization representing industrial heritage and is special adviser to the International Council on Monuments and Sites (ICOMOS) on industrial heritage (Njuguna, Wahome, and Deisser, 2018, p. 26). The Charter recognized that the buildings and structures, processes and tools associated with industrial activities, "along with all their other tangible and intangible manifestations" and surrounding towns and landscapes "are of fundamental importance." Moreover, it stressed that the "meaning and significance" of industrial heritage "should be probed and made clear for everyone," and it therefore recommended that "the most significant and characteristic examples should be identified, protected, and maintained. . . . for the use and benefit of today and of the future" (The Nizhny Tagil Charter for The Industrial Heritage, 2003). As the Charter (2003) noted:

> Industrial heritage is of social value as part of the record of the lives of ordinary men and women, and as such it provides an important sense of identity. It is of technological and scientific value in the history of manufacturing, engineering, construction, and it may have considerable aesthetic value for the quality of its architecture, design, or planning.

The Charter further recommended that "the meaning and value of industrial sites" should be explained "through publications, exhibitions, television, the Internet and other media" and "sustainable access to important sites" should be enabled "by promoting tourism in industrial areas" (The Nizhny Tagil Charter for The Industrial Heritage, 2003).

This chapter raises questions about the practical implications of the Charter and its recommendations. Specifically, it asks whether preservation and physical and virtual access to industrial heritage through museums and tourism initiatives at deindustrialized sites have adequately probed the meaning and significance of the social "value" of industrial heritage,

DOI: 10.4324/9781003308324-37

Uncovering Gender Tracks

what values have been conveyed through industrial heritage initiatives (Smith and Campbell, 2017), how they relate to the plethora of "objects, structures, landscapes, and historical practices" that it encompasses (Morin, 2014), and what specific "sense of identity" has been and is being transmitted. As a corollary, it explores meanings that remain to be probed as part of industrial heritage initiatives, particularly in relation to gender.

To explore which meanings and identities are being spread by industrial heritage initiatives in different parts of the world, the chapter focuses on rail transport, its infrastructure, and machinery, which have consistently been included among definitions of industrial heritage and industrial heritage tourism initiatives. Albeit not as prominent in industrial heritage scholarship as sites associated with manufacturing and extractive industries (Kerley, 2010; Bence, 2012; Bhati, Pryce, and Chaiechi, 2014; Gould, 2015), railways and their associated tangible heritage are an ever-present feature of industrial transport heritage initiatives. Indeed, for Muriel-Ramirez (2017), the terms "industrial heritage and railway heritage" are virtually synonyms because "their meaning is very close, with railways being just a particular kind of industry." As Njuguna, Wahome, and Deisser (2018, p. 22) pointed out, "a railway creates its own narratives and significantly transforms a society by exposing it to the rest of the world. It creates new social, economic, and political relations as a form of intangible heritage."

This chapter argues that the "technological and scientific value in the history of manufacturing, engineering, construction" (The Nizhny Tagil Charter for The Industrial Heritage, 2003) dominates this rail transport domain of industrial heritage as demonstrated by the privilege and priority given to technological hardware and operations. These features are most prominent in conservation efforts related to deindustrialized/decommissioned sites and interpretation displays through which value and meaning of rail transport's heritage is explained by means of a variety of mechanisms and media. This orientation has immense implications for the recognition, or more precisely lack of recognition, of gender in rail-related industrial heritage initiatives and memoryscapes.

It is through "the genre known as 'industrial railway heritage attractions'" (Bhati, Pryce, and Chaiechi, 2014, p. 113) that railways provide "a source of heritage tourism assets and experience," which "can be in the form of railway museums, preserved rail tracks and rail journeys in original carriages, engines and buildings" (Bhati, Pryce, and Chaiech, 2014, p. 117). Importantly, scholars have argued that visits to such heritage attractions offer opportunities for "reaffirmation of identity" and, as importantly, since "both heritage and identity form a strong relationship with tourism, then heritage tourism inevitably becomes an issue of politics." As Bhati, Pryce, and Chaiechi (2014, p. 122) put it, "[t]his relationship between heritage and identity adds further complexity to the issues surrounding heritage railway attractions."

To demonstrate how initiatives to preserve, manage, and interpret the tangible and intangible dimensions of railway industrial heritage in a wide range of countries fail to probe the meaning of identity related to the heritage on display, the chapter examines how 'Things' and social relations are entangled in authorized heritage discourse relating to rails and rail heritage. By focusing on "What is 'said'" and "what is 'unsaid,' but taken as given" (Smith and Campbell, 2017, p. 28), I aim to highlight the gender politics that frame rail industrial heritage and rail heritage tourism and in doing so to show that the extensive, albeit, not universal, changes in gendered norms, which have occurred around the world since the 1970s, have been, and continue to be, disregarded in rail memoryscapes.

To provide an overview of the most prominent aspects of railway industrial heritage, the chapter begins with a listing of numerous rail industrial heritage preservation and access initiatives in many different national contexts. The point of this listing is to demonstrate the global extent of rail industrial heritage initiatives in deindustrialized locales and to provide a basis for identifying their commonalities. In this way, the chapter will demonstrate that such commonalities have rendered gender invisible in rail memoryscapes, effectively erasing it from rail heritage sites and rail heritage tourism regardless of location. A conceptual framing of gender vis-à-vis rail industrial heritage initiatives is then presented to help explain how such heritage initiatives convey traditional industrial-era gendered assumptions, stereotypes, and representations. The discussion explains how this orientation ensures a close association between rail heritage memoryscapes and hegemonic masculinity, which invariably serves to sustain outmoded gendered norms across the world and across generations.

Railways as industrial heritage

According to Llano-Castresana, Azkarate, and Sánchez-Beitia (2013, pp. 61–62): "Railways are one of the most valuable heritage assets from the second industrial revolution" and "also part of our heritage and our memory, silent witnesses of our closest industrial past." Included as part of rail industrial heritage are (i) infrastructure in the form of rail tracks, engineering structures, and a wide range of different types of buildings and structures, such as rail and freight stations, locomotive and tram depots, manufacturing and maintenance workshops, guardhouses at level crossings, and signal boxes; (ii) railway rolling stock, such as locomotives, carriages, freight, and related wagons, tramways, and a myriad of machines, tools, and equipment used to build and maintain all the hardware; (iii) smaller objects, such as station clocks, tickets, and the devices to print and distribute them to passengers, as well as the work wear of those employed in railway systems, historic photographs, and a range of other artifacts. In addition, the occupations and skills that supported rail operations and the safety of rail workers and passengers are often included in railway heritage memoryscapes (Falser, 2001; Gould, 2015). The focus on these tangible and intangible aspects of rail industrial heritage has shaped and arguably also constrained rail heritage memoryscapes.

In effect, railways, rail infrastructure, and their material remains are ubiquitous in many "industrial" heritage initiatives stretching across many countries in Africa, Asia and the Middle East, Australia and New Zealand, Europe, the UK, and North, Central, and South America. For the most part, these emphasize the steam era and its buildings, technological hardware, and operations. To give an indication of the global spread of such heritage initiatives, the following listing gives examples from different continents.

In Africa, they include the rail museum in Nairobi, Kenya (Njuguna, Wahome, and Deisser, 2018) and Jackel House, the Nigerian Railway Corporation's mini museum at its headquarters in Ebutte-Metta, Lagos, and the Lagos-Ibadan standard gauge rail line (Editor Guardian Nigeria, 2019; Sulaimon, 2019). In the Middle East and Asia, heritage initiatives include rail buildings and movable heritage in Turkey (Yazar, 2013; Ekimci, Ergincan and Inceoglu, 2019; Seyrek and Omay Polat, 2024)), the Hijaz Railway in Saudi Arabia (Orbaşli and Woodward, 2008; Saudi Government, 2023), the National Rail Museum in Chanakyapuri, New Delhi, India (Ebert, 2011) among many rail heritage sites in that country (Joshi, 2017, 2018; Joshi and Johri, 2023), the Railway Museum in Omiya, Japan (Huang, 2007), the Taipei Railway Workshop in Taiwan (Chen et al., 2020), the Lampang Railway station buildings, yards, and locomotive and freight sheds in northern Thailand (Yiamjanya, 2020), the Penang Hill Railway in Malaysia (Bhati, Pryce, and Chaiechi, 2014), the Malaysia–Singapore line, and the Tanjong Pagar Railway Station in Singapore (Henderson, 2014; Singapore

Government, 2022). Among others in various Australian states, notable examples include the Puffing Billy Railway in Victoria, the Kuranda Railway and the Ipswich Workshops Rail Museum in Queensland (Bhati, Pryce, and Chaiechi, 2014; Queensland Government, n.d.), and the NSW Rail Museum located within the historic town of Thirlmere south of Sydney (Transport Heritage NSW, 2024). In New Zealand, the Glenbrook Vintage Railway is prominent among several (Reis and Jellum, 2014; Glenbrook Vintage Railway, n.d.).

European examples include the Spoorwegmuseum in Utrecht in the Netherlands (Gwynne, 2009), the Rio Tinto heritage railway in Andalusia (Muriel-Ramirez, 2017), the Basque Railway Museum at the old Azpeitia Station (Llano-Castresana, Azkarate, and Sánchez-Beitia, 2013; Iron Route in the Pyrenees, n.d.), the Ciernohronska Forest Railway in Slovakia (Krešáková, 2021), the Railway Museum at Jaworzyna Śląska in Poland (Gerber, 2013), the Gyor-Veszprem railway line and the Magyar Vasúttörténeti Park Railway Museum in Hungary (Bence, 2012), and the Rhaetian Railway in Switzerland (Boksberger and Sturzenegger, 2014). In England, the National Rail Museum in York (Figures 26.1 and 26.2) and STEAM, the Museum of the Great Western Railway in Swindon, figure among an extensive number of rail heritage sites across the UK (Taksa, 2003, 2006, 2017; Railway Museum, n.d.; STEAM Museum of the Great Western Railway, n.d.).

In the Americas, rail heritage is also extensive. Canada features the Exporail Canadian Railway Museum and the Toronto Rail Museum, among others, and in the US, the California State Railroad Museum in Sacramento (Figures 26.3 and 26.4) and the Railroaders Museum in Altoona, Pennsylvania are prominent among a wide-ranging number of rail

Figure 26.1 National Railway Museum, York, UK, Locomotives. (Copyright: Lucy Taksa, 2007)

Figure 26.2 National Railway Museum, York, UK, Rail Clocks. (Copyright: Lucy Taksa, 2007)

heritage sites (Taksa, 2006, 2008; California State Railroad Museum, n.d.[a]; The Railroaders Memorial Museum, n.d.).

Notable examples are also to be found in Central and South America, prominent among which are the Locomotive Repair Building in Aguascalientes in Mexico (Collazo, 2017), the Trelew railway station in the province of Chubut, the La Trochita narrow gauge railway in Argentina's Patagonia region (Oliveira and Ferrari, 2015), and the Estrada de Ferro in Araraquarense and the Devil's Railway in Brazil (de Lima Lourencetti, 2021; Sherwood, 2010). It is impossible to include a complete or exhaustive listing of the immense number of such sites around the world. Nonetheless, those included here indicate that rail industrial heritage initiatives are truly a global phenomenon.

Although there are many reasons why railways have spawned so many heritage sites, a couple are of utmost significance. First, the rise of modern railways in the UK in the nineteenth

Figure 26.3 California State Railroad Museum Locomotive, Sacramento USA. (Copyright: Lucy Taksa, 2002)

century had a major historical impact by helping to propel the industrial revolution, an energy revolution, economic growth, and mass employment, which spread through imperialism well beyond Europe to the Americas, the Ottoman Empire, a range of countries in Africa, Asia, and Australia and New Zealand, becoming the dominant mode of transport around the world between the 1830s and 1950s and in some places into the 1970s (Chandler, 1965; Taksa, 2017). Second, this multifaceted impact spawned a long-standing emotional connection to railways and specifically the steam locomotive, dating back to the boom period between 1845 and 1847 that Wolmar (2007, p. 86) referred to as 'railway mania.' A century later, according to Samuel (1996, p. 236), there arose a "railway preservation mania" in response to the "modernization and rationalization" that accompanied the "extinction of branch railways and narrow-gauge lines" and the replacement of steam with diesel locomotives in the UK in the early 1950s. For Coulls, Divall, and Lee (1999, p. 4) "the whole story" from the mid-twentieth century "has been one of slow decline, at least in terms of route mileage." It was against this background that the "mass historical enthusiasm" for rail heritage grew exponentially, catching "the public imagination in a very big way, calling up childhood memories . . . and offering historical rides in the most picturesque parts of the country" (Samuel, 1996, p. 186). Indeed, the closure of rail lines and cessation of rail operations in many places, as part of deindustrialization, has inspired investment in preservation activities and the setting up of museums and other rail heritage tourist activities across

Figure 26.4 California State Railroad Museum Carriage, Sacramento USA. (Copyright: Lucy Taksa, 2002)

the world. In other words, rail deindustrialization, as I have argued elsewhere (Taksa, 2017) has not been a linear, uni-direction process; rather it connects the shift away from industrial manufacturing towards the service economy. As the foregoing listing of rail heritage sites and museums in so many different countries shows, deindustrialization of rail operations has not dissipated emotional connections to industrial era railways, their infrastructure, and their hardware nor to the demand for their conservation. Indeed, it can be argued that the symbolism associated with the railways fulfils "associational and psychological needs," which provide continuing rationale for the conservation of the railway's tangible remains (Njuguna, Wahome, and Deisser, 2018, p. 24).

Hence, despite the diversity of regional, national, economic, social, and cultural contexts in which rail heritage initiatives are found, they are remarkably similar. Indeed, close examination through a gendered lens highlights significant consistencies in approach to the construction of rail memoryscapes in deindustrialized locales. In the first place, working people are a negligible feature in these places and in virtual exhibitions. Even when men and women who worked in or were engaged with rail operations are acknowledged at these places (Figures 26.5 and 26.6), prominence tends to be given to male workers and often to 'great men,' notably the inventors, the engineers, and leading managers.

Women are rarely included, and in cases where they are, the focus is on an emblematic woman, with the Rosie the Riveter trope (California State Railroad Museum, n.d.[b])

Figure 26.5 California State Railroad Museum Sacramento USA. Male rail workers. (Copyright: Lucy Taksa, 2002)

standing in for the role of women in war particularly in the US (Union Pacific Railroad Museum, n.d.). Little recognition is given to the broader gendered dimensions of rail operations generally or during wartimes when large numbers of women were engaged in rail work in many countries resulting in complicated gender relations (Taksa, 2019). In effect, no efforts are made to recognize, acknowledge, or question the gender culture associated with rail-related industrial work in these places, nor the links between technology, industrial machinery, and masculinity (Taillon, 2001; Taksa, 2005). It can be argued that two particular interconnected factors contribute to the erasure of gendered dimensions of rail heritage, namely (i) obsession with technological infrastructure and hardware and (ii) technological determinism.

Obsession with 'big things,' such as trains, related rolling stock and railway buildings, is prevalent at sites of railway heritage and tourism. In Africa, tourism opportunities to generate revenue are evident in Ebutte-Metta, Lagos at the headquarters of the Nigerian Railway Corporation's mini museum and the Nigerian government's initiative to set up a rail museum and to "rehabilitate about 3,505 kilometers of the entire narrow gauge" between Lagos and Ibadan. Indeed, at the Jackel House Museum (named after a former [male] superintendent), the focus centers on railway artifacts and steam locomotives and carriages "gathered in the premises in the railway compound." The potential for "rehabilitation of a couple of steam locomotives for tourists' use" is represented as a way of capitalizing on the "huge

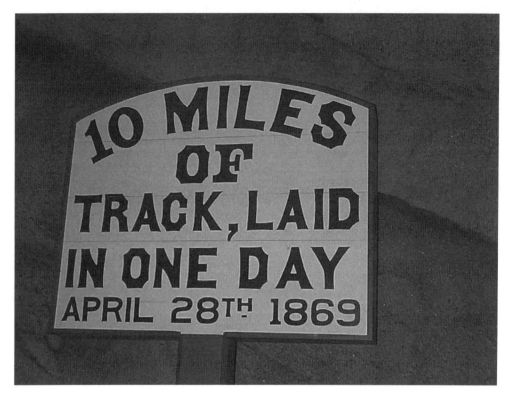

Figure 26.6 California State Railroad Museum Sacramento USA. Historical sign regarding the laying of tracks. (Copyright: Lucy Taksa, 2002)

international market for heritage steam in other countries" and as a basis for further rail modernization (Sulaimon, 2019; Ugwu, 2010). Likewise, in New Zealand's Goldfields heritage railway, which starts at Waihi, the preserved station building and yard infrastructure includes a goods shed, six railway houses and ancillary buildings, along with steam and diesel locomotives, passenger carriages and freight wagons, and a Cowans-Sheldon 10-tonne railway crane. Here, NZ Online encourages potential visitors to "Travel back in time and enjoy a ride on a heritage train with Goldfields Railway" (Goldfields Railway, n.d.; Goldfields Heritage Railway, n.d.). Further north, another significant heritage railway site and museum is located in Whangarei, Northland (Whangarei Steam & Model Railway Club, n.d.) (Figures 26.7–26.10).

Another example is provided by Saudi Arabia's Hijaz Railway, which ran between Medina and Tabuk (Orbaslı and Woodward, 2008). In Medina's restored historic Ottoman railway station, the Hejaz Railway Museum includes a "treasure trove of artefacts, manuscripts and photographs from a bygone era" and several engines and pieces of rolling stock on display, while in Tabuk, a preserved station includes a restored locomotive and freight car, as well as "other period relics" (Saudi Government, 2023).

This obsession with rail technology and infrastructure, or what Stuart (1992, p. 140) referred to as "object fetishism," clearly conveys values and meanings that serve to sustain

Figure 26.7 Whangarei Steam Club. Whangarei Museum and Heritage Park, Northland, New Zealand. (Copyright: Lucy Taksa, 2004)

the technological determinism of the industrial era with its belief in the progressive march of technology, reflecting the presumption of linear evolution from steam to diesel to electric power and the dominance of "man" over nature (Passmore, 1974). It has been argued that this notion of "mastery over nature" "remains a powerful emblem of technology," as well as of science and engineering also evident "in wider culture." Indeed, as Faulkner (2001, p. 82) pointed out, symbolic links between "[a]chieving control and domination over nature," modern technology and hegemonic masculinity, call for technology to be understood "as a 'masculine culture'." Yet, as Faulkner also stressed,

> [i]t is useful to distinguish between gender in technology and gender of technology. In the former case, gender relations are both embodied in and constructed or reinforced by artifacts to yield a very material form of the mutual shaping of gender and technology. In the latter, the gendering of artifacts is more by association than by material embodiment. . . . One aspect of the gendering by association lies in the symbolism that attaches to technology.
>
> *(Faulkner, 2001, p. 83)*

In this regard, she noted that "[t]he symbolic gendering of technology extends beyond the artifactual but may still have material consequences" and that "the association between masculinity and technology . . . operates largely at the level of the image technology holds for outsiders," which she argued contributes to "continued male dominance" (Faulkner, 2001,

Figure 26.8 Railway Memorabilia Museum, Northland, New Zealand. (Copyright: Lucy Taksa, 2004)

Figure 26.9 Whangarei rail artifact. Whangarei Museum and Heritage Park, Northland, New Zealand (Copyright: Lucy Taksa, 2004)

Uncovering Gender Tracks

Figure 26.10 Whangarei diesel. Whangarei Museum and Heritage Park, Northland, New Zealand. (Copyright: Lucy Taksa, 2004)

p. 85). This view is particularly apt for both rail technology and rail industrial heritage. It is therefore:

> important to explore the various ways in which artifacts are gendered, because it serves to underline the otherwise (to many) improbable point that even the "nuts and bolts" of technology warrant a feminist gaze.
>
> *(Faulkner, 2001, p. 84)*

A number of examples of the nexus between object fetishism (Figure 26.11) and technological determinism provide a useful way of highlighting what Cockburn (1983, p. 17) depicted as "[t]he prevailing belief" that technology "is neutral," and for establishing the basis for a gender framing of rail industrial heritage.

One case in point is provided by the heritage initiatives related to the Basque Railway Museum at the old Azpeitia station, whose website proclaims, "The railway is one of the great achievements of the Industrial Revolution. Steam, iron and steel came together to create a means of transport that revolutionized society" (Iron Route in the Pyrenees, n.d.). Importantly, the relationship between this combination of elements and linear technological determinism is reflected in the Museum itself, which has a collection of "over seventy vehicles, from smoking steam locomotives to silent electric trains, along with passenger carriages, freight wagons, tramways or trolleybuses," its power plant retaining "the original transformers from 1925" that "plunge us in that world of Futurism . . . of a hundred years ago!" Here too, a mechanical shop, described as "a veritable museum of the machine-tool sector" contains "16 engines driven by a single electric motor by means of a complex system of pulleys, bushbars and belts." Meanwhile, the station building includes "an exhibition of over

The Routledge Handbook of Deindustrialization Studies

Figure 26.11 California State Railroad Museum Sacramento USA. Technological artifact. (Copyright: Lucy Taksa, 2002)

200 clocks that the railways used to teach the world how to measure the passing of time" (Iron Route in the Pyrenees, n.d.); a passing that is explicitly informed by the assumption of linear progress.

Another example can be found in Brazil, where the "Francisco Aureliano de Araújo" Railway Museum in the renovated premises of the old Railway Station includes restored "original features" such as ticket booths, a nineteenth-century clock, work and ID cards, photographs of employees and of stations and locomotives, exhibitions of tools, lamps, and "objects from the wagons (lamp, washbasin parts, door locks, heavy tools, lanterns, lanterns)." And while the "Immigrant Memorial Room" recognizes the cultural diversity of the Italian, Japanese, and Portuguese people who worked in Araraquara, a key feature is "a 7.5-meter panel 'LINE OF TIME,'" which presents the history of the railroad, from the 1930s until today, with an overview of the railroad in Araraquara, in Brazil and in the world (Railway Museum of Araraquara Francisco Aureliano de Araújo, n.d.).

In a similar vein, at the Canadian Railway Museum, "located near the very first railroad in Canada," visitors can "admire over 400 railway artifacts," the largest railway collection in Canada and "among the largest of its kind in the world." Paying "homage to the workers who built the railroads," this museum gives witness to "how the railroad went from a dream to a reality, in terms of both its technological innovations and social dimensions, to develop Canada and all of its communities." Certainly, issues of race were acknowledged through a

448

2011 exhibit that explored "the fascinating story of the Chinese laborers who contributed to the construction of the Canadian Pacific Railway." However, virtual capsules available via smartphones including vignettes dealing with railway work and "the physical characteristics of the vehicles or their use" focus on enhancing understanding of "how the devices in the vehicles work" rather than giving attention to the workers, their work, or their relations. In short, the museum fulfils "its mission by developing, preserving, and showcasing a collection of Canadian railway heritage objects and allowing the public to live the railway experience on its site" (Tourisme Montréal, n.d.). No reference is given to the workers' identities, and the gendered culture of rail work during the nineteenth and most of the twentieth centuries is completely ignored.

The Railway Museum in Omiya in the Japanese city of Saitamaapan adopts an analogous trajectory. Located in an old diesel train workshop, which became obsolete after the conversion of diesel to electric railcars, the museum is designed to tell the story of the railway industry and the progress of railway systems through its 610,000 artifacts and by running displayed cars on some of the tracks and routes in the workshop that have been preserved and maintained. In this way it fulfils its mission to "introduce the principles and mechanisms of railways and the latest technologies" (Huang, 2007). At the Rolling Stock Station, "the largest exhibition area" in the museum, 36 different rolling stock are displayed, from "the first locomotive to run" in Japan "in 1872, to the Shinkansen, which boasted the world's fastest cutting-edge technology." Here, according to the website: "you can experience the tremendous size and power of rolling stock, and feel first hand the dynamism of these trains when they were in operation, through a production using video, audio, lighting, and ICT" (East Japan Railway Company, n.d.).

These examples demonstrate the way that the tangible remains of the industrial era are neutered, severed from identities of and relations between the men and women who worked on the railways, and the gendered cultures that shaped their relations. No efforts are evident to probe meanings and identity. In cases where attention is given to the latter, the focus is on empire, nation, or region.

Gendering memoryscapes

Although scholars have increasingly recognized that "stories of deindustrialization and industrial heritage are profoundly gendered" (Berger and High, 2019, p. 5), gender issues are blatantly disregarded at all the aforementioned sites, and as far as I have been able to ascertain, all other initiatives to preserve and make accessible rail industrial heritage at deindustrialized sites. It could be argued that such erasure of gender can be explained by the difficulties of presenting in a digestible manner, the complexities of gender, beyond traditional dichotomics and dualistic premises, and of the need to account for fluidity and hybridity (Frances and Paechter, 2015; Reading, 2015; Wilson, 2018). However, to my mind this is a lame excuse and a problematic one given that silences regarding gender serve to reproduce and legitimize stereotypical "gender identities and the social values that underpin them" (Smith, 2008, p. 161). In light of the overview and examples presented earlier, I argue that railway industrial memoryscapes presented through rail heritage initiatives sustain this reproduction and legitimation through their almost exclusive focus on the tangible material culture associated with steam-era technologies and hardware and by extension initiatives related to diesel- and electric-powered rail technologies. This failure to give any, let alone critical recognition to gendered norms and gendered relations that formed a central feature of rail operations and rail work during the steam era and after it, is of utmost significance since it ensures that the nexus between gender and technology is overlooked at rail heritage sites. In effect, this serves to cast outmoded norms and relations in aspic, extending their longevity not only in the present but also as a legacy for the future. However, as Cockburn noted over 40 years ago, technology is "neither neuter nor neutral" (Cockburn, 1983, p. 17). On the contrary, she stressed that contemporary technology expresses and embodies:

> values that have on the one hand developed out of patriarchy, and on the other have developed to make patriarchy what it is in modern society. The relations surrounding technology continually renew and extend male hegemony over the rest of us. The growth of industrial technology has to be seen as part and parcel of the historical development of gender difference.
>
> *(Cockburn, 1983, p. 18)*

In fact, the nexus between gender, changes in rail technologies (Taksa, 2005, Walsh, 2002, 2007), and steam-related icons and artifacts at deindustrialized sites of steam heritage in different parts of the world (Taksa, 2017) have been noted, especially in relation to the 'romance-of-steam' narrative and its international currency via literary and other media. And while there have been efforts made relatively recently at sites of rail industrial heritage to shift the focus from railway men to include railway women (Robinson, n.d.; Enss, 2021), they are by no means widespread across the globe. Moreover, it must be said that simply adding women to the historic record or to displays does little to obviate the traditional, dichotomous gendered assumptions that both explicitly and implicitly prevail in rail heritage initiatives. In what amounts to an authorized heritage discourse that frames such initiatives, masculinity continues to "stand in for the general" without the need for "explicit naming"; it literally "goes without saying" (Salzinger, 2004, p. 13) thereby ensuring the endurance of hegemonic masculinity in rail heritage memoryscapes.

How can these gender dimensions of rail heritage be interrogated? Butler's conceptualization of gender performativity is pertinent here. As she has stressed, "gender is prompted by obligatory norms" and "there is no gender without this reproduction of norms" (Butler, 2009, p. 1). Of particular relevance here is her argument that "[t]he performativity of gender is thus bound up with the differential ways in which subjects become eligible for recognition" (Butler, 2009, p. iv). In short, it "has everything to do with 'who' can become produced as a recognizable subject, a subject . . . whose life, when lost, would be worthy of mourning" (Butler, 2009, p. xii). However, before gendered memoryscapes can be interrogated as "a discursive practice or 'performance'" (Cockburn and Ormrod, 1993, p. 7; and generally, Butler, 1990), additional points need to be made about gender to enable a departure from the traditional gender blindness that has dominated transport history and heritage, primarily because of the focus on machinery, technological processes, modes of transport, and operations of rail organizations that have traditionally targeted mainly male audiences (Walsh, 2002).

Feminist scholars of technology have long demonstrated that a gendered perspective encourages us to recognize the nexus between technology relations and social relations (Wajcman, 1991; Cockburn and Ormrod, 1993; Lohan and Faulkner, 2004). Specifically in terms of the gendered dimensions of industrial heritage memoryscapes, it becomes important to focus attention on gender symbolism as "a fundamental category within which meaning, and value are assigned" (Harding, 1986, p. 57 cited in Cockburn and Ormrod, 1993,

p. 6). As Cockburn and Ormrod argued, for gender to be "read as 'a discursive practice or performance'," gender symbolism needs to be viewed "in terms of representations and meanings" (Cockburn and Ormrod, 1993, p. 7). In this regard, they drew attention to "projected identity" as this relates to the "potential, actual or desired gendered identities as others perceive or portray them." Identifying these dimensions makes it possible to explore the way rail heritage continues to this day to be a bearer of hegemonic masculinity.

Human geographer, Liz Bondi offers one more valuable avenue for relating gender symbolism and projected gender identities to the doing of gender at rail heritage sites. Focusing on the "apparent interplay between changing gender identities and changing urban landscapes," Bondi (1992, p. 158) was specifically interested in reading "the urban landscape for statements about, and constructions of, femininity and masculinity" to identify "what versions of femininity and masculinity are being articulated" (Bondi, 1992, p. 157). Her concern was to examine "largely shared systems of general beliefs" specifically about gender differences, which "are associated with the built environment" and "which are partially created and sustained by design" (Bondi, 1992, p. 157). Bondi was, in fact, highly critical of the tendency for simplistic relationships to be drawn between architectural styles and gender dichotomies, whereby "masculinity is recognized in what is large, solid and powerful, and in what is linear and vertical" (Bondi, 1992, p. 158). In her view, such crude biological definitions of what is masculine and what is feminine in appraisals of architectural style purvey dichotomous gender coding and differences as unchanging and universal (Bondi, 1992, p. 160). Nevertheless, she showed that such gender coding was evident in popular imagery, noting for example how "skyscrapers symbolize power through the use of verticality" and that such symbolism has "been created and sustained in a variety of cultures operating 'via a key symbol of masculinity'" (Bondi, 1992, p. 160). In effect, she pointed out that "buildings operate as symbolic representations of gender" and that the failure of professional and lay interpretations to "explore the relationship between these representations and the lives of women and men inhabiting, working in or moving around these environments," and "to question dominant representations of gender, implicitly endorse and sustain patriarchal gender relations" (Bondi, 1992, p. 161). Her conclusion that such representations "bear the impress of former ideas about gender identities" and that painstaking renovations in effect recuperate them (Bondi, 1992, p. 164) is particularly pertinent to rail heritage initiatives and memoryscapes across the globe.

Yet the overt erasure of gender at sites of railway heritage is not the prime focus of the scholarship on erasure relating to heritage. For the most part, the latter has concentrated on the destruction of "material traces of the past of national or regional importance" associated with "cultural heritage" and also endangerment, disappearance, and preservation of intangible heritage. Increasingly, this literature has also focused on "impermanence, and renewal that build on local traditions and practices that are still alive and perpetuated by living communities," particularly vis-à-vis Indigenous communities (Alivizatou, 2011; Holtorf and Kristensen, 2015; See also Bharucha, 2000). In this context, museums and other heritage initiatives "amplify" certain voices and identities while erasing others (Lim, 2021). Of course, erasure of gender from railway industrial heritage and its memoryscapes does not involve the same acts as depicted by these accounts of erasure, particularly that relate to Indigenous pasts. Nonetheless, I use the term insofar as it suggests processes by which the favoring of certain representations serve to nullify and 'blot out' others, obviating the need to probe meanings and identities. We see this not only in regard to artifacts and displays but also in language and speech acts (Pennycook, 2004; Yaghoubi-Notash et al., 2020). One example is "the Old Patagonian Express, better known as 'La Trochita'," which has been represented as "one of the most famous trains in the world. It's a unique historical and cultural heritage, drawing railroad fans from all parts of the globe." In this case riding on the Express is depicted as being "like neglecting the passing of time and losing oneself in a children's tale of the early twentieth century" (Contenidos Patagonia, n.d.). How does this representation relate to gender symbolism?

According to Taillon (2001), children's rail tales are replete with gender-specific metaphors that convey gendered assumptions, norms, and performances. Reverend W. Awdry's Thomas the Tank Engine stories and characters are a good case in point since they provide insight not only into these norms but equally into their transmission. Probing these stories using a gendered lens illustrates that traditional industrial-era gender norms form a consistent thread woven through metaphors, symbols, and codes in the stories from their first appearance in 1945 to the last one in 1972, enduring to this day in rail memoryscapes and tourist collateral (Taksa, 2017). One recent example is provided by 'A Day Out with Thomas" hosted by the NSW Rail Museum (2024), which invited steam and rail heritage lovers in Australia to "'Pop' on board a train ride adventure with Thomas & Friends" over six days in March 2024.

These stories reflect on the progressive linear march of rail technology by highlighting the tensions between different masculinities brought to the fore by the gradual demise of steam and the rise of dieselization. They also give an indication of the impact that the employment of women in the railways in England had in the decades after the Second World War. For instance, throughout the stories, steam engines Thomas, Edward, Gordon, Henry, James, and Toby (Awdry, 1996) are depicted as honest and hardworking. By contrast, diesels, which appeared from 1957, provide a stark contrast to the former's 'respectable' masculinity. Initially depicted in male form, they are referred to as "diseasals" and devious, sneaky creatures that "purred" with "an oily voice" (Awdry, 1996, pp. 205–206, 209, 211, 320). However, in 1961, Daisy the Diesel enters center stage. For Awdry, Daisy was not like Annie and Clarabel, the emotionally sensitive coaches that "ran happily behind" Thomas, Edward, Gordon, Henry, and James. Daisy was "hard to please. She shuddered at the engine shed. 'This is dreadfully smelly,' she announced. 'I'm highly sprung, and anything smelly is bad for my swerves'" (Awdry, 1996, p. 253). "'Look at me!' she purred to the waiting passengers. 'I'm the latest Diesel, highly sprung and right up to date'" (Awdry, 1996, p. 254). A decade later, in 1972, Mavis, the diesel, appeared (Awdry, 1996, p. 398). Depicted as "young" and "full of her own ideas," she was soon spoken to "severely" by The Manager for being "a very naughty engine." As he put it: "You have no business to go jauntering down Toby's line instead of doing your work." Only later in the tale, after her mischievous behavior had been circumvented and Mavis had apologized and accepted that Toby had far more knowledge and experience than her, was Mavis a welcome visitor in the shed. As Awdry (1996, pp. 402, 404–405) concluded this story: "She is still young and still makes mistakes; but she is never too proud to ask Toby, and Toby always helps her to put things right." These projected gender identities reflect the challenges to the gender order and dominant masculinities that were occurring during the 1960s, a time of technological change and deindustrialization. They also very clearly sought to reinforce the established gender order in which women were subordinate to men, knew their place, and conformed to norms of femininity. Significantly, Daisy and Mabel have been excluded from authorized heritage representations at sites of rail heritage and related tourist collateral, where the dominant versions of masculinity represented by the steam engines, most prominently Thomas the Tank Engine, prevail to this day alongside the positive emotional dimensions that were captured by Awdry's celebration of steam.

This emotional effect extends beyond these stories and is evident in railway heritage initiatives in different parts of the world. As the 'Old Patagonian' Express website tells it:

> La Trochita passengers are special . . . These tourists are as special as the train itself: they know the history of each machine, which the original wagons are and the stories of each railway line. That is why the emotion they feel when they are in front of the old locomotives, born at the beginnings of the past century, is unequalled.
>
> *(Contenidos Patagonia, n.d.)*

Here we see how "heritage has the power to evoke intense emotions" (Linn-Tynen, 2020, p. 260). It is precisely this emotional connection to big rail objects and what passes as their 'cultural heritage' that sustains traditional gendered meanings and identities as part of rail industrial memoryscapes. If we listen closely, we can hear the voices emanating not from rail hardware or the infrastructure per se but instead from "culturally and historically defined schema of coding and decoding" (Erikson, 2006, p. 5) in "What is 'said' in a text" and "what is 'unsaid,' but taken as given" (Smith and Campbell, 2017, p. 28). The coding explicit in the rail heritage initiatives earlier listed not only allows "individuals in the present to connect with the past" but also provides a "means by which to confirm and communicate identity." Yet, as Linn-Tynen (2020, p. 260) notes, if things are missing from "Historic sites, memorials and other forms of cultural heritage" or if "that heritage . . . is misrepresented, this can have profound impacts on the collective memory and society in the present."

Now it is generally thought that ascribing objects with heritage value and endowing their "representations of the past with meaning" involves imposing "present-day extant beliefs, ideologies, or norms (socio-economic, political or cultural) onto them. Simply put, their meaning is determined by the concerns of the present." However, I would argue that by creating shrines to the technology of the industrial past, rail industrial heritage initiatives sustain concerns from the past. By aestheticizing, sanitizing, and romanticizing rail industrial processes (Samuel, 1996, p. 303; Summerby-Murray, 2002, p. 50), rail heritage initiatives denude them of the messiness of the gendered cultures that were central to rail work around the world for over two centuries. In doing so, such initiatives fail to engage with present-day gender politics and the now extensive appreciation of a wide range of masculinities. Instead, these initiatives and their memoryscapes explicitly and implicitly support outmoded rail industry cultures, which "embodied" the norms of hegemonic masculinity during the industrial era (Connell and Messerschmidt, 2005, p. 832) and which were maintained through: "Cultural consent, discursive centrality, institutionalization, and the marginalization or delegitimation of alternatives" (Connell and Messerschmidt, 2005, p. 846). These same processes can be seen in rail industry memoryscapes around the world today, where gender coding and differences are explicitly and implicitly conveyed as unchanging and universal (Bondi, 1992, p. 160).

Conclusion

According to van den Dries and Schreurs (2020, p. 289), the bequest is among "the principal motives of heritage management," it is the legacy for future generations that inspires preservation. The overview of numerous rail heritage initiatives in different parts of the world presented here indicates that the legacy is remarkably consistent, regardless of national, regional, economic, or cultural differences.

If, as Holtorf (2020, p. 309) argues "the most important question in studying cultural heritage is now not what it is, but what it does," then we have little choice but to conclude that rail industrial heritage in deindustrialized locales sustains traditional industrial era-gendered norms and hegemonic masculinity through the overarching obsession with objects that places greatest value on technology, engineering, and aesthetics of rail-related architecture and hardware and the potential that this has for revenue from rail heritage tourism. Its "social value as part of the record of the lives of ordinary men and women" and as an "important sense of identity," is rarely recognized in other-than-homogenized, national or masculine terms regardless of location. Its "meaning and significance" has not been "probed and made clear for everyone. . . . for the use and benefit of today and of the future" (The Nizhny Tagil Charter for The Industrial Heritage, 2003). While heritage scholarship has recognized the profound changes in assumptions about gender, gender identity, and gender relations that have been evolving since the closing decades of the twentieth century (Reading, 2015; Shortliffe, 2016; Smith, 2008), more recent understandings of gender have been ignored and excluded in representations of rail industrial heritage. Holtorf (2020, p. 309) recently argued that we should "no longer consider cultural heritage in terms of what it was, but rather of what it could become." The failure to probe gender identities and the meaning of industrial-era gendered norms and cultures as part of rail industrial heritage initiatives and memoryscapes in deindustrialized sites suggests that gendered understandings and insights are blowing in the wind as the heritage steam whistle echoes across the globe.

Reference list

Alivizatou, Marilena. (2011). Intangible Heritage and Erasure: Rethinking Cultural Preservation and Contemporary Museum Practice. *International Journal of Cultural Property*, 18(1), pp. 37–60.

Awdry, Rev and Wilbert, V. (1996). *Thomas the Tank Engine: The Complete Collection*. London: Heinemann Young Books.

Bence, S. (2012). The Role of Railway, as a Heritage of Industrial History, in Tourism, with Conclusion on Quality of Life *Journal of Tourism Challenges and Trends*, V(2), pp. 85–102.

Berger, S. and High, S. (2019). (De-)Industrial Heritage: An Introduction. *Labor: Studies in Working-Class History of the Americas*, 16(1), 1–27.

Bharucha, Rustom. (2000). Beyond the Box. *Third Text*, 14(52), pp. 11–19.

Bhati, A., Pryce, J. and Chaiechi, T. (2014). Industrial Railway Heritage Trains: The Evolution of a Heritage Tourism Genre and Its Attributes. *Journal of Heritage Tourism*, 9(2), pp. 114–133.

Boksberger, Philipp and Sturzenegger, Martin. (2014). The Rhaetian Railway in the Albula/Bernina Landscapes: A Masterpiece of Railway Engineering. In Conlin, Michael V. and Bird, Geoffrey R. (eds.) *Railway Heritage and Tourism: Global Perspectives*. Bristol, UK: Channel View Publications, pp. 201–213.

Bondi, Liz. (1992). Gender Symbols and Urban Landscapes. *Progress in Human Geography*, 16(2), pp. 157–170.

Butler, Judith. (1990). *Gender Trouble: Feminism and the Subversion of Identity*. London: Routledge.

Butler, Judith. (2009). Performativity, Precarity and Sexual Politics. *AIBR. Revista de Antropología Iberoamericana*, 4(3), pp. i–xiii.

California State Railroad Museum. (n.d.[a]). https://www.californiarailroad.museum/visit/exhibits (Accessed: 6 July 2023).

California State Railroad Museum. (n.d.[b]). Rosie the Riveter. https://www.californiarailroad.museum/store/rosie-the-riveter (Accessed: 27 July 2023).

Chandler, Alfred D. (1965). *The Railroads: The Nation's First Big Business*. New York: Harcourt, Brace and World.

Chen, Yu-Hsun et al. (2020). Object Investigation of Industrial Heritage: The Forging and Metallurgy Shop in Taipei Railway Workshop. *Applied Sciences*, 10(7), Article 2408.

Cockburn, Cynthia. (1983, November). Caught in the Wheels: The High Cost of Being a Female Cog in the Male Machinery of Engineering. *Marxism Today*, pp. 16–20.

Cockburn, Cynthia and Ormrod, Susan. (1993). *Gender and Technology in the Making*. London: Sage.

Collazo, Alejandro Acosta. (2017). Recognition of Industrial Heritage in Aguascalientes, Mexico. *WIT Transactions on Ecology and the Environment*, 226, pp. 407–416.

Connell, R.W. and Messerschmidt, J.W. (2005). Hegemonic Masculinity: Rethinking the Concept. *Gender & Society*, 19(6), 829–859.

Contenidos Patagonia. (n.d.). *Old Patagonian Express "La Trochita"*. https://www.patagonia-argentina.com/en/old-patagonian-express-la-trochita/ [Online] (Accessed: 24 June 2022).

Coulls, A., Divall, C. and Lee, R. (1999). *Railways as World Heritage Sites*. Technical Report. ICOMOS, Paris, France.

de Lima Lourencetti, Fernanda. (2021). Enhancing the Cultural Value of Railways in the Western Region of São Paulo State (Brazil). *e-Phaistos*, IX(2). http://journals.openedition.org/ephaistos/8696 (Accessed: 26 May 2022).

East Japan Railway Company. (n.d.). *The Railway Museum*. https://www.railway-museum.jp/e/ [Online] (Accessed: 8 January 2023).

Ebert, Anne-Katrin. (2011). The National Rail Museum: Chanakyapuri, New Delhi, India. *Transfers: Interdisciplinary Journal of Mobility Studies*, 1(2), pp. 141–145.

Editor. (2019, September 20). FG Moves to Preserve Railway Heritage. *Guardian Nigeria*. [Online] https://guardian.ng/news/fg-moves-to-preserve-railway-heritage/ (Accessed: 20 September 2019).

Ekimci, B., Ergincan, F. and Inceoglu, M. (2019). Railroad Buildings of Eskişehir: Challenges and Opportunities for Industrial Heritage. *Heritage*, 2(1), pp. 435–451.

Enss, Chris. (2021). *Iron Women: The Ladies Who Helped Build the Railroad*. Lanham, Maryland: Rowman and Littlefield.

Eriksen, Anne. (2006). The Murmur of Ruins: A Cultural History – Le murmure de ruines: une histoire Culturelle. *Ethnologia Europaea*, 36(1), pp. 5–20.

Falser, M. (2001). *Industrial Heritage Analysis: World Heritage List and Tentative List*. UNESCO World Heritage Centre. https://whc.unesco.org/archive/ind-study01.pdf (Accessed: 24 June 2022).

Faulkner, Wendy. (2001). The Technology Question in Feminism: A View from Feminist Technology Studies. *Women's Studies International Forum* 24(1), pp. 79–95.

Francis, Beckie and Paechter, Carrie. (2015). The Problem of Gender Categorisation: Addressing Dilemmas Past and Present in Gender and Education Research. *Gender and Education*, 27(7), pp. 776–790.

Gerber, Piotr. (2013). New Forms of Protection of Industrial Heritage in Poland. The Museum of Silesian Industry and Railways in Jaworzyna Slaska. In Areces, Miguel Ángel Álvarez (ed.) *Paisajes culturales, patrimonio industrial y desarrollo regional*. Centro de Iniciativas Culturales y Sociales, CICEES: Ayuntamiento de Gijón: Gobierno del Principado de Asturias, pp. 79–85. ISBN 978-84-939924-5-3.

Glenbrook Vintage Railway. (n.d.). About Us. https://www.gvr.org.nz/about-us [Online] (Accessed: 6 July 2023).

Goldfields Railway. (n.d.). Waihi, New Zealand. https://www.waihirail.co.nz/ [Online] (Accessed: 27 July 2023).

Goldfields Heritage Railway. (n.d.). Waihi, New Zealand. https://www.newzealand.com/au/plan/business/goldfields-railway-inc/ [Online] (Accessed: 27 July 2023).

Gould, Shane. (2015). The Rolt Memorial Lecture 2012: Industrial Heritage at Risk. *Industrial Archaeology Review*, 37(2), pp. 73–92.

Gwynne, Robert. (2009). The Railway Museum Reinvented: The Cité du Train (Mulhouse) and the Nederlands Spoorwegmuseum (Utrecht). *Technology and Culture*, 50(4), pp. 876–882.

Harding, S. (1986). *The Science Question in Feminism*. Ithaca, NY: Cornell University Press.

Henderson, Joan C. (2014). Railways as Heritage Attractions: The Malaysia-Singapore Line. In Conlin Michael V. and Bird Geoffrey R. (eds.) *Railway Heritage and Tourism: Global Perspectives*. Bristol, UK: Channel View Publications, pp. 190–200.

Holtorf, Cornelius. (2020). 'Cultural Heritage is Concerned with the Future': A Critical Epilogue. In Apaydin Veysel (ed.) *Critical Perspectives on Cultural Memory and Heritage Construction: Construction, Transformation and Destruction.* London: UCL Press, pp. 309–312.

Holtorf, Cornelius and Kristensen, Troels Myrup. (2015). Heritage Erasure: Rethinking 'Protection' and 'Preservation'. *International Journal of Heritage Studies,* 21(4), pp. 313–317.

Huang, Yu Yu. (2007). *The Railway Museum in Omiya, Japan.* https://anih.culture.tw/index/en-us/inventory/69424 (Accessed: 23 June 2022).

Iron Route in the Pyrenees. (n.d.). *Basque Railway Museum – Azpeitia. A Travel Back in Time.* https://ironrouteinthepyrenees.com/re/basque-railway-museum/ [Online] (Accessed: 6 July 2023).

Joshi, M. (2017). *Report: Inventory of Industrial Heritage in India, Volume 1.* https://www.spacematters.in/inventory-of-industrial-heritage (Accessed: 5 July 2022).

Joshi, M. (2018). The Industrial Heritage Inventory of India. *TICCIH Bulletin,* 79, p. 1. https://ticcih.org/wp-content/uploads/2018/01/TICCIH-B79-1Q18.pdf (Accessed: 6 July 2024).

Joshi, Moulshri and Johri, Somya. (2023). *National Report 2018–2022: The International Committee for the Conservation of the Industrial Heritage, India.* TICCIH. https://ticcih.org/wp-content/uploads/2023/11/TICCIH-India-National-Report-2022.pdf (Accessed: 6 July 2024).

Kerley, Amanda. (2010). Saving Puffing Billy – Heritage Values in 1950s Melbourne. In Nichols, David et al. (eds.) *Green Fields, Brown Fields, New Fields: Proceedings of the 10th Australasian Urban History, Planning History Conference.* Melbourne, Victoria: The University of Melbourne, pp. 313–325.

Krešáková, V. (2021). Reflections on Industrial Heritage Transformation in Slovakia (Case Study: Forest Railway Cierny Balog). *Politeja.*18(74), pp. 193–203.

Lim, Imogene L. (2021). Erasure 2.0: Gatekeepers. *Heritage BC.* https://heritagebc.ca/resources/racism-do-not-let-the-forgetting-prevail/erasure-2-0-gatekeepers/ (Accessed: 23 June 2022).

Linn-Tynen, Erin. (2020). Reclaiming the Past as a Matter of Social Justice: African American Heritage, Representation and Identity in the United States. In Apaydin, Veysel (ed.) *Critical Perspectives on Cultural Memory and Heritage Construction, Transformation and Destruction.* London: UCL Press, pp. 255–268.

Llano-Castresana, Urtzi, Azkarate, Agustín and Sánchez-Beitia, Santiago. (2013). The Value of Railway Heritage for Community Development. *WIT Transactions on The Built Environment,* 131, pp. 61–72.

Lohan, M. and Faulkner, W. (2004). Masculinities and Technologies: Some Introductory Remarks. *Men and Masculinities,* 6(1), pp. 319–329.

Morin, Bode. (2014). Industrial Heritage in Archaeology. In Smith, Claire (ed.) *Encyclopedia of Global Archaeology.* New York, NY: Springer, pp. 3864–3873.

Muriel-Ramirez, M.J. (2017). Institutional Foundations of Heritage Railways: The High Cost of Low Trust in the Preservation of Merit Goods. *Journal of Economic Issues,* 51(3), 663–687.

The Nizhny Tagil Charter for The Industrial Heritage. (2003). https://www.icomos.org/18thapril/2006/nizhny-tagil-charter-e.pdf [Online] (Accessed: 23 June 2022).

Njuguna, Mugwima Bernard, Wahome, Ephraim W. and Deisser, Anne-Marie. (2018). Saving the Industry from Itself: A Case of the Railway Industrial Heritage in Kenya. *Historic Environment: Policy & Practice,* 9(1), pp. 21–38.

NSW Rail Museum. (2024). *Thomas & Friends: A Day Out with Thomas.* https://www.nswrailmuseum.com.au/day-out-with-thomas?mc_cid=d791de59a7&mc_eid=4639dcf328 [Online] (Accessed: 11 February 2024).

Oliveira, Eduardo and Ferrari, Monica. (2015). Convergences of the Railway's Historical Process and Management of Railway Heritage (Brazil and Argentina). In *XVIth International TICCIH Congress 2015 Proceedings.* http://ticcih.org/ticcih-congress-proceedings-now-available-online/ (Accessed: 23 June 2022).

Orbaşli, Aylin and Woodward, Simon. (2008). A Railway 'Route' as a Linear Heritage Attraction: The Hijaz Railway in the Kingdom of Saudi Arabia. *Journal of Heritage Tourism,* 3(3), pp. 159–175.

Passmore, John Arthur. (1974). *Man's Responsibility for Nature. Ecological Problems and Western Traditions.* London: Gerald Duckworth and Co., Ltd.

Pennycook, Alastair. (2004). Performativity and Language Studies. *Critical Inquiry In Language Studies: An International Journal,* 1(1), pp. 1–19.

Queensland Government. (n.d.). *The Workshops Rail Museum*. https://www.theworkshops.qm.qld.gov.au/ [Online] (Accessed: 6 July 2023).

The Railroaders Memorial Museum. (n.d.). https://www.railroadcity.org/museum.html [Online] (Accessed: 6 July 2023).

Railway Museum. (n.d.). https://www.railwaymuseum.org.uk/ [Online] (Accessed: 6 July 2023).

Railway Museum of Araraquara Francisco Aureliano de Araújo. (n.d.). https://www.araraquara.sp.gov.br/governo/secretarias/cultura/paginas-cultura/museu-ferroviario-de-araraquara [Online] (Accessed: 6 July 2023).

Reading, Anna. (2015). Making Feminist Heritage Work: Gender and Heritage. In Waterton, Emma and Watson, Steve (eds.) *The Palgrave Handbook of Contemporary Heritage Research*. Basingstoke: Palgrave Macmillan, pp. 397–410.

Reis, Arianne C. and Jellum, Carla. (2014). New Zealand Rail Trails: Heritage Tourism Attractions and Rural Communities. In Conlin, Michael V. and Bird Channel, Geoffrey R. (eds.) *Railway Heritage and Tourism: Global Perspectives*. Bristol, UK: View Publications, pp. 90–104.

Robinson, A. (n.d.). *Women's History Month: Women in Rail*. https://ribblesteam.org.uk/news/womens-history-month-women-in-rail/ [Online] (Accessed: 24 June 2022).

Salzinger, Leslie. (2004). Revealing the Unmarked: Finding Masculinity in a Global Factory. *Ethnography*, 5(1), pp. 5–27.

Samuel, Raphael. (1996). *Theatres of Memory: Volume 1, Past and Present in Contemporary Culture*. London: Verso.

Saudi Government. (2023). *A Bygone Era Discover the Hijaz Railway*. https://www.visitsaudi.com/en/do/culture/the-hijaz-railway (Accessed: 5 January 2023).

Seyrek, Şeyma and Omay Polat, Elvan Ebru. (2024). Learning from Swindon Railway Town: A Comparative Study with Alsancak Railway Campus. *Megaron*, 19(2), pp. 161–183.

Sherwood, Louise. (2010, November 27). Brazil's Devil's Railway Gets New Lease of Life. *BBC News*. https://www.bbc.com/news/world-latin-america-11578463 (Accessed: 24 June 2022).

Shortliffe, Sarah Ellen. (2016). Gender and (World) Heritage: The Myth of a Gender Neutral Heritage. In Bourdeau, Laurent and Gravari-Barbas, Maria (eds.) *World Heritage, Tourism and Identity: Inscription and Co-production*. Abingdon: Routledge, pp. 107–120.

Singapore Government. (2022). *Former Tanjong Pagar Railway Station*. https://www.roots.gov.sg/places/places-landing/Places/national-monuments/former-tanjong-pagar-railway-station (Accessed: 1 May 2023).

Smith, Laurajane. (2008). Heritage, Gender and Identity. In Graham, Brian and Howard, Peter (eds.) *The Ashgate Research Companion to Heritage and Identity*. Farnham: Ashgate, pp. 159–79.

Smith, Laurajane and Campbell, Gary. (2017). The Tautology of 'Intangible Values' and the Misrecognition of Intangible Cultural Heritage. *Heritage and Society*, 10(1), pp. 26–44.

STEAM Museum of the Great Western Railway. (n.d.). https://www.steam-museum.org.uk/ [Online] (Accessed: 6 July 2023).

Stuart, Iain. (1992). Stranger in a Strange Land: Historical Archaeology and History in Post Contact Australia. *Public History Review*, 1, pp. 136–147.

Sulaimon, N. (2019, September 20). Nigerian Govt Moves to Preserve Railway Heritage. *News Nigeria*. https://pmnewsnigeria.com/2019/09/20/nigerian-govt-moves-to-preserve-railway-heritage/ (Accessed: 6 July 2023).

Summerby-Murray, Robert. (2002). Interpreting Deindustrialised Landscapes of Atlantic Canada: Memory and Industrial Heritage in Sackville, New Brunswick. *The Canadian Geographer/Le Géographe canadien*, 46(1), pp. 48–62.

Taillon, Paul Michel. (2001). 'To Make Men Out of Crude Material': Work Culture, Manhood, and Unionism in the Railroad Running Trades, c.1870–1900. In Horowitz, Roger (ed.) *Boys and Their Toys? Masculinity, Technology and Class in America*. New York: Routledge, pp. 33–54.

Taksa, Lucy. (2003). 'Hauling an Infinite Freight of Mental Imagery': Finding Labour's Heritage at the Swindon Railway Workshops' STEAM Museum. *Labour History Review (UK)*, 68(3), pp. 391–410.

Taksa, Lucy. (2005). 'About as Popular as a Dose of Clap': Steam, Diesel and Masculinity at the New South Wales Eveleigh Railway Workshops. *Journal of Transport History (UK), Third Series*, 26(2), pp. 79–97.

Taksa, Lucy. (2006). Australian Attitudes to Industrial Railway Heritage in Global Perspective. In Oliver, Bobbie and Bertola, Patrick (eds.) *The History of the Westrail Midland Railway Workshops*. Perth: University of Western Australia Press, pp. 260–280.

Taksa, Lucy. (2008). Globalisation and the Memorialising of Railway Industrial Heritage. *Historic Environment – Special Issue: 'Thinking Rail: Lessons from the Past, the Way of the Future*, 21(2), pp. 11–19.

Taksa, Lucy. (2017). Romance of the Rails: De-Industrialisation, Nostalgia and Community. In High, Steven, MacKinnon, Lachlan and Perchard, Andrew (eds.) *Deindustrialization and Its Aftermath*. Vancouver: University of British Columbia Press, pp. 126–151.

Taksa, Lucy. (2019). 'Hidden in plain sight': Uncovering the Gendered Heritage of an Industrial Landscape. In De Nardi, Sarah, Orange, Hilary, High, Steven and Koskinen-Koivisto, Eerika (eds.) *The Routledge Handbook on Memory and Place*, Abingdon: Routledge, pp. 203–213.

Tourisme Montréal. (n.d.). *Exporail, the Canadian Railway Museum*. https://www.mtl.org/en/what-to-do/museums-and-culture/exporail-canadian-railway-museum[Online] (Accessed: 27 July 2023).

Transport Heritage NSW, NSW Rail Museum. https://www.nswrailmuseum.com.au/ (Accessed: 12 May 2024).

Ugwu, Chidi. (2010, May 21). Nigeria: Restoring Railway Artefacts. *Daily Champion (Lagos)*. https://allafrica.com/stories/201005210611.html (Accessed: 6 July 2023).

Union Pacific Railroad Museum. (n.d.). *"Move Over, Sir!" Women Working on the Railroad*. https://www.uprrmuseum.org/uprrm/exhibits/traveling/women-railroad/index.htm [Online] (Accessed: 27 July 2023).

van den Dries, Monique and Schreurs, José. (2020). A Glimpse into the Crystal Ball: How Do We Select the Memory of the Future? In Apaydin, Veysel (ed.) *Critical Perspectives on Cultural Memory and Heritage Construction, Transformation and Destruction*. London: UCL Press, pp. 289–306.

Wajcman, Judy. (1991). *Feminism Confronts Technology*. North Sydney: Allen and Unwin.

Walsh, Margaret. (2002). Gendering Transport History: Retrospect and Prospect. *Journal of Transport History: Special Issue, Gender and Transport History*, 23(1), pp. 1–8.

Walsh, Margaret. (2007). Gender in the History of Transportation Services: A Historiographical Perspective. *The Business History Review*, 81(3), pp. 545–562.

Whangarei Steam & Model Railway Club. (n.d.) https://railheritage.org.nz/buildings/whangarei-station/ (Accessed: 14 July 2024).

Wilson, Ross J. (2018). The Tyranny of the Normal and the Importance of being Liminal. In Grahn, Wira and Wilson, Ross J. (eds.) *Gender and Heritage Performance, Place and Politics*. Abingdon and Oxon: Routledge, pp. 1–21.

Wolmar, Christian. (2007). *Fire and Steam: A New History of the Railways in Britain*. London: Atlantic Books.

Yaghoubi-Notash, Massoud, Nejad Mohammad, Vahid and Soufiani, Mahmoud. (2020). Language, Gender and Subjectivity from Judith Butler's Perspective. *Philosophical Investigations*, 13, pp. 305–315.

Yazar, Nadide Ebru. (2013). *Railway Heritage of Roundhouses in Turkey*. Rust, Regeneration, Romance Conference Proceedings, Ironbridge, York UK.

Yiamjanya, Siripen. (2020). Industrial Heritage Along Railway Corridor: A Gear Towards Tourism Development, a Case Study of Lampang Province, Thailand. *E 3S Web of Conferences*, 164, p. 03002. Topical Problems of Green Architecture, Civil and Environmental Engineering 2019 [TPACEE]. https://doi.org/10.1051/e3sconf/202016403002 (Accessed: 19 June 2022).

27

INDUSTRIAL HERITAGE FROM THE SOUTH

Decolonial Approaches to the Social Construction of Heritage and Preservation Practices

Marion Steiner*

Introduction

The experience of industrialization and deindustrialization are uneven around the world, and the same is true for the social realities that are linked to these processes on the ground. This chapter takes a closer look at the concepts and methods we need to be able to cope with the specific intellectual and political challenges that arise from deindustrialization in different places and continents with regard to the social construction of heritage and preservation practices.

First, I present some general reflections on how industrial heritage has emerged as a concept in the 1970s and 1980s in European countries that faced economic and social crises due to the translocation of industrial production to other parts of the world at the time. In the following three subsections, I present specific cases and projects from Latin America and Asia and the experiences of people who are fighting on the ground for an independent interpretation of what industrial heritage actually means for them and should mean for the common good in their respective areas.

Their critical, post and decolonial views stem from the observation that industrial heritage preservation concepts and methods have been transferred from Europe to other world regions without much questioning of whether this was (and is) at all appropriate given the traditional focus of the North on self-referential narratives of technical and economic innovations and superiority that supposedly brought progress and growth to supposedly 'underdeveloped' countries, where local development paths often came to an abrupt and too often violent end with the arrival of European-style modernity, industrialization, and the extractivist business model.

---

* I want to express my profound gratitude to Pamela Fuentes and Esperanza Rock in Chile, Magdalena Novoa in the US, and Moulshri Joshi in India for their inspiration over the past years. Their impressive work and example are my most fundamental motivation to keep going and keep writing even in very tough times. I also thank them for having accepted to revise this text and share their critiques and suggestions on very short notice. Our bounds are substantial, our will to explore the unknowable is unbroken, and our mission continues.

DOI: 10.4324/9781003308324-38

Eventually, I want my (English-speaking) readers to understand what are the driving motivations behind the hard work that is being done in the so-called Global South, particularly by women, when it comes to the (re)interpretation of their communities' pasts and the (re)construction of their future. I also want readers to get inspired and learn from the ways these people suggest moving forward toward the collective and grounded creation of just, inclusive, and resilient industrial heritage narratives and preservation practices.

Last but not least, I hope that this account will also have some impact on the process of remaking international post-Second World War organizations such as TICCIH, ICOMOS, and UNESCO. In TICCIH in particular, with a new generation on board of professional women some of whom get quoted here, we are already, slowly but steadily, working on a revised version of the 2003 Nizhny Tagil Charter on Industrial Heritage.

Thinking Industrial Heritage From the South

To set the frame for the experiences I discuss in the main body of this chapter, I will first present three fundamental convictions that are shared by the people I introduce later on: (i) Heritage is a social construction and a political battlefield; (ii) Industrial Heritage is a Eurocentric concept that has to be decolonized; (iii) TICCIH needs to move on to become a truly global organization.

Heritage and Human Rights

There are still people who think that heritage is about the past, but it's not so at all. Heritage is about how, in our present day, human communities collectively negotiate their respective understandings of the past and visions for the future. This means that heritage is all about decisions and selections, and these depend on interests and motivations that are as different as are people, places, and things (Capel, 2014; Bogner et al., 2018; Meier and Steiner, 2018, 2023). Crucial questions in the social negotiation process on what we consider heritage or not are these: Why do we find something worth to be protected? What do we actually want to demonstrate or prove? What are the messages that we see behind historical legacies, and why and for whom would these be of any use for the future? Are our interpretations inclusive and diverse, or do they tend to be exclusive or even potentially xenophobic? Do they foster collaboration or competition? Is the collective aim to prove the supposed superiority of someone's supposedly own nation, technology, or people, or is it about creating more social peace, mutual human understanding, and solidarity?

Heritage can be an answer to real social needs and reassure collective identities in times of crisis. It is always political; it's exposed to manipulation, and it can get instrumentalized for ideological goals. Heritage will always express ideological convictions and beliefs; heritage is, in fact, a political battlefield. Homogenous master narratives obscure the fact that different people have different interpretations of the past and the future, while "agonistic" views (Berger, 2019, 2022; Berger and High, 2019) shed light on this diversity and enable us to think about more democratic ways to construct heritage. Traditionally, the focus in cultural heritage has been on the powerful and elites, and also in industrial heritage the dominant master narratives concentrate on smart white men bringing progress, technology, and welfare to the world (Meier and Steiner, 2018, 2023). Migrant stories, female voices, first nations perspectives, and others that imply conflicting interpretations of the past, evoking conflicts, suffering and political fights, are still too often, consciously, or unconsciously, omitted.

460

'Critical' heritage stems from the motivation to pay tribute to these people, and 'insurgent' heritage is these people themselves standing up to defend their rightful understanding of the past and the future. This reflection also leads us to a first definition of 'decolonial' heritage: fundamentally, it's about putting on the table the global power relations and hierarchies that confine the interactions between groups of people as well as between humans and nature, with the motivation to fight for and defend people, places, and things that would otherwise get omitted, oppressed, or "discarded" (Liboiron and Lepawsky, 2022). To make their voices heard, loud and clear, as a matter of human respect no matter how hard this may be, implies that heritage work can also be really dangerous, depending on the political context on the ground.

Concluding on my first point: heritage is not only a social construction, but it is also hard social and political work defending basic human cultural rights, and decolonial heritage is a fight for social justice on a local, national, and in particular on the global scale. This is particularly relevant when it comes to industrial heritage, as industrialization has been a global phenomenon since its very beginning. Deindustrialization processes also cannot fully be understood without considering global contexts, in particular the translocation of industrial production from one part of the world, or regions, or continents, to others. Despite all the ground-breaking intellectual work that has been done on concepts like the Modern World System since the 1950s (Wallerstein, 2004), this question of scale in global power relations still tends to be overlooked regularly, and this leads to my second introducing statement on industrial heritage as a Eurocentric concept.

Industrial Heritage and Decolonization

Industrial heritage as a concept emerged in the 1970s in Europe, from the specific context of the social and economic crisis in Europe and Northern America that resulted from deindustrialization processes there as a consequence of the global shifts in industrial production. In this decade, TICCIH – The International Committee for the Conservation of Industrial Heritage – was founded with the First International Congress on the Conservation of Industrial Monuments being held in 1973 in Ironbridge, UK, the second one in 1975 in Bochum, West Germany, and the third one in 1978 in Sweden,[1] with participants from different European countries and Northern America.

The urgent need for the field of industrial heritage to have its own defining documentation was, decades later, also the background to the elaboration of TICCIH's *Nizhny Tagil Charter on Industrial Heritage* (TICCIH, 2003), as there was much confusion over terminology and little in the way of an established academic approach to provide the theoretical basis to situate industrial heritage within the field of cultural heritage. Published in July 2003, the charter emerged as an initiative of TICCIH's president at the time, Eusebi Casanelles, the then-director of the National Museum for Science and Technology of Catalonia, situated in Terrassa, Spain. The draft was written by James Douet and drawn from *The Historic Scotland Guide to International Charters* (1997); it was then reviewed by the TICCIH Board, commented on by national representatives and ratified at the World Congress 2003 in Nizhny Tagil, Russia (Stuart, 2023). The same urgency motivated the elaboration of the best practice handbook *Industrial Heritage Re-Tooled: The TICCIH Guide to Industrial Heritage Conservation* (Douet, 2012), which is still a useful tool today, also for teaching worldwide.

Both the charter and the book were important to anchor industrial heritage as a specific thematic field in the canon of cultural heritage and to make clear that dealing with the legacies of (de)industrialization requires specific methods, concepts, and criteria of its own. In that sense, the Nizhny Tagil Charter has set a precedent and was very successful throughout its 20 years of existence. It has also inspired further institutional cooperation work, for example, with ICOMOS on the *Joint ICOMOS-TICCIH Principles for the Conservation of Industrial Heritage Sites, Structures, Areas, and Landscapes* (ICOMOS and TICCIH, 2011), and the debate probably also inspired at least partially the 2013 update of the Australian *Burra Charta for Places of Cultural Significance* dating from 1979 (ICOMOS Australia, 2013).

However, both the 2003 TICCIH Charter and the 2012 handbook are very limited in geographical scope, and until today concepts, methodologies, and criteria tend to be transferred from Europe to other world regions without much questioning of whether this is (and was) at all appropriate. Unfortunately, this is also due to the often-unreflected adoption of theoretical frameworks by experts in the Global South who continue to think that all leading things come from Europe or Northern America or are still too shy to express divergent opinions and develop models that fit better with their social realities and necessities on the ground.

TICCIH and Its Global Scope

Criticisms of the TICCIH Charter, both conceptual and methodological, have existed from the beginning even within the organization's board (Stuart, 2023; Casanelles, 2012). There is awareness about the fact that the complexity and diversity of different cultural contexts, languages, and social realities around the world, very specific to each place, are not reflected in the charter or the handbook. Long-serving TICCIH officials acknowledge that there hasn't been enough time back then in the early 2000s to organize a broader discussion on the Charter draft, but we need to also consider that interactive and global communication possibilities were still very limited back then compared to today's standards. A particular side note for the younger generations: One still had to dial into the Internet over telephone landlines back then and emailing had just started, paper mail was still the rule, and there were no cellphones yet nor instant messaging, online meeting tools or live streaming platforms.

However, in the early 2010s, crucial critiques have been raised from Asia, via the declarations on industrial heritage conservation of the Modern Asian Architecture Network (mAAN, 2011) and the Asian Network for Industrial Heritage (ANIH, 2012). Also, Latin American colleagues expressed critiques; for instance, Cuban colleagues never tire to state that the global industrial business model based on domination, exploitation, and extractivism as we know it today, had actually started with the European colonization of the world and that the invention of the steam engine or the so-called Industrial Revolution are far from being so important from a global perspective as Eurocentric interpretations suggest (Steiner, 2020, 2022a; Rigol and Rojas, 2012).[2] They call on paying more attention to global power relations, the role of traditional local manufacturing as potential kick-offs for industrialization processes, and to rediscuss the definition of time range that has been imposed by Eurocentric perspectives (Contreras, 2024).

There is also a critical awareness of this in Europe, which in Germany, for example, has been repeatedly articulated through the Working Group on Theory and Education in Heritage Conservation e.V. (AKTLD) whose annual conferences provide a good opportunity for that kind of debate (Bogner et al., 2018; Meier and Steiner, 2018, 2023; see also Steiner 2022b). Similar issues have also been discussed on the international level for many years in scientific communities such as the Association for Critical Heritage Studies (ACHS) or, more recently, the DéPOT project.[3]

In this kind of forums where colleagues from the North and the South, the West and the East come together to discuss agonic heritage constructions in the context of historical power relations and center–peripheries divides, we eventually come to understand that in fact there is no such thing as 'the Global South'; the South can be anywhere (in Sweden, e.g., the north is the south), and that the classical North–South-divide dichotomy can be misleading and should at the least be complemented by a parallel reflection on East–West relationships. The titling of my program parts at the 2022 TICCIH World Congress in Montreal as "Industrial heritage from global perspective" (session) and "Sharing industrial heritage glocally" (roundtable) was also a result from that kind of discussions.[4] However, we could think about 'the South' as a linguistic *truque*, taken from the ordinary expression 'it all went south' used by English native speakers to describe situations in which things didn't go at all as they should have gone. That is what I decided to do for this text.

Having previously tried to deepen the discussion with the 2012 World Congress in Taiwan, titled 'Post-Colonialism and Reinterpretation of Industrial Heritage,' the debate gained new momentum at the 2022 World Congress in Montréal, Canada, with a special commission having been set up by the TICCIH Board after the General Assembly, whose task consists of critically revising the Nizhny Tagil Charter (Steiner, 2022a; Stuart, 2023) from less Western viewpoints. These discussions also address "the basic problem that is inherent to the [World Heritage] concept: namely, that a World Heritage based on superlatives tends to be exclusionary and centered on elites, as well as foster competition (not least among the nation-states it is supposed to transcend)" (Meier and Steiner, 2023).

I will get back to this in the final remarks at the end on the basis of the inputs from and discussion of the experiences that compose the main body of this text.

Making Industrial Heritage From the Grounds

In the following three subsections, I explore specific professional and personal experiences that retrace the intellectual and political endeavors of five women born in the decade between 1975 (me) and 1986, who work between research and activism on industrial heritage in Germany, Chile, the US, and India. By initial formation, we have a geographer, an anthropologist, an ethno historian, an artist who then became an urban planner, and an architect, who all work moving back and forth between continents and languages, which allows for enriching switches between North–South, South–North, and South–South perspectives. The field cases I present illustrate diverse historical, (geo)political, cultural, and social realities on the ground and touch different kinds of deindustrialization and heritage related to electricity, mining, and the chemical sectors.

The selection of these places and people relies on the good insights I have into the "situated knowledges" (Haraway, 1988) of dear female colleagues I work with since years due to current and former professional contexts, right now with my ESPI Lab Valparaíso in Chile and in addition serving as TICCIH's Secretary General.

El Sauce y La Luz: Postcolonial Industrial Heritage and Glocal Communities

The first place I introduce you to is the El Sauce y La Luz hydroelectric complex that was built by Berlin firms in the first decade of the twentieth century in the outskirts of Valparaíso with the aim to provide electric street lighting and tramway systems to what was then the most important port city and financial center on South America's west coast. The El Sauce power plant was inaugurated in May 1906, and a year later constructions of the La Luz water reservoir started, which was completed in 1910. The site as a technological system also includes former workers' houses, tunnels, aqueducts, electrical posts, and so on and was decommissioned in 1997. None of its elements counts with any legal protection as of today. The site is currently in a very poor condition and still widely unknown to the local population and authorities, also due to the power plant's remote location in the back of a valley. However, its rediscovering started around 2005, when local people from the Placilla Cultural Center came across it by coincidence and started to research and document the place. From an international comparative perspective, the site is very important in terms of historical heritage values, because being a hydroelectric system built by the AEG-Deutsche Bank group, this is the great exception from the general rule of these actors selling coal-fueled electrical systems to the world, as I was able to demonstrate in my thesis and subsequent research.[5]

I moved to Valparaíso in 2018 with the motivation to support the industrial heritage activists in Placilla and to create "glocal" historiographies that can connect the industrial heritage communities in Valparaíso and Berlin (Steiner and Fuentes, 2024). Also, I wanted to put at the local museum's service the knowledge that I had created for my PhD thesis, which is in German, and I felt that dissemination in Spanish on the spot was necessary to make it accessible for the local community. And I had a slight worry, because when we first met and went on our first field trip together in 2014 (see Figure 27.1), I had noticed a slight tendency that colonial-style narratives around brave German men contributing to local development were in

Figure 27.1 The machine hall of the El Sauce hydropower plant in the outskirts of Valparaíso, Chile. (Photo: author, 2014)

the making in Placilla, too. So my wish to help constructing more critical narratives became a lasting motivation to finalize my dissertation in which I analyzed in detail the historical power relations and the big business that were behind the Berlin electrification of Valparaíso and Santiago de Chile. Before publishing the book in 2019, I started to work as a geography professor at a local university, and from August 2018 onward, I worked with the museum people on a regular basis. For that, it was of course helpful that I knew Chile from previous visits since the 1990s and had even written my graduate thesis about urban planning in Valparaíso.[6]

The first project we did together was the creation of an exhibition and a series of fact sheets on the different elements that compose the El Sauce y La Luz hydroelectric complex with my students in 2019 (Steiner, 2023). The portrayed sites included not only the system's main technological elements in the hinterland of Valparaíso but also sites in the inner city that explain the role of international finance for the implementation of large-scale electrification, the shift from coal to water as energy source, and the use of electricity for the modernization of urban infrastructure. Also, of course, we included information on the local museum highlighting its pioneering role in the social process of local heritage construction. My interactions with the heritage activists in Placilla eventually confronted me with an intellectual challenge, as I came to understand that my own scientific knowledge interest was in fact motivated by the German industrial heritage discourse and its lack of more critical, and in particular anti-capitalist, anti-imperialist, and postcolonial aspects.

This interest determined a research focus that my MUHP friends found interesting and complementary to theirs while also stating that it was not their main interest, which was of course frustrating for me to hear in the first place. Then, I self-critically reflected that my approach was naturally conditioned by my personal background of having been engaged with the Third World Movement from a very early age, since my time at school in a region that was a hotspot of the Solidarity with Chile movement in West Germany soon after the military coup on September 11, 1973. Thus, thanks to continuous conversations with the local heritage activists, I came to understand that my approach is still Western-centered but in postcolonial terms, which also means that "the South" and "the peripheries" remain very important categories for me, because despite wanting to overcome the artificial North–South divide, I still need them to describe unfair power relations within what is called the Modern World System, which continues to be a useful concept today for that same reason (Wallerstein, 2004). At the same time, I started to explore my friends' specific local perspectives on industrial heritage and got more confident over time, as I realized that my intellectual work is indeed an important contribution, because it helps to argument historical heritage values that can make a difference in the process of attaining legal protection for the El Sauce y La Luz hydroelectric complex.

Also, I realized that, as the German Latin Americanist Olaf Kaltmeier put it: "While in Western European countries, heritage has been transformed into a depoliticized lifestyle factor, heritage in postcolonial contexts has become a battleground on the interpretation of history and its projection into the future" (Kaltmeier, 2017, p. 13). In Placilla, this starts with the fact that the MUHP is a community museum, which is very unusual in the Chilean museum context. It was founded in 2009 by the Placilla Cultural Center that was created by people from the local neighborhood in 2006 who started to rediscover their place's role in the industrialization and urban development processes of the traditional world port city of Valparaíso. The museum is financed exclusively with competitive public funds, with the sole exception of the space, which is state property, its provision with electricity and water and the very humble salary of its director, who is a municipal employee. Self-management and volunteer work from the neighborhood and the members of the cultural center are the

Figure 27.2 The Historical Museum of Placilla after its expansion. (Photo: Francisco Rivero, 2021)

basis of the museum work, which on the positive side means that it is able to operate quite independently. Even the expansion works and the construction of a new second floor in 2021 were financed with a public grant (see Figure 27.2). Apart from constantly preparing applications for public funding, the museum's main activities focus on permanent and temporal exhibitions, workshops with the neighborhood, regular walks especially for families and school children dedicated to cultural and environmental education, and research projects focused on the local history and heritage.

Thus, the museum pays particular attention to the social and environmental dimensions of heritage and on issues that might appear more intangible at first sight, like the memories of former hydroelectricity workers and their family histories, applying anthropological methodologies such as oral history and the collection and digitalization of family albums but that also translate into tangible things like Western-style industrial culture and the continuing destruction of nature by human activities. I learned a lot about my friends' distinctive reflections on human–nature relations and integrated heritage when working with Pamela on our book *Light for Valparaíso. The El Sauce y La Luz Hydroelectric Complex: A Shared Industrial Heritage Between Placilla de Peñuelas and Electropolis Berlin* (Steiner and Fuentes, 2021), which is the final result of a FONDART research project that was awarded to the Placilla Cultural Center by the Chilean Ministry for Cultures, Arts and Heritage and in which I participated as a co-researcher.[7] In four chapters, the book combines our respective research approaches and results, with the first chapter dedicated to the entangled global history of electrification in Valparaíso and chapter 3 focusing on the stories of the people who operated the system and for generations had lived in the El Sauce and La Luz sites, interviewed by CCP members.

The book project was another intellectual challenge as our research interests are different and do not necessarily come together. Wouldn't we have cared for each other, we could have walked right past each other (Steiner, 2021). To avoid this is in fact a constant effort that represents hard care work and also 'decolonial' work, which starts with accepting that your own knowledge is limited and that there are things just impossible to understand simply because they are beyond your imaginative power coming from a different place and culture. These frontiers of knowledge are only human, and that's precisely why ethnographic methods such as 'immersion to the field' and 'active listening' are so important, as they allow to gradually extend your understanding beyond the human limitations of knowledge. The concept of "situated knowledges," as explained by Donna Haraway in 1988 and others, helps to be more patient with oneself and more open to listen closely to local people in other parts of the world.

That process of pushing the frontiers of the knowable and of intercultural understanding actually never ends. In our case, a new opportunity is now on with the FONDECYT research project that was awarded to me by the Chilean state in 2023, hosted by the University of Chile and implemented in cooperation with the Bauhaus University Weimar, the Technical University Berlin, and the Berlin Center for Industrial Heritage. The project focuses on the technical, economic, and cultural history of the German urban electrification in Metropolitan Chile in comparison with Mexico and Brazil[8] but also includes a heritage dimension that allows us to continue our efforts of constructing a 'glocal' community of care for the shared heritage of Elektropolis in Overseas from a decolonial perspective. This can be particularly interesting as it opens up important strategic opportunities for the organization of international support for our case.

Another pending research question in Valparaíso refers to the clash between different ontologies and visions of being-in-the-world in connection with Indigenous realities. The construction of hydroelectric systems as such, and hydrodaming, is also colonialism (Liboiron, 2018), and in our case it is very likely that the valleys of what is today the La Luz water reservoir have been Indigenous territories that were then occupied by a powerful group of people forcing the native people to abandon their use of these places because of flooding. Descendants of these dispossessed people may even still live close by today (see Figure 27.3).

Figure 27.3 Aerial view of the La Luz water reservoir built 1907–1910 by Berlin companies. (Photo: Francisco Rivero, 2021)

The Routledge Handbook of Deindustrialization Studies

This topic is also important to better explain the ruptures that the introduction of a new industrial logic to these territories brought with it: The European-style industrialization and urbanization of lands was a modernization introduced to Chile by the national and European-born elites through the global port city of Valparaíso and from there invaded the hinterlands and pushed the borders of even the national territory ever more south and north. It's noteworthy that this type of development was not intrinsic to the local paths; it came from the outside and was too often installed violently with brutal force.

Lota: Radical Nostalgia and Insurgent Heritage

This topic of colonization in postcolonial contexts becomes even more obvious in the South of Chile, so next I take you to the Biobío Region, also called *Wallmapu* in *mapudungún*, the local native language. When Chile got independence from Spain in 1810, these were factually still Indigenous lands inhabited by *Mapuche* peoples (see Figure 27.4). During the nineteenth century, when the new Chilean Republic pushed its frontiers ever more

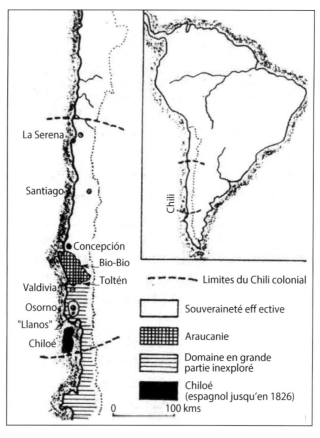

Figure 27.4 Map of Chile around 1810, before the national territory was expanded to the South and the North. (Source: Steiner, 2019, vol. 1, p. 105; taken from Blancpain, 1974, p. 4, also in Bilot, 2010, p. 7)

south and north with the ambition to integrate new areas into their national territory, railway connections were built into *Wallmapu* as a part of the state's expansion to the south. The occupation of lands resulted in any kind of possible conflict with the *Mapuche* peoples and also the neighboring state Argentina to the east (Rock, 2022a, 2022b; Novoa, 2022b).[9] Similar conflicts arose in the north, too, in territories that were claimed by Chile, Peru, and Bolivia at the same time (Steiner, 2019, vol. 1, pp. 104–114).

By the 1880s, the Chilean colonization had reached *Wallmapu*, with the Biobío River representing an important frontier and a direct interface between the native peoples' territories and their cosmologies and European-style large-scale industrialization systems that followed an extractivist logic. Local Indigenous people were involved as workforce while also bringing in settlers from abroad, especially from Southwest Germany, to cultivate the lands, forcing Indigenous people to migrate into restricted areas, dispossessing them of their lands, and cutting them off from their traditional life sources (Rock, 2022a, 2022b).[10] In San Rosendo, this is particularly well visible until today in the landscape marked by the presence of a huge railway complex on the intersection of the Biobío and Laja Rivers (see Figure 27.5; Rock and Torres, 2024). Some 100 kilometers to the west, on the Pacific Ocean's coast, Lota and Coronel became very attractive for extracting coal, to supplying huge parts of the energy the country needed for its territorial expansion, industrialization, and urbanization processes.

The closing of the Lota coal mines in 1997 caused huge parts of the local population to be set off from their traditional jobs after generations. As a result of this deindustrialization, the social and economic situation in Lota is very difficult still today. Lota is one of the poorest cities in Chile and in addition suffers from a very bad reputation. However,

Figure 27.5 Railway heritage on Indigenous lands: San Rosendo railway complex on the confluence of the Biobío and Laja Rivers. (Photo: Sebastián Orellana, CreaSur Photographical Archives, 2023)

born precisely from these difficulties and from the local community, grassroots heritage and tourism initiatives started to emerge, striving for the social recognition and rights of the working class (Novoa, 2021a, 2025) and lately also promoting the nomination of the 'Lota Mining Complex' as a UNESCO World Heritage site, which made an important step forward when it was inscribed on the Chilean tentative list in 2021. The main driving forces behind this are the women who already in the late 2000s had set up the *Mesa Ciudadana de Cultura, Patrimonio y Turismo de Lota*, the Citizens' Roundtable for Culture, Heritage, and Tourism of Lota (Novoa, 2021b, 2022a; Rock et al., 2024). In parallel, from the academic field, pioneering research on Lota and its industrial heritage was pushed forward in particular by women, including Alejandra Brito Peña, María Isabel López, and María Dolores Muñoz Rebolledo.[11] Today, doing research on Lota has become mainstream, a fact that can, at least partially, be attributed to the effects of the successful community mobilization for a future recognition by UNESCO. This is basically a good thing because there is still so much knowledge to be (re)created and good governance to be implemented. Among the researchers' experiences that exist, I want to talk here in some more detail about two female colleagues who have particularly inspired my intellectual and political reflections. They both work with specifically 'decolonial' approaches on Lota's industrial heritage, have both dedicated their PhD thesis to this, and have a strong commitment with the local community.

I first got to know Magdalena Novoa Echaurren, in July 2021 during the pandemic, as I had to review her paper proposal for the TICCIH World Congress 2022 in Canada 'Gendered nostalgia: grassroots heritage tourism and (de)industrialization in the coal region of Chile' (Novoa, 2025). I was so fascinated by her work that I invited her to join my session at the TICCIH Congress and also the one I organized at the congress of the Chilean Society of Geography SOCHIGEO in Valparaíso in October 2021.[12] Magdalena works on community development "with the unique perspective of an artist who found a pathway into planning via cultural heritage studies and historic preservation."[13] She first came in touch with Lota while she was working for the Chilean National Council of Monuments at the Chilean Ministry for Cultures, Arts and Heritage in Valparaíso for two years, given the fact that Lota counts with an extraordinary amount of listed monuments despite being socioeconomically poor. Desperate about the fact that not much could be done for Lota from the official governmental side, she decided to switch back to the academic field and started a PhD in architecture at the University of Texas at Austin, which she finalized in 2020 with her thesis titled 'Insurgent Heritage: Grassroots Movements and Citizenship in Chile.' For this research, she worked with the citizens' roundtable 'Mesa de Lota' and in particular the women in Lota, living with them for several months twice.

As she told us at the SOCHIGEO Congress, when she first arrived at Lota, her initial idea was to create a collaborative map. To her great frustration, this approach was not attractive at all for the local women she wanted to work with and who criticized it as "colonial" and even the typical kind of "academic extractivism," where no benefit would come out from for their local community (Sletto, Novoa and Vasudevan, 2023).[14] This critique of a map not being an adequate format to support the local heritage community was a particularly fascinating point to put on the table in a geography congress. During that early phase of her fieldwork, she came to understand the critiques of the Mesa women of the official heritage narratives that were constructed by the state and a private NGO in Lota since the late 1990s and that focus on celebratory narratives on capitalist development, while the local women wanted to tell their own stories, including the painful experiences of the past and the suffering of the working class in the history of mining, and in particular the female perspective on that and the specific suffering of women from oppression and gender violence in a male-dominated industrial system. These topics cannot be represented appropriately on a map because of their intrinsic intangible dimension, so Magdalena started to look out for better formats to tell the stories the women actually wanted to tell and share with her.

Eventually, her immersion in the field by research residencies enabled Magdalena to find a more appropriate approach. Actively listening to the suggestions that came from the community, she discovered an artistic format that is deeply rooted in the local tradition. The *Arpillera Urbana* (urban burlap) was, already during the dictatorship in Chile (1973–1989), a specific tool for the Lota women to self-organize political resistance as a community, organize international support, and thus even to generate some income. Together they decided to use this particular format to talk about heritage in a series of workshops that Magdalena then organized reviving methodological skills from her earlier profession as an artist and paying for the coffee, cookies, and also the time the women spent working with her on the collective fabrication of an *Arpillera*, which ended up being called *Memorias de la Mujer Lotina* (Memories of the Lota Woman) (see Figure 27.6).[15]

Magdalena's endeavors as a researcher in the field show how important the notions of 'progressive nostalgia,' 'radical tourism,' and 'insurgent heritage' are for a reorientation of both theory and methodology. The *Arpillera* example also makes it very clear that 'decolonial' is fundamentally about *how* you do things, about how much you are able to actually

Figure 27.6 The Arpillera "Memories of the Lota Woman": presentation at the international congress in Concepción in October 2023. (Photo: Sebastián Orellana, CreaSur Photographical Archives, 2023)

listen to what local people want to talk about, want to share, and do with you. And these approaches are of course also relevant for reinventing urban planning modes that still tend to be very exclusive, particularly in countries like Chile, providing residents with critical tools to envision alternatives for the development of their cities (Sletto, Novoa and Vasudevan, 2023; Novoa, 2025).

Only months after having known Magdalena, I received an email from María Esperanza Rock Núñez at the end of February 2022, when the academic year in Chile started with great stress as we were returning to the classrooms after the pandemic. She would then just not stop calling me up on the phone at my university in Valparaíso until I contacted her back, and we met for the first time online on April 5. One outcome of this was her writing an article for the German journal *Industriekultur* (Rock, 2022a) and another one for the *TIC-CIH Bulletin* (Rock, 2022b). A second outcome was that I joined the Southern researchers' network NUDISUR codirected by her,[16] and a third one was that I found out that Esperanza and Magdalena did not know each other; so in July 2022, we had a first meeting online the three of us.

Esperanza had started researching on Lota with a focus on the creation of an oral history archive and is particularly intrigued by identifying persisting Indigenous traditions in the local mining and industrial culture (Rock, 2016). As a child, she had lived the impacts of deindustrialization on the local society from very close, as her father was engaged with setting up a manufacturing project in Coronel, and an important percentage of the new factory's staff with whom her family shared their lives were actually former miners who had lost their jobs when coal mining ended in Lota. It might be because of these personal experiences that she eventually became an ethnohistorian. Today, she lives with her architect husband and two kids in a small place outside the regional capital Concepción, in close contact with nature and the local Indigenous communities.

Her work impresses and inspires me because her life mission, in a similar way to my own, is to connect academic research and community work. In addition to teaching at the local university, she is an unpaid (!) director of the CreaSur Cultural Center, the arts and crafts project Casa Taller, the OTEC Cultura y Territorio that offers capacitation workshops for municipal staff and other professionals, and the aforementioned NUDISUR network.[17] Continuing the research that she had started for her PhD (Rock, 2016), in her current research project, 'Memories of Urban and Cultural Transformations of Deindustrialization in the Global North and South: A Comparative Study of the Coal Basin in Southern Chile and the Ruhr Region in Germany,' financed by Chile's National Agency for Research and Development ANID for three years (2023–2026), she continues to develop an oral history archive, now incorporating a comparative analysis of industrial heritage narratives in Lota and the Ruhr region in Germany.[18] One fundamental reflection here is that in south Chile, as in other parts of the world outside Europe, industrialization is not something that has 'naturally' evolved from the local grounds but was imposed from the outside and by outsiders, may they have been European imperialists (and North Americans from the 1920s onward) or the national Chilean elite, often exercising power and violence, and dispossessing native peoples of their lands. Despite this, however, memories, cosmogonies, and beliefs from before having survived and remain living in Lota, have mixed up with others from Palestinian, Italian, Aymara, Spanish, English ancestries in an extraordinary cultural diversity, and they all form part of the local mining culture.

It is also important to state that local *Mapuche* people not only opposed or resisted the arrival of the new industrial model to their lands, but quite some of them also appreciated the promises of modernization and progress and came to integrate the new system, thus shaping Lota as it is today (Rock, 2022a, 2023). I find this point particularly interesting because it highlights that there is, in fact, a difference between capitalism and colonialism. Max Liboiron (2018) explains this well:

> The United Nations Declaration of Rights of Indigenous Peoples (UNDRIP) clearly states that Indigenous groups have the right to development. . . . This can mean mining. It can mean aquaculture. It can mean hydrodaming. It can mean pollution and waste. Such development is an Indigenous *right*. Indigenous peoples are rightsholders, not stakeholders, on their Land. Often, this doesn't sit well with people. They want to support the rights of Indigenous peoples, but not *that* right. . . . The right for Indigenous people to pollute their own Land, should they so choose, . . . does mean that self-determination and sovereignty can and do take many forms, and that these are first and foremost the routes to anti-colonialism and decolonization.

An important connecting point between Magdalena's and Esperanza's intellectual and methodological work is the particular attention they both pay to finding horizontal, collaborative, and decolonial ways to think and make industrial heritage, living with the people whose history and memories they research on, actively learning from them, and also working *for* them, trying to find humble and supportive ways to move on, caring about giving something back to the local community, and not to fall in the pitfalls of academic extractivism. I think a lot can be learned from these approaches, in human and also in conceptual terms, when it comes to the construction of heritage and (new) narratives that allow for including all kinds of different human experiences related to industrialization and deindustrialization processes: the hopes for a better future, may they have come true or not, the suffering and the pain, and the dreadful experiences of violence, domination, and oppression.[19]

Bhopal: Toxic Heritage, Healing, and Networks of Care

The third place I take you to is Bhopal in central India, where in 1973 a chemical plant for the production of fertilizer was opened by the US company Union Carbide. This was part of the national policies for rural development India focused on after its independence from Britain in 1947, and these were often financed with multinational investments. The alpha-naphthol plant in Bhopal was "the largest of this design anywhere in the world. The factory produced agricultural pesticides with a promise of a 'greener and better India' and used hazardous chemicals like phosgene, chlorine and methyl isocyanate that lay stocked in abundance at the site" (Joshi, 2008, p. 1). Around midnight and during the first hours of December 4, 1984, a leak occurred, and the gas invaded neighborhoods and the city downhill in silence. It was not an accident; warnings have been there in the months and even days before the disaster but were ignored. This catastrophe was described as the most severe chemical disaster in human history so far, causing an unknowable number of immediate deaths that go in the thousands or tens of thousands depending on the source and perspective.[20] Today, 40 years later, "an uncertain number carry this contamination in their bodies while over half a million remain formally registered for medical support" (Joshi, 2023, p. 714).

Figure 27.7 Women survivors at Bhopal fighting for Justice and Repair in 2022, 38 years after the tragedy. (Source: International Campaign for Justice in Bhopal (ICJB), https://www.bhopal.net)

As I write, the site is still not cleaned up and "[t]he waste of the Bhopal Gas Tragedy remains the most lasting legacy of the disaster. In nasty ways," to quote my TICCIH Board colleague Moulshri Joshi, "four decades since it ceased operation, the pesticide plant continues to produce chemicals, the company continues to occupy the land and the past continues to live violently in the present" (Joshi, 2023, p. 714). The principle, to which many Europeans got used in the past decades, that who contaminates has to pay for the cleaning up of the site (in German called 'Verursacherprinzip') is not on in India nor many other parts of the South, and only in very recent times we have been seeing some cases where local NGOs start to win trials at the international courts for Human Rights against huge international companies who violate their right to live in healthy environments. In Bhopal, the local survivors and particularly women grouped together and are fighting since 40 years now for appropriate repair and justice (see Figure 27.7).

The Bhopal site can thus be considered a "dark" industrial heritage where "the old rendering plant is a visible reminder of the . . . disaster while the invisible, persistent chemicals in the soil and groundwater continue to occupy the city" (Joshi, 2023, p. 714). There is an illusion that pollution is restricted only to the inside of the site, but of course it affects a much wider area and "[t]he factory above and soils below (are in fact) connected through a toxic stream of leaching chemicals" (Joshi, 2023, p. 714). In 2005, the government organized an open competition to design a memorial at the 67-acres site with attractive prize money; a contamination map had been previously elaborated with NGOs between 1999 and 2003 (see Figure 27.8). The decision of what the memorial should be – a sculpture, a hospital, a park . . . – was left to the participating architects' imagination, as Moulshri told me, and

Industrial Heritage From the South

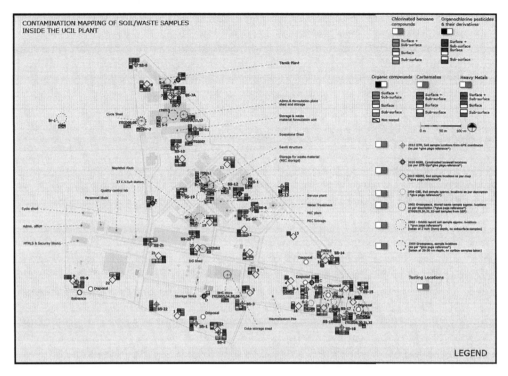

Figure 27.8 Contamination mapping of soil and waste samples at the former Union Carbide India Ltd. site in Bhopal. (Source: SpaceMatters, 2017, p. 15)

many participants suggested redeveloping the land for its large size and location, proposing institutions or even housing with a symbolic, grand "memorial."[21]

The proposal that finally won the competition was the one made by Moulshri Joshi and her team from SpaceMatters, and they were then also commissioned to be architects for implementing the project.[22] Their proposal was the only one that suggested not to tear down but to keep the old rendering plant and to make it the central icon of a memorial park. They submitted a masterplan for the site that included a landscape strategy and a cultural agenda for the revival of the contaminated land. The factory was the central iconic memorial in their scheme, preserved in its rusted state with the entire industrial landscape. This was a year or so before the team came across TICCIH's Nizhny Tagil Charter; so industrial heritage is not yet in the language of the proposal but very much there in spirit. Together with mAAN and TICCIH, SpaceMatters then started off an international workshop and symposium as an action-research initiative in Bhopal, which took place there between January 23 and February 4, 2011 and "explored the significance of the Union Carbide industrial site – its heritage as the site of the Bhopal gas tragedy, its present condition as an abandoned industrial brownfield site and its relevance as a future site for commemoration of the victims of the world's greatest industrial disaster" (Ballal et al., 2012).

In 2017, SpaceMatters mapped the existing vegetation on the site localizing the native trees, and from there on, the team developed their proposal to remediate toxic soil and water using Indigenous plants and in situ technologies, knowing that bioremediation processes use various types of plants and microbes to move, transfer, stabilize, and/or destroy contaminants in soil and groundwater (SpaceMatters, 2017). Stemming from that basis, they concretized the landscaping strategy for the site, defining different uses for different zones: areas of public access would be cleaned to avoid contamination through the accessible food chain; in the memorial area, soils with high toxicity would be contained and stored in sealed containers for public display; in staff areas not open to the public, soils with medium toxicity would be capped under a layer of fresh soil; permeable reactive barriers would intercept and filter groundwater as it passes through the site to the low-lying areas to the east; throughout the site, control stations would monitor contamination levels in all the methods used for remediation all across the site; pumping stations would extract groundwater for analysis, as well as phytoirrigation; and with regard to phytoremediation, a number of different types of vegetation are proposed that fulfill different functions (see Figure 27.9). Today, the decontamination process is underway, and the future memorial park will be a powerful resource and asset for creating awareness, especially on issues of industry and ecology (Joshi, 2024). From its very start, the project is based on the reflection that toxic waste as a historic document is a heritage that has a tremendous potential for education. A second compelling conviction, which aligns with more recent theoretical reflections such as those formulated by Max Liboiron in *Pollution is Colonialism* (2021), is that toxic waste should be dealt with on the site instead of carrying it to other places and thus expose other communities to pollution, too (Joshi, 2022).

More general questions arise from the Bhopal case with regard to its message and legacy for the world: How to deal with toxic heritage and how to heal the wounds in human

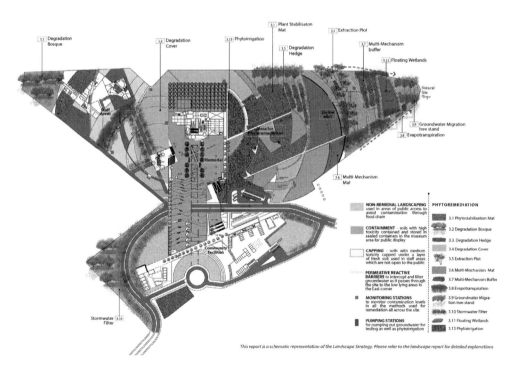

Figure 27.9 Conceptual landscape strategy for the future Bhopal memorial site. (Source: SpaceMatters, 2017, p. 64)

souls and natural environments. One key message that is at the heart of the SpaceMatters project team is that we, as humanity, have to learn how to live with the pollution that we produce and that we should cope with our moral obligation to cope with it in our own front yards instead of permanently trying to take the waste to other, generally more fragile communities and thus violate their rights to live in healthy environments. The Bhopal Memorial Site project revindicates to learn how to frame risks and become more preventive for the future. That also determines new ways of doing the work, collaboratively and caring about people and communities, and redefining policies and political frameworks and goals, because "Garbage is Infrastructure, Not Behaviour," as Liboiron put it: "The way a problem is defined forecloses on the types of solutions that make sense" (Liboiron, 2014), as we can see here.

On this ethical basis, Bhopal also connects to other sites around the world that have a tremendous educational potential for future generations building global networks of care and solidarity. Links have been made, for example, with nuclear disaster sites such as Chernobyl or Nagasaki, and Auschwitz or Buchenwald as testimonial sites of major human catastrophes of industrial scale (Ballal et al., 2012). Together, these sites represent the memories of man-made catastrophes that exist across the world and that all call on a joint human vision of a future that should be free of such disasters.

A Shared Mission: Building Decolonial Futures

The three cases I have presented here featuring a community museum, a citizens' roundtable, and survivors' NGOs as genuine 'rightsholders' can be considered action-research initiatives that explore new horizontal and collaborative ways of working together, with academics supporting organized local communities. Their specific methods include immersion in the field, active listening to the situated knowledges, and the creation of joint projects from the grounds (bottom-up) that can make a substantial contribution to structural change while in parallel sensitizing public institutions and students on how to work and address their future professional lives in less "participative" and more "decolonial" ways.[23]

Another crucial point is that all three cases challenge the classic European-centered perspectives on industrial heritage because they question the classic focus on the material conservation of the physical remains of industrialization in at least two ways. One critical point to consider is 'Heritage imperialism,' that is the fact that countries that have more money than others are more likely to be able to safeguard their material heritage, which in industrial heritage contexts poses the question of a new kind of imperialism, one that after the domination of the world by European-style development models is now repeated on the heritage conservation stage. This feels particularly bad in competitive contexts like World Heritage nominations, which follow national logics on an international stage and tend to focus on superlatives and celebratory narratives.

The second point to consider is that the basic reason why we should preserve heritage is actually not to fill up our cities and landscapes with monuments but to make people think, learn, and reflect about the processes that are behind material expressions. In industrial heritage, this means that once and for all we have to look into the details of the negative impacts of industrialization. As Moulshri Joshi put it: "We should no longer normalize disasters, erase narratives of pain and shame or fester wounds of environmental contamination, as these are not simply a side effect of development but a moral obligation" (Joshi, 2023). She urges us not to exclude "Stories of pollution and people, of pain and shame and of destruction and dispossession . . .

from the narrative of industrialization," because "perhaps for their absence, we continue to recreate the colonial paradigm in the service of the nation till date" (Joshi, 2023).

Another common point between the projects presented here seems particularly relevant to me, as the same is true for many other cases around the world: the key driving forces are women, and that is not at all a coincidence. Decolonial heritage work is about the protection and development of healthy, sustainable, and fair environments, and this requires careful communication, trustful relationships, and horizontal teamwork which is extremely time-intensive and hard social and political work that in most cases is badly paid or not paid at all. The gender care and pay gap thus also applies to heritage work, but if women don't do it, probably nobody would. We thus make a difference in nurturing local communities of care, creating networks of mutual empowerment, and building deep friendships across continents, which will last.[24] Our individual actions will of course not save the world, but they are expressions of an ethic that lead to other actions that do scale (Liboiron, 2014). However, this means very hard work without the guarantee to receive financial or academic reward for that. The volunteer work Aulikki Pollak does in Limache is a particularly impressive example for female heritage activism in the Chilean ultra neoliberal context, where a professional journalist and networker is at the core of a strong organized local community fighting against real estate speculation, misguided models of capitalist development, and the construction of high-rise buildings in historic townscapes, who won their case with an official heritage designation and even in a trial against the local mayor's team (Pollak, 2023).

On the academic side, the four women I have introduced here, we have all made the experience of being discarded in painful and unexpected ways from good and stable work positions at universities. I got set off from my university in Valparaíso after four years in an unjustified and ridiculous but traumatizing way; Moulshri has been set off from her university, too, even after having won a great prize; Esperanza struggles to be with the Chilean academic system because her priorities are on community empowerment and not on publishing indexed papers with no public access; and Magdalena left Chile for academic exile in the US, where she found better conditions to research, teach, and develop her career. Our and other experiences show that that current academic system in the South has a particularly severe problem with activist heritage women, and although new conceptualizations such as "Discard Studies" help to understand the structural problem behind that (Liboiron and Lepawsky, 2022), and although one of course always makes her way through and finds even better jobs, the decolonial work of critical industrial heritage women is hindered by an academic system that is not able to properly address real social needs.

Global Industrial Heritage: Networks of Care and Solidarity

The cases I have presented here revindicate the definition of new concepts and criteria to understand heritage and assess heritage sites and demonstrate that people able to apply horizontal, collaborative, and decolonial work methods are needed to construct (global) heritage futures from local grounds (community-led) and to create healthier, fairer, and more sustainable environments.

This has direct implications also for the work of international heritage organizations such as UNESCO and TICCIH. As for UNESCO's World Heritage program, one main point is to question the state of conservation as a Eurocentric Western criterion that is still dominating the program, which means that it should be reconsidered how relevant 'authenticity' and

Industrial Heritage From the South

'integrity' as criteria for assessing Outstanding Universal Value should still be in the future, in particular given that a new global heritage imperialism is already in the making. Many experiences from the South challenge the classic definitions of material authenticity and integrity and move toward more process-oriented criteria focused on the social dimension and meanings, affection, and collective processes to safeguard heritage. If one looks for other narratives, these social practices can be a core argument, as "the outstanding also emerges through everyday practices" (Meier and Steiner, 2023).

As for TICCIH, the process of critically revising key theory, concepts, methodology, criteria, narratives, and communication formats is officially on the way with the Commission on the Nizhny Tagil Charter having been set up after the last General Assembly in Montreal (Steiner, 2022a). In addition, TICCIH has become more global, younger, and more female in recent years, as new colleagues from different continents were elected to the board at the same Assembly in 2022.[25] By the way, five of the six new board members are women, and of course the work as TICCIH board member is an honorary unpaid work – and if you want to make a real change, remake the organization, and transform it into a more diverse, accessible, and truly global organization, and in addition you have to manage the change, then that is a really lot of work. But it is also rewarding because this is our common platform and global community where we can care for each other and share our thoughts and where we empower and support each other mutually to keep moving on. We thus even started thinking about a volume 2 of the TICCIH Handbook (Douet, 2012), which is still a good tool today but has a very limited geographic scope, and our next World Congress 2025 in Kiruna in northern Sweden will be another milestone in the process of transforming TICCIH into a truly global membership organization.[26]

Acknowledgments

This work was supported by the National Agency for Research and Development (ANID) of the Republic of Chile, research project Fondecyt de Iniciación 11230957, whose responsible researcher is Dr Marion Steiner.

Notes

1 Note how the name "TICCIH" was evolving over this period, broadening meanings from "monuments" to "heritage" and consolidating the network from a sequence of "congresses" to "committee" (more in Douet, 2012).
2 See also our Cuban colleague Karen Sanabria's lecture 'Borrando límites: por un patrimonio regional de la producción' at the X Latin American TICCIH Congress in Monterrey, Mexico, on October 24, 2023. https://www.youtube.com/watch?v=fcxkwubJYGs
3 Website ACHS: https://www.criticalheritagestudies.org; website DéPOT: https://deindustrialization.org
4 The session presentation text can be found here: https://sites.grenadine.uqam.ca/sites/patrimoine/en/ticcih2022/home updated version will be published in the congress proceedings that are currently being edited by Lucie Morisset and Juliette Passilly and will be published before the next TICCIH World Congress 2025 in Kiruna, Sweden.
5 See Steiner (2019); Steiner and Fuentes (2021); and Steiner (2025, in print).
6 My first visit to Chile was in 1995/1996 with a scholarship from the Carl Duisberg Foundation and the Land NRW to work for three months with children in the poblaciones of Puerto Varas and Puerto Montt. My graduate thesis is Marion Steiner (2001) *Stadt am Wasser? Stadtplanerische*

Ansätze zur Revitalisierung der Waterfront in der chilenischen Hafenstadt Valparaíso (unpublished manuscript). Institute of Geography, Humboldt University of Berlin.

7 FONDART Regional research project 2020 no. 551999. http://espi.rhondda.de/complejo-hidroelectrico-el-sauce-y-la-luz/

8 ANID-FONDECYT INICIACIÓN 11230957 (2023–2026). http://espi.rhondda.de/luz-poder-y-progreso/

9 See also Novoa. (2021). *Wounded Landscapes: Race, Gender, and Grassroots Preservation in Wallmapu,* Online Lecture for the Women & Gender in Global Perspectives Program, University of Illinois, 5 November. https://wggp.illinois.edu/spotlight/event/faculty-affiliate-lecture-wounded-landscapes-race-gender-and-grassroots

10 The Chilean state even created special institutions with the declared goal to 're-educate' Indigenous people to make them 'real' citizens; the German reform of the Chilean education system at the turn to the twentieth century also played a shocking role here.

11 See, for example, the ANILLO research project 'Patrimonio industrial: formas de habitar colectivo en el sur de Chile' led by Alejandra Brito and its pioneering closing publication: (Brito et al., 2018).

12 See Novoa. (2021). *Perspectivas de género en la interpretación y construcción social del patrimonio minero de Lota, Chile.* Online Lecture for the 'Global perspectives on industrial heritage' session organized by Marion Steiner at the SOCHIGEO congress 2021, Pontifical Catholic University of Valparaíso, 22 October. http://espi.rhondda.de/mesa-coordinada-sochigeo/; https://www.youtube.com/live/fYCuNf_9XRY?feature=shared&t=10041

13 Interview with Novoa. (2021). *Educator and Change Agent: Welcome, Dr. Magdalena Novoa! University of Illinois, 21 January.* https://urban.illinois.edu/about-us/news/educator-and-change-agent-welcome-dr-magdalena-novoa/ (Accessed: 17 March 2024).

14 Interview with Novoa. (2021). *Educator and Change Agent: Welcome, Dr. Magdalena Novoa!, University of Illinois, 21 January.* https://urban.illinois.edu/about-us/news/educator-and-change-agent-welcome-dr-magdalena-novoa/ (Accessed: 17 March 2024).

15 A short video on the elaboration of the Arpillera is available here, with English subtitles: https://vimeo.com/460719545

16 Nucleo de Investigación del Sur (NUDISUR). https://nudisur.org/. NUDISUR later signed a cooperation agreement with TICCIH and together we implemented the IV International and Interdisciplinary Cultural Heritage Congress on "Industrial Heritage, Social Issues and Challenges for a New Governance" in Concepción, Chile, in October 2023 (Rock and Steiner (2023); Rock et al. (2024)).

17 CreaSur: https://creasur.cl/; Casa Taller: https://www.casa-taller.cl/; OTEC: https://www.culturayterritorio.cl/

18 ANID-FONDECYT INICIACIÓN 11230309, original title in Spanish: "Memorias de las transformaciones urbanas y culturales de desindustrialización del norte y sur global: Estudio comparado de la cuenca de carbón del sur, Chile, y región de la Ruhr, Alemania," see https://www.relatosdelcarbon.cl

19 Human emotions and in particular artists and artisans also played a key role during the international Industrial Heritage Congress in Concepción, Chile, in October 2023 (Rock et al. (2024); Bretti López (2024)).

20 See the website of the International Campaign for Justice in Bhopal (ICJB), which also contains a detailed description of what happened in Bhopal in 1984 from the survivors' perspective: https://www.bhopal.net

21 Exchange with Moulshri Joshi on WhatsApp on March 12, 2024. See also the project report by SpaceMatters (2017).

22 See their original proposal here: https://architexturez.net/doc/az-cf-122776. Read more in Joshi (2024).

23 See Rock et al. (2024), chapter 4 on the Certificate program "Collaborative Methodologies for Heritage Projects with a Critical Approach," for an inspiring example of how collaborative and decolonial methodologies can be adapted in cultural heritage projects by local municipal and other professional staff.

24 On that kind of reflection, from the Chilean context, see also Alejandra Brito's recent ANID-FONDECYT Regular research project 1200806 (2020–2023) called "Industries and women

Industrial Heritage From the South

in southern Chile. Labor inclusion and social reproduction (1940–1982);" original title in Spanish: "Industrias y mujeres en el sur de Chile. Inclusión laboral y reproducción social (1940–1982)." On the concept "cuidadoras de memoria" (memory careworkers), see Brito Peña (2023).

25 See the composition of the TICCIH board for the current period 2022–2025 here: https://ticcih.org/about/board/

26 See https://ticcih2025-kiruna.se

27 All TICCIH bulletins are available open access at https://ticcih.org/ticcih-bulletin/. All my texts are available open access on my website: www.patrimoniocritico.cl/ Publicaciones. For other texts that I know are available open access on the Internet, I provide the URL.

References List[27]

ANIH. (2012). *The Taipei Declaration for Asian Industrial Heritage*. https://ticcih.org/about/charter/taipei-declaration-for-asian-industrial-heritage/

Ballal, A., af Geierstam, J. and Joshi, M. (2012). *Bhopal 2011 – Landscapes of Memory*. New Delhi: Space-Matters, mAAN, Norwegian University of Science and Technology and University of Gothenburg.

Berger, S. (2019). Industrial Heritage and the Ambiguities of Nostalgia for an Industrial Past in the Ruhr Valley, Germany. *Labor*, 16(1), pp. 37–64. https://doi.org/10.1215/15476715-7269314

Berger, S. (2022). Erinnerungen an Deindustrialisierung im Ruhrgebiet im globalen Vergleich: Welche Erinnerung gestaltet welche Zukunft? In Landschaftsverband Rheinland (LVR) and Landschaftsverband Westfalen-Lippe (LWL) (eds.) *FUTUR 21. kunst, industrie, kultur: Katalog zur Konferenz und zum Festival des Landschaftsverband Rheinland/Landschaftsverband Westfalen-Lippe 2022*. Köln: Wienand Verlag, pp. 150–153.

Berger, S. and High, S. (2019). (De-)Industrial Heritage: An Introduction. *Labor*, 16(1), pp. 1–27. https://doi.org/10.1215/15476715-7269281

Bilot, F. (2010). *Allemandes au Chili*. Rennes: Presses universitaires de Rennes.

Blancpain, J.-P. (1974). *Les allemands au Chili (1816–1945)*. Köln/Wien: Böhlau.

Bogner, S., Franz, B., Meier, H.-R. and Steiner, M. (eds.). (2018). *Monument – Patrimony – Heritage. Industrial Heritage and the Horizons of Terminology*. Holzminden: Mitzkat, Heidelberg: arthistoricum.net. https://doi.org/10.11588/arthistoricum.374.531

Bretti López, M.J. (2024). The "Arts in Ruins" Festival: An Affective Encounter with the Intangible Dimension of the Biobío Region's Industrial Heritage. In Rock, E. et al. (eds.) *Initiating Transformations* (see below). Concepción: Centro Cultural CreaSur, pp. 243–263.

Brito Peña, A. (2023). Cuidadoras de Memorias: las mujeres y la defensa del Patrimonio Industrial-Minero en el sur de Chile. *Revista EURE – Revista De Estudios Urbano Regionales*, 50(150). https://doi.org/10.7764/EURE.50.150.03

Brito Peña, A., Cerda, G., Fuentes, P. and Pérez, L. (eds.). (2018). *Industria y Habitar colectivo. Conjuntos habitacionales en el sur de Chile*. Concepción: Stoq Editorial.

Capel, H. (2014). *El patrimonio: la construcción del pasado y del futuro*. Barcelona: El Serbal.

Casanelles, E. (2012). TICCIH's Charter for Industrial Heritage. In Douet, J. (ed.) *Industrial Heritage Re-Tooled: The TICCIH Guide to Industrial Heritage Conservation*. Lancaster: Carnegie Publishing, pp. 228–232.

Contreras, C. (2024). Aprendizajes y cavilaciones a partir del X Coloquio Latinoamericano para la Conservación del Patrimonio Industrial. *Arqueología Industrial*, (90), pp. 32–33.

Douet, J. (ed.). (2012). *Industrial Heritage Re-Tooled: The TICCIH Guide to Industrial Heritage Conservation*. Lancaster: Carnegie Publishing.

Haraway, D. (1988). Situated Knowledges: The Science Question in Feminism and the Privilege of Partial Perspective. *Feminist Studies*, 14(3), pp. 575–599. https://doi.org/10.2307/3178066

ICOMOS and TICCIH. (2011). *The Dublin Principles. Joint ICOMOS-TICCIH Principles for the Conservation of Industrial Heritage Sites, Structures, Areas, and Landscapes*. https://ticcih.org/about/about-ticcih/dublin-principles/

ICOMOS Australia. (2013). *The Burra Charter. The Australia ICOMOS Charter for Places of Cultural Significance*. https://australia.icomos.org/publications/burra-charter-practice-notes/

Joshi, M. (2008). Case for Salvaging the Remains of the World's Worst Industrial Disaster at Bhopal. *TICCIH Bulletin*, (43), pp. 1, 8.

Joshi, M. (2022). *Maps and Mutual Aid. How Bhopal Can Inform a Critical View of Heritage.* Unpublished Script of the Conference Held at the INCUNA Congress 2022 in Gijón, Spain. https://youtu.be/6GDwAgsN6C4?si=U-jPbSvjZlYSXH2R

Joshi, M. (2023). Cómo la catástrofe de Bhopal puede aportar una visión crítica del patrimonio industrial. In Álvarez Areces, M.A. (ed.) *Patrimonio Mundial. Sitios industriales y obra pública. De lo local a lo universal,* 2 vols. Gijón: CICEES (=Los Ojos de la Memoria, Vol. 30), pp. 714–723.

Joshi, M. (2024). Enacting the Past. *Landscape. La Journal of Landscape Architecture,* 77, pp. 61–69.

Joshi, M. and Ballal, A. (2011). Bhopal Gas Tragedy. Dissonant History, Difficult Heritage. *Context: Built, Living and Natural,* 8(2), pp. 7–14. https://www.dronah.org/wp-content/uploads/2017/03/context-14_r.pdf

Kaltmeier, O. (2017). On the Advantage and Disadvantage of Heritage for Latin America: Heritage Politics and Nostalgia between Coloniality and Indigeneity. In Kaltmeier, O. and Rufer, M. (eds.) *Entangled Heritage. Postcolonial Perspectives on the Uses of Past in Latin America.* London and New York: Routledge, pp. 13–36.

Liboiron, M. (2014, January 23). Against Awareness, For Scale: Garbage is Infrastructure, Not Behavior. *Discard Studies Blog.* https://discardstudies.com/2014/01/23/against-awareness-for-scale-garbage-is-infrastructure-not-behavior/

Liboiron, M. (2018, November 1). Waste Colonialism. *Discard Studies Blog.* https://discardstudies.com/2018/11/01/waste-colonialism/

Liboiron, M. (2021). *Pollution is Colonialism.* Durham: Duke University Press.

Liboiron, M. and Lepawsky, J. (2022). *Discard Studies. Wasting, Systems, and Power.* Cambridge: The MIT Press. https://doi.org/10.7551/mitpress/12442.001.0001 (open access).

mAAN. (2011). *The Seoul Declaration on Industrial Heritage in Asia.* https://www.academia.edu/1580547/mAAN_Seoul_Declaration_2011_on_Industrial_Heritage_in_Asia

Meier, H.-R. and Steiner, M. (2018). Monument – Patrimony – Heritage. Industrial Heritage and the Horizons of Terminology. Introduction to the Conference Topic. In Bogner, S. et al. (eds.) *Monument – Patrimony – Heritage.* Holzminden and Heidelberg: Mitzkat, arthistoricum.net, pp. 16–35. https://doi.org/10.11588/arthistoricum.374.c5415

Meier, H.-R. and Steiner, M. (2023). Jenseits von Superlativen, oder: vom World zum Global Heritage? In Engelberg-Dočkal, E.V., Hönig, S. and Herold, S. (eds.) *Alltägliches Erben.* Holzminden and Heidelberg: Mitzkat, arthistoricum.net, pp. 30–35. https://doi.org/10.11588/arthistoricum.1254.c17544

Novoa, M. (2021a). Gendered Nostalgia: Grassroots Heritage Tourism and (De)industrialization in Lota, Chile. *Journal of Heritage Tourism.* Special Issue. https://doi.org/10.1080/1743873X.2020.1867561

Novoa, M. (2021b). Decolonizing Heritage: Class and Gender in Deindustrialized landscapes. In Mace, J. and Zhu, Y. (eds.) *Notions of heritage.* Québec: Presses de l'Université du Québec, pp. 55–81.

Novoa, M. (2022a). Insurgent Heritage: Mobilizing Memory, Place-based Care and Cultural Citizenships. *International Journal of Urban and Regional Research,* pp. 1016–1034. https://doi.org/10.1111/1468-2427.13143

Novoa, M. (2022b). Wounded Landscapes: Theorizing Spaces of Exclusion and Oblivion in the Americas (Part of the Research Article What Frameworks Should We Use to Read the Spatial History of the Americas). *Journal of the Society of Architectural Historians,* 81(2), pp. 134–153. https://doi.org/10.1525/jsah.2022.81.2.134

Novoa, M. (2025, in print). Mobilizing Gendered Nostalgia through Grassroots Heritage Tourism in the Chilean Coal Basin: The Case of Lota and Pilpilco. In Morisset, L. and Passilly, J. (eds.) *Industrial Heritage Reloaded | Le patrimoine industriel rechargé. Proceedings of the XVIIIth TICCIH World Congress 2022 in Montréal.* Montréal: Patrimonium.

Pollak, A. (2023). La lucha por la identidad de San Francisco de Limache: resistencia contra el avance del "concreto" y la defensa del Patrimonio Cultural. In Venegas Espinoza, F. et al. (eds.) *Travesía patrimonial: Avenida Urmeneta de San Francisco de Limache, joya arquitectónica de Chile central.* Concepción: Editorial Universidad de Concepción, pp. 268–293.

Rigol, I. and Rojas, Á. (2012). *Conservación patrimonial: teoría y crítica.* Havana: Editorial UH.

Rock, E. (2016). Memoria y oralidad: formas de entender el pasado desde el presente. *Diálogo andino,* 49, pp. 101–112. https://doi.org/10.4067/S0719-26812016000100012

Rock, E. (2022a). Das Erbe des Kohlereviers von Lota. *IndustrieKultur*, 100, pp. 16–17. http://espi.rhondda.de/lota-ik100/

Rock, E. (2022b). A Critique of the Industrial Heritage of the Global South. *TICCIH Bulletin*, 97, pp. 20–22.

Rock, E. (2023). Reflexiones sobre patrimonio y perspectiva decolonial en estudios postindustriales en comunidades del hemisferio sur. *Revista Gerónimo De Uztariz Aldizkaria*, 37. https://doi.org/10.58504/rgu.37.5

Rock, E. and Steiner, M. (2023). Industrial Heritage, Social Issues and Challenges for a New Governance: The IV International and Interdisciplinary Cultural Heritage Congress in Chile. *TICCIH Bulletin*, 102, pp. 5–8.

Rock, E., Steiner, M., Stewart, D. and Torres, A. (eds.). (2024). *Initiating Transformations. Industrial Heritage as an Asset for Regional Development. Critical Views from and for the Global South.* Concepción: Centro Cultural CreaSur. https://www.creasur.cl/en/gore-program/industrial-heritage-as-an-asset-for-regional-development/

Rock, E. and Torres, A. (2024). Das industrielle Erbe der Eisenbahn in San Rosendo. *Industriekultur*, 108, pp. 48–51. http://espi.rhondda.de/ik-san-rosendo/

Sletto, B., Novoa, M. and Vasudevan, R. (2023). 'History Can't be Written without Us in the Center': Colonial Trauma, the Cartographic Body, and Decolonizing Methodologies in Urban Planning. *Environment and Planning D: Society and Space*, 41(1), pp. 148–169. https://doi.org/10.1177/02637758231153

SpaceMatters. (2017). *Detailed Project Report – Site Development and Remediation, Bhopal Gas Tragedy Memorial Project by SpaceMatters.* New Delhi: SpaceMatters.

Steiner, M. (2019). *Die chilenische Steckdose. Kleine Weltgeschichte der deutschen Elektrifizierung von Valparaíso und Santiago de Chile, 1880–1920*, 2 vols. Weimar: Bauhaus-Universität Weimar. https://doi.org/10.25643/bauhaus-universitaet.3925

Steiner, M. (2020). Hello from Your New Secretary General. *TICCIH Bulletin*, 88, pp. 2–4.

Steiner, M. (2021). Reflexiones postcolonialistas acerca de la percepción de Berlín como ciudad modelo de la modernidad técnica. In Balbontín, C. and Rodríguez, L. (eds.) *Historia, Trauma, Memoria*. Santiago: Libros del amanecer, pp. 37–61.

Steiner, M. (2022a). Retooling TICCIH: 2022 General Assembly and our Work Program for the next year. *TICCIH Bulletin*, 98, pp. 19–20.

Steiner, M. (2022b). Industrie 'kultur' oder Barbarei der Mächtigen? Kritische Überlegungen aus Sicht des Globalen Südens. In Landschaftsverband Rheinland (LVR) and Landschaftsverband Westfalen-Lippe (LWL) (eds.) *FUTUR 21. kunst, industrie, kultur: Katalog zur Konferenz und zum Festival des Landschaftsverband Rheinland/Landschaftsverband Westfalen-Lippe 2022.* Köln: Wienand Verlag, pp. 154–157.

Steiner, M. (2023). Patrimonios desde la PUCV: Miradas cruzadas entre Educación, Construcción y Geografía. In Agrupación de las Universidades Regionales de Chile (eds.) *Cartografías de los patrimonios para un nuevo Chile*. Valparaíso: Ediciones Universitarias de Valparaíso, pp. 77–91.

Steiner, M. (2025, in print). Electropolis Berlin – A New Urban Vision Fuelled by Coal and Imperial Ambitions. In Moss, T. (ed.) *Grounding Berlin. Ecologies of a Technopolis, 1871 to the present.* Pittsburgh, PA: University of Pittsburgh Press, Series History of the Urban Environment.

Steiner, M. and Fuentes, P. (2021). *Luz para Valparaíso. El Complejo Hidroeléctrico El Sauce y La Luz. Un patrimonio industrial compartido entre Placilla de Peñuelas y la Elektrópolis Berlín.* Valparaíso: Centro Cultural Placilla.

Steiner, M. and Fuentes, P. (2024). Glocal Historiographies and Critical Industrial Heritage. Striving for a Critical Heritagization of the El Sauce y La Luz Hydroelectric Complex in Valparaíso, Chile. *TICCIH Bulletin*, 103, pp. 30–33.

Stuart, I. (2023). Time to Update the Nizhny Tagil Charter!. *TICCIH Bulletin*, 100, pp. 4–5.

TICCIH. (2003). *The Nizhny Tagil Charter for the Conservation of the Industrial Heritage.* https://ticcih.org/about/charter/

Wallerstein, I. (2004). *World-Systems Analysis. An Introduction.* Durham and London: Duke University Press. https://sociologiadeldesarrolloi.wordpress.com/wp-content/uploads/2014/11/223976110-26842642-immanuel-wallerstein-analisis-de-sistemas-mundo.pdf.

CONCLUSION

Tim Strangleman, Sherry Lee Linkon, Steven High,
Jackie Clarke, and Stefan Berger

Deindustrialization Studies as a Field

Over the last four decades or so, the study deindustrialization has rapidly expanded. Across multiple disciplines and interests we can now talk of a coherent field of study. The field itself is rooted in historical understandings of industry – how it developed, matured, declined, and ended. From the start of the modern period of deindustrialization it would have been impossible to see these trends of decline in anything other than international perspective. The 'run-away shop' was moving elsewhere after all. Globalization and international competition were an integral part of deindustrialization; but it is worth noting that historically global political and economic pressures have shaped where and when industry gets done. The Cold War for instance played a huge part in the reindustrialization of Japan after the Second World War, and equally the development of the so-called Tiger economies was a by-product of postwar geopolitics. Equally, the end of the Cold War saw the collapse of industry in Eastern Europe.

Deindustrialization is also marked in a different way by history, by the legacy and imprint the industrial past leaves on individuals, communities, places, regions, and nation-states. One of the profound issues that continues to resurface in the study of industrial change is how memory is created, reproduced, held, and erased over time. For individuals caught up in the process of displacement, memory might take simple forms – the box of keepsakes stored in an attic, photos of coworkers or industrial memorabilia placed proudly on display. Many industrial workers took physical reminders of their workplaces when industry was shuttered, just as retirees often do. On a wider scale, communities seek to remember their industrial past through statement artwork evoking industry. The best examples for instance in the UK are the pit head wheels or giant Davey Lamps mounted at the entrance to former coal settlements. More formal still are the museums and heritage sites which seek to preserve aspects of what once was there.

Memory, as we have seen countless times in this volume, is complex and shifting. Memory is not a static thing but becomes a muse for different groups for different purposes. What is remembered, valued, and celebrated about the industrial past is as important as what is forgotten, lost, and erased. Who gets to remember, who gets to form a part of the story, and

DOI: 10.4324/9781003308324-39

Conclusion

who does not is a choice, a selection, an active decision made across time and space. Over two decades ago, Cowie and Heathcott warned their readers against descending into what they labeled 'smokestack nostalgia,' an uncritical wallowing in an industrial past. They reminded us quite rightly that industrial jobs were difficult, dangerous, and were often the best paid, least bad option for those who did them. At that time, the dangers of such nostalgia were seen as health and environmentally related, but in the intervening years we could add to that list of dangers the corrosive nostalgia that attaches to a political celebration of the industrial past which laments a variety of other ills – loss of control, of identity, for example. Here is the value of a critical field like deindustrialization studies where the complexities of the past are understood and worked on and worked with. One of the fascinating ways in which the field has emerged and developed is in the constant questioning of safe interpretations of the past. This includes the way many people were excluded from narratives of industry – female workers, ethnic minorities, and queer people. Also, we can see how the role and importance of industry itself are challenged by new ways of thinking. The most obvious example here is over debates about shifts to net zero. The environment affords us with many opportunities to think not only about the present and future but also about communities that fought so hard to keep polluting jobs and industry in the past. This might allow us to think about the importance of just transitions today and tomorrow.

Thinking Through the Half-Life of Deindustrialization Studies

The concept of the half-life of deindustrialization has been central to many of the contributions to this volume as it has to the field as a whole. Its importance here is that it identifies that the process of deindustrialization is long-lived and open-ended. It also highlights in this openness that outcomes are not fixed. They are subject to change and modification, to policy interventions and other moves. The importance is that as a field, deindustrialization studies deploys its historical imagination in thinking about both the present and more especially the future. Recently, there has been a renewed interest in the field of sociology in thinking about the future. Traditionally, social scientists shy away from thinking about the future, less still making predictions. But in their edited special issue, Halford and Southernton (2023) make an argument that sociologists and social scientists have an urgent need to think about the future, how the social might unfold. They make the argument that if academics stand back from such debates, the vacuum will be filled by journalists and other commentators with far less of an evidence base to build on in discussing the shape of future society. Deindustrialization studies similarly needs to think about how our collective knowledge of industry and its decline and helps shape our expectations of the future – both how the half-life will continue to unfold and how insights from deindustrialization can help us think about the future of work, community, class, and politics. The point of this field then, at least in part, must be to inform and help shape debates about the future of society.

Reference List

Halford, S. and Southernton, D. (2023). What Future for the Sociology of Futures? Visions, Concepts and Methods. *Sociology*, 57(2), pp. 263–278.

INDEX

Note: Page numbers in *italics* indicate figures, and page numbers in **bold** indicate tables.

abandonment: of community 25, 37, 84; industrial 173, 211, 289–290, 301; of social norms 66; urban 83–84, 98, 121–122
Abrams, Philip: *Historical Sociology* (1982) 67
abstract ideas 9, 15, 33
academic: articles 54, 255, 279–280; debate 11, 43, 53, 174; research 12, 138, 172, 470, 472–473
Acheson, T.W. 128
Acres International 134
ACT UP 268
action: collective 19, 70, 155, 234, 236, 352; research 371, 382–383, 421, 475, 477
activism: anti-nuclear 34; environmental 223; heritage 369, 373, 478; memory 5, 288–289, 301, 368–369; narratives 126, 128, 134; political 65, 96, 131, 174
addiction 37, 110, 298
AfD *see* Alternative for Germany
affective: history 191, 195; legacy 196–197; life 189, 191–193, 198; practice 184, 190–193, 198–199
affects 4, 173, 190, 198–199, 209, 269
Africa 57; underdevelopment 120
African American workers 79, 208
age: of climate crisis 172, 321; coming of 170, 222, 224; discrimination 206; industrial 67, 108, 322, 386
agency: auditing 353–354; political 143, 174
agglomeration 237, 384, 392, 407
Agnew, Terese: *Portrait of a Textile Worker* 347
AGORA 389
agriculture 49–51, 58, 132–133, 174
Ahmad, Riaz 211

AI (artificial intelligence) 10
AIDS 262, 266, 268–272
Air Canada 131
Airbnb 112
airports 211
Aitken, Keith 147
alcohol 3, 227, 232, 241, 289
Alexander, Brian 119
alienation 87, 324, 327, 329–331
alliances 175, 364, 369, 386
Alternative for Deutschland (AfD) party 3, 143, 368
Althusser, Louis 67
Amalgamated Textile Workers' Union 206
Amazon 104
Ambassador-in-Residence Program 291
ambivalence 172, 212, 223, 331, 339
ambivalent nostalgia 88, 322
American: Democrats 103; Dream 289; ghetto 98, 209–210, 234–236, 290; hegemony 105–108; Midwest 1, 24–25, 81, 141–142, 208, 268; military bases 120, 131; New Left 26, 103
American Rust Belt: mixed race neighborhoods 122
Americana 66
Amin, Samir 105, 109
analysts 34, 57
Anand, Shriya 349
Anchor Hocking 119
Anderson, Benedict 127
Andre the Giant 293–294
anger 38, 41, 86, 165, 198, 341, 421–422
anthropology 219, 413

Index

anxiety 34, 85–86, 195, 227, 239
Anzieu, Didier 192
Apel, Dora 5, 280–281, 283–284, 286
Apple 106
ARBED steel group 389
Arbeit macht frei placards 288
Archer, Dennis 290
Archer, Rory 141, 222
Area Redevelopment Administration for
    Appalachia 99, 127
Argentina 57, 440, 469
art projects 287, 290, 292
Arthurson, Kathy 235–236
Ashington Group 321
Asia 19, 25, 43, 56, 203–205 *see also* South Asia
assumptions: moral 66, 99, 139, 240, 422;
    racial/gendered 15, 123, 182, 438, 450,
    452; regarding redevelopment 148, 170,
    245, 328; silent or unspoken 19
Astibo fashion industry 223
Athabasca, Canada 321, 328, 330–332
atmosphere: concept of 335; deindustrializing
    340–341, 344; political 134, 240; pollution
    110, 232
atomic bomb 38
Attlee, Clement 69
attraction: cultural 290, 382, 392; heritage 437;
    tourist 407 *see also* tourism
Australia: cultural capital 420, 422–423, 425,
    427; feeling communities 250–251; industrial
    heritage 365, 373, 375–376, 429, 452; labor
    market 56–57, 249; territorial stigma 233
autoethnography 34, 143, 265
automobile industry: assembly plants 118, 208,
    337; autoworkers 118, 142; decline of 97,
    171, 288; manufacturing 1–2, 19, 142 *see
    also* Detroit
Avraamov, Arseny 337
Aziz, Ammar 353–354

Baccini, Leonardo 142–143
Bachelet, Pierre (singer) 256
backlash politics 142
Bacon, Robert 54, 140
Bailey, Marlon M.: *Butch Queens Up in Pumps*
    (2013) 269
Bailkin, Jordanna 210
Bair, Jennifer 352
Balay, Anne: *Steel Closets* 262, 268
Bangladesh: climate crisis 174; garment industry
    347, 349, 351–354; industrial output 58,
    104, 109
bankruptcy 129, 160, 220, 225–226, 288,
    292–293, 344
banlieues (urban outcasts) 83, 98, 210 *see also*
    ghetto

Barrow, Clyde W. 103, 107–108
Barthos, Karl 337
Bassler, Gerhardt 131
Baumol, William 51–52, 56
BBC (British Broadcasting Company) 236,
    238, 244
BBC (British Broadcasting Corporation) 233,
    238, 244
Beaton, Kate: *Ducks: Two Years in the Oil Sands*
    5, 281, 283, 320–324, *325*, 327–331; *Hark!
    A Vagrant* 320–321
Beckert, Sven 203
Bederman, Gail 193
behavior 70, 116, 330, 350, 452
Beissel, Adam 255
Belgium **23**, **55**, 156, 159–160, 163, 166
Bell, Daniel: *The Coming of Postindustrial Society*
    1973 11, 18, 52, 95, 170, 175, 375
Belleville, Pierre 157
Belt Publishing 42
Benanav, Aaron 171
Benefits Street (reality television) 185, 233,
    236, 238
Benefits Streets (British TV) 233, 238
Benn, Tony 54, 146, 197
Bennett, Jane: *Vibrant Matter: Towards a
    Political Ecology of Things* 237
Beresford, Melissa (et al 2022) 70–71
Berger, Stefan 5, 22, 41, 97, 126–127, 316,
    374
Bernes, Jasper: *The Work of Art in the Age of
    Deindustrialization* (2017) 285
Bérubé, Allen 268
betrayal 141, 143, 263
Bettis, Pamela J. 79–80, 82
Beveridge, William 69
Beynon, Huw 96, 145
*Beyond the Ruins: The Meaning of
    Deindustrialization* (Cowie/Heathcott)
    2003 13, 27, 35
Bhramba, Gurminder 87, 264
Billy Elliot (film) 271
Black: communities 80, 84, 98, 208, 338;
    culture 301; deprivation 123; empowerment
    122; ghetto 98, 209–210, 233–236, 294;
    majority 4, 98, 122; music 299, 338;
    pathologization 85, 121; radical tradition
    116; representation 123; spatial agency
    287–288; women 80–81; workers 78–80,
    118–119, 122, 284, 373
Black and ethnic minority (BAME) 209
Black Lives Matter movement 88
Blackaby, Frank 54, 140, 148
blackness 85
Blade Runner (1982-film) 232
Blake, William 66, 335

Index

blast furnace 35, 190, 232, 237–238, 340, 366, 382, 389–390, 394, 407
blue-collar work 79, 81, 219–221, 227, 251, 255, 340
Bluestone, Barry 2, 11, 13, 19, 25–27, 29, 96, 103, 141, 170, 205, 266
body count 12, 102
Bole, David 383
Böll, Heinrich 305–307, 316
Bollywood 347, 350–351
Bolton, George 146
Bonilla-Silva, Eduardo 77
Bosnia-Herzegovina 220–221
Bost, François 22
Bottà, Giacomo 5, 251, 280, 282, 284
Botte, Marie-Claire 338
Bourdieu, Pierre 234, 424
BP (British Petroleum) 145
Brauer, Juliane 250
Brazil 2, 57, 440, 445, 467
breadwinner 184, 194–196, 252, 264, 352, 354
Brewer, Rose M. 80–81
Brexit: "spirit of citizenship" agenda 138; politics 142, 145, 197; support for 85–87, 138, 184, 191, 197, 368
Bright, Geoff 43, 184
Britain 49; government services 54; Labour Party 52, 138, 146–148
British Aluminum 64, 69
British National Party 143, 211
British Steel Corporation 145, 237
Bronfiglioli, Chiara 4, 185
Brown, Katy 138
Brunswick Mining and Smelting 133
built environment: deterioration of 35, 37–38, 342; and gender differences 451; redevelopment 42
Burrill, Fred 4, 98
Byrne, David 63–64

Cabaret Voltaire 338
Cairncross, Alec 22, 140
Cairns, Kate 234
Cambodia 104
Cambridge Guide to Literature in English 33
Canada/Atlantic Canada: economic development 4, 99, 126–127; Fort McMurray 320–324, 328–331; interwar year 129–130; left-nationalism 23–24, 95, 103, 131; literature 323; Maritime Provinces 111; oil patch 320–321, 323; oil sands 320, regionalism 127–129, 134, resource dependency 24
Canadian Broadcast Corporation 131
Canadian Golden Horseshoe 142
cancer 34, 330, 354

Cape Breton: any job is a good job 324; culture 323
capital: accumulation 102, 108, 130, 239; flight 19, 25, 29, 41, 55, 83, 95–96, 103, 106, 108, 169, 263; mobility 22, 77, 127, 355; organic composition 107, 109
capitalism: forms 77, 366, 376; fundamentals 10, 28, 98, 102, 109; global 4, 20, 349, 351, 354; industrial 19, 24, 63, 77, 85, 107, 116–117, 169–170, 265–266; neoliberal failure 296; violence 38, 99, 282, 352
capitalist: accumulation 109; development 97, 107, 128, 169, 173, 175, 471, 478; monopolies 162; society 10, 76, 96; world-system 105, 107, 110, 155, 219
carbon emissions 169, 174
Caribbean 23, 78, 98, 116, 121, 203–204
caring services 203, 212, 354, 473, 477
cartoons 20, 25, 308, 310, 312, 321, 323
Casey, Velda 204
Cattell, Nicole 291
Catteral, Steven 64
CDP *see* Community Development Project
Center for Working Class Studies (CWCS) 64
centrality 20, 23, 29, 40, 48–49, 97–98, 285, 453
centralization 107, 128
CFDT *see* French Democratic Confederation of Labour
challenges: cultural 40, 263, 394, 452; employment 80, 129, 148, 206, 351–352, 354, 392; environmental 3; of just transitions 14; military 131, 204; political 1, 219, 401; racial 88, 121; supply chain 105
Chambers-Letson, Joshua 267
change: agents of 382; cultural 65, 306; employment 52, 55; resistance to 67; structural 51, 96, 149, 281, 365, 375, 381–382, 384, 401, 477
Chargesheimer (Hargesheimer, Karl-Heinz): *Im Ruhrgebiet* 306–307; photographer 305, 316
Chatham Dockyard 38
Chatterjee, Piyusha 5, 280–281, 284–285
Chauncey, George: *Gay New York* 265
chemical: industry 173–174, 238, 402; spill 165
Chéreque, Jacques 163
Chernobyl 34, 477
Chicago 34, 79–80, 83–84, 119, 203, 208, 234–236, 265, 296, 337–339
children: child labor 105, 118; education 119, 121–122; of industrial workers 35–36, 40, 79, 190, 222–225, 251, 279, 430; providing for 149, 155, 157, 193, 195
China: Iron Rice Bowl 104; job skills 106; state-owned steel factory 141; trade liberalization 12, 24, 104, 106–107, 109

Index

Chinai, Alisha: *Made in India* (pop song) 349

Chobani yogurt 43

Chocholle, René 338

Chowdhury, Elora Halim 353

Chrysler 79, 209, 248, 288

citizen: citizenship 65, 69, 138, 150; industrial 124, 141; ordinary 185, 218; second-class 210; working-class 218, 224

civil rights movement 83, 342, 423

Clark, Andy 37–38, 148, 150

Clark, Colin: *Conditions of Economic Progress* (1953) 51–52, 56

Clarke, Jackie 4

class: consciousness 10; fragmentation 102, 108; identity 64, 105, 186, 249, 373, 420, 427; structure 108; struggle 13, 24, 76, 126, 130, 148, 254, 316, 351; theory 234

climate change 3, 110, 149, 169, 171–174, 321, 394

Climate Emergency Services 172

closure, factory/plant: consequences 2

coal: crisis 306–307, 384, 400; industry 68–69, 129, 159, 175, 205, 384

coal mining 22; communities 96, 145, 149; deposits 402; expansion 384; state-owned 22, 401

Cohen, Elie: *L'Etat brancardier. Politiques du declin industriel* (1989) 22

Cold War 11, 51, 103, 141, 156–157, 266, 341, 400, 484

Cole, George Douglas Howard 69, 132

collective effervescence 240

collective memory 139, 148, 222, 320, 322, 381, 392, 453

colonial legacy 78

colonialism 77, 99, 117, 120, 173, 205, 330, 371, 467

color line 118–120

commodity 48–49, 57, 105–106, 111, 186

communication: intergenerational 424–426, 429–431

Communist Party of Great Britain (CPGB) 145–146

community 4; art projects 287, 290, 292; assets 64; emotional 249, 253; feelings communities 249–250; response 14, 67; sense of 248; vitality 112

Community Development Project (CDP) 207, 209, 211

competition: cutthroat 148; foreign 25, 55, 138; intense 11, 24; interurban 84

competitiveness 58, 69, 155

Confederation 127, 129, 131, 134

conflict: closure related 156; generational 38, 40, 198, 432; open 130; power struggles 38,

41; racial 77, 86–87, 119; resolution 162; social 71, 130, 154, 158, 162, 284

Conrad, Margaret 129

conscious change 19

conservative position 54, 123, 197, 422–423

construction: economic 408; identity 181, 369, 451; postwar 11, 18, 79, 95, 130, 391; social 116, 371, 459–461

consumption 10, 84, 110, 157, 162, 227, 250, 253, 264, 281, 342, 344

contaminants: heavy metals 35, 250; soot 35, 305, 310

contraction 4, 54–55, 58, 79, 84, 87, 139, 164

Contrepois, Sylvie 105

Cooer, Melinda 264

Cook, Tim 106

COP26 172

Cope, Mitch 292

copper mine 223

corporate: dominance 23; greed 25, 95, 145; multinational corporations 23, 95, 138, 238, 353; responsibility 38, 83, 164

corruption 37, 369, 405

Coventry Transport Museum 172

COVID-19 46

Cowie, Jefferson 12–13, 19, 27, 29, 35, 43, 89, 96, 103, 263, 266, 322, 404, 485

craft-skill community 38–39

Crawford, Douglas 145

crime: organized 37; violent 235, 240

criminal activity 107–108, 220, 290

criminality 107

criminalization 108

crisis: AIDS 266, 268–269; ecological 169–170 *see also* climate change; economic 129; financial 96, 224, 248; industrial 134, 158–159; oil 336; outmigration 129; unemployment **159**; urban 210

Croatia 141, 219–224, 226–227

cultural: connection 126, 323; forms 64, 67, 203; justice 287, 299–301; producers 34, 52, 249, 270, 299, 336, 342, 344; representation 34–35, 41, 183–183, 322, 331, 335, 351; scientists 383

culture 13; material 186, 270, 413, 449; popular 64–65, 71–72, 323, 327; of power 64, 285; urban 312, 386

Cumbler, John 97

curator 34, 225, 419–420, 423–424, 429

Curator-in-Residence Program 291

Curits, Ben 69–70

Cvek, Sven 219

Cvetkovich, Ann: archive of feelings 186, 270

Czechoslovakia 402, 413

Index

D'Emilio, John 265–266
Daewoo 163
Darcy, Michael 235–236
Daumas, Jean-Claude 22
Davidson, Tony J. 342
Davis, Meryl (figure skater) 249
Davis, Miles 300
Debraggio, Andrew 42
decarbonization 72, 174
decay: history of 248; moral 218, 233–234, 238; urban 248, 250
decision-makers 165, 382, 386, 393
decline: economic 35, 55, 79, 85–86, 127, 140, 157, 203, 211, 220, 287, 301, 307, 392, 399; industrial 22, 66, 78, 85, 89, 98–99, 110, 134, 162–163, 209, 281, 301, 389; social 233, 307
decolonization 86, 210, 212, 473
deindustrialization: chronology 10–11, 13, 43, 89, 162; complexity 12, 35, 89; consequences 33, 76, 81–82, 84, 89, 154, 250, 252, 256–257, 285, 307–307, 310; controversy 12, 288; defining the concept 9, 22; effects of 14, 33–36, 41, 43, 64, 181, 189–191, 194, 263, 270, 295, 298; history of 4; impact 4, 69, 80, 145–146, 151, 189 *see also* affect; gender; implications 4, 182, 190, 197, 218, 349; injures 35–36, 38, 42, 86, 142; is harmful 34; language of 22; life after 222; modern meaning 11; musical response 339, 342–343 *see also* music; polycrisis 336, 339, 341, 344; premature 48, 57; process of 1, 20, 28; representations 5, 34, 182, 265, 283, 285, 287, 306, 316, 322; scholarship of 139; tariff induced 24; theoretical approach 15; thesis 23; vulnerability 141
Deindustrialization and the Politics of Our Time (DéPOT) project 30n18, 98, 142, 462
deindustrialization as a breaching experiment 15
Deindustrialization of America: Plant Closings, Community Abandonment and the Dismantling of Basic Industry, The (Bluestone/Harrison) 1982 2, 11, 13, 26–27, 96, 98
deindustrialization studies: contributions 81; field of 86, 103, 107, 126–127, 186, 266, 322, 404; heart of 3, 322; moral economy 64
Delaunay, Jean-Claude 52
Delelis, André 255
Democratic Party 37, 103, 143
demoralization 87, 224
Denmark 57
Denning, Michael 108
Denton, Nancy A. 82
Department of Tourist Development 134
dependency theory 23, 29, 103

deprivation 66, 83, 88, 123–124, 150, 185, 208
deregulation 77, 83
destruction: of communities 96, 171, 330; delayed 38; property 211, 329, 331, 451; symbolism 64, 72
Detroit Lions (football team) 249
Detroit Sound Conservancy 300
Detroit, Michigan: impacts of deindustrialization 78–79, 83, 98; motor city 97, 171, 185, 208–209, 248, 287; unemployment rate 1, 208–209, 211
devastation 36, 111, 149, 192, 289, 349
develop or perish slogan 131
Devitt, Liam 5, 186
devolution 70, 139, 144–147, 150
Dey, Aditi 349
Dey, Deblina 351
Dhobi Weatherlux 202
Dickens, Charles 339
Dicks, Bella 374, 431
Didley, Bo 337
Die Krupps 338
Diggs, Isaac: photographer 298, 300–301; Sterling Toles 299
Diggs, Issac 298–301
disintegration 85, 102, 108, 110, 192
disinvestment 25–26, 79, 82–83, 89, 116, 142, 181, 205, 289, 331
dislocation 173; economic 210.29; industrial 105, 143, 173; social 20, 67, 203
disposal sites 34
documentary 238, 244, 279–282, 284, 291, 309, 347, 353–354
dominant class 18, 367
Dominion Steel and Coal Company Ltd 130
Dominion Textile 104
Dotty Wotty House 290, *291*
downsizing 1, 9, 69, 254, 405, 408
drug: availability 37, 232, 234–235; industry 37; treatment programs 84
Du Bois, W.E.B. (William Edward Burghardt) 117, 124n1
Dudley, Kathryn Marie 2
Dugrand, Raymond: *Villes et Campagnes en Bas-Languedoc* (1963) 22
Dumans, Bruno 255
Duplessis, Maurice 130
Durkheim, Émile 240

ecological crisis 169–170
economic: defeat 22; devastation 36, 111; division 23, 48; forecasting 170; growth 46, 51, 53, 56, 130–131, 156, 185, 218, 226, 290, 349, 370, 441; impact 1, 141; miracles 50; production 63, 139; recession 54, 336, 384; reductionism 67; survivability 84; theory 49, 108

490

Index

economic change: effects of 40, 42, 279, 280, 284, 341, 349; structural 131, 335

economic crisis 129, 159, 206, 307, 340, 461

economic development: modern 51; regional 127, 130–131, 134

economic restructuring: cultural influences 284, 339, 348; policy 169, 355; premise 35, 77, 81, 85; transformations 182, 212

economists 19, 23, 48, 51–52, 54, 56, 96, 103, 109, 131, 138, 140, 383

Ecumenical Coalition 96

Edgerton, David 50

education: formal 50, 56, 204, 210; lack of 3, 51, 79–80; after-school programs 84, 291

elections: general/governmental 57, 132–133, 143, 145–148, 159; presidential 37, 85, 138, 142, 162, 310

electrical industry 19, 384

Elliot, Rebecca 172–173

Eltis, Walter 54, 140

Eminem (musician): *Lose Yourself* 248–251

emissions, net zero 169, 174

emotions: history of 4, 71, 186, 249–250; human 71, 227, 248, 251, 256, 270, 421

employment: by country, 1970/2016 1–2, **23**; data 139; discrimination 80, 123; law 141; layoffs 78–79, 141, 161, 184, 190, 192; policy 13; radio stations 161–162; rates 80, 159, 209, 220, 238, 240, 400; seniority 78–79; *Tour de France* 161; working conditions 78, 118, 157–158, 184, 206, 284, 352–353

Engels, Friedrich 10, 107

Enlightenment-era 51

entertainment 239, 244, 250, 284, 295, 398, 408

Entin, Joseph: *Living Labor: Fiction, Film, and Precarious Work* (023) 285

entrepreneurs 84, 123, 129, 285, 293, 337, 348, 350, 370, 398, 411

environmental: challenges 132, 242, 245, 320, 365, 410; deterioration 35–38, 287, 324, 327; harm 36, 88, 111, 142, 173, 223; just transition 148; justice 76, 173–175; productivity 58; stigma 233, 242, 244

environmental impact 321–324, 330

Equal Employment Opportunity Commission 79

Equal Opportunities Program 133

equalization 104, 130–131

eradication 10–11, 164

erasure 10, 39–40, 65, 343, 410, 443, 449, 451

Eribon, Didier 143

Erikson, Kai 194

Escobar, Arturo 175

ethics 15, 70, 118, 174, 239, 329

ethnic: diversity 184, 426; dominant (background) 423–424, 426 *see also* ethnicity; minority 4, 185, 203, 205, 209

ethnicity 4, 15, 80, 86, 199, 373

EU *see* European Union

European Capital of Culture 315–316, 388, 390, 393, 398, 407

European Free Trade Area 145

European Union (EU) 138, 143, 145, 197, 220, 222, 224, 364, 376, 385, 407

evolution 48, 66, 68, 155, 164, 184, 445

exclusion 39, 233, 240–241, 288, 296, 423 *see also* racial; social

exploitation: colonial 203–204; forms of 107–108, 111, 116, 124, 284, 329, 344, 388, 409, 462; justification 116–118

export: commodity 53, 57, 148, 323, 349, 352; jobs for export 25, *26*

expulsion 107

extension 19, 69, 123, 386, 410, 449

extraction: exhaustion of 111; resource 24, 131, 133, 320, 322–323, 330–331

Facebook 222

factory: closures 19, 22–23, 154, 165, 170, 175, 218, 222, 226, 322, 348; dismantling 37, 146, 158, 389, 399; lay-offs 1, 37, 78–79, 81, 141, 161, 184, 190–192, 291

failings 53, 87, 138, 159

Fair Housing Act 1968 83

fallout: cultural 263–264; economic 320; shelter 38–39

family: breadwinners 184, 194–196, 252, 264, 352, 354; investment in 88, 109; members 142–143, 353, 424, 430–431; nuclear 264–265; tradition 132, 182, 184, 222–222, 265, 312

fantasy 10, 40, 65, 111–112, 184, 192–194, 197, 285

Federated Press 20

Feinberg, Leslie: *Stone Butch Blues* (2014) 265, 268

feminine: feminist 175, 263, 267, 447; feminist sector 224, 227–228

Ferns, James 184

figural economy 85, 281, 285

filmmakers 35, 154, 157, 161, 335, 337, 340, 355, 363

filmmaking: exploitation of women 351–352; garment industry 347–349, 351–355; production process 348

financial: development 204, 368; economic status 110, 132; funding 50, 388, 408, 465–466, 473 *see also* grants

financialization 102, 107–109, 163–164, 285

Findlay, Neil 150

Index

Fisher, Alan George Bernard: *Clash of Progress and Security* (1935) 51
Fishermen's Protective Union, Newfoundland 129
fishing industry: decline 99, 129, 321, 323, 328–329; fish canning 219, 224, 226, 228; fish stocks 111; labor shares **50**; modernization 131–133
Fleming, Robin 10
Flür, Wolfgang 337
Folkwang School 308–309
Fontaine, Marion 3–4, 28, 97, 99, 255–256, 282, 374, 392
food stamps 110
football clubs 186, 239–240, 249, 253–256
Forbes, E.R. 132
Forbes, Malcolm 119
Ford Motor Co 208, 248, 288, 337, 344
Fordism (system of mass production) 1, 14, 83, 264, 269, 401
foreign: competition 25, 55, 138; direct investment 23, 401; imports 25; workers 25, 105, 210 *see also* migrant workers
Fortune Global Forum 106
fossil fuel 99, 149, 171, 174–175, 321
Foster, John Bellamy 110
France: industrial decline 22, **23**, **50**, 66, 105, 120, 185–186; labor movements 154, 156, 158, 165–166; migration/migrant workers 204–205, 210; mining cities 157–158, 382, 391; mining industry 96–97; unemployment **159**, 160–161
Frank, André Gunder 24, 95, 105
Frank, David 129
Frank, Miriam 268
Franklin, Aretha 301
Fraser, Alistair 37–38
free-trade 53, 102, 145
French Communist Party 156, 158
French Democratic Confederation of Labour (CFDT) 156, 160, 162–164
Frenkel, Michael 24
Front National/Rassemblement National (France) 3, 394
Fukushima 34
Fullilove, Mindy 121
futurology 14, 16n2, 308

Gadrey, Jean 52
Gandy, Matthew 335
Ganser, Karl 314–315
garment industry: anti-sweatshop campaign 347; KiK (German) 353–354; poor working condition0s 353
Garruccio, Roberta 142
Gater, Richard 196–197

Gaye, Marvin 301
Gelsenkirchener Bergwerks AG (GBAG) 388
gender 3; dynamics 186; hierarchies 81, 88, 182; representation 186, 437, 450–451; workforce composition 52, 227, 264, 271, 351
General Agreement on Tariffs and Trade (GATT) 19, 95
General Confederation of Labour (CGT) 156, 158, 160–164
General Motors 248, 288, 296
genocide 146, 289
gentrification 41, 181, 186, 233, 235, 239, 268–268, 284, 287
geography: cultural fallout 263; economic 19, 105; importance of 27, 29; of poverty 238; weaponization of 96
Geography of De-Industrialization, The (1986) 27
German Democratic Republic (GDR) 398, 400, 403, 409–410, 413
Germany: mine sites 97, 254, 383 *see also* Ruhr, Germany; postwar 11, 53; restructuring (strukturwandel) 22, 29; reunification 400m 403–404; Rhenish capitalism 98, 367; unification 22, 49
Gershuny, Jay 12
Gest, Justin 86
Gholz, Carleton 300
Giardina, Michael 255
Gibbs, Ewan: *Coal Country: The Meaning of Deindustrialization in Postwar Scotland* 4, 69, 96, 99, 148, 150
Gilbert, Dan (real estate developer) 292–295
Gildart, Keith 64, 69–70
global: capitalism 4, 20, 349, 351, 354; employment 46; supply chains 105, 148, 348, 352; warming 4 *see also* climate change
Global North: deinvestment in production capacity 102, 104, 205, 349 *see also* offshoring; heritage imperialism 371–372; make work projects 111; racism 117, 120–121, 124, 202
Global South: decolonial perspectives 370–371, 374, 376–377; investments 109–110; manufacturing industry/competition 206, 347–351, 353–355; runaway factory destination 1, 5, 29, 120
globalization 2, 25, 56–57, 85, 105, 109, 155–156, 285
Glodwick, Greater Manchester, England 202, 207, 209, 211
Goffman, Erving 233–235, 240
Golden Age (c.1960–1973) 49, 58, 411
Gordon, Avery 43, 184
Gordy, Barry 301, 337
Götz, Norbert 68

492

Index

graffiti artists 141, 288, 293, 295, 309
grants 112, 292, 466
Great Depression 11, 129
Great Financial Crash 46
Great Migration 82, 203
Green New Deal 175
Greenspan, Hank 71
grief 5, 36, 225, 336, 373, 421–422
Grönemeyer's, Herbert: *Bochum* 251
gross domestic product (GDP) 56–57, 112, 170, 220
Grütter, Heinrich Theodor 306
Guinness 64, 69
Gutman, Herbert 42, 279
Gutu, Dinu 253
Guyon, Tyree 290, *291*, 291–292

Hackworth, Jason 4, 77, 83–84, 98
half-life: concept of 4, 14, 36; of deindustrialization 33, 35–37, 39–40, 43, 64, 70, 142, 173, 197, 241, 245, 280, 285, 363, 485; measuring 34; metaphor 33, 36–38, 42; in nuclear physics 34; visibility 41
Haliburton, E.D. 132
Hall, Stuart 18, 77, 81, 254, 281
Hamera, Judith: *Unfinished Business: Michael Jackson, Detroit, and the Figural Economy of American Deindustrialization* (2017) 85, 281, 283, 285, 322
Hamilton, Alexander 49
Hamilton, Scott 66
Haritaworn, Jin 268–269, 272
Harrison, Bennett 2, 11, 13, 19, 25–27, 29, 96, 98, 103, 141, 170, 205, 266
Harvey, David 84, 104, 303n15
Hayden, Dolores 39
Hayes, Issac 301
HBO: documentary *(Come Unto Me: The Faces of Tyree Guyton)* 291
Healey, Dennis 54, 140, 148
health: community 289; conditions, chronic 298; insurance 265, 405; mental 35, 225, 341; occupational 252
health care 56, 208, 222, 238, 289–290, 369, 405
Heathcott, Joseph 12–13, 27, 35, 89, 103, 263, 322, 404, 485
Hebert, Guillaume 393
Heidelberg Arts Leadership Academy 291
Heidelberg Project 290–292, 301
Heinrich, Michael 105
heritage: actors 363–364, 374; railway 5, 372, 374, 437–443, 449–454; safeguards 393, 477, 479; tangible/intangible 404, 437, 451
heterosexuality 255, 262, 264–265

hierarchies: employment 211; gender 81, 88, 182; racial 81, 85, 88, 210, 212, 281; social 141, 281
High, Steven 3–4, 11, 38–42, 55, 76, 102, 118, 128, 131, 183, 186, 202, 210, 269
Hillel, Edward: United Sound Systems Recording Studios 298–301
Hiller, James 129
Hinshaw, John 87
historiography 2, 4, 105, 263, 316
history: casualties of 10, 65; labor 96, 264, 267–26, 373, 420, 423–428; politics of 403; theory 5, 403; working-class 42, 66, 348, 373, 421–422, 427, 432
History Workshop 65, 67
Hobsbawm, Eric 49, 103
Hochschild, Arlie Russell 86
hockey 252, 257
Home Owners Loan Corporation 290
Homeless Action Network 298
homes/houses: abandoned 112, 290, 296, 301; equity-positive 122; foreclosed 292; private 82; public 121, 234; stately 422, 426
homes/housing: property values 121, 210, 235, 290, 292
homesickness 323, 404
Hook, Peter 343
Hooker, John Lee 300
hooks, bell 267
hooligan 253
Hoque, Mashukul 207
HoSang, Daniel 77, 85
Hossain, Rubaiyat: *Made-in-Bangladesh* (film) 351–352
hostility 10, 65, 87, 198
Housos (Australian TV) 235–236
Howell, Colin 129
Huck, Gary 25
Hudson, Ray 96, 145, 240, 251
human: condition 68, 70, 112, 343; development 18; history 10, 473; relations 237, 301; rights 461
humanities 2, 14–15, 266
hurt 198, 248, 349
Husbandry 48
Hütter, Ralf 337

IBA *see* International Building Exhibition
identity: otherness 83, 85; sexual 265; working-class 64, 105, 186, 249, 253, 255, 269, 373, 420, 427
Illitch, Mike 293, 295
imaginaries 3, 77, 85, 336, 339–340, 353
IMF (International Monetary Fund) 65, 120, 219

Index

immigrants 38, 78, 82, 156, 185, 203, 207, 210, 234, 264, 388
Imperial Chemical Industries (ICI) 237–238, 242
imperialism 78, 104, 173, 370–371, 441, 477, 479
incarceration 83, 123, 294
incentives 24, 112, 123
inclusive/inclusion 2, 79, 86, 175, 196, 290, 420, 432, 460
income: accounting 48, 51; elasticity 52; loss of 81; low-income workers 78, 174, 235, 252, 301
independence: national 139, 402, 468; political 127; support for 144–145, 147–148
Independent Socialist Canada 23
India: consumer goods market 109, 237; economic success 349–351; Glodwick neighborhood 207; industrial trajectory 53, 56–57; migrants 57; Oldham textile industry 206; toxic heritage 371, 463, 473–474
Indian Workers' Association (IWA) 209
Indigenous: communities 235, 328, 330, 451, 472; nations 330; people 128, 211, 330, 371, 469, 473
industrial: capital 102, 105, 108, 111, 170; capitalism 19, 24, 63, 77, 85, 88, 116–117, 169–170, 265–266; citizen/citizenship 69, 124, 141; communities 145, 173, 184, 186, 189, 191, 195–197; culture 13, 15, 39, 43, 63–65, 68, 71–72, 383, 385, 394, 413, 466, 472; decline 22, 66, 78, 85, 89, 98–99, 110, 134, 163, 281, 301, 389; destabilization 349; era 28, 40, 122, 148, 198, 255, 311, 327, 363, 386, 399, 438, 442, 452 *see also* post–industrial; labor 5, 38, 57, 219, 224, 249, 252, 262, 266, 271, 279, 285, 398, 404–405; life 64, 186, 283, 327, 348, 411; loss 11–12, 85, 172; output 46, 58, 140, 171, 220; overcapacity 170–171; performance 53; practice 106; productivity 34, 46, 58; reserve army 108–109; restructuring 83, 99, 162; revolution 28, 46, 49, 71, 95, 127, 134, 204–205, 337–338, 438, 441; ruination 173, 363; society 3, 48, 50–52, 105, 170, 175, 219, 227, 314, 336, 375, 406; sounds 337–339; systems 63, 471
industrial heritage 34, 126; global comparison 5; initiatives 453; interpretation 364–367, 371; parallel development 402; railway 437, 440, 447, 450, 453–454
industrial production: decline 28, 222, 344; demand for 48, 56; increase 46, 58, 461; translocation 459, 461
industrial structure: of feeling 3–4, 108, 185, 222; structural change 365, 381–382

industrial workers 2; current 227–228; family of 35, 222; former 224, 227
industrialism 10, 18, 28, 52, 65, 98–99, 165
industrialization: dependent 24, 95; half-life metaphor 43; interconnections with deindustrialization 43, 81; levels of 48; narrative 15, 46, 58, 191, 477; politics of 3, 10; process of 14–15, 462; state-guided 49
industry: automotive 97, 160, 164, 185; coal 68–69, 129, 134, 159, 163, 175, 205, 384; energy 321; expansion 46; heavy 11, 36, 99, 126, 149, 154, 158, 183–185, 190, 196, 307, 402, 409, 411; loss of 11–12, 82, 88; mining 11, 255, 391; modern 121; paper 161; petrochemical 42, 173–174, 238; rise of 116–117, 120–121, 124; service sector 52, 110, 112
inequality 19, 55, 76–77, 88, 96, 99, 116, 141, 184, 210, 370
inflation 220, 401
influencers 65
information society 52
infrastructure: civic 211; existing 174, 394, 408; industrial 383; rail 438, 442–444 *see also* railway; transport 389, 393; urban 465
inhumanity 161
injury 39, 42, 330, 349
injustice 99, 173, 244, 268, 353, 373, 421
inner city: economic decline 211; neighborhoods 82–83, 123, 208–209
Innis, Harold 131
innovation 19, 42, 104–105, 161, 351, 370, 448, 459
insurrectionary conspiracies 10, 65
intellectual: challenges 459, 465, 467; history 19; transformation 48
interaction 71, 127, 186, 203, 212, 336, 366, 461, 465
International Building Exhibition (IBA) Emscher Park: campaign 312, *314*, 314–315, 365, 385; initiation of 385–386, 388; inspiration 393, 409–410
international competition 2, 56, 58, 205, 464, 474, 484
International Women's Day 221
intervention: charitable 256; economic 120, 131; political 25; state 83, 133–134
investment: capital 19, 84, 107, 109, 128; cycles 105; direct/foreign direct 23, 132, 401; foreign 11, 26, 106; industrial 132; private 54, 306
iron: industry 388; mines 96–97, 158
Iron and Steel Trades Confederation 147
ironworks 222–223, 402
Irving, K.C. 133
Isle of Sheppey 12

494

Index

Italian Communist Party (center-left) 22
Italy 22, **23**, **55**, 97, 138, 142, 156, 166, 226, 308, 341
Iuga, Liliana 5, 365–366, 370, 374
Ivčić, Snježana 219
Ivenson, Gabrielle Mary 252

Jameson, Fredric 344
Japan: Japanese competition 55
Jary, David 9
Jary, Julia 9
Jinenez, Luis 194
job blackmail 171
job loss: experience 40, 139; industrial 1, 12, 54, 80, 147; manufacturing 79, 84, 140, 142–143
joblessness 108
Joel, Billy: *Allentown* 250
Johnson, Christopher 11, 97, 205
Jones, Andy 252
Jordano, Dave: *Detroit – Unbroken Down* 296; *Michael, Poletown, Detroit* (2011) 296–297, *297*; *Woman Sleeping in a Parking Lot, Eastside, Detroit* 297, *298*
Jospin, Lionel 163
journalist 12, 34, 104, 138, 157, 162, 202, 308, 478, 485
Journey to Nowhere: The Saga of the New Underclass (Maharifge/Williamson) 1985 64
Jovanović, Deana 223
Joy Division 342–343
justice: economic 3, 424, 432; environmental 76, 173–175; notions of 70; queer labor 268

Kahn, Albert 288
Kaldor, Nikolas 53–54
Kalra, Virinda 78, 80, 82, 88
Kashmir 204
Katariya, Sharat: *Sui Dhaaga; Made in Inda* (film) 350–352
Katowice Climate Conference 169
Kaur, Ravinder 350
Kazi, Mansoor 206
Kernaghan, Charles 347
Kessler-Harris, Alice 264
Keynes, John Maynard: Keynesian theory 69, 103, 140, 162
Khatoon, Saeeda: known as mother Courage 354
Kideckel, David 183, 220, 404
kidnapping 158, 165
Kinsman, Gary 266
Kirk, Richard 338, 340
Kleinman, Arthur (et al 1997) 194
Kohei, Saito 111
Koistinen: *Confronting Decline* 11

Kojanić, Ognjen 219
Kraftwerk (German band) 337–338
Kryder-Reid, Elizabeth 173
Kumar, Krishan 12
Kuznet, Simon: *Modern Economic Growth* (1966) 51

labor 48; confederation 160, 164; feminized labor 351; history 96, 263–264, 267–268, 420, 423–428; power 106–111; union 24, 78, 155; unpaid workers 352, 479
labor market: changes 182, 196, 351–352; competition 120; discrimination 79–80; marginalization 80; polarization 56; statistics 236, 238
labor movement: organized 154–155; origins 70, 119–120, 146, 154–156, 169; supporters 147, 376
Labour/Le Travail (Canadian journal) 128
Laframboise, Lauren 355
Land Bank Association, Detroit 291
landscape design 314, 389, 393
Latin America 19, 23, 29, 57, 95, 120, 400, 459, 462, 465
Latino workers 79–80
Latvia 131–132
Lawrence, D.H. 66
Lawson, Christopher 4, 184–185
Laxer, Gordon 23
Laxer, Jim 24, 103
Laxer, Robert 95
layoffs/laid-off workers 1, 78–79, 141, 184, 190, 192
Leary, John Patrick 301
Leatherface (British rock band): Dead Industrial Atmosphere 335
left-wing: movements 19–20; party 155, 157, 162, 342, 368; politics/politicians 103, 145, 255
legacy: colonial 78, 204; foreign 399, 412; masculine 196; mining 381, 394; poverty 181, 287; slavery 204, 373
legitimation 66
leisure activities 4, 186, 250, 252–253, 310
Lengelle, Maurice 51
Lennon, Myles 175
Lesbians and Gays Support the Miners (LGSM) 262, 268
Levi factory 165
Levitt, Kari Polanyi 23
Lewis, Clive 147
Lewis, Joe 249
Lewis, W. Arthur 56–57
LGBTQ 186, 262–263, 268
Li, Junxin 141
liberalization 2, 24, 58, 104, 109, 141–142, 401

Index

Linkon, Sherry Lee: *Steeltown USA: Work and Memory in Youngstown: The Half-Life of Deindustrialization: Working-Class Writing About Economic Restructuring* 4–5, 14, 34–36, 40, 64, 142, 173, 212, 241, 263, 265, 271, 348, 363
liquidation 161, 237 *see also* bankruptcy
List, Friedrich 49
literary: clubs 223; representation 265, 306; texts 66, 309
literature: contemporary 55; deindustrial 13–14, 40, 55, 68, 72, 224, 251; nostalgic 323; pop culture 323; well-established 70
Little Caesar's Pizza 293
Liu, Petrus 267
lived experiences 35–36, 88, 175, 185, 224, 264, 267, 347–348
Location, Location, Location (British TV) 233, 236, 240
longue durée 105, 107, 399
Los Angels International Airport (LAX) 294
loss, sense of 86, 143, 183, 348–349, 355, 430–431
Louvres-Lens Museum 393
Lowndes, Josheph E. 77, 85
lumpenization 102, 107–108, 110
lumpenproletariat (underclass) 107–108
Luxembourg, Germany 5m 374, 381–384, 388–389
Lynd, Staughton 96

MacDonald, Edward 134
Macdonald, Graeme 322
MacDonald, Robert 238
MacEachern, Alan 134
Mackinnon, Lachlan 4, 99
macroeconomics 54, 58
Mah, Alice: *Industrial Ruination, Community, and Place* (2012) 4, 88, 99, 173, 222, 322, 348
Maharidge, Dale 64
Mahon, Rianne 24
Major, John 69–70
Makedonka cotton plant 223
Makin-Waite, Mike 87, 143
male: Black 79–80; white heterosexual 264; workers 15, 77–78, 80, 172, 194, 202, 212, 264, 330, 442
Mallach, Alan 83
Mallon, Ray 244
manual labor 184, 196–197, 328
manufacturing: decline 80, 83, 88, 143, 146, 170; employment 35, 46, 54, 79–80, 140, 143, 181; global 104, 171; history 436–437; new 148; relocation 350
Marchand, Ives 296

Maritime Provinces 11, 1291
Maritime Rights Movement 129
Maritimes 24, 128, 131
market: embeddedness/disembeddedness 68; logic 12; socialism 218–220; values (real estate) 118, 290, 292, 350
Marshall, T.H. 69
Martha and the Vandellas 337, 344
Martin, Andy 335
Martin, Ron 22, 27
Marx, Karl 10, 102, 107–111, 244
Marxism 103, 105, 266–267
Marxist theory 4, 67, 98, 102–103, 112, 130, 403
masculinity 38; crisis of 75; father, identity of 265; hegemonic 438, 445, 450–451, 453–454; male sense of failure 194; practices 190, 195, 252, 265, 452; working-class 181–182, 255, 262, 264
Massé, Pierre 157
Massey, Doreen: *Spatial Division of Labour* 1984 19, 29, 82, 96–97, 104, 348
Matera, Marc (et al 2023) 212
materiality of objects 237
May, Sarah 173
May, Theresa 138
Mayer, Jeremy 86
Mazar, Alissa 250
McChesney, Robert 110
McDowell, Linda 196
McGahey, Michael 146
McGeever, Brendan 86
McGuirk, Pauline 254
McKay, Ian 29
McKenzie, Lisa 235
Medicaid 110
Meffre, Romain 296
memoir: graphic 281, 320, 331; reviews 327–330
memory 34; activism 5, 288, 363, 368–369, 374; importance of in representation 322; intergenerational 349; storehouse 39
memory activists 363, 366–367, 374, 376
metallic vitalities 185, 237, 240, 245
metaphor: abstract idea 33–34; gender-specific 452; half-life 34, 36–41, 43; rust belt 185
metropole: colonial 203, 210; family structure 268–268, 271; imperial 210, 212; international 310, 312
Michelin tire group 163
Michigan Department of Transportation 300
middle-class: home ownership 121, 300, 420; imposters 2; minority 198, 207; workers 265
Middlesbrough: Benefits Street 238–239; as blemishes place 240–242; environmental stigma 242–244; molecular politics 240;

Index

predominately white 4, 185, 232, 237; steelmaking town 237

migrant: lived experience 350; Mirpuris 204, 206–207; post-colonial 210; undocumented 105; workers 78, 104, 106, 139, 156, 182, 210, 264, 373, 388 *see also* ethnic minority

migration: ethnic 122; forced 110; outmigration 112, 129, 131, 323, 327, 331

mill closures 23, 35, 37, 96, 265

Millar, Grace 69

miner: coal 280, 312; former 254, 256, 328, 404, 472; miners' strike 147, 160, 271

mining: history 390, 392; industry 11, 255, 385, 391

minority: communities 185, 205, 208; disadvantaged 82, 210; workers 79, 203

Mission Bassin Minier 393

Mitterrand, François 162

Modell, Judith 87

modernity 10, 49, 157, 185, 218, 238, 243–244, 307, 350, 371, 459

modernization theory 105

Modolov, Alexander: *The Iron Foundry* 337

Moe, Jens 134, 262

Mondon, Aurelien 138

Montenegro 220

Montgomery, Alesia 293

Montreal, Canada 38, 40, 104, 121, 128, 203, 463, 479

Moore, Andrew 296

Moore, Steve 24

moral: assumptions 66; economy 4, 63–69, 71–72, 86, 89, 104, 155; interpretation 67

Morgenthau Plan 53

Morris, William 66

Mosbach, Catherine 393

Moslov, Alexander: *The Iron Foundry* 337

motor city 1, 97, 171, 185, 208–209, 248, 287

motorcycles 252

Motown 248, 298, 301, 337, 339, 342

Motown (record label) 298, 301, 337, 339, 342

Moulinex factory 165

Mount Allison University 320

Mount Pleasant 119

Mozart 51

Mrozowicki, Adam 141

Mulroney, Brian 211

multinational company (MNC) 120

multinational corporations 23, 95, 138, 238

Muñoz Rebolledo, María Dolores 4

Munoz, Jose Estaban 270

Munro, Kirstin 111

mural 41, 293–296

murder 117, 145, 269, 341

Muschg, Adolf 316

museum: MOMA (Museum of Modern Art) 338; rail 438–439, 443, 452; Ruhr Museum 306, 309; Tale Art 338

music: connection with work 339; displacement 339; festivals 344; folk revival of the 1960's 337; genres 250; healing element of 251; punk rock 339; punk rock/hardcore punk 282, 284, 335, 339–343; song writing 147, 159; vanishing mediator 336, 343–344; visual and narrative dimension 336, 340

Musić, Goran 222

musicians 5, 248, 282, 295, 298–299, 336–339, 343

Muslim women 354

Musso, Stefano 97

Nagasaki 477

narrative: of decay 301; historical 126, 151; of industrialization/deindustrialization 58, 119, 126, 169, 411, 477; queer labor 267–268; racist 117

Natarajan, Radhika 210

National Coal Board (NCB) 69, 146

National Energy Conference 146

National Institute of Economic and Social Research 1978 22

National Maritime Union 25

National Political Economy 49

National Rail Museum 438–429

National Union of Mineworkers (NUM) 70, 146

National Union of Mineworkers Scottish Area (NUMSA) 146

nationhood 138–139, 142–143, 145

Nayak, Anoop 4, 185–186, 196–197, 253

Nazi 288, 307

Negazione 341

negotiations 41, 158–159

Neilson, David 109

neo-capitalism 220

neoliberalism 69, 83, 105, 211

Netherlands 48, **55**, 439

New Deal era 77, 211

New Democratic Party 103

New Industries program 131–132

New Left organization 26, 66, 103, 266

New Zealand 51, 438–439, 441, 444

Newfoundland 111, 129, 131–132, 324, 329

Newfoundland Radio Hour 324

Newman, Joshua 255

Newman, K.S. 87

next generation 22, 33, 37, 195, 199

Nine Inch Nails 338

Nitzer Ebb 338

Nixon, Darren 196

Nixon, Richard *20*, 23–24

Index

Nixon, Rob 38, 43
noise: classifications of 336; industrial 336–339; specific features of, in music 338
Nord/Pas-de-Calais 383, 391–392, 394
norms: economic 69; gender 372, 437–438, 449, 452, 454; religious 351; social 66, 347, 350, 352, 355; visual 309
North America: capitalist economy 18, 23, 29; community/queer community 249, 262–263, 265; employment shift/transformation 51, 55, 95, 170, 181, 222; moral economy 64, 117, 121, 202–203, 205; political economy 103, 109–110, 134, 143
Northern Recording 251
nostalgia: ambivalent 88, 173, 322, 331; angry nostalgia 404; forms of 5, 427–428; industrial 13, 173, 185, 224; progressive 368, 372–373, 405, 431, 471; queer 269; romantic 298
novelist 154, 337
nuclear family 264–265
NUM. *see* National Union of Mineworkers
Núñez Seixas, Xosé M. 127

O'Brien, Brontierre 66
O'Hanlon, Seamus 250
Obama, Barack 293
observations 10, 19, 69, 171, 424–425, 431
obsolescence 10, 19, 86
obsolete 10, 65, 68, 342, 386, 449
occupational health 72, 252
OECD (Organization for Economic Co-operation and Development) 47, 51–51
Offer, Avner 70
Office of National Statistics (ONS) 236, 238
offshoring 2, 104, 108, 348
oil industry 54
oil sands: destruction of Indigenous communities 330–331; environmental implications 320–324, 327–328; workers 329–330
Oldham Weekly Chronicle 202, 211–212
Oliver, Melvin 79
Olsen, Tillie 284
Opel car factory 311
optimism 42, 88, 285
oral history/historians 55, 102, 139, 142, 148, 183, 269–271, 282, 309, 466, 472
organized crime 37
Ostrava-Karviná mines 402
outmigration 112, 129, 131, 232, 237, 331
outsiders 192–193, 234, 328, 445, 472
overlap 19, 43, 121, 174, 206, 227, 321, 364, 407
OxyContin 110

Packard Motor Car Co 208, 288, *289*, 290, 301
Pager, Devah 123
Pahl, Ray: *Divisions of Labour* 1984 12
Pakistan 349, 353–354
Palmer, Bryan 66
Panting, Gerald 128
Paprocki, Kasia 174
paradox 29, 35–36, 51
Paris, Dan 149
Paris, France 161–162, 210, 256
Paris, Illinois 234, 373
Parker, Charlie 300
Parks, Virginia 79
Parliament 300
passivity 4, 237
Passoli, Lisa 133
Past & Present (journal) 64
Patz, Christopher 353–354
pauperization 99, 108–109
Peck, Jamie 69
Pehe, Veronika 401
Penney, Matthew 4, 98
Perchard, Andrew 4, 12, 15, 69–70
Pere Ubu: *The Modern Dance* (1978) 340
Perera, Sonali: *No Country: Working-Class: Writing in the Age of Globalization* (2014) 285
Pernau, Margrit 249
Perry, Kennetta 210
pessimism 87
petrochemical industry 173–174, 237–238, 242
Petrovi, Tanja 226, 405, 412
Petty, William 48
phenomena 34, 64, 105, 184, 199, 226, 234, 249, 323, 336, 399
Philadelphia 208, 234
Phillips, Jim 69–70, 148, 184
photography 5, 280, 287, 298, 301, 306, 308–309, 336, 347
physical: disorder 123; environment 3, 34, 252, 255, 383; remains 371, 383, 391–392, 477, 484; work 190, 252, 407
Pickering, Paul 22, 126
Pike, Andy 29, 349
pillage 116–117, 124, 225
Pine, Francis 406
Pittsburgh Steelers (American football) 254–255
place: loss of 172; meanings of 182, 185, 191; place-based stigma 4, 185, 232
Plan International UK 241
planners: role of 382–383, 386; scientific 121; urban 5, 170, 300, 365, 393, 463
plant closure 2, 15, 25, 79, 96, 129, 141, 146, 240, 264
Pleasant, Emma 38–40, 43

poem 245, 284
poetry 10, 66, 285
Poland 63, 175, 368–370, 399, 408–411, 413, 439
Polanyi, Karl 23, 63, 65, 67–69, 71
Poliakov, Sviatoslav 252
policing 108, 110, 123, 150, 235–236, 294
policy: climate 174; employment 13; foreign 127; government 24, 53, 141, 236; responses 15, 99, 127, 130, 134; traditional 163
policymakers 34, 64–66, 68, 198, 413
political: actor 49, 83–84; consciousness 64, 147; corruption 37; effects 34, 281; engagement 233; imaginary 183, 269; intervention 25; movement 86, 103, 370; trends 68
political economy: concepts 127–129; critique 102, 107, 110; Marxist 102–103; national/international 19, 139; radical 96
politics: anti-union 11; divisive 3; far right 76, 86–87, 138, 142–143, 151, 316; molecular 240, 245
pollution: air/water 310, 385; environmental 88, 223; toxic 170–171, 173–174
Pont Saint-Charles 40–42
populist politics 36, 76, 87
Portelli, Alessandro 279–280
post-communist 5, 253, 367, 369–370, 374, 376
post-industrial future 5, 123, 283, 306, 316, 365, 368, 382
post-socialism 218–220, 226, 400
post-socialism/post-socialist 185, 218–222, 224, 226, 398–400, 406, 410–412
posterity 10, 65, 271
Potkonjak, Sanja 222
poverty: high rates of 80, 82, 170; legacy of 204, 209, 238–239, 287; racialization of 84, 97, 288, 290, 296; theoretical 24
Power House Productions 292, 301
precariat 141, 211
preferential treatment 119, 210, 390
pregnancy, teenage 232, 241, 245
prejudice 10, 117, 123, 327
preserve/preservation: cultural heritage 301, 365, 477; industrial structure 382, 390, 402, 412, 437; of memory 39–40, 284, 367, 381
Prince Edward Island 129, 133–134
Pringle, Kevin 148
prisons 108
privatization: industrial 22, 68, 146–147, 211; process 220–221, 228; of public spaces 288, 295; of state-owned enterprises 401, 405
production 10; cultural 249, 270, 342, 344; ethical 347; garment 117, 347, 350, 352

see also industrial production; just-in-time 106–107, 355; rationalization 145, 208; social 63
productiveness 48–49
profitability 105, 117
progress: downward spiral 289–290; human 18, 336; material 51; modernization 111, 170, 210, 388, 403; scientific 41, 373
progressive: ideas 157; movement 19; nostalgia 368, 372–373, 405, 431, 471; parties 3
Progressive Alliance 25, 96
Progressive Conservative Party 132–133
property: relations 64, 84, 108, 233; values 84, 121, 210, 290, 292
prosperity 48–49, 111, 172, 222, 242, 288–289, 301, 328, 385, 400
protection: of children 105, 155; environmental 174, 365; heritage 402–403; lack of 78–79; legal 25, 39, 53, 203, 464–465; rent control 295
protest: labor related 156–159, 162, 165, 206; moral 70, 72; political 301, 354, 411
public: art 5, 281, 284m 287; health 72; opinion 154, 157, 165; service reform 69–70, 289; utilities 47; welfare 227
Purdue Pharma 110

quarry/quarrying 47, 143, *144*, 238
queer: ephemeral 270; faces 267; gay community 265, 268; gay liberation movement 262, 266; historians 263, 266; history 186, 262, 266–271; lifestyle 269–270; Others 268; politics 268–269; representation 265; sex 266; study 269; working-class 269
queer theory: communism of incommensurability 267; methodological straightness 186, 264, 270–271
Quicken Loans 293–294

race: categories 77–78; hierarchies 81, 83–85, 209, 281; modalities 89, 116; race-making 85
racial: capitalism 76–77, 99, 116; conflict 86–87; diversity 203; exclusion 82, 118–119, 124; inequalities 76, 81, 181; politics 86, 426; stigma 85
racialization 76–77, 85, 116, 185, 235–236, 288
Račic, Jasna 219
Racing Club de Lens (RC Lens) 186, 254–257
racism: historically specific 77–78, 124; immigrant 206–207, 288, 316, 342; institutionalized 80, 87, 99, 116, 118–120
racist narratives 25, 82, 118, 123, 142, 197, 207, 293, 298
radical: politics 3, 23, 96, 139, 142; tourism 471

Index

radio stations 161–162
radioactive waste 34, 39, 41, 241, 263
radioactivity half-life 39–40, 173
Radolović, Karlo 226
Raggi, Pascal 164
railway: bridges 344; families 64; heritage 5, 372, 374, 437–438, 443, 449, 451, 453; ironstone 237; job losses 140; museum 437; nationalized 69–70; ownership (Indigenous) 212
rally 161
Rammstein 338
rape 117, 329
RCA (Radio Corporation of America) 19, 96
Reagan, Ronald 12, 159
real estate: agent 84; development 292–293, 295, 343, 478 *see also* construction; market values 290; transactions 220
recession 54, 129, 139, 237, 249, 257, 288, 336, 384, 400
recomposition 108, 164
Redcar steelworks 232, 237–240, 244
redevelopment: myth 296; strategies 5, 381, 383; urban 81, 84, 89, 389
reflection: critical 411, 429; cultural 15, 191; storytelling 183–184, 202, 316
reform: economic 311, 315, 400–401; neoliberal 84, 295
refugees 43
regeneration 140, 186, 196, 233, 243, 251 *see also* urban renewal
Regent Park (Toronto, Canada) 234
regional development 4, 98–99, 131, 233, 245, 370, 382, 384, 386, 412
regional economic development 127, 134
regionalism 126–128, 130
regulatory agency 34
Rehberg, Gerhard 256
Rehling, Nicola 253
Reicher, Christa 5, 365–366, 370, 374
Reichert, Gina 292
Reid, Jimmy 145–146
Reill, Guido 142
reindustrialization 148–149, 349, 375, 392, 484
reinvention 10, 351
relative surplus 107–108
religious: diversity 410; institutions 64; life 88, 351, 373
Renault 163
Reny, Tyler 86
repairs/renovations 112, 198, 209, 451
repertoires of collective action 155
reporters. *see* journalist
representation: cultural 34–35, 41, 182–183, 322, 331, 335, 351, 392; visual 5, 288, 306–307, 336

reproduction 63, 109–111, 116, 121, 164, 309, 350, 449–450 *see also* social reproduction
Republican Party 142–143
repurpose 37, 250, 392–394
resentment 35, 37–38, 42, 85–87, 89, 142, 198
resilience 42, 184, 233, 297, 336
resistance: acts of 233, 289, 301; forms of 130, 164, 185; politics 99, 240; working-class 4, 98–99, 245
resource: cultural 39, 41, 289; extraction 24, 133, 320, 322, 330–331; financial 11, 83; heritage 382, 412; industrial past 306, 315–316; political 220, 432; public 83, 295; resource-switching 84
retrenchment 11, 83
revolution: agricultural 18, 204; energy 441 *see also* industrial revolution; neoclassical 49, 103; psychological 131, 299
rhetoric 33, 69, 85, 131, 138, 161, 207, 280–281, 285
Rhodes, James 4, 15
Rich, Adrienne 263
right to work states 19, 24, 111
right-wing populism 4, 22, 76, 86–88, 99, 111, 138, 142, 368, 422
rigidity 67, 192
Rind, Esther 252
riots 119, 211, 289
rites of passage 2
Roberts, Steven 196, 198
Robichaud, Louis 133
Robinson, Cedric 118
Robinson, Smokey 301
robotization 104, 311, 336
Rock and Roll Hall of Fame 343
Rock Ventures 293
Rodney, Walter 120
Rodrik, Dani 57
Rogaly, Ben 86
Rogers, Dallas 235–236
Romania 183, 253, 404
Rowe, David 254
Rowell-Sirois Commission 130
Rowthorn, Bob 22, 27
Royal Commission on Dominion Provincial Relations 130
Rugby 254
Ruhr Museum 306, 308–309
Ruhr, Germany: demographic diversity 385; discovery of 305, 316; Emscher Landscape Park 386; heritage 307; industrial cultural landscape 384; International Garden Exhibition 388; *Kommunalverband Ruhrgebiet (KVR)* 310, *311–312*, 312, *313*; negative portrayal 307, 310; North

500

Index

Rhine-Westphalia 385; perception of 307; regional association 308

ruination: anticipatory 174; core of 296; forms of 368, 381 *see also* industrial ruination

runaway plants/shops 2, 19–20, *21*, 22, 24–26, 141

runaway shop 22, 24–25, 141

Runrig (folk-rock band) 147

Russo, John: *Steeltown USA: Work and Memory in Youngstown* 34–36, 40, 44n4, 64

Russolo, Luigi: *L'arte dei Rumori* (The Art of Noise) 1967 336

Rust Belt: Canadian 70; Chinese 104; class identity 255, 264, 322; memorabilia 42; organized deprivation 83; pollution 233; racialized dimensions 78–79, 82–83, 97, 120, 122; resource redirection 84, 238

Safford, Sean 122

Sager, Eric 128

Sahaviriya Steel Industries (SSI) 237, 239

Saint Etienne, France 160–161, 164, 255

Salmond, Alex 146, 148–149

Samuel, Raphael 65, 428, 441

Samuelson, Robert J. 23

Save Our Steel (SOS) 239

Save Scottish Steel campaign 145

Savoie, Donald 131

Sayer, Andrew 63, 65, 67–71, 424

Scargill, Arthur 146

Schalke 04 (German football) 186, 254–257

Schindler, Seth (et al 2020) 104

Schmidt, Uta C. 308

Schneider, Flrian 337

scholar/scholarship: deindustrialization 3, 29, 95–96, 112, 139–141, 182, 269, 285, 349; literary 13–14, 19, 63, 280, 306

Schulan, Sarah: *Gentrification of the Mind* (2012) 268

Scotland: colliery closures (coal mine) 145–146; devolution 139, 147–150; economy of 144–147; just transition 175; moral economy 70, 96, 99; organized crime study 37

Scott, James C.: *The Moral Economy of the Peasant; Rebellion and Subsistence in Southeast Asia* 63, 65, 68, 70–72

Scott, Ridley 232, 245

Scottish: employment *144*; labor movement 146

Scottish Government 148–150

Scottish Greens 148–149

Scottish National Party (SNP) 139, 145

Scottish Nationhood 143, 147

Scottish Parliament 139, 144, 147, 149–150

Scottish Trades Union Congress (STUC) 146–147

security: economic 78–79, 141, 400, 406; job 182, 185, 222, 224, 227; threat to 192

Seger, Bob 300

segregation: hypersegregation 82; residential 79, 81–82, 89, 185, 288

Selective Employment Tax 54

self-determination 70, 198–199, 473

self-reliance 292, 350

Senjković, Reana 224

Serbia 219–221, 223–224, 405

service sector 50–52, 56–58, 80, 108, 170, 197, 375

sewing machine 347, 350

sexual: assault/violence 240, 320–321, 323, 329–331; normativity 265

sexuality: gender and 5, 143, 186, 266–267; heterosexual 255, 262, 264–265; homosexual 271

Shadow of the Mine: Coal and the End of Industrial Britain, The (Beynon/Hudson) 96

Shapiro, Thomas M. 79

sharecropping 203, 209

Shaw, Walter R. 134, 207, 235

Shepard Fairey 293–294, *294*

Shildrick, Tracy 238

shipbuilding industry: collapse of 128–129, 138, 144–145, 147, 237; communities 173, 254; dry dock 335; male-dominated 219, 224, 226–228

shoe industry 160, 219, 280

shortages 369, 406

shutdowns 13, 33, 36–38, 43, 98, 102, 105, 129, 285, 339

Sibley, David 233

Sides, John 78

Siedlungsverband Ruhrkohlenbezirk (SVR) 307–308

Simpsons, The (American TV) 262

Singer Sewing Machine factory 87

Singh, Ajit 54

Sivanandan, Ambalavaner 78

Skeggs, Beverly 39

Skinner, Dennis 146

Škokić, Tea 222

Slater, Lorna 149

slavery: forced labor 77, 117, 175; legacy of 204, 373; modern 197–198, 203; racial exploitation 120; slave trade 117, 203, 422

Slovenia 220, 224–226

Smallwood, Joey 131–133

Smiles, Mika 241

Smith, Adam (G.I.) 48–49, 133

Smith, Adrian 257

Smith, Laurajane 5, 368, 372–374, 422, 427

Smith, Neil 104

smog 232, 238, 242–243, 245

501

smokestack nostalgia 223, 404, 485
social: actors 38, 279, 281, 284, 376; conservatism 3; convention 68; devastation 111, 219, 307; disturbance 10, 65, 211; division 13; dysfunction 107; effects 34, 111, 341, 409; exclusion 424–425, 431; fallout 264, 320; haunting 184; justice 103, 287, 296, 301, 372–373, 376, 431, 461; mobility 79, 253; problems 37, 156, 225, 234, 421; process 9, 348, 465; production 63; protection 169, 182, 227; provision 81; relations 13, 43, 68, 104–105, 107, 267, 270, 349, 370, 437, 450; reproduction 106, 111, 266; structure 52, 77, 205, 211–212, 220, 266, 280, 383; suffering 194, 198; violence 96, 184
Social Democratic Party 143
socio-spatial division 76, 84
socioeconomic change 25, 28, 143, 210, 340, 343–344, 381, 383–385, 393, 411
solidarity: acts of 224, 240, 262, 266; cross-racial 86, 203; job security 182, 185, 222, 224, 227
South America 2, 438, 440, 463
South Asia: films 5, 281, 284–285, 347–349, 351–355; migrant workforce 204, 206–207, 209–211; wage disparity 78, 80, 117
South Korea 2, 104
South Wales/New South Wales 96, 145, 147, 184, 254
Southcott, Joanna 10, 65
Soviet Union 49, 218–220, 222, 252, 337–338, 400, 406
spatial: inequality 19, 76, 96, 206; restructuring 19, 96
sports: leisure career 252–253; sporting events 251; sports clubs 182, 227, 252–253, 255, 257; ultra fan groups 253–254
Springorum, Dietrich 308
Springsteen, Bruce 35, 64, 250
SSI *see* Sahaviriya Steel Industries
St. Laurent, Louis 130
Standing, Guy 141
Stanfield, Robert 132–133
Stanley, Neil 253
Stanton, Cathy 29, 419
staples theory 131
steam engines 410, 452, 462
Steedman, Carolyn 65
steel industry: conflicts 160, 268; lay-offs 37; racial dimension 77–79; recomposition 164–165, 237; steelmill 147; steelworkers union 240; steelworks 141, 147, 158, 232–233, 237–239, 241, 365, 389–390, 407; toxins 34–36, 316

Steeltown USA: Work and Memory in Youngstown (2002) 44n4, 64
Stein, Judith 66
Steiner, Marion 5, 370–372, 374, 479
stereotypes 70, 107, 132, 234, 248, 251, 283, 308, 350, 438
stigma: environmental 185, 233, 242, 244–245; forms of 85, 233, 235–236, 240–242; place-based 4, 185, 232; territorial 83, 99, 182, 232–236, 241, 245; transnational literature 233
stopgaps 110–111
Storm, Eric 127
Strangleman, Tim 28, 43, 67, 69–70, 172, 195, 348, 368
structure: economic 77, 140, 143, 150, 205, 264, 308; industrial 3–4, 37, 52–53, 108, 145, 185, 222, 382, 390, 392
Stubbs, Frankie 335
Stubbs, Mike 172
Stubbs, Thomas 109
STUC *see* Scottish Trades Union Congress
Studdert, David 197
student loans 283, 327–328
Students for a Democratic Society 26
Sturgeon, Nicola 149–150
Subileau, Jean-Louis 393
subjectivities 77, 85–89, 263
suburbanization 81–84, 89
Suchma, Philipp C. 257
Sugrue, Thomas: *The Origins of the Urban Crisis* (1996) 78, 82, 97, 118–119, 211
Sumlin, Hubert 337
Sunderland brewery 335
Super Bowl (football) 250, 258
surveillance 108, 294
survivors 71, 194, 353, 474, 477
sustainability 170, 174–175, 194, 238, 371, 381–383, 388–389, 392, 408, 436, 478
Sutcliffe-Braithwaite, Florence 70
Sweden 55, 371, 461, 463, 479
Switzerland 55, 439
Sydney Steel Corporation 133
symbolism 64, 72, 442, 445, 450–452

Taft-Hartley Act 19, 24
Taiwan 2, 104, 106, 438, 463
tangible goods 47, 49, 52–53, 79, 109, 158, 401
Tanzania 1
tax revenues 81, 256
taxi driver 80, 172, 235
technology, modern 11, 104, 185, 311, 445, 449–450
television production 19, 157, 185, 233, 235, 285, 327

Index

termination of industrial activities 383, 404, 406

territorial stigmatization 83, 99, 185, 233, 235

textile industry: heritage 78; industrial retrenchment 11; international competition 205–206; racial dimension 80, 155; social relations 104; tariff-induced decline 24

Thatcher, Margaret 12, 22, 54, 69–70, 96, 99, 140, 146, 149–150, 154, 159, 202, 268

theft 25, 240

Thielman, Sam 321

Third World countries 53

Thomas, David 340

Thompson, Alex 202

Thompson, Dorothy 66

Thompson, Edward Palmer (E.P.): Customs in Common (1993) 68; *The Making of the English Working Class* 10, 65–66; *Poverty of Theory* (1978) 4, 10, 14, 63–64, 67m 69–72

Thompson, Heather Ann 123

Thompson, Peter 5, 280–281, 283–284

Thompson, Stacy 339

Three Mile Island 34

Tickell, Adam 69

Tilly, Charles 155

Tito, Josip Broz 141, 219

Tomann, Juliane 5, 367–370, 374

Tomlinson, Jim 4, 10–11, 22–23, 68–70, 98, 103, 140, 148, 182, 184, 212

Tooze, Adam 139

torture 109, 117

tourism: heritage 283, 315, 343, 365–366, 411, 437–438, 454, 470; reliance on 84, 226; state intervention 134; sustainable 392; tourist destinations *387*

toxic: effects 35, 142; harm 173; pollution 170, 173; variations 36; waste 34–35, 476

toxicity 35–40, 173, 194, 241, 476

toxins 35, 160, 173, 205, 238, 473–474

trade: liberalization 24, 104, 109; unions 20, 22, 25, 96, 182, 192, 203, 363, 373, 375, 382, 421

Trade Union Act 1937 130

tradition: authoritarian 66; black radical 98, 116; family 265, 312; marketable forms of 350–351, 399; working-class 193, 202, 248, 337

transfer 19, 107–108, 110, 118, 349, 389, 476

transgender 268

transition: energy 175, 394; fossil fuel 175; industrial 46, 123, 172–175, 227, 394, 409, 437; just transition 4, 99, 149, 169, 175

transport/transportation: improved/modern 196, 389; industrial 437; modern 389; modes of 441, 447, 450; networks 128, 391

trauma 160, 172, 184, 191, 194, 198, 271, 299, 411

trends: political 68, 111, 144; productivity 11, 56, 170, 219

Trump, Donald J. 3, 37, 85, 87, 138, 142, 269, 368

Turner, Chris: *The Patch: The People, Pipelines, and Politics of the Oil Sands* (2017) 321

Ulrich, Kay 147

uncertainty 10, 169, 173

Unemployed Workers Centre 209

unemployment: among blacks 80–82; high rates of 1–2, 54, 84, 129, 141, 146, 149, 159, 209, 211, 220; low levels 206; youth 238

UNESCO World Heritage 382, 386, *387*, 391, 393–394, 470

uneven development 102, 104–105, 108–109, 127

Union for Radical Political Economics 25, 103

Union of Radical Political Economics 25

unionization 2, 24, 82, 164

United Auto Workers (UAW) 26, 118

United Electrical, Radio and Machine Workers of America (UE) 20, 25

United Kingdom (UK) 1; the "British disease" 22; Coventry, city of 171–172, 209–210, 257; exclusion stigma 241; government 145–146, 149–150 *see also* Brexit; half-life communities 14; historical narratives 96, 98, 103, 126, 139, 191; immigrant labor/ housing 78, 82–83; industrial employment rates/growth **23**, 46, 51, **55**, 80; interwar era 11, 205; marginalization 86–88; miners strike 154, 161; Office of National Statistics 236; privatization of state assets 69

United States of America (USA): corporate greed 25; employment rates/trends 1, 27, 47, 55–56, 59, 80, 96, 108, 159; government policy 24, 141, 236; hegemony 105–108; interwar period 55; labor history 264, 373, 420, 423–424; New Deal era 77; racial diversity 203; Supreme Court 24–25; trade union/labor movement 20, 99

University of Essen 308

University of Hull, Middlesbrough 241

University of Pittsburgh 25

University of Toronto 131

Upper Clyde Shipbuilders (UCS) 145

urban: atmosphere 335; decay 248, 250; dwellers 234; governance 83–84, 233; loss 41; planning 5, 365, 386, 393, 463, 465, 472; redevelopment 81, 84, 89, 389; regeneration 243, 245, 250, 382, 393; renewal 121, 243, 288, 300

Index

Utica, New York 42–43
utopian artisan 10, 65

Valdmanis, Alfred 132
values: emotional 252, 254; market 282, 290, 350; middle-class 372; political 68, 420–421, 423–424, 431; property 121, 210, 290, 292; social 421, 425, 449; working-class 154
Vergara, Camilo Jose 196
Vernon, James 211
victim: blaming 293; compensation 353–354; passive 165, 347; of violence 320, 341
Vietnam 58
Vigna, Xavier 3–4, 28, 97, 99, 183
violence: domestic 289, 298, 352; economic 38, 41; gender 471; physical 38, 255, 352; sexual 320–321, 323, 329–331; social 96, 184; structural 18, 38, 41, 99
Virdee, Satnam 86
virtues 26
visual: arts/artists 285, 335, 337, 340; representation 5, 288, 306–307; style 321, 323, 332
Vodopivec, Nina 225

Wacquant, Loïc: *Urban Outcasts* (2008) 83, 98, 185, 210, 233–236, 239, 242, 245
Waffle Movement 23–24, 95, 103
Wagner, Helen 5, 280–281, 283–284, 286
Wales 69–70, 150, 184, 190, 197–198, 241, 252 *see also* South Wales
Walkerdine, Valerie 4, 182, 184–185, 194
Wallerstein, Immanuel 103, 105–107, 371
Walley, Christine: *Exit Zero* 34, 36, 265
Walmart 104, 110
Wambach, Julia 4, 186
Waring, Marilyn 354
Waters, Muddy 337
Watkins, Mel 23, 95, 103
Wawrzyniak, Joanna 401, 405–406
wealth 105, 117, 122, 124, 161, 203, 239, 289, 349
Weber, Max: *Protestant Ethic and the Spirit of Capitalism* (1905) 344
welfare: benefits 110, 183, 210, 222, 225, 235, 245, 400; economics 69; rights 66; state 58, 69–70, 77, 156–157, 159, 182
well-being 68, 170, 251, 255, 289, 419, 421, 431
Well, Debi 24
West Germany **55**, 219, 400, 461, 465
Weymouth, Stephen 142–143
Whatley, Warren C. 119
White: elites 122, 450; majority 120, 122–123; men/males 15, 77–80, 142, 202, 212,

253, 264, 460; privilege 76, 235 *see also* preferential treatment; resentment 86; women 78, 80, 235
white-collar workers 81, 253
Whiteness 85; methodological 87, 264; politics of 76
Whitfield, Jenenne 291–292
Wicke, Christian 97, 126
Widdick, Branko 118
Williams, Jody 337
Williams, Raymond 4, 15, 19, 43, 63–64, 71, 103, 222, 266, 270
Williamson, Michael 64
Willoughby, Roger 192, 196
Wilson, David 84
Wilson, Greg 127
Wilson, Harold 140
Wilson, William Julius 80, 205, 209–210
Winant, Gabriel 77–79, 81, 116, 238
Wishart, Pete 147
Wolfe, Billy 145
women: devaluation of 224–225; industrial labor 218–219; minoritized 81; night-shift workers 224–225
Wordsworth, William 66
work: meaning of 13
worker: betrayal and despair 263; dangerous working conditions 118; disempowerment 164, 220; displaced 2, 14, 22, 28, 33, 36–38, 80, 169, 279, 283, 327; ethnic minority 203; foreign 25, 105, 210; male manual 141, 193–194, 206, 221; male, older 194; non-white 78, 117–120, 124; nostalgia 224; self-management 160, 185, 218, 221; strike 119 *see also* miner; white male 15, 77–78, 202, 212, 264
Workers Educational Association 66
workforce: development programs 103, 134, 409; worker -owned/women-led 42
working-class: culture 43; families 35
Working-Class Studies Association (WCSA) 13, 15, 34, 202, 364
World Bank 120, 204, 401
World Health Organization (WHO) 242
World Heritage Site. *see* UNESCO
World War I 50, 129, 402, 407
World War II 11, 55, 78–79, 119, 130–131, 140, 183, 205, 208, 218, 248, 264, 367, 391, 407, 452, 484
world-system 102, 105, 107–108, 110–111, 371
Worley, Matthew 339
wounds of class 102, 110–111
Wright, Erik Olin 69
Wright, Fred: cartoonist 20, *21*, 25, *26–27*

Index

Wright, Valerie 69, 148, 184
writers 35, 160, 165, 233, 282, 323, 363

Yezbick, Julia 290
Young Christian Workers 156
Young, Coleman 290
Youngstown 34–37, 64, 84, 86, 96, 141, 250, 269
Youngstown State University 64
Yousaf, Humza 148
YouTube 248, 251

Yugoslavia 4, 141; Borovo shoe factory 219; break from Soviet Bloc 219; DITA factory workers 221; foreign debt 219; gross industrial output, decline 220; plant closures/ruination 222; socialist model of 218; workers strike 141, 219
Yusoff, Kathryn 175

Zazzara, Gilda 22, 36, 38, 41
Zimmerman, Jeffrey 84
zones 81–82, 104–105, 109, 250, 476